External Liberalization
in Asia, Post-Socialist Europe,
and Brazil

External Liberalization
in Asia, Post-Socialist Europe,
and Brazil

Edited by

Lance Taylor

OXFORD
UNIVERSITY PRESS

2006

OXFORD

UNIVERSITY PRESS

Oxford University Press, Inc., publishes works that further
Oxford University's objective of excellence
in research, scholarship, and education.

Oxford   New York
Auckland   Cape Town   Dar es Salaam   Hong Kong   Karachi
Kuala Lumpur   Madrid   Melbourne   Mexico City   Nairobi
New Delhi   Shanghai   Taipei   Toronto

With offices in
Argentina   Austria   Brazil   Chile   Czech Republic   France   Greece
Guatemala   Hungary   Italy   Japan   Poland   Portugal   Singapore
South Korea   Switzerland   Thailand   Turkey   Ukraine   Vietnam

Published by Oxford University Press, Inc.
198 Madison Avenue, New York, New York 10016

www.oup.com

Oxford is a registered trademark of Oxford University Press

Library of Congress Cataloging-in-Publication Data

External liberalization in Asia, post-socialist Europe, and Brazil / edited by Lance Taylor.
   p.   cm.
ISBN-13: 978-0-19-518932-2
ISBN-10: 0-19-518932-9
1. Free trade—Asia.   2. Asia—Economic policy.   3. Free enterprise—Asia.   4. Free trade—Europe, Eastern.
5. Europe, Eastern—Economic policy.   6. Free enterprise—Europe, Eastern.   7. Free trade—Brazil.
8. Brazil—Economic policy.   9. Free enterprise—Brazil.   10. International finance.   11. International economic
integration.   12. Globalization.   I. Taylor, Lance, 1940–
HF2294.E98 2005
382'.3—dc22   2005005900

Printed in the United States of America
on acid-free paper

Acknowledgments

The papers presented in this volume were supported by a grant from the Ford Foundation to the Center for Economic Policy Analysis (CEPA) at New School University in New York, with Manuel (Butch) Montes ably serving as program officer. Project meetings were held at the Institute of Economic Growth in Delhi, the Development Research Center in Beijing, and the Development Strategy Institute in Hanoi with the assistance of the relevant Ford Foundation country offices and local hosts.

Matias Vernengo, Nelson Barbosa-Filho, and Jeff Sussman at CEPA handled the administration, and Mona Ali (especially), Per Gunnar Berglund, and Codrina Rada helped out with the editing. Terry Vaughn and Catherine Rae at Oxford University Press guided the publication process.

Our thanks to them all.

Contents

Editor and Contributors

Iwan J. Azis, Cornell University, United States

Carlos C. Bautista, College of Business Administration, University of the Philippines

Korkut Boratav, Turkish Social Science Association, Turkey

Tan Eu Chye, Faculty of Economics & Administration, University of Malaya

Amitava Krishna Dutt, Department of Economics and Policy Studies, University of Notre Dame

Shantong Li, Department of Development Strategy & Regional Economy, State Council, China

Joseph Y. Lim, School of Economics, University of the Philippines

Bhanupong Nidhiprabha, Faculty of Economics, Thammasat University, Thailand

Gábor Oblath, Monetary Council, National Bank of Hungary

Le Anh Tu Packard, Ministry of Finance on Diagnostic Audit, Vietnam

Leon Podkaminer, The Vienna Institute for International, Economic Studies

J. Mohan Rao, Professor, Department of Economics, University of Massachusetts

Jomo K. S., University of Malaya and Asia Research Institute, National University of Singapore

Lance Taylor, Center for Economic Policy Analysis, New School University

Mun-Heng Toh, Department of Business Policy, National University of Singapore

Matias Vernengo, Department of Economics, University of Utah

Alexander Yu. Vorobyov, Gazprom, Moscow

Erinc Yeldan, Department of Economics, Bilkent University, Turkey

Jong-Il You, Korean Development Institute

Stanislav V. Zhukov, Institute of World Economy and International Relations, Moscow

External Liberalization
in Asia, Post-Socialist Europe,
and Brazil

1

External Liberalization in Asia, Post-Socialist Europe, and Brazil

Lance Taylor

This volume is about the experiences of fourteen countries with external liberalization and related policies, based on papers written by national authors following a common methodology. The focus is on transition and Asian economies, with Brazil as an illuminating comparator. The authors provide "thick descriptions" à la Geertz's (1973) famous Balinese cockfight about how diverse economies responded to rather similar "reform" packages, and offer lessons about ongoing institutional change. They also suggest policy shifts that may help make economic performance better in the future than it has been in the past.

Somewhat arbitrarily, the countries can be classified into five groups:

Steady-growth economies: China, India, Singapore, and Vietnam

Asian crisis economies: Indonesia, South Korea (hereafter, Korea), Malaysia, and Thailand

Cyclical stagnation: Philippines and Turkey

Inflation stabilization paramount: Brazil and Russia

Post-socialist transitions: Hungary and Poland

Liberalization of trade and external capital flows in developing and post-socialist countries has been in full swing at least since the late 1980s and in some cases long before. Some of the Asian economies just listed were "early reformers." Prior to the 1997–1998 crisis, growth and distribution in most of them appeared to be outstanding (the Philippines and Turkey being notable exceptions). However, the steadily growing Asian economies also performed well and were scarcely paragons of reform. They also managed to avoid the crisis, in part because they had *not* fully liberalized their capital and trade accounts.

From vastly different initial conditions, formerly socialist economies also opened dramatically in the 1990s. Their histories make interesting contrasts to those of the Asians, as also does Brazil's—a case of a "late reformer" with a substantial industrial base. Another dimension to the story is provided by the fact that Brazil, Turkey, and Russia engaged in drastic "exchange rate–based" attempts to stabilize high inflations with open capital markets. Their subsequent financial crises in many ways resemble the ones a few years earlier in East Asia.

Crises aside, the liberalization packages also had important implications for the generation of effective demand within economies, their patterns of productivity and employment growth (or, in some cases, the lack of same), and income distribution. The country case studies shed light on these questions as well.

Methodology

The studies are all "before and after" in the sense that they attempt to trace through the effects of liberalization over time in a specific national context. Depending on data availability, the authors carried out decompositions of shifts in effective demand and movements across sectors and time in labor productivity growth and employment. The algebraic details appear in Appendix II at the end of this chapter, but in brief the methodology of the decompositions goes as follows.

Effective Demand

In any national economy, the level of activity is determined by effective demand. It is the outcome of the balance between demand "injections"—private investment in fixed capital and inventories, public spending, and exports—and "leakages," which are private saving, taxes, and imports. In terms of the standard national income and product accounts (NIPA), the supply of goods and services that results is equal to the total value of goods and services produced (the gross domestic product, or GDP) plus imports.

Following Godley (1999), one can ask hypothetically "what would have been" the level of supply had it been determined exclusively by an injection and leakage from just one of the three main sectors—private, government, and the rest of the world. For example, the government's injection of government spending is G and the corresponding leakage into taxation is tX, where t is the tax rate and X the total value of supply. If injections and leakages came only

from the public sector, then since total injections must equal total leakages, we would have $G = tX$, or $X = G/t$. Similar calculations may be made for the private and foreign sectors. For the private sector alone, investment would have to equal savings, $I_P = s_P X$ or $X = I_P/s_P$, where s_P is the savings rate. For the foreign sector alone, exports would have to equal imports, $X = mX$ or $X = E/m$, where m is the propensity to import.

In practice, X will be a weighted average of these terms, with the weights depending on the leakage rates s, t, and m. Since a financial deficit in one sector has to be balanced by a surplus elsewhere, macro financial balances have to satisfy the identity

$$(I - sX) + (G - tX) + (E - mX) = 0$$

Sectoral Productivity Growth

A fairly consistent pattern across countries has been an acceleration of productivity growth in traded goods following liberalization, but low or negative employment growth in the sector which can be traced to real appreciation and a shift in demand toward non-traded goods. Employment in non-tradeds went up or down according to the relative strengths of higher demand and (typically) slow or negative productivity growth.

To see the details, we can begin with a productivity decomposition. Suppose that one has data on employment and output for several sectors over time. Let $\theta_i = X_i/X$ be the share of sector i in real output, with $\sum_i X_i = X$. Similarly for employment: $\lambda_i = L_i/L$ with $\sum_i L_i = L$. The level of labor productivity in sector i is X_i/L_i with a growth rate $\varepsilon_i = \hat{X}_i - \hat{L}_i$ (with a "hat" over a variable signifying its growth rate).

After a bit of manipulation, an expression for the growth rate ε_L of economy-wide labor productivity emerges as

$$\varepsilon_L = \sum_i [\theta_i \varepsilon_i + (\theta_i - \lambda_i)\hat{L}_i]$$

Overall productivity growth decomposes into two parts. One is a weighted average $\sum_i \theta_i \varepsilon_i$ of sectoral rates of productivity growth. The weights are the output shares θ_i. The other term, $\sum_i (\theta_i - \lambda_i)\hat{L}_i$, captures "reallocation effects" (Syrquin 1986). A sector with relatively high labor productivity will have a higher share of output than of the labor force, $\theta_i > \lambda_i$, so that if its employment growth is positive, $\hat{L}_i > 0$, reallocation of labor toward the sector generates a positive contribution to productivity growth economy-wide.

Two generalizations emerge when the productivity decomposition is applied to liberalizing economies.

If one disaggregates into traded and non-traded goods, the productivity growth rate in the former is higher, and (as noted above) it tended to speed up after many countries liberalized. Insofar as non-traded sectors acted as labor sinks, their productivity growth rates declined.

With some exceptions, reallocation effects on productivity tended to be small, upsetting at least some traditional development economics dogmas.

Given these findings on productivity, it is tempting to look at growth rates of employment, which after all are driven by changes in productivity and demand. Very broadly following Pasinetti (1981), one can put together a two-step employment decomposition over time in terms of these forces.

Let P stand for the population, E the economically active population, L the total of people employed, and U the total unemployed, or $U = E - L$. The participation rate is $\eta = E/P$ and the unemployment rate is $v = U/E$. The overall employment rate is $L/E = 1 - v = \phi/\eta$ with $\phi = L/P$ as the employed share of the population. Evidently, we have $E = L + U$. Dividing by P lets this expression be rewritten as $\eta = \phi + \eta v$. Taking growth rates and a bit of algebra show that

$$0 = (1-v)(\hat{\phi} - \hat{\eta}) + v\hat{v} = -(1-v)\hat{\eta} + v\hat{v} + (1-v)\hat{\phi}$$

The terms after the first equals sign state that changes in the rates of employment and unemployment must sum to zero. The formula furthest to the right decomposes this condition in terms of the participation rate, η; the unemployment rate, v; and the employed share of the population, ϕ.

In a second step, ϕ provides a useful tool to analyze job growth across sectors. Along with the ratios defined above, let $x_i = X_i/P$ or sectoral output per capita. The labor/output ratio in sector i can be written as $b_i = L_i/X_i$, and let $\phi_i = L_i/P$. Then we have

$$\phi = \sum (L_i/X_i)(X_i/P) = \sum b_i x_i$$

Transforming to growth rates gives

$$\hat{\phi} = \sum \phi_i(\hat{x}_i + \hat{b}_i) = \sum \phi_i(\hat{x}_i - \varepsilon_i)$$

so that the growth rate of the overall employment ratio is determined as a weighted sum across sectors of differences between growth rates of output levels per capita and labor productivity (the weights ϕ_i do not add up to one because they are ratios of each sector's employment to total population).

The last equation provides a framework in which sources of job creation can usefully be explored. In expanding sectors (relative to population growth), productivity increases do not necessarily translate into reduced employment; in slow-growing or shrinking sectors, higher productivity means that employment declines. Under liberalization, the interaction of non-traded and traded sectors can be traced in this fashion, along with the behavior of sectors acting as "sources" or "sinks" for labor (agriculture has played both roles recently, in different countries). The most common outcome is that productivity growth has exceeded output growth in traded goods sectors, to the detriment of the creation of high-end jobs.

Stylized Scenarios

Based on experiences of the preceding decade, generalizations about the effects of external liberalization began to appear around the year 2000.[1] The main points go as follows.

Capital Account Liberalization

With regard to the capital account of the balance of payments, countries liberalized for several reasons — to accommodate external political pressures (Korea and other Asians), to find sources of finance for growing fiscal deficits (Turkey and Russia), or to bring in foreign exchange to finance the imports needed to hold down prices of traded goods in exchange rate–based inflation stabilization programs (Brazil and other countries in Latin America).

When they removed restrictions on capital movements, most countries received a surge of inflows from abroad. They came in subject to the accounting restriction that an economy's *net* foreign asset position (total holdings of external assets minus total external liabilities) can only change gradually over time through a deficit or surplus on the current account. Hence, when external liabilities increased as foreigners acquired securities issued by national governments or firms, external assets had to jump up as well. The new assets typically showed up on the balance sheets of financial institutions, including larger international reserves of the central bank. Unless the bank made a concerted effort to "sterilize" the inflows (selling government bonds from its portfolio to "mop up liquidity," for example), they set off a domestic credit boom. In poorly regulated financial systems, there was a high risk of a classic mania-panic-crash sequence along Kindleberger (2000) lines—the famous crises in Latin America's Southern Cone around 1980 were only the first of many such disasters.

When the credit expansion was allowed to work itself through, interest rates could be low. At times, however, other factors entered to push both levels of and the spread between borrowing and lending rates upward. One source of widening spreads is related to asset price booms in housing and stock markets, which forced rates to rise on interest-bearing securities such as government debt. Another source playing a role at times originated from central banks trying to sterilize capital inflows, and so pushing up rates as well. Finally, in non-competitive financial markets, local institutions often found it easy to raise spreads. High local returns pulled more capital inflows, worsening the overall disequilibrium.

Unsurprisingly, exchange rate movements complicated the story. In countries with high inflation, the exchange rate was used as a "nominal anchor" in anti-inflation programs. Its nominal level was devalued at a rate less than the rate of inflation, leading to real appreciation. In several cases, the effect was rapid, with traded goods variable costs in dollar terms jumping upward immediately after the rate was frozen.

The same outcome also showed up via another channel. As countries removed capital controls and adopted "floating" rates, they lost a degree of freedom in policy formulation. From standard macroeconomic theory we know that in a closed economy the market for bonds will be in equilibrium if the money market clears as well. When proper accounting restrictions (including a fixed level of net foreign assets in the short run) are imposed on portfolio choice in an open economy, this theorem continues to apply (Taylor 2004). That is, an open economy has just one independent "asset market" relationship, say an excess supply function for bonds of the form

$$B - B^d[i, i^*, (\varepsilon/e)] = 0$$

In this equation, B and B^d are bond supply and demand respectively. The latter depends positively on the domestic interest rate, i; negatively on the foreign rate, i^*; and on expected depreciation, ε, as normalized by the current spot rate, e.[2] Total bond supply, B, will change slowly over time as new paper is issued to cover corporate and (especially) fiscal deficits.

Similar considerations apply to the well-known uncovered interest rate parity (UIP) formula,

$$i = i^* + (\varepsilon/e) + \rho$$

tying the domestic interest rate to the foreign rate, the expected growth rate of the nominal exchange rate, and a "risk premium," ρ, which at times can amount to thousands for basis points. For given i^*, ε, and ρ, this arbitrage equation predicts an inverse relationship between e and i. For given i^*, e, ε, and ρ, in an open capital market, it strongly suggests that the domestic interest rate, i, is unlikely to fall below the sum of the terms on the right-hand side, which can amount to tens of percentage points.

The inverse relationship from both equations means that if i tended to rise, then e would appreciate or fall. Or, the other way around, if the exchange rate strengthened over time, then interest rates would be pushed upward. This tendency would be amplified if real appreciation stimulated aggregate demand in the short run—the other side of the coin of the well-known possibility that devaluation can be contractionary in developing economies (Krugman and Taylor 1978). Abandoning capital controls made the exchange rate/interest rate trade-off far more difficult to manage. Some countries—notably in Asia—did succeed in keeping their exchange rates stable and relatively weak, though as discussed below that benefit ultimately fed into external crisis.

Current Account Liberalization

Current account deregulation basically took the form of the transformation of import quota restrictions (where they were important) to tariffs, and then the consolidation of tariff rates into a fairly narrow band, for example between 0 and 20 percent. With a few exceptions, export subsidies were also removed. There were visible effects on the level and composition of effective demand, and on patterns of employment and labor productivity.

Demand composition typically shifted in the direction of imports, especially when there was real exchange appreciation. In many cases, national savings rates also declined. This shift can be attributed partly to an increased supply of imports at low prices (increasing household spending, aided by credit expansion following financial liberalization), and partly to a profit squeeze (falling retained earnings) in industries producing traded goods. The fall in private savings sometimes was partially offset by rising government savings where fiscal policy became more restrictive. Many countries showed "stop-go" cycles in government tax and spending behavior.

Especially when it went together with real appreciation, current account liberalization pushed traded goods producers toward workplace reorganization (including greater reliance on foreign outsourcing) and downsizing. If, as assumed above, unskilled labor is an important component of variable cost, then such workers would bear the brunt of such adjustments via job losses. In other words, traded-goods enterprises that stayed in operation had to cut costs by generating labor productivity growth. As discussed above, unless demand for traded goods grew rapidly, higher productivity growth meant that their total employment levels could easily fall.

The upshot of these effects often took the form of increased inequality between groups of workers, in particular between the skilled and unskilled.[3] With liberalization stimulating productivity increases leading to a reduction of labor demand from modern, traded-goods production, primary income differentials widened between workers in such sectors and those employed in non-traded, informal activities (e.g., informal services) and the unemployed.

Crises

More than half the economies considered herein went though external crisis. The basic pattern is familiar. A high internal return on financial assets is needed to bring capital from abroad. But then inflows surge and debt-financed public (Turkey or Russia) or private (Mexico pre-1994, or the Asian economies pre-1997) spending follows in turn. The exchange rate appreciates. The central bank builds up reserves and attempts to sterilize them by cutting back on the domestic component of the money supply, with further upward pressure on interest rates. Eventually the bubble bursts, hot money flees the country, and

onerous macro adjustment follows. The usual ingredients are very high real interest rates, big devaluations, and severe retrenchment of aggregate demand.

Although "basic," this scenario is a theme subject to notable national variations. Some countries did not have significant real appreciation prior to their crises; others kept interest rates under control. A relatively stable nominal exchange rate did appear to be a common element, as did mismatches in domestic financial institutions' balance sheets—especially between relatively short-term liabilities denominated in foreign currencies and long-term assets in national money. When, as was often the case, the short-term liabilities exceeded the central bank's foreign reserves, the situation was ripe for capital withdrawals and massive devaluation.

Additional Observations

The country studies add interesting (and at times conflicting) details to the scenarios just discussed. They include the following.

Non-liberal Policies

The first point worth making is that liberalization was incomplete. Of the four steadily growing economies, three (China, India, and Vietnam) retained strong controls on capital movements. Malaysia, Hungary, and Poland (in its more rapid growth period prior to 1995) also had policies in place to regulate capital flows. All four steady growers as well as Malaysia, Thailand, Korea, and Poland in the early 1990s also utilized industrial and export promotion policy interventions.

Demand Decomposition

Results from the demand decompositions varied across countries. One interesting question is whether there was a "typical" demand story about the Asian and other crises. As a prelude, it makes sense to look at shifts in real exchange rate as a major influence on demand. Among the nine sample countries hit by crises, there was prior real appreciation in six: Thailand, Philippines, Turkey (2000–2001), Russia (1998), Brazil (1999), and Hungary (1995). But Indonesia, Korea, and Malaysia all had real depreciation going into 1997–1998.

For the Asians, one can compare total supply (X) with private (I_P/s_P), government (G/t), and foreign

(E/m) contributions to demand, bearing in mind that X fell sharply after the crisis, then recovered. The leading sources of demand (contributing factor $\gg X$) were as follows:

Country	Pre-crisis	Post-crisis
Indonesia	I_P/s_P	E/m, G/t drops
Korea	I_P/s_P	E/m, G/t
Malaysia	G/t	E/m, I_P/s_P drops
Philippines	I_P/s_P and G/t	I_P/s_P and G/t
Thailand	I_P/s_P and G/t	G/t, E/m, and I_P/s_P drop

Prior to the crisis in each country, demand was led internally by the private sector and/or the government. After the crisis in most cases, the external accounts swung into strong surplus while leading domestic sources of demand fell off. Malaysia, Philippines, and Thailand were partial exceptions. Indonesia was the clearest case of adverse demand effects of post-crisis fiscal contraction, while Philippines had no foreign response.

Among the other countries that had crises, in Hungary there were booms in I_P/s_P and G/t before 1995. Thereafter, these contributing factors dropped below X while E/m rose in line with strong real depreciation. Turkey has had a consistent external deficit after an export surge expired in the late 1980s. I_P/s_P tracks X fairly closely so demand is led by G/t with strong tendencies toward financial instability. Finally, demand in Brazil was led by E/m during 1980–1995, then private demand I_P/s_P became the major contributor leading into the 1999 crisis.

There can also be crisis when the current account situation is apparently favorable. In Russia, E/m consistently leads demand and I_P/s_P drags it down (with a low I_P and high s_P). G/t was expansionary until 1998, then contractionary after the crash.

Among other post-socialist economies, demand in Vietnam is strongly private sector led, with a very low level (negative in earlier years) of s_P. Poland had low I_P/s_P early in the 1990s and a higher level later, while E/m followed an opposite track along with real appreciation late in the decade. Consistently the Polish government demand position G/t exceeds X. China was led by E/m in the 1990s, with I_P/s_P lying consistently below X. As in Russia, an internal private sector financial surplus was linked with an external surplus. China's real exchange rate has been relatively stable.

Elsewhere, India's demand has been led by G/t for decades. E/m has recently declined relative to X, with real appreciation late in the 1990s. Finally, Singapore over the long term presents an interesting transformation. Until the mid-1980s, demand was led by I_P/s_P and G/t with an external deficit, and thereafter $E \gg mX$ with a strong private financial surplus.

Foreign Direct Investment

Foreign direct investment (FDI) has been the focus of liberalization in countries seeking to raise such inflows. Singapore is the classic case, pursuing FDI aggressively since the 1960s. Total flows into China since 1980 range around $300–400 billion, or a third of current GDP. Shares of cumulated FDI in GDP are of similar size (or larger) in Vietnam, the Asian economies, and Hungary. Elsewhere, as in Brazil and India, the ratio is substantially less.

Several questions arise with regard to FDI that are not adequately addressed by most countries' data. The FDI numbers are financial, typically recording equity positions exceeding a certain percentage (often 10 percent of shares outstanding) of the companies concerned that are held for a certain period of time (at least a year). The linkage between such financial flows and annual gross fixed capital formation within an economy can be obscure. Econometric attempts to quantify this relationship (as in the paper for Brazil) frequently fail. The same observation applies to attempts to link FDI to productivity growth.

Another question is how much value-added within an economy is generated by FDI. Detailed studies do not seem to be readily available, but if the foreign investment is largely directed toward assembly operations with a high import content, then its contribution to domestic value-added (or GDP) is likely to be a small percentage (in the single digits?) of the volume of exports it generates. Especially when profit remittances are taken into account, the contribution of FDI to the current account may be low or negative. Chinese, Vietnamese, and Thai data presented in the country papers substantiate this point.

Capital Flight

In a few of the countries, capital flight has been of major concern. China and Russia have private saving flows that substantially exceed private investment. Capital flight under such circumstances can be an attractive financial option, and indeed estimates of its level in both countries range upward to 10 percent of GDP. "Hot money" (Volatile Capital Movements) exacerbates the problem—the reversal of total capital flows in Turkey in 2000–2001 was almost 20 percent of GDP!

Labor Productivity Growth

As described above, the basic approach is to compare productivity growth patterns in "traded" and "non-traded" sectors. The general expectation is that productivity will rise more rapidly in the former. However, there are complicating factors. In Asia in particular, should agriculture be treated as traded or non-traded? The general presumption is the latter. Also, patterns of productivity growth were strongly affected by movements into labor sinks such as agriculture and non-traded services in the crisis.

China has had double-digit reported productivity growth in the (traded) industrial sector. Other sectors including agriculture reported generally positive results. Hungary's and Poland's productivity growth has also been led by the traded sector.

India has had almost equal rates of productivity growth (more than 5 percent per year) in industry and non-agricultural non-traded, and somewhat less in agriculture. Indonesia likewise had productivity growth exceeding 5 percent in both sectors through 1996. Thereafter, both rates declined, but much more sharply in the non-traded sector, which served as a labor sink in the crisis. Thailand had relatively high productivity growth in agriculture in the 1990s, with other non-traded as the lagging sector. As in Indonesia, non-tradeds served as a labor sink in the crisis, with negative productivity growth.

Philippines has grown slowly in comparison to its neighbors, lurching in and out of macro booms and ever more serious busts. The traded sector generally leads, but there are large movements of labor in and out of agriculture, leading to big "reallocation" effects. Vietnam's agricultural and service sectors have had relatively low (at times negative) productivity growth in the 1990s, with more rapid growth in industry.

Finally, Singapore is an interesting contrast— since the mid-1980s, productivity growth has run at about 3 percent per year in the non-traded sector versus 1.5 percent in traded.

Labor Reallocation across Sectors

The results can be anticipated on the basis of productivity growth patterns. As noted above, labor will move into a sector when its growth rate of output per capita exceeds its rate of labor productivity growth. A few country results are given here.

Hungary's story is complicated by a shrinking population. In general, however, the non-traded sector acted to stabilize employment, especially in the first part of the 1990s when productivity in the traded sector grew rapidly.

In Indonesia in the early 1990s, the growth rate of output per capita in non-tradeds exceeded that in tradeds—that pattern reversed sharply with the crisis. Productivity growth was high in both sectors before 1997 (somewhat faster in traded goods). The upshot is that for most of the 1990s, there was positive employment growth in the non-traded sector, and negative in the traded. The overall employment/population ratio did not fall in the wake of the crisis, signaling a degree of labor market flexibility.

In Philippines during 1988–2000, output rose by 45 percent and the overall unemployment rate by 1.8 percent. This jobless growth largely reflected rapid productivity increases in the traded sector during upswings. With a fluctuating tendency for people to move out of agriculture, services acted as the main labor sink.

In Vietnam during the same period, most employment growth occurred in agriculture and services, consistent with the productivity trends mentioned above.

Summary of Employment and Distributive Outcomes

The effects of liberalization on employment and distribution are discussed in detail in the country vignettes that follow. In preparation, I summarize the major conclusions on a cross-country basis.

As noted just above, employment reallocation across sectors results from the interaction of trends in growth of output per capita coming from the demand side and productivity growth reflecting forces of supply. In summary, traded sector output growth failed to keep up with productivity so that the overall employment structure shifted toward the non-traded sector in seven cases (Brazil, Hungary, India, Philippines, Poland, Singapore, and Turkey), consistent with a broad tendency toward real appreciation in these countries. In China, Korea (late in the period), Thailand, and Vietnam, there was a shift in employment toward traded goods, consistent with their successful export performances. No overall data were available for the other three countries.

Also as noted above, liberalization tends to shift the employment structure toward more highly skilled workers. In seven cases—Brazil, Hungary, India, Korea, Philippines, Poland, and Vietnam—this outcome was observed. Among the countries for which data were available, Turkey was the only one in which the share of unskilled employment rose.

Four countries—Brazil, India, Thailand (at the end of the period), and Turkey—reported increased "informality" of employment.

Skilled/unskilled, urban/rural, and formal/informal pay differentials tended to rise, with increases in some or all such measures in Brazil, China, India, Indonesia (prior to the crisis, with a reversal thereafter), Poland, Thailand, Turkey, and Vietnam.

Consistent with worldwide trends toward growing income inequality, increases in the Gini coefficient and/or shifts against labor in the functional income distribution showed up in China, India, Singapore, Malaysia, Philippines, Russia, Poland, and Hungary. The Gini decreased in Thailand in the decade prior to the 1997 crisis.

Finally, the effects of liberalization on income poverty as measured by headcount ratios are complicated. The story in India is difficult to follow because of controversy over how poverty should be measured, but it seems clear that rising food prices and slow agricultural growth did little to benefit the rural landless—the core poverty group of the subcontinent. The rapidly growing Asian economies of Korea, Indonesia, Malaysia, and Thailand all saw reductions in poverty incidence of tens of percentage points in the decades prior to the Asian crisis, and then sharp increases thereafter (especially in Indonesia). Poverty rose in Turkey during its series of financial crises in the 1990s. After their brusque liberalizations early in the 1990s, Hungary, Poland, and (very markedly) Russia had rising headcount ratios.

Country Experiences

To savor fully the impacts of liberalization, one has to delve into the country studies. Brief summaries follow, which can be supplemented with data presented in Appendix I at the end of this chapter, periodized according to the country authors' delineation of phases of the liberalization experience.

Steady Growth Economies

China, India, Singapore, and Vietnam maintained steady, moderate-to-high growth rates through the 1990s, in sharp contrast to most of the rest of the non-industrialized world. These economies are all relatively *dirigiste* in their style of national management. In their own ways, all regulate international capital flows. On the whole they avoided the real exchange rate appreciation observed elsewhere and maintained productivity growth in both traded and non-traded sectors.

China

China, in fact, reports economy-wide productivity growth of more than 10 percent per year in the mid-1990s (with 15 percent in industry). Insofar as they are credible, such numbers can be attributed to several factors acting upon a large and diverse economy with a total GDP of around $1.1 trillion at current exchange rates and a population of 1.3 billion.

One was opening to international trade, with import and export shares of GDP rising from around 5 percent to more than 20 percent between 1978 and 2000 (average tariffs fell from around 40 percent to 15 percent during the 1990s). Roughly half of this foreign trade takes the form of "re-export" or export-oriented processing and assembly activities.

There was also a controlled liberalization of capital inflows. During the period 1985–2000, foreign debt increased almost ninefold, from $16 billion to $146 billion. By the year 2000, the total of accumulated FDI was $346 billion, or 32 percent of GDP (with perhaps a quarter of the total representing the "round-tripping" of funds by mainland enterprises; another large portion coming from Hong Kong, Macao, and Taiwan; and the balance coming "from abroad"). After 1997, "foreign funded enterprises" (mostly re-export operations) began to run a trade surplus of around $2 billion per year, or 10 percent of the total.

Despite these developments, external opening was selective. Capital controls remain in place, and this firewall insulated China from the 1997 financial crisis in East Asia. China devalued by about 20 percent in 1994 when a managed float replaced a dual exchange rate system. Although there was subsequent appreciation, the relatively weak real exchange rate (along with export subsidies in the form of tax rebates) helped maintain a positive current account balance on the order of $20 billion per year at the end of the 1990s.

Unsurprisingly, massive capital inflows and a current account surplus fed into both reserve accumulation (despite attempts at sterilization) and capital flight. On the latter count, net negative errors and omissions in the balance of payments fluctuated in the $10–20 billion range during the 1990s. One estimate put total flight in 1999 at $60 billion! Meanwhile, foreign reserves increased from 11 to 38 percent of the supply of base money between 1992 and 1998. Growth in the money supply correlated with a jump in the inflation rate to 24 percent in 1994 and 17 percent in 1995. To curtail monetary expansion, the central bank raised interest rates and reduced loans to domestic financial institutions, which in turn slashed credits to state-owned enterprises (SOEs). In a context of massive industrial restructuring, the results included layoffs of 8 percent of the SOE labor force, a source of substantial political unrest.

Except for 1993 when its net borrowing $(I_p - s_p X)$ was positive, the private sector was a net lender to the rest of the economy during the past decade—exactly reversing its role in the 1980s. As already observed, there was a strong external surplus throughout the 1990s (again reversing the situation in the 1980s) while the public sector ran a steady deficit. The government financed its moderately expansionary fiscal policy by issuing debt to domestic borrowers— by 1999, the total of its outstanding obligations was around 5 percent of GDP.

These shifts in demand composition were directly related to liberalization. Before the drive to open the economy, the government was the major saver and investor, mandating the investment programs of the SOEs. After opening, resources were redistributed toward the private sector. Government revenue fell from over 30 percent of GDP around 1980 to 11 percent in 1996 and 15 percent in 2000. The personal income share rose from 50.5 percent in 1978 to 80.9 percent in 1997. Personal real income has grown in the 7–8 percent annual range, with consumption increasing at about 6 percent.

The slower growth of consumption than income shows that in the presence of SOE layoffs and the absence of adequate pension and health insurance schemes, households have maintained high savings rates. Private investment, meanwhile, has been low as banks (largely controlled by the state) held back on new credit because of past accumulation of non-performing loans to SOEs. The upshot was a large private financial surplus that financed the current account surplus and the government deficit throughout the 1990s.

Broadly speaking, employment shares have been reduced in agriculture (from 70 percent to 50 percent of the labor force between 1980 and 2000) and in urban SOEs. Overall employment growth was around 1 percent per year in the 1990s, with job destruction in traded sectors and job creation in non-tradeds.

There is still positive employment growth in the low-productivity agricultural sector, so it contributes a negative "reallocation" effect to productivity growth economy-wide. The main engine for productivity increases has been the industrial sector (reported growth on the order of 15 percent during the 1990s), contributing to the labor shedding in traded goods just mentioned. The other sectors had positive productivity growth rates as well.

Rising income inequality accompanied liberalization. Non-wage income accounts for 55 percent of the total in urban areas, largely flowing toward high-income households (though there are also small transfer flows to former SOE workers). The urban Gini coefficient as estimated by the World Bank rose from 0.23 in 1990 to 0.30 in 1999; the rural values were 0.30 and 0.34 respectively. The ratio of urban to rural household incomes declined from 2.57 in 1978 to 1.82 in 1983 (as the initial phases of deregulation favored agriculture) but then rose again to 2.79 in 2000. Income differentials across provinces also widened.

These changes were caused by several factors: an increasing share of non-wage incomes (as already noted), widening wage differentials by skill groups, layoffs in traditional industries and SOEs, differential effects of liberalization across regions, a shift in the terms of trade against grain-producing agriculture, relatively slow urbanization, and a likely increase in illegally obtained income flows.

India

India is comparable to China in terms of population (a bit more than a billion people) but its GDP of about $500 billion is considerably less. The average GDP growth rate was around 6 percent in the 1980s and 1990s, tailing off toward the end.

Sporadic steps toward reducing state control and raising external openness date to the late 1970s, but much more decisive action came after a balance-of-payments crisis in mid-1991 (in part in response to pressure from the international financial institutions). There was an immediate effort at stabilization, followed by implementation of a package of "reforms."

Devaluation weakened the real exchange rate by about 10 percent after the crisis, with modest real appreciation subsequently. Most non-tariff restrictions on capital and intermediate goods imports were removed. Import duties as a share of imports fell from 45 to 25 percent by the end of the decade, and export incentives were broadened and simplified. "Negative lists" of restricted imports (including defense- and health care–related imports, and some consumer and capital goods) were drawn up and subsequently shortened. The byzantine industrial "license raj" was dismantled and the financial sector deregulated. Portfolio and FDI flows were liberalized, though until 2001–2002 strong controls remained in place on commercial borrowing and capital outflows. As in China, exchange controls helped insulate India from the Asian crises.

Using 1991 as the reference year, before-and-after comparisons suggest that the effects of the reforms have been decidedly mixed. The economy did open to foreign trade, with export and import shares rising several points to about 11 and 14 percent of GDP respectively (numbers broadly comparable to China's if its re-export trade and overall trade surplus are not taken into account). The compositions of the import and export baskets have not changed, and the trade deficit rose in the 1990s.

Cumulated FDI in the 1990s was $15 billion, a pittance compared to China's inflows. At the end of the decade about 40 percent of FDI took the form of mergers and acquisitions of existing firms, without apparent technological spillovers. Annual portfolio investment was in the $1–3 billion range in the 1990s. There were stock market and real estate price excursions early in the decade, but they later subsided. Real appreciation appears to be associated with inflows as in the mid-1990s, but the trend later reversed. The central bank has attempted to lean against the capital inflow wind, but with indifferent success because of the limited ability of local bond

and stock markets to absorb government securities. Purchases of dollars by the bank have led to substantial increases in international reserves.

In 1990–1991, the combined central and state government budget deficit was over 11 percent of GDP. As a consequence of the stabilization program, this number fell to 7.5 percent in 1996–1997, but then grew again to over 10 percent at the end of the decade. Contributing factors were interest payments on government debt (up from 3.8 to 4.7 percent of GDP) and a fall in indirect tax revenues of about 1.6 percent of GDP. Lower tariffs were a major factor behind this loss, which was partly offset by an increase of 0.7 percent in the GDP share of direct taxes.

Compared to the 1980s, gross fixed investment rose as a share of GDP in the 1990s. Since growth did not accelerate, the implication is that capital productivity has fallen. As a consequence of the fiscal squeeze, capital formation by the central government fell from 5.6 percent of GDP in 1990–1991 to 2.6 percent in 1999–2000. Much of such investment is in infrastructure, and it may well "crowd in" private investment. Lack of infrastructure is looming increasingly large as a constraint on economic growth.

Price inflation was somewhat lower in the 1990s than the 1980s, though it was rising toward double-digit annual rates during 1998 and 1999 before falling again to around 5 percent. The terms of trade shifted toward agriculture, consistent with its lagging performance discussed below. The real interest rate fluctuated in the 5–10 percent range.

Effective demand, unsurprisingly, was led by government spending, with $G > tX$ since the 1980s. The private demand contribution has closely tracked output, and foreign transactions have been contractionary. There was positive labor productivity growth in 1993–2000 in all one-digit sectors, with job losses in the primary sectors of agriculture and mining, utilities, and social services.

Specific problem areas include agriculture and employment. Despite an unusual run of favorable monsoons, the trend growth rate of the index of agricultural production fell from 3.4 percent in the 1980s to 2.2 percent in the 1990s. Part of the problem can be traced to the shortfall of public infrastructure investment. Also, no attempt has been made to modify the institutions that generate landlessness and poverty in the countryside, where labor force participation rates have declined.

Elsewhere, there has been increasing inform-alization of labor markets and expansion of low-wage female employment. Potentially tradable sectors such as parts of agriculture and manufacturing have not generated significant employment growth; rather, non-tradables have seen the biggest employment and output gains.

Inequality has risen in both the personal and functional distributions of urban and rural incomes. Because of changes in methodology in the National Sample Surveys, there has been substantial debate about whether the incidence of poverty was affected by the reforms. The poor in India are concentrated among the rural landless, scheduled castes and tribes, and households in which all members are illiterate. Poverty tends to be reduced by labor-intensive non-agricultural output and employment growth in rural areas; all the poor are hit by higher food prices. The benefit from public food distribution and employ-ment-generation schemes, but spending on such programs as a share of GDP did not increase in the 1990s.

Singapore

Singapore, in one sense, is a successful long-term capital liberalization experiment, relying on FDI to deliver real resources and technological upgrading. On the other hand, its success has little to do with laissez-faire. The government has intervened continually in the foreign investment process, providing incentives and infrastructure for foreign firms and aggressively pursuing export promotion. The outcome has been annual GDP growth in the 7–9 percent range begin-ning in 1960 and continuing until 2000 (growth slowed thereafter), supported by a social contract under which the government devotes great effort to stimulating production while providing a package of social services to keep the labor force in line.

Singapore became a sovereign state in 1965 (se-ceding from the Federation of Malaysia), accompa-nied by substantial social unrest. Import substitution was practiced under an Economic Development Board (EDB) that had been set up in 1961. With independence, the EDB's emphasis switched to export-led industrialization spearheaded by foreign investment attracted by an absence of restrictions on ownership or borrowing, enforced labor discipline, and public participation in setting up operations. Between 1961 and 1978, GDP increased by more

than four times, and the manufacturing share rose from 15 to 27 percent of GDP. Growth continued through 1985, when the city-state was hit by severe recession. More incentives for transnational corpo-rations were put into place and labor costs were re-duced, setting off a new round of growth.

Leaving out re-export and entrepôt activity, there was a consistent trade deficit until 1985, with the government and the private sector alternating in providing stimulus to demand (the private sector's excess of investment over saving was especially im-portant in the 1970s). The configuration switched markedly thereafter, with a trade surplus rising to nearly 20 percent of GDP. The balancing "twin sur-plus" within the system was the private sector's excess of saving over investment. Capital inflows continued, and some were transformed into Singapore's own foreign holdings abroad.

The "participation rate" in Singapore was 59 percent in 1995, reflecting the fact that an estimated 30 percent of the labor force is made up of foreign workers. In the 1970s and 1980s, the manufacturing sector was the major source of employment generation, with output growth exceeding labor productivity growth of around 4 percent per year. In the 1990s the service sectors gen-erated the bulk of new jobs. Historically, manufacturing has been the major source of productivity growth economy-wide, with financial services becoming im-portant in the 1980s and 1990s.

The Gini coefficient as estimated on the basis of labor force surveys fell from 0.48 to 0.44 between 1973 and 1982, but since then has trended upward to 0.5. One cause is increasing wage differentials for skilled workers. The estimates do not take into ac-count housing subsidies and wealth distribution schemes for citizens that the government has put into place.

Vietnam

Vietnam went through a prolonged economic crisis in the 1980s, which catalyzed a 1989 Doi Moi package of external and domestic reforms. They placed the economy on the road to a market system, albeit one subject to strong state control. The pro-gram started with austerity aimed at curbing inflation, 90 percent devaluation, and liberalization. In rather non-standard fashion, devaluation and high interest rates may have been anti-inflationary because they encouraged portfolio shifts away from gold toward dong-denominated assets and created incentives for dishoarding of commodities including rice.

External liberalization covered the current but not the capital account, saving the country from the volatility that swamped its neighbors. Even current account liberalization was incomplete; for example, in 2001 the International Monetary Fund (IMF) ranked Vietnam at 9 on a scale of 10 for trade restrictiveness. FDI was encouraged by Singapore-style legislation, and cumulated to $32 billion between 1988 and 1999 (GDP in 2001 was at about the same level). Over half of the inflow came from Asian countries, and was directed toward oil and gas production, import-substituting industries, and export sectors such as garments and footwear. Despite its export dynamism, however, the "FDI sector" in 1998 still had a $685 million trade deficit (the deficit was $2.14 billion overall). Exports of petroleum products and of textiles, garments, and footwear each make up 20 percent of the total of about $10 billion.

In comparison to post-socialist Eastern Europe and the former USSR, Vietnam went through a rapid transformation to steady growth at 7 percent per year in the 1990s, expansion of the external sector, and improvements in living conditions for many people. Total trade (including re-export) rose from 25 percent of GDP in 1988 to 111 percent in 2000. From 1993 to 1998, the proportion of people living below the poverty line fell from 58 to 37 percent.

"Externalization" intertwined with greater market orientation deserves partial but not full credit for Vietnam's strong macroeconomic performance during the Doi Moi years. The development of offshore oil resources, and favorable shifts in the geopolitical environment including domestic institutional changes in East Asian economies, also played critical roles. The initial package was especially potent because the economy was operating well below its potential during the pre-1989 period. Existing resource underutilization and misallocation were so great that the reforms produced substantial increases in output without requiring much by way of additional inputs. In the 1980s, output growth was constrained by a scarcity of imported inputs due to the international economic boycott ("before"), while the Doi Moi era was marked by changes in the post–Cold War international balance of power and Vietnam's more conciliatory foreign policy stance ("after"). The decision by non-socialist countries to end the trade embargo probably contributed as much to the rapid expansion

of exports and imports as Vietnam's actual lowering of trade barriers.

Aggregate demand was led by the private sector, especially before 1990 when estimated private saving was negative. By 2000, saving and tax leakage parameters were around 0.2 each, and the import coefficient was 0.6.

As in other countries that liberalized trade and shut down state enterprises, not many jobs were created in the higher value-added sectors of the economy because output growth could not compensate for the productivity increases that Vietnamese firms needed to survive the more competitive environment of the 1990s. The low-productivity primary sector accounted for 60–80 percent of Vietnam's employment growth, with significant contribution from the services sector during the 1992–1997 period.

At the same time, geopolitical sea change and significant resource underemployment help to explain why the U.S. dollar value of Vietnam's exports grew at an annual average rate of over 26 percent from 1989 to 2000, even though after the initial devaluation through 1995 there was a trend rise in the relative price of non-traded to traded goods. There was enough slack, despite widely reported shortages of skilled labor, to accommodate both greater export demand and greater growth of the non-traded goods and services sectors.

Overall income inequality increased marginally, with the Gini coefficient rising from 0.33 in 1992–1993 to 0.35 in 1997–1998. Theil T decompositions suggest that inequality rose in urban areas and fell in rural ones. Simulations with computable general equilibrium models suggest that upper-income urban households have reaped a major share of the gains generated from sustained economic growth.

Asian Crisis Economies

The economies that fell into crisis shared common features—notably, liberalized capital markets—but their histories are by no means uniform with regard to exchange rate movements, demand and productivity growth patterns, and other factors. The contrasts are as interesting as the similarities.

Korea

Korea, of course, was a superstar performer among developing economies in the second half of the last century. It also followed the conventional wisdom that the sequence of liberalization should go from trade to domestic finance to the capital account. Korea's experience shows, however, that following the "correct" sequence by no means guarantees success.

Trade liberalization began in the early 1980s when the country narrowly avoided a debt crisis along the lines of Mexico, Argentina, and Brazil. But the process was gradual and went in stages. Strategic protection of selected industries such as agriculture and automobile continued, and various non-transparent regulations were retained. Financial deregulation also went slowly, but did include privatization of the largely state-controlled commercial banks, entrance of new commercial banks and non-bank financial institutions (NBFIs), partial deregulation of interest rates, and a gradual opening of the financial market. Meaningful opening up to capital flows did not occur until the 1990s.

Nonetheless, the financial liberalization of the 1980s produced an important change in the financial structure—explosive growth of NBFIs such as securities, insurance, and investment trust companies. While the commercial banks were still effectively under government control, the unregulated NBFIs could offer higher interest rates and attract deposits away from the banks. Increasingly, financial resources came to be managed by the industrial conglomerate or chaebol groups that owned the NBFIs. The groups thereby obtained independent power to raise funds without the approval of the government. This meant a fundamental change in the Korean model of development. Checks on chaebol management by creditors and institutional investors were lacking, and the previously widespread government regulation regime was retreating. With the pace of liberalization gathering speed in the 1990s, the problem worsened.

The overriding policy theme for the 1990s was "responding to globalization." In practice, that meant accelerating liberalization and deregulation. The last pockets of protection such as rice, financial services, retailing, and automobiles were liberalized. Industrial policy was wound down, with policy loans phased out and entry restrictions lifted by the mid-1990s. Additional financial liberalization, including interest rate deregulation and the relaxation of entry barriers to financial activities, was undertaken. Finally and most importantly, controls on capital inflows were greatly weakened.

These measures proved disastrous. With chaebol groups controlling much of the NBFIs, intensification of competition in finance did not result in enhanced market discipline. The corporate governance system of chaebol groups, the affiliates of which are interlinked through a nexus of cross-investment and cross-debt guarantees, created a bias toward over expansion. With the regulation of the developmental state dismantled, they engaged in an investment race as exemplified by Samsung's entry into automobiles and Hyundai's into steel making.

Capital account liberalization and the relaxation of entry barriers to financial industry served to create much better access to financial resources for the chaebol and, thereby, much greater risks. Meanwhile, the government failed to apply prudential regulation and supervision that had become all the more important as a result of liberalization. NBFIs were especially poorly supervised. In the end, liberalization policies led to a rapid buildup of bad assets in the financial system and foreign debt that culminated in the exchange crisis of 1997.

In effect, the crisis was caused by an international bank run, triggered by a perception of bankruptcy risks of the major Korean banks. There was a steep increase in external debt in the mid-1990s. At the end of 1996, gross external liabilities were $164 billion, up two and a half times from the end of 1993 and five times from the end of 1990. But the real source of vulnerability was that too large a proportion of the external debt was short term, amounting at the end of 1996 to 2.8 times foreign exchange reserves, leaving the financial system highly vulnerable to a run.

The rise in foreign debt was closely tied to capital account liberalization and the ensuing rise in capital inflows. From the end of 1992 to the end of 1996, foreign exchange liabilities of the commercial banks rose from about $62 billion to $140 billion, and those of the merchant banks from less than $5 billion to about $19 billion. A large part of the short-term capital inflow was used to finance long-term projects and risky investment abroad. Outflow of portfolio investment was also dramatic, as the financial institutions expanded their business in international finance including the extremely risky derivatives and junk bond markets. Foreign portfolio assets rose from only $0.5 billion in 1993 to almost $6 billion in 1996. The resulting buildup of risk only could happen in the presence of capital market liberalization and the absence of strict prudential regulation and an improved supervisory system. There were no guidelines on foreign exchange liquidity and risk management, and virtually no supervision of the foreign exchange dealings by merchant banks and the foreign branches of the commercial banks.

Finally, an underlying crisis of accumulation helped transform the bank run into a full-blown financial crisis. Falling profitability, rising corporate indebtedness, *chaebol* bankruptcies, and deteriorating bank balance sheets were all surface manifestations of a failure in the accumulation regime. Rapid industrialization and growth since the early 1960s had been based on a symbiotic combination of authoritarian politics, industrial policy based on government control of finance, and the *chaebol* system. Having produced miraculous economic expansion, this system was running into inherent limitations by the late 1980s.

Corporate profitability had exhibited a declining trend in Korea since the early 1970s, driven mostly by a decline in the output/capital ratio that was particularly pronounced in two periods of high capital formation: 1976–1980 (related to the heavy and chemical industrialization drive) and 1988–1996 (associated with the mismanaged liberalization).

Despite falling profitability, firms continued to invest heavily. As a consequence, corporate indebtedness rose. The ratio of the corporate debt to GDP continuously increased from 1.09 in 1988 to 1.63 in 1996. The debt/equity ratio of the Korean companies rose from around 2.5 in 1989, to above 3.0 in the first half of the 1990s, to over 4.0 in 1997. Given their falling profitability and deteriorating balance sheets, the downturn in the economy since 1996 caused serious financial troubles for many firms. According to some estimates, the ratio of nonperforming loans to total loans increased from around 15 percent during 1988–1990 to 26 percent in 1997. At the end of 1996, the ratio of nonperforming loans to capital for the merchant banks was as high as 31.9 percent while the ratio was 12.2 percent in the commercial banking sector.

In a sense, the liberalization policy was an attempt to meet the challenge posed by falling capital productivity, extremely high investment (37 percent of GDP during 1990–1997), and financial deterioration. More market-oriented allocation was expected to generate greater efficiency. However, liberalization only served to enhance *chaebol* power, and misallocation problems became more severe. Furthermore, the

chaebol responded to the steep increases in wages and unionization in the late 1980s not so much by productivity enhancement as by resorting to subcontracting and outsourcing, taking advantage of the large wage differential between *chaebol* firms and smaller subcontracting firms. With most subcontracting firms' survival dependent on orders from the *chaebol*, they fought to survive on the margin and failed to develop into a technically progressive and innovative sector. The productivity gap between the *chaebol* firms and smaller firms kept increasing in the 1990s.

Moreover, the very success of the authoritarian regime in delivering rapid growth undermined the social basis of authoritarian politics by strengthening various social groups. As democratic transition began in 1987, the politics of finance also changed. Under the authoritarian regime, the government used discretionary powers to allocate financial resources to favored industries and to help out favored firms. Such powers were greatly diminished as a result of winding down the industrial policy and financial liberalization measures. While cast as economic liberalization measures, these policy reforms were as political as they were economic in nature. Democratization made it increasingly difficult for the government to control resource allocation, while external pressures were very instrumental in bringing about external liberalization policies.

The crisis hit Korea in November 1997, causing a V-shaped recession and recovery. The growth rate was –6.7 percent in 1998 (worsened by contractionary interest rate hikes and fiscal austerity imposed even more mindlessly than usual by the IMF). It rebounded to 10.7 percent in 1999 but then slowed thereafter. Meanwhile, labor productivity growth continued at about a 4 percent annual rate while real wage growth stagnated, shifting the functional income distribution against labor. On the other hand, spending on the social safety net was increased dramatically, from 5.1 percent of GDP in 1997 to 7.5 percent in 1999. It is noteworthy that this shift in social policy took place as Korea was being forcefully integrated into the world economy.

Leading into the crisis, the private sector's contribution to demand consistently exceeded total supply, accompanied by an external deficit and a neutral contribution by government. After the crisis, demand was supported by both government and an external surplus, with the private sector I_p/s_p falling sharply in 1997 and gradually recovering thereafter. Investment hovered around 27–28 percent during 1999–2001, or ten percentage points below its level earlier in the 1990s.

The unemployment rate jumped from 2.6 percent in 1997 to 6.8 percent in 1998 and 6.3 percent in 1999. With the participation rate falling by 1.3 percent in 1998 and 1.5 percent in 1999, the economy moved sharply away from its earlier "full employment" (2–3 percent unemployment rate) situation. Manufacturing and construction suffered the brunt of the job losses, while agriculture employment rose by 6.7 percent in 1998. As in many other countries, lower-skilled workers disproportionately lost employment and the ratio of "non-regular" to "regular" employees rose. The average wage of non-regulars is about half that of regulars, and they have poor job security. The wage differential by education (an important explanatory factor for observed inequality) had been narrowing until 1993, then stabilized and rose visibly with the crisis.

Given these shifts in the wage structure, the shift in the functional income distribution mentioned above, and the spike in interest rates in 1997, it is not surprising that overall income inequality went up. Average monthly income in the bottom decile (of all persons receiving some labor income) fell by 6 percent 1997–2000, while that of the top decile rose by 19 percent. The lower five deciles all lost income, while the upper five gained. Various studies show that the share of households in poverty roughly doubled.

Post-crisis policy reforms included attempts to enhance transparency and accountability in corporate management, increased financial regulation, a move toward corporatism via a tripartite labor/employer/government commission, and expansion of the social security programs. It remains to be seen how successful these changes will be in reining in the *chaebol*, establishing an effective state regulatory apparatus, reinvigorating economic growth, and reconstructing a social consensus on the distribution of income and power.

Indonesia

Indonesia had largely decontrolled its capital account as early as 1970. Other liberalizing moves came in the 1980s in response to the oil price reduction in 1983. There were devaluations in the 30 percent range in 1983 and 1986, and in the latter year moves were made to liberalize trade and investment, with the goal of boosting non-oil exports. Tariffs were reduced, and legal restrictions on ownership and foreign investment were relaxed or removed. Bank deregulation came in 1988, though a few large banks linked to industrial groups continued to dominate the sector.

GDP growth at an average rate of 8 percent per year between 1987 and 1996 followed the policy changes. Capital inflows were a major driving factor, combined with a relaxed monetary policy at the end of the 1980s. Expansion of base money was supported by net foreign asset accumulation, and year-on-year growth rates of domestic credit exceeded the inflation rate by double-digit margins. Using a variety of tools, the central bank attempted to sterilize the inflows and restrict credit expansion in the first part of the 1990s. It basically failed, because off-budget borrowing by the government was monetized, and emission of export credits in foreign currency fed into growth of the money supply.

While all this was happening, there was slow depreciation of the real exchange rate, measured in terms of the differential between domestic and foreign inflation rates and the nominal depreciation rate. Domestic interest rates were driven along UIP lines by foreign rates and the Indonesian risk premium.

From the early 1980s until 1994, effective demand was led by foreign and government deficits (with the latter partly financed by foreign borrowing). The private sector provided net lending to the others. This situation reversed dramatically during 1994–1997, with the private sector pumping demand into the system. The private sector's saving rate fell from around 16 percent in 1996 to 9 percent in 1999, as its debt level soared. After the crisis in 1998–1999, plummeting demand was supported by the external and private sectors in the face of strong fiscal contraction.

Consistent with overall depreciation, prices and wages in tradable sectors rose relative to those of non-tradables until 1997, reflecting the fact that tradables had been heavily subsidized prior to liberalization. The employment share of tradables declined from the late 1980s through 1997, when the trend reversed. The employment share of agriculture was still 55 percent in 1985 but had dropped to 44 percent in 1995. As a consequence, services were the main sources of employment growth during the post-liberalization boom.

In more detail, prior to 1997 output per capita grew faster in the non-tradable than tradable sector.

This pattern drastically shifted when the crisis hit, with non-tradable output falling by more than 20 percent in 1998. Productivity growth was higher in tradables and fell by "only" 10 percent in 1998, while non-tradable productivity growth was –20 percent that year. The non-tradable sector was therefore the major job generator before the crisis, with the pattern reversing thereafter.

The overall income distribution was fairly stable during the liberalization boom, although the data underrepresent the high income population, suppress regional differentials, and ignore cleavages between small business owners and conglomerates and the ethnic Chinese minority. Prior to the crisis, the poverty headcount ratio fell from 22 percent in 1984 to 11 percent in 1996, with roughly equal reductions in both urban and rural areas. Directed government policies (pricing policy for basic consumption goods, education, health, and infrastructure investment) helped support these trends.

For Indonesia, the major causes of the 1997 crisis were financial, especially the mismatch between short-term foreign debt and the availability of international reserves. Despite apparently solid "fundamentals" (rapid growth, low fiscal deficit, slow inflation, and real devaluation) leading into the crisis, its effects were devastating. GDP growth was –14 percent in 1998, and the exchange rate collapsed in the face of very high interest rates. Inflation surged by almost eighty points.

The poverty headcount ratio nearly doubled in 1998, offsetting the gains of a decade. Real wages fell sharply, but employment stayed stable (largely supported by job creation via reverse migration back to agriculture). Real consumption levels declined across the income distribution, with the biggest real reduction of 24 percent suffered by the top income quintile. In other words, the urban middle class was especially hard hit by the crisis.

Malaysia

Malaysia has run an open economy since colonial times, a policy stance that continued after the peninsula became independent in 1957, an expanded federation was formed in 1963, and Singapore seceded in 1965. Selective tariff protection was utilized for two rounds of import-substituting industrialization (ISI)—for consumer goods in the 1960s and for heavier industries such as automotive in the 1980s. The capital account has also been relatively open,

although the regulatory authorities did not allow easy access by nationals to foreign bank borrowing. In the crisis period, short-term loans were less of the problem in Malaysia than in Indonesia, Korea, and Thailand. The authorities also resorted to capital controls in two periods—to regulate destabilizing inflows in 1994 and outflows in 1998.

There is a long-standing policy to attract FDI in manufacturing, with 84.5 percent of exports coming from that sector in 1999. As usual, there are questions as to how much value-added is generated by manufactured exports, owing to their high import content, but no recent empirical investigations seem to be available. Profit remittances are substantial, amounting to 3–4 percent of GDP in the mid-1990s (more than offset by new FDI capital inflows). Prior to the 1997 crisis, the merchandise trade account was usually in surplus to the tune of 1–2 percent of GDP, while the current account ran a somewhat larger deficit. With broad balance between flows in both directions, the ringgit dropped against the dollar with the Plaza Accord in 1985, and then tended to weaken gradually until the crisis when it depreciated strongly.

The propensity to import has risen steadily since the 1970s, while tax revenues are less than 10 percent of total supply and the ratio tends to drift downward. Private saving fluctuates in the 20+ percent range. The government deficit, largely financed by domestic borrowing, has stimulated demand since the 1970s. Before 1997, there tended to be a private, sector surplus and an external deficit. Post-crisis, private, and external stances changed signs, and after a brief period of fiscal contraction the government became a bigger net borrower.

Since the mid-1980s, manufacturing and services have generated employment growth with agriculture as the major supplier. Productivity growth has been balanced across traded and non-traded sectors.

Overall inequality declined in the 1980s and rose in the 1990s, with the Gini coefficient fluctuating between 0.45 and 0.5. With sustained growth, poverty incidence fell from 40 percent in 1976 to 6.8 percent in 1997, and then rose a point or two thereafter. Social policy has traditionally been biased in favor of the predominantly Muslim Malay Bumiputera—or indigenous—community, but liberalization has diluted its force. Agricultural support programs continue to exist.

As noted above, Malaysia's 1997 crisis was softened by pre-existing restrictions on foreign borrowing (external liabilities did not exceed available reserves, as in other countries) as well as mechanisms for prudential regulation put into place after a banking collapse in the late 1980s. On the other hand, high levels of portfolio investment going into the crisis forced the Kuala Lumpur stock exchange to plummet when it started to flee. In effect, Malaysia was less beholden to its banking system than were its neighbors, and the system was in less trouble anyway. Recovery was not as spectacular or sustained as Korea's but was stronger than in Thailand and Indonesia.

Thailand

Thailand switched its development strategy from ISI in the 1960s to export promotion through subsidies and investment strategy thereafter. Imports were liberalized, with the ratio of tariff revenues to total imports falling from 18 percent in 1970 to less than 4 percent in 2000. The ratio of total trade to GDP rose from 27 percent in 1970 to 120 percent in 2000. FDI was encouraged, with an annual inflow of $2 billion in 1990 rising to $7 billion in 1998 (around 7 percent of GDP), when foreign investors acquired ailing Thai banks at fire sale prices. Before that, a representative destination was the electronics industry, which accounted for about 35 percent of exports and 1.5 percent of total employment in 2000. The value of exports from the sector was 22 percent of GDP, but its value-*added* was probably closer to 3 or 4 percent. In effect, a great deal of FDI was directed toward assembly operations without high skill content.

Capital controls were relaxed in 1991 when Thailand accepted IMF Article VIII. In 1993, financial institutions were permitted to offer offshore banking facilities to domestic borrowers, in an attempt to establish Bangkok as a regional financial center. The ratio of capital inflows to GDP was 2 percent in 1970, then was 10 percent in 1990, and peaked at 12 percent in 1995, before collapsing at –13 percent in 1998. Maturity and currency mismatches in borrowing were severe by the mid-1990s.

Despite a current account deficit, capital inflows were large enough to raise international reserves to almost $40 billion prior to the crisis. Thin local bond markets precluded sterilization, so reserve increases fed into credit creation at annual rates in the 20–30 percent range. Asset prices rose sharply in 1994–1995 and the exchange rate appreciated.

Thailand's import propensity rose from 0.2 in 1985 to nearly 0.4 ten years later. Saving and tax propensities stayed fairly flat at about 0.2 and 0.13 respectively. Prior to the crisis, both private sector and government contributions to effective demand were slightly above the level of total supply; the external sector ran a deficit. These sectoral roles switched after the crisis, with the external sector propping up demand and the private sector strongly reducing it.

In a bit more detail, between 1991 and 1996 the real effective exchange rate appreciated by about 0.7 percent per year. It then depreciated by 10.6 percent on average in 1997 and 1998. Relative prices of traded and non-traded goods followed a similar pattern. The productivity differential between the two sectors moved in line with the real exchange rate. Between 1991 and 1998, labor productivity in the traded sector rose faster than in the non-traded. This pattern reversed (with substantial labor shedding in the non-traded sector), along with real depreciation post-crisis. Reverse migration also led to negative agricultural productivity growth in the late 1990s.

There was a substantial reduction in overall inequality between 1988 and 1998, with the Gini coefficient dropping from 0.48 to 0.41. The poverty headcount ratio was 32.6 percent in 1988, 11.4 percent in 1996, and then 15.9 percent in 1999. Poverty alleviation was aided by a steady increase in the agricultural terms of trade in the 1990s and by a modest extension of social service programs.

Cyclical Stagnation

In different ways, the Philippines and Turkey have stagnated as a consequence of repeated business cycles tied to external liberalization. The malaise has affected the Philippines for decades and Turkey since the late 1980s.

Philippines

Philippines, among the populous Southeast Asian economies, is the one that has hewed most faithfully to traditional, conservative economic policy as advocated by the Bretton Woods institutions. It also has by far the worst record for economic growth. In 1960, Philippine per capita GDP was almost twice as high as Korea's and Thailand's. On the basis of its growth spurt in the 1950s and 1960s, Korea overtook the Philippines in the mid-1970s. Thailand pulled ahead in the late 1980s, and widened the gap with rapid growth prior to the Asian crisis while the Philippines went through a series of bust-recovery cycles.

The story traces to the 1950s, a prosperous decade based upon ISI following a balance of payments crisis in 1949 that was offset by import and exchange controls. However, the rigidities of the ISI regime, corrupt politics, an agricultural sector still recovering from the war, and overvaluation led to another crisis in 1960. Trade and exchange liberalization got underway in 1962, with the IMF playing an increasingly important role in designing economic policy. There were eighteen stand-by agreements with the Fund between the mid-1960s and the mid-1980s, perhaps a world record for the time (the willingness of the IMF to deal with the Philippines was, of course, related to the ascendance of the Washington-friendly Ferdinand Marcos regime in 1965).

Nevertheless, crisis-recovery cycles continued to recur, becoming steadily more frequent and with weaker recoveries. The economy deteriorated in the late 1970s and early 1980s due to corrupt, inefficient allocation of public investment financed by foreign debt, the second oil price shock, and the Volcker interest rate shock. GDP growth was negative in the mid-1980s (-7.6 percent growth in 1984 and 1985), 1991–1993, and 1997 with the Asian crisis. The 1984–1985 collapse led to intensified trade and capital market liberalization, which evidently did not succeed in boosting growth.

The Philippine 1997 crisis scenario followed the general pattern of countries in the region, in somewhat subdued fashion. The capital market was fully liberalized by 1993, and a familiar pattern of capital inflows associated with exchange appreciation and booming asset prices followed in train. GDP growth in the mid-1990s was in the 5 percent annual range; after the crisis, output contraction was less than in the other countries.

Throughout the 1980–2000 period, effective demand was led by the government and (especially in the 1990s) the private sector. There was a consistent external deficit, aggravated by a steady upward trend in the import coefficient that accelerated in the 1990s. The saving rate trended downward during the same period.

From 1988 through 2000, bust periods displaced labor but recovery brought very little employment absorption. This led to a long-run trend for the unemployment rate to rise. Lack of employment absorption in the growth phases had to do with (1) low business confidence in some periods, (2) the need to improve labor productivity in the tradable (manufacturing) sector due to the higher exposure to external competition, and (3) high import dependence that created biases against using domestic resources and inputs. Labor productivity in most sectors falls during recessions and increases during boom times, with negligible trend growth over time.

In the 1990s the service sector absorbed more labor than manufacturing, which had to boost productivity because of its increasing exposure to competition brought about by real appreciation and external liberalization. Agriculture is declining in terms of output and employment because of little genuine agrarian reform as well as neglect of infrastructure and investment in rural areas. Increasing output and employment shares of services, relatively constant shares of industry and manufacturing (since the late 1980s), and falling shares of agriculture can be explained by labor productivity and employment movements during the recession-recovery cycles of the economy. Because of the rising importance of services, low productivity growth in that sector increasingly drags down the growth rate overall.

In terms of distribution, an increasing share of income goes to the corporate sector after every bust-recovery transition. The informal household sector's operating surplus has fallen with external liberalization and as labor moves out of agriculture. Government income inevitably improves during the growth periods and as a result of painful tax reforms. However, during bad times of recessions and sharp currency devaluation, the contraction in imports and incomes reduces significantly tax revenues and results in the deterioration of the fiscal position. The general trend of tariff reductions aggravates this problem.

There is evidence of moderate but discernable shifts in labor employment from low-skilled workers to middle-level as well as managerial and professional workers. Together with the fall in real wages in the 1990s, this points to some deterioration in the income distribution within the household and labor sectors.

Turkey

Turkey witnessed severe fluctuations in its aggregate macroeconomic performance over the 1990s. In per capita terms its GDP had been left almost stagnant at its 1990 level by the end of the decade. Persistent disequilibria and ongoing price inflation for more than two decades finally led to the initiation of a comprehensive disinflation program in 2000, aimed at restructuring the domestic economy to fit the needs of external finance capital.

That effort took the form of an exchange rate–based anti-inflation package like those applied in Brazil and Russia, in this case designed, engineered, and monitored by the IMF. Unlike Brazil's Real Plan and others around the world in 1990s, it dramatically failed in the short run. The causes lay with a financial cycle driven via a liberalized capital account—Turkey went through four such oscillations in the 1990s. The basic pattern resembles the one sketched above, featuring real appreciation and high domestic interest rates leading into the bust.

The unsuccessful stabilization package followed this pattern. With inflation running between 60 and 70 percent in 1999 (with the WPI rate below the CPI), the program targeted rates in the 20–25 percent range at the end of 2000. Various restrictions on central bank activities effectively forced it to act as a mild currency board. A nominal devaluation rate of 20 percent was pre-announced as in the infamous Argentine *tablita* of the late 1970s.

Non-resident capital inflows totaled $15.5 billion in the first ten months (in a $150 billion economy). Risk premia narrowed and on UIP grounds, internal interest rates fell. The current account deficit was $9.5 billion at year's end, driven by deterioration in the trade balance. The bigger deficit was associated with real appreciation because prices rose between 30 and 40 percent over the year (in contrast to the pre-announced 20 percent nominal devaluation). The ratio of short-term debt to central bank reserves rose from 101 percent at the beginning of the year to 152 percent in December.

The IMF began to worry aloud about the macro situation in November, and non-resident investors responded by withdrawing assets rapidly. The central bank's reserves fell by $7 billion in two mid-November weeks. The bank broke its agreement to act as a currency board and provided Turkish lira liquidity to the banks. Emergency IMF funds were mobilized but failed to stabilize the economy. A political skirmish between the president and prime minister led to another attack on the lira in February 2001. In the final analysis, there was a capital flow reversal of almost $28 billion between the first ten

months of 2000 and the eight months that followed—almost 20 percent of GDP!

Turkey got into its present situation after widely trumpeted initial success as an "early reformer," with a liberalization push coming on the heels of an external crisis in the late 1970s. Developments in the 1980s and 1990s make an interesting contrast, as initial current account and labor market deregulation set up a jerky transition toward liberalized external and internal capital markets. The early 1980s witnessed a major export push, facilitated by rapid demand growth in Turkey's major trading partners and pushed on the domestic front by devaluation, aggressive export subsidies, and policies aimed at cutting real wages and the agricultural terms of trade (in contrast to India, higher agricultural prices appear to benefit—not harm—low-income peasant proprietors in the countryside). Despite rapid export growth, investment in traded goods sectors did not increase, so that capacity limits helped choke off the boom later in the decade. Moreover, higher exports were matched by imports so that demand was not externally led.

More fundamentally, the model broke down as repression of wages and the terms of trade could no longer be sustained—there was a wage explosion in 1988 accompanied by a marked political shift toward "populism" à la Turk. However, the government was unwilling or unable to raise taxes to fund its higher expenditures. Liberalizing the capital account was the expedient adopted to permit higher public borrowing. The pattern was for the banking system to borrow in external markets, and then relend the money to the government with a handsome interest rate spread. Along the lines discussed above, the rapid financial boom-bust cycles of the 1990s took over.

Throughout the 1990s, effective demand was led by the government, with private and external contractionary effects alternating in importance in tune with the cycle. Productivity growth has been slow, and fairly evenly balanced between traded and non-traded goods. Labor force participation has risen, accompanied by informalization and widening of wage spreads between skilled and unskilled labor. Although data are scarce, it is likely that poverty has increased. Shifts toward and away from populism on the political front were dramatic and the sequence of deregulation efforts was non-standard, but otherwise Turkey exemplified the most familiar adverse effects of external liberalization.

Inflation Stabilization

Reducing "high" inflation (annual rates in the two- to four-digit range) under a liberalized capital account was a principal goal in the 1990s in many countries. Besides Turkey, the ones considered here are Brazil and Russia—each a large economy with a significant industrial base. Both succeeded in reducing high inflations, but then fell into financial crisis.

Brazil

Brazil enjoyed GDP growth of about 7.5 percent per year for more than three decades prior to the international debt crisis triggered by the Mexican default in 1982. Foreign finance dried up immediately, and to meet debt service obligations Brazil had to transform a trade deficit of 2.2 percent of GDP in 1980 to a surplus of 5.9 percent by 1984. This massive macroeconomic shift required currency devaluation (itself inflationary in an "indexed" economy where most current prices were tied to lagged overall price indexes), demand contraction, and (arguably) steadily rising prices as a means for cutting back on real spending via "forced saving."

In the 1980s—a "lost decade"—growth averaged 3.3 percent with an annual inflation rate (GDP deflator) of about 340 percent. Growth was 0.8 percent during 1990–1994 and inflation reached 1645 percent. The successful Real Plan stabilization in 1994 drastically cut inflation to 9 percent for the rest of the decade, with growth at 2.6 percent. However, the Real Plan also ushered in an international financial crisis in 1999, from which the economy is still recovering.

The success of the anti-inflation package was directly tied to capital market liberalization. It shared many elements with half a dozen "heterodox" programs that had been attempted beginning in 1986. Deindexation was achieved by introducing a new nominal non-inflationary unit of account tied to three price indexes; the unit was ultimately transformed into the real, which was pegged to the dollar. Residual inflation persisted so there was some real appreciation, but the major impetus for spiraling prices had been removed. The operation worked precisely because there was no pressure on the balance of payments. Capital inflows turned positive in 1990, and by 1995 they had reached a level of $30 billion per year (in a $500 billion economy).

The Real Plan exercise had been preceded by several years of relatively tight fiscal policy, with primary surpluses of around 2–3 percent of GDP and operational surpluses (including interest payments) of –1 or –2 percent. But anti-inflationary success was *not* accompanied by concurrent fiscal austerity. Primary surpluses were near zero in 1995–1997 and rose to about 3 percent in 1999–2000. Operational surpluses, however, were consistently negative as public debt rose from $30 billion in 1995 to $50 billion in 2000 (and much higher thereafter). High internal interest rates, largely driven by external rates and risk premia along UIP lines, were the principal cause of the fiscal deterioration. The liberalized capital market that was essential for inflation stabilization carried its own seeds of fiscal destruction.

On the side of trade, from the 1960s onwards policies such as a crawling peg devaluation regime and export subsidies had been utilized to promote external competitiveness. Reduction of import barriers intensified in the late 1980s while there was still high inflation. During the 1980s demand was strongly export led, with E/m running three times as large as X. This situation rapidly reversed as imports grew at 14 percent per year in the 1990s while exports grew at 6 percent. It is difficult to separate public and private saving and investment accounts in Brazil, but after 1994 demand was clearly domestically led, probably with private investment and government consumption as the main contributing factors.

Brazilian proponents of liberalization argued that FDI and the importation of "modern" (that is, foreign-made) intermediate and capital goods would lead to a jump in productivity, leading to export expansion. As already noted, the export surge did not happen. The productivity growth rate did rise from 1 percent before the Real Plan to 2.6 percent in the second half of the 1990s. Both developments are consistent with real appreciation under a liberalized trade regime. FDI increased to about $5 billion per year by the end of the decade, but econometric tests suggest that it had negligible effects on productivity growth and domestic capital formation.

The 1999 crisis was followed by real depreciation and (still) higher interest rates, in the usual fashion. The output contraction was less sharp than in East Asia and Russia, and prior bank restructuring kept financial disruption to a minimum. However, the recovery that began in 2000 remains weak.

Liberalization-cum-appreciation were associated with deindustrialization. In metropolitan São Paulo, the industrial heart of the country, in 1990 48.7 percent of private sector workers were employed in industry, with the figure falling to 32 percent in 1999. The employment share of services correspondingly increased. Relative service sector as well as skilled wages also rose.

In six major metropolitan regions, total unemployment ("open" and "hidden") went from 10.3 percent in 1990 to 17.7 percent in 2000. As in other countries, demand growth was insufficient to offset faster productivity growth so there was negative net job creation. Informality in the labor market also increased.

Russia

The Russian transition doubtless has more acts to play, perhaps as dramatic as the ones that have already been staged. The opening act featured orthodox liberalization shock therapy in 1992. The outcomes were a huge drop in output, rapid inflation as a vehicle for limiting demand by slashing real incomes, chaos in the public finances, distortion of the financial system, and an explosion of enterprise arrears. There were massive and often corrupt redistributions of property rights, resources, and political commitments.

The second act was "depressive stabilization." The inflation rate declined from almost 1000 percent in 1993 to 10 percent in 1997 in response to a tightly maintained exchange rate corridor and negative or zero growth. As in Turkey, the fiscal deficit was not monetized but rather financed by short-term bonds, with a large proportion sold abroad. The exchange rate became overvalued and there was capital flight on the order of $25–30 billion per year (larger than the trade surplus and almost 10 percent of Russia's $300 billion GDP). In the mid-1990s came a series of internal financial bubbles and Ponzi games.

External financial crisis hit in August 1998, as foreign funds that had been invested in government bonds and the stock market abruptly departed. GDP fell by 4.6 percent that year, and the nominal exchange rate went from 5.96 rubles per dollar at the end of 1997 to 20.65 at the end of 1998.

Act 4 was more pleasant. Devaluation helped slow and possibly reversed deindustrialization, and higher world energy prices boosted the current account surplus from $2–3 billion to around $20 billion. Due in part to tighter enforcement, capital flight fell to the $5 billion range. GDP growth rose to 5.4 percent in 1999, 9 percent in 2000, and 5.1 percent in 2001.

Demand was led by foreign transactions as the government swung toward fiscal balance. Russia's high saving rate (about 30 percent of GDP) and lagging investment demand meant that the private sector was the economy's net lender.

Can the late 1990s recovery be sustained? There are clouds on the horizon. GDP growth continued to slow in 2001–2002. Four-fifths of exports are raw materials (primarily fuels and metals), making the economy highly dependent on sales into markets susceptible to big price fluctuations. Various estimates suggest that if the price of oil drops by one dollar per barrel, GDP growth might slow by 0.5 percent, investment growth by 1 percent, and budget revenue by 1 percent. Profits are far higher in the energy-related sector than in other sectors, a symptom of the Russian version of Dutch disease that pervades the whole economy. Government finances remain fragile, with taxes hovering around 15 percent of GDP and interest obligations in the 3–5 percent range, leaving little room for spending initiatives. Monetary policy has to concentrate on sterilizing the petrodollar inflow. Investment demand remains mired at 60–70 percent of saving supply (and fell well below 20 percent of GDP for all of the 1990s). Much of the capital formation that occurs takes place in the raw material export sectors, worsening prospects for reindustrialization.

Real wage and pensions payments suffered through the first three phases of liberalization described above. By 1997 they had fallen to one-half of their levels in 1991, and by 1999 to one-third. Slow recovery began in 2000, but its prospects obviously depend on future growth of GDP. The overall Gini coefficient is near 0.4, and in 1998 over 40 percent of the population had incomes below the official poverty line.

More fundamentally, prior to its demise, the Soviet system had two main proto-classes, the *nomenklatura* in charge of the party/state governing apparatus and the rest of the population. The (former) *nomenklatura* were the clear gainers from liberalization, as in connection with the criminal "mafia" they seized control of the major productive assets in a blatantly rigged privatization process, and engaged in massive capital flight. The only Russians whose real earnings rose (the so-called new Russians) were people in upper-income strata who benefited from forced saving and the rapid, corrupt privatization. The production structure shows sharp duality between activities that may survive under the new economic regime and those that will not, and while

Soviet-style industrial organization has been obliterated, a truly market-based system has not emerged in its place. At best, it will be many years before globalization and liberalization in Russia produce happy results for the population at large.

Post-socialist Transitions

In their own historical contexts, Hungary and Poland shared much of Russia's fate of the 1990s. But the phasing and repercussions of shock therapy were milder, following non-Soviet paths.

Poland

Poland in the 1980s had already taken steps toward a market system, with a multifaceted pricing system based on diverse values and/or rationing for the "same" commodity in different markets. This crutch was reinforced by the fact that agriculture had never been collectivized, leaving a farmer population with a significant social role.

The economy was pulled out of the initial contractionary effects of shock therapy in 1991 by fiscal stimulus, devaluation, and a strong export response. Moreover, "liberalization" during 1992–1995 was incomplete. Imports were controlled through tariffs and other means; exports were (clandestinely and selectively) promoted by subsidies. Real appreciation was avoided via a managed nominal exchange rate and partially controlled capital movements. Real interest rates were moderate. In contrast to Russia, investment went up, pulling the economy out of its initial post-shock recession. Higher economic activity meant that public sector deficits could decline without reductions in spending.

After 1995, the story was different. Policy shifted toward steady liberalization of imports along with strongly reduced levels of support for exports. Less controlled capital inflows failed to bring down domestic interest rates. The still shallow forex market was given a bigger role in setting the exchange rate. Unsurprisingly there has been strong real appreciation. Growth slowed, and recently crossed the threshold of contraction. Unemployment has risen, and foreign debt has accumulated. A "supply-side" fiscal policy misfired, resulting in big public deficits. Financial crisis may lurk in the wings.

The effective demand configuration also reversed around the transition year 1995. The government's demand contribution G/t has consistently exceeded the supply level X, falling until 1996 and increasing thereafter. The financial counterpart shifted from monetization to borrowing from the private sector, with the interest burden now running at 3 percent of GDP. In the latter part of the 1990s the trade surplus evaporated due to rising imports, and the private sector became a net debtor to the rest of the world and lender to the government. Post-1995, GDP growth slowed by a percentage point on average.

Overall income inequality did not increase in the pre-1995 "illiberal" period, and rose significantly thereafter. Farmers' incomes rose before 1995, but confronted with import competition from Western Europe, they became the main losers thereafter in both relative and absolute terms. Retirees and the unemployed also suffered. Generally, the overall position of wage earners improved but wage inequality increased strongly in the post-1995 "liberal" period. Employers and the self-employed fared well in both periods, but certainly better under liberalization. In the late 1990s there had been a visible increase in poverty, largely due to rising unemployment.

There has been positive productivity growth, the consequence of high capital formation in previous years and the overall evolution of ownership structure, management practices, and so on. So falling employment (and strongly rising unemployment) in recent years reflects an overall slowdown in effective demand. The fundamental causes include reduced protection against imports and less support to exports. Indirectly, the expansion of trade and current account deficits prompted macro policy adjustments (both fiscal and monetary) that magnified the tendency for domestic demand to slow.

Labor productivity rose faster during the "illiberal" years 1992–1995 than the "liberal" years 1995–1999, for both tradables and non-tradables. The sectoral differential widened in the "liberal" period. The share of the tradable sector in employment did not change much in the first period and declined significantly in the second. Low-skill employment in the non-tradable sector rose after 1995. While it is difficult to single out any clear productivity leader, in both periods agriculture was certainly the lagging sector. The foreign-owned sector—which has exhibited impressive rates of growth of output and employment—appears to have been a productivity laggard. Reallocation of labor from domestic to foreign-owned corporations has reduced the overall productivity gain.

Hungary

Hungary's liberalization during the 1990s concentrated on the current account. Adverse impacts of large capital inflows were mitigated by sterilization and partial, gradual deregulation of the capital account. The country escaped the kind of "big bang" experienced by Poland and Russia. The mode of external liberalization, as well as the implementation of institutional changes in Hungary in the early years of the transition, may best be characterized as "shock therapy in slow motion," followed by true shock therapy in a stabilization package in 1995. As elsewhere, the outcomes of liberalization were deeply intertwined with both the accompanying economic policies and exogenous shocks at the time.

Hungary opened up its formerly strictly controlled trade system in 1989 without any temporary protection whatsoever, and combined the liberalization of imports with significant real appreciation. With the aim of "establishing a full-scale market economy" as soon as possible, abrupt changes in the institutional and legal framework surrounding companies were implemented. They included the introduction of strict legislation on bankruptcy procedures, driving potentially viable companies out of business. (The ones most affected, due to the real appreciation, were those operating in the traded-goods sector.)

In practice, liberalization turned out to be an economic time bomb, which exploded in 1993. Its adverse effects on the trade balance were concealed because the Hungarian economy suffered a deep ("transformational") recession between 1990 and 1992. In 1993, as the recession began to subside, the trade balance and the current account deteriorated very sharply.

Demand decomposition exercises reveal that the fall in output had a close relationship with the fall in exports due to the collapse of trade with Eastern European partners, with whom Hungary had a special trading framework. The jump in the external deficit in 1993–1994 had to do with deterioration of the fiscal position and an increase in private investment. But the mode of external liberalization—in particular, the associated real appreciation—had an important role in the expansion of the external gap.

By 1994, the deterioration of the current account reached such proportions that a correction became inevitable. The stabilization package of 1995 involved trade and exchange rate policy measures

(import surcharge, devaluation, and the introduction of a crawling peg) that could have been introduced initially. Fiscal measures aimed at cutting social benefits had some minor influence in increasing income inequalities. However, the direct importance of these steps was negligible compared to a ten-point jump in the inflation rate, with a corresponding drop in real wages and social transfers. Employment in traded sectors fell by 10 percent, and wage differentials widened.

In the partly deregulated capital account, FDI increased (with gross flows possibly amounting to 7–8 percent of a $50 billion GDP in the late 1990s) and apparently fed into higher gross domestic capital formation. Potential negative effects on monetary developments, the exchange rate, and the external balance were more or less avoided by maintaining a crawling peg with a narrow (± 2.25 percent) band, by the sterilization of excessive inflows, and, in particular, by refraining from the full-scale liberalization of the capital account (the latter explains why sterilization could be effective).

While there were benefits from FDI inflows—growth in investments, exports, and GDP—disturbing inequalities and strains also emerged within Hungary. The emergence of excessive regional and sectoral disparities has been closely related to the presence (extent) of foreign capital. While the central and western part of Hungary that received large FDI inflows has been prospering since 1996, counties in the northeast—only recently penetrated by FDI—have been characterized by high unemployment, slow growth, or recession. By 1999–2000, however, the sharp divergence in regional performances had started to subside.

Also by 1999, real GDP had returned to its level of the late 1980s, with consumption a bit over 60 percent of GDP (unchanged from its earlier share), investment at 26 percent (up from 16 percent), and government spending at 14 percent (down from 18 percent). The economy is quite open, with import and export GDP shares in 2000 of 65.6 percent and 61.6 percent respectively.

Between 1992 and 2000, traded goods output grew by 5.3 percent per year, and non-traded by 2.2 percent. During the same period, employment in traded goods fell at a 3.3 percent rate, and grew at 0.8 percent in non-tradeds. Labor productivity nearly doubled in traded goods over the period, but increased by only 12 percent in non-tradeds. The traded goods employment/population ratio fell by 25 percent in 1992–1995, and then gradually rose by about 5 percent (in part due to a population decrease of 2 percent, 1992–1998). In non-traded goods, the ratio grew by 35 percent over 1992–1998. This increase made up for about one-third of the employment loss in the traded goods sector.

During the 1970s and 1980s, the ratio between income levels of the highest and lowest deciles of the population was around 4 or 5. It reached a level of 5.8 in 1988, 7.1 in 1992, and 7.5 in 2000. The Gini coefficient is now around 0.33. Entrepreneurship and level of education are the most evident determinants of inequality. Around 10 percent of the population is below the national poverty line, concentrated among households headed by a single person, elderly females, and the Gypsy (Roma) population.

On a final note, macro policy in 2001 switched toward reducing a 10 percent annual inflation rate using the currently popular set of tools—exchange rate appreciation and fully opening the capital account. The liberalization measures are in line with recommendations/requirements made by the EU (as well as international financial institutions), and, in the optimistic case, they may contribute to the convergence of Hungary's inflation to that of the euro region. However, it is by no means clear whether it will also support the country's real convergence—maintaining its relatively high growth rate—as well. As noted repeatedly above, exchange rate–based stabilizations carry their own perils.

Conclusion

The liberalization packages we have discussed all represent attempts at the integration of diverse developing and transition economies into the evolving world capitalist system. Under the aegis of the vintage-1980s Washington Consensus and later reformulations, all nations not members of the "old" Organization for Economic Cooperation and Development (OECD; as it stood before the entry of Mexico, Poland, South Korea, Turkey, et al.) faced great and increasing pressure to adopt a set of "good policies" together with "good institutions." As we have seen, good policies included a conservative macroeconomic stance, liberalization of the international trade and capital flows, privatization, and deregulation. Good institutions meant "sound"

banking and financial policies with prudential regulation, protection of property rights, market-oriented governance, and transparent accountability of government bodies.

Outcomes were decidedly mixed. Of the fourteen countries discussed herein, only four managed steady growth of a period of a decade or more, and (attempts at prudential financial regulation notwithstanding) nine went through financial crises. In general, growth and productivity performances were subpar by historical standards.

With regard to employment and distribution, the record was also mixed. In at least seven country cases, output per capita in the traded goods sector grew less rapidly than labor productivity, forcing the overall employment structure to shift toward less attractive jobs in the non-traded sector (consistent with a broad tendency toward real appreciation). The shift went the other direction in four countries that had successful export performances.

Similarly, liberalization tends to shift the employment structure toward more highly skilled workers, an outcome observed in seven countries. Where data were available, there was just one exception.

Four countries reported increased "informality" of employment.

Skilled/unskilled, urban/rural, and formal/informal pay differentials tended to rise, with increases in some or all such measures in eight countries.

Consistent with worldwide trends toward growing income inequality, increases in the Gini coefficient and/or shifts against labor in the functional income distribution showed up in eight cases, with one exception.

Contrary to all these findings, orthodox neoclassical theory asserts that increased integration of world commodity and capital markets is conducive to growth and is expected to improve welfare. On the side of trade, standard comparative advantage arguments are interpreted to mean that liberalization will raise economic efficiency and thereby growth. But mainstream commentators rarely acknowledge that the assumptions underlying standard trade theory—in particular, Say's Law and a pre-determined trade balance—are not satisfied in practice (Ocampo and Taylor 1998). In their absence, liberalization is likely to mean demand slumps and job losses in traded-goods sectors, perhaps exacerbated by productivity gains on the part of previously protected firms that manage to survive lost protection. As has been emphasized, these adverse effects are often worsened by real exchange rate appreciation, a possibility not contemplated in standard models that presume all goods are traded.

Capital flows are supposed to expand investors' possibilities for portfolio diversification, while simultaneously enabling households to smooth their consumption-saving decisions over their life cycle. Historical experience suggests otherwise. The recent crisis episodes across Latin America and Asia demonstrate the dangers of deregulation, which in practice subjects weak indigenous financial systems to short-term foreign capital, which is excessively liquid, excessively volatile, and always subject to herd psychology.

Besides liberalization aimed at raising developing and transition economies' integration with global commodity and capital markets, they are also asked to adopt or maintain contractionary monetary and fiscal policies. The goal is to secure investor confidence and international creditworthiness (Grabel 1996). Central banks are supposed to be "autonomous" and concentrate all their efforts on "inflation targeting." Fiscal policies are to be directly focused on the objective of "budget with a primary surplus." As Rodrik (2000) argues, this policy mix signifies reduced political autonomy in the developing world in exchange for market access to the industrialized North, and is itself a bad bargain as far as development is concerned. Robust growth is not likely to emerge in an economy perpetually subject to contractionary policy and in which the government is forced to eschew any attempt at creating a developmentalist state.

Alternative institutions such as developmentalism and policies such as intelligent capital controls, directed protection coupled with industrial policy, maintenance of sensible levels of macro prices (such as real interest rate, real wage, and real exchange rate), and judiciously expansionary macro policy are of course possible—at least in principle. Whether principle can become practice in the coming years will depend on many factors. The two most important are greater possibilities for autonomous action on the part of governments in non-wealthy countries, and the ability of national economic policy makers to respond to the challenges that great autonomy would present. The constellation of forces will not be completely under the control of "emerging" nation-states, but they certainly can play some role in influencing its shape.

Appendix I: Summaries of Country Results

Key

++	Strong increase
+	Increase
+/0	Slight increase
−−	Strong decrease
−	Decrease
0/−	Slight decrease
+/−/+	Fluctuating trend
+/−	Up, then down
−/+	Down, then up
0	No change
n.a.	Not available
no data	No data in paper

(continued)

Appendix I: (*continued*)

Brazil	Transition	Liberalization	Post Real Plan
Growth, Employment, and Inequality	1981–1989	1991–1994	1995–2000
Growth rate	3.3%	0.8%	2.6%
Real exchange rate (+ = real appreciation)	−−/+	−/+	+/−−
Employment rate (+ = fall in unemployment)	−−/+	−	−
Wage share in GDP	−−	+/0	−−
Real wages	−−	+/0	0/−
Income Inequality			
Per capita household income	−	−	0
Primary incomes (labor force)	−	−	−
Skilled/unskilled	−/+	++	++
Formal/informal	−/+	++	++
Employment Structure			
Traded/non-traded	−	−−	−
Skilled/unskilled	+	++	++
Formal/informal	−	−−	−−
Aggregate Demand Decomposition	1981–1989	1991–1994	1995–2000
Aggregate demand	−−	−/+	−
Direct Multiplier Effects			
Investment/savings	−−	−/+	+
Exports/imports	++	−−	−/+
Effect of Leakages on Demand			
Savings	−−	−/+	+
Taxes		−	+
Imports	−−	+	+
Productivity and Employment	1981–1989	1991–1994	1995–1998
Productivity Growth[a]	0.6%	1.0%	2.6%
Overall growth in employment	13.9%[b]	−8.0%	−3.0%
Employment sector reallocation effects	n.a.	n.a.	n.a.
Labor Supply Changes			
Participation Rate Growth	0.21%	0.18%	0.11%
Unemployment Rate	5.4%	5.0%	6.5%
Macroeconomic Variables	1981–1989	1991–1994	1995–2000
Trade deficit	−−/+	+	++
Domestic credit	+	−−	−/+
Changes in reserves	−	++	+/−−
Real interest rate	+/−	+/−	++/−
Interest rate spreads	+	+/−	++
Imports/GDP	−−	++	−
Exports/GDP	+	−	−/+
Imposition of export incentives	+	−	+

a. Manufacturing sector only.

b. 1985–1989.

(*continued*)

Appendix I: (*continued*)

China	Starting Up	Adjustment	Acceleration	Post-Crisis
Growth, Employment, and Inequality	1979–1987	1988–1991	1992–1997	1998–2001
Growth rate	9.9%	7.2%	11.2%	7.8%
Real exchange rate (+ = real appreciation)	−−	+/−	+/−/+	0/−
Employment rate (+ = fall in unemployment)	n.a.	n.a.	n.a.	n.a.
Wage share in GDP	−/+/−	0	0/−	+/0
Real wages	−/+/−	+/0	++/0	0/+
Income Inequality				
Per capita household income	++	+/−	+	+
Primary incomes (labor force)	n.a.	n.a.	n.a.	n.a.
Skilled/unskilled	n.a.	n.a.	n.a.	n.a.
Urban/rural	−−	0	+/−	+
Employment Structure				
Traded/non-traded	+		+/0	−
Skilled/unskilled	n.a.	n.a.	n.a.	n.a.
Aggregate Demand Decomposition	1982–1987	1988–1991	1992–1997	1998–1999
Aggregate demand	11.97%	7.04%	11.54%	7.48%
Direct Multiplier Effects				
Investment/savings	+/−	−	+/−	0
Government/tax	0	+	+/−	+
Exports/imports	−/+	+	−/+	−
Effect of Leakages on Demand				
Savings	−/+	+	+/0	−
Taxes	+/−	−	−/0	+
Imports	+/0	0/+	+/−	0
Productivity and Employment	1979–1991	1987–1991	1992–1997	1998–2001
Productivity Growth				
Overall	6.63%	1.69%	10.21%	6.86%
Agriculture	4.60%	1.30%	5.46%	2.64%
Industry	5.27%	7.69%	14.76%	16.15%
Construction	0.75%	1.29%	6.54%	5.44%
Service	4.97%	3.26%	2.61%	6.26%
Overall growth in employment	3.09%	2.54%	1.20%	0.74%
Traded	1.96%	2.28%	−0.42%	−1.22%
Non-traded	8.25%	3.42%	6.64%	1.46%
Employment sector reallocation effects	n.a.	n.a.	n.a.	n.a.
Labor Supply Changes				
Participation rate	n.a.	n.a.	n.a.	n.a.
Unemployment rate	n.a.	n.a.	n.a.	n.a.
Employment rate	n.a.	n.a.	n.a.	n.a.
Macroeconomic Variables	1990–1992	1993–1994	1995–1996	1997–1998
Trade deficit	+	−−	−−	−
Changes in reserves	+/−/+	+	++	+
Real interest rate	n.a.	n.a.	n.a.	n.a.
Interest rate spreads	n.a.	n.a.	n.a.	n.a.
Imports/GDP	+	+	+/0	+
Exports/GDP	+	+	+	+

(*continued*)

Appendix I: (*continued*)

Hungary	Transition	Initial Stage	Stabilization	Growth
Growth, Employment, and Inequality	1990–1992	1993–1994	1995–1996	1997–1998
Growth rate	–6.3%	1.1%	1.4%	4.7%
Real exchange rate (+ = real appreciation)	++	0/–	––	–
Employment rate (+ = fall in unemployment)	––	––	0/+	+
Wage share in GDP	++	+	––	–
Real wages	–4.7%	1.5%	–8.7%	4.2%
Income Inequality				
Per capita household income	–2.3%	–1.1%	–2.7%	2.2%
Skilled/unskilled		+	+	0
Employment Structure				
Traded/non-traded	77.5%	65.3%	61.9%	63.2%
Skilled/unskilled	83.0%	85.5%	91.2%	94.0%
Aggregate Demand Decomposition	1990–1992	1993–1994	1995–1996	1997–1998
Aggregate demand	–4.7%	2.0%	3.3%	7.0%
Direct Multiplier Effects				
Investment/savings	––	++	–	++
Government/tax	+	++	–	+
Exports/imports	–	––	+	0
Effect of Leakages on Demand				
Savings	–	–/+	+/0	0
Taxes	–	+/–	+	–
Imports	0/–	+	0	++
Productivity and Employment	1990–1992	1993–1994	1995–1996	1997–1998
Productivity Growth				
Overall	2.1%	6.8%	2.8%	4.0%
Traded	n.a.	13.5%	8.3%	6.1%
Non-traded	n.a.	2.8%	0.1%	2.9%
Overall growth in employment	–8.3%	–4.2%	–1.4%	0.6%
Employment sector reallocation effects	n.a.	small	none	small
Labor Supply Changes				
Participation rate	58.6%	55.0%	52.1%	51.5%
Unemployment rate	6.0%	11.3%	10.1%	8.3%
Employment rate	47.7%	38.8%	36.9%	36.8%
Macroeconomic Variables	1990–1992	1993–1994	1995–1996	1997–1998
Trade deficit	0/–	++	––	+
Domestic credit	––	–	–/+	+
Reserves	+	+	++	+
Real interest rate	++	–/+	+	0
Interest rate spreads				
Imports/GDP	+	++	–	++
Exports/GDP	+	–	++	++

(*continued*)

India	Pre-Reform	Post-Reform
Growth, Employment, and Inequality	1981–1991	1991–1999
Growth rate	5.9%	7.0%[c]
Real exchange rate (+ = real appreciation)	−/−−	−−/+/0
Employment rate (+ = fall in unemployment)	+	0/+
Wage share in GDP	−	−
Real wages	+	+/0
Income Inequality		
Per capita household income	+	+
Primary incomes (labor force)	+	+
Skilled/unskilled	+	+
Urban/rural	−	+
Formal/informal	+	+
Employment Structure		
Traded/non-traded	−	−
Skilled/unskilled	+	n.a.
Formal/informal	0	−−
Aggregate Demand Decomposition	1981–1991	1992–1999
Aggregate demand	no data	no data
Direct Multiplier Effects		
Investment/savings	0/−	−/+/−
Government/tax	++	++
Exports/imports	−−/−	−−
Effect of Leakages on Demand		
Savings	+/0	+/−/+
Taxes	+	−
Imports	0/−	−−/0
Productivity and Employment	1981–1991	1992–1999
Productivity Growth		
Overall[d]	3.3%	2.8%
Traded[e]	n.a.	4.8%
Non-traded[f]	n.a.	5.6%
Overall growth in employment	2.0%	0.8%
Employment sector reallocation effects	none	0.5%
Labor Supply Changes		
Participation rate	+	+
Unemployment rate	−	+
Employment rate	−	0/+
Macroeconomic Variables	1981–1991	1992–1999
Trade deficit	−	++
Domestic credit	0	+
Changes in reserves	−	++
Real interest rate	0/−	++/−−/+
Interest rate spreads	0	+/−
Imports/GDP	0/+	++/0
Exports/GDP	0/+	+/0
Imposition of export incentives	+/0	−

c. Excluding crisis year 1991. If 1991 is included, then the figure is 6.1 percent.

d. Total factor productivity growth.

e. Labor productivity growth, 1993–2000.

f. Labor productivity growth, 1993–2000.

(continued)

Appendix I: (*continued*)

Indonesia	Stabilization	Pre-Crisis	Post-Crisis
Growth, Employment, and Inequality	1983–1986	1987–1996	1997–1999
Growth rate	6.2%	8.0%	−6.6%
Real exchange rate (+ = real appreciation)	−	+	−−
Employment rate (+ = fall in unemployment)	−/0	−/0	0
Wage share in GDP	+	+	+
Real wages	+/0	+/0	−−
Income Inequality			
Gross domestic income per capita	+	+	−
% change primary incomes, wage	+/0	++	−
Tradeables/non-tradeables			
Employment	+/−	+	−
Wage	+	−	+
Skilled/unskilled (wage)	−	+	−
Urban/rural (wage)	+	+	−
Aggregate Demand Decomposition	1983–1986	1987–1996	1997–1999
Aggregate demand	4.5%	8.4%	−11.1%
Direct Multiplier Effects			
Investment/savings	−	−/+	−−
Government/tax	++	+/−	−−
Exports/imports	−	+	−
Effect of Leakages on Demand			
Savings	+	0/+	+
Taxes	0	+	+/−
Imports	−	0/+	+/−
Productivity and Employment	1983–1986	1987–1996	1997–1999
Productivity Growth			
Overall	8.4%	5.7%	−4.1%
Traded	n.a.	5.2%[g]	−1.1%
Non-traded	n.a.	5.3%[h]	−7.3%
Overall growth in employment	−2.7%	2.2%	1.0%
Labor Supply Changes			
Participation rate	+/0	+/0	+
Unemployment rate	+	+/−	+/−
Employment rate	+	+/−	+/−
Macroeconomic Variables	1983–1986	1987–1996	1997–1999
Trade deficit	−/+	−/+	−−
% change	−	+/−	++
Domestic credit	+	++	+/−
Changes in reserves (− = increase)	−/+	−−	++
Real interest rate	+	−	++/−
Interest rate spreads	+/−	−/+	+
Imports/GDP	−	−/+	+/−
Exports/GDP	0	+	+/−
Imposition of exports incentives	+/0	++	+

g. 1988–1996.

h. 1988–1996.

(continued)

Appendix I: (*continued*)

Malaysia	Parity Growth	Pre-Crisis
Growth, Employment, and Inequality	1971–1987	1988–1999
Growth rate	6.8%	7.6%
Real exchange rate (+ = real appreciation)	+	
Employment rate (+ = fall in unemployment)	−	−
Wage share in GDP	no data	no data
Real wages		
Income Inequality		
Per capita household income	+/−	++/−−
Primary incomes (labor force)	no data	no data
Skilled/unskilled	n.a.	+^{i}
Urban/rural	−^{i}	0/−^{k}
Formal/informal	n.a.	n.a.
Employment Structure		
Traded/non-traded	no data	no data
Skilled/unskilled	no data	no data
Aggregate Demand Decomposition	1971–1987	1988–1999
Aggregate Demand	no data	no data
Direct Multiplier Effects		
Investment/savings	−	−/−−
Government/tax	0/+	+
Exports/imports	+/−/+	+/0/++
Effect of Leakages on Demand		
Savings	0	+/0
Taxes	0	+
Imports	0/−	−−/−
Productivity and Employment	1971–1987	1988–1999
Productivity Growth		
Overall	+	+
Traded	+	+
Non-traded	+	+
Overall growth in employment	+	+
Employment sector reallocation effects	n.a.	n.a.
Labor Supply Changes		
Participation rate	+	+
Unemployment rate	−/+	−−/+
Employment rate	+	+/−
Macroeconomic Variables	1971–1987	1988–1999
Trade deficit	−	+/−
Domestic credit	n.a.	n.a.
Changes in reserves	+/−	++/−−
Real interest rate	n.a.	n.a.
Interest rate spreads	n.a.	n.a.
Imports/GDP	0/+	++/+
Exports/GDP	no data	no data
Imposition of export incentives	n.a.	n.a.

i. 1994–1996.

j. 1970–1987.

k. 1989–1997.

(*continued*)

Philippines	Crisis	Liberalization	Pre-Crisis	Post-Crisis
Growth, Employment, and Inequality	1980–1985	1985–1993	1993–1997	1997–2000
Growth rate	–1.1%	3.2%	5.0%	3.0%
Real exchange rate (+ = real appreciation)	––/0	0/+	++	––/0
Employment rate (+ = fall in unemployment)	––	++/–/0	+	––
Wage share in GDP	–	+/0	0/+	0
Real wages	–	+/–	–	–
Income Inequality				
Per capita household income	+	–/+	–/+	+
Primary incomes (labor force)	n.a.	n.a.	n.a.	n.a.
Skilled/unskilled	n.a.	n.a.	n.a.	n.a.
Urban/rural	n.a.	n.a.	n.a.	n.a.
Employment Structure				
Traded/non-traded	n.a.	–	–	–
Skilled/unskilled	n.a.	+	+	+
Urban/rural	+	+	+	+
Aggregate Demand Decomposition	1980–1985	1985–1993	1993–1997	1997–2000
Aggregate demand	–1.4%	5.0%	9.0%	1.0%
Direct Multiplier Effects				
Investment/savings	–	++	+	–
Government/tax	––	+/–	+	0
Exports/imports	–/+/–	+/0	+	0/–
Effect of Leakages on Demand				
Savings	+/0	+	0/–	0
Taxes	0	0	+/0	+/0
Imports	–/+	–	––	+
Productivity and Employment	1980–1985	1985–1993[1]	1993–1997	1997–2000
Productivity Growth				
Overall	n.a.	+/–	+	–/+
Traded	n.a.	+/–	+	–/+
Non-traded	n.a.	+/–	–	0/+
Overall growth in employment	n.a.	2.75%[m]	3.7%	1.1%
Employment sector reallocation effects	n.a.	to services, agriculture	to services	to services
Labor Supply Changes				
Participation rate	n.a.	0/–	+/0	0
Unemployment rate	++	––/+	––	++
Employment rate	––	++/–	++	––
Macroeconomic Variables	1980–1985	1985–1993	1993–1997	1997–2000
Trade deficit	+/––	–/++	++	––
Domestic credit	+/––	++	+	+/–
Changes in reserves	––/++	++/––/+	+	–/++
Real interest rate	++	––/+/–	–	+/–
Interest rate spreads	+	0/–/+/–	+/–/+	+/–
Imports/GDP	––	++	++	––
Exports/GDP	+/–/+/–	++	++	––
Imposition of export incentives				

l. 1988–1993.

m. 1989–1993.

(continued)

Appendix I: (*continued*)

Poland	Closed	Open
Growth, Employment, and Inequality	1992–1995	1995–2000
Growth rate	5.3%	5.1%
Real exchange rate (+ = real appreciation)	+	++
Employment rate (+ = fall in unemployment)	−	++/−−
Wage share in GDP	−	+
Real wages	0.0%	6.2%
Income Inequality		
Per capita household income	3.2%	4.7%
Primary incomes (labor force)	2.9%	3.8%
Skilled/unskilled	0	0
Urban/rural	−	++
Formal/informal	n.a.	n.a.
Employment Structure		
Traded/non-traded	−	−−
Skilled/unskilled	0	+
Urban/rural	0	0
Formal/informal	n.a.	n.a.
Aggregate Demand Decomposition	1991–1995	1995–2000
Aggregate demand	7.2%	7.7%
Direct Multiplier Effects		
Investment/savings	0	++
Government/tax	0	−
Exports/imports	0	−−
Effect of Leakages on Demand		
Savings	0	−
Taxes	0	−
Imports	+	++
Productivity and Employment	1992–1995	1995–1999
Productivity Growth		
Overall	4.9%	3.4%
Traded	9.0%	6.5%
Non-traded	2.2%	1.0%
Overall growth in employment	0.0%	1.4%
Labor Supply Changes		
Participation rate	−	−
Unemployment rate	0	−/++
Employment rate	−	++/−−
Macroeconomic Variables	1992–1995	1995–2000
Trade deficit	−	++
Domestic credit	+	+
Changes in reserves	0	++
Real interest rate	−/+	++
Interest rate spreads	0	0
Imports/GDP	0	++
Exports/GDP	0	+
Imposition of export incentives	+	−−

(*continued*)

Russia	Post-Gaidar	Crisis	Recovery
Growth, Employment, and Inequality	**1994–1997**	**1998**	**1999–2001**
Growth rate	–4.8%	–4.6%	6.5%
Real exchange rate (+ = real appreciation)	++	––	++
Employment rate (+ = fall in unemployment)	––	–	+
Wage share in GDP	–	0	––/0
Real wages	–/++	–	––/+
Income Inequality			
Per capita household income	0/+	––	–/+[n]
Primary incomes (labor force)	no data	no data	no data
Skilled/unskilled	no data	no data	no data
State/private and mixed	++	0	+
Employment Structure			
Traded/non-traded	no data	no data	no data
Skilled/unskilled	no data	no data	no data
State/private and mixed	no data	no data	no data
Aggregate Demand Decomposition	**1994–1997**	**1998**	**1999–2001**
Aggregate demand	no data	no data	no data
Direct Multiplier Effects			
Investment/savings	––/–	––	––
Government/tax	++/+	0	––/0
Exports/imports	+	+	++
Effect of Leakages on Demand			
Savings	+	+	–
Taxes	–	0	–/+
Imports	0	0	–
Productivity and Employment	**1994–1997**	**1998**	**1999–2001**
Productivity Growth			
Overall	no data	no data	no data
Traded	no data	no data	no data
Non-traded	no data	no data	no data
Overall growth in employment	no data	no data	no data
Employment sector reallocation effects	no data	no data	no data
Labor Supply Changes			
Participation rate	no data	no data	no data
Unemployment rate	9.1%	11.9%	10.2%
Employment rate	––	–	+
Macroeconomic Variables	**1994–1997**	**1998**	**1999–2001**
Trade balance	–	+/0	++
Domestic credit	n.a.	+	–/0
Changes in reserves	0/–	–	++
Real interest rate	no data	no data	no data
Interest rate spreads	no data	no data	no data
Imports/GDP	–	––	––/+
Exports/GDP	––	––	++
Imposition of export incentives			

n. 1999–2000.

(*continued*)

Appendix I: (*continued*)

Singapore	Inward Looking	Outward Looking	Restructuring	Post-recession
Growth, Employment, and Inequality	1960–1965	1966–1978	1979–1985	1986–2000
Growth rate (by decade, annual average)	5.7%	10.5%	7.2%	8.0%
Real exchange rate (+ = real appreciation)	n.a.	n.a.	+	−/+
Employment rate (+ = fall in unemployment)	0/−	+	+	−
Wage share in GDP	n.a.	+/0	++	−/+
Real wages	0	+	++	−/+
Income Inequality				
Personal income (Gini coefficient)		−	+	+
Primary incomes (labor force)	n.a.	n.a.	n.a.	n.a.
Skilled/unskilled	n.a.	n.a.	n.a.	n.a.
Formal/informal	n.a.	n.a.	n.a.	n.a.
Employment Structure				
Traded/non-traded	n.a.	+	−/+	−
Skilled/unskilled	n.a.	n.a.	n.a.	n.a.
Formal/informal	n.a.	n.a.	n.a.	n.a.
Aggregate Demand Decomposition	1960–1965	1966–1978	1979–1985	1986–2000
Aggregate demand	5.7%	10.5%	7.2%	8.0%
Direct Multiplier Effects				
Investment/savings	0	+/−−	0/−	0/−
Government/tax	+	0/−	−/+	−−
Exports/imports	−	++	+/−	++
Effect of Leakages on Demand				
Savings	−−	+/0	+/−	−/+/−
Taxes	+	0	+	+
Imports	+	0/−	−/+	0
Productivity and Employment		1973–1975	1976–1985	1986–2000
Productivity Growth				
Overall[o]		3.5%	3.1%	4.3%
Traded (contribution to overall)		0.8%	0.8%	2.1%
Non-traded (contribution to overall)		1.6%	1.7%	2.2%
Overall growth in employment[p]		1.0%	0.6%	0.0%
Employment sector reallocation effects[q]		4.2%	4.0%	3.6%
Labor Supply Decomposition[r]				
Participation rate		0.94%	1.28%	1.02%
Unemployment rate		−0.10%	0.04%	0.02%
Employment rate		1.04%	1.24%	1.00%
Macroeconomic Variables	1960–1965	1966–1978	1979–1985	1986–2000
Trade deficit	−	++/−−	0/−	−−
Domestic credit	n.a.	+	+	+
Changes in reserves	n.a.	+	+	+
Real interest rate	n.a.	−/+	+	−/+
Interest rate spreads	n.a.	−	+/−	+
Imports/GDP	−	+	+	+
Exports/GDP	−	+	+	+
Imposition of export incentives	+	+	+	+

o. Average annual growth rate during period.

p. Average annual growth rate during period.

q. "Reallocation" plus "interaction" effects.

r. Average annual change in percentage points.

(continued)

Appendix I: (*continued*)

South Korea	Capital Flows	Pre-Crisis	Crisis	Aftermath
Growth, Employment, and Inequality	1993–1996	1996–1997	1997–1998	1998–2000
Growth rate	7.4%	5.0%	–6.7%	10.1%
Real exchange rate (+ = real appreciation)	+/–	–	– –	+
Employment rate (+ = fall in unemployment)	+/0	0/–	– –	+
Wage share in GDP	–/+	+	– –	+
Real wages	+	+/0	– –	+
Income Inequality				
Per capita household income	0	+	++	0/–
Primary incomes (labor force)			– –	++
Skilled/unskilled	0	0	++	–
Urban/rural	n.a.	n.a.	n.a.	n.a.
Employment Structure				
Traded/non-traded	+/0	–	– –	++
Skilled/unskilled	+	++	++	+
Urban/rural	+	+	–	+
Permanent/contingent	0/–	–	0/–	–
Aggregate Demand Decomposition	1993–1996	1996–1997	1997–1998	1998–2000
Aggregate demand	++	+	– –	++
Direct Multiplier Effects				
Investment/savings	+	0	– –	++
Government/tax	0	0	+	–
Exports/imports	0/–	+	++	–
Effect of Leakages on Demand				
Savings	+	+	–	+
Taxes	+/0	0	++	+/–
Imports	–	–	0	– –
Productivity and Employment	1993–1996	1996–1997	1997–1998	1998–2000
Productivity Growth				
Overall	no decomposition in paper			
Traded	no decomposition in paper			
Non-traded	no decomposition in paper			
Overall growth in employment	2.4%	1.4%	–5.6%	2.6%
Employment sector reallocation effects	no decomposition in paper			
Labor Supply Changes				
Participation rate	+/0	+/0	–	0/–
Unemployment rate	0	+/0	++	0/–
Employment rate	+	+/0	– –	+
Macroeconomic Variables	1993–1996	1996–1997	1997–1998	1998–2000
Trade deficit	++	+	– –	– –
Domestic credit	++	+	– –	+
Changes in reserves	++	– –	– –/+	++
Real interest rate	+	0	++/–	–
Interest rate spreads	+	0	++	–
Imports/GDP	+	+	–	+
Exports/GDP	+	+	++	–
Imposition of export incentives				

(continued)

Appendix I: (*continued*)

Thailand	Trade Lib.	Financial Lib.	Crisis
Growth, Employment, and Inequality	1981–1990	1991–1996	1997–2000
Growth rate	no data	no data	no data
Real exchange rate (+ = real appreciation)	−	0/+	−−/0
Employment rate (+ = fall in unemployment)	−/+	+/0	−−/+
Wage share in GDP	+/−	+	0
Real wages	no data	no data	no data
Income Inequality			
Gini index	+/−	0	0
Primary incomes (labor force)	no data	no data	no data
Urban/rural	+	+/−	+
Formal/informal	no data	no data	no data
Employment Structure	no data	no data	no data
Traded/non-traded	n.a.	+	+
Urban/rural	no data	no data	no data
Formal/informal	+	+	0/−
Aggregate Demand Decomposition	1981–1990	1991–1996	1997–2000
Aggregate demand	no data	no data	no data
Direct Multiplier Effects			
Investment/savings	−/+	0/+	−−/+
Government/tax	−/0	+	++
Exports/imports	−	−−	+/0
Effect of Leakages on Demand			
Savings	+	0	−
Taxes	+	0	−
Imports	0/++	+/−	++
Productivity and Employment	1981–1990	1991–1996	1997–2000
Productivity Growth			
Overall	−/+	0	−−/+
Traded	0	0/+	−−
Non-traded	0/+	−	−−/+
Overall growth in employment	3.7%	0.7%	−0.2%
Employment sector reallocation effects	n.a.	n.a.	n.a.
Labor Supply Changes			
Participation rate	n.a.	n.a.	n.a.
Unemployment rate	+/−	0/+	++/−
Employment rate	−/+	+/0	−−/+
Macroeconomic Variables	1981–1990	1991–1996	1997–2000
Trade deficit	0/+	++/−	−−
Domestic credit	+	++	−−
Changes in reserves	+	++	−−
Real interest rate	+	++	−−
Interest rate spreads	+	++	−−
Imports/GDP	++	+	++
Exports/GDP	++	+	++
Imposition of export incentives	+	+	−

(continued)

Appendix I: (*continued*)

Turkey	Export prom., Liberalization	Liberalization and Crisis	Flows and Contagion
Growth, Employment, and Inequality	**1980–1988**	**1989–1994**	**1995–2000**
Growth rate (real GNP)[s]	4.9%	4.0%	2.7%[t]
Real exchange rate (+ = real appreciation)	– –	++/–	+
Employment rate (+ = fall in unemployment)	n.a.	n.a.	n.a.
Wage share in GDP	20.9%	30.2%	27.1%
Real wages[u]	–	++/– –	0/–
Income Inequality			
Per capita household income	n.a.	n.a.	n.a.
Primary incomes (labor force)	n.a.	n.a.	n.a.
Skilled/unskilled	+	+	+
Formal/informal	+	+	+
Employment Structure			
Traded/non-traded	+	–	–
Skilled/unskilled	–	–	–
Urban/rural	0/–	–	0/–
Formal/informal	–	–	0
Aggregate Demand Decomposition	**1980–1988**	**1989–1994**	**1995–2000**
Aggregate demand	5.40%	4.00%	6.60%
Direct Multiplier Effects			
Investment/savings	–/+	0	+/–
Government/tax	+	+	++
Exports/imports	+	–	–
Effect of Leakages on Demand			
Savings	+	+	0
Taxes	+	–/+	– –
Imports	–	–	– –
Productivity and Employment	**1981–1988**	**1989–1993**	**1994–1997**
Productivity Growth[v]			
Overall	11.6%	10.8%	0.7%
Traded	8.8%	11.7%	–2.0%
Non-traded	12.7%	8.5%	3.2%
Overall growth in employment	n.a.	n.a.	n.a.
Employment sector reallocation effects	small	small	small
Labor Supply Changes			
Participation rate	54%[w]	55%	51%
Unemployment rate	8.4%[x]	7.8%	8.0%
Macroeconomic Variables	**1980–1988**	**1989–1994**	**1995–2000**
Trade deficit	–	–	–/+
Domestic credit	+	–	+
Changes in reserves	– –	+	++
Real interest rate	–	++	++/–
Interest rate spreads	–	+	++
Imports/GDP	+	+	++
Exports/GDP	++	–/+	+/0
Imposition of export incentives	++	0	0

s. Growth rates are calculated in log-exponential form.

t. 1995–2001. Note that 2001 is a "crisis" year.

u. Numerically: –2.5 percent, 7 percent, and –6 percent.

v. Manufacturing sector only.

w. 1988.

x. 1988.

(continued)

Vietnam	Closed	Liberalization	Hesitancy	Fall in FDI
Growth, Employment, and Inequality	1981–1988	1989–1993	1994–1997	1998–2000
Growth rate	5.6%	6.5%	9.0%	5.8%
Real exchange rate (+ = real appreciation)	+/−−	++	−/0	0/−
Employment rate (+ = fall in unemployment)	+	+	+	+
Wage share in GDP	−/+	+	0	0
Real wages	−−/++	++	+	+*
Income Inequality				
Per capita household income	n.a.	+	+	+
Primary incomes (labor force)	no data	no data	no data	no data
Skilled/unskilled	0	+	+	+
Urban/rural	0	+	+	+
Employment Structure				
Traded/non-traded	n.a.	+	−	+
Urban/rural	+/0	+	+	−
Aggregate Demand Decomposition	1986–1988	1989–1993	1994–1997	1998–2000
Aggregate demand	no data	no data	no data	no data
Direct Multiplier Effects				
Investment/savings	+	−−/+	0	0
Government/tax	0	−−	−−	−
Exports/imports	+/−	++	+	+/0
Effect of Leakages on Demand				
Savings	−−	−	0	−
Taxes	++	0	+	+
Imports	−	+	−	+
Productivity Growth	1981–1988	1989–1993	1994–1997	1998–2000
Overall	2.3%	3.3%	5.9%	3.7%
Agriculture	n.a.	−1.3%**	−1.2%	−0.3%
Industry	n.a.	0.2%**	0.2%	0.4%
Construction	n.a.	0.0%**	0.2%	0.0%
Services	n.a.	0.5%**	1.4%	0.5%
Employment	1981–1988	1989–1993	1994–1997	1998–2000
Overall growth in employment	3.3%	3.2%	3.1%	2.1%
Employment sector reallocation effects	n.a.	−0.6%	0.6%	0.6%
Labor Supply Changes				
Participation rate	no data	no data	no data	no data
Unemployment rate	no data	no data	no data	no data
Employment rate	+	+	+	+
Macroeconomic Variables	1981–1988	1989–1993	1994–1997	1998–2000
Trade deficit	++	−	+	−−
Domestic credit	+	++	0/−	++
Changes in reserves	no data	no data	no data	no data
Real interest rate	n.a.	+	n.a.	n.a.
Interest rate spreads	no data	no data	no data	no data
Imports/GDP	+	−	++	−−
Exports/GDP	++	++	+	−−
Imposition of export incentives		+		

Appendix II: Productivity and Demand Decompositions

Because macro data are available for discrete periods of time (typically years), the analysis is set up with variables for period beginning at time t, indicated by a subscript. For simplicity, equations are stated with t taking only the values 0 and 1 corresponding to the beginning and end of a period respectively.

To begin with a productivity decomposition, suppose that one has data on employment and output for several sectors over time. Let $\theta_0^i = X_0^i/X_0$ be the share of sector i in real output in period 0, with $\sum_i X_0^i = X_0$. Similarly for employment: $\lambda_0^i = L_0^i/L_0$ with $\sum_i L_0^i = L_0$. The level of labor productivity in sector i is X_0^i/L_0^i with a growth rate of

$$\varepsilon_L^i = (1 + \hat{L}^i)^{-1}(\hat{X}^i - \hat{L}^i) \approx \hat{X}^i - \hat{L}^i$$

in which $\hat{X}^i = (X_1^i - X_0^i)/X_0^i$ and similarly for other variables with "hats." The term $(1 + \hat{L}^j)^{-1}$ captures "interaction" effects on growth rates arising from their calculation in discrete time.

After a bit of manipulation, an exact expression for the rate of growth of economy-wide labor productivity emerges as

$$\varepsilon_L = (1 + \hat{L})^{-1} \sum_i [\theta_0^i(\hat{X}^i - \hat{L}^i) + (\theta_0^i - \lambda_0^i)\hat{L}^i] \quad (1)$$

Another expression for ε_L comes out after some manipulation of (1),

$$\varepsilon_L = (1 + \hat{L})^{-1} \sum_i [\lambda_0^i(\hat{X}^i - \hat{L}^i) + (\theta_0^i - \lambda_0^i)\hat{X}^i] \quad (2)$$

In (2), sectoral productivity growth rates are weighted by employment shares, and the reallocation effect is stated in terms of output growth rates. The message is basically the same as in (1).

Growth rates of employment are driven by changes in productivity and demand. The relevant decomposition (expressed in terms of continuous time for simplicity) appears in the text.

The decomposition procedure for effective demand draws on Godley (1999).

At the one-sector level (ignoring intermediate outputs and sales along with the distinction between wage and profit income flows), the aggregate supply of goods and services available for domestic use (X) can be defined as the sum of total private income (Y_p), net taxes (T), and "imports" or (for present purposes) all outgoing payments on current account (M):

$$X = Y_P + T + M \quad (3)$$

In NIPA categories, we have GDP $= Y_P + T = X - M$ so the accounting in (10) is non-standard insofar as X exceeds GDP. The aggregate supply and demand balance can be written as

$$X = C_P + I_P + G + E \quad (4)$$

that is, the sum of private consumption, private investment, government spending (on both current and capital account) and "exports" or incoming foreign payments on current account. It is convenient to define leakage parameters relative to aggregate supply, yielding the private savings rate as $s_P = (Y_P - C_P)/X$, the import propensity as $m = M/X$, and the tax rate as $t = T/X$.

From all this, one gets a typical Keynesian income multiplier function

$$X = (I_P + G + E)/(s_P + t + m) \quad (5)$$

which can also be written as

$$X = (s_p/\lambda)(I_P/s_p) + (t/\lambda)(G/t) + (m/\lambda)(E/m) \quad (6)$$

in which $\lambda = s_P + t + m$ is the sum of the leakage parameters, and I_P/s_P, G/t, and E/m can be interpreted as the direct "own" multiplier effects on output of private investment, government spending, and export injections with their overall impact scaled by the corresponding leakage rates (respectively, savings, tax, and import propensities). That is, aggregate supply is equal to a weighted average of contributions to demand from the private sector, government, and the rest of the world. If two of these contributions were zero, then output would be equal to the third.

Another representation involves the levels of $I_P - s_P X$, $G - tX$, and $E - mX$, which from (6) must sum to zero. Moreover, the economy's real financial balance can be written as

$$\dot{D} + \dot{Z} + \dot{A} = (I_P - s_P X) + (G - tX) + (E - mX) = 0 \quad (7)$$

where $\dot{D}(= dD/dt)$, $\dot{Z}$, and $\dot{A}$ stand respectively for the net change per unit time in financial claims against the private sector, in government debt, and in foreign assets.

Equation (7) shows how claims against an institutional entity (the private sector, government, or rest of the world) must growing when its demand contribution to X exceeds X itself. So when $E < mX$, net foreign assets of the home economy are declining, while $G > tX$ means that its government is running up debt. A contractionary demand contribution from the rest of the world requires some other sector to be increasing liabilities or lowering assets, for example, the public sector when $G > tX$. Because from (7) it is true that

$$\dot{D} + \dot{Z} + \dot{A} = 0,$$

such offsetting effects are unavoidable.

Notes

1. See, for example, Taylor (2001) and Vos, Taylor, and Paes de Barros (2003).

2. Scaling the expected change in the exchange rate by its current level puts the quantity ε/e—the expected rate of return from capital gains on foreign securities—on a comparable footing with the two interest rates.

3. As discussed endlessly in the literature, this outcome runs counter to predictions from the Stolper-Samuelson (Stolper and Samuelson 1941) theorem. But since that theorem presupposes Say's Law and ignores the real exchange rate and the distinction between traded and non-traded goods, there is no reason to expect it to apply.

References

Geertz, Clifford. 1973. *The interpretation of cultures.* New York: Basic Books.

Godley, Wynne. 1999. *Seven unsustainable processes: Medium-term prospects and policies for the US and the World.* Annandale-on-Hudson, N.Y.: Jerome Levy Economics Institute, Bard College.

Grabel, Ilene. 1996. Marketing the Third World: The contradictions of portfolio investment in the Global Economy. *World Development* 24 (11): 1761–76.

Kindleberger, Charles P. 2000. *Manias, panics, and crashes: A history of financial crises,* 4th ed. New York: John Wiley.

Krugman, Paul, and Lance Taylor. 1978. Contractionary effects of devaluation. *Journal of International Economics* 8:445–56.

Ocampo, Jose Antonio, and Lance Taylor. 1998. Trade liberalization in developing economies: Modest benefits but problems with productivity growth, macro prices, and income distribution. *Economic Journal* 108:1523–46.

Pasinetti, Luigi L. 1981. *Structural change and economic growth.* Cambridge: Cambridge University Press.

Rodrik, Dani. 2000. The global governance of trade as if development really mattered. Paper presented at the UNDP Meetings, New York, October 13–14.

Stolper, Wolfgang F., and Paul A. Samuelson. 1941. Protection and real wages. *Review of Economic Studies* 9:58–73.

Syrquin, Moshe. 1986. Productivity growth and factor reallocation. In *Industrialization and growth,* edited by Hollis B. Chenery, Sherman Robinson, and Moshe Syrquin. New York: Oxford University Press.

Taylor, Lance. 2001. Exchange rate *in*determinacy in portfolio balance, Mundell-Fleming, and uncovered interest rate parity models. *Cambridge Journal of Economics,* 28:205–27.

———, ed. 2001. *External liberalization, economic performance, and social policy.* New York: Oxford University Press.

Vos, Rob, Lance Taylor, and Ricardo Paes de Barros. 2003. *Economic liberalization and income distribution: The case of Latin America.* Northhampton, MA: Edward Elgar.

2

Belindia Goes to Washington:
The Brazilian Economy after the Reforms

Matias Vernengo

1. Introduction

Taylor and Bacha (1976) developed the Belindia[1] model to portray the evolution of certain developing economies that were large enough to support integrated domestic markets. According to the authors, this process was characterized by changes in the structure of production (the share of consumer durables and intermediate goods in total production increased), worsening income distribution, an increasing gap between the wages of skilled and nonskilled workers, and the dominance of multinational corporations in domestic production. In other words, industrialization beyond the production of simple goods was possible as a result of increasing wage inequality and considerable foreign capital participation.[2] Brazil was, as the authors themselves noted, one of the countries that well fit the pattern of development formalized in the Belindia model.

The development strategy followed by Brazil in the post-war period up to the debt crisis in 1982 is generally described as import-substitution industrialization (ISI). High levels of import tariffs and a relatively high dispersion of the tariff structure protected domestic production. Overvalued exchange rates discriminated against the exports of primary goods and favored intermediate and capital goods imports. As a result, the rate of growth was highly dependent on the expansion of domestic demand.

The debt crisis led to a revision of the conventional wisdom on development that culminated in the so-called Washington Consensus. According to this view, inward-oriented strategies produced tremendous inefficiencies, associated with excessive state intervention, leading to lower rates of growth and increased inequality. The successful experience of the East Asian countries led many, including the World Bank (World Bank 1993; Edwards 1995), to conclude that outward-oriented development strategies were conducive to rapid and sustainable development.

Brazil, however, was a late convert to the liberalization, deregulation, and privatization creed of the

Washington Consensus. Only after the Real Plan of July 1994 did Brazil clearly adopt the set of policies promoted by Washington, even though trade and capital account liberalization started in the early 1990s under the Collor administration.[3] A peculiarity of the Brazilian reform process in the early 1990s was the coexistence of trade and capital liberalization with high inflation. This might, in part, explain the excessive zeal in the use of the exchange rate as a stabilization instrument and the disregard for the consequences of exchange rate overvaluation in the context of trade liberalization.

Indeed, reform-minded authors such as Franco (1999) favor an overvalued exchange rate, for it reduces the cost of imported goods, leading to a rise in the imports of intermediate and capital goods.[4] Increased imports, in turn, lead to increased productivity and, as a result, rising exports and growth rates. The export boom makes the initial trade deficits sustainable in the longer run perspective. It was also expected that market-friendly reforms would lead to an increase in foreign direct investment (FDI) that would again translate into higher rates of growth. In particular, it was argued that FDI would generate a positive macroeconomic externality and lead to an increase in domestic investment.

By and large, the expectation was that post-reform growth would be higher and led by exports. The greater emphasis on exports together with a more efficient use of imports would produce larger trade surpluses. An important complement of the reform package would be labor market deregulation that would maintain real wages and keep unemployment relatively low. As a result, the reforms would lead to higher growth and productivity, with a relatively low level of unemployment.

This expectation proved to be the Achilles' heel of the arguments in favor of reforms: since the trade deficits persisted, rates of growth have been modest and unemployment is on the rise. In fact, in a recent evaluation of the macroeconomic performance, sponsored by the Banco Nacional de Desenvolvimento Econômico e Social (BNDES), Pinheiro, Giambiagi, and Gostkorzewciz (1999, 13) argue that it is difficult not to agree with the proposition that the 1990s have been a second lost decade. In their view, the only important achievement was stabilization. Yet they argue that reforms might lead to higher rates of growth in the future, and the solution for economic woes is speeding up the reforms, particularly fiscal

reform. Specifically, reforms should force the reduction of fiscal deficits, since "[fiscal] deficits reduce saving and investment" (Dornbusch 1997, 13).

Critics of the stabilization process, such as Delfim Netto (1998) and Tavares (1999), have argued that one of the consequences of foreign exchange appreciation in particular, and of the reforms in general, is higher unemployment and reduced international competitiveness. This, in turn, implies higher trade deficits, making the economy extremely dependent on short-term capital flows, and leading to increasing balance of payments vulnerability. Finally, for some authors, the high interest rates needed to attract capital flows are the most important cause of the soaring budget deficits. The crisis of January 1999, even though lacking the depth of the Mexican or Asian crises, put on display the fragility of the reforms.[5]

This paper discusses the effects of the reforms on macroeconomic performance, growth, employment, wage differentials, income distribution, and poverty in Brazil. The results are compared with recent evaluations of the effects of the reforms in other Latin American countries. The next section discusses the effects of the debt crisis and the move toward the reforms. The succeeding section analyzes the growth performance of the Brazilian economy, before and after the reforms. The following sections examine the effects of the reforms on the labor market, on income distribution, and on poverty. The last section pulls the results together for an evaluation.

2. Late Stabilization and Reforms

The international debt crisis triggered by the Mexican default in August 1982 had a severe impact on the Brazilian economy. High levels of inflation and stagnant growth rates marked the macroeconomic performance during the 1980s, the so-called lost decade. The average rate of inflation in the 1980s was around 341 percent per year, and the peak annual inflation was 2596 percent as measured by the GDP price deflator (see table 2.1). Looking at the whole post-war period, one must conclude that the growth performance of the Brazilian economy is divided in two periods, before and after the debt crisis. The real GDP growth was, on average, 7.45 percent from 1948 to 1980, and it slowed down to only 2.47 percent in 1981 to 2000. The real rate of growth in the 1980s was 3.3 percent if we exclude 1980, and 3.94 if we

TABLE 2.1 Inflation, Growth, and Labor Productivity

Years	Inflation (GDP Deflator)	Real GDP Growth	Real GDP per Capita Growth	Productivity Growth
1948–1980	45.3	7.45	4.40	4.1
1981–1989	341.2	3.30	1.28	0.6
1990–1994	1643.6	0.79	−0.77	1.0
1995–2000	8.9[a]	2.62	1.24	2.6[b]
1990–2000	757.8	1.78	0.33	1.7[b]

Source: FGV Dados (n.d.), Bonelli (1994).

a. Figure for the 1996 to 1999 period.

b. Figure goes up to 1998.

include it. Growth has been even lower in the 1990s: 1.78 percent for the whole decade, 2.69 if we exclude the 1990 recession, and 2.62 for the period after stabilization. Table 2.1 also shows the differences between the first part of the 1990s and the post-stabilization period. Inflation decreased drastically, but the rates of growth recuperated only slightly. As far as growth rates are concerned, the 1990s—and not the 1980s, as one would expect—is the lost decade.

Table 2.1 also shows that labor productivity growth was higher in the 1990s, in both subperiods, in comparison with the 1980s. However, the rate of growth of productivity is still considerably below the level of the import-substitution period. This is not surprising since there is a well-established positive correlation between output and productivity growth.[6]

The results in table 2.1 show that the effects of the debt crisis were powerful. Yet the crisis did not immediately lead to a dramatic change in policy orientation in Brazil, at least in the direction of liberalization. Arguably, the extremely successful growth performance of the post-war period (with an average rate of growth of 7.45 percent) led to considerable inertia in policy formulation. The 1980s were marked by heterodox stabilization plans that built on the structuralist explanations of inflation, according to which inflation was caused mainly by balance of payments constraints, and propagated by generalized indexation (Arida and Lara-Resende 1985). According to this view, both a fixed exchange rate and deindexation were crucial for successful stabilization. All the heterodox plans (Cruzado, Cruzado II, Verão, and Bresser) froze domestic prices and eliminated wage indexation rules in order to eliminate inertial inflation.[7]

According to the structuralist view, two problems still remained elusive in the early 1990s and made any attempts at stabilization problematic. First, indexation prevented incomes from being eroded, but also tended to freeze the pre-existing set of relative prices. This set of relative prices did not necessarily correspond to the equilibrium set, that is, the one that was desired by economic agents. Hence, a price freeze and the elimination of indexation rules also tended to freeze an out-of-equilibrium relative price structure. When the freeze was removed, prices exploded as agents tried to impose their incompatible income claims. In this case, Amadeo (1994) suggests a social pact is needed if stabilization is to succeed.

The second problem was the outflow of capital caused by the debt crisis. In fact, the debt crises not only eliminated external finance but also reversed the direction of capital flows, forcing a huge drain of resources from Brazil to developed countries (Cardoso and Fishlow 1988). Figure 2.1 shows the large trade surpluses (positive *BT*) that were generated in order to pay for the service of the foreign debt, and the variation in the real exchange rate (*E*) needed to obtain those surpluses. A trade deficit of 2.2 percent of GDP in 1980 was transformed into a trade surplus of 5.9 percent of GDP in 1984. It must be emphasized that this was achieved through large devaluations (expenditure switching) and also by a reduction in the rate of growth (expenditure changing).

In 1987 the foreign exchange shortage led to the suspension of external debt service payments. The episode was short lived and Brazil resumed payments in 1988. Not long after the Brazilian moratorium, in

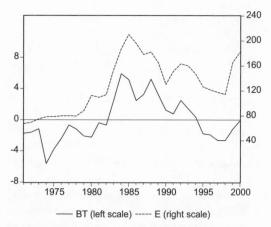

FIGURE 2.1 Trade Balance and Real Exchange Rate

Source: FGV Dados (n.d.).

March 1989 the U.S. government announced the Brady Plan. Recognition that the existing debt could not be serviced on its original terms led to the major program of restructuring the terms of obligations. The Brady Plan and the structural adjustment loans of the World Bank were negotiated on the basis of Brazil's capacity to repay, which, in turn, was seen as being dependent on the implementation of the reforms. This indicates that, although it may take some time, debt crises are instrumental in forcing countries into restructuring their economies along market-friendly lines.

In the early 1990s, contemporaneously with the Brady negotiations, capital flows returned to Latin America, and brought along with them the new problem of how to cope with increasing and volatile capital inflows (Agosin and French-Davis 1996). Figure 2.2 shows that the resumption of capital flows, represented by the change in the sign of the capital account (KA), led to an unprecedented accumulation of foreign reserves (FR). Foreign reserves went from being less than $10 billion after the default to approximately $60 billion in the late 1990s. According to Calvo, Leiderman, and Reinhart (1993), the central reason for the reversion in the direction of capital flows was external, namely, the recession in the United States and the reduction in U.S. interest rates.

The main problem in the early 1990s was whether to implement the reforms after or simultaneously with the stabilization of the economy. Stabilization was not seen as a pre-condition for the actual

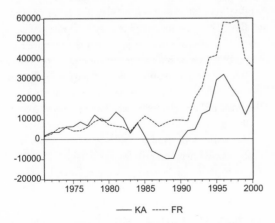

FIGURE 2.2 Capital Account and Foreign Reserves

Source: Banco Central do Brazil (n.d.).

execution of the reforms.[8] In fact, one of the arguments for trade liberalization was that it would have a stabilizing effect on the price of tradable goods. The Collor Plan, implemented in March 1990, was the last of six heterodox stabilization plans, all of which failed in bringing down the rates of inflation to reasonable levels. As with all previous plans, stability was short lived. The generally accepted conclusion was that heterodoxy failed, and a great deal of orthodoxy was needed to solve the inflationary problem.

The failure of the plan and of trade and financial reform was accompanied by a considerable increase in the central bank foreign reserve levels. As shown in figure 2.2, it is only in the aftermath of the Collor Plan that foreign reserves start to be accumulated. This accumulation of reserves allowed a successful exchange rate–based stabilization plan in 1994, along the lines of plans implemented in other Latin American economies. The Real Plan was designed to follow the consensus on shock therapy, which appeared to include some of the lessons from the heterodox plans of the 1980s. According to Bruno (1993, 7), "The root of high chronic inflation, like hyperinflation, turns out to lie in the existence of a large public-sector deficit, the quasi-stability of the dynamic process...[comes] from an inherent inertia strongly linked with a high degree of indexation or accommodation of the key nominal magnitudes (wages, the exchange rate, and monetary aggregates) to the lagged movements of the price level."

The adoption of a fixed exchange rate regime would eliminate the propagation mechanism, but successful stabilization would require fiscal reform. In general, the explanation for the advantages of exchange rates as anchors is rooted in the literature on credibility and time consistency rather than on inertial inflation (Edwards 1995, 101). With respect to exchange rate regimes, this debate has been translated into the consensual view that fixed exchange rate systems create environments that are more prone to producing fiscal discipline and low inflation. The argument is that if foreign central banks were committed to price stability, then a worldwide concerted assault on inflation would be successful. In this sense, fixing the exchange rate might be a good strategy for fighting inflation. This was the basic argument in favor of the exchange rate–based stabilization policies in Latin America, in particular in the Southern Cone stabilization plans of the 1970s and in the Convertibility Plan in Argentina.

Interestingly enough, the Brazilian exchange rate–based stabilization plan seems to be more related to the heterodox plans of the 1980s than what is generally assumed.[9] First, the deindexation process was engineered in a way that resembles the so-called Larida proposal of the mid-1980s. A new unit of account that corrected for inflation by the average of three different inflation indexes was introduced. Inflation accelerated in the old currency, while the new unit of account was unaffected by inflation. This process had a great advantage over the previous price freezes, since it allowed relative prices to change before the monetary reform. The adjustment of relative prices in the transition period increased the distributive neutrality of monetary reform.[10]

Second, and most importantly, Brazil never proceeded with the fiscal adjustment that was crucial for the consensus therapists. In fact, as a quick inspection of Table 2.2 shows, in the first half of the 1990s primary fiscal surpluses (revenue minus spending excluding interest payments) were obtained and coexisted with high inflation, and the primary deficit only increased after the Real Plan. In contrast, the operational deficit had been high all through the 1990s, with the exception of 1993 and 1994, but exploded after the Mexican crisis of December 1994. In other words, the fiscal results worsened after stabilization.

Furthermore, the Mexican crisis forced interest rates up, directly impacting debt servicing and leading to an operational deficit of 9.4 percent of GDP in 1999. The hike in interest rates and the relatively lower rates of growth associated with the need to reduce current account deficits led to the increase in net public debt from 29.2 percent of GDP in 1994 to

almost 50 percent in 1999. These negative trends have since been reversed to a considerable extent. Growth resumed in the aftermath of the 1999 depreciation, and interest rates were reduced from more than 40 percent on an annual basis to 16.5 percent. Yet, despite the recent improvement, the evidence clearly shows that the public deficit, especially the operational deficit, and public debt increased after the stabilization. The fiscal results indicate that the fiscal problems are the result of the stabilization process and not the cause of inflationary pressures.[11]

Bacha (1994) argues that the fiscal deficits in Brazil are repressed, and that a better measure of the deficits would be what he calls the potential deficit. According to this view, Brazilian inflation does indeed have its fundamental cause in a fiscal imbalance. Potential deficit is measured as the actual deficit inserted in the official budget approved in Congress. Potential deficits are extremely large, and according to the estimates quoted by Bacha (1994, 9), it would be around 10 percent of GDP in 1991, when the operational deficit was at 1.4 percent of GDP. Inflation is the mechanism that represses the potential deficit, since the budget calculations assume a lower rate of inflation than the actual rate of inflation. As a result, spending is eroded, while all revenues are indexed. This result implies the existence of an inverse Olivera-Tanzi effect, that is, a negative relationship between inflation and deficits.

Looking at the operational deficit and the GDP deflator evolution in the 1990s, there is some evidence of the existence of a negative Olivera-Tanzi effect. A cursory look at the data shows that in the early part of the 1990s, the operational deficit fell while the inflation rate soared after the failure of the Collor Plan. The reverse is true after the Real Plan, when the rates of inflation approached international levels but the operational deficit increased steadily.

The fact that operational deficits have soared after the Real Plan, and continued increasing even after the crisis of January 1999, leads one to suspect that it is the financial component of the deficits that is problematic. One way to evaluate whether the potential deficit hypothesis or the financial hypothesis is the correct one is to look at various federal government spending categories. This would give us a more accurate picture of the composition of government spending. The potential deficit hypothesis implies that after stabilization, those spending categories that were repressed would rise. According to this view,

TABLE 2.2 Public Surplus, Public Debt (% GDP)

Year	Primary Surplus	Operational Surplus	Net Public Debt
1991	2.8	−1.4	37.9
1992	2.3	−2.2	37.2
1993	2.7	0.3	33.0
1994	5.3	1.4	29.2
1995	0.4	−4.9	30.5
1996	−0.1	−3.8	33.3
1997	−1.0	−4.3	34.5
1998	0.01	−7.5	42.4
1999	3.2	−9.4	49.5
2000	3.5	−1.2	49.5

Source: Roberto Macedo (2000) and Banco Central do Brazil (n.d.).

TABLE 2.3 Federal Government Spending by Category (%)

Year	Interest on Domestic Debt	Wages and Salaries	Transfers to States and Cities
1991	0.10	32.2	25.2
1992	10.9	32.3	24.0
1993	16.2	29.7	20.4
1994	7.1	38.3	19.3
1995	7.8	39.3	20.3
1996	10.2	37.9	19.7
1997	8.4	35.2	19.3
1998	12.5	31.9	18.2
1999	15.0	30.6	20.4
2000	10.0	22.6	15.6

Source: FGV Dados (n.d.).

federal transfer to states and cities, and wage and salary expenses, would rise, since those categories are considered problematic. On the other hand, according to the financial hypothesis, the interest payments on debt would increase.

Table 2.3 reveals that the financial component of the deficit is increasing in the second part of the 1990s. It can be seen that interest payments on debt service rise from 7.1 percent of total government spending in 1994 to 15 percent of government spending in 1999. In the first part of the 1990s, as a result of the Collor Plan, interest payments fluctuated a great deal. On the other hand, wages and salaries expenses have been remarkably constant, while transfers to states and cities have been falling steadily. The evolution of fiscal policy shows that the conventional view—according to which sound fiscal policies and the increased openness promoted by the reforms are the backbone of macroeconomic stability—do not seem to have empirical foundation in the case of Brazil.

It is correct to argue that reforms were influential in the reversion of capital flows in the 1990s, and capital inflows were crucial for the exchange rate–based stabilization program. In that respect, reforms were instrumental for price stability. However, the reforms and the capital inflows created several further imbalances. The high rate of interest needed to attract capital flows worsened fiscal deficits, and led to the appreciation of the exchange rate. This, in turn, led to recurrent problems of balance of payments sustainability.

In addition, the combination of current and capital account liberalization has imposed considerable adjustment pressures in particular on the ability of the government to use both monetary policy and fiscal policy for domestic purposes. The stabilization-cum-liberalization had severe effects on the ability to grow without generating unsustainable current account deficits, and led to increasing unemployment and worsening income distribution, as far as wage differentials are concerned (Amadeo 1996). The following sections deal with those imbalances.

3. Openness and Growth

The notion that trade liberalization is an optimal development strategy has become a dominant feature of mainstream economics. In addition, the notion that capital openness leads to higher rates of growth is also part of conventional wisdom. Above all, the contrasting experiences of the relatively closed Latin American economies and the relatively open East Asian countries have led many authors (e.g., World Bank 1993; Edwards 1995) to argue that outward-oriented development strategies are more conducive to growth.[12]

However, the literature on the advantages of economic openness is far from being consensual. Measures of openness do not seem to be consistent across studies (Pritchett 1996). Taylor (1991b, 100) argues that structuralist models of both commodity and capital flows suggest that "openness or a hands-off policy in either market will not necessarily lead to faster growth or less costly adjustment to external shocks." Further, Rodriguez and Rodrik (1999) find little evidence that open trade policies are significantly associated with higher growth. In their recent study on the effects of structural adjustment reforms in Latin America, Stallings and Peres (2000) find that capital and current account liberalization had a significant but small effect on growth.

At first glance, the Brazilian experience lends little support for the notion that there is a positive correlation between openness and growth. If one classifies the 1948 to 1980 period as inward oriented, 1981 to 1989 as the crisis or transition period, and the 1990s as outward oriented, then one must conclude that import substitution was quite successful (see table 2.1).[13] In Brazil's case, at least, it is difficult to agree with Edwards's (1995, 41) view, according to which "the ever-growing presence of the state in the 1950–80 period eventually stifled efficiency and growth."

According to the conventional view, the protectionist policies that dominated the agenda in Latin American economies generated an anti-export bias that discouraged both the growth and diversification of exports. Two channels were responsible for the relatively poor export performance. First, tariffs and quotas increased the cost of imported intermediate and capital goods used to produce exportable goods. Second, protectionist policies were, in general, complemented by overvalued real exchange rates that reduced the competitiveness of exports.

In Brazil's case it is clear that at least from the late 1960s onwards, there has been a concern with maintaining a relatively competitive exchange rate regime in order to promote exports.[14] On the other hand, the reduction of tariff and non-tariff barriers was only intensified in the late 1980s. That is, trade liberalization started in the period of high inflation.

Figure 2.3 shows the reduction of average tariffs for consumption (TCG), capital (TKG), and intermediate goods (TIG), and the reduced dispersion of the tariff structure. Note that by the late 1980s, tariffs were already lower than in the 1960s and were considerably lower than the tariff levels during the oil shocks and the debt crisis. This suggests that the main restriction to imports after the debt crisis was the shortage of foreign exchange rather than protectionism per se (Resende 2000).

Note that tariffs reached their highest levels during the two oil shocks and the debt crisis. One would expect that during this period of reduced openness, domestic demand forces would be the main forces driving output growth, while in the 1990s growth would be export led.[15] Following the decomposition of effective demand presented by Berg and Taylor (2000), however, one finds that the opposite is true. In fact, the early 1980s up to 1994 may be characterized as a period of export-led stagnation, while the post-stabilization period has been a domestic demand–led stagnation.

As figure 2.4 shows, up to the debt crisis, growth was led by domestic demand, where the domestic stance (DS) is given by public and private investment over the national savings rate. This has also been true since 1994, whereas the period from the debt crisis in 1982 to the Real Plan in 1994 was export led. The foreign stance (FS) is defined as exports over the import propensity, and X represents aggregate supply.[16]

Breaking down the components of the domestic stance is a difficult task, since data on public and private investment are usually presented together in the Brazilian national accounts. There is some evidence that the bulk of the reduction in total investment in the 1980s was caused by the reduction of public investment, especially investment carried out by public enterprises (Carneiro and Werneck 1993, 66–69). Also, there is evidence that public investment continued to be depressed in the 1990s, a reason that has been frequently used to defend the necessity of the privatization process. Hence, it is reasonable to

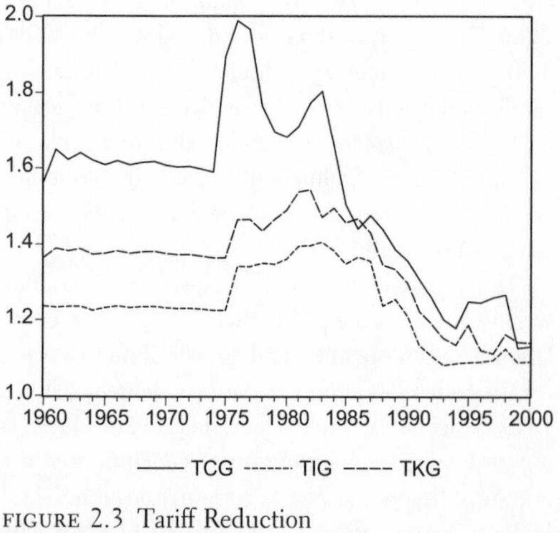

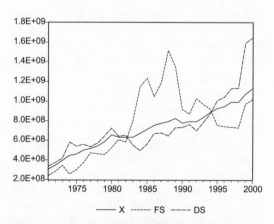

FIGURE 2.3 Tariff Reduction
Source: SECEX (n.d.).

FIGURE 2.4 Demand Decomposition
Source: FGV Dados (n.d.) and author's calculations.

assume that the domestic stance in the 1970s was led by public investment and in the 1990s was dominated by private investment, which, however, did not reach the levels of the 1970s.

For consumption, however, the story is reversed with an increase in government consumption in the mid-1980s. Government consumption increased from around 10 percent of GDP in the 1970s to 18 percent in the 1990s. Private consumption, in contrast, was around 70 percent in the 1970s and stands at a little bit more than 60 percent in the 1990s. Private consumption fell in the high inflation period, but it never recovered the levels of the 1970s. Furthermore, there is no indication that the liberalization process led to a considerable change in the level or the (private and public) composition of consumption.

In short, the evolution of the domestic stance shows that while in the 1970s government investment and private consumption were the crucial components of demand, in the late 1990s private investment and government consumption became more significant. It is also important to note that the swings in the domestic stance have been considerably smaller than the changes in the foreign stance. The foreign stance swings are related to the debt crisis and the Real Plan, changing signs in 1982 and 1994. Those swings in the foreign stance show the difficulties in restoring and maintaining economic growth in the face of external imbalances.

In fact, it appears that the liberalization process increased import penetration without reducing the anti-export bias of the Brazilian economy. Table 2.4 shows the evolution of the rates of growth of export and import volumes from the 1980s onwards. In the 1990s there is clearly an explosion in the rate of growth of the volume of imports. The rate of growth of the volume of exports, on the other hand, is lower on average in the 1990s than in the 1980s. That is, in the 1980s the rate of growth of exports averaged 11.5 percent, whereas in the relatively more open 1990s the rate of growth of exports was 5.8 percent.

TABLE 2.4 Exports and Imports (% Growth)

	Exports	Imports
1970–1980	15.5	~2.1
1981–1989	11.5	~1.4
1990–2000	5.8	14.3

Source: IPEA Data (n.d.).

The increase in import penetration, in conjunction with the sluggish rate of growth of exports, in the context of a relatively open economy spells trouble for the sustainability of the current account. Furthermore, the exchange rate stabilization plan—which meant appreciated and relatively fixed exchange rates—implies that lower rates of growth are instrumental in keeping the current account under control. These lower rates of output growth explain the fall in the rate of growth of imports.

One may conclude that trade liberalization intensified the balance of payments restrictions imposed on the economy. Following Amadeo (1996), we develop a simple framework to analyze the restrictions on economic growth imposed by external imbalances. We assume that the balance of trade (BT) is a negative function of the rate of growth of domestic output (G) and a positive function of the real exchange rate (E).

The BT line in figure 2.5 represents the equilibrium in the trade account for a given rate of growth and real exchange rate, and for a given degree of openness. As correctly pointed out by Amadeo (1996, 6), the liberalization process leads to a movement of the BT line to the southeast from BT0 to BT1.[17] In other words, an economy in the surplus region (below BT0) would be in the deficit region (above BT1) after liberalization, even if it remained at the same initial position (constant growth and real exchange rate). The stylized trajectory of the economy in countries that implemented stabilization-cum-liberalization plans indicates that initially the rate of growth

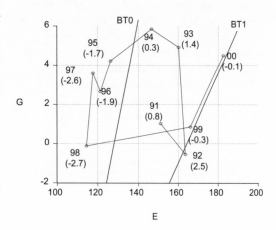

FIGURE 2.5 Trade Deficits and Growth

Source: FGV Dados (n.d.).

increases and the exchange rate appreciates. Eventually, the unsustainable size of the trade deficit leads to a combination of low rates of growth and depreciation. The dilemma is whether to move higher growth by promoting a nominal depreciation (Brazil and Mexico) or by domestic deflation (Argentina).

The actual evolution of the Brazilian economy closely follows the stylized pattern described above. Figure 2.5 shows the rate of growth of real GDP and the real exchange rate, and the data in parentheses represent the balance of trade deficit $(-)$ or surplus $(+)$ as a proportion of GDP. The rate of growth has consistently been falling after the Real Plan, and even after the depreciation of January 1999, growth has remained at relatively low levels for the trade deficit to be sustainable.

Furthermore, there is some evidence that the BT curve moved to the southeast and is more flat in the post-stabilization period. Figure 2.5 shows that the position in 2000 would have represented a surplus position in the early 1990s, whereas now it is in the deficit position, showing the movement of BT to the southeast. Also estimating the income and price elasticities of BT, I found that after liberalization, the trade account has become more sensitive to real GDP than to the real exchange rate. Table 2.5 shows the income and price elasticities of BT and imports (M).[18] As can be seen, the income elasticity is higher in both cases in the post-stabilization period, while the opposite is true for the price elasticity.

We also included the more conventional estimates of the income and price elasticities of imports, since they give a more clear understanding of the impact of liberalization. The income elasticity of imports increased from 0.81 to 2.34 in the two periods.[19] The main consequence of the rise in the income elasticity of imports and the reduction of the price elasticity (from 0.06 to 0.03) is that in order to grow faster without generating trade deficits, the real exchange rate would have to be considerably more devalued than it currently is. The impossibility of maintaining a

depreciated currency in an economy that is more open to capital flow movements may very well imply that the economy will be trapped in stop-go cycles in the near future. That is, relatively low levels of growth continue to be instrumental in the achievement of a sustainable trade account deficit.

Yet one suspects that the defenders of the liberalization process expected the rise in the income elasticity of imports. In their view, the structural change promoted by a higher degree of openness would have certain costs, but those costs would be overweighed by the benefits. Furthermore, trade liberalization, represented by the reduction of tariffs and the elimination of non-tariff barriers, would have to be complemented with the opening of the capital account. This was done in 1991 when the participation of non-residents in domestic financial markets was regulated by law (Annex IV, Resolution 1289/87).[20]

The benefits from capital account opening depended on two events, according to conventional wisdom. First, capital account opening would lead to an inflow of long-term inflows of foreign direct investment (FDI) rather than short-term volatile portfolio flows. Second, it was argued that the inflows of FDI would have a positive impact on productivity, and hence on growth and export performance, allowing the economy to grow faster without incurring balance of payments problems.

The increase in FDI flows relative to portfolio flows was confirmed, at least since 1995, as can be seen in figure 2.6, in which both flows are measured in proportion to GDP. Regarding the positive effects of FDI on growth, the evidence is controversial and more difficult to ascertain.

The theoretical justification for the benevolent view of the role of FDI is based on the notion that transnational firms are the main vehicles for the introduction of new techniques of production and new products into developing economies for which domestic firms do not have the know-how. In this view, FDI should raise efficiency, expand output, and lead to higher economic growth in the host country (Moran 1998, 20). In contrast, the maligned model of FDI and development assumes that instead of filling the gap between savings and investment, FDI may lower domestic savings and investment by driving domestic firms out of business and using imported inputs (Moran 1998, 21).[21]

Dutt (1998, 283) develops a North-South model in the structuralist tradition in which "one should

TABLE 2.5 Income and Price Elasticities

Elasticity	1971–1989		1990–2000	
	BT	M	BT	M
Income	−0.01	0.81	−0.05	2.34
Price	0.06	−0.26	0.03	−0.08[a]

a. Statistically insignificant.

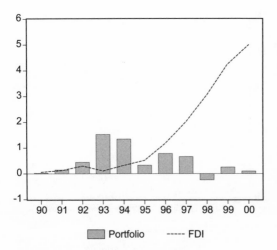

FIGURE 2.6 Capital Flows (% GDP)

carefully distinguish between different types of *FDI* before concluding that the effects of *FDI* on Southern development are good or bad." The model assumes that there are two countries, North and South, and two goods produced under fix-price and flex-price conditions along Kaleckian lines. According to the model, FDI flows from the northern to the southern country would have a positive impact on growth in the South if foreign investment goes to the production of the northern good, which is produced under oligopolistic conditions (fix price). The reverse is true if FDI goes to the production of the southern good that is produced under competitive conditions (flex price).

In the same vein, Agosin and Mayer (2000) developed a theoretical model that identifies whether FDI crowds out or crowds in domestic investment. The authors run a regression of the domestic investment to GDP ratio on the rate of growth of output (acceleration principle), and on the FDI to GDP ratio, both variables with several lags. They verify that FDI is not directly correlated with GDP. Their results show that the positive impacts of FDI on domestic investment are not assured. In the case of Latin America, the results show that FDI has had a negative effect on domestic investment. In the case of Asian countries, however, FDI has crowded in domestic investment.

In Brazil's case, their results are statistically insignificant. Following Stallings and Peres (2000, 86–87), I run a regression of the rate of domestic investment on capacity utilization, FDI, and some indicators of macroeconomic instability,[22] namely, the variation of the real exchange rate, $D(E)$, and a dummy for high inflation. The results are summarized in table 2.6.

A first glance, Table 2.6 shows that capacity utilization has a positive impact on domestic investment, as would be expected. Also, FDI has a positive impact on the domestic investment ratio, which runs against the other results in the literature. Finally, the macroeconomic instability variables have the expected signs, with the change in the real exchange rate and high inflation having a negative effect on investment, but are generally not significant in statistical terms.

TABLE 2.6 Determinants of Domestic Investment (1971–2000)

Independent Variable	(1)	(2)	(3)	(4)	(5)
Constant	2.8 (39.1)	2.8 (33.9)	−5.66 (−1.4)	−5.2 (−3.9)	2.7 (112.7)
Capacity	0.15 (4.1)	0.13 (3.6)	1.91 (2.3)	1.92 (6.7)	1.6[a] (31.1)
FDI	0.05 (1.3)	0.05[a] (2.3)	0.05 (2.2)	0.05 (6.6)	0.02 (2.5)
$D(E)$		−0.03 (−1.4)	−0.06 (−3.4)		
High Inflation	−0.05 (−0.6)				
Trend				−0.02 (−15.3)	
R^2	0.65	0.81	0.72	0.95	0.98
Adj. R^2	0.59	0.74	0.66	0.94	0.98

Source: FGV IMF Dados (n.d.), and IBGE (*t* statistics shown in parentheses). The dependent variable is the domestic investment to GDP ratio in (1) to (4), and domestic investment to capital stock ratio in (5). Capacity is measured as the rate of growth of GDP in (1) and (2). Capacity utilization is measured as the gap between actual and potential GDP in (3) and (4). Several measures of potential GDP were estimated, and the one used was estimated with a Hodrick-Prescott filter. Finally, capacity was measured as the output to capital stock ratio in (5). FDI is also divided by the current dollar value of GDP in (1) to (4), and as a ratio to the stock of capital in (5). The high inflation dummy is 0 for rates of inflation lower than 400, and 1 otherwise. Other inflation values were used with similar results.

a. Variable with a one period lag.

The results of the effects of macroeconomic instability on domestic investment should be read with caution. The effects of exchange rate variation and high inflation are not robust, despite the fact that in regression (3) the coefficient for $D(E)$ is significant. This seems to indicate that instability does not affect investment in a meaningful way. This result contradicts most econometric studies on the subject.

The coefficient for FDI is significant in four of the five regressions presented in table 2.5, and the size and statistical significance are relatively insensitive to the model specification and to the lag structure adopted. This result, however, should not be taken as a complete vindication of the positive effects of FDI. In the first place, the effects of FDI on domestic capital accumulation are relatively small. An increase of FDI of 5 percent would have an impact of somewhere in between 0.25 and 0.1 percent in domestic investment. Second, this analysis says nothing about the effects of FDI on the balance of payments.

Arguably, only greenfield FDI would have a positive effect on domestic investment and growth, since it will not compete directly with already established firms in the host country. On the other hand, mergers and acquisitions (M&A) or brownfield FDI inflows could have a negative effect on domestic investment.

Around 30 percent of all FDI inflows go to the privatization process, 20 percent correspond to M&A, and the rest go to the modernization of already established multinational firms or new multinational firms. That is, around half of FDI inflows imply only a change in the ownership. Arguably, this change in ownership might lead to an improvement in management and an eventual increase in productivity. Moreira (1999, 343) argues that foreign ownership (defined as foreign ownership of the majority of the voting capital) has a positive effect on labor productivity.

The weight of the evidence indicates that, although positive, the effects of FDI have been negligible. Another result from the equations in table 2.6 is that the principle of acceleration is significant and probably the driving force of domestic investment. In that sense, domestic investment did not recover to the levels of the 1970s, mainly because output growth or capacity utilization did not recover either. In addition, the main reason for lower rates of growth in the second part of the 1990s has been associated with the need to keep the balance of trade under control. Yet, the combination of current account liberalization

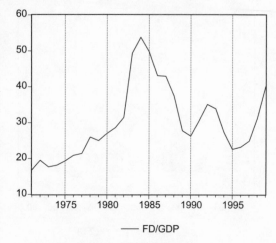

— FD/GDP

FIGURE 2.7 Foreign Debt Instability

Source: IPEA and FGV Dados (n.d.).

with an exchange rate–based stabilization program and the consequent appreciation of the domestic currency led to a perverse structural change and the persistence of relatively high trade deficits during the second half of the 1990s.

As is well known, current account deficits imply the need to attract capital flows to finance the deficit. In other words, the deficit country becomes a debtor. The increase in foreign debt (FD) to GDP ratio can be seen in figure 2.7. The foreign debt to GDP ratio started growing after the Real Plan and reached 40 percent in 1999 (that corresponds to the debt crisis). Since the depreciation, with the reduction in the current account deficit and the higher rates of growth of GDP, one can see that foreign debt to GDP ratios are stabilizing.

Two important conclusions may be derived from the Brazilian experience that shed light on the growth and openness debate. On the one hand, it is clear that a relatively depreciated—more depreciated than before the reforms—currency is essential to maintain growth and a balanced current account. The main consequence of the need for a depreciated currency is a rate of inflation higher than the rest of the world. In fact, in 2000 the Consumer Price Index was 6 percent, and the GDP deflator was 7.4 percent. These rates will pose difficulties for the Central Bank that is adopting a strategy of inflation targeting (Bogdanski, Tombini, and Werlang 2000). In fact, the accumulated inflation in the first quarter of 2001 already encompasses half of the total target for the year.

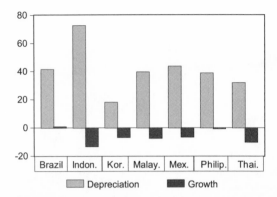

FIGURE 2.8 Contractionary Devaluation

On the other hand, the Brazilian experience is peculiar, since depreciation did not lead to a considerable contraction as in most developing countries. In general, depreciation leads to a contractionary adjustment if the economy has a trade deficit or if it redistributes income to capitalists (Krugman and Taylor 1978). That is, if the volume of imports is high and its value increases, the contraction of output may be the only way to reduce the trade deficit. Also, if the redistributive effect of depreciation increases the income of low spending groups, then, too, a contraction of output follows. The evidence on nominal exchange rate depreciation and real growth presented in figure 2.8 shows that in all cases, a steep recession follows depreciation.

This raises the question of what is different about the Brazilian case that accounts for the relatively painless depreciation. If one looks at balance of payment (BoP) crises through the perspective of the so-called Frenkel-Neftci (N-F) cycles described by Taylor (2004), one obtains some insight. In particular, according to the N-F logic, a BoP crisis depends on a relatively fixed and appreciated exchange rate, a deregulated domestic financial system, and a liberalized capital account. Furthermore, high interest rates in the domestic market vis-à-vis returns to foreign assets and the consequent capital inflows lead to portfolio positions that are usually long on domestic assets and short on foreign holdings. The mismatch is twofold. Maturities are different and revenues and debts are denominated in different currencies, carrying foreign exchange risk.

In this environment, depreciation occurs when no local interest rate is high enough to attract more capital inflows. The effects are magnified beyond the

usual contractionary effects, since liability dollarization leads to widespread defaults, which, in turn, lead to a debt-deflation spiral. Additionally, this has negative effects on the finance, insurance, and real estate (FIRE) sector, leading to costly bailouts with negative fiscal consequences.

Although the Brazilian economy presented almost all of the above-mentioned characteristics of the N-F cycle, there were some conspicuous differences. First, the bailout of the banking sector preceded the 1999 depreciation. Most banks profited from the high inflation years, since indexation meant that the use of checking deposits was widespread despite high inflation. But banks could maintain interest on a large part of demand deposits below inflation, since most people would accept some compensation rather than none. Further, the federal government compensated the banking sector for holding public debt with extremely high rates of interest. Stabilization wiped out these profitable opportunities, and as a result the banking sector share of GDP fell from 12.7 percent in the 1990–1994 period to 6.9 percent in 1995 (Carvalho 1998).

Additionally, in the midst of the stabilization plan, the central bank drastically increased reserve requirements to reduce credit and contain demand pressures. The collapse of Economico and Nacional, two of the largest national banks, and the fears of a systemic banking crisis led the government to launch the Programa de Estímulo à Reestruturação e ao Sistema Financeiro Nacional (PROER). The program promotes the financing of the bad loans of problem banks by imposing the absorption of them by healthy institutions along the lines that the Federal Reserve Board used later in the case of long-term capital management (LTCM).

Second, Brazilian regulations do not allow deposits in foreign currency (dollars) in domestic institutions. That measure and the widespread use of indexation during the high-inflation period imply that Brazil has a relatively small degree of liability dollarization. As a result of these two characteristics, debt-deflation processes were relatively weak in Brazil.[23] However, if it is true that Brazil did not suffer a major recession after devaluing, it is also true that the economy was growing relatively slowly before. All in all, the effects of openness have been lower rates of growth and persistent current account deficits.

Furthermore, the incipient recovery of 2000 may be less robust than is usually assumed, since investments in infrastructure have been minimal in the last decade. The 4.5 percent growth of real GDP in 2000 put on display the limitations of the policies pursued in the last decade. Investment in energy production and distribution has been below the level needed to maintain potential growth. As a result, the federal government is imposing severe restrictions on energy consumption. On average, industrial users will reduce their energy consumption by 20 percent in 2001. In some sectors (e.g., aluminum and cement), the reduction will be as much as 25 percent.

In sum, both the persistent current account deficits and the supply-side constraints associated with the lack of investment in infrastructure during the last decade imply that the economy is stuck in a low-level equilibrium trap. This poor macroeconomic performance has had, as one would expect, a negative impact on the labor market performance, as I discuss in the following section.

4. Unemployment, Income Distribution, and Poverty

Note that when discussing the effects of liberalization and stabilization on the labor market, most economists tend to agree that the elimination of the inflation tax and the redistribution toward wages would cause demand pressures to build up. In the absence of a negotiable social pact, contractionary demand policies were then seen as the only alternative. In other words, in a wage-led economy, if stability leads to higher wages, then contractionary fiscal and monetary policies are advisable.[24]

Yet, when we look at the long-term evolution of the real minimum wage (see figure 2.9) or the average wage for workers in the formal labor market (see figure 2.10), we find that real wages are lower in the 1990s than in the high-inflation period of the 1980s. Furthermore, real wages were higher in the import-substitution period. Hence, real wages were compressed both in the period of inflation acceleration and in the stabilization phase. There is no clear relation between increasing real wages and higher inflation, although there is a clear relation between higher real wages and a higher growth of real output in the import-substitution period.[25]

In the 1980s, real wages fluctuated a great deal—as a result of the stabilization shocks and inflation resumption—but they fell overall, since indexation

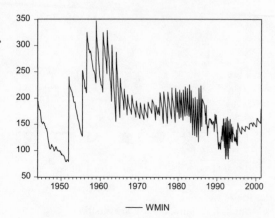

— WMIN

FIGURE 2.9 Minimum Wage

Source: IPEA Data (n.d.).

was less than perfect. In the 1990s, the average real income of workers, as represented in figure 2.10, increased until the middle of the decade and then fell to roughly the same level as at the beginning of the decade. However, the minimum wage, as seen in figure 2.9, displays the exact opposite behavior. It was cut down in the first part of the decade, and it grew back to its initial level during the second half of the decade.

A second set of questions may be asked about the behavior of relative wages in the post-liberalization period. The effects of liberalization on the relative wage structure may be understood with the help of a simple structuralist model with a fix-price/flex-price market distinction (Taylor 1991a, 2001). The fix-price

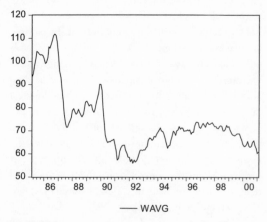

— WAVG

FIGURE 2.10 Average Wage

Source: IPEA Data (n.d.).

sector corresponds to the tradable sector, where markups are assumed to be relatively constant and output and employment are determined by effective demand. In the non-tradable sector, the flex-price market, the labor market works as a buffer absorbing excess supply or demand for labor in the tradable sector. Productivity in the non-tradable sector is considerably lower than in the tradable sector.

Liberalization switches demand toward imports leading to trade deficits and reducing output in the tradable sector. In addition, real appreciation weakens the tradable sector even more. Workers are then absorbed in the non-tradable sector, so that the overall rate of unemployment, at least initially, does not increase much. Assuming for simplicity's sake that the tradable sector corresponds to the industrial sector, and that services are the non-tradable sector, one may conclude that liberalization leads to a process of deindustrialization. Using the data on the metropolitan area of São Paulo, Brazil's industrial core, we find that in 1990 48.7 percent of all workers in the private sector were employed in the industrial sector, whereas in 1999 only 32 percent were employed in the industrial sector. The reverse is true in the case of services, with an increase from 32.9 to 48.8 percent of total employed workers. This tends to confirm Pieper's (2000) argument that Brazil is an acute case of output deindustrialization.

In addition, the increasing exposure to foreign competition implies that there is a change in relative prices against the tradable sector. According to conventional wisdom, the rise in the price of non-tradable goods relative to tradable goods might lead to a fall in the real wage in the non-tradable sector and hence to an increase in the demand for labor in that sector. In other words, the fall in real wages allows labor demand to increase and reduces unemployment. According to the structuralist view, the level of employment in the non-tradable sector also depends on effective demand. If effective demand is increasing in the non-tradable sector, then the capacity to increase employment is enhanced. To the extent that wages are able to keep pace with prices, wages in the non-tradable sector may or may not rise relative to wages in the tradable sector.

Once again, if we use the data for the metropolitan area of São Paulo, we can see in figure 2.11 that the average income of the non-tradable sector (WNT) is rising against the average income of the industrial sector (WT). The data contradict the conventional

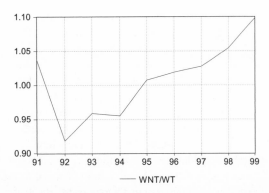

FIGURE 2.11 Relative Wages

Source: SEADE.

view, since there seems to be a positive correlation between employment and wages. That is, the relative increase in the level of employment in the services sector is accompanied by a relative increase in wages.

Furthermore, according to the conventional view based on the factor price equalization theorem of the Hecksher-Ohlin (H-O) model, it is commonly argued that liberalization would narrow the skilled-unskilled wage ratio in the South, and widen it in the North. Figure 2.12 shows the relative wages of workers with a college degree or more (skilled, WSK) relative to workers with unfinished primary school (unskilled, WNSK). As can be seen, the result contradicts the H-O model. This result confirms what Wood calls the Latin American challenge to the East Asian conventional wisdom, that is, greater trade openness in Latin America has been accompanied by rising wage inequality.

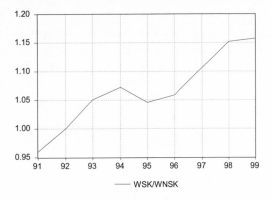

FIGURE 2.12 Relative Wages

Source: DIEESE (n.d.).

The structural change caused by liberalization led to a rising wage gap between skilled and non-skilled workers. One possible explanation is that by introducing new technologies, the process of liberalization increases the bargaining power of skilled workers (Amadeo 1996). Another possible explanation, put forward by Wood (1997), is that the entry of low-wage Asian countries (e.g., Bangladesh, China, India, Indonesia, and Pakistan) altered the competitive advantage of middle-income countries like Brazil.

In addition to the wage gap, it must be noted that the quality of jobs created in different sectors diverges greatly. Amadeo and Pero (2000) argue that the quality of jobs created in the services sector is worse than that in the industrial sector. In that sense, they suggest that unemployment is not a good measure of labor market conditions. Table 2.7 shows that even unemployment, a relatively poor indicator of the labor market, considerably worsens in the latter half of the 1990s. Open unemployment increased more than 80 percent from 1995 to 1999 from 4.6 to 8.4 percent, before falling in 2000.

Furthermore, when we look at the data on hidden or disguised unemployment for the metropolitan region of São Paulo we find a similar pattern, with rates of unemployment soaring in the second part of the decade.[26] In other words, in the first part of the decade, when unemployment rates were increasing and decreasing as part of the cycle, the rate of unemployment was, at best, a poor indicator of the labor market performance. However, in the second part of the decade, it is clear that the economy has accommodated to a situation with higher rates of unemployment.

The higher rates of unemployment reflect the relatively poor performance of the economy in the post–Asian crisis period. However, it is important to note that the increase in unemployment cannot be completely blamed on cyclical or short-run factors. In the first half of the 1990s, unemployment was, on average, lower despite the negative effects of the recession of 1990. One possible explanation is that in the post-stabilization period, the intensification of the liberalization process led to higher rates of unemployment in the long run. If this is the case, the recovery from the 1998–1999 crisis will not be sufficient to reduce unemployment to pre-reform levels.

Figure 2.13 shows that the participation in São Paulo had a slight increase from around 60 percent to 62.5 percent. Hence, the increase in unemployment throughout the 1990s from around 10 to almost 18 percent has to be blamed on the fall of the employed share of population.

The increase in unemployment in the second half of the 1990s, in particular after 1997, masks the different sectoral evolution of employment. Figure 2.14 shows the indexes for employment levels in the economy as a whole (L), the industrial sector (LI), the commerce sector (LC), and the service sector (LS). It is clear that industrial employment has been falling all through the liberalization period, starting in the late 1980s. Employment in the commerce and service sectors, on the other hand, has followed a cyclical pattern. It recovered from the early 1980s recession and fell as much as industrial employment

TABLE 2.7 Unemployment

Year	Open Unemployment[a]	Hidden Unemployment[b]	Total Unemployment[b]
1990	4.3	2.9	10.3
1991	4.5	3.1	10.9
1992	5.8	6.0	15.2
1993	5.3	6.0	14.6
1994	5.5	5.3	14.2
1995	4.6	4.2	13.2
1996	5.4	5.1	15.1
1997	5.7	5.7	16.0
1998	8.1	6.5	18.2
1999	8.4	7.2	19.3
2000	7.8	6.6	17.7

Source: IBGE and DIEESE (n.d.).

a. Data for the six metropolitan regions of Recife, Salvador, Rio de Janeiro, Belo Horizonte, São Paulo, and Porto Alegre.

b. Data for the metropolitan region of São Paulo.

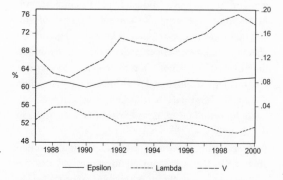

FIGURE 2.13 Labor Decomposition

Source: DIEESE (n.d.).

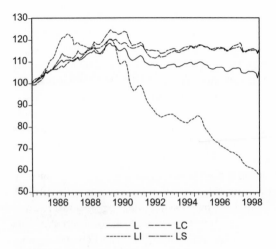

FIGURE 2.14 Employment

Source: DIEESE (n.d.).

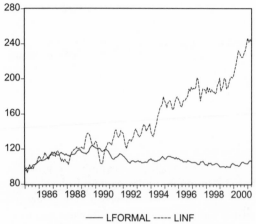

FIGURE 2.15 Formal and Informal Employment

Source: DIEESE (n.d.).

during the recession of the early 1990s. Yet, in contrast with industrial employment, during the 1990s non-industrial employment also fluctuated with the cycle, increasing after the recession in the mid-1990s and falling after the external shocks of the Tequila and Asian crises.

The 1995 to 1997 period, between the Tequila and the Asian crises, is particularly interesting. Industrial employment fell in these two years, but the increased employment in the commerce and service sectors was more than enough to compensate for that fall. As a result, employment in the economy as a whole was relatively constant. This explains why, in contrast with the Argentine experience of exchange rate–based stabilization, unemployment did not immediately increase in Brazil.

Notice that liberalization was marked by another clear trend in the labor market, namely, an increase in the degree of informality of labor relations. Figure 2.15 shows the indexes of workers employed in the formal and informal sectors. According to Amadeo and Pero (2000, 127), the reduction in the share of formal wage earners is associated with the downsizing strategies pursued in the industrial sector after the liberalization process.

In summary, the process of liberalization led to a pronounced decrease in industrial employment and a shift toward the service sector. Also, the increase in informality signals the deterioration of employment conditions. In particular, increasing informality has led some authors to conclude that institutional

reforms are needed in order to improve the quality of the jobs created. In this view, the costs imposed by the payment of benefits on formal contracts are too high and force many firms into hiring in the informal market. Benefits may add 25–30 percent to the costs of manufacturing employment, a range that is within international standards and that cannot justify the massive increase in informality. In short, the main reason for the increase in precarious jobs is the lack of good jobs, and this, in turn, is partially explained by the process of liberalization.

In addition, the effects of the stabilization plan and the reforms in labor markets had repercussions on income distribution. In fact, the improvement in income distribution with the reduction of the inflation tax was considered one of the most important features of stabilization by several government officials (Franco 1999).

In fact, looking at the Gini or Theil T coefficients in the post-stabilization period, one notices a slight improvement with respect to the pre-stabilization period (see table 2.8). Interestingly enough, this trend precedes the Real Plan and dates back to the early 1990s.

This might indicate that the stabilization plan has not contributed significantly to the improvement of income distribution as measured by the Gini coefficient. On the other hand, some authors associate the reduction of almost 25 percent of the poverty rate with the stabilization (Amadeo and Neri 1999).

TABLE 2.8 Income Distribution and Poverty

	1990	1993	1995	1996	1997	1998	1999
Gini	0.62[a]	0.58	0.57	0.57	0.57	0.56	0.58
Theil T	0.78	0.77	0.73	0.73	0.74	0.74	0.72
Poverty	44.2	44.1	33.2	34.1	34.1	33.4	34.9

Source: IBGE (2000).

a. Figure for 1989.

Two factors relating to the evolution of income distribution in the last decade must be emphasized. First, the improvement in income distribution was relatively small, since progress in the base of the distribution is insufficient to improve the Gini coefficient, which is driven by the behavior of the middle quintiles (Rocha 2000, 3). Second, when we look at alternative measures, it is not clear that income distribution did in fact improve during the 1990s.[27] For instance, the share of wages in total income was approximately 51.4 percent in 1993 and only 40.7 percent in 1999. The flip side of the reduction in the share of wages is the increase in the net operational surplus (interest, profits, rents, etc.) from 35.4 to almost 46 percent in the same period.

The reduction in the share of wages in total income indicates that liberalization and increased unemployment dramatically reduced the bargaining power of workers. Furthermore, the maintenance of high interest rates (as part of the exchange rate–based stabilization program) allowed an increase in the remuneration of capital, despite increasing competition from abroad. These results show a considerable worsening in income distribution, in contrast with the picture presented by the Gini coefficient. Part of the explanation for this apparent ambiguity is that both the Gini and the Theil indexes are calculated on the basis of wage income. Hence, the relatively small reduction in inequality in the 1990s reflects a reduction in overall wage inequality, while the share of wages in total income has been compressed. It must also be emphasized that real wages in the 1990s are lower in comparison to the 1980s and the import-substitution period.

A second type of question not directly connected to the discussion of whether the Real Plan improved income distribution is about the relationship between income distribution and poverty. The effects of reduced inequality, as measured by the Gini coefficient, have had negligible effects on poverty reduction. In

fact, Rocha (2000, 6) shows that poverty also fell considerably after the short-lived period of stability during the Cruzado Plan in the mid-1980s, a period in which income distribution was deteriorating. One may conclude that price stability was the main explanatory variable in poverty reduction.

Poverty rates, however, have been falling since the 1970s, according to Rocha (2000). Hence, sources other than price stability are also important for poverty reduction. Output growth is the obvious candidate, but it cannot explain all poverty reduction, since poverty also fell in the first part of the 1980s, a period in which the economy stagnated as a result of the debt crisis. In retrospect, the reduction of poverty was a consequence of industrialization and the consequent migration from rural to urban areas.[28] All in all, cities provide greater access to electricity, treated water, medical care, and public schools. In that respect, Amadeo and Neri (1999) argue that the increases in the minimum wage in the post-stabilization period, that is, after 1994, were sufficient to substantially reduce urban poverty. In short, the increase of the minimum wage in an environment of price stability proved to be an important factor in the reduction of poverty.

The argument, however, is not completely convincing from a long-run perspective, since real minimum wages were constant in the 1970s and falling in the 1980s while poverty was decreasing throughout that period. Hence, a higher real minimum wage is only part of the explanation.

The minimum wage increased by almost 55 percent in real terms from its lowest point in 1994 to 2000, but it is still below the level of the pre-debt crisis period and well below the level of the import-substitution period. The question, then, is why increases in the minimum wage have not been higher. According to the conventional view, the limits imposed on the federal government by social security payments are the main reason for not increasing the minimum wage (Giambiagi and Além 1999). It must be noted that high interest rates and low rates of growth also worsen the fiscal stance, and yet that has not prevented the current administration from pursuing both in its attempt to achieve external equilibrium. This shows that there is a double standard, according to which the increase in the minimum wage is tied to fiscal stability, but interest rate increases are only conditional upon external accounts, irrespective of the fiscal stance. One may conjecture

that social policies are relegated to a secondary position, and that the liberalization policy is the priority
of the current administration. Not surprisingly, the
results on employment and income distribution reflect the government priorities.

5. Policy Alternatives

Brazil's relatively poor performance in terms of growth
rates, unemployment, and income distribution begs
the question of why the government pursued the current strategy. The consensus to pursue liberalization
has foreign and domestic sources. On the foreign front,
the recurring balance of payments problems that were
intensified with the development of the euro-dollar
market and the oil and interest shocks of the 1970s led
to an increasing consensus that outward-oriented
strategies were the only solution. In fact, the United
States used the debt crisis of the early 1980s to impose
liberalization as part of the conditionality agreements
to reschedule the debts of developing countries.

Also, mainstream defenders of outward orientation tended to argue that export-led growth was behind the successful experience of the Asian countries.
Export-led growth was equated with greater integration into the world economy and a laissez-faire approach to trade policy that would lead to a better
allocation of resources and higher rates of growth.[29]
(This argument reached its high point with the
World Bank's [1993] East Asian report, according to
which East Asian economies implemented market-
friendly policies. Several authors have shown the
limitations of the World Bank position.)

On the domestic front, the inability to tame the
inflationary pressures during the 1980s and the failure of the heterodox plans led to the notion that only
orthodox stabilization strategies would work. Thus,
fiscal conservatism complemented outward orientation as part of the lessons of the lost decade.

With respect to outward orientation, despite their
strong export orientation, the East Asian economies
were not fully integrated with the world economy.
Import substitution was an integral part of the East
Asian strategy in the 1950s and 1960s. The equalization of export orientation with free trade is also misleading. At least in the Korean case, the state heavily
intervened in the economy. Besides, the East Asian
financial markets were relatively closed compared to
other underdeveloped regions such as Latin America.

The difference between East Asian and Latin
American economies is of particular interest, since
the former are normally associated with export-led
growth strategies, while the latter are connected with
inward-oriented strategies. While it is true that the
East Asian trade regime was more open that that of
Latin America, the opposite is true when one looks at
the financial regime.[30] Capital flows were much
more heavily regulated in Asian economies at least
until the 1990s. This is the primary reason for the
greater resistance to financial crises displayed by the
Asian economies until the late 1990s, when financial
liberalization was well underway.

One possible implication of the above discussion
is that the nature of the financial regime rather than
the trade regime is more relevant to understanding
the perils of development. In other words, it is not the
difference between inward- and outward-looking development strategies that matters, but the difference
between closed and open financial regimes. Opening
the capital account is supposed to bring financial
inflows that will stimulate investment and productivity growth. This part of the liberal credo remains
wishful thinking in Brazil's case. On the contrary,
liberalization has led to the need to maintain low
rates of growth to keep (or at least try to keep) the
current account under control. One of the consequences of low growth rates has been an increase in
unemployment rates since 1997. The improvement
after the depreciation of 1999 may be short-lived, as
has been dramatically shown by the constraints in
energy supply and the persistent current account
deficit.

Additionally, rising capital inflows following liberalization led to real exchange rate appreciation,
offsetting liberalization's incentives for traded goods
production and increasing the inequality between the
wages of workers in the tradable and non-tradable
sectors. Appreciation, in turn, was linked to high real
interest rates that added to production costs and to
the financial costs of the public debt.

Policy alternatives in an increasingly interdepen-
dent world are difficult to implement. It is true that
the current account liberalization has been consolidated in a series of multilateral and bilateral trade
agreements, in particular the Mercosul, in accordance
with the World Trade Organization (WTO). Thus,
the scope for changes in trade policies, even when
desirable, is limited. However, the recent discussions
on the Brazilian AIDS policies, and the favorable

ruling by the WTO on the Brazilian dispute with Canada over subsidies to EMBRAER, the Brazilian airspace company, show that there is some room for alternative policies. In addition, capital account liberalization has been incomplete in Brazil, and the possibilities for change are open, in particular, after the wave of criticism that the Asian and Russian crises engendered. In our view, the main advantage of a relatively more closed financial regime would be the ability to control interest rates for domestic purposes.

Lower interest rates would reduce the financial components of fiscal deficits and would free resources for social policies. A reduction in the share of interest, profits, and rents in total income and an increase in the share of wages may lead to an increase in effective demand and higher rates of growth and employment. Furthermore, higher rates of growth tend to stimulate productivity growth, leading to virtuous circles of cumulative growth. No change in the direction of the economic policy under the current administration has occurred. Low levels of growth, relatively high unemployment, and stagnant or worsening income distribution continue.

6. Summary of the Results

In the last twenty-five years, Brazil has suffered a debt crisis and a long period of stagnation and high inflation. As a result, parts of the Belindia model were abandoned, in particular the process of state-led industrialization. On the other hand, wage inequality continued to increase through the 1990s, and income distribution remains one of the hallmarks of Brazilian society. Table 2.9, below, summarizes the results of the reforms pursued during the 1990s, and also of the post–Real plan period when reforms were intensified. Reforms are compared to the ISI (1950–1980) and the crisis (1981–1989) periods.

The results show that the reforms and the Real Plan only led to increases in domestic investment and

productivity when compared to the crisis period. Worse than that is the fact that rates of growth and employment were even better during the so-called lost decade. The ISI period stands as the Golden Age of Brazilian development. The effects on income distribution are ambiguous and depend on the measure that one emphasizes. It is clear, however, that Brazil remains a highly unequal society.

All in all, if Belindia stood for a model of industrialization concomitant with increasing inequality, the Washington Consensus reforms have been associated with deindustrialization and have been accompanied by the maintenance of high levels of inequality. In Brazil, "Belgium" is not doing well, and "India" perseveres and survives.

Notes

1. "Belindia" refers to the duality of the Brazilian economy: the modern or industrial sector being "Belgium" and the backward or rural sector being "India."

2. To a certain extent, the Belindia model formalizes ideas developed in Furtado (1972) and Tavares (1972). According to this view, the concentration of income in the upper middle class generated a demand for consumer durables that allowed the economy to continue to grow after the recession of the early 1960s.

3. Many Latin American countries such as Argentina and Chile initiated the reforms in the 1970s, only to revoke them temporarily. Others, like Mexico, started in the mid-1980s. However, in almost all the other countries, reforms were well underway by the early 1990s. According to Stallings and Peres (2000), Brazil may be classified, along with Colombia, Costa Rica, Jamaica, and Mexico, as a cautious reformer, while Argentina, Bolivia, Chile, and Peru are aggressive reformers. The main source of the difference, according to the authors, is related to the country's previous economic performance. That is, countries that did well in previous periods were more reluctant to adopt the reforms.

4. According to Franco (1999, 53), the higher productivity of the Brazilian economy in the early 1990s

TABLE 2.9 Effects of the Reforms and the Real Plan

	Growth		Investment		Productivity		Employment		Equity	
	1990s	Real	1990s	Real	1990s	Real	1990s	Real	1990s	Real
1950–1980	~	~	~	~	~	~	n.a.	n.a.	~	~
1981–1989	~	~	+	+	+	+	~	~	$\tilde{+}/$	$\tilde{+}/$

Source: Author's calculations.

meant that a certain degree of appreciation was desirable. In contrast, other pro-reform authors disagree on the role of exchange rate policy. Other authors claim that trade liberalization calls for real depreciation and a fall of the wage in dollars. See Rodrik (1999).

5. In fact, according to Rodrik (1999, 2), "the talk in Washington turned towards 'second-generation reforms,' 'governance,' and 'reinvigorating the state's capability.'" The reason for this change is, according to Rodrick, the widespread dissatisfaction with market-oriented reforms.

6. Several authors, such as Bonelli (1994) and Franco (1999), refer to this as the Verdoorn Law or effect. In fact, the Kaldor-Verdoorn effect was related to a long-term correlation between productivity and growth. The majority of empirical studies on the Kaldor-Verdoorn effect use cross-section analysis, thus smoothing out cyclical variations. The time series analysis, however, picks up both cyclical and long-term effects. The simple regression below shows the cyclical effect of output growth (G) on productivity growth (λ).

$\lambda = -3.87 + 0.53G + T^2$		Twenty-eight Observations	
Independent Variable	Coefficient	Standard Deviation	T Statistics
Constant	-3.87	1.68	-2.29
G	0.53	0.11	4.63
T^2	0.002	0.0008	2.37
$R^2 = 0.46$		Adj. $R^2 = 0.42$	

The regression shows that an increase in output growth of 1 percent would have an impact of 0.53 in labor productivity growth. Labor productivity is defined as output per employed worker, hence the above result implies that employment would increase around 2.13 percent, with the same increase of 1 percent in output growth. This cyclical result is in fact what is generally known as the Okun Law. Interestingly enough, the Okun effect in Brazil is similar to that of the United States and other developed nations.

7. The Collor Plan is more difficult to classify. Prices were frozen for only one month, but the main measure of the plan was the blocking of all financial assets for eighteen months, reducing the holdings of M4 by almost 70 percent.

8. In contrast with the Brazilian government, economists in general viewed stability as a pre-condition for the implementation of the reforms. Rodrik (1995) argues that high and variable inflation distorts the signals transmitted by relative prices, and notes that the

devaluation that should accompany the liberalization would have an inflationary effect.

9. The case of Mexico, where a social pact was crucial for stability, also contains some heterodox features. Argentina and Chile, on the other hand, represent the typical orthodox stabilization programs.

10. The Real Plan created a parallel currency—the unidade real de valor (URV)—that was indexed to three widely used inflation indexes. While prices in cruzeiros reais changed, absolute price in URVs was relatively constant, and relative prices were allowed to change. Finally, the monetary reform of July 1, 1994, fixed the parity between cruzeiros reais, URVs, and reais—the new currency—at CR\$2,750 = 1 URV = 00R\$1. As prices in URVs were already stable, prices in reais were also stable.

11. Latin American structuralists developed the notion that fiscal deficits are endogenous in a high-inflation environment. For a description of structuralist views on the role of fiscal deficits, see Câmara and Vernengo (2000).

12. In general, the terms "outward orientation" and "openness" are used without distinction. Note, however, that openness refers to the absence of restrictions to trade and capital flows, whereas outward orientation means emphasizing the role of foreign markets as an outlet for domestic production.

13. Rodrik (1999, 71) argues along similar lines. For him, "contrary to received wisdom, ISI-driven growth did not produce tremendous inefficiencies on an economy-wide scale. The inescapable conclusion is that most countries in Latin America and the Middle East had productivity growth records prior to 1973 that look quite favorable in comparison with those in East Asia." This result stands by itself, and does not depend on Rodrik's view on the importance of the domestic institutions of conflict management.

14. From 1967 onwards, Brazil promoted a reduction in tariffs and a crawling peg system that maintained the relatively depreciated exchange rate. This liberalizing experience was partially successful in increasing the levels of manufacturing exports.

15. This decomposition is based on the notion that growth is demand led, as in many structuralist models, rather than supply constrained, as in neoclassical theory.

16. Aggregate supply (X) is defined as the sum of total consumption (C), total investment (I), and exports (E_X):

$$X = C + I + E_X$$

In the absence of reliable data on government and private investment, the leakage parameters relative to aggregate output are defined for national rather than private savings. The national savings rate is defined as

$s = (Y - C)/X$, and the import propensity is given by $m = M/X$. The fiscal and foreign stances are then given by

$$X = \frac{s}{(s+m)} \cdot \frac{I}{s} + \frac{m}{(s+m)} \cdot \frac{E_X}{m}$$

The own multipliers depict the effects of the different components of aggregate demand on output.

17. Amadeo (1997) seems to imply that BT moves to the southeast without rotating. In my view, that would be the case only if the liberalization process had no impact on the income and price elasticities of BT. In fact if we define BT in logs as:

$$\ln(BT) = \alpha - \beta 1 \, ln(G) + \beta 2 \ln(E)$$

if liberalization leads to an increase in the income elasticity, $\beta 1$, and/or a decrease in the price elasticity, $\beta 2$, then the BT line would become more flat, as shown in graph 1.

18. Regressions used quarterly data on exports, imports, domestic GDP growth, consumer prices as a proxy of domestic prices and industrial prices as a proxy for international prices, and a weighted average of GDP for ten Brazilian trading partners.

19. Chow's breakpoint test ($F_{18,6} = 4.22$) rejects the null hypothesis that the coefficients are the same in the two subsamples.

20. Note that during most of the 1990s Brazil maintained a tax on financial operation levied on capital flows. However, the motivation was less to put sand in the wheels of the international financial system than to obtain fiscal revenues.

21. Some authors argue that foreign capital inflows decrease domestic savings and investment. Their critique was, however, directed to all types of capital inflows. The dependency school criticism of multinational enterprises (MNEs) is more directed to FDI inflows. In this sense the maligned model of FDI can be traced back to the dependency school criticism of the role MNEs, according to which profit remittances by MNEs weakened the balance of payments position of the host country.

22. The effects of macroeconomic shocks may be crucial in explaining the variance in growth performance across countries. It has now become conventional wisdom to include measures of shocks or instability in the investment functions. Yet the results are mixed at best.

23. Note that the argument pursued here suggests that devaluations were contractionary in Asia because of their effects on the banking sector and the subsequent debt-deflation processes that resulted from banking crises.

24. This section is based on Vernengo (2002).

25. The rate of inflation is clearly related to the re-adjustment period of the minimum wage as described by the inertialist theories of inflation (Taylor 1991a).

26. The 'open unemployed' refers to those workers who were unable to find a job in the last week. The 'hidden unemployed' includes workers that have irregular and discontinuous jobs as well as those who, discouraged, dropped out of the labor force. Total unemployment in table 6 is the sum of hidden unemployment and open unemployment in the metropolitan region of São Paulo, which is not shown in the table.

27. Barros and Corseuil (2001, 288) also argue that trade liberalization had a smaller impact than capital account liberalization on income inequality. Their conclusion that continued external liberalization would not create greater benefits or costs for social welfare, however, is more difficult to support, in particular, given the dismal performance in terms of job creation. Unless one believes that unemployment does not hurt social welfare, their conclusion is incorrect.

28. The problem of rural poverty was associated with uneven regional development. Furtado (1958) describes the problems created by the decay of the export oriented plantation system and the development of a subsistence system in the Brazilian northeast.

29. Some mainstream authors have toned down this view. Rodrik (1999, 1) admits, "the relationship between growth rates and indicators of openness ... is weak at best."

30. Arguably, some Asian countries—notably, Indonesia, Malaysia, and Thailand—did open their capital accounts as early as Latin America. The second-tier tigers were less successful than the more financially closed among the first-tier tigers (South Korea and Taiwan).

References

Agosin, M., and R. French-Davis. 1996. Managing capital inflows in Latin America. *Office of Development Studies Discussion Paper* no 8.

Agosin, M., and R. Mayer. 2000. Foreign investment in developing countries: Does it crowd in domestic investment? *UNCTAD Discussion Papers* no 146.

Amadeo, E. 1994. *Institutions, inflation and unemployment*. Aldershot, UK: Edward Elgar.

———. 1996. The knife-edge of exchange rate based stabilization. *UNCTAD Review* 1–25.

Amadeo, E., and M. Neri. 1999. Politica macroeconomic y Probreza en Brasil. In *Politica Macroeconomica y Pobreza en America Latina y el Caribe*, edited by E. Ganuza, L. Taylor, and S. Morley. New York: PNUD.

Amadeo, E., and V. Pero. 2000. Adjustment, stabilization and the structure of employment in Brazil. *Journal of Development Studies* 36 (4): 120–48.

Arida, P., and A. Lara-Resende. 1985. Inertial inflation and monetary reform in Brazil. In *Inflation and indexation*, edited by J. Williamson. Washington, D.C.: Institute for International Economics.

Bacha, E. 1994. O Fisco e a Inflação. *Revista de Economia Politica* 14 (1).

Banco Central do Brasil. n.d. Selected data. www.bcb.gov.br/.

Barros, R. P., and C. Corseuil. 2001. Apertura Económica y Distribución en Brasil. In *Liberalización Desigualda y Pobreza*, edited by E. Ganuza, R. P. Barros, L. Taylor, and R. Vos. Buenos Aires: Eudeba.

Berg, J., and L. Taylor. 2000. External liberalization, economic performance, and social policy. CEPA Working Paper, no. 12, February.

Bogdanski, J., A. Tombini, and S. Werlang. 2000. Implementation of inflation targeting in Brazil. Banco Central do Brasil, Working Paper no 1.

Bonelli, R. 1994. Productivity growth and industrial exports in Brazil. *CEPAL Review* 52 (April): 71–89.

Bruno, M. 1993. *Crisis, stabilization, and economic reform: Therapy by consensus*. Oxford: Clarendon Press.

Calvo, G., L. Leiderman, and C. Reinhart. 1993. Capital inflows and real exchange rate appreciation in Latin America. *IMF Staff Papers* 40 (1).

Câmara, A., and M. Vernengo. 2000. The German balance of payments school and the Latin American neo-structuralists. In *Credit, interest rates and the open economy*, edited by L-P. Rochon and M. Vernengo. Cheltenham, UK: Edward Elgar.

Cardoso, E., and A. Fishlow. 1988. *The macroeconomics of the Brazilian external debt* (in Portuguese). São Paulo: Brasiliense, 1989.

Carneiro, D., and R. Werneck. 1993. Obstacles to investment resumption in Brazil. In *Savings and investment requirements for the resumption of growth in Latin America*, edited by E. Bacha. Washington, D.C.: IADB and Johns Hopkins University Press.

Carvalho, F. 1998. The real stabilization plan and the banking sector in Brazil. *Banca Nazionale del Lavoro Quarterly Review*: 291–326.

Delfim Netto, A. 1998. *Cronica do Debate Interditado*. Rio de Janeiro: Topbooks.

DIEESE. n.d. Departamento Intersindical de Estatística e Estudos Sócio-Econômicos. www.dieese.org.br/ped/ped.html.

Dornbusch, R. 1997. Brazil's incomplete stabilization and reform. *Brookings Papers on Economic Activity* 1 (1997): 367–94.

Dutt, A. 1998. Direct foreign investment and North-South trade. In *Development Economics and Policy*, edited by D. Sapsford and J. Chen. London: Macmillan.

Edwards, S. 1995. *Crisis and reform in Latin America: From despair to hope*. Washington, D.C.: World Bank.

FGV Dados. n.d. Fundação Getúlio Vargas. http://fgvdados.fgv.br/.

Franco, G. 1999. *O Desafio Brasileiro*. São Paulo: Editora 34.

Furtado, C. 1958. *The economic growth of Brazil*. Berkeley: University of California Press.

———. 1972. *Análise do 'Modelo' Brasileiro*. Rio de Janeiro: Civilização Brasileira.

Giambiagi, F., and A. Além. 1999. O Ajuste do Governo Central. In *A Economia Brasileira nos Anos 90*, edited by F. Giambiagi and M. Moreira. Rio de Janeiro: BNDES.

IPEA Data. n.d. Instituto de Pesquisa Econômica Aplicada. http://ipeadata.gov.br/ipeaweb.dll.

Krugman, P., and L. Taylor. 1978. Contractionary effects of devaluation. *Journal of International Economics* 8: 445–56.

Macedo, R. 2000. Privatization, asset and income distribution in Brazil. Mimeo. São Paulo.

Moran, T. 1998. *Foreign direct investment and development*. Washington, D.C.: Institute for International Economics.

Moreira, M. 1999. Estrangeiros em uma Economia Aberta. In *A Economia Brasileira nos Anos 90*, edited by M. Giambiagi and M. Moreira. Rio de Janeiro: BNDES.

Pieper, U. 2000. Deindustrialization and the social and economic sustainability nexus in developing countries. *Journal of Development Studies* 36 (4).

Pinheiro, A., F. Giambiagi, and J. Gostkorzewicz. 1999. O Desempenho Macroeconomico do Brasil nos anos 90. In *A Economia Brasileira nos Anos 90*, edited by F. Giambiagi and M. Moreira. Rio de Janeiro: BNDES.

Pritchett, L. 1996. Measuring outward orientation in LDCs: Can it be done? *Journal of Developing Economics* 49: 307–35.

Resende, M. 2000. Crescimento Economico, Disponibilidade de Divisas e Importação Total por Categoria de Uso no Brasil. *Texto para Discussão* no. 714. Brasilia: IPEA.

Rocha, S. 2000. Pobreza e Desigualdade no Brasil. *Texto para Discussão* no. 721. Rio de Janeiro: IPEA.

Rodriguez, F., and D. Rodrik. 1999. Trade policy and economic growth: A skeptic's guide to the cross-national evidence. *NBER Working Paper* no. 7081. Cambridge, Mass.: NBER.

Rodrik, D. 1999. The new global economy and developing countries: Making openness work. *Overseas Development Council Policy Essay* no. 24. Washington, D.C.

SECEX. n.d. Ministério do Desenvolvimento, Indústria e Comércio Exterior. www.mdic.gov.br/indicadores/default.htm.

Stallings, B., and W. Peres. 2000. *Growth, employment and equity*. Washington, D.C.: Brookings.

Tavares, M. C. 1972. *Da Substituição de Importações ao Capitalismo Financeiro*. Rio de Janeiro: Zahar.

———. 1999. *A Destruição Não Criadora*. Rio de Janeiro: Record.

Taylor, L. 1991a. *Income distribution, inflation and growth: Lectures on structuralist macroeconomic theory*. Cambridge, Mass.: MIT Press.

———. 1991b. Economic openness: Problems to the century's end. In *Economic liberalization: No panacea*, edited by T. Banuri. Oxford: Clarendon Press.

———. 2001. Outcomes of external liberalization and policy implications. In *External liberalization, economic performance, and social policy*, edited by L. Taylor. New York: Oxford University Press.

———. 2004. *Restructuring macroeconomics*. Cambridge, Mass.: Harvard University Press.

Taylor, L., and E. Bacha. 1976. The unequalizing spiral: A first growth model for Belindia. *Quarterly Journal of Economics* 90: 197–218.

Vernengo, M. 2002. External liberalization, macroeconomic instability and the labor market in Brazil. Working paper. Geneva: International Labor Office.

World Bank. 1993. *The East Asian miracle*. Policy research report. New York: Oxford.

3

External Liberalization, Growth, and Distribution in China

Shantong Li

Introduction

China underwent trade liberalization at the end of 1978. Since then the country[1] has witnessed tremendous social and economic changes. Per capita GDP rose from 379 yuan in 1978 to 7,078 yuan in 2000,[2] an increase of 5.58 times in real terms. Openness was accompanied by economic development. This included an improvement in technology and management, increased competition, and a rise in labor productivity. While people have greatly benefited from the country's successful economic performance, concurrently, several new problems have emerged. Among these are an increased rate of unemployment, the slowdown of income growth for rural households, and increased income disparity among regions and between urban and rural areas.

The main purpose of this study is to examine the effects of external liberalization on China's economic growth, employment, and income distribution. This paper is organized as follows. Section 1 describes China's macro environment following trade liberalization. Section 2 reviews China's experience with liberalization. Section 3 analyzes the macro impact of liberalization through a decomposition of aggregate demand. Section 4 focuses on the distributive effects of liberalization though a decomposition of employment and productivity. The social impact of liberalization is dealt with in sections 5 and 6.

1. The Macro Environment of China's Trade Liberalization

While China is pushing forward with trade liberalization, it has enforced efficient and fruitful reforms in finance, banking, planning, investment, state-owned enterprises, and government institutions. After twenty years of reform, China's market economy has preliminarily been established. The private sector is

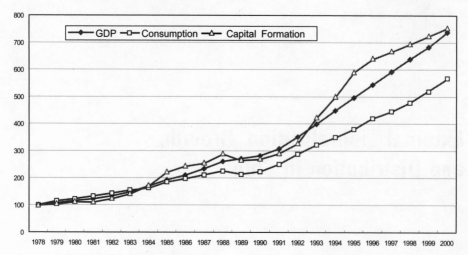

FIGURE 3.1 Expansion of GDP, Final Consumption, and Capital Formation

becoming an organic part of China's economy. Government institutions have been substantially streamlined and their direct intervention in the economy has gradually declined.

The changes in the macro environment brought about with trade liberalization involve a whole host of factors. This discussion is mainly centered on the growth of output, the growth of domestic demand, the functions of external departments, the stock and flow of foreign investment, changes in commodity prices, changes in actual exchange rates, and macroeconomic policies.

1.1. Quantitative Descriptions of Macroeconomic Performance

Since 1978 China's economic scale has been expanding very rapidly (see figure 3.1). From 1978 to 2000, calculated on the basis of constant prices, China's GDP rose by 6.4 times, final consumption rose by 4.7 times, and capital formation increased by 7.5 times.

While China's economy is expanding, connections between China and the global economy have been deepening. As we can see from figure 3.2, the dependence of China's economy on foreign trade has

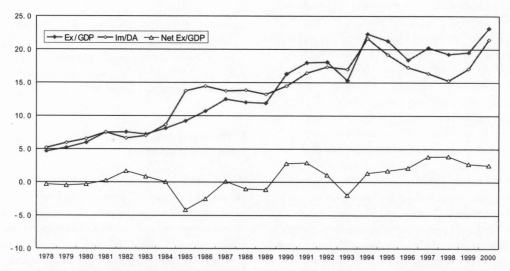

FIGURE 3.2 The External Trade Dependence Ratio

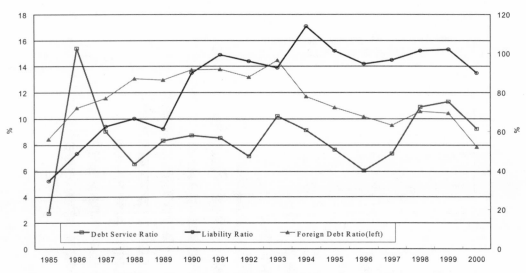

FIGURE 3.3 Changes in China's Foreign Debt Status since 1985

shown an upward trend since 1978. During 1978–2000, the ratio of exports to GDP went up from 4.6 to 23.2 percent, rising by 18.6 percentage points. The ratio of imports to domestic final demand went up from 5.2 to 21.5 percent, increasing by 16.3 percentage points.

Alongside strengthened external relations, China's foreign debt has also increased. During 1985–2000, the foreign debt balance increased from $15.8 billion to $145.7 billion, rising by 8.2 times. The debt service ratio and the liability ratio of foreign debt fluctuated, but their average levels were higher in the 1990s than in the 1980s. Their levels in 2000 were respectively 6.5 and 8.3 percentage points higher than those in 1985; after rising from 56 percent in 1985 to 96.5 percent in 1993, the foreign debt ratio dropped to 52.1 percent in 2000 (see figure 3.3).

The continued increase in foreign direct investment is yet another expression of the uninterrupted deepening of China's external economic relations. By 2000, accumulated foreign direct investment amounted to $346.637 billion. The ratio of the annual flow of foreign direct investment to GDP grew from 0.4 percent in 1984 to 6.2 percent in 1994 before dropping to 3.8 percent in 2000. The ratio of accumulated foreign direct investment to GDP went up year after year from 1.0 percent in 1984 to 32.1 percent in 2000, rising by 31.1 percentage points (see figure 3.4).

Since 1979, there have been fiscal deficits most years. Nevertheless, the level of China's fiscal deficit

is not high and is comparatively stable. Over twenty years, the highest fiscal deficit level was only 3.4 percent of GDP, and the deficit level of most years was around 1.0 percent of GDP. Since 1994, the government has mainly relied on the issue of government bonds to finance its deficits. The Chinese government's debt level has not grown rapidly. During 1979–2000, the proportion of government debt to GDP went up from 0.9 to 4.7 percent. By the end of 2000, the outstanding stock of debt was 1,302.2 billion yuan, or 14.6 percent of GDP (see figure 3.5).

From 1978 to 1997, China's general price index constantly grew. The consumer price index (CPI) rose by 3.8 times. Over these twenty years, several severe inflations took place. Inflation first occurred in 1985, when the inflation rate reached 11.9 percent; it struck again in 1988, and the rate went up to 18.8 percent; and once again in 1994, when the inflation rate hit 24.1 percent. After late 1997, China's general price indices decreased (see figure 3.6).

Through the 1980s and early 1990s, China's nominal exchange rate index (against the U.S. dollar, same as in figure 3.7) had been going up (i.e., currency devaluation); the exchange rate in 1994 was four times that of 1981. Since 1994, China's nominal exchange rate index has been decreasing. As a result of a few severe inflations occurring since the reforms, changes in China's real exchange rate index were not as great as in the nominal rate index.

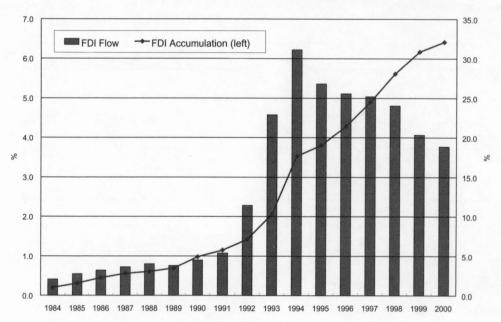

FIGURE 3.4 Growth in Foreign Direct Investment

1.2. The Policy Phases of Liberalization

Although China's external liberalization is a gradual process, we may roughly divide it into four major phases. Since the reforms, economic performance has fluctuated to some extent, sometimes drastically so (see figure 3.8). Each fluctuation has brought about adjustments in macroeconomic policies. The four major phases and adjustments are as follows.

1.2.1. 1979–1987: The Starting-Up Phase

In this phase, the following measures toward external liberalization were taken:

- Reforming the highly concentrated foreign trade system
- Reintroducing the practice of retaining a share of foreign exchange earned and permitting enterprises to adjust foreign exchange with each other
- Establishing special economic zones in Shenzhen, Zhuhai, Shantou, and Xiamen, and then opening up fourteen port cities and other coastal areas
- Encouraging the utilization of foreign capital and lifting some restrictions on foreign funded enterprises

1.2.2. 1988–1991: The Time of Adjustment

In this phase, the following measures were taken in China's external liberalization.

- Instituting the contractual foreign trade "responsibility" system and the export rebates system, abolishing the mandatory export plans
- Completing the legislation concerning foreign-funded enterprises and further loosening restrictions on them
- Establishing foreign exchange swap markets in various provinces, autonomous regions, and municipalities
- Establishing the Hainan Special Economic Zone and opening up Pudong in Shanghai

1.2.3. 1992–1997: The Acceleration Phase

From 1992 to 1994, the major step toward external liberalization was the opening up of four cities along the Yangtze River and the capital cities of eleven inland provinces.

The characteristics of economic performance were as follows:

- Domestic investment demand quickly expanded.
- The utilization of foreign capital dramatically increased.

From 1994 to 1997, the following steps toward external liberalization were taken:

- Implementing foreign exchange settlements by banks and establishing a unified national interbank foreign exchange trading market. After the end of the dual exchange rate arrangement, the new exchange rate was subject to a single managed floating system based on market supply and demand.
- Realizing the convertibility of the Renminbi (RMB) under the current account.
- Given the huge amount of foreign capital inflows, setting guidelines for industries involved in foreign investments.

From 1994 to 1996, the central government implemented financial and banking policies conforming to the principle of austerity, and finally realized a soft landing in 1996. In 1996, China's GDP increased by 9.6 percent and the growth rate of retail prices dropped from a peak of 21.7 percent in 1994 to 6.1 percent.

1.2.4. 1998–2001: Adjustment after Financial Crisis

In this period, China joined the World Trade Organization and more thoroughly merged into the world

economy. The government's pursuit of active fiscal policy to cope with deflation and the slowdown in foreign capital inflows were other characteristics of economic performance. China's economy continued on the track of high growth and low inflation. However, growth in domestic demand showed a clear downward trend. To cope with the problem, the central government recommended stimulating domestic demand by switching from a restrained to an active fiscal policy.

2. Liberalization: A Review

The end of 1978 should be considered the real starting point of China's external liberalization. During the thirty years between 1949 and 1978, China pursued a socialist economic development strategy. Before 1978, China's foreign economic relations were limited to foreign trade and aid to other countries. Moreover, its foreign trade sector grew at a very slow pace because of the blockade imposed by Western countries, the severance of Sino-Soviet relations, and the Cultural Revolution, among other factors. The ratio of China's exports to the world's total dropped from 1.23 percent in 1953 to 0.75 percent in 1978. In the global ranking of foreign trade, China's place fell from seventeenth to thirty-second.

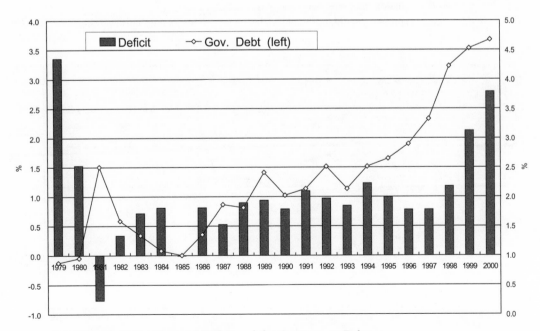

FIGURE 3.5 Changes in the Financial Deficit and the Government Debt

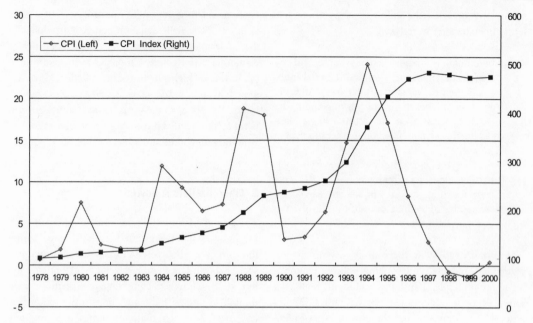

FIGURE 3.6 Changes in China's Commodity Prices since 1978

The economic development strategy pursued before 1978 was successful. Despite three years of serious natural disasters and the political turmoil that occurred during the Cultural Revolution, China still achieved an average annual economic growth rate of 6 percent (see figure 3.9) from 1952 to 1978. Despite sharp fluctuations, the inflation rate was very low most of the time, and the period was unblemished by enormous government deficits or balance of payments imbalances. Measured in outputs of electricity, cement, and rolled steel, the industrial basis of China at the end of the 1970s was on par with that of Japan and the Soviet Union in the 1960s. Furthermore, its income distribution and social development record was better than that of the middle-income countries. In practice, China's emphasis on self-reliance meant

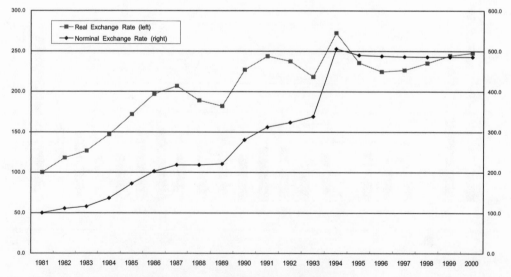

FIGURE 3.7 Changes in China's Nominal and Real Exchange Rate Index

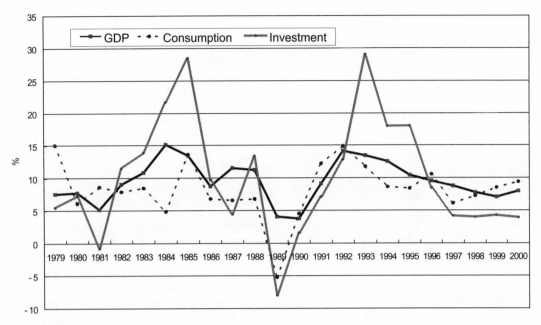

FIGURE 3.8 Fluctuations in China's Economy since 1978

that it had virtually no foreign debt upon entering the reform period.

China had much lower economic growth than several of its East Asian neighbors in the 1960s and early 1970s (see table 3.1). Moreover, as it had closed itself to the rest of the world in the thirty years before 1978, it had made little technical progress in many key areas. Chinese leaders became increasingly aware

that unless effective measures were taken to eliminate the technological gap between China and its neighboring countries, the gap in output would only widen.

At the end of 1978, the 11th Central Committee set up the task of pursuing the reform and opening-up policy, developing the national economy, and speeding up the socialist modernization drive. It also

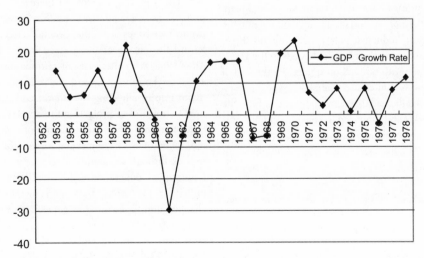

FIGURE 3.9 Economic Growth before Reform

Source: Issues of *China Statistics Yearbook*.

TABLE 3.1 Growth Rates of Some Economies, 1960–1976

	GNP	Per Capita GNP
South Korea	9.6	7.3
Singapore	9.5	7.5
Japan	9.1	8.0
Taiwan	9.0	6.2
Hong Kong	8.7	6.4
Thailand	7.7	4.6
Malaysia	6.7	3.9
Pakistan	6.1	3.2
China	5.7	3.6
Philippines	5.4	2.4
Indonesia	5.2	3.1
India	3.5	1.2

Source: Bell, Khor, and Kocchar (1993, 8).

explicitly stated that it was necessary to foster foreign economic cooperation and to adopt advanced technology. This socialist reform and opening-up policy represented a significant change in Chinese economic strategy and laid the ideological and theoretical foundations for external liberalization.

2.1. Foreign Trade

2.1.1. Foreign Trade before Reform

Before 1978, China's foreign trade was handled by state-owned foreign trade corporations (FTCs). FTCs traded according to the quotas set by the central plan, with all of their profits and losses incorporated into the state budget. Productive enterprises with no direct access to foreign markets supplied goods to the FTCs in accordance with production quotas. By the end of 1978, China had fifteen specialized FTCs. This system separated the tradable commodity sector from the foreign market and subjected the balance of payments to foreign trade plans. According to a World Bank survey in 1986, this "separation layer" brought about the following problems:

- Low export efficiency: exports were not determined according to China's comparative advantage. Some export commodities incurred heavy losses.
- An irrational export pattern: as international prices failed to be transmitted to producers, profitable exports could not be encouraged,

whereas money-losing ones could not be discouraged.
- The lack of information: the "separation layer" deprived Chinese enterprises of many opportunities to obtain technical assistance in product design, new product development, quality control, and many other areas.
- The lack of competition from imports: import control and high tariffs protected the backward technology of domestic enterprises, operations, and management.

2.1.2. Foreign Trade Reforms and Tariff Cuts

There were several aspects to reforming China's foreign trade system. First, foreign trade operations were delegated to lower levels and, along with the existing mandatory and guidance plans, market regulation was allowed. Second, a contractual operational responsibility system within the foreign trade sector was instituted and a foreign trade agent system was introduced under which foreign trade enterprises offered all kinds of services to importers and exporters. Third, starting from canceling financial subsidies to exports, efforts were made to enable autonomy and fair competition in the foreign trade sector.

China implemented a highly protective tariff policy in the thirty years from the establishment of the People's Republic to the initiation of the reform and opening-up drive. After the planned economic system was established in the late 1950s, planned control served as the mainstay in the import sector, with tariffs playing the role of increasing state revenues. From 1951 to 1983, tariff rates were revised twenty-two times with the general tendency being toward the raising of the average import tariff rate. After 1980, with the onset of reforms, opening up, and the relaxation of import controls, tariffs played a major role in adjusting the import and export commodity mix and in protecting the domestic industry. Since the early 1990s, in the course of negotiating its restoration of GATT status and joining the WTO, as well as through its membership in the Asia-Pacific Economic Cooperation (APEC), China has committed to promoting trade and investment liberalization and to lowering its general tariff rate.

In 1992, China began a significant reduction of tariff rates. Before December 1992, its average tariff rate was 43.2 percent. In January 2001, its average tariff rate plunged to 15.3 percent, declining by 64.6 percent (see table 3.2).

TABLE 3.2 Adjustments in China's Tariffs

	Adjusted Tax Items	Average Tariff Rate after Adjustment (%)
December 31, 1992	3,371	39.9
December 31, 1993	2,898	35.9
April 1, 1996	4,898	23
October 1, 1997	4,874	17
January 1, 1999	1,014	16.73
January 1, 2000	819	16.44
January 1, 2001	3,462	15.3

Source: *Economic Daily*, March 13, 2001.

2.1.3. The Outcome of Foreign Trade Reforms

Since China initiated the reform and opening-up drive, its trade sector has seen unprecedented expansion and development. In the 1980s, trade grew at an average annual rate of 11.5 percent. Trade has grown even faster since the beginning of the 1990s. From 1980 to 1999, total imports and exports soared from $38.14 billion to $360.63 billion, growing at an average annual rate of more than 15 percent (see figure 3.10). High trade growth has rapidly uplifted China's status in and share of world trade. At the end of 2000, China became the seventh highest ranked trade power in the world.

From the early 1980s onward, China's foreign trade dependency ratio has risen substantially. It peaked at 43.61 percent in 1994, much higher than the U.S. ratio of 17.8 percent and Japan's ratio of 14.7 percent at the same time. China's foreign trade dependency fell in subsequent years, but the ratio stayed above 34 percent. For a big country, such a high foreign trade dependency ratio is very unusual. This demonstrates that China's foreign economic activity constitutes a high share of the national economy. Yet it is not accurate to use the foreign trade dependency ratio to measure the degree of China's opening up. Calculating according to purchasing power parity puts China's 1990 GDP at roughly US$1.25 trillion, China's trade value in 1990 at $111.5 billion, and its foreign trade dependency ratio at only 9 percent. If per capita GDP (which was $2,598) is used for calculation, China's GDP in 1990 would total $2.9 trillion, with its foreign trade dependency ratio standing at only 4 percent.

Moreover, a considerable part of China's trade growth since the beginning of the 1980s actually belonged to the growth of processing trade. Here export and imported input growth occurred simultaneously,[3] thus exaggerating China's foreign trade dependency ratio. Furthermore, processing trade has a minor impact on the domestic economy.[4] Excluding processing trade, the degree of China's opening up is lower than the international average.

In fact, China's opening up is asymmetrical in structure. The degree to which China has opened up

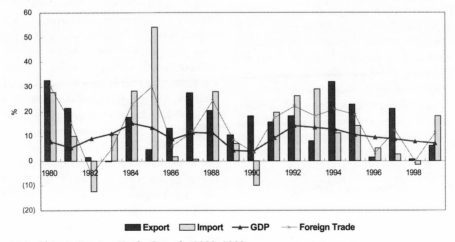

FIGURE 3.10 China's Foreign Trade Growth, 1980–1999

Source: Issues of *China Statistics Yearbook*.

commodity trade is much greater than the degree to which it has opened up the financial sector. Within the financial sector, China is relatively lax about allowing the influx of foreign capital, primarily FDI (there are still restrictions on the inflow of foreign investments in the domestic securities market), and is relatively strict when it comes to controlling the outflow of capital. Compared with some developing nations in Latin America and Asia, this asymmetrical opening strategy is successful in some respects because it enables China to avoid an excessive external impact—this became most evident during the Asian financial crisis—while using foreign trade and capital to speed up its economic development.

2.2. Foreign Exchange

2.2.1. Circumstances before Reforms

In 1953 China became a planned economy. With the completion of the socialist transformation of the private financial sector, the Bank of China began to monopolize foreign exchange handling. All foreign exchange earnings of enterprises and individuals were to be sold to the state, and when the private sector was in need of foreign exchange, the state would approve forex allocation according to plan.

In 1958, China retained a share of foreign exchange earned. Local foreign trade enterprises were permitted to retain 6 percent of their foreign exchange export earnings (in other words, foreign exchange retained by enterprises would be sold to a designated bank at government-set exchange rates). Meanwhile, enterprises received foreign exchange quota certificates. When in need of foreign exchange, they could, on the basis of the quotas, buy foreign exchange at a designated bank at government-set exchange rates. The practice of retaining a share of foreign exchange earned was repealed during the Cultural Revolution. The foreign exchange control system played a significant role in keeping international payments in balance and stabilizing exchange rates.

2.2.2. Changes in the Foreign Exchange Managerial System

After 1979, the government carried out a series of reforms in the foreign exchange managerial system. As a result, foreign exchange control gradually shifted from highly planned controls to indirect market regulation. In 1994, the dual exchange rates were merged, and the bank's foreign exchange settlement system was officially introduced. In December 1996, China accepted the obligation as prescribed by the IMF to realize the convertibility of yuan under the current account.

Before 1978, planned management had assured the stability of China's financial sector and prices. The exchange rate was also by and large stable. To prioritize the development of the heavy industry, the cost of using foreign exchange was lowered, resulting in the serious overvaluation of Chinese currency. Before 1971, the exchange rate was invariably kept at one U.S. dollar against 2.4618 yuan.[5] Only when a certain foreign currency devalued or appreciated was the value of the yuan adjusted accordingly, giving up its function to adjust imports and exports.

In 1981 China began reforming its exchange rate system by introducing the dual exchange rate system. One rate referred to the internal trading settlement price, which was set according to the nation's average cost of earning foreign exchange from exports in 1978, that is, one U.S. dollar against 2.8 yuan. The other rate was the official quoted rate used for internal non-trade settlement.[6] The internal trading settlement rate was abolished in 1985, but the exchange rate remained overvalued to the detriment of export expansion. The quota adjustment was permitted in 1986, giving rise to the new dual exchange rate system under which the official exchange rate and the foreign exchange adjustment price coexisted. But the adjustment price was still subject to official control, and the trading in quotas was not brisk. In 1988, foreign exchange adjustment prices were decontrolled on the foreign exchange swap market, resulting in a premium jump of about 80 percent.

As of January 1, 1994, a single, managed floating system based on market supply and demand was introduced. Meanwhile, the official exchange rate and the market exchange rate were merged to one U.S. dollar to 8.70 yuan. Since then, because of China's sustained international balance of payments surplus, the supply of U.S. dollars on the foreign exchange market has exceeded demand, so that the yuan has appreciated slightly.

The depreciation of the yuan in 1994, as well as the export rebates, greatly promoted the rapid growth of China's exports. However, in recent years, China's export growth has mainly been driven by its improved trade structure, the speedy development of processing trade, and the greater competitiveness of export enterprises. During the Asian financial crisis, the yuan stayed stable while the currencies of neighbors drastically depreciated. To date, China has always controlled its capital account. It is precisely because of this firewall that when the Asian financial crisis broke out in 1997, China was able to keep itself away from the direct damage caused by the crisis. Although capital account convertibility was the explicit objective of the next phase of reforms, China still needed to make great efforts to meet the necessary preconditions.

2.2.3. Foreign Exchange Reserves

Before China's foreign exchange control system was reformed in 1994, its foreign exchange reserves consisted of two parts: the state foreign exchange balance and the foreign exchange balance operated by the Bank of China. After reform, the balance of foreign exchange earned by designated foreign exchange banks using their own funds to operate foreign exchange was deducted from state foreign exchange reserves. China's foreign exchange reserve structure was now in basic line with internationally accepted practice.

Since the early 1990s, particularly since 1994, China's foreign exchange reserves have been growing rapidly. Such reserves amounted to US$105 billion at the end of 1996 (see table 3.3), ranking China's reserve supply as the second highest in the world, next only to Japan.

The substantial increase in China's foreign exchange reserves in recent years is the result of the following two reasons. First, policy change was the immediate factor contributing to a substantial increase in reserves. In 1994, the state stopped retaining a share of foreign exchange earned and banks were authorized to settle and sell foreign exchange. As a result, the foreign exchange accumulated, operated, and turned over by foreign trade corporations for years upon years was replaced with the quick settlement of foreign exchange. Previously, the banks'

function as second-tier reserve was subject to various kinds of restrictions. This meant that banks could not play the role of absorbing and cushioning foreign exchange. After reform, the great pressures of settling large amounts of foreign exchange were speedily attended to by the central bank via the foreign exchange market, resulting in a whopping 143 percent increase in state foreign exchange reserves that year. This unprecedented increase in China's foreign exchange reserves did not stem from its enhanced international competitiveness, but merely from the change in its foreign exchange accounting form.

Second, twin surpluses brought about a sustained growth in foreign exchange reserves. Since 1994, the above effect of the policy change has diminished gradually. The major factor contributing to the substantial increase in state foreign exchange reserves has been the twin surpluses in both the current and the capital account. There are two reasons for this situation. On the one hand, cheap domestic production and preferential policies for foreign investors have promoted an inflow of large amounts of FDI. This has resulted in a large surplus in the capital account. On the other hand, the foreign trade policy pursued by China to promote exports since 1994 and the depreciation of the exchange rate have also resulted in the continued surplus in the current account. In table 3.4 we can see that during 1993–1994, a reversal took place in China's trade situation, that is, a deficit of $12.2 billion changed speedily into a surplus of $5.4 billion. In the meantime, the capital account balance changed from a deficit of $250 million in 1992 into a surplus of $23.5 billion in 1993, and $32.6 billion in 1994. Meanwhile, in order to maintain the exchange rate at the level of about one U.S. dollar against 8.3 yuan, the People's Bank of China buys U.S. dollars at the daily rate of $100 million from the open market and sells yuan in large amounts. This has also given rise to a marked increase in China's foreign exchange reserves.

There is some debate about the right amount of foreign reserves. Some scholars think that China's

TABLE 3.3 Changes in China's Foreign Exchange Reserves in 1990s (in Billion US$)

	1990	1992	1994	1995	1996	1997	1998	1999	2000
Foreign exchange reserves	11.09	19.44	51.62	73.59	105.03	139.89	144.96	154.67	165.57

Source: *China Statistics Yearbook* (2001).

TABLE 3.4 China's Balance of Payments in 1990s
(US$1 Million)

	Current Account Balance	Capital and Financial Account Balance	Reserve Assets	Net Errors and Omissions
1990	11,997	−2,774	−6,089	−3,134
1991	13,271	4,580	−11,091	−6,760
1992	6,401	−251	2,102	−8,252
1993	−11,904	23,474	−1,767	−9,803
1994	7,658	32,644	−30,527	−9,775
1995	1,618	38,675	−22,463	−17,830
1996	7,242	39,967	−31,662	−15,547
1997	36,963	21,015	−35,724	−22,254
1998	31,471	−6,321	−6,426	−18,724
1999	15,667	7,642	−8,505	−14,805
2000	20,519	1,922	−10,548	−11,893

Source: Issues of *China Statistics Yearbooks.*

current foreign reserves are too high, and for a country with capital scarceness, maintaining such a large amount of low-return foreign reserves is a waste of resources. But the mainstream opinion is that the large scale of foreign reserves keeps up a stable financial system during capital account liberalization and helps maintain confidence in the economy. However, the rapid growth of foreign reserves occurred under strict foreign exchange regulation that could not reflect real demand and supply in the market, and the demand from enterprises and households may increase dramatically now that regulation has loosened. Furthermore, the impact of the Asian financial crisis increased the government's desire to maintain foreign reserves.

Even as China retains a trade surplus, actual resources introduced from abroad have flowed out in the form of official reserves and errors and omissions, and through other channels, so that China has become a de

facto capital exporter. Capital flight has become a major problem (see page 165). Tian (2001) estimates the scale of China's capital flight. Her estimation includes two types of capital flight. One type directly transfers out capital through illegal channels, for example, through smuggling and the forgery of import and export bills. The other type transfers illegal capital in the name of legal channels; for example, capital outflows belonging to the capital account transferred under the current account (see table 3.5).

The greatest impact of foreign exchange reserves on the domestic economy lies in their effect on the monetary supply mechanism. Foreign exchange reserves had a vital impact on China's inflation and deflation in the 1990s. During 1984–1993, of the total base money supply of the People's Bank of China, loans extended to financial institutions usually accounted for 70–90 percent. This meant that loans extended to financial institutions during this period constituted a major channel for the base money supply. After 1994, with the change in the foreign exchange control system, a change took place in the major channel for monetary supply, with money held in foreign exchange constituting the most important part of the base money supply.

From table 3.6 we can see that the ratio of money held in foreign exchange to the base money jumped from 9.8 percent in 1993 to 25.8 percent in 1994 and continued to rise year by year before reaching 38.3 percent at the end of 1998. A better explanatory category is the ratio of the increased amount of money held in foreign exchange to the yearly increase in the base money supply (shown in the last column of the table). The ratio stood at 67.8 percent in 1994, indicating that more than two-thirds of increased base money that year came from increased money held in foreign exchange. The ratio in 1998 was 57.6 percent, still very high.

TABLE 3.5 Estimation of China's Capital Flight

	1990	1991	1992	1993	1994	1995	1996	1997	1998	1999
Traditional means of capital flight	122.66	60.26	163.38	−72.5	174.43	249.81	96.39	364.74	386.37	238.3
Capital flight in the name of current aggregate	40.64	47.7	66.01	86.78	197.96	254.4	290.2	310.31	314.18	364.61
Total	163.3	107.96	229.39	14.28	372.39	504.21	386.59	675.05	700.55	602.91

Source: Tian (2001).

TABLE 3.6 Ratio of Money Held in Foreign Exchange to Base Money (100 Million Yuan)

	Money Held in Foreign Exchange (F)	Base Money (B)	F/B	Increase of F (ΔF)	Increase of Base Money (ΔB)	ΔF/ΔB
1992	1,072.26	9,029.9	0.114	−83.40	1,526.8	−0.054
1993	1,221.46	12,458.5	0.098	149.20	3,428.6	0.044
1994	4,448.97	17,217.8	0.258	3,227.5	4,759.3	0.678
1995	6,145.86	20,759.8	0.296	1,696.8	3,542.0	0.479
1996	8,732.32	26,888.5	0.324	2,586.4	6,128.7	0.422
1997	11,596.60	30,632.8	0.378	2,864.3	3,744.3	0.765
1998	12,001.38	31,335.3	0.383	404.78	702.5	0.576

Source: Calculation according to issues of *China Financial Yearbook*.

The increase in money held in foreign exchange directly fueled high inflation in 1994 and 1995 (see figure 3.11). China's economy began to show signs of overheating in the first half of 1992, with investments in fixed assets jumping by 42.6 percent and the GDP shooting up by 14.3 percent. Consequently, banks were forced to increase money supply, leading to the rapid accumulation of inflationary pressure. In the second half of 1993, the government decided to strengthen macroeconomic regulation and controls. But the sharp increase in money held in foreign exchange made it impossible to exercise effective controls over base money, so that the inflation rate peaked at 24 percent in 1994 and hit 17 percent in 1995.

To ensure implementation of the moderately tight monetary policy and to cater to a substantial increase in foreign exchange reserves, the central bank adopted a number of sterilizing measures to reduce loans to domestic financial institutions. The central bank's net claims on financial institutions began to fall in the first quarter of 1994. This continued until the second quarter of 1998, when the domestic economy showed signs of deflation. The central bank's net claims on financial institutions started to rise rapidly. In this process, money supply grew in a sustained manner. Essentially, money supply was not materialized via increased loans extended to the financial sector, but flowed to the economy via transactions in foreign exchange.

This structural change in money supply had a noticeable impact on the macro economy as a whole. The money supply targets of Chinese financial institutions were primarily state-owned enterprises,

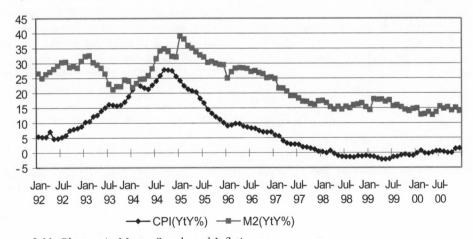

FIGURE 3.11 Changes in Money Supply and Inflation

Source: National Bureau of Statistics of China, Central Bank.

mostly oriented to the domestic economy. The ability of SOEs to obtain loans had a direct bearing on their production and the increase in their employees' wage incomes. The shrinkage of domestic credits was thus an enormous burden upon such enterprises.[7] The difficulties faced by SOEs affected the demand for domestic capital goods, consumer goods, as well as the general price level.

As for the foreign trade enterprises that were capable of earning foreign exchange, these firms were concentrated in coastal areas, border areas, or special economic zones. In terms of their scale, they constituted a small proportion of the national economy. The increase in the wage incomes of their workers and staff did not have a great impact on China's general price level. In particular, a considerable part of their foreign exchange revenues was held by foreign-funded enterprises, whose participation in the domestic market was much less and which did not play a great role in expanding domestic demand. Therefore, the change in the money supply mechanism caused by money held in foreign exchange curbed, to some extent, the growth of the total domestic demand. It is one of the factors contributing to the deflation that has affected China since 1997.

2.3. Utilization of Foreign Capital

2.3.1. The Process of Utilizing Foreign Capital

Absorbing and utilizing foreign capital are major aspects of China's reforms and external liberalization, and serve as important symbols of the degree of China's opening up.

Initially, China's foreign investment policy showed a strong regional orientation. To make full use of the regional advantage of the coastal areas in attracting direct investments from Hong Kong and Macao, the Chinese government granted preferential terms to these areas. In the 1980s, foreign borrowing was the major form of foreign capital. FDI mainly came from Hong Kong and Macao, and concentrated in the Guangdong and Fujian Provinces. The majority of foreign capital was put into hotel and travel service projects, and labor-intensive processing projects. After 1989, although foreign loans plunged to almost zero, most Western countries imposed economic sanctions against China,[8] and many Western enterprises withdrew investments from China, foreign direct investment still increased. This was largely

owing to a substantial rise in foreign direct investment from other Asian countries and regions. In particular, the Taiwanese authorities relaxed restrictions on investments in China's mainland, resulting in a marked increase in investments from Taiwan.

In the early 1990s, foreign investments contributed to an increase in productive and export-oriented projects and a drop in the ratio of hotel and travel service projects. Investment areas and industries were expanded, and Taiwanese investments rapidly expanded. In terms of the investment structure as a whole, foreign loans were still in the dominant position (accounting for 60 percent of total foreign investment). The proportion of foreign direct investment climbed to 30 percent. In 1992 China created a new plan for opening up and restructuring the economy. The State Council decided to open up six cities along the Yangtze River, six inland border cities, and eighteen inland provincial capitals. This opened up China's economy at many levels, improved the investment environment, and elevated foreign investments to new heights. Actual direct foreign investment topped $11 billion in 1992 and shot up to $27.5 billion in 1993 (see figure 3.12). Between 1992 and 1994, contractual foreign investment and actually utilized foreign investment were 4.8 times and 3.1 times the figures for the previous thirteen years, respectively.

Alongside a sustained increase in actually utilized foreign direct investments, contractual foreign direct investments peaked in 1993 before declining to $81.4 billion in 1994, primarily because of the adjustment in domestic policy. Owing to the sustained growth of its economy during 1992–1993, China faced mounting inflationary pressure. The government pursued an austere financial and monetary policy.

While foreign investments were increasing, the government began to pay close attention to the quality of such investments and no longer encouraged foreign investment in real estate and the processing industry. As a result, the ratio of foreign investment in real estate to the total foreign investment fell from its peak of 39.3 percent in 1993 to 28.7 percent in 1994 and dropped further in subsequent years. Since those investing in real estate were mostly enterprises from Hong Kong, the ratio of foreign investment from Hong Kong to total foreign direct investment decreased accordingly and, for the first time, fell below 60 percent in 1994. Transnational companies from Europe and the United States, however, increased their

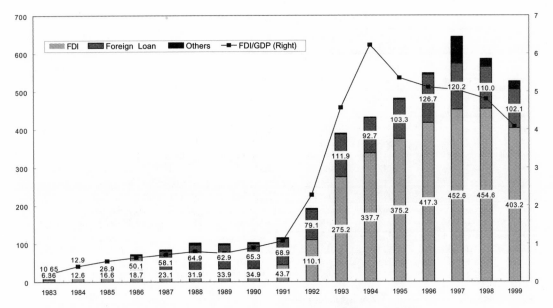

FIGURE 3.12 Actually Utilized Foreign Capital (in Hundreds of Millions of Dollars)
Source: *China Statistics Yearbooks.*

involvement in the Chinese economy. In 1994, the average scale of foreign investment was $1.7 million; this jumped to $3.3 million in 1996 before declining to $2.43 million in 1997.

Capital and technology-intensive FDI projects also rose noticeably in this phase, and the layout of investment regions began to extend from the coastal areas to the vast central and western regions. Foreign investments were directed to a variety of industries and sectors. In particular, the tertiary industry including the aviation, transport, and insurance sectors and the accounting offices began to use foreign investment. Investments from large transnational companies also rose steadily. Statistics show that of the world's top *Fortune* 500 companies, 300 have invested in China.[9]

2.3.2. Foreign Capital's Contribution to the Economy

China began to attract FDI on a large scale after it initiated its reform and opening-up drive. From 1984 to 1991, its FDI stood at around 30 percent of foreign capital utilized. After 1992, the ratio rose rapidly to about 70 percent and approached 80 percent in 1994, 1995, 1996, and 1998. From 1993 to 1998, China was the second largest FDI absorber in the world, next only to the United States. In 1999, China's uti-

lization of FDI ranked at 4, only less than that of the United States, the UK, and Sweden. From 1979 to 1999, the total amount of FDI flowing to China exceeded $30.6 billion, the second largest in the world, making up roughly 10 percent of the global FDI flow. The FDI absorbed by China took a high share in total FDI flowing to developing countries, varying from one-third to one-half during the 1990s. In 1995, China's share reached 40 percent. For the seven successive years from 1993 to 1999, China was the largest FDI absorber in developing countries.

But many scholars warn that the amount of FDI that China has attracted may be overestimated. On the one hand, the quality of China's statistics is debatable. On the other hand, a large part of foreign investment in China is domestic capital. This is because some domestic enterprises register a company abroad before returning to China to make investments, for the purpose of taking advantage of the preferential policies offered by the Chinese government to foreign investors. This type of direct investment is called "round tripping," which may account for about 25 percent of all FDI. Another reason for overestimation is that the numbers are actually fabricated by local governments to show off their success or by some enterprises to take advantage of the preferential policy.

TABLE 3.7 Foreign Capital's Share in Fixed Asset Investment

	FAI Grouped by Source of Funds						
Year	State Budgetary Appropriation	Domestic Loans	Foreign Investment	Fundraising and Others	Domestic Investment	Total	Foreign Investment/Total
1981	269.76	122.00	36.36	532.89	924.65	961.01	0.038
1985	407.80	510.27	91.48	1,533.64	2,451.71	2,543.19	0.036
1989	366.05	762.98	291.08	2,990.28	4,119.31	4,410.39	0.066
1990	393.03	885.45	284.61	2,954.41	4,232.89	4,517.50	0.063
1991	380.43	1,314.73	318.89	3,580.44	5,275.60	5,594.49	0.057
1992	347.46	2,214.03	468.66	5,049.95	7,611.44	8,080.10	0.058
1993	483.67	3,071.99	954.28	8,562.36	12,118.02	13,072.30	0.073
1994	529.57	3,997.64	1,768.95	11,530.96	16,058.17	17,827.12	0.099
1995	621.05	4,198.73	2,295.89	13,409.19	18,228.97	20,524.86	0.112
1996	625.88	4,573.69	2,746.60	15,412.40	20,611.97	23,358.57	0.118
1997	696.74	4,782.55	2,683.89	17,096.49	22,575.78	25,259.67	0.106
1998	1,197.39	5,542.89	2,617.03	19,359.61	26,099.89	28,716.92	0.091
1999	1,852.14	5,725.93	2,006.78	20,169.80	27,747.87	29,754.65	0.067
2000	2,109.45	6,727.27	1,696.24	22,577.14	31,413.86	33,110.10	0.051

Source: Calculation according to issues of *China Statistics Yearbook*.

Note: Domestic investment = state budgetary appropriation + domestic loans + fundraising and others. Total = domestic investment + foreign investment. "Fundraising" refers to funds received by construction enterprises from higher authorities or local governments, or monies raised by enterprises or institutions themselves for the purpose of investment in fixed assets during the reference period. Others refer to funds received during the reference period that are not included in the above-mentioned sources.

Aside from whether or not the foreign investment figures are accurate, foreign investments, especially FDI, have become very important to China's economy. Since employment in foreign-funded enterprises grew very rapidly, the contribution of foreign-funded enterprises to urban employment growth reached 12.5 percent in the 1990s. By the end of 2000, foreign-funded enterprises accounted for 24 percent of total value-added and 27 percent of total sales revenue in the industrial sector (which absorbed two-thirds of total FDI).

Foreign Investment and Domestic Capital Formation   One direct impact of FDI on China is the increase in the country's production capital. We can compare foreign investment in fixed assets with local investment in fixed assets.

In table 3.7, foreign investment was not divided into FDI and other types of foreign capital, but after 1992, FDI made up the absolute majority of foreign investment. As of 1997, the share of foreign investment in the source of total fixed assets investment (FAI) decreased (see table 3.8). This might be due to three reasons: first, after the Asian financial crisis, the growth of foreign capital utilization slowed down; second, less foreign capital went toward fixed asset investment; and third, the government pursued positive fiscal policy, thus fiscal investment and investment by state-owned enterprises grew quickly. However, in 2000, the fixed asset investment made by foreign-funded enterprises made up 7.9 percent of total FAI, bigger than the share taken by foreign capital in FAI sources (5.1 percent). This fact shows that FDI could spur some domestic supporting investment. Therefore, contributions by FDI to China's capital stock are positive in value.

FDI and Foreign Trade   The relation between FDI and exports usually be classified into two types: trade creation and trade substitution. Generally speaking, if a transnational company comes to China for the purpose of utilizing China's inexpensive raw materials and labor, such FDI is normally regarded as trade substitution. However, FDI in China may be the trade-creation type. In addition, a lion's share of exports from foreign-funded enterprises is due, to some extent, to the behavior of the Chinese government. The Chinese government imposes many restrictions on foreign investors, such as requirements on export performance and the requirement on striking a balance between foreign exchange revenues and spending. All this compels foreign-funded enterprises to increase exports. Apart from granting universal preferential taxation treatment to exports, the Chinese government offers some other preferential policies to exports from foreign-funded enterprises.

Wang (1999) divides foreign-funded enterprises in China into two market orientation types, that is, export oriented and domestic market oriented. According to his analysis, FDI from Hong Kong and Macao, usually of a lower technical level, shows obvious export orientation. As newly industrialized regions, Hong Kong and Macao's technical levels are just a little higher than China's, but they have international marketing and networking experience. Hong Kong and Macao transferred their labor-intensive industries to China and, in particular, to sectors that were relatively advantaged in China. Therefore, these foreign-funded enterprises exported the majority of their products to the international market. At the beginning of the opening-up period, FDI from Hong Kong and Macao accounted for 80 percent of total FDI received by China: however, its share has continuously decreased in recent years. At the end of 2000, its share dropped to 60 percent of the total cumulative FDI. In 2000, 44.56 percent of the FDI absorbed by China came from Hong Kong and Macao. FDI from Western countries, usually with higher technical levels, went into the import-substitution sectors promoted by the Chinese government. So U.S.-, European-, and Japanese-funded enterprises were mostly domestic market oriented.

The rapid import and export growth of foreign-funded enterprises serves as a major growth area in the development of China's foreign trade. In 1980, imports into and exports from such enterprises accounted for 0.11 percent of China's total imports and exports. In 1992, the ratio of imports into and exports from such enterprises to China's total imports and exports surged to 26.24 percent, with exports climbing to 20.43 percent of China's total exports and imports to 32.72 percent of China's total imports. In 1998, the ratio rose further to 48.68 percent, with exports shooting up to 44.06 percent and imports to 54.73 percent. But as machines, equipment, and large amounts of raw materials needed for investment by foreign companies have to be imported, despite sizable exports, in most years, these enterprises still have a deficit in the balance between their own imports and exports.

The speedy development of *processing* trade handled by foreign-funded enterprises constitutes a major source of the rapid growth of foreign trade of such enterprises. Export in *regular* trade does not constitute a high ratio to the total export of such enterprises. The trade in processing materials supplied by clients is also the greatest trade form for these enterprises, with its ratio to the total export of these enterprises reaching as high as about 80 percent.

While advancing imports and exports, the trade growth of foreign-funded enterprises has also promoted

TABLE 3.8 The Share of Actually Utilized Foreign Capital Used in FAI

	Foreign Capital Used in FAI (100 Million Yuan)	Actual Foreign Capital (100 Million USD)	Exchange Rate (Average Rate)	Actual Foreign Capital (100 Million Yuan)	Share
1985	91.48	46.47	293.66	136.46	0.67
1989	291.08	100.59	376.51	378.73	0.77
1990	284.61	102.89	478.32	492.14	0.58
1991	318.89	115.54	532.33	615.05	0.52
1992	468.66	192.02	551.46	1,058.91	0.44
1993	954.28	389.60	576.20	2,244.88	0.43
1994	1,768.95	432.13	861.87	3,724.40	0.47
1995	2,295.89	481.33	835.10	4,019.59	0.57
1996	2,746.60	548.04	831.42	4,556.51	0.60
1997	2,683.89	644.08	828.98	5,339.29	0.50
1998	2,617.03	585.57	827.91	4,847.99	0.54
1999	2,006.78	526.59	827.83	4,359.27	0.46
2000	1,696.24	593.56	827.84	4,913.73	0.35

Source: Calculation according to issues of *China Statistics Yearbook*.

Note: Figures of foreign capital used in FAI are taken from the "Foreign Investment" column in Table 3.7.

TABLE 3.9 Foreign-Funded Enterprises and China's Foreign Trade (100 Million US$, %)

	Share in Exports and Imports	Share in Exports	Share in Imports	Trade Balance of China	Balance of Foreign-Funded Enterprises
1980	0.11	0.05	0.17	−19.00	−0.26
1985	3.39	1.08	4.89	−149.00	−17.67
1990	17.43	12.58	23.07	87.40	−44.93
1991	21.35	16.77	26.51	80.50	−48.60
1992	26.42	20.43	32.72	43.50	−90.15
1993	34.27	27.51	40.24	−122.20	−165.96
1994	37.04	28.69	45.79	54.00	−182.21
1995	39.10	31.51	47.65	167.00	−160.67
1996	47.30	40.72	54.46	122.20	−140.97
1997	46.94	40.98	54.59	404.20	−28.21
1998	48.68	44.06	54.73	435.90	42.44
1999	48.39	45.47	51.83	292.30	27.44
2000	49.91	47.93	52.10	241.10	21.69

Source: China Statistics Information Consulting and Service Center and *China Statistics Yearbook* (2001).

the optimization of the import and export commodities mix. Statistics show that in most years, the proportion of finished manufactured goods in the exports of such enterprises was higher than the nation's average. In other words, foreign-funded firms play a major role in increasing the proportion of finished manufactured goods in exports. The percentage of such enterprises in China's total export of mechanical and electrical products was 37.14 percent in 1993, and it jumped to 57.87 percent in 1997. Of China's high-tech exports, foreign-funded enterprises account for more than 70 percent.

At the same time, domestic enterprises have greatly increased their competitiveness in the global market. From table 3.9, we find that domestic exporters were the main source of China's trade surplus. From 1994 onwards, domestic exporters contributed more than $20 billion to the trade surplus each year. After China's entry into the WTO, with the greater utilization of improved low-cost techniques, the exports of domestic enterprises will continue to grow at a high rate.

3. Decomposition of Aggregate Demand

3.1. Decomposition of Foreign and Domestic Sectors

China has witnessed an economic boom as well as strong export growth since its opening up to the rest of the world. According to figures provided by the

International Financial Statistics Yearbook (IFS), China's export volume was US$15.44 billion in 1977 and US$152.44 billion in 1998 (at 1990 US$ prices), a 900 percent increase and an 11.52 percent annual growth rate. In 1977 China's GDP was 564.7 billion yuan, and by 1998 it was 4,133.4 billion yuan (in 1990 RMB prices), a 600 percent increase and a 9.94 percent annual growth rate. These figures comply with those of other export-oriented countries. But is foreign trade the only source of China's continued expansion? What role did domestic government and private (non-government) sectors play in the growth in output?

Following Berg and Taylor's (2000) method, I decompose aggregate demand. The decomposition is a two-step process. The first step is distinguishing the foreign sector from the domestic (see table 3.10 and figure 3.13). In the second step, domestic demand is decomposed into government and non-government sectors.

In the gross domestic product by expenditure approach, China's GDP is divided into three parts: consumption, investment, and net exports. Consumption is subdivided into household consumption expenditure and government consumption expenditure. However, the investment part does not differentiate government from households and enterprises. Besides, the *China Statistical Yearbooks* do not include the annual series of private income, Y, and net taxes, T. All these data need to be worked out in the second step.

The following is the result of the calculation: China's economy has not shown a definitive export orientation in the 1980s, as figure 3.13 indicates. E/m

(the contribution of exports to GDP) was higher than total supply or X in 1982, 1983, and 1987, and vice versa in the other years. However, E/m was always higher than X in the 1990s, except for the year 1993. The trend becomes more obvious since 1995, showing a greater contribution of exports to the output. Experts have attributed this to the following reasons: the government's consistently pro-export policy in the 1990s, greater tax rebounds for export, and the sharp depreciation of the RMB in 1994. As a result, China has maintained a large margin of favorable balance while its trade volume continues to rise, with the balance hitting US$29.23 billion in 1999.

3.2. Further Decomposition

In the second step, I decompose domestic demand in a bid to test the respective roles of government expenditure and private investment. In doing so, investment is divided into government investment and individual investment. In China, the state has always been the biggest investor, accounting for 69.4 percent of the total investment in 1981. Despite a continuous decline in state investment, its share in total

investment was 53 percent in 1999. This implies that "private investment" contains large amounts of investment made by state-owned units.

Because the National Statistics Bureau has included the daily expenditure of extrabudgetary expenditures as part of government consumption in the gross domestic product by expenditure approach, the government expenditure (G) includes not only the budget expenditure (not including debt interest payments) but also the extrabudgetary expenditures. G ought to be calculated by removing transferred payments (including pensions, social and relief funds, and price subsidies) from the total government expenditure. In order to work out T and Y, we have adopted a method similar to that used by Oblath in this volume. That is, private revenues (Y) equal GDP minus T, while net taxes (T) is the result of government budget revenues (not including domestic and foreign debt income) minus transferred payments, adding extrabudgetary revenues. Government investment (Ig) is the result of G minus government consumption (Cg); and private (non-government) investment (Ip) is total capital formation minus government investment.

TABLE 3.10 Decomposition of Foreign and Domestic Sectors

	X = GDP + M (100 Million Yuan)	m = M/X	s = (GDP − C)/X	I/s (100 Million Yuan)	E/m (100 Million Yuan)
1982	5,846.9	0.06	0.32	5,559.2	7,335.5
1983	6,485.5	0.06	0.32	6,325.2	7,290.5
1984	7,786.8	0.08	0.32	7,782.7	7,802.5
1985	9,988.9	0.12	0.30	11,202.8	6,924.9
1986	11,416.3	0.11	0.31	12,227.6	9,146.6
1987	13,231.9	0.11	0.33	13,196.7	13,330.9
1988	16,564.0	0.11	0.32	17,032.4	15,218.0
1989	18,452.1	0.11	0.32	19,031.3	16,728.3
1990	20,553.5	0.11	0.34	19,045.3	25,248.1
1991	24,170.8	0.12	0.34	22,336.0	29,335.1
1992	29,934.5	0.14	0.33	29,102.2	31,961.3
1993	40,167.6	0.14	0.36	42,073.5	35,351.5
1994	56,306.6	0.17	0.35	54,511.9	60,019.5
1995	69,807.9	0.16	0.36	67,005.8	75,978.4
1996	81,144.8	0.16	0.35	76,964.5	90,384.6
1997	88,549.2	0.15	0.35	80,469.8	111,413.8
1998	92,738.3	0.15	0.35	84,056.9	116,042.5
1999	98,385.2	0.16	0.33	91,670.6	113,260.7

Source: Issues of *China Statistical Yearbook*.

Note: GDP: gross domestic product by expenditure approach. C: final consumption expenditure. I: gross capital formation. (C and I are directly taken from the "Gross Domestic Product by Expenditure Approach Table" in *China Statistical Yearbooks*. M: import of goods and services. E: export of goods and services. (M and E are both from the international balance of payments. The original data in US$ has been converted to RMB according to the average exchange rate.)

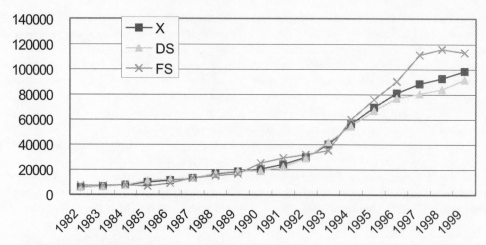

FIGURE 3.13 Decomposition of Foreign and Domestic Sectors
Source: Calculation according to issues of *China Statistical Yearbook*.

It can be inferred from figure 3.14 that for most of the 1980s (except 1982 and 1983), private investment's contribution *Ip/s* was greater than *X*, giving a strong impetus to China's economic growth. However, the situation changed completely in the 1990s, so that *Ip/s* was lower than *X* in every year except 1993, proving that private investment (in terms of demand) was no longer the main expansionary factor driving output growth. The government expenditure's contribution *G/t* was smaller than *X* for almost all of the 1980s. The government budget deficit was very small in this period, and if we take extrabudgetary revenues and expenditures into account, total government revenues were even larger than expenditures. However, *G/t* was always greater than *X* all through the 1990s except for 1993. The budget deficit rose from −14.65 billion yuan in 1990 to −174.36 billion yuan in 1999, expanding more than ten times. In short, government expenditure has become an important expansionary factor pushing China's economic growth. This trend is even more prominent in recent years.

3.3. Resource Gaps

I have worked out the share of Ip-Sp, G-T, and E-M in GDP in another decomposition. The resource gaps tell the same story as in figure 3.14. Figure 3.15 may give us a clearer idea of the features of China's economy in different time periods.

China's economy developed steadily in the 1982–1984 period, recovering from the contraction in the beginning of the 1980s. The national economy became overheated after the fourth quarter of 1984: bank credit loans and investment expanded quickly, and imports increased sharply. This led to a huge investment-savings gap and a trade deficit in 1995. The government initiated contractionary fiscal and credit policies in 1985, leading to the industrial output slide in the first half of 1986. Then, at the end of 1986, the government loosened restrictions on credit loans. For the next few years, investment demands were always in bloom.

But then rampant inflation occurred in 1988 owing to panic buying caused by price reforms. The government began to take administrative measures to restrict investment and consumption in 1989, leading to rapid investment and consumption shrinkage. Investment was much less than savings in both 1990 and 1991. Economic growth also dropped significantly. China's economic growth rate was a mere 3.8 percent in 1990, the lowest it had been in twenty years.

China's exports rapidly increased in 1990 and 1991. However, the contraction of the domestic economy restricted the growth of imports. The result, of course, was a large favorable trade balance. *G* was greater than *T* from 1990 onwards, but the difference between the two was small.

China speeded up its reform and opening up after Deng Xiaoping's 1992 speech on his South China Tour, and domestic investment heated up once again. In 1992–1993, China witnessed rapid growth in its domestic investment and foreign capital utilization,

TABLE 3.11 Contributions of Investment, Government Expenditure, and Exports to Output

	$s = Sp/X$	$M = M/X$	$t = T/X$	Ip/s (100 Million Yuan)	G/t (100 Million Yuan)	E/m (100 Million Yuan)	$X = GDP + M$ (100 Million Yuan)
1982	0.14	0.06	0.31	5,550.5	5,684.6	7,335.5	5,846.9
1983	0.12	0.06	0.33	6,473.0	6,334.2	7,290.5	6,485.5
1984	0.12	0.08	0.33	7,910.1	7,739.9	7,802.5	7,786.8
1985	0.10	0.12	0.32	15,418.5	9,509.5	6,924.9	9,988.9
1986	0.12	0.11	0.31	14,133.8	11,172.9	9,146.6	11,416.3
1987	0.15	0.11	0.29	14,012.6	12,806.6	13,330.9	13,231.9
1988	0.16	0.11	0.26	17,985.1	16,254.3	15,218.0	16,564.0
1989	0.16	0.11	0.27	19,558.2	18,464.0	16,728.3	18,452.1
1990	0.19	0.11	0.25	17,183.8	21,125.2	25,248.1	20,553.5
1991	0.21	0.12	0.25	20,778.2	24,520.5	29,335.1	24,170.8
1992	0.22	0.14	0.23	28,406.6	30,166.3	31,961.3	29,934.5
1993	0.33	0.14	0.13	41,677.9	41,468.4	35,351.5	40,167.6
1994	0.34	0.17	0.12	53,209.9	59,871.7	60,019.5	56,306.6
1995	0.34	0.16	0.12	65,318.3	74,134.6	75,978.4	69,807.9
1996	0.31	0.16	0.13	74,981.1	84,737.1	90,384.6	81,144.8
1997	0.33	0.15	0.12	78,563.8	92,178.5	111,413.8	88,549.2
1998	0.32	0.15	0.13	80,964.2	98,561.9	116,042.5	92,738.3
1999	0.30	0.16	0.14	85,842.7	108,945.8	113,260.7	98,385.2

Source: Calculation according to *China Statistical Yearbook*.

Note: GDP: gross domestic product by expenditure approach. G = budgetary expenditure + extrabudgetary expenditure − transfer payments. T = budgetary revenues + extrabudgetary revenue − transfer payments. $Ig = G − Cg$; Ig: government investment; Cg: government consumption expenditure. $Ip = I − Ig$; I: gross capital formation; Ip: private investment. $Sp = GDP − T − Cp$; Sp: private savings; Cp: household consumption expenditure. Because adjustments on the coverage of extrabudgetary revenues and expenditures were made in 1993, the extrabudgetary revenue and expenditure figures were less than the previous year's. This adjustment affected G, T, and t, but had little effect on G/t.

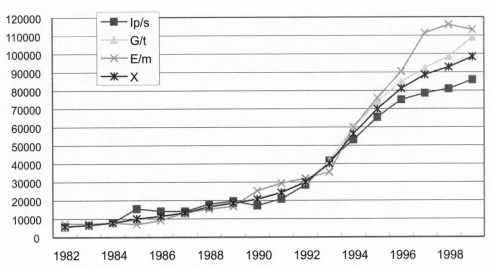

FIGURE 3.14 Contributions of Investment, Government Expenditure, and Export to Output

Source: Calculation according to issues of *China Statistical Yearbook*.

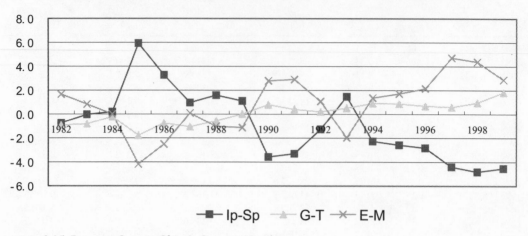

FIGURE 3.15 Resource Gaps in China's Opening-Up Phase

Source: Calculation according to issues of *China Statistical Yearbook*.

leading to a huge growth in imports. An investment-savings gap and trade deficit appeared in 1993, the only time in the 1990s.

In 1994, China's CPI inflation rate hit 24.1 percent and the government began austerity measures once again. However, this time the government mainly relied on monetary policies. From July 1993 to July 1995, the government increased interest rate three times: this had a restraining effect on investment. The fixed asset investment growth rate was 61.8 percent in 1993, 30.4 percent in 1994, and 14.8 percent in 1996. The fiscal deficit also declined.

Meanwhile, China carried out major reforms in its foreign exchange system in 1994 and the exchange rate depreciated by almost 50 percent, promoting huge export growth. In the years that followed, China maintained a high favorable trade balance because of pro-export policies and the enhanced competitiveness of its export goods.

The Asian financial crisis in 1997 had huge negative effects on China's economy, leading to a rapid decline in the export growth rate. However, China maintained a favorable trade balance because the drop in its import growth was even greater. Meanwhile, non-government investment increased slowly because of a structural oversupply caused by years of repetitive construction, large amounts of unused production capacity, and restrictions on private ownership enterprises (in terms of their financing channels). At the same time, bank loans were much less than bank deposits, leaving huge deposit balances in the banking system.

Active fiscal policies became the most direct and effective way to stimulate China's economy. Deflation has persisted since 1997, and although the central bank has lowered the interest rate several times, it has failed to effectively stimulate the expansion of investment. Nor can the demand for consumption rise by large margins because citizens are unclear of their future income and expenditure after reform. In light of such conditions, government expenditure has become the most powerful tool to prop up economic growth, especially the government investment in capital construction. In 1997, the government expenditure for capital construction was 101.95 billion yuan. The number increased to 138.77 billion in 1998 and 211.66 billion yuan in 1999. The gap between government expenditures and revenues was mainly covered through issuing public debt. Consequently, the amount of government debt has also expanded greatly (see table 3.12).

In the 1990s (especially after 1994), the government began to issue public debt on a large scale. As institutional investors were permitted to enter the bond market, they replaced individuals as the main holders of government debt. Because the interest rate on treasury bonds was higher than on bank deposits, individuals and SOEs were actively purchasing treasury bonds (see table 3.13). And because the profitability expectations of most enterprises were not encouraging, commercial banks tended to buy large volumes of treasury bills and bonds instead of giving loans.

TABLE 3.12 Government Debt Issuance (100 Million Yuan)

	Total	Domestic Debt	Foreign Borrowing	Other Domestic Debts
1982	83.86	43.83	40.03	
1983	79.41	41.58	37.83	
1984	77.34	42.53	34.81	
1985	89.85	60.61	29.24	
1986	138.25	62.51	75.74	
1987	223.55	63.07	106.48	54.00
1988	270.78	92.17	138.61	40.00
1989	407.97	56.07	144.06	207.84
1990	375.45	93.46	178.21	103.78
1991	461.40	199.30	180.13	81.97
1992	669.68	395.64	208.91	65.13
1993	739.22	314.78	357.90	66.54
1994	1,175.25	1,028.57	146.68	
1995	1,549.76	1,510.86	38.90	
1996	1,967.28	1,847.77	119.51	
1997	2,476.82	2,412.03	64.79	
1998	3,310.93	3,228.77	82.16	
1999	3,715.03	3,702.13		12.90
2000	4,180.10	4,153.59	23.10	3.41

Source: *China Statistical Yearbook* (2001).

In the 1990s (except for 1993), a big private sector surplus financed the government deficit expansion and the trade surplus. The direct reason for this situation was the rapid growth of private sector savings and relatively insufficient private sector investment. However, the underlying reason for this lies in the economic reform.

Before the reform and the opening-up drive, the government received the majority of the national income and became the main source of savings. SOEs had no authority to invest autonomously. The government made decisions to distribute investments and became, by de facto, the primary investor in the economy. However, after the reform and opening-up drive, national income distribution was skewed in favor of individuals, and households became the main source of savings. Because of the inadequate social security system and uncertain future expectations, household savings rates were very high. Thus, continuing economic growth pushed the household savings growth to 30 percent per year.

However, economic reforms gave enterprises the freedom to make investment decisions, and enterprises became the main investors. In China, direct finance was not as yet well developed. The main channel between savings and investment was the banking system that was dominated by state-owned banks. After the commercialization of state-owned banks, strict control on bad loan ratios made banks more cautious. Duplicated constructions of the past led to oversupply in many industries; thus, profitable investment opportunities were hard to find. At the same time, some growing and profitable privately owned enterprises and small business had difficulties getting loans from state-owned banks. All the above factors restrained the growth of investment, leaving a big surplus in the private sector. Part of the surplus has flown out in the form of trade surplus, and the other part has financed government deficits through treasury bond purchases.

4. Employment and Labor Productivity

4.1. Employment Growth

Since the reform and opening-up policy, there was a continuous growth in employment. In 1978, the total number of employed persons was 401.52 million. In 2000, employment was up to 711.5 million, a net increase of 309.98 million. The annual employment growth rate averaged 2.9 percent from 1979 to 1990. Thereafter, the growth rate gradually stabilized to 1.1 percent (1991 to 2000).

TABLE 3.13 Structure of Treasury Bonds Holders (%)

	Individuals	SOEs	Non-Banking Financial Institutions	Life Insurance Funds	Commercial Banks
1981		100			
1982–1990	80	20			
1991–1993	75	10	10	5	
1994–1995	75	5	10	5	5
1996	30	15	20	15	20

Source: www.ChinaBond.com.cn.

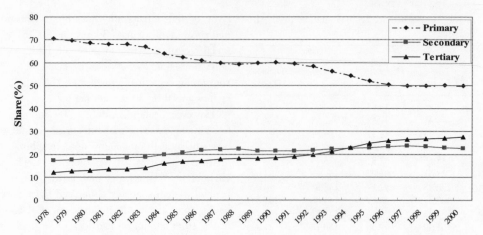

FIGURE 3.16 Changes in the Employment Structure, 1979–2000

4.2. Changes in Employment Structure

The structure of employment in China shows two significant changes.

4.2.1. Labor Moves away from the Primary Industry

As shown in figure 3.16, the agriculture sector share of the total employed persons declined from 69.8 percent in 1979 to 50 percent in 2000, a reduction of nearly 20 percent. Meanwhile, the labor force share engaged

in the secondary sector increased from 17.6 percent in 1979 to 22.5 percent in 2000, an increase of about 4.9 percent. The tertiary sector labor share grew from 12.6 percent in 1979 to 27.5 percent in 2000, an increase of about 15 percent. These trends reflect and are consist with industrialization.

4.2.2. Employment in the Non-state Units Remains High

As shown in figures 3.17 and 3.18, owing to the transformation of the economy, the adjustment in the

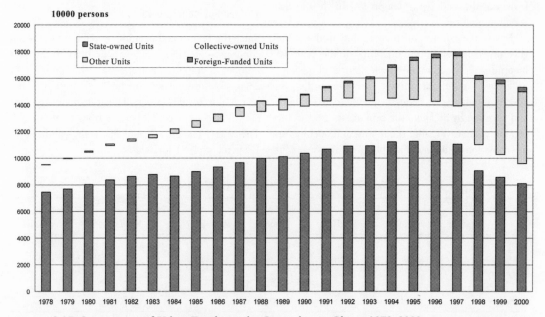

FIGURE 3.17 Composition of Urban Employees by Ownership in China, 1978–2000

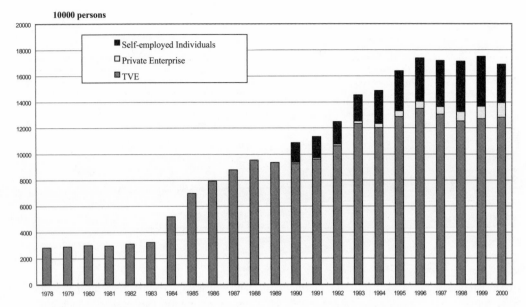

FIGURE 3.18 Composition of Rural Employees by Ownership in China, 1978–2000

industrial structure, and the SOE reform, the SOE's capacity to absorb labor force became increasingly weaker. The employment growth rates of the state and collectively owned enterprises have been declining. Especially from 1997 to 2000, negative growth rates have been the norm. In this period, collectively owned urban enterprises also faced austerity measures. From 1992 to 2000, the average annual growth rate for the state and collectively owned enterprises in towns dropped to –0.63 and –10.44 percent respectively.

The non-state-owned sectors played an increasingly important role in stabilizing employment. The share of the urban employed in the non-state-owned sectors increased from 0.16 percent in 1978 to 25.3 percent in 2000. Enterprises with foreign funds or with funds from Hong Kong, Macao, or Taiwan have been the fastest in developing. In 1985 there were only 60,000 employees working for these enterprises, while in 2000 this number had jumped to 6.42 million (accounting for 3 percent of total urban employment): an annual growth rate of 36.6 percent. The next biggest growers were the private enterprises and town and village enterprises (TVEs). Employees in these enterprises rose from 150,000 in 1978 to 34.02 million in 2000 at an annual rate of 27.9 percent.

4.3. Labor Productivity

International trade and the opening of the domestic market have played increasingly important roles in regulating China's internal industrial profits, restructuring as well as labor flows, and ultimately this will affect productivity in various sectors. Here we follow Berg and Taylor's decomposition technique to identify the main drivers of productivity growth.

4.3.1. Overview

With more than twenty years of foreign investment and participation in the international scientific and technological community, China not only has imported technologies and key equipment but also, by learning from foreign enterprise management experience, has introduced excellent human resource management and intensified competition among enterprises. In short, the country has greatly boosted its general industrial, technological, and management level.

Labor productivity has maintained a relatively high growth rate, with an average annual growth rate of 5.97 percent in 1979–1990 and 9.09 percent in 1991–2000. Productivity grows at different rates in different sectors. Industrial sector productivity is the fastest growing: a 9.91 percent average annual

TABLE 3.14 Contributions of Sectoral Productivity Growth to Overall Productivity

	Growth Rate of Overall Productivity (%)	Σ	$\left(\frac{X_i}{X}\right)_{t-1} \hat{P}_i$			
			Agriculture	Industry	Construction	Service
1979	4.17	5.49	1.39	3.86	−0.19	0.43
1984	14.31	10.34	4.62	5.96	−0.65	0.42
1988	9.08	8.28	0.17	5.85	0.19	2.07
1991	7.52	6.91	−0.03	5.32	0.32	1.29
1992	13.41	11.43	1.27	7.92	0.61	1.64
1998	7.44	7.63	0.59	3.88	0.84	2.32
2000	7.27	6.17	0.50	4.25	0.13	1.28
1979–2000 Annual Average Growth Rate (%)		6.77	3.92	9.91	3.43	4.30

Source: Calculations based on *China Statistical Yearbook* (various years).

growth rate was achieved in 1979–2000. During the same period, the service sector came in second at 4.30 percent, and agricultural and construction productivity growth rates were 3.92 and 3.43 percent respectively. Table 3.14 shows that sectoral productivity growth, particularly in the case of the industrial sector, plays an important role in the improvement of overall productivity.

4.3.2. The Effect of Employment Reallocation

With its large farming sector, China is a prime example of transition from a planning to a market economy. The reallocation effect of transition on employment is especially noticeable with respect to aggregate productivity growth. From table 3.15, we find that the absolute value of the sectoral reallocation effect was especially high in the industrial and agricultural sector. The agricultural sector's reallocation effect has been negative for twenty-plus years, but its absolute value shows a declining trend. The negative effects of the employment gains of the agricultural sector on overall productivity will grad-

ually weaken. In contrast, the industrial sector shows the reverse trend. The positive effects on overall productivity will become more and more notable in industry.

Since the reform and opening up, TVEs, private enterprises, foreign-funded enterprises, and other non-state-owned enterprises have vigorously developed. This has created a large number of new jobs and further boosted labor shifts from the primary to the secondary and tertiary sector. Structural adjustment, industrialization, and industrial upgrading have also had a similar effect on labor shifts. During the early period of external liberalization (1979–1983), the effect of employment reallocation on the growth of overall productivity was negative only in the agriculture sector. With the process of reform and opening, the positive effect was gradually strengthened (see table 3.16).

After 1984, with the development of a market economy, TVEs and private enterprises entered the transition period of structural adjustment and innovation, and economic growth gradually stabilized. The employment absorptive capacity of non-agricultural

TABLE 3.15 The Sectoral Reallocation Effect (%)

$(X_i/X-L_i/L)_{t-1}$ (%)	1979	1984	1988	1991	1992	1994	1998	2000
Agriculture	−42.43	−34.04	−33.20	−26.33	−29.48	−31.30	−28.47	−29.82
Industry	29.17	24.10	20.64	21.80	22.06	25.07	28.06	29.92
Construction	1.69	1.80	1.05	0.84	0.87	2.00	1.50	1.83
Service	11.57	8.14	11.51	14.91	16.49	13.50	7.42	9.53

Source: Calculations based on *China Statistical Yearbook* (2001).

TABLE 3.16 Employment Reallocation Effect on the Growth of Overall Productivity

| | Growth Rate of Overall Productivity (%) | Σ | $\left(\frac{X_i}{X} - \frac{L_i}{L}\right)_{t-1} \hat{L}$ | | | |
			Agriculture	Industry	Construction	Service
1979	4.17	1.32 (31.7%)	−0.47	0.99	0.12	0.68
1984	14.31	3.97 (27.7%)	0.31	1.74	0.53	1.40
1988	9.08	0.80 (8.8%)	−0.61	0.70	0.05	0.66
1991	7.52	0.61 (8.1%)	−0.65	0.56	0.02	0.67
1992	13.41	1.98 (14.8%)	0.14	0.60	0.06	1.18
1998	7.44	−0.19 (−2.6%)	−0.12	−3.75	−0.05	0.05
2000	7.27	0.10 (1.6%)	0.12	−0.45	0.08	0.36

Note: The figure within parentheses refers to the contribution of employment reallocation in that sector to the growth of overall productivity.

sectors decreased in the middle and late 1980s, and in the early 1990s labor began to move back into the agricultural sector. The number of employed persons in agriculture increased by 38.26 million from 1985 to 1991, with an average annual growth rate of 1.95 percent. The negative effects of employment growth in this sector on overall productivity are apparent once again, and the contributions of sectoral productivity growth to the improvement of overall productivity show a declining trend.

In 1992 alone, the number of direct investment projects by investors in foreign countries, Hong Kong, Macao, and Taiwan hit 48,764, 2.8 times higher than that in 1991. Foreign investment also maintained high growth in the following years. The construction of coastal development zones and the "three comings and one compensation"[10] enterprises greatly promoted the development of export-oriented processing and trading enterprises, TVEs, and foreign-funded enterprises.[11] In addition, the development of the commercial service industry and construction in big and medium-sized cities has produced urgent demands for relatively cheaper rural labor. During this period, employment in the industrial, construction, and service sectors grew at an average annual rate of 1.71, 6.39, and 7.3 percent respectively. The number of employed persons in agriculture fell by 1.38 percent during 1992–1996. The effect of employment growth on overall productivity in the agricultural sector had become positive.

The Asian financial crisis in 1997 affected the economic growth of many countries in Asia and the world, exerting a notably negative influence on China's exports and the development of TVEs.

Because China's economic expansion slowed down, along with the strengthening of reforms in state-owned enterprises, lots of workers were laid off. From 1997 to 2000, the average annual employment growth rate slumped to –6.06 percent in industry, 0.98 percent in construction, and 1.58 percent in the service sector. This had a negative effect on general productivity. Employment in agriculture increased for three consecutive years since 1997 with an increase of 5.83 million from 1996 to 1999. Employment in 2000 was less than that in 1999, but was still 4.45 million more than that in 1996. The reallocation of labor across sectors shows negative effects on overall productivity from 1997 to 1999; however, this situation eased in 2000.

5. External Liberalization and Income Distribution

Since 1979, the pattern of income allocation among the state, enterprises, and individuals has drastically inclined toward individuals. The ratio of government revenue to GDP declined from 31.2 percent in 1978 to 10.9 percent in 1996, and the ratio of personal incomes to GDP soared from 50.5 percent in 1978 to 80.9 percent in 1997. Although government revenue began to rise after 1997 and its ratio to GDP rose to 15.0 percent in 2000, because of the increasing regulation of taxation, generally speaking, the ratio of government revenue to GDP has sharply decreased comparing to the beginning of reform and opening up. The government's control over the economy has weakened and enterprises have been released of their social obligations. These have affected changes in household income distribution to some extent.

5.1. The Characteristics of Household Income Distribution after Liberalization

5.1.1. Household Income Increases Substantially

The reform and opening up have brought unprecedented prosperity to China's economy and also enabled Chinese urban and rural households to enjoy such prosperity. From 1978 to 2000, per capita GDP grew annually at a rate of 8.1 percent while per capita household consumption grew from 184 yuan to 3,397 yuan. From 1985 to 2000, annual per capita consumption grew especially sharply at a rate of 5.86 percent in constant prices.

Since 1978, wages have risen substantially. The average worker's wages were only 615 yuan in 1978 and surged to 9,371 yuan in 2000. Farmers have also scored a substantial increase in their earnings. From 1978 to 2000, the per capita net income of China's rural families surged from 133.6 yuan to 2,253.4 yuan. Not accounting for price increases, rural income grew at an average annual rate of 7.35 percent.

5.1.2. The Diversification of the Source of Household Income

A marked change has taken place in the income structure of urban households. A survey conducted by the National Bureau of Statistics shows that with the reform of the income distribution system, the share of wage incomes fell substantially while non-wage incomes rose year by year. According to the survey, the share of non-wage incomes of urban workers from their workplace jumped from 8 percent in 1978 to 32.8 percent in 1997 (with the number excluding various in-kind compensations by workplaces and non-wage incomes from units other than workplaces). In 1999, wage income accounted for 44.5 percent of the total income of urban households, 43 percentage points lower than in 1981 and 23 percentage points down from 1990. Non-wage incomes—such as property income, net income from individual operations, and transfer incomes—made up 55.5 percent of the total income of urban households. Yet analysis indicates that wage income remains a primary source of the stabilization of family incomes and that it has always played the key role in equalizing incomes.

Non-wage incomes are concentrated in high-income households, thus aggravating the inequality of income distribution. Social relief funds and living expenses issued to laid-off workers constitute a large share of the income of low-income earners and narrow the income gap to some extent, but their impact is still small.

5.1.3. The Inequality in Household Income

In terms of universal income growth, the Chinese have not enjoyed the prosperity brought about by economic growth on an equal footing. As far as the overall state of national income distribution is concerned, since the initiation of the reform and opening up, the gap in household incomes has by and large steadily increased and China's income distribution has become increasingly unequal.

China's Gini coefficient has continually increased since the initiation of the reform and opening policy. Calculations by the World Bank show that in 1967, the Gini of personal urban household income in China was 0.15, almost the lowest in the world. In 1980, the World Bank estimated the Gini coefficient of China's mainland households' income at 0.33. The income disparity as a whole was not extensive, and income distribution was quite equal within urban and rural areas. In 1988, the Gini drawn from both urban and rural areas rose to 0.382. Since the beginning of the 1990s, household income disparity has further widened. Statistics from the National Bureau of Statistics show that the Gini coefficient drawn from both urban and rural areas hit 0.425 in 1996 and climbed further to 0.456 in 1998. However, the Gini may be inaccurate because of statistical errors in the data. For example, some people may underreport their incomes. Problems also exist in the selection of samples.

Table 3.17 shows that although the national Gini coefficient may decrease if the price difference between urban and rural areas is taken into account, we can see that since the beginning of the 1990s, the Gini coefficient has been rising steadily.

5.1.4. The Characteristics of Widening Household Income Disparity

The widening household income disparity is manifested in the rising income gap between urban and rural areas, between regions, among urban households,

TABLE 3.17 Gini Coefficient

	Rural Gini	Urban Gini	National CLD = 0	National CLD = 10%
1990	29.87	23.42	34.84	33.34
1993	33.70	27.18	41.96	40.18
1996	32.98	28.52	39.80	38.16
1997	33.12	29.35	39.79	38.21
1998	33.07	29.94	40.30	38.70
1999	33.91	29.71	41.64	39.97

Source: World Bank.

Note: Given that the price level is lower in rural areas than in urban areas, the purchasing power of money is stronger in rural areas. Therefore, in order to calculate the national Gini coefficient at comparable prices, incomes are adjusted according to the 10% difference in the price level between urban and rural areas.

TABLE 3.18 Per Capita Annual Income of Urban and Rural Households

Year	Per Capita Annual Net Income of Rural Households (Yuan)	Per Capita Annual Disposable Income of Urban Households (Yuan)	The Ratio of Urban to Rural
1978	133.6	343.4	2.57
1979	160.2	387.0	2.42
1980	191.3	477.6	2.50
1983	309.8	564.0	1.82
1984	355.3	651.2	1.83
1985	397.6	739.1	1.86
1990	686.3	1,510.2	2.20
1995	1,577.7	4,283.0	2.71
1996	1,926.1	4,838.9	2.51
1997	2,090.1	5,160.3	2.47
1998	2,162.0	5,425.1	2.51
1999	2,210.3	5,854.0	2.65
2000	2,253.4	6,280.0	2.79

Source: *China Statistical Yearbook* (2001).

between industries, and between units of different ownership types.

1. The income gap between urban and rural households has been widening steadily.

   In 1978, the ratio of the per capita disposable income of urban households to the per capita net income of rural households was 2.5:1. From 1980 to 1983, as a result of rural land system reform, the living standards of farmers rose substantially and their per capita net income posted sustained growth. After 1984, however, the income gap between urban and rural households steadily widened. Especially since the 1990s, the increase in the per capita net income of rural households has been far lower than the per capita disposable income of urban households. Moreover, the increase in farmers' income has been slow, further widening the income gap between urban and rural households. Furthermore, given that a large part of the net income of rural households is used for production and the fact that urban households enjoy various kinds of financial subsidies in housing, medical care, and education, the actual income gap between urban and rural households is even wider. Table 3.18 shows the income disparities between rural and urban households from 1978 to 2000.

2. The gap between regions has continued to grow: since China initiated the reform and opening up, all provinces had growth rates exceeding those before the reform.

   Figures 3.19 and 3.20 below show that regional disparity in per capita GDP narrowed

during the 1980s and began to increase in the early years of the 1990s. The disparities in per capita consumption among regions decreased transitorily in the beginning of the 1980s and maintained a slowly rising trend, but fell in the last two years. Meanwhile, the gap in per capita consumption among regions is lower than that of per capita GDP, which shows that transfer payments from the government are effective in narrowing consumption disparity among regions. However, figure 3.19 also shows that the gap in per capita GDP is becoming close to that of per capita consumption, which also shows that the ability of the central government to adjust incomes has weakened.

Figure 3.20 shows that the consumption disparity of rural households across regions is higher than that of urban households. Second, as far as the overall trend is concerned, the consumption gap among rural households has been widening with fluctuations. After 1990, at first, the gap dramatically increased and then widened steadily. Third, the consumption disparity of urban households gradually increased in the early 1980s, decreased from 1983 to 1985, and increased again after 1988. But the two most recent years have seen a slowly decreasing trend.

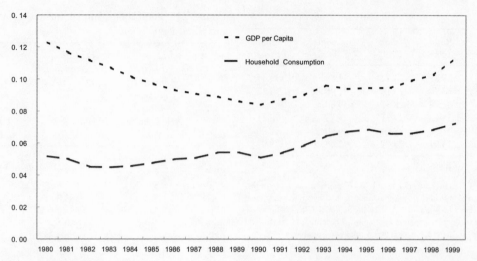

FIGURE 3.19 Variation Coefficient of per Capita GDP and Household Consumption across Provinces (Calculated at 1980 Prices)

These features can also be seen in the comparison of per capita net income. In 1978, Shanghai (which had the highest average rural household income) had an average per capita net income of 290 yuan, whereas Hebei (which had the lowest average rural household income) had an average per capita income of 91.5 yuan, a ratio of 3.2:1. In 2000, Shanghai (which was still the highest ranked in terms of the income of rural households) had an average per capita net income of 5,596 yuan, whereas Guizhou (which now had the lowest rural per capital income) had an average per capita income of 1,374 yuan, a ratio of 4.07:1. At the same time, the income gap among rural households in the eastern region, the central

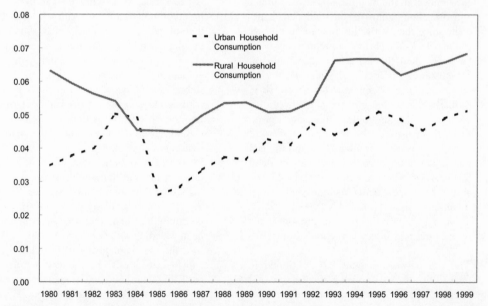

FIGURE 3.20 Variation Coefficient of Urban and Rural Household Consumption per Capita across Regions

Note: Without weighted population.

region, and the western region noticeably widened.[12]

From the perspective of urban households, the consumption gap among regions gradually increased at the beginning of the 1980s and then decreased from 1983 to 1985. After 1988, the gap increased again. But it has exhibited a slowly decreasing trend in the last two years. In 1978, the ratio of the highest provincial per capita disposable income of urban households to the lowest one was 1.62:1, and this ratio surged to 2.48:1 in 2000. Comparing the per capita disposable income of urban households in three regions, in 1980, the central region and western region matched 92.5 and 94.4 percent of the income of the eastern region, respectively. But the ratios plummeted to 68.3 and 72.5 percent, respectively, in 1998. Within eighteen years, they had plunged by 24.2 percentage points and 21.9 percentage points, respectively.

Income and wealth polarization are quite obvious among urban households. While the income and wealth of high-income households continues to increase, decreasing income for low-income groups has become a very serious problem. A survey conducted by the National Bureau of Statistics shows that in 1998, the per capita annual income of the highest-income earners (accounting for 20 percent of urban households) was 10,962 yuan, whereas that of the lowest-income earners (accounting for 20 percent of urban households) was only 2,447 yuan. The income of the highest-income households was 4.5 times that of the lowest-income households. The growth rate of the income of the highest-income group (accounting for 10 percent of urban households) was 5 percentage points higher than that of the lowest-income group (accounting for 10 percent of urban households). In other words, social wealth is increasingly concentrated in high-income households.

3. The income gap between different industries has kept rising.

The industrial gap primarily refers to the gap in the incomes of people employed in different industries. Restricted by the data, we mainly compare the wages of workers in different industries. Since 1978, the gap in the wage level among different industries has further widened. Meanwhile, a marked change has taken place in the income rankings of different industries.

In 1978, the wage gap among various sectors was not wide, with the ratio of the industry with the highest average annual wage income to the industry with the lowest average annual wage income being only 1.66:1.

After the initiation of the reform and external liberalization, on the one hand, distribution began to incline toward industries with a high content of science and technology as well as the newly emerging industries. Wage levels in the traditional manual labor industry, the labor-intensive industries, and highly competitive industries plunged relative to the wage levels in high-tech and newly emerging industries, which have been growing substantially. A striking example of this trend is that of the mining industry. The wage level of workers employed in mining was the highest ranking among all industries in 1990, and yet plummeted to the third-lowest rank in 2000. By comparison, the wage level employed in computer application services in 2000 was 28,333 yuan, ranking first among all industries, and far above the national average level of 9,371 yuan.

On the other hand, the wage gap between the monopoly industries and non-monopoly industries has widened since 1990. In 1991, the average wages of workers in the production and supply of electricity, gas, and water were 2,922 yuan; those of workers in finance and insurance were 2,255 yuan; and those of workers in manufacturing were 2,289 yuan, the ratio among the three being 1.28:0.93:1.0. In 2000, the average wages of workers in the electricity, gas, and water industry were 12,830 yuan; those of workers in finance and insurance were 13,478 yuan; and those of workers in manufacturing were 8,750 yuan, with the ratio among the three being 1.48:1.55:1.0. In 2000, the average wages of workers in air transport and post and telecommunication services were 23,454 yuan and 16,359 yuan, ranking second and third highest respectively (after computer application services).

4. The gap between the average wages of workers in different ownership units has been widening.

In 1985, the ratio among average wages of workers in state-owned units, urban collective-owned units, and other units was 1:0.8:1.18. However, the ratio increased to 1:0.74:1.31 in 1990 and to 1:0.67:1.32 in 1996. After 1996, this ratio fluctuated without much change. From this we can see that the income gap

TABLE 3.19 Earnings Differentials between Average Wages of Units of Different Types

	1985	1990	1991	1992	1993	1994	1995	1996	1997	1998	1999
State owned	1,213	2,284	2,477	2,878	3,532	4,797	5,625	6,280	6,747	7,668	8,543
Collective owned	967	1,681	1,866	2,109	2,592	3,245	3,931	4,302	4,512	5,331	5,774
Other units	1,436	2,987	3,468	3,966	4,966	6,303	7,463	8,261	8,789	8,972	9,829
Foreign funded	2,144	3,411	3,918	4,347	5,315	6,533	8,058	9,383	10,361	11,767	12,951

Source: *China Statistical Yearbook.*

between workers in urban collective-owned units, workers in state-owned units, and workers in other units has increasingly widened.

From table 3.19 we can see that the wage level in foreign-funded enterprises is far higher than the overall average wage level. Workers and staff in such enterprises enjoy a very high income, and the income gap between them and workers in other types of enterprises has been rising.

5.2. An Analysis of the Increasingly Widening Income Gap

Unbalanced income distribution in China has both internal as well as external reasons. China's domestic reform program has fundamentally worsened income distribution. On the other hand, China's external liberalization is by no means the definite cause of the imbalance in the income distribution. However, in practice, external liberalization has some impact on income distribution. The following factors are the main contributors to the widening income gap.

1. Reform of the income distribution system has widened the income gap.

    Since China's reform and opening to the outside world, the transformation of the economic system has resulted in high growth rates as well as a change in the profit and income distribution pattern. In the new market economy, the ethos of "to each according to his work" prevails and various productive factors jointly partake in distribution. In the course of market competition, the formation and expansion of the income gap are inevitable because of competitive differences between social members and economic organizations, and the disparity between labor contributions and other factor inputs.

2. The development of factor markets further widens the income gap.

The income level is defined not only by working time but also by production factors, such as capital, technique, management, and risk, that widen the income gap. In terms of the link between income and education, (after reform) a worker's income is in direct proportion to her level of education. In 1997, college degree holders had an average annual income of 10,364 yuan. Junior college degree holders earned an average of 8,944 yuan. Technical secondary school graduates' average earnings were 8,071 yuan, and senior high school graduates, on average, earned 7,229 yuan. Junior high school graduates' average earnings were 6,811 yuan, and elementary school graduates earned an average annual income of 6,468 yuan. The income ratio of those with a primary school education to those with a university education was 1:1.6.

External liberalization also accelerated the transformation of the income structure. In order to attract a more talented workforce in an increasingly competitive environment, many domestic enterprises have widened the income gap between employees with different posts or ranks. The variable part of one's wage has an increasingly larger share in the total wage, and is now widely recognized as the key element comprising the income gap. Along with wage structure rationalization, people are increasingly earning non-wage incomes, the effect of which has significantly widened the income gap. Income from property plays an increasingly important role in total income.

The development of the domestic economy and the increased utilization of foreign capital along with external liberalization helped accelerate the development and expansion of China's capital market. An increased availability of personal financial products has provided more opportunities for households to gain incomes from financial investments. In 1990, the annual capital income of an urban resident was 15.6 yuan. By 2000, this number had increased to 128.38 yuan. Although this type of income plays a relatively minor role in one's total disposable income, it is the source of serious imbalances among households. According to a 1999 investigation of the income sources of high-income families in urban areas, the average annual income of these households was 109,702 yuan. However, the average capital income was 6,528 yuan, accounting for about 6 percent of the total average income, and the average income from doing business was 37,112 yuan, accounting for about 33.8 percent of the total income. This high-income group, which accounted for merely 6 percent of the total population, enjoyed 60 percent of total capital income. It is true that capital income did not contribute much to the total income, but it did contribute to the worsening income disparity.

3. The reform of state-owned enterprises (SOEs) and the adjustment of the industrial structure have changed the income distribution pattern.

The reform of SOEs has exposed these enterprises to intense market competition. At the same time, the increase in import-oriented and foreign-funded enterprises accompanying the expansion of external liberalization has intensified market competition. Consequently, many domestic enterprises have suffered losses in the face of intensifying competition: some have had to downsize their staff; and some enterprises, especially those that suffer from long-term losses, insolvency, or unsustainable deficits, have been forced into bankruptcy. As a result, many workers have lost their jobs or their incomes have been reduced dramatically.

Moreover, increased competition has promoted greater productive efficiency (with the goal of eliminating excess production capacity) and accelerated the development of high-tech and capital-intensive industries. All this will bring about numerous changes in labor flows, and higher unemployment rates will be inevitable. Meanwhile, the upgrading of the industrial structure has given rise to the change in the structure of labor demand. As a result, society has increased its demand for high-quality labor and decreased its demand for low-quality labor. The change in the demand structure has increased the wage rate of technicians and reduced the wage rate of non-technicians, leading to the worsening of the income gap.

The reform of the ownership structure took a much greater toll on traditional SOEs relative to dynamic non-state enterprises. With their out-of-date operating systems, SOEs found it difficult to adapt to the market. Non-state-owned enterprises, however, enjoyed rapid development and expanded their scale with the introduction of foreign capital and the growth of foreign trade. Their profits are generally far more inspiring than those of the SOEs. Workers in non-state enterprises also enjoy a higher level of wages relative to those in SOEs. This is especially apparent in foreign-funded or joint venture enterprises, where skilled workers are concentrated and whose wage levels are far greater than those in other enterprises. With the unfolding of competing demands for professionals between foreign-funded and domestic enterprises, skilled workers are more likely to benefit. As external liberalization deepens, the wage level of Chinese high-tech talents and senior management personnel will also gradually converge to international standards. However, foreign capital has little impact on workers from traditional sectors or SOEs. Workers from these sectors will maintain their relatively low-income levels, and this will help further widen the already existing income gap.

4. Unbalanced regional economic development.

Owing to its relatively advanced development, environmental conditions, regional advantage, and government support, the eastern region has achieved rapid economic growth. In the course of its leading the country in opening to the outside world, the gap between it and the central and western regions has widened (see table 3.20). It is true that the eastern region's utilization of foreign investment will attract labor, create jobs, and help increase household incomes. But the skewed geographic distribution of overseas investment has furthered the already existing gap between different regions in China. There are obvious regional differences in terms of the degree and the timing of external liberalization. These differences, along with the uneven regional distribution of foreign investment and wide regional disparities in

TABLE 3.20 Foreign Investment by Region (%)

	1979	1985	1990	1995	1999
Eastern region	100	95.9	94.6	88.1	87.6
Central region	0	4.1	3.5	8.9	9.5
Western region	0	0	2.3	3.0	2.9

terms of foreign trade, have aggravated regional inequality in economic development.

5. The declining trend in agricultural prices worsens the income of farmers.

In recent years, China's rural economy has suffered a slowdown. China has an underdeveloped agriculture sector. Compared with other countries, China's agriculture products are high cost and less competitive in the production of land-intensive products. Since 1997, Chinese grain prices have tended to rise steadily. As for the long-term trend, because of resource restraints and supply-demand relations, China's domestic grain prices will probably be higher than grain prices in the international market. After external liberalization, China's traditional agriculture can barely compete against large-scale foreign farms. In the international market, awash with cheap agriculture products, the prices of Chinese products will inevitably make its agricultural products less competitive.

6. Lagging urbanization slows down the increase in rural income levels.

The transformation from agricultural to non-agricultural labor is the precondition for the improvement of productivity and the increased scale of agriculture production and operation. However, China's urbanization level still ranks with those of low-income countries. According to World Bank statistics, China's urbanization level was merely 32 percent in 1999, 14 percent lower than the world average. Lagging urbanization has weakened the ability to absorb rural surplus labor, thereby preventing the further transformation of labor from agriculture sector to non-agriculture sector and limiting the development of agricultural industrialization as well as the increase in farmers' incomes. Not surprisingly, the income gap between rural and urban areas has increasingly grown.

7. The existence of monopolies.

Since competitive market institutions have not been fully established, monopolies still exist in some industries, such as telecommunications, banking, insurance, and railways. The average wages of workers employed in these monopoly industries have experienced rapid growth relative to competitive industries. From 1978 to 2000, the growth rate of the national average wage was 13.2 percent, while that in the insurance industry was 15.1 percent. In short, monopolies have greatly contributed to the widening income gap between different industries.

8. Unlawful and corrupt activities intensify the income unbalance.

Among all the problems faced by China in its transition from a planned to a market society, overhauling the legal system was yet another hurdle, and weaknesses and loopholes in the law still remain. Unfair competition and corruption are common and have deleterious effects on income distribution. Some people use their franchises to seek "rental" and gray incomes. This illegal means of income has a very negative influence on income distribution and further intensifies the income imbalance.

In summary, external liberalization has had some positive effects on income distribution. For example, China has a comparative advantage in labor-intensive industries. Increased exports will promote the speedy development of labor-intensive industries such as manufacturing, and will therefore help create a huge number of job opportunities. This will enable surplus rural laborers to transfer from the primary to the secondary or the tertiary industry. The transformation of agricultural labor to non-agricultural labor will increase the overall income level of rural households. The development of foreign trade and investment introduces new techniques and advanced management experience into the domestic environment. This helps strengthen the competitiveness of domestic enterprises. Besides, external liberalization has also facilitated the labor flow. All these factors have benefited income distribution. However, when the distribution of investment is unbalanced, and the degree of foreign trade differs from one place to another, foreign investment does not promote fair results for everyone. At the same time, foreign investments are more likely to enter competitive fields that promote a more equitable income distribution. So far, all of the elements mentioned above have resulted in an increasingly widening income gap.

6. Poverty

6.1. The Poverty Relief Program

The poverty relief program was put forward and implemented on a large scale only after the initiation of the reform and external liberalization. From 1978 to 2000, this program underwent the following three stages.

TABLE 3.21 Rural Poor Population and Impoverishment Rate

	1978	1985	1993	2000
Rural poor population (million)	250	125	80	30
Rural impoverishment rate (%)	30.7	14.8	8.7	3

Structural Reform Promotes Poverty Relief (1978–1985)

In this phase, farm production was improved thanks to rural land reform. As a result, the number of poverty-stricken people fell by 17.86 million annually, on average (see table 3.21).

Large-Scale Development-Oriented Poverty Relief Drive (1986–1993)

To further strengthen poverty relief, the Chinese government adopted a series of important measures since 1986, such as setting up special help-the-poor work units and allocating special funds for the poor. During this period, the number of the rural poor fell, with an annual decrease of 6.4 million on average, and at an average annual rate of 6.2 percent.

Tackling Key Problems of Poverty Relief (1994–2000)

This phase was marked by the promulgation and implementation of the Seven Year Priority Poverty Alleviation Program in March 1994. This program clearly stipulated that China should concentrate on building its human, material, and financial resources.

The program also intended to mobilize people from all walks of life in the effort to solve the food and clothing problems of the rural needy by the end of 2000. It was the first action program for development-oriented poverty reduction with clear and definite objectives, targets, and measures, as well as a time limit.

6.2. The Current State of Poverty in China

The current state of poverty in China may be characterized by the following three aspects:

1. The coexistence of absolute and relative poverty.

Solving the food problem for rural households marks, in a sense, the easing of the state of absolute poverty in China. Yet at the same time, relative poverty—which is on the rise—has become another salient characteristic of the state of China's poverty. The widening gap between the rich and the poor is the strongest expression of relative poverty.

2. The coexistence of rural and urban poverty.

Before China initiated the reform and external liberalization drive, China's poverty was concentrated in its rural areas. Urban poverty was little known before the 1990s. However, in the course of industrialization and urbanization, redundant rural laborers inevitably flocked to cities. The overwhelming majority of these migrants and their families joined the mass of the urban poor. Also part of the urban poor are those who have lost their jobs as a result of the economic restructuring. Weakened profitability (as competition intensifies), increased losses, and bankruptcy are the most direct reasons for the formation of the urban poor. In line with different price indices and living standards, different cities have different poverty lines. According to the analysis by the National Bureau of Statistics, China's urban poor numbered 11.7 million in 2000.

3. The coexistence of regional and individual poverty.

China's rural poverty has evident regional characteristics. Spatially, the poor are extensively distributed yet also relatively concentrated. All provinces, autonomous regions, and municipalities under the direct administration of the central government house poor populations, 80 percent of whom are distributed in province-level areas in the central and western regions. 45.7 percent of China's poor are concentrated in the western region alone.

The main difficulties faced by China in the field of poverty alleviation are as follows. First, although the income of the poor has obviously improved, the current standard of poverty relief is very low. Second, restricted by unfavorable natural conditions (soil, water, natural resources, etc.) and a weak social insurance system, people who now have enough to eat and wear may easily sink back into poverty. Third, although the poverty reduction drive has greatly reduced poverty and poor social conditions for many, there has been no qualitative change either in the production and living conditions of poverty-stricken farmer households, or in the development of social, economic, and cultural conditions in the affected areas. Fourth, because of its large population, China will face employment constraints for many years to come. This pressure is bound to adversely affect employment opportunities for the impoverished and will lead to new populations of the urban poor. Besides, farmers operating on a small scale in impoverished rural areas can hardly keep up with the new market competition. Moreover, the environmental damages incurred during the course of development in impoverished rural areas will be difficult to recover. In short, poverty alleviation in China will be very complicated, arduous, and long-term work.[13]

Notes

1. China is a populous country and is vast in territory with a land area of 9.6 million square kilometers. Its population was 1.27 billion in 2000. According to the official average exchange rate, the total volume of China's GDP is more than 1,000 billion U.S. dollars and its GDP per capita exceeds US$850. Nonetheless, China is still a comparatively low-income country. According to the World Bank's 2002 *World Development Report*, China's gross national income (GNI) per capita in 2000 was $840. This was equivalent in level to 16.3 percent of the world average and 3.1 percent of the average level of high-income countries. Even if converted on the basis of purchasing power parity, China's GNI per capita in 2000 was only US$3,940, equivalent to 53.6 percent of the world average level and 14.4 percent of the average level of high-income countries.

2. Equivalent to $855 according to the official exchange rate.

3. The value of processing exports is the sum of imported inputs and value added by processing.

4. According to the customs statistics, in 2001, imports by processing trade amounted to $94.01 billion and exports amounted to $147.53 billion, with a total of US$241.54 billion, or 47 percent of China's foreign trade value.

5. With the devaluation of the U.S. dollar in 1971, the exchange rate was adjusted upward to one U.S. dollar against 2.2673 yuan.

6. With the U.S. dollar's appreciation, the official rate rose from 1.448 yuan against one U.S. dollar in 1980 to 2.7963 yuan in early 1985.

7. According to the statistics of the Ministry of Labor and Social Security, workers laid off from SOEs numbered 6.57 million in 2000. Laid-off workers accounted for 8.3 percent of the total number of those employed in SOEs in 2000.

8. After the Tian An Men event.

9. Among them are General Motors, Exxon Mobil, and Ford Corporation of the United States; the Matsushita Electric Industrial Company and the Mitsubishi Heavy Industries of Japan; the Volkswagen Company of Germany; and the Philips Company of the Netherlands.

10. Enterprises that process raw materials on clients' demand, assemble parts and process materials according to the clients' samples, and engage in compensation trade.

11. Especially in the southeast coastal areas, including the southern part of Jiangsu province, Wenzhou, southern Fujian province, and the Pearl River Delta area.

12. In 1978, the ratio of per capita net income of rural households among the eastern, the central, and the western region was 1.36:1.09:1 respectively. This ratio increased to 1.59:1.18:1 in 1985 and to 2.23:1.65:1 in 1995. After 1995, the ratio decreased some and was 2.13:1.35:1 in 1999. However, the absolute income gap is still very large.

13. Two poverty measures exist in China, given the large gap between urban and rural households. The standard of rural poverty was first calculated by the National Statistics Bureau in 1986, on the basis of investigations of the consumption expenditures of 67,000 rural households. The poverty line was determined as 206 yuan in per capita net income in rural areas in 1985. This was equivalent to 300 yuan in 1990 and 625 yuan in 2000 (about US$75.50) according to the price index changes. The urban poverty line was calculated according to different provinces, given that Chinese provinces have a huge population and vary greatly in terms of their living standards, patterns of consumption, and prices. Based on the 1998 data from the urban household survey conducted by the National Statistics Bureau, the provincial poverty lines ranged from 1,484 yuan (in Qinghai) to 3,636 yuan (in Shanghai) per capita income per year. The national urban poverty line is 2,310 yuan, which is a weighted average of provincial lines, with weights equal to provincial population shares.

References

Bell, Michael W., H. E. Khor, and Kalpana Kocchar. 1993. China at the threshold of market economy. IMF Occasional Paper, no. 107. Washington, D.C.: International Monetary Fund.

Berg, Janine, and Lance Taylor. 2000. External liberalization, economic performance, and social policy. CEPA Working Paper Series 1, no. 12, New York; Center for Economic Policy Analysis.

Cline, William R. 1997. *Trade and income distribution*. Washington, D.C.: Institute for International Economics.

Wang, Mengkui, ed. 1999. *The review and prospect of Chinese economic development*. Beijing: China Financial and Economics Publishing House.

4

Opening Up the Hungarian Economy: Conditions and Consequences of Liberalizing Trade and Capital Flows in Hungary

Gábor Oblath

Introduction

This chapter addresses four interrelated issues[1]:

- The external liberalization of current and capital transactions in Hungary—a review of controls on international transactions, the timing and sequencing of their removal, institutional changes, and the possible effects of liberalization measures;
- the macroeconomic history of Hungary during and after external liberalization—a description of general macroeconomic developments based on official statistics;
- decomposing changes in important macroeconomic variables (demand and employment)— this requires the construction of macroeconomic data from incomplete official statistics; and
- major social developments (in particular, changes in income distribution) during the period under review.

The first topic is the focal issue, as well as the point of departure, of our analysis: what type of controls on international transactions existed prior to external liberalization, how they were eased, and what the consequences of the liberalization measures were. The second and the third topics are clearly interrelated and represent two approaches to understanding macroeconomic developments and the effects of economic policies pursued in different subperiods. The only reason for making a distinction between the two approaches is that while one relies upon official statistics, the other uses data constructed for the present study.

Before touching upon the fourth topic, a warning is in order. I shall try to identify the economic and social implications of external liberalization. But it should be clear from the outside that in Hungary, just as in other countries of Central and Eastern Europe, trade liberalization in the early 1990s coincided with the fundamental transformation of the overall political, economic, and social system.[2] In Hungary, trade liberalization had been launched in 1989, a year before political transformation and the accompanying economic changes, but by the time the effects of liberalization would have become apparent, the more fundamental (economic and social) consequences of general systemic change already dominated the macroeconomic landscape. Therefore, it is extremely difficult to distinguish empirically between the implications of general changes in the system (involving domestic liberalization in several spheres of the economy) and those related to external liberalization proper.

These difficulties are even more pronounced when one turns to *social issues*, in particular income distribution. Although liberalization is likely to have had specific social effects, the drastic fall in output, employment and real incomes, as well as the emergence of *open* unemployment in the early 1990s, was due to the transformation of the overall economic system. Thus, it is not really possible to sort out which component of this change resulted from trade liberalization. I have to admit in advance that while reviewing major social changes as well as shifts in income distribution, I lack the points of reference and techniques for identifying the contribution of external liberalization to these changes.

Returning to the economic effects of trade liberalization, in addition to the difficulties mentioned so far, a special case of international macroeconomic interdependence has to be taken into account as well. Soon after the start of external liberalization in Hungary, profound systemic changes took place (involving similar liberalization measures) in other former socialist countries as well. Before the changes, Hungary had maintained very close economic links and special trade arrangements with these countries, under the framework of the CMEA (also referred to as COMECON). For several reasons—partly by design (i.e., political reasons), partly by default (inadequate coordination)—these links were very abruptly cut in the early 1990s. Besides the developments that were not directly related to external liberalization as well as the political and economic developments, changes in the country's important trading partners (including the demise of the CMEA) also affected the trade and overall economic performance of Hungary. (Naturally, the changes in Hungary simultaneously affected the country's eastern trading partners.)

There are two basic problems with identifying the effects of trade liberalization in Hungary. First, while liberalizing external transactions, the domestic economic system was fundamentally transformed, which initially resulted in a sharp decline in domestic output and employment. Second, the country's most important former trading partners liberalized their trade and transformed their economic system at the same time, which—via trade diversion—also had a negative effect on trade and output in the countries concerned.[3]

The period covered by this analysis involves the years 1989–1998 (though I also touch upon developments in 1999–2000). Over these ten years, the liberalization of trade (and other items in the current account) was fully implemented and capital flows were also substantially—though not fully—liberalized in Hungary. The remaining controls on capital flows were removed in a single step in June 2001. I shall discuss the potential effects of the last round of capital account liberalization only briefly, as they are beyond the scope of the present analysis.

This study primarily addresses issues related to trade (current account) liberalization. This is explained by the fact that while the liberalization of capital flows did not lead to serious macroeconomic problems in Hungary, trade liberalization did. This experience is in sharp contrast with that of several other countries that were also opening up their economies. As described in this study, the lack of major adverse effects of large capital inflows is partly due to the relatively efficient sterilization of the inflows, but also because of the partial and rather gradual liberalization of the capital account—at least until mid-2001.

Finally, some remarks on the statistics underlying my analysis, as well as on the conceptual difficulties of reconstructing macroeconomic data are necessary. As I focus on the quantitative description of macroeconomic and certain sectoral (social) developments, the quality of our analysis strongly hinges upon the quality of official Hungarian statistics.[4]

First, the accuracy and reliability of official statistics increase over time; in other words, figures for the late 1980s and early 1990s are generally less comprehensive and reliable than those for the second half of the 1990s. Second, as already mentioned, I was unable to quantify some of the basic macroeconomic identities from available official data. In order to carry out the decomposition exercises, I had to (re)construct certain macroeconomic statistics.

Briefly put, Hungarian national accounts, balance of payments, and fiscal statistics are inconsistent. Moreover, national accounts are incomplete (they only partially cover the general government and the external sector) and due to two major revisions in the accounting system, consistent time series (at current prices) are not available for the period under review. However, when attempting to overcome these shortcomings by constructing macroeconomic data to fit in the framework suggested by Berg and Taylor (2000) for decomposing aggregate demand, I ran into several conceptual difficulties, unrelated to the quality of official statistics.

Actually, the reconstruction of national accounts in accordance with macroeconomic identities turned out to be the most intricate phase of the study. I had to cope with two conceptual problems: the definition of the external balance and that of the fiscal balance. First, if the external balance is understood as net exports (of goods and services), the fiscal balance has to be redefined so as to exclude net interest payments on foreign public debt. If, in turn, the difference between net taxes and government expenditures is understood as a concept approximating the *actual* fiscal balance, then the external balance has to be redefined as (approximating) the current account (i.e., net exports plus net interest). As explained in the text, I chose the former interpretation. The second problem relates to the treatment of the inflationary component of domestic interest payments on public debt at a time of relatively high inflation. (In the period reviewed, inflation in Hungary varied between 10 and 35 percent.) As the component of interest payments that compensates for the inflationary erosion of public debt represents amortization rather than actual income transfer, we deducted the inflationary compensation from nominal interest payments on domestic public debt. Naturally, these two kinds of adjustments will affect the size/ratio of the calculated public deficit, as well as the relative share of the private and the government sector in GDP. As a result of these adjustments, some of the macroeconomic magnitudes in the standard analysis (based on official statistics) will be different from those in the decomposition exercises (based on reconstructed data).

The chapter is structured as follows: first, I present an overview of the main issues related to external economic liberalization in Hungary, focusing on the liberalization of trade. This is followed by a review of macroeconomic developments in the country over the past decade. Next, after dealing with the conceptual and statistical difficulties involved, decomposition exercises are performed regarding changes in aggregate demand and employment; at the end of this analysis, macroeconomic characteristics of different subperiods are discussed. The following section treats social changes and shifts in income distribution. Finally, the different lines of analysis are brought together and conclusions drawn regarding the mode of external liberalization in Hungary. It is in this section that I briefly touch upon the full-scale liberalization of capital transactions in mid–2001.[5]

1. External Liberalization in Hungary: Overview of Major Issues

While discussing external liberalization in Hungary, two distinct lines of the liberalization process have to be drawn. On the one hand, foreign trade was abruptly opened up in 1989, without any contingency planning in the event of unexpected developments. On the other hand, the liberalization of capital flows was introduced in a cautious, gradual manner (mainly after 1995). The non-trade transactions in the current account (i.e., services, in particular the supply of currency for travel) were also liberalized step by step. It was understood that there was no clear dividing line between the current and the capital account transactions in a period of dismantling the foreign exchange controls of central planning. While trade liberalization was introduced in a formally structured but substantively unregulated manner, capital account liberalization was implemented under policy control with very close monitoring and a continuous attempt to correct its potentially destabilizing macroeconomic effects. I shall argue that this major difference in policy attitudes regarding the two components of external liberalization has an important role in explaining why trade liberalization (along with other factors) almost lead to a balance of payments crisis, while major disruptions were avoided during the process of liberalizing the capital account. In the following, I first discuss questions related to trade (current account) liberalization; I return to the liberalization of financial transactions at a later point.

Trade liberalization in Hungary was to wind up becoming a peculiarly restrictive system that differed from international trade controls practice in several crucial ways. The import regime of the 1970s and 1980s was not explicit and did not rely on instruments applied in developed or developing market economies. However, it was more liberal than the trade regimes of the traditional centrally planned economies of Eastern Europe. (The Hungarian foreign trade regime corresponded to the general features of the overall system: unofficially, it used to be referred to as a system based on "neither plan, nor market".)[6] There were very few openly declared quotas, and import tariffs were not conspicuously high in Hungary. Controls on imports were imposed *directly* by the Licensing Department of the Ministry of Foreign Trade. However, *indirectly*, the entire "semicentrally planned" system of the 1970s and 1980s—as well as the state monopoly on foreign trade and the system responsible for its administration—also contributed to the filtering of imports.[7]

International experience regarding the liberalization of import regimes based on *open* quantitative restrictions (i.e., quotas) could not offer clear directions as to the ways and means of eliminating implicit restrictions based on informal rules. In particular, the experience of the IMF and the World Bank, gained under stabilization/liberalization programs, was not directly relevant for Hungary.

The situation was complicated by a further consideration. Hungary's options for liberalizing imports were seriously constrained by the fact that the actual operation of this rather complex and obscure system was utterly different from the one presented to the international public and to the country's relevant foreign partners. The Hungarian administration at that time "sold" international organizations (GATT and the World Bank, among others) the notion that the Hungarian import regime was fully liberalized (with customs duties only, and a licensing system used exclusively for registration purposes). The target audience—especially international organizations—accepted this presentation, although they very well knew that the Hungarian import regulation was based on informal administrative controls.[8]

The reason why this circumstance reduced the Hungarian government's options was that some of the suggested liberalization methods would have involved the disclosure of the actual workings of the Hungarian import regime internationally. The government ought to have acknowledged that the system was different from the picture earlier shown to the world. This would, no doubt, have implied many inconveniences, yet at that time, revealing the state of affairs was not without precedent: the actual size of the external debt was made public in the same period (in 1989).

Let us now turn to the main proposals regarding the ways and means of liberalizing imports. One of the proposals focused primarily on what commodity groups to liberalize and in what order. The other proposal primarily sought the techniques for transforming, as a first step, implicit quantitative restrictions into market-type instruments (tariffs and/or import surcharges) and envisaged the further stages of liberalization as the dismantling (reduction) of these tariffs/surcharges. (According to the latter concept, the "second best" alternative to the transformation of quantitative controls into customs duties could have been compensated devaluation, that is, the correction of the exchange rate to offset the effects of the removal of existing controls.)[9] The government shunned potential international inconveniences and commercial policy conflicts that could have followed from efforts to have the tariffs accepted internationally. It opted for gradual import liberalization (implemented over three to four years), based on progressively extended positive lists, without temporary compensation.

The criteria applied to the composition of these lists were the following: the first to be liberalized were machinery and components considered necessary for the modernization of production, as well as inputs to current production, while competitive imports would have followed later. These principles, however, were not strictly followed: consumer goods were included in the list in the first year, and by 1991, more than 90 percent of imports had been liberalized, instead of the envisaged 70–80 percent. The remaining restrictions mainly applied to agricultural (food industry) products and some consumer goods (with the imports of the latter governed by a so-called global quota).

The outcomes of liberalization did not only depend on the way in which it was implemented. Simultaneously with import liberalization, the Hungarian economy suffered fundamental macroeconomic shocks (albeit with differing sectoral impacts), and this makes it difficult to distinguish between developments related to, and those unrelated to, import liberalization at the micro, sectoral, and macroeconomic levels.

In spite of the economic and some fundamental methodological difficulties, in an earlier study

(Oblath 2000), I attempted to quantify the effects of trade liberalization on the composition of inputs and the level of output in industry at a product-group/ branch level. The analysis suggested a positive relationship between the rate of liberalization and the level of import penetration. However, it also indicated a negative relationship between the rate of liberalization and the extent of output change in 1991. Of course, when interpreting the findings, the effects of several other factors have to be borne in mind. The country suffered a major exogenous shock accompanied and followed by several endogenous ones in the years of rapid import liberalization. The external shock was related to the demise of COMECON and the almost total collapse of the country's eastern markets (in 1990–1991, the volume of Hungary's exports to former socialist countries cumulatively fell by 55 percent). The internal shocks were generated by the so-called transformational recession, and some were due to the radical cuts in production and consumption subsidies, as well as the emergence of a market economy (involving the elimination of permanent excess demand)—the latter, at least, may have been unavoidable. However, other internal shocks were the result of the hasty introduction of certain institutional changes, without practically any regard for their impact on the real economy. One key instance of this "institutional shock therapy" was the implementation of the Bankruptcy Act and the Financial Institutions Act that undermined the financial position of even those companies whose current business results would have otherwise been positive.[10]

The macroeconomic and institutional shocks had different consequences in the short and medium term. In the short run, they reduced production and domestic absorption and also contributed to the fall in imports.[11] In the early 1990s, the development of imports gave the impression that (in contrast with some fundamental economic considerations and contrary to international experience) the Hungarian economy had special features or capabilities. These features were considered to have been responsible for the fact that despite the almost full-scale liberalization of imports over three years—not accompanied by temporary protection, but on the contrary, accompanied by the marked real appreciation of the forint—imports did not grow. This notion, which ultimately turned out to false, emerged because the factors listed above (and discussed in section 2.3)

temporarily neutralized the direct effects of import liberalization on the volume of imports.

It was not until the end of 1992 that, parallel with the end of domestic recession, imports started to grow rapidly (in 1993, the volume of imports rose by 21 percent), and the expansion continued in 1994 (when the volume of imports increased by 10.5 percent). This huge growth was later attributed to fiscal expansion and to loose monetary policy. Although both factors may have had a role in the increase in imports (but not in its magnitude), the fall in exports could not be explained by the mildly expansive stance of economic policy at that time. In this interpretation, the delayed effects of the manner of import liberalization contributed significantly to the vigorous growth of imports and the expansion of the external deficit in 1993 and 1994 (to almost 10 percent of GDP). Once the economic recession ended, imports entered the country almost unhindered. Thus, the fact that import liberalization was implemented without temporary protection (and concurrent with the real appreciation of the national currency) hit back four years after the launch of the trade liberalization program: first as a sharp deterioration of the external balance, then as the need for stabilizing the economy.

While emphasizing the difficulty of retrospectively identifying the delayed effects of import liberalization, it should be clear that the stabilization package introduced in March 1995 might easily be interpreted as the subsequent admission of the inadequacy of the import liberalization strategy (and the exchange rate policy accompanying it). The package included a 9 percent nominal devaluation of the forint, the introduction of a crawling peg exchange rate regime (with a rather large initial rate of crawl), and the implementation of an import surcharge of 8 percent. These measures were proposed prior to— more precisely, in order to prevent—the imbalance in the external accounts. This interpretation implies that the import liberalization plan had serious shortcomings that had to be remedied later on, as part of the stabilization program, at more serious costs.

In view of the above, we may ask whether the 1995 stabilization package (especially some of its measures aimed at curbing domestic demand) could not have been prevented had the initial import liberalization been prepared more thoroughly and implemented as part of a comprehensive economic policy. An unhistorical question merits an unhistorical answer: some of these drastic steps could perhaps have been avoided had import liberalization taken place with more deliberation, in the context of a lucid program, accompanied by the increase of tariffs and/or real depreciation of the domestic currency.

Let us now turn to the liberalization of capital flows, which was a rather long process. Inward flows, especially those involving FDI, were already permitted in the 1980s (this was the basis of "East-West joint ventures" at that time), but their importance remained limited until the 1990s. Controls on foreign credits of the corporate and banking sector were eased in the first half of the 1990s, but relatively strict regulations on outward capital flows remained until the second half of the decade. The gradual removal of outward flow restrictions began after 1995, and inward flows of short-term capital and portfolio investments were also liberalized to a large extent, except for three important areas. The market for short-term government papers (treasury bills) as well as the Hungarian forward and other derivative markets remained legally closed to non-residents. In addition, non-residents were not permitted to raise credits in Hungarian currency. Of course, just as all controls, these regulations could be circumvented but doing so entailed significant transaction costs. In any case, the maintenance of these defense lines turned out to be extremely useful in the short periods of speculative attacks against the forint, in particular at the time of the Russian crisis in 1998. As mentioned earlier, these controls—together with the ones affecting outward flows—were abolished in mid-2001.

The surge of capital inflows other than FDI began in the second half of 1995 when the stabilization program turned out to be politically sustainable, and its early economic effects were revealed in the sharp improvement of the current account and the fiscal balance.[12] The large inflows, however, had little to do with liberalization measures taken at that time. Rather, expectations regarding the sustainability of the crawling peg exchange regime (with a narrow band) and the huge interest premium deriving from domestic monetary tightening were the major "pull" factors of capital inflows. Although the interest premium eventually decreased, it still remained considerable and continued to be a driving force of further capital inflows.

In Hungary, the interest-rate sensitive and partly or fully speculative inflows, in contrast with several other countries' experience, did not involve adverse

monetary and other macroeconomic effects (e.g., unwarranted credit expansion and sharp deterioration in the current account). The main reason was that the bulk of these inflows were sterilized relatively efficiently, without unreasonably high macroeconomic costs.[13] The efficiency of sterilization, in turn, indicates that the liberalization of the capital account was only partial.

While the adverse impact of capital inflows could be avoided, the positive macroeconomic effects of FDI inflows were realized in the form of significant increments to the productive capital of the country. The growth in these capacities contributed to the overall growth of the economy, in particular, to the increase in exports.

Although these developments entailed several structural and regional problems, pointing toward the emergence of a dual economy (some of these features are addressed in the concluding section), it can be safely concluded that the liberalization of capital inflows did not result in macroeconomic disruptions in Hungary. However, there was a side effect of the cautious policy pursued in the second half of the 1990s: inflation stuck at around 10 percent. This was the reason for the change in policy regarding the monetary/exchange rate regime in mid–2001—another issue to be taken up in the last chapter.

2. Macroeconomic Developments in the 1990s

The following brief and highly selective overview of the country's macroeconomic developments covers the evolution of output and components of domestic demand, the role of the external sector, stocks and flows related to external and internal balance, the rate of inflation, and changes in indicators of the real exchange rate. Other aspects of macroeconomic development (in particular, employment, unemployment, productivity, wages, and income shares) will be discussed in the next chapter, in the context of decomposing aggregate demand and changes in employment. It should be stressed that the following table (see table 4.1) and charts display official statistics, while those in the next section are generally based on my own estimates, calculations, or revisions of the official figures.[14]

In the early years of the decade, the country—like practically all of the transition economies—experienced a very sharp and deep recession (between

TABLE 4.1 Selected Macroeconomic Indicators

	1990	1991	1992	1993	1994	1995	1996	1997	1998	1999	2000
	Volume Change Relative to the Previous Year (%)										
GDP	-3.5	-11.9	-3.1	-0.6	2.9	1.5	1.3	4.6	4.9	4.2	5.2
Domestic absorption	-3.1	-9.1	-3.6	9.9	2.2	-3.1	0.6	4.0	7.8	4.0	5.1
Household consumption	-3.6	-5.6	0.0	1.9	-0.2	-7.1	-3.4	1.7	4.9	4.6	4.1
Investments	-7.1	-10.4	-2.6	2.0	12.5	-4.3	6.7	9.2	13.3	5.9	7.7
Exports[a]	-5.3	-13.9	2.1	-10.1	13.7	13.4	8.4	26.4	16.7	13.1	21.8
Imports[a]	-4.3	-6.1	0.2	20.2	8.8	-0.7	6.2	24.6	22.8	12.3	21.1
Net exports' contribution to change in GDP[a]	-0.5	-2.9	0.6	-10.6	0.5	4.9	0.7	0.6	-2.9	0.1	0.0
Consumer price index	117.0	135.0	123.0	122.5	118.8	128.2	123.6	118.3	114.3	110.0	109.8
	% of GDP										
Exports[a]	31.1	32.8	31.4	26.4	28.9	36.9	38.9	45.5	50.6	53.0	61.6
Imports[a]	28.5	33.7	31.7	34.6	35.4	38.2	39.9	45.5	52.7	55.5	65.6
Net exports[a]	2.6	-1.0	-0.3	-8.2	-6.5	-1.3	-1.1	0.0	-2.1	-2.5	-4.0
Gross foreign debt	60.7	62.7	61.7	65.6	65.1	69.5	58.7	50.4	50.7	58.0	59.1
Net foreign debt (A)[b]	45.5	40.3	37.6	39.4	42.7	34.9	28.9	22.6	21.4	18.9	18.0
Net foreign debt (B)[b]	45.5	40.3	37.6	39.4	42.5	34.4	28.2	21.8	18.8	15.1	12.5
FDI stock	1.6	5.8	9.9	15.1	16.5	29.0	33.4	36.0	37.9	42.4	42.3
FDI inflow		4.4	4.0	6.2	2.8	10.1	4.0	4.0	3.0	3.4	2.9
Current account	0.4	0.8	0.8	-9.0	-9.4	-5.5	-3.7	-2.1	-4.8	-4.4	-2.9
Net foreign interest payment	4.3	4.0	3.3	2.9	3.1	3.6	2.6	2.1	2.0	1.6	1.6
Net foreign interest + profit repatriation	4.4	4.1	3.4	3.1	3.4	4.0	3.2	3.0	4.0	3.4	3.4
Fiscal balance (GFS definition)	0.5	-3.0	-7.2	-6.6	-8.4	-6.4	-3.0	-4.8	-4.8	-3.7	-3.7
Gross public debt	66.3	74.1	78.5	89.5	86.6	85.2	71.9	62.9	61.1	60.4	55.3

Source: Central Statistical Office (CSO), National Bank of Hungary (NBH), and Ministry of Finance (MF).

a. Goods and services.

b. (A): total net foreign debt; (B): net foreign debt in foreign exchange.

1989 and 1993, GDP fell by 18 percent), with investments falling almost as much as output, while consumption also decreased, but to a smaller extent. By 1993, the gap between the change in output and domestic absorption resulted in a large external deficit. Output and investment started to increase in 1994, but the external imbalance remained excessive, which led to the stabilization package in early 1995. Stabilization brought about a further steep fall in consumption and a temporary drop in investment, but due to a sharp increase in net exports GDP did not fall. Since 1997, output has been increasing at an annual rate of 4.5–5 percent, with extremely rapid growth in investment and modest increases in consumption. In 1999, when the volume of GDP reached its pre-transition level, consumption was still much lower (by about 7.5 percent) while investment was 25 percent higher than a decade earlier.

Between 1996 and 2000, the investment rate grew from 21.5 to 24 percent (due to relative price changes, the increase in the share of investments was larger at constant prices: 4 percentage points). The annual contribution of FDI inflows to fixed capital formation in this period was around 20 percent. This points to the importance of the external sector in Hungary's macroeconomic developments. The relative size of exports and imports (of goods and services) is large and has been increasing rapidly. Therefore, even small variations in their relative growth rates (the change in net exports) could have powerful macroeconomic effects. Indeed, in 1993–1994 the sharp deterioration in net exports and the current account resulted in the stabilization crisis mentioned above. Since 1995 the external balance has basically been under control.

One of the most onerous legacies of the pre-democratic era was the huge external debt accumulated during the 1980s. In 1990, the gross foreign debt was 60 percent and the net debt was 45 percent of GDP. These ratios may appear to be "normal," but at that time the ratio of exports to GDP was half of its present level, and net interest payments abroad used up more than 4 percent of GDP, while output was falling at unprecedented rates. Since 1995, the ratio of net foreign debt to GDP has been decreasing rapidly and the relative magnitude of net foreign interest payments has also been falling. However, due to the increase in FDI, the repatriation of profits has been increasing.

If we compare developments in the stock of FDI[15] and net foreign debt, we find that a kind of (implicit)

debt-equity swap took place in Hungary in the second half of the decade. While total net foreign liabilities did not change much relative to GDP, its composition changed significantly: the share of net debt decreased, while that of foreign equity increased since 1994. This was partly due to privatization (the peak in 1995 was because of a jump in privatization revenues). FDI inflows stabilized by around 3–4 percent of GDP in the last couple of years, at a time when privatization proceeds declined steadily (in 2000, revenues from this source were nil). However, since official statistics underestimate the size and do not reveal the actual macroeconomic importance of FDI in Hungary, I elaborate on issues related to foreign direct investments in Appendix 1 at the end of this chapter.

Turning to fiscal developments, after an initial improvement (mainly due to radical cuts in subsidies), both the fiscal deficit and public debt began to increase rapidly. The imbalance grew (despite policy attempts to cut the deficit) because of the fall in activity (the tax base shrank, employment fell, and unemployment increased). But the reason for the jump in public debt (from about 65 percent of GDP to almost 90 percent) was not only the large and increasing deficit, but also the transfer of private debt to the government (particularly in the form of bank consolidations). It should be noted that the fiscal balance in table 4.1 *is not* corrected for inflation.[16] Since 1995 the debt ratio has been decreasing, and after a sharp improvement in 1995–1996 the fiscal deficit was 4–5 percent of the GDP. However, the primary balance shows a surplus, as interest payments on public debt, albeit with a decreasing trend, were still around 6–7 percent of GDP at the end of the decade. Again, with a declining trend, the bulk of interest payments were nominal, as they mainly compensated for the inflationary erosion of public debt. (I shall have more to say on the fiscal position and the inflationary component of the deficit when estimating net taxes in the context of demand decomposition.)

The last remark leads to the question of inflation in Hungary. In the early years of the transition, inflation jumped to 30–35 percent (from 15–17 percent in the late 1980s). Until 1994, a gradual decline could be observed (to under 20 percent), which, referring to the previous topic, contributed to fiscal difficulties in that period.[17] The stabilization package in 1995 resulted in another leap in inflation (to almost 30 percent). Between 1996 and mid-1999, the inflation rate steadily decreased, but then it got stuck at a rate of around 10 percent. This led to the abandonment of both the crawling peg exchange rate regime (with a switch to an almost floating rate within a ±15 percent band), and to the introduction of a monetary policy regime based on inflation targeting in mid–2001.

Having reviewed the evolution of output, the components of demand, the trade balance and current account, FDI, the fiscal position, and inflation, a final important piece of information is necessary to bring these elements of macroeconomic developments together, which is the behavior of the real exchange rate (see figure 4.1).

The notion underlying figure 4.1 is that there is no such thing as *the* real exchange rate (RER). There are several indicators; I selected four of these. The first two are based on relative price indices (CPI and producer price index, or PPI, relative to the weighted average of partner countries' CPI and PPI, adjusted for the change in the nominal effective exchange rate). The third is based on relative unit labor costs (ULC, the relative ratio of gross labor costs per employed persons to value-added per employed persons). The fourth is a "hybrid" indicator: the ratio of the RER based on PPI to that based on ULC. It can be shown that the latter corresponds to the relative ratio of the producer real wage to productivity, which,

under certain assumptions, is an indication of relative profitability.[18]

The first point is that figure 4.1 shows the path of various RER indices, but one does not know anything for sure about the "correct" level/path of these indicators. So, by simple observation, one cannot tell whether a change in a certain direction was economically justified. One has to infer this from other pieces of information presented above.

The second point is that while the indices based on relative prices behave rather consistently, there were extremely large swings in the RER indices based on ULC and relative profitability. The RER based on CPI shows an almost continuous and significant real appreciation (with a temporary reversal in 1994–1996); the one based on PPI, in turn, lacks any trend (though the cycle of 1994–1996 is present in its case as well). The different longer-run behavior of the two types of RERs can be explained partly by real factors, partly by policy measures. The PPI includes traded goods, the domestic prices of which—in a very open economy, after complete trade liberalization—are strongly affected by foreign prices of similar goods and the nominal exchange rate. Therefore, the RER based on PPI does not contain much information on changes in the international competitiveness of the country—an important reason why one may have an interest in changes in the real exchange rate.

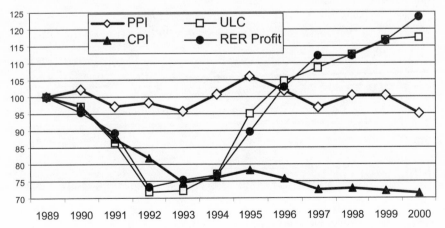

FIGURE 4.1 Indicators of the Real Effective Exchange Rate (1989 = 100). A fall indicates a real appreciation.

Source: NBH.

As for the RER index based on CPI, since it includes the prices of non-traded goods with a large weight, it could be a better indicator of excessive (economically unjustified) changes in the real exchange rate. However, in Hungary, as in other transition economies, the RER index based on CPI, as well as its difference relative to the one based on PPI, was influenced by two important factors unrelated to international competitiveness. One has been the gradual removal of subsidies and administrative controls on consumer prices, a process that still continues. The other is related to the so-called Balassa-Samuelson effect, involving a differential in the growth rate in the productivity of sectors supplying traded and non-traded goods and an equilibrium real appreciation of the RER based on CPI.[19] This factor has been relevant for Hungary since 1996.

This leaves us with RER indices based on ULC and relative profitability, the ones displaying large movements in the period under review. These two generally moved together, as the RER based on PPI did not change significantly. Between 1989 and 1993, there was a massive real appreciation according to the RER based on ULC and relative profitability (almost 40 percent and 35 percent, respectively), the extent of which is certain to have been excessive. On the one hand, the external balance (both the balance on goods and services and the current account) deteriorated

sharply in 1993 (see figures 4.2 and 4.3). Still, this could have been due to other elements of macroeconomic mismanagement (in particular, fiscal expansion—see figure 4.4). But, on the other hand, a very sharp reversal in the latter two indicators of the RER could be observed after 1993. This reversal can be seen in the case of RER indices based on relative price indices as well: an adjustment correcting the overshooting (excessive real appreciation) began in 1994 according to all indicators of the real exchange rate.

It is also clear, however, that the stabilization package in 1995 simply reinforced adjustments in the RER that had started earlier, but were not sufficiently strong to counteract the simultaneously negative effects of trade liberalization and the upturn in economic activity on the external balance.

Finally, it should be noted that since 1994, the real exchange rate based on ULC (similarly to the one based on relative profits) has been depreciating almost continuously. It is quite possible that just as the real appreciation between 1989 and 1993 turned out to be excessive, the real depreciation between 1994 and 2000 may also have led to an overshooting, but in the opposite direction. If so, this has been corrected by the widening of the exchange rate band in mid-2001, and the accompanying nominal appreciation of the domestic currency (about 15 percent real appreciation in 2001–2002 based on ULC).

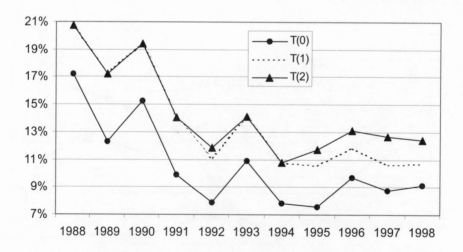

FIGURE 4.2 Net Taxes in % of GDP (the Government's Income Share) under Three Definitions Notation: T(0): including total interest payments; T(1) excluding net external interest payments; and T(2) excluding net external interest and domestic inflationary compensation.

Source: Table 4.2.

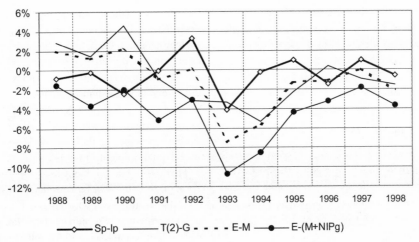

FIGURE 4.3 Net Private Savings, the Balance of the Public Sector, and Net Exports (% of GDP)
Source: Author's calculations based on CSO and NBH data.

3. Decomposition of Aggregate Demand and Employment

In the following, I first discuss the conceptual and statistical problems surrounding the decomposition of aggregate demand, and review the necessary adjustments of official statistics (section 3.1). Next, I perform the decomposition exercises regarding aggregate demand and employment (sections 3.2 and 3.3). Based on the decompositions and other information, I review the characteristic features of subperiods of the 1990s.

3.1. Conceptual and Statistical Questions

For reconstructing Hungarian macroeconomic data in accordance with the framework recommended by Berg and Taylor (2000), I had to make several

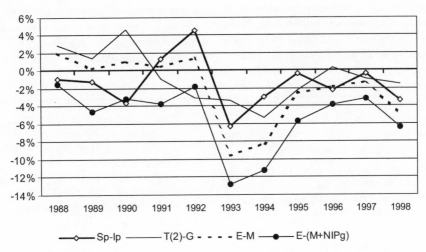

FIGURE 4.4 The Ratio of Net Private Savings, the Balance of the Public Sector, and Net Exports to GDP at Constant (1988) Prices
Source: Table 4.3.

adjustments on the official figures. Therefore, the statistics underlying the decomposition of aggregate demand are different from the ones on which the previous macroeconomic overview was based. The reasons for, and the nature of, the adjustments are presented below.[20]

3.1.1. Conceptual Issues

The major conceptual problem I encountered was that when deriving the relationship between the net positions of the private, government, and external sectors from the components of aggregate supply and demand (see Berg and Taylor 2000, 16), we get

$$(Sp - Ip) + (T - G) = E - M$$

that is, that the difference between private savings ($Sp = Yp - C$) and investments (Ip) plus the fiscal balance ($T - G$) equals net exports ($E - M$).

However, the sum of the two domestic items on the left-hand side corresponds to the current account, rather than to net exports. To make the identity meaningful, one either has to alter the definition of the right-hand side (deduct net primary and secondary income transfers made to the rest of the world from $[E - M]$), or change the definitions of the left-hand side. In the latter case, mainly $(T - G)$, thus T, has to be redefined so as to exclude net interest payments on foreign public debt. As explained later, I chose the latter solution.

The other important conceptual problem relates to the treatment of the inflationary component of interest payments on domestic public debt. If this component is included in Yp, a false representation of developments in income shares (in the ratio of Yp to T) may emerge. Therefore, I estimated $(T - G)$ so as to exclude that part of nominal interest payment on domestic public debt, which compensates for the inflationary erosion in its real value.

If a country makes significant net factor payments abroad (because it is heavily indebted and/or it has benefited from large FDI inflows, thus profits are repatriated from the country), a decision has to be made on the interpretation of private incomes (Yp) and net taxes (T). These may correspond to GDP, GNI (gross national income), or GNDI (gross national disposable income). In the first case, in the definition of aggregate supply ($X = Yp + T + M$), M indicates imports of goods and services, and Yp and T correspond to domestic incomes (they still include

net interest payments and profits payable to non-residents). In the second case, Yp and T indicate resident incomes (thus, net interest payments and profit transfers due to non-residents are deducted), and M corresponds to imports of goods and services plus primary income transfers made to non-residents. Although aggregate supply (X) may be (but, as I show, not necessarily is) invariant to the above choices, its composition—that is, the ratio of M to $(Yp + T)$—can be quite different in the two cases.

There is yet a third possibility for interpreting $(Yp + T)$: this sum can be considered to correspond to GNDI. In this case, both Yp and T are corrected for both primary and secondary (i.e., unrequited) net income transfers abroad, and M indicates imports of goods and services plus primary plus secondary net income transfers made (or received from) abroad.

While all of the three interpretations make sense, from the point of view of "conceptual clarity" the third one is preferable: expenditures and savings are made from disposable income. Still, in my statistical analysis, focusing on the real side of the economy (i.e., factors affecting changes in output and employment), I took the first approach, where the sum of Yp and T corresponds to GDP. However, I have to call attention to the fact that other approaches may lead to different results.

3.1.2. Technical and Statistical Problems

The major problem with Hungarian macroeconomic statistics is that they do not "close": although, as we have seen, a considerable amount of data on macroeconomic developments are available, some of the most important ones are either inconsistent or incomplete.

1. There are no official statistics on the components and the total of Yp (thus on T).
2. Data on exports and imports of goods and services are significantly different in the balance of payments (BOP) statistics and in the national accounts (NA). The national accounts only partly incorporate income transfers to and from the rest of the world.
3. Furthermore, those income transfers that are included in both statistics are accounted differently in the two (therefore, the size of these items is also significantly different in the two statistics).
4. Finally, the construction of time series at constant prices also raised several problems.

As I do not have space to discuss the solutions of these problems and the difficulties involved, the interested reader can contact me.

3.2. Decomposition of Aggregate Demand

3.2.1. Basic Statistics at Current and Constant Prices

The basic statistics underlying the decomposition exercises (relative to GDP) are given in table 4.2.[21]

As I computed public income (i.e., net taxes, T) from the fiscal balance, and private incomes (Yp) were derived as ($GDP - T$), some explanations of the table above should be useful. In the first step, I (temporarily) identified T with the sum of the adjusted[22] fiscal balance and G $[T(0) = (T(0) - G) + G]$. However ($T - G$) may be interpreted in several ways, and for the purposes of this analysis two major adjustments had to be made. First, external interest payments were deducted from ($T(0) - G$), as I was interested in factors affecting domestic output (GDP) and aggregate demand (GDP + M), rather than national income (GNI or GNDI). This is how I got $T(1)$. Second, the nominal compensation for the inflationary erosion of domestic public debt also has to be deducted from public interest payments; as a result of the second adjustment, I get $T(2)$—which, in my interpretation, is the relevant indicator of public income. The measure of private income with which I continue the calculations is $Y(2)$ [$= GDP - T(2)$]. Thus, private savings (Sp, row 11) are given as $Y(2) - Cp$.

Before proceeding to the discussion of net positions of the private and the government sector, I take a look at the evolution of the share of the government's (and, implicitly, the private sector's) income share according to the three interpretations (see figure 4.2).

The distance between $T(0)$, $T(1)$, and $T(2)$ in the graph indicates the evolution of the relative importance of net foreign public interest payments and the compensation for the erosion of domestic public debt in government income (net taxes). It can be clearly seen that until 1994, it was only the foreign interest payments that increased this share, but from 1995 on, the inflationary component of domestic interest payments also had such a role. The difference between the share of $T(0)$ and $T(2)$ was similar at the base and the end period (3.5 and 3.2 percentage points respectively), but in the meantime it once increased to 5 percent (in 1989)—only due to foreign

interest payments—and at the end of the period, foreign interest payments and the inflationary compensation together had similar importance.

As Yp is the mirror image of T, the above figure also indicates how the share of $Y(0)$, $Y(1)$, and $Y(2)$ changed over time. The share of $Y(2)$ was 79 percent in 1988, it reached 89 percent in 1994 and fell to 87.5 percent in 1998.

Figure 4.3 shows how the ratio of the twice-adjusted fiscal balance $[(T(2) - G]$ (referred to as "domestic real fiscal balance" as it excludes foreign interest payments and domestic "inflation prime"), net exports, and net savings ($Sp - Ip$) to GDP evolved over the period reviewed. As a memorandum item, I add net exports plus net public interest payments abroad as a rough approximation of the current account's ratio to current GDP.

Some important tendencies can be identified from the ratios presented above. On the one hand, there is a clearly deteriorating trend in the fiscal balance between 1990 and 1994, an improvement between 1995 and 1996, and a slight increase in the deficit thereafter. On the other hand, net exports also decreased in the first period and improved in the second, but when observing annual shifts in these ratios, no direct relationship can be established between the two. The reason is that net private savings ($Sp - Ip$) fluctuated rather strongly in this period.

The data and the figure above, however, represent only a starting point to the actual quantification of multiplier effects on output of different components of demand. For the latter type of analysis, one needs aggregates at fixed prices. I chose to use prices of the base period, which means that levels of the end period are strongly scaled downwards (between 1988 and 1998, the GDP deflator increased by roughly 580 percent). The opposite holds for relative shares of some major aggregates, most importantly exports, imports, and, by implication, aggregate demand (supply). At 1998 prices, the ratio of imports to GDP was 26 percent in 1988 and close to 53 percent in 1998. In contrast, at 1988 prices, the same ratio was 35 percent in 1988 and 70 percent in 1998 (see table 4.3). Of course, the relative change in the two ratios does not depend on the choice regarding the application of base-period or end-period prices, but in terms of percentage points, there is a significant difference (27 points in the first case and 35 in the other). The reason why I finally decided to use 1988 prices was that significant changes in the trade

TABLE 4.2 Macroeconomic Aggregates at Current Prices: 1988–1998 (% of GDP)

	1988	1989	1990	1991	1992	1993	1994	1995	1996	1997	1998
X [1 + 2 + 7 = 3 + 4 + 5 + 6]	134.9	135.1	129.4	133.7	132.5	135.9	136.9	138.2	139.9	145.5	152.7
Yp(0) [1]	82.8	87.7	84.7	90.1	92.1	89.1	92.2	92.5	90.3	91.2	90.8
T(0) [2 = 8 + 5]	17.2	12.3	15.3	9.9	7.9	10.9	7.8	7.5	9.7	8.8	9.2
Cp [3]	63.2	64.1	64.0	69.9	72.4	73.9	71.6	66.3	63.7	61.7	62.3
Ip [4]	16.9	18.9	19.0	16.1	12.4	16.1	17.9	21.0	24.7	24.6	25.9
G [5]	17.9	15.8	14.8	15.0	15.0	17.5	16.1	13.9	12.7	13.6	14.0
E [6]	36.8	36.3	31.6	32.8	32.6	28.4	31.4	36.9	38.9	45.5	50.6
M [7]	34.9	35.1	29.4	33.7	32.5	35.9	36.9	38.2	39.9	45.5	52.7
T(0) − G [8 = 2 − 5]	−0.7	−3.5	0.4	−5.1	−7.1	−6.6	−8.3	−6.4	−3.0	−4.9	−4.8
T(1) [2/a]	20.7	17.2	19.5	14.1	11.1	14.1	10.8	10.6	11.9	10.6	10.7
Y(1) [1/a]	79.3	82.8	80.5	85.9	88.9	85.9	89.2	89.4	88.1	89.4	89.3
T(1) − G [8/a = 8 + 10/a]	2.9	1.4	4.6	−0.9	−3.9	−3.3	−5.3	−3.3	−0.9	−3.0	−3.3
T(2) [2/b]	20.7	17.2	19.5	14.1	11.9	14.1	10.8	11.7	13.1	12.7	12.4
Y(2) [1/b]	79.3	82.8	80.5	85.9	88.1	85.9	89.2	88.3	86.9	87.3	87.6
T(2) − G [8/b = 8/a + 10/ba]	2.9	1.4	4.6	−0.9	−3.1	−3.3	−5.3	−2.2	0.4	−1.0	−1.5
Memo (fiscal indicators)											
Operational fiscal balance [8/c = 8 + 10/ba]	−0.7	−3.5	0.4	−5.1	−6.3	−6.6	−8.3	−5.3	−1.7	−2.8	−3.1
Primary balance [9 = 8 − 10]	2.9	1.4	4.6	−0.9	−2.6	−3.0	−2.7	2.1	4.4	2.8	1.6
Net interest payments [10]	3.5	4.9	4.2	4.2	4.5	3.6	5.6	8.5	7.4	7.6	6.4
o/w: − foreign (NIPg) [10/a]	3.5	4.9	4.2	4.2	3.2	3.2	3.0	3.1	2.1	1.9	1.5
−domestic [10/b]	0.0	0.0	0.0	0.0	1.3	0.4	2.7	5.5	5.3	5.8	4.8
O/w − inflationary erosion [10/ba]	0.0	0.0	0.0	0.0	0.8	0.0	0.0	1.1	1.3	2.0	1.7
−real interest [10bb]	0.0	0.0	0.0	0.0	0.5	0.4	2.7	4.4	4.0	3.7	3.1
Sp = Y(2) − Cp [11 = 1/b − 3]	16.0	18.7	16.6	16.0	15.7	12.0	17.7	22.0	23.2	25.6	25.3
Sp − Ip [12 = 11 − 4]	−0.9	−0.2	−2.4	−0.1	3.3	−4.1	−0.2	1.0	−1.5	1.0	−0.6
T(2) − G [8/b]	2.9	1.4	4.6	−0.9	−3.1	−3.3	−5.3	−2.2	0.4	−1.0	−1.5
E − M [13 = 6 − 7]	2.0	1.2	2.2	−1.0	0.2	−7.4	−5.6	−1.3	−1.1	0.0	−2.1
E − (M + NIPg) [13/a = 13 − 10/a]	−1.5	−3.7	−2.0	−5.2	−3.1	−10.7	−8.5	−4.3	−3.2	−1.8	−3.6

Source: Author's calculations based on CSO and NBH statistics.

Notation: X: aggregate demand (GDP + imports = domestic demand + exports); Yp: private income; T(0): government income *after* having paid the compensation for the inflationary erosion of domestic public debt; Cp: private consumption; Ip: private investment; G: public consumption and investment; E and M: exports and imports of goods and services (national accounts definition); T(1): government income *before* paying net interest on foreign public debt; and T(2): government income *before* paying net interest on foreign public debt *and net of* compensation for the inflationary erosion of domestic public debt.

TABLE 4.3 Major Macroeconomic Aggregates at Constant (1988) Prices: 1988–1998 (% of GDP)

	1988	1989	1990	1991	1992	1993	1994	1995	1996	1997	1998
X	134.9	136.9	135.4	135.5	137.3	145.5	148.5	148.0	150.3	159.9	170.2
Cp	63.2	65.6	64.4	66.4	68.2	69.8	67.5	61.2	58.0	56.2	56.5
Ip	16.9	17.4	18.1	15.9	12.8	17.9	20.9	24.3	28.1	28.6	31.6
G	17.9	16.7	16.5	17.3	17.6	21.9	19.9	17.0	15.7	16.4	16.8
E	36.8	37.2	36.4	36.0	38.7	35.9	40.2	45.4	48.5	58.7	65.3
M	34.9	36.9	35.4	35.5	37.3	45.5	48.5	48.0	50.3	59.9	70.2
T(2)	20.7	18.1	21.1	16.4	14.5	18.5	14.5	14.8	16.0	15.5	15.2
Y(2)	79.3	81.9	78.9	83.6	85.5	81.5	85.5	85.2	84.0	84.5	84.8
T(2) − G	2.9	1.4	4.6	−0.9	−3.1	−3.3	−5.3	−2.2	0.4	−1.0	−1.5
Memo: operational balance	−0.7	−3.5	0.4	−5.1	−6.3	−6.6	−8.3	−5.3	−1.7	−2.8	−3.1
Primary balance	2.9	1.4	4.6	−0.9	−2.6	−3.0	−2.7	2.1	4.4	2.8	1.6
Foreign net interest payment (NIPg)	3.5	4.9	4.2	4.2	3.2	3.2	3.0	3.1	2.1	1.9	1.5
Domestic net real interest payments	0.0	0.0	0.0	0.0	0.5	0.4	2.7	4.4	4.0	3.7	3.1
Sp = Y(2) − Cp	16.0	16.3	14.5	17.3	17.3	11.6	17.9	24.0	26.0	28.3	28.3
Sp − Ip	−0.9	−1.2	−3.6	1.3	4.5	−6.3	−2.9	−0.4	−2.1	−0.3	−3.4
T(2) − G	2.9	1.4	4.6	−0.9	−3.1	−3.3	−5.3	−2.2	0.4	−1.0	−1.5
E − M	2.0	0.2	1.0	0.4	1.4	−9.6	−8.3	−2.6	−1.8	−1.3	−4.9
E − (M + NIPg)	−1.5	−4.7	−3.2	−3.7	−1.8	−12.8	−11.2	−5.7	−3.9	−3.1	−6.4

Source and notations: See table 4.1.

regime (liberalization of imports) were implemented in the late 1980s. Since very significant changes in relative prices occurred during the 1990s, if I observed volume changes at prices of the second half of the decade, the extent of actual developments in the critical period—the early 1990s—could have been obscured.

Table 4.3 shows the ratios presented in table 4.2 at 1988 prices. This table contains fewer items than the former one: mainly, those displayed are used in the decomposition of aggregate demand.

Even a casual comparison of the two tables reveals that the ratios measured at current and constant prices differ significantly. Figure 4.5 summarizes some of these differences.

Figure 4.5 is meant to give an idea of the magnitude and direction of changes in relative prices from 1998 to 1998. An upward shift in any of the lines indicates an increase in the relative price of a particular item (i.e., relative to the average "price" of the GDP in 1988); a downward change points to the opposite. The figure shows that radical changes in the

price structure took place between 1988 and 1998. Regarding domestic demand, the most profound shifts in relative prices occurred in the early period of the transition (between 1989 and 1991): the price (deflator) of consumption (thus, the CPI) increased considerably; the relative price of other components of domestic demand tended to fall. While the relative prices of private investments fell more or less continuously, this was not the case for government expenditures, relative prices of which began to increase after 1993. The most important shift in relative prices had to do with external transactions. The declining trend in the relative prices of both exports and imports can clearly be identified in the figure. This indicates a rather significant real appreciation of the domestic currency (measured by the GDP deflator and the CPI). The wedge between the relative price of exports and imports, in turn, indicates changes in the terms of trade. The latter was more or less continuously positive in this period.

It is interesting to observe that the major adjustment in the nominal exchange rate in 1995 had

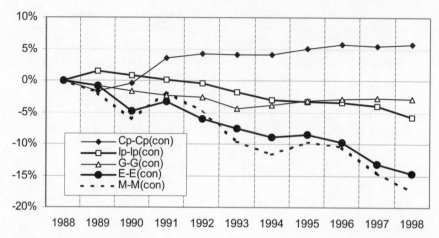

FIGURE 4.5 The Difference in Ratios to GDP at Current and Constant (1988) Prices (The Scope and Direction of Changes in Relative Prices)

Source: Tables 4.2 and 4.3.

relatively limited impact on the real exchange rate in this year. Though the trend changed temporarily, the extent of the real adjustment is concealed by the above figure: the magnitude of the real depreciation is indicated by the real exchange rate based on unit labor costs (see figure 4.1).

As a result of the changes in relative prices, the identity between net exports, on the one hand, and the sum of net private savings and the fiscal balance, on the other, holds at different levels at fixed (1988) prices than at current ones.

The comparison of figures 4.3 and 4.5 indicates that at constant prices (in volume terms), the deterioration of the external balance in 1993 was more abrupt and larger than at current prices. (At 1988 prices, the ratio of net exports to GDP decreased by 11 percentage points in a single year; at current prices, the same change was 7 percentage points). Shifts in the opposite direction are also more pronounced at fixed prices: between 1993 and 1996, the ratio of net exports increased by 8 percentage points, while at current prices by 6.5 points. That is to say, at fixed prices the amplitude of swings in the relative size of macroeconomic balances is larger than at current prices (this holds for net private savings as well). The message is that—in contrast to what one may rightly expect at a time of high inflation—in Hungary's case, the use of constant prices tends to "blow up" the relative importance of certain macroeconomic changes.

(Or rather, at current prices, certain real fluctuations are dampened.) This counterintuitive outcome is likely to be explained by the fact that those macroeconomic aggregates (exports and imports) displayed the most pronounced swings, whose price (relative to the "price" of the GDP), as discussed above, changed to the largest extent.

3.2.2. Aggregate Demand: Multiplier Effects and Leakages

I begin by presenting the direct multiplier effects of investment, government spending, and exports (of goods and services). This is followed by a review of "leakages" and the effects of specific components of demand on output. The computations are based on ratios of aggregates at constant prices (see table 4.4).

The first part of table 4.4 shows the evolution of the ratio of private savings, net taxes, and imports to aggregate supply (the private savings rate, the tax rate, and the import propensity, respectively). The second part indicates the ratio of private investments to the savings rate, the ratio of government expenditures to the tax rate, and the ratio of exports to import propensity. The latter are interpreted as the direct multiplier effects ("stances") of private investments, government expenditures, and exports on aggregate supply. If savings, taxes, and imports are interpreted as "leakages," the third part of the table shows how

TABLE 4.4 Contributions to Aggregate Demand: "Leakages" and Multiplier Effects ("Stances") of Components of Demand (in % and HUF Billion at Prices of 1988)

	1988	1989	1990	1991	1992	1993	1994	1995	1996	1997	1998
I.											
s_p ($=Sp/X$)	11.9%	11.9%	10.7%	12.7%	12.6%	8.0%	12.1%	16.2%	17.3%	17.7%	16.6%
t ($=T/X$)	15.4%	13.2%	15.6%	12.1%	10.6%	12.7%	9.8%	10.0%	10.7%	9.7%	9.0%
m ($=M/X$)	25.8%	27.0%	26.2%	26.2%	27.2%	31.3%	32.7%	32.4%	33.5%	37.5%	41.2%
II.											
Ip/s_p (1)	2,179.4	2,267.3	2,525.5	1,648.9	1,299.7	2,857.7	2,277.5	2,012.7	2,209.0	2,294.6	2,834.2
G/t (2)	1,780.9	1,949.5	1,577.0	1,885.0	2,134.6	2,192.1	2,675.4	2,282.4	1,991.4	2,413.2	2,788.3
E/m (3)	2,182.8	2,128.7	2,074.0	1,810.0	1,826.3	1,466.3	1,622.1	1,874.9	1,968.7	2,222.3	2,356.7
X ($4=5+6+7$)	2,065.7	2,114.8	2,018.1	1,787.5	1,759.3	1,858.0	1,956.4	1,982.4	2,040.3	2,270.5	2,533.3
III.											
$s_p/(s_p+t+m)$	22.4%	22.8%	20.4%	25.0%	25.0%	15.4%	22.1%	27.6%	28.2%	27.3%	24.9%
$t/(s_p+t+m)$	28.9%	25.4%	29.8%	23.7%	21.0%	24.5%	18.0%	17.1%	17.4%	14.9%	13.4%
$M/(s_p+t+m)$	48.7%	51.8%	49.9%	51.4%	54.0%	60.1%	59.9%	55.3%	54.5%	57.8%	61.7%
IV.											
$Ip/s_p*s_p/(s_p+t+m)$ (5)	488.2	517.1	514.5	411.4	325.3	439.5	504.3	555.9	621.8	626.5	704.4
$G/t*t/(s_p+t+m)$ (6)	515.5	494.8	469.2	446.2	448.2	536.7	480.5	389.4	346.0	359.6	373.9
$E/m*m/(s_p+t+m)$ (7)	1,062.0	1,102.8	1,034.5	929.9	985.8	881.8	971.6	1,037.1	1,072.4	1,284.4	1,455.0

Source: Author's calculations based on CSO and NBH statistics.

Notation: See table 4.2.

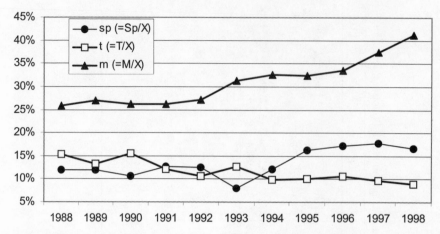

FIGURE 4.6 The Private Savings Rate, the Tax Rate, and Import Propensity (Ratios to Aggregate Supply, %)
Source: Table 4.4.

the relative importance of particular forms of leakages changed over time. Finally, the fourth part demonstrates the combined effect of "stances" and corresponding leakages on aggregate supply (which is equal to the sum of the last three items in the table).

On reviewing contributions to, and leakages from, aggregate demand, I shall proceed in the order of items presented in table 4.4. For identifying longer-term developments, and separating the latter from short-term variations, the evolution of each item is presented in graphical form as well.

Figure 4.6 shows how the savings rate, the tax rate, and import propensity evolved in the period 1988–1998.

It is interesting to observe that in the first three years after import liberalization (between 1990 and 1992), the import propensity was almost constant (especially compared to the fluctuations in the tax and the savings rate). However, after 1992 there was a sharp increase, which was only temporarily halted by the stabilization program in 1995: from 1997, the increase continued at an accelerated rate. Between 1988 and 1998 the ratio of imports to aggregate supply increased by 12.5 percentage points. The tax rate fluctuated in the first five years (in 1993, the year of the sharp deterioration of the trade balance, there was an increase), and the stabilization program did not significantly modify it. Through these fluctuations,

the tax rate declined by 6.5 percentage points over the ten years reviewed.

The private savings rate showed the greatest variation in this period. The jump in the external deficit was accompanied by a fall in the savings rate in 1993, but in both 1994 and 1995 it grew very sharply. This was followed by a slowdown (until 1997) and a slight fall in 1998.

Having reviewed developments in "leakages," I now turn to the evolution of "stances" on output of components of demand (see figure 4.7).

The most striking feature of figure 4.7 is the extreme volatility in the stance of private investments. In the first two years there was an increase, followed by a very sharp decrease in the period of the transformational recession. An abrupt growth in 1993 (in the year of large increase in the external deficit) was followed by a fall until 1995, and again a sizable increase from 1996. Between 1988 and 1992 the symmetrical fluctuations in the stances of government expenditures and private investments ensured that changes in E/m very closely followed those in aggregate supply (i.e., the external balance was maintained). The change in 1993 was due to the fact that in this year the stance of private investments became strongly expansionary, which was magnified by the continuing slightly expansive stance of government expenditures.

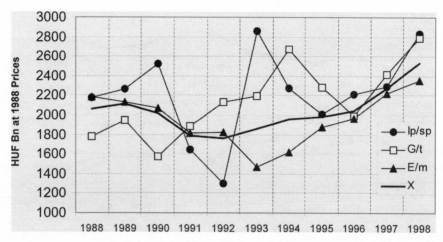

FIGURE 4.7 The Stance of Private Investments, Government Expenditures, and Exports (in HUF Billion at 1988 Prices)
Source: Table 4.4.

There are two important lessons from this analysis regarding the early years of transition. One is that that between 1989 and 1991, the (downward) movements in X and E/m were almost completely synchronised, which—as m was practically constant in this period—may lend some support to the notion that the transformational recession could have been export led (see section 2.2.1). The other is that the sudden collapse of the external balance cannot simply be attributed to the emergence of the "twin deficits"[23] but rather to the decline in savings and the end of the transformation recession, that is, the increase in private investment activity. In 1994, however, the fiscal stance indeed became expansionary (it was an election year), and though the gap between X and E/m lessened somewhat, it still remained rather wide.

The figure clearly shows the channels through which the stabilization package of 1995 worked: it involved a contractionary fiscal stance (G/t fell in two consecutive years) and a temporarily reduction in Ip/sp. In 1997 and 1998 both government expenditures and investments contributed to the sizable growth of domestic demand, but this time, the widening of the gap between aggregate supply and stance of exports was much less significant than in 1993–1994. This can mainly be attributed to the growth in export capacities and the improvement in the international competitiveness of the country (supported by the devaluation in 1995 and the introduction of a

downward crawling peg). This interpretation is reinforced by figure 4.7: between 1996 and 1998, import propensity grew by almost 8 percentage points. The only way that an unsustainable external deficit could be avoided under such circumstances was a parallel expansion in exports.

I close this decomposition exercise of aggregate demand by taking a brief look at shares of its separate components in "total leakages" and the ratio of individual components of domestic demand to "total leakages."

In figure 4.8, the ratio of Sp, T, and M is given not with respect to X (as in figure 4.9), but relative to (Sp + T + M). The major difference in the two types of presentations of the same story relates to developments after 1994. In figure 4.9, import propensity increases almost monotonically; the stabilization program does not appear to have influenced its trend. Figure 4.8, however, shows that there was a temporary decline in the relative impact of the import propensity in 1995 and 1996. On the other hand, figure 4.9 clearly displays the decline in the relative importance of sp and t after 1996.

Finally figure 4.9 presents an overview of the "normalized" stances of components of aggregate demand. "Normalization" here means that stances are scaled by the relative shares of corresponding leakages so that the sum of normalized stances of the components equals aggregate demand.

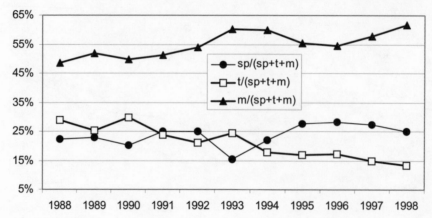

FIGURE 4.8 The Relative Share of Private Savings, Taxes, and Imports
Source: Table 4.4.

The total of the gray, white, and black parts of the bars represents aggregate demand (supply). The change in its composition over time offers some additional information to what we have already learned from the foregoing figures. In particular, beyond the variations reviewed, the longer-term trends stand out extremely clearly. These are the increasing role of the external sector, the slowly (but by far not monotonically) decreasing importance of government spending, and—after a temporary drop between 1990 and 1992—the growing contribution of private investments.

3.3. Decomposition of Changes in Employment and Productivity

In what follows, I perform some of the decomposition exercises suggested by Berg and Taylor (2000)

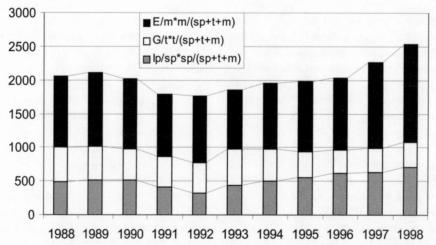

FIGURE 4.9 "Scaled" Stances in Components of Aggregate Demand (Billions of HUF at Prices of 1988)
Source: Table 4.4.

regarding the factors contributing to changes in employment/unemployment and labor productivity in the traded and non-traded goods sectors. Unfortunately, there is a break in the official time series on sectoral employment (and overall unemployment) in 1992: the figures before and after 1992 are not compatible and non-comparable. Therefore, I had to choose 1992 as a base year for sectoral decompositions. This certainly narrows the timespan of the analysis, but, as we saw earlier, the macroeconomic effects of trade liberalization were revealed only after 1992. Thus, the limitations of comparable data are not likely to affect the results of the analysis.

Table 4.5 presents changes in output, employment, and productivity relative to 1992 in the traded sector, the non-traded sector, and sectors as a whole.[24] It should be noted that output (and its change) measured as the value-added of all sectors does not match GDP (its change). The reason is that the sum of the sectoral figures does not include two important adjustments necessary to reach GDP: the correction for FISIM[25] and for direct (product) taxes.

Since 1994, there was a continuous increase in the output of the traded-goods sector and, with the exception of a single year (1995), in that of the non-traded goods as well. This exception indicates that the stabilization program of 1995 involved not just a change in relative prices, income shares, and relative output, but also a downward adjustment in the output of the non-tradable sector.

Between 1992 and 2000, total value-added increased by 3.3 percent per annum (by 2.8 percent between 1992 and 1998), that in the traded goods sector by 5.3 percent (4.9 percent); and in the

non-traded sector by 2.2 percent (1.8 percent). Total employment, although at a slowing rate, continuously declined until 1997 (by almost 10.5 percent); thereafter it began to gradually increase. *The loss in employment was primarily due to the huge fall in the traded goods sector*; in the other composite sector, the number of employed persons did not change significantly until 1998; and thereafter it started to increase rather rapidly. As a result of these developments, by 2000, labor productivity of all sectors was 37 percent higher than in 1992: it doubled in the traded goods sector, while productivity in the non-traded sector increased by a mere 12 percent. The divergence in productivity growth resulted both from different changes in output and employment in the two sectors, but to see the relative importance of these factors, I made a very simple calculation.

I did not meddle with quantifying the exact formulae for productivity growth, but took a much simpler route. First, I calculated the contribution of output and employment growth in the traded and non-traded goods sector, respectively, to the change in total output and employment. Next, I considered the differences in the respective contributions in output and employment growth as an approximation of contributions to total productivity growth.

Formally,

$$(\Delta X^T/X_0 + \Delta X^{NT}/X_0) - (\Delta L^T/L_0 + \Delta L^{NT}/L_0) \approx P^*$$
$$= [(\Delta X/X_0 + 1)/(\Delta L/L_0 + 1) - 1]$$

where X is output (at constant prices), L is employment, and P is labor productivity ($=X/L$); Δ and "$*$," respectively, indicate an absolute and relative

TABLE 4.5 The Cumulative Change in Value-Added, Employment, and Productivity in the Traded and Non-traded Goods Sector (1992 = 100)

	1993	1994	1995	1996	1997	1998	1999	2000	Annual Growth Rate (%)	
									1992–1998	1992–2000
GDP—traded	100.4	104.9	111.2	114.9	125.2	133.3	141.4	151.5	4.9	5.3
GDP—non-traded	100.7	104.8	102.8	104.4	107.1	111.1	114.8	119.2	1.8	2.2
GDP—total	100.6	104.8	105.4	107.7	112.8	118.0	123.1	129.3	2.8	3.3
Employment—traded	85.7	81.5	76.2	76.1	76.2	78.4	78.5	76.6	−4.0	−3.3
Employment—non-traded	99.4	99.1	99.8	98.5	98.4	99.0	103.7	106.6	−0.2	0.8
Employment—total	93.7	91.9	90.1	89.4	89.3	90.6	93.4	94.3	−1.6	−0.7
Productivity—traded	117.1	128.7	145.9	151.0	164.2	170.0	180.3	197.8	9.2	8.9
Productivity—non-traded	101.3	105.7	103.0	106.0	108.8	112.2	110.7	111.8	1.9	1.4
Productivity—total	107.3	114.1	117.0	120.6	126.3	130.3	131.9	137.1	4.5	4.0

Source: Author's calculations based on CSO data.

change: T and NT (upper) indices, respectively, are the indicators of the traded and non-traded goods sectors; and characters without upper-case indices refer to the economy as a whole. The lower-case index 0 refers to the base period. Again, I stress that this is not an exact formulation of the respective relationships (I omitted the "correction term" linking first differences to growth rates). However, the empirical importance of the correction term is negligible: the cumulative difference between the total growth rate of productivity calculated from the right-hand side and the left-hand side is only 2 percentage points for the period 1992–2000 (35 versus 37 percent; 0.2 percentage points per year). Therefore, I use the formula on the right-hand side for decomposing components of productivity growth between 1992 and 2000.

Table 4.6 shows the contributions of changes in output and employment in the traded and non-traded sector to total productivity growth in terms of both percentage points ("absolute contributions") and percents ("relative contributions").

The increase in the productivity of the tradable sector contributed to the growth in overall productivity (roughly 35 percent) by about three-fourths (26 percentage points); the contribution of productivity increase in the non-tradable sector was about one-fourths (9 percentage points). In the tradable sector, the decline in employment had a very significant role in the expansion of productivity of that sector, and its contribution to total productivity

TABLE 4.6 The Contribution to Total Productivity Growth of the Change in Output and Employment in the Traded and Non-traded Goods Sectors between 1992 and 2000 (Percentage Points and Percent)

	T	NT	Σ
	Percentage Points		
X	16	13	29
L	−10	4	−6
P	26	9	35
	Percent		
X	46	37	83
L	−29	11	−17
P	74	26	100

Source: Calculations based on CSO data.

Notations: T, traded goods; NT, non-traded goods; X, output; E, employment; and P, labor productivity.

growth was almost 30 percent (10 percentage points). In the non-traded goods sector, in turn, employment increased; the contribution of the latter to total productivity growth was about 10 percent (4 percentage points).

Overall, the increase in total output and the loss in total employment, respectively, contributed to productivity increase by 83 percent (about 29 percentage points) and 17 percent (6 percentage points). Thus, over the period as a whole, the non-traded sector could make up for about one-third of the employment loss in the traded-goods sector. This development, however, is solely due to changes in 1999–2000, when employment started to increase. Figure 4.10, below, shows how employment and unemployment evolved in the two sectors between 1992 and 1998.

In the non-tradable sector, employment was almost constant until 1998, and unemployment from this sector[26] decreased rather slowly. In the traded-goods sector, in turn, the decline in employment stopped in 1996, and the number of unemployed decreased rapidly from the peak of 1993. Figure 4.9 shows that the decline in unemployment (between 1993 and 1997) is not due to increases in employment, but rather because of the fall in the participation rate (and partly because of the decline in population).

I now turn to the decomposition of employment ratios in the two sectors. The growth in the employment ratio of a sector is given by the ratio of the growth in output/capita to the growth in labor productivity of the sector, that is, $L'/P' = (X'/P')/(X'/L')$, where L is employment, P is the population, X is output, L is employment, and ($'$) indicates an index number.

Figure 4.11 shows the differential performance of the two sectors regarding the composition of changes in employment ratios. To be sure, this way of presenting developments concerning output, employment, and productivity does not add much to what we have already found, except for the fact that changes in the population are also taken into consideration. Between 1992 and 1998, the population of Hungary decreased from 10.337 to 10.135 million (almost 2 percent).

Figure 4.11 tells us that relative to the total population, output increased both in the traded and non-traded sector, but in the former relative growth was much more significant (the figures presented in table 4.5 are somewhat scaled upwards because of the

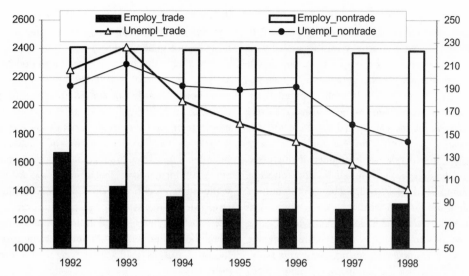

FIGURE 4.10 Employment (Left Scale) and Unemployment (Right Scale) in the Tradable and Non-tradable Sectors, 1992–1998 (1,000 Persons)

Source: CSO (2001).

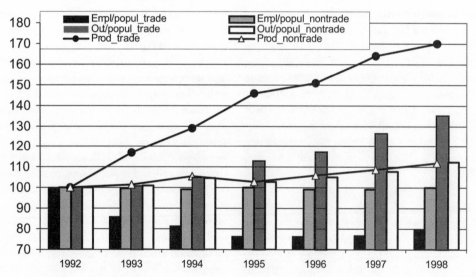

FIGURE 4.11 Decomposition of Changes in Employment Ratios in the Tradable and Non-tradable Sector, 1992–1998 (1992 = 100)

Source: CSO (2001); and author's calculations.

shrinking population). In the traded-goods sector, two phases can be distinguished: between 1992 and 1996, the rapidly growing productivity was associated with a marked decrease in the employment/population ratio. Thereafter, this tendency appears to have reversed (again, partly due to the fall in population): still, productivity continued to increase at a relatively high rate. As for the non-traded goods sector, the employment/population ratio was almost constant during the whole period, while productivity increased rather moderately (it actually fell in 1995, and this was accompanied by a small decline in the output/population ratio in this sector).

Overall, the non-traded goods sector acted as an important stabilizer of employment—dampening the fall in overall employment during a very large fall in the number of employed persons in the traded-goods sector. As emphasized at the outset, it is extremely difficult to establish which part of the employment loss in the traded-goods sector can be attributed to general systemic changes, on the one hand, and to trade (import) liberalization, on the other. Although trade liberalization is likely to have had a significant impact on the fall in employment in the traded-goods sector (especially due to the peculiar conditions of liberalization in Hungary), two important factors have to be taken into account. One is the collapse of trade with the CMEA: this entailed a significant drop in the output and employment of the traded-goods sector, quite apart from trade liberalization. The other factor is the relative underdevelopment of the service sector under socialism; this meant that the share of this sector was bound to increase during the economic and social transformation of the former system.

The final decomposition exercise relates to "reallocation effects" of employment on productivity. Here the question to be answered is the following: did the growth of employment (output) in sectors with high output/labor ratios, or the loss of employment (output) in sectors with low output/labor ratios (and vice versa), have a significant impact on the change in overall labor productivity? I did not perform the detailed decomposition, since by reviewing the "reallocation weights" $[(Xi/X - Li/L)_{t-1}]$, the volume index of output, as well as the change in employment and productivity in different sectors, one can see whether such reallocation effects had an impact on productivity growth. When addressing this issue, it is useful to break down the two broad sectors

discussed above into subcategories. Table 4.7 shows the factors affecting productivity in agriculture, industry, construction, and services.

Except for the beginning of the period (1993–1994) and its very end (1998), employment reallocation effects do not appear to be significant in affecting productivity. In 1993–1994 the loss of both employment and output in agriculture—the sector with the lowest "reallocation weight"—had a considerable impact on productivity, but later on this effect subsided, just as that of other sectors, as the reallocation weights (both on the positive and negative side) substantially decreased. However, a positive effect can be identified at the end of the period, when both output and employment increased in industry, and its reallocation weight also became positive.

3.4. Characteristics of Subperiods

What have we learnt from the foregoing analysis? To answer the question, in table 4.7 I summarize the results of the decomposition exercises along with values or tendencies of other macroeconomic variables (reviewed in section 2) relevant for assessing developments in subperiods following trade liberalization (1989–1991) and the increase in capital inflows (since 1995). The figures, combined with the qualitative information in the table, indicate a cycle with falling output (employment) and relatively stable external balance in the beginning, followed by a slight increase in economic activity and a radical deterioration in the external balance. The latter led to a harsh stabilization package, which reduced domestic absorption, but not output, as the increase in net exports more than compensated for the fall in domestic demand. As the effects of the stabilization subsided, mainly as a result of large inflows of FDI (and fixed capital formation due to FDI), the Hungarian economy started to grow rapidly. The most characteristic feature of this growth path is that it entails much larger increases in aggregate output than in GDP (the share of imports increases), but as exports also grow rapidly, the external balance remains more or less under control.

In the following, we discuss the main attributes of the four subperiods identified (see table 4.8).

1989–1992 (liberalization, transformational recession, and stable external accounts). The first period

TABLE 4.7 Reallocation Weights and the Change in Sectoral Output, Employment, and Productivity (Percentage Points and Index Numbers)

	1993	1994	1995	1996	1997	1998
Agriculture						
$(Xi/X - Li/L)_{t-1}$[a]	−3.6	−2.3	−1.7	−1.0	−1.4	−1.7
X/X_{t-1}	92.1	99.5	102.7	104.1	99.5	98.6
L/L_{t-1}	75.9	93.8	90.1	102.5	95.2	96.9
$(X/L)/(X/L)_{t-1}$	121.3	106.1	114.0	101.6	104.5	101.8
Industry						
$(Xi/X - Li/L)_{t-1}$[a]	−2.1	−1.9	−2.0	−0.2	−0.1	1.3
X/X_{t-1}	103	105.9	106.9	103.2	111.4	108.3
L/L_{t-1}	89.4	95.5	94.6	99.1	101.7	104.6
$(X/L)/(X/L)_{t-1}$[a]	115.3	110.9	112.9	104.1	109.6	103.5
Construction						
$(Xi/X - Li/L)_{t-1}$[a]	0.9	0.3	0.1	−0.9	−1.3	−1.0
X/X_{t-1}	94.5	104.7	100.2	92.8	108.2	105.8
L/L_{t-1}	95.5	97.1	108.1	100.2	100.7	104.9
$(X/L)/(X/L)_{t-1}$	98.9	107.9	92.7	92.6	107.5	100.9
Services						
$(Xi/X - Li/L)_{t-1})$[a]	5.1	4.1	3.7	2.1	2.9	1.6
X/X_{t-1}	101.1	104.1	97.9	102.3	102.2	103.6
L/L_{t-1}	99.4	99.8	100.6	98.8	99.9	100.6
$(X/L)/(X/L)_{t-1}$	101.8	104.3	97.3	103.6	102.3	102.9
All sectors						
X/X_{t-1}	100.6	104.2	100.5	102.2	104.7	104.7
L/L_{t-1}	93.7	98.0	98.1	99.2	100.0	101.4
$(X/L)/(X/L)_{t-1}$	107.3	106.4	102.5	103.1	104.7	103.2

Source: Calculations based on CSO (2001).

a. In percentage points.

covers the implementation of trade liberalization, and the years of the "transformational recession." The annual decline in GDP was 6.3 percent on average, employment fell to a very large extent (these were the years of the emergence of open unemployment), and real wages/household incomes also decreased, but not as significantly as output. Thus, along with the vast decline in investments (see the sign of the stance of *I/s*), the share of wages increased in GDP. Productivity increased somewhat, as the fall in employment was larger than the decrease in output.

In spite of the radical liberalization of imports, the loss of markets of former socialist countries, and a massive real appreciation of the domestic currency, there was only a slight deterioration in the trade balance. This can be explained partly by the recession itself, partly by the restrictive stance of monetary policy combined with a relatively tight fiscal policy. ("Relatively tight" here means that though the stance of *G/t* was not restrictive, compared to the extent of the decline in output, it was far from being expansive.)

1993–1994 (end of the transformational recession and deterioration in the external balance). In these two years, the "hidden" external imbalance became explicit, as investments picked up, and the transformational recession ended. The trade deficit soared, in spite of the fact that the real appreciation of the currency halted (in 1994 there was a slight real depreciation). Real wages increased somewhat, while the fall in employment continued.

There was a large shift in employment shares toward the non-traded goods sector, as employment in sectors producing traded goods radically decreased. The stance of both investments and government spending was strongly positive, while that of exports (partly because of the decline in exports in 1993, partly due to the increase in import propensity) became strongly negative. Monetary policy eased somewhat in this period, and though international reserves did not fall (and even increased), this was solely due to the "overfinancing" of the large current account deficit by drawing on foreign credits and increasing

TABLE 4.8 Summary of Macroeconomic Developments in Hungary

	1990–1992	1993–1994	1995–1996	1997–1998
Growth, Employment, and Inequality				
Growth rate (average annual change in real GDP)	−6.3	1.1	1.4	4.7
Real exchange rate (ULC based) (+ = real appr.)	++	0/−	−−	−
Employment rate (+ = fall in unemployment)	−−	−−	0/+	+
Wage share in GDP	++	+	−−	−
Real wages (real wage/earners)	−4.7	1.5	−8.7	4.2
Income inequality				
Per capita household income	−2.3	−1.1	−2.7	2.2
Skilled/unskilled		+	+	0
Employment structure				
Traded/non-traded	77.5	65.3	61.9	63.2
Skilled/unskilled	83.0	85.5	91.2	94.0
Aggregate Demand Decomposition				
Aggregate demand	−4.7	2.0	3.3	7.0
Direct multiplier effects				
I/S	−−	++	−	++
G/T	+	++	−	+
E/M	−	−−	+	0
Effect of leakages (average growth)	−	−/+	+/−	
Savings	−	−/+	+/0	0
Taxes	−	+/−	+	−
Imports	0/−	+	0	++
Productivity and Employment				
Productivity growth				
Overall	2.1	6.8	2.8	4.0
Traded		13.5	8.3	6.1
Non-traded		2.8	0.1	2.9
Overall growth in employment	−8.3	−4.2	−1.4	0.6
Employment sector reallocation effects	n.a.	small	none	Small
Labor supply changes				
Participation rate	58.6	55.0	52.1	51.5
Unemployment rate	6.0	11.3	10.1	8.3
Employment rate	47.7	38.8	36.9	36.8
Macroeconomic Variables				
Trade deficit (goods and services)	0/−	++	−−	+
Domestic credit	−−	−	−/+	+
Reserves	+	+	++	+
Real interest rate	++	−/+	+	0
Interest spreads				
Imports/GDP	+	++	−	++
Exports/GDP	+	−	++	++

Source: CSO (2001), (NBH), and author's calculations.

Key: ++ strong increase, + increase, +/0 slight increase, −− strong decrease, − decrease, 0/− slight decrease, +/− up then down (or vice versa), 0 no change, and n.a. not available.

gross foreign public debt. The deficit of the current account reached 10 percent of the GDP by 1994.

In this interpretation, the lagged effects of trade liberalization, combined with the real appreciation of the currency, were revealed in this period. Though both fiscal and monetary policy are likely to have contributed to the increase in the external imbalance, the changes in sectoral employment structure and productivity point toward the delayed impact of trade liberalization.

1995–1996 (stabilization). These two years are characterized by a strong fiscal contraction, the real depreciation of the domestic currency, a fall in real wages, a significant shift in income shares toward profits, and an improvement in the external balance. It is in this period that capital flows were liberalized to a large extent (though not fully), and a considerable amount of capital—portfolio investments, FDI, and short-term capital—flew into the country. These net inflows had a moderate effect on domestic monetary conditions and the current account, as, for the major part, they were sterilized.

1997–1998 (–2000) (rapid growth and balanced external accounts, with increasing import-propensity). Since 1997, the economy has been growing rapidly, at a rate close to 5 percent. The increase in production was supported, from the supply side, by a significant enlargement of productive capacities since 1996, a moderate growth in employment, and large gains in productivity. From the demand side, the expansion of private investments was the main driving force (mainly financed by FDI inflows) but the stance of government spending also became more supportive of economic growth. Real wages and household incomes started to increase, but less than GDP: the decline in the share of wages, though at a slower rate than in the previous period, continued. The large inflow of foreign capital (just as its sterilization) also continued; it resulted in a mild increase in domestic credit (in real terms), and real interest rates did not fall significantly. This period of economic growth, however, is characterized by the impact of a particular component of capital inflows, namely, FDI. The effects of the latter show up in structural changes in the real economy, rather than in domestic monetary developments. The most pronounced macroeconomic transformation relates to the continuous increase in the import propensity, a development clearly revealed by the divergence in aggregate output and total value-added (GDP). However, exports also grew rapidly, while a part of capital inflows were used for the reimbursement of foreign public debt; thus, the external balance was kept under control. Another important feature of the growth path since 1997 is that it did not involve a considerable increase in employment. Although the rate of unemployment decreased, this mainly had to do with the continuing fall in the participation rate. Recently, however, the employment rate also started to increase.

Before summing up the implications of external liberalization in Hungary and touching upon the recent full-scale liberalization of the capital account in 2001, I will briefly review changes in income distribution and some of the social developments in the 1990s.

4. Social Implications: Changes in Income Distribution in the 1990s

4.1. Changes in Inequality

In Hungary, just as in other transition countries, the economic and social developments of the 1990s resulted in pronounced changes in income distribution, pointing toward an increase in inequality. The magnitude of these changes does not appear to be as drastic as in some other Central-East European countries, and they are certainly smaller than those characterizing Southeast Europe and the CIS countries. But I shall only touch upon international comparisons to show that in relative terms, the growth in social inequalities was modest in Hungary.[27] I also leave aside the question of whether or not actual income differences in the pre-democratic era were accurately revealed by official Hungarian statistics. I focus instead on developments in the 1990s, relying on official data and the analyses of research institutes that measure social changes.

For measuring income inequalities, first, the changing ratio of the top and the bottom income deciles and, second, the changing patterns shown by the Gini coefficient will be considered.

During the 1970s and 1980s, the average ratio between the richest and the poorest income decile group was around 4 to 5. This ratio hit 5.8 in 1988, and by the early 1990s the top decile was about seven times richer than the poorest 1 million people. During the 1990s, a further 0.5 to 1 percentage point

TABLE 4.9 Average Net Monthly Household Income Per Capita According to Income Deciles (In HUF)[a]

	1992	1993	1994	1995	1996	1997	1998	1999	2000
The poorest decile	4,432	4,721	5,200	5,994	6,566	7,309	8,637	10,463	12,206
2nd	6,015	7,007	7,855	8,932	10,047	11,385	13,428	16,259	18,266
3rd	6,847	8,134	9,311	10,591	12,292	14,103	16,202	19,757	22,294
4th	7,534	9,020	10,445	12,021	14,075	16,111	18,507	22,891	25,693
5th	8,189	9,867	11,525	13,356	15,752	18,046	21,016	25,523	28,782
6th	8,934	10,852	12,708	14,720	17,143	19,770	23,328	27,976	31,629
7th	10,010	12,153	14,284	16,498	19,070	21,812	25,817	30,827	35,321
8th	11,525	13,949	16,638	19,116	21,606	24,771	29,391	35,272	40,819
9th	14,166	17,173	20,577	23,984	26,793	30,283	35,146	44,036	50,222
The richest decile	31,274	29,081	36,631	42,087	46,251	57,257	62,475	84,515	91,730
Average	10,858	12,190	14,511	16,722	18,940	22,091	25,384	31,729	35,675
highest/lowest	7.06	6.16	7.04	7.02	7.04	7.83	7.23	8.08	7.52

Source: Kolosi et al. (2000).

a. Weight added according to the personal weight of the head of the household.

increase in the ratio can be identified (see table 4.9). This is generally interpreted in two ways: either as evidence of the slow, though continuous, increase in income inequalities, or as the relatively small shift of 0.5 percent due to the 1995 restrictions, soon after which the level of inequality stabilized. Because of measurement uncertainties admitted by the data source, as well as the utterly hectic nature of decile ratios over the latest years, it difficult to decide which interpretation is the correct one.

A more detailed analysis of all decile groups could highlight finer tendencies. During the early 1990s, due to the general economic decline, and especially because of the soaring unemployment rate, the income of the bottom deciles was decreasing most rapidly compared to other groups. In the course of the mid-1990s, the condition of the middle deciles slowly worsened. The large cuts in government spending on social goals around 1995 pushed the middle 50–60 percent down, while those below or above the third to eighth decile groups remained relatively unaffected. The income share of households belonging to the top decile continuously grew throughout the decade (from 20.9 percent in 1989 to 25.3 percent in 1999; see Kolosi et al. 2000). Toward the end of the decade, upper-middle decile groups also changed their positions parallel to the top decile. Apparently, in the late 1990s, the lowest decile group's income also stopped falling behind the rest. Its share in total personal incomes grew from 3.2 percent in 1996 to 3.6 percent in 1999 (though it has not regained its portion of 4.5 percent in 1989).

In sum, the size of inequalities (measured by the ratio of the income share of the highest to the lowest decile) almost doubled by the end of the decade, as compared to the average of the 1970s and 1980s. The most crucial change was certainly experienced during the early 1990s, at the time of the transformational recession, but the present state cannot be explained by either the prevailing economic trends of the 1980s (Atkinson et al. 2000) or the shift to the market economy in itself (Kolosi et al. 2000).

In Hungary, the Gini coefficient remained around 0.22 to 0.26 throughout the 1980s. By this measure, Hungary's concentration of income was higher than that of the Nordic states but lower than the Western European average.[28] Among Central and Eastern European states, income distribution figures have always shown sharper inequality for Poland and Hungary than for the other countries; and by 1989, Hungary's Gini coefficient was already 0.29. After the systemic change, however, the concentration of income did not grow as rapidly as in most of the post-socialist bloc. Consequently, with its present 0.33–0.34 coefficient, Hungary is in the middle range of transition economies (European Bank for Reconstruction and Development [EBRD] 2000). Data shown in table 4.9 have led some analysts to expect a halt in further income concentration, but it is too early to identify any longer stability.

Hungary's current Gini ratio is close to that of the United States, but it is higher than that of a number of EU countries. Of course, Hungary's average income level is much lower than these countries', but

Greece or Portugal, with similar per capita GDP, show relatively higher rates of income inequality.

The distribution of different types of incomes changed differently during the 1990s (see table 4.9). The concentration of market incomes increased the most significantly; within the latter, inequalities in capital incomes grew more sharply than those in earnings. Table 4.10, below, also shows that state redistribution has played a significant role in diminishing unequal market incomes at the level of households throughout the 1990s. As social security benefits are mostly important in substituting for incomes during unemployment or retirement in proportion to prior earnings, the potential of state redistribution in reducing income inequity can be seen in its capacity in providing social incomes (family subsidies and support, etc.) for those in need. In this respect, while pensions, sick pay, and child-related benefits constitute a decreasing part of the budget of all social groups, and the losses in the case of the poor are above the average, the state still shows some relative success in Hungary, when compared to other post-Soviet countries.

4.1.1. Social Dimensions of Income Inequality

Numerous recent analyses have tried to identify the substantial dimensions of income inequalities (for example, Tóth 2000; Kolosi et al. 1998; Kolosi et al. 2000). Among the basic social factors explaining the dispersion of income, *entrepreneurship* and *level of education* are most significant. Regarding the level of earnings, neither the blue-collar–white-collar distinction nor belonging to the Gypsy-Roma minority proved to be significant in themselves. Unemployment plays a significant role only in the case of those out of the labor market for more than a year. Among employees working in the competitive (non-public) sector, no significant difference can be identified between those who work in state-owned and those who work in privately owned companies. Companies that have foreign ownership tend to provide higher salaries for their workers. In addition, there is a large gap between salaries of employees with the same level of education in the public sector vis-à-vis the competitive sector. In sum, if a complex factor of nine variables is generated,[29] 41 percent of income dispersion can be explained (of which the first three factors explain almost 30 percent). This relatively high level implies a static and strongly structured system of income inequalities.

4.2. Patterns of Poverty in Hungary

4.2.1. Absolute Poverty

The number of poor was already growing during the 1980s, but with the rapid increase in unemployment, poverty grew at a faster rate in the beginning of the 1990s. According to an absolute line of poverty, which extends the national poverty line of 1992 to further years, the increasing trend did not stop during the 1990s, as the number of poor reached 19.9 percent in 1996, and 31.1 percent of the total population in

TABLE 4.10 Gini Coefficients 1991–2000

	1991–1992	1992–1993	1993–1994	1994–1995	1995–1996	1996–1997	1997–1998	1998–1999	1999–2000
Market income (1)	46.6	47.1	49.9	50.6	50.1	51.6	52.6	53.7	54.8
Other (non-state) income (2)	64.3	68.7	71.9	68.9	65.8	67.8	70.1	75.8	70.1
Net income before redistribution (1 + 2)	47.2	48.0	50.5	51.0	50.4	52.2	54.1	55.6	55.4
Social incomes (3)	37.3	35.6	36.6	36.7	37.9	40.1	40.8	45.1	40.6
Social security benefits (4)	31.8	35.2	35.4	36.1	37.9	36.7	37.6	39.8	37.1
(1 + 2 + 3)	45.1	45.6	47.9	48.7	48.4	50	51.2	53.7	53.3
Total household incomes (1 + 2 + 3 + 4)	29.5	27.8	29.5	31.6	30.8	30.8	32.0	34.3	33.0

Source: Kolosi et al. (2000).

TABLE 4.11 The Share of the Population Living below the National and the International Poverty Line (%)

	Survey Year	Population below the National Poverty Line (%)	Population below $1 a Day (%)	Poverty Gap at $1 a Day (%)	Population below $2 a Day (%)	Poverty Gap at $2 a Day (%)
Bulgaria	1995	—	<2		7.8	1.6
Czech Republic	1993	—	<2	<0.5	<2	<0.5
Slovak Republic	1992	—	<2	<0.5	1.7	0.1
Slovenia	1993	—	<2	<0.5	0.5	0.1
Poland	1993	23.8	5.4	4.3	10.5	6
Romania	1994	21.5	2.8	0.8	27.5	6.9
Russian Federation	1994	30.9	—	—	—	—
Hungary	1993	8.6	<2	<0.5	4	0.9

Source: World Bank (2000).

1998.[30] We also have to notice that, parallel to the increase in the number of the poor, the proportion of people living below both national and international poverty lines was not growing as fast in Hungary as in CIS countries or in Poland. Hungary, more or less, followed the trend characterizing Central European transition economies throughout the 1990s (see table 4.11).

4.2.2. Relative Poverty

Looking at relative poverty lines, however, with the stabilization of employment and the decrease in unemployment in the late 1990s, the increase in the number of the poor seems to have halted. This latest, most generally accepted, view can be modified a bit by an extended interpretation of poverty that also takes into account the relative poor, defined by those living below 40 or 60 percent of median income (Kolosi et al. 2000). On the one hand, this shows that the decline in the number of the relative poor between 1992 and 1994 was not so evident. On the other hand, it also suggests that the increase after the restrictions in 1995 was not much sharper, compared to the general trend since the 1980s.

The figures unanimously show that the number of poor began to fall after 1997, but in the latest years, some moderate increase can be identified (see table 4.12.a). While the number of poor seems to be stabilizing or slightly growing today, the gap between the share of people below and above different relative poverty lines stopped widening (see table 4.12.b).

4.2.3. Social Dimensions of Poverty

Due to the concentration of factors intensifying the risk of poverty, a couple of social groups are much

TABLE 4.12.a Poverty Lines

Years	Share of the Poor (in % of the Total Population)		
	Below the 50% of the Average	Below the 50% of the Median	Absolute Poverty (Number of People Living below the 1992 Poverty Line, Corrected for Inflation)
1991–1992	12.8	10.2	10.1
1992–1993	10.4	6.6	—
1993–1994	12.1	7.4	8.6
1994–1995	15.8	9.0	—
1995–1996	18.3	12.8	19.9
1996–1997	17.8	12.4	—
1997–1998	12.8	9.1	31.1
1998–1999	13.8	10.3	—
1999–2000	14.6	9.1	—

TABLE 4.12.b Poverty Gap (the Average Distance in % from the Poverty Line among the Poor)

	Below the 50% of the Average	Below the 50% of the Median	The Poorest Quintile
1991–1992	33.2	31.3	30.9
1992–1993	26.5	27.0	25.0
1993–1994	26.3	26.7	26.2
1994–1995	29.0	33.4	27.9
1995–1996	29.8	29.9	31.2
1996–1997	31.1	32.6	30.8
1997–1998	29.2	30.7	27.8
1998–1999	27.6	25.3	26.7
1999–2000	25.3	26.3	25.5

Source: Kolosi et al. (2000); and Ferge (1998).

more severely affected than the average. Table 4.13 highlights the share of the poor in groups usually regarded as the most vulnerable in this respect. The conditions of these groups clearly deteriorated between the early and mid-1990s.

However, the chances for becoming poor may be explained by other, more fundamental, socio-demographic variables (see the impact factors of income inequality in section 4.1). Analyzing the risk factors of poverty, we find that poverty ratios are much higher among households headed by a single person under forty or over sixty and households with at least three children. Ratios are also higher among the female elderly (mostly pensioners) living alone. (It should be mentioned, however, that the risk of elders becoming poor was close to the average of the total population in 1992, and since then it has become half of that.) The level of education, as mentioned earlier, probably plays the most significant role in avoiding both casual and long-term poverty. Those with less

TABLE 4.13 Proportion of the Relative Poor (below 50% of the Average Income) in Some Typically Vulnerable Groups (%)

	1992	1997
Children 0–2 years	15	35
Children 3–6 years	14	28
Villages	13	20
Gypsy-Roma population	46	58
Unemployed	17	37
Northeastern Hungary	14	26

Source: Ferge (1998, 561).

than eight years or with eight to twelve years of schooling have the highest chance of holding irregular connection with, or becoming expelled from, the labor market. Exclusion from the labor market proves to be most crucial just before reaching the age of retirement (this also explains the sharply growing number of disabled and early pensioners at the beginning of the 1990s).

The foregoing review of changes in income distribution was meant to sketch major developments in this field, but it did not aim at establishing or testing casual links or quantitative relationships between external liberalization and income distribution. The country experienced so many fundamental shocks in the 1990s that it would not make much sense to attribute any quantitative effects of specific social changes to foreign economic liberalization. However, that the main channel through which the radical mode of opening the Hungarian economy to imports (in combination with the collapse of trade with Eastern Europe) is likely to have affected social developments is fairly clear. Namely, the exceptionally sharp fall in employment (and the accompanying increase in unemployment), particularly in the traded-goods sector, was (directly and indirectly) related to the specific form of trade liberalization in Hungary. However, the evolution of income differences between the traded and non-traded goods sectors (and within these sectors) does not appear to be closely related to external liberalization. I return to this issue in the concluding section.

5. Summing Up: Hungary's Experience with External Liberalization and Recent Developments

In conclusion, I will summarize some of the lessons of external liberalization in Hungary and touch upon developments and prospects related to the full-scale opening of the capital account in mid-2001.

Although the international literature on economic transformation in Central and Eastern Europe generally treats Hungary as an example of "gradualism" (see, e.g., Bokros and Dethier 1998; World Bank 1976; UN Economic Commission to Europe [ECE] 2000), as we hope we have demonstrated, this interpretation rests on several misunderstandings. True, the country escaped the kind of "big bang" experienced by (and recommended for) several transition economies at the outset of economic transformation. However, the mode of external liberalization, as well as the implementation of institutional changes in Hungary in the early years of the transition, may best be characterized as "shock therapy in slow motion",[31] followed by the actual shock therapy of the stabilization package in 1995.

It is important to emphasize that Hungary's experiences with opening up the current and the capital account have at least as much to do with the specific policies that accompanied liberalization measures as with external liberalization per se. That is to say, it is impossible to reflect on the effects of external liberalization in Hungary without considering the policy measures taken (and those that could or should, but were not, taken) at the time of opening up the economy. Therefore, the Hungarian experience does not provide general lessons regarding the macroeconomic effects of liberalization. The lessons of this experience are limited: *if* a country opens up its trade under those policy (and other) conditions that characterized Hungary in the late 1980s and early 1990s, similar negative consequences can be expected. (This also holds for the country's relatively favorable experiences regarding the gradual and controlled opening of its capital account.) The emphasis on the policy environment is a corollary to the caveat made in the introduction and elaborated upon in section 2: at the time of external (trade) liberalization, several other fundamental external and internal shocks affected the country. Thus, the outcomes of liberalization were deeply intertwined with both the accompanying economic policies and the exogenous shocks of the time. This implies that the interpretation of developments following external liberalization in Hungary rests on judgments regarding the relative importance of several simultaneous factors. It is no wonder that, even a decade after the launch of the liberalization program, there is no consensus on its actual macroeconomic impact.

As for the associated policy measures, the country opened up its formerly strictly controlled trade system in 1989 without any temporary protection whatsoever, and combined the liberalization of imports with a significant real appreciation of the domestic currency. At the same time, with the aim of "establishing a full-scale market economy" as early as possible, abrupt changes in the institutional and legal framework of companies were implemented. These included the introduction of strict legislation on bankruptcy

procedures, driving potentially viable companies out of business. (The most affected companies, due to the real currency appreciation, were those operating in the traded-goods sector.)

While the opening of trade was conceived as a formally structured and efficiently sequenced process (positive lists were announced and extended annually—without sizable effects on the trade balance until 1992), the mode of trade liberalization actually turned out to be an economic time bomb, which finally exploded in 1993. The main reason why the effects of liberalization on the trade balance were concealed was that the Hungarian economy suffered a deep ("transformational") recession between 1990 and 1992. In 1993, as the effects of the recession began to subside, the trade balance and the current account deteriorated very sharply.

Our decomposition exercises revealed that the fall in output was closely tied to the fall in exports from the collapse of trade with Hungary's Eastern European partners. Although the jump in the external deficit in 1993–1994 had to do with the deterioration of the fiscal position as well, the increase in private investments had a more important role. However, the importance of supply-side factors in the expansion of the trade deficit is revealed in that Hungarian exports lost market shares in Western Europe. The combination of the sudden jump in imports and the fall in exports in 1993 indicates that the mode of external liberalization—in particular, the associated real appreciation—had an important role in the expansion of the external deficit.

In 1994, the deterioration of the trade balance and the current account reached such proportions that, especially with the Mexican crisis in the background, a correction became inevitable. The stabilization package of 1995 involved trade and exchange rate policy measures (import surcharge, devaluation, and the introduction of a crawling peg) that should have been introduced at the outset of trade liberalization. The fiscal measures of the stabilization program, aimed at cutting social benefits, had some minor negative influence on income distribution (i.e. in increasing inequalities). However, the direct importance of these steps was negligible compared to the jump in the inflation rate, involving a steep fall in the real value of wages and social transfers.

The nature of trade liberalization is likely to have affected employment and income distribution as well. Employment in the traded-goods sector fell radically, to a greater extent than in comparable Eastern European countries, in particular the Czech Republic. The impact of the mode of external liberalization, as well as the inflow of foreign capital, shows up in the large wage differentials between the sectors supplying traded goods and public services, as well as between wages in foreign- and domestic-owned companies.

In contrast with trade liberalization, Hungary did not experience major negative effects from capital account liberalization. On the contrary, the country realized important benefits from capital inflows that speeded up after 1995—as a result of steps in liberalizing both inflows and outflows of foreign capital. The positive influence of these inflows is revealed by the increase in fixed capital formation due to FDI.[32] The potential negative effects (on monetary developments, the exchange rate, and the external balance) were more or less avoided by maintaining the crawling peg with a narrow ($\pm$ 2.25 percent) band and the sterilization of excessive inflows, and, in particular, by refraining from the full-scale liberalization of the capital account (the latter explains why sterilization could be effective).

While experiencing the benefits of FDI inflows—the rapid growth in investments, exports, and GDP—disturbing inequalities and strains also emerged within Hungary. The emergence of excessive regional and sectoral disparities has been closely related to the presence of foreign capital. While the central and western parts of Hungary, receiving large FDI inflows, have been prospering since 1996, counties in the northeast—only recently approached by FDI—have been characterized by high unemployment, slow growth, or depression. In 1999–2000, however, the sharp divergence in regional performances began to subside. This development is due to the fact that, more recently, economic growth in Hungary has become somewhat more broadly based than in the period following the stabilization program: besides exports and investment, domestic household incomes and demand have also started to increase.

5.1. Postscript on Policy Changes in Mid-2001

The changes in 2001 mark a fundamental turn in monetary and exchange policy, as well as in the overall policy attitude toward capital inflows. In an attempt to radically cut inflation, stuck at about 10 percent since mid-1999, monetary policy switched to a regime based on inflation targeting; the fluctuation band of the exchange rate was widened from $\pm$ 2.25 percent to $\pm$ 15 percent, while all remaining controls on capital movements were lifted. The widening of the band, in the absence of central bank intervention, resulted in a nominal appreciation reaching 10–12 percent and a real appreciation of about 15 percent in 2001–2002.

The real appreciation is certain to have hurt the traded-goods sector, but the implications are not yet clear. As shown in the paper (see, in particular, section 2), according to ULC-based real exchange indices, there was a significant real depreciation of the Hungarian currency since 1995. An optimistic reading of developments since mid-2001 suggests that the nominal and real appreciation of the currency is a correction of its former undervaluation.

Swings in the nominal and real exchange rate are likely to have been amplified by the combination of the effective float and the full-scale liberalization of the capital account. The vulnerability of the currency to speculative attacks or to "contagion" effects has certainly increased.[33] The liberalization measures implemented in 2001 are in line with recommendations/requirements made by the EU (as well international financial institutions), and, in the optimistic case, they may contribute to the convergence of Hungary's inflation with that of the euro region. However, it is by no means clear whether it will also support the country's real convergence—maintaining its relatively high growth rate—as well.

Although I have no specific forecasts on the possible effects of the recent liberalization measures, there are evident similarities between the mode of trade liberalization in 1989 and the full-scale liberalization of the capital account in mid-2001. I simply hope that the commonalities end here and that this time the adverse effects can be avoided.

Appendix: FDI Inflows and Their Macroeconomic Impact

The problem with the measurement of FDI is that the Hungarian balance of payments does not include reinvested earnings, which is an important component of foreign direct investments. In table 4.14, I present some calculations regarding the absolute and relative size of FDI, taking into consideration reinvested profits, reported by the CSO (2001).

Although there may be several problems with comparing (and adding up) figures from different

TABLE 4.14 Indicators of FDI Flows 1995–1999 (Billion EURO and %)

	1995	1996	1997	1998	1999
Gross FDI (CB) billion EUR	3.47	1.82	1.92	1.82	1.85
Net FDI (CB) billion EUR	3.44	1.82	1.53	1.39	1.61
Reinvested profits billion EUR	0.78	1.09	1.57	1.74	1.87
Gross FDI (AB) billion EUR	4.25	2.91	3.49	3.56	3.72
Net FDI (AB) billion EUR	4.21	2.91	3.10	3.13	3.48
	In % GDP				
Gross FDI (CB)	10.1	5.0	4.7	4.3	4.1
Net FDI (CB)	10.0	5.0	3.8	3.3	3.6
Reinvested profits	2.3	3.0	3.9	4.2	4.1
Gross FDI (AB)	12.3	8.1	8.6	8.5	8.3
Net FDI (AB)	12.2	8.1	7.7	7.5	7.7
Current account/GDP (CB)	–5.5	–3.7	–2.1	–4.9	–4.3
	In % Gross Capital Formation (GCF)				
Gross FDI (CB)	50.2	23.6	21.3	18.4	17.2
Net FDI (CB)	49.7	23.6	17.0	14.0	14.9
Reinvested profits	11.2	14.1	17.5	17.6	17.3
Gross FDI (AB)	61.4	37.7	38.8	36.0	34.5
Net FDI (AB)	60.9	37.7	34.5	31.7	32.3

Source: NBH (CB-figures) and CSO: National Accounts (1998–1999).

Note: CB: cash flow basis; AC: accrual basis.

sources, I had no choice in this case. The NBH does not report data on reinvested earnings, while the CSO does, when presenting the components of the differences between GDP and GNI (gross national income). Cash flow statistics (of the NBH) on FDI are based on data reported by commercial banks; reinvested earnings are based on tax returns of the corporate sector. Therefore, the FDI figures on "accrual basis" (AB) in table 4.14 are only meant to give a rough idea of the approximate magnitude of the underestimation of annual FDI due cash flow statistics. I would definitely like to avoid the impression that these calculations have anything to do with the FDI (and, thus, current account) figures that the NBH will publish, if and when it starts reporting FDI on an accrual basis.

Having made these caveats, we may observe that by 1999, reinvested earnings, as reported by the CSO, reached the size of gross FDI in the balance of payments. Even if we consider the CSO figure as an overestimation of the size of reinvested profits, there is no question that the actual magnitude of FDI in Hungary (on accrual basis) is much closer to the AB than to the CB (official) figures in the table. Thus, in the last few years, the actual ratio of gross FDI to GDP is likely to have been closer to 8 percent, rather

than around 4 percent, as shown by official statistics. The reason why this question is important for managing capital inflows is that total profits from former FDI are potential sources of outflows. The fact that earnings were reinvested on a large scale in Hungary indicates that there was an implicit inflow, disregarded by official statistics.

While the interpretation of the calculated (AB) FDI figures relative to GDP do not involve fundamental conceptual problems, their ratio to real investments do: these figures (in the last block of the table) have to be handled with care.[34] This is so, because about one-third of the cumulative 19.1 billion EUR FDI inflow to Hungary until 1999 consisted of privatization revenues that had little do with real capital formation. These proceeds, as already pointed out, were mainly used for redeeming foreign public debt. The importance of privatization revenues within total FDI is shown in table 4.15, in which we reproduce the middle part of table 4.8 (ratios to GDP) net of privatization proceeds accounted as FDI.[35]

While the ratios in table 4.15 (inclusive of privatization revenues) show a clearly declining trend for FDI inflows on a cash-flow basis, and a somewhat uncertain direction on an accrual basis, table 4.16

TABLE 4.15 Indicators of FDI Flows Net of Privatization Revenues (Accounted as FDI) (% of GDP)

	1995	1996	1997	1998	1999
Gross FDI (CB)	3.2	3.8	4.1	4.3	4.1
Net FDI (CB)	3.1	3.8	3.2	3.3	3.6
Reinvested profits	2.3	3.0	3.9	4.2	4.1
Gross FDI (AB)	5.4	6.8	8.0	8.5	8.3
Net FDI (AB)	5.4	6.8	7.0	7.5	7.7

Source: NBH and CSO.

presents a different picture. It indicates that, net of privatization revenues, there was a more or less general upward shift in all indicators of FDI inflows, but this shift is much more obvious in the case of indicators based on the accrual, than on the cash flow interpretation.

To assess the actual macroeconomic impact of FDI, we leave aside both BOP statistics and our rough adjustments of the official figures, and turn to data based on tax returns, as reported by the CSO (2001).

As it turns out, the importance of FDI in the Hungarian economy is much more significant than what is revealed by BOP statistics. Table 4.16, relating to the non-financial corporate sector, shows the contribution of companies with more than 10 percent foreign ownership to the performance of this sector.

As shown by the table, the role of companies with (partial or full) foreign ownership has been continuously increasing in foreign trade. Their role in value-added and investments had been increasing until 1997; since then, they have maintained their relatively high share. Two other features of the foreign ownership sector stand out. First, its share is higher in investments than in value-added, and its share in

TABLE 4.16 The Contribution of Companies with Foreign Ownership to Indicators of the Corporate Sector (%)

	Value Added	Investments	Exports	Imports
1994	39	48	54	57
1995	39	55	58	63
1996	43	52	69	70
1997	49	58	75	74
1998	49	57	77	74
1999	49	57	80	76

Source: CSO (2001).

foreign trade is higher than in investments. Second, while in the mid-1990s, the share of this sector was higher in imports than in exports; by the end of the decade, its role has been reversed.

It should be emphasized that the characteristics of the sector with more than 10 percent foreign ownership actually apply to companies with full (or at least above 50 percent) foreign participation, as these are the ones that provide the bulk of value-added, investments, and foreign trade of companies with foreign ownership.

We may conclude that investments from FDI flows have become an integral and extremely dynamic part of the Hungarian economy and their actual macroeconomic impact cannot be measured by FDI inflows recorded in the balance of payments.

Notes

1. I would like to thank Márton Oblath, Gábor Pula, and Tamás Révész, who provided valuable input and research assistance.

2. The transformation involved the change of the "socialist" (or "communist") system into a "capitalist" one. I wish to avoid the related terminological issues. Kornai (1992), who presented the most comprehensive review of the pre-transformation system, refers to it as "socialist," which is what the government called itself.

3. "Trade diversion" may appear to be a misnomer in this case, as the forty-year existence of the CMEA itself involved trade diversion (from traditional Western partners toward the Soviet Union and other CMEA countries; see, e.g., Brada 1992). However, given the *existing* trade links in the late 1980s, trade liberalization resulted in a large fall in intraregional trade within Eastern Europe, which was initially only partly compensated by the growth of trade with the West.

4. These remarks are not meant to discredit Hungarian macroeconomic statistics, which are among the best in Central and Eastern Europe. Still, I have to call attention to the difficulties I encountered in my work.

5. This is a heavily abridged version of my original paper. Due to limitations of space, several parts, especially the ones devoted to the detailed treatment of statistical/conceptual problems, are omitted.

6. For a comprehensive review of the "Hungarian type" of reformed socialist economy that functioned, with several modifications, between 1968 and 1989, see Kornai (1986) and Szamuelly (1996).

7. On the workings of this system, see Gács (1993).

8. See Oblath (1991).

9. The alternative proposals for import liberalization in Hungary are discussed in Oblath (1992).

10. Lajos Bokros—a few years before becoming the minister of finance who implemented the stabilization program of 1995—termed the legal package including these acts as "shock therapy à la Hongroise."

11. The volume of commodity imports barely increased (by 1 percent in 1989), and then it decreased by 5 percent in 1990, to rise by a mere 5.5 percent in 1991 and to decline again by 7.5 percent in 1992.

12. Naturally, the almost immediate improvement of the current account and the fiscal balance was not directly related to the essence of the stabilization package. The short-term improvement in the current account was mainly due to the return of flight capital (that left the country in the form of current account transactions). However, the jump in the rate of inflation, as a result of the devaluation, significantly increased fiscal revenues.

13. On the costs of sterilization in Hungary, see for example Szapáry and Jakab (1998) and Oblath (1999).

14. Some basic information on the country: Hungary is a small country, with a territory of 94,000 km² and a population of 10.07 million (as of 1999). Its GDP at the official exchange rate was somewhat above 50 billion dollars in 2000; but at purchasing power parity (PPP), it was about 2.3 times higher, that is, 115 billion dollars. Thus, per capita GDP at PPP is above 11,400 dollars (about 52 percent of the European Union's average); the ratio of GDI (gross domestic income) to GDP was around 96–97 percent, indicating that the country makes significant net income transfers abroad.

15. Table 4.1 reports a very rough (and economically inadequate) statistical approximation of the liabilities stemming from inflows of FDI. The effect of changes in exchange rates is, but reinvested profits are not, taken into account. On the measurement of FDI and its actual macroeconomic impact, see appendix 1 of this chapter.

16. For the background and details of fiscal problems in the early years of the transition, see Oblath (1995).

17. See Oblath and Sebestyén (1998) on the importance of seigniorage in the 1990s.

18. For details on the RER based on relative profitability, see for example Lipschitz and McDonald (1993).

19. See Balassa (1964) and Samuelson (1964) on the original proposition, and Halpern and Wyplos (1977) and ECE (2001), ch. 6, on its relevance for the transition economies.

20. This section had to be significantly shortened.

21. Because of adjustments for the foreign trade of tax-free zones, the figures for exports and imports for the first half of the 1990s differ from those presented in table 4.1.

22. The adjustment took care of the fact that foreign interest payments were made by the central bank, and in the year when the sum of foreign public interest payments abroad and the officially published primary balance did not cover the published deficit, the latter was increased so as to include net interest payments made by the central bank.

23. See for example the Bokros and Dethier (1998) volume, in particular Dethier and Orlowski (1998).

24. I included industry and agriculture in the traded-goods sector, and all other branches into the non-traded sector. Of course, this is simplification, as the output of agriculture is "semitradable" while several types of services are internationally traded. This categorization serves as a rough approximation.

25. Financial intermediary services indirectly measured. On the role of FISIM, see System of National Accounts (SNA; 1993).

26. The number of unemployed persons whose last occupation was in that sector.

27. See for example Aghion and Commander (1999), Milanovic (1999), and Ferreira (1999).

28. The Gini coefficient, a general indicator of income distribution, is derived from the cumulative distribution of earnings across population and is defined as one-half of the mean difference between any two observations in the earnings distribution divided by average earnings. Its value is 0 for total equality, and 1 for the situation if all income is concentrated in the hands of one person. For well-known methodological problems (Atkinson et al. 2000), the Gini coefficient calculated for different countries (and for different periods) cannot be directly compared. Still, it is generally accepted that a value of Gini around 0.20–0.25 indicates a relatively equal society, while a level of 0.4–0.5 points to considerable inequality. Most Western European societies belong to the first group, while countries of the former Soviet Union (CIS countries) are examples for the latter.

29. Consisting of the level of education, entrepreneurship, and workplace position with major significance, and foreign owner of workplace, ability to speak foreign languages, gender, and age with minor significance (Tóth 2000).

30. See Ferge (1998). Note, however, that the method of calculation (the adjustment of the 1992 poverty line for overall inflation) is rather problematic.

31. I owe this paradoxical phrase, which I find most expressive of the nature of gradualism in Hungary, to my colleague, Kamilla Lányi.

32. See Appendix 1 of this chapter.

33. This possibility materialized at the time of the crisis in Argentina in 2001.

34. Actually, there is a problem with measuring FDI flows at current exchange rates (just as with any item in foreign currency) relative to GDP: the official exchange rate is significantly undervalued relative to Purchasing

Power Parity (PPP). According to OECD-EUROSTAT calculations, Hungary's GDP at official exchange rate was about 43 percent of its GDP at PPP in 1999. (The exchange rate deviation index—ERDI—was around 2.3.) Thus, the relative size of any foreign currency item (in percent of GDP) would have to be scaled downwards by more than 50 percent, if expressed in proportion to GDP at PPP. I simply mention this point, but do not elaborate on it, as it is tangential to the actual topic.

35. I emphasize that here I consider only privatization revenues recorded as FDI. In 1997, the bulk (and since 1998, practically all) of the privatization revenues were recorded as portfolio investments.

References

Aghion, P., and S. Commander. 1999. On the dynamics of inequality in the transition. *Economics of Transition* (2).

Atkinson, A. B., et al. 2000. *Handbook of income distribution*. Vol. 1. Amsterdam: Elsevier Science BV.

Balassa, B. 1964. The purchasing power parity doctrine: A reappraisal. *Journal of Political Economy* (December).

Berg, J., and L. Taylor. 2000. External liberalization, economic performance, and social policy. CEPA Working Paper Series, no. 12, February. New York: Center for Economic Policy Analysis, New School University.

Bokros, L., and J. J. Dethier, eds. 1998. *Public finance reform during the transition: The experience of Hungary*. Washington, D.C.: The World Bank.

Brada, J. 1992. Regional integration in Eastern Europe: Prospects for integration within the region and with the European Union. In *New Dimensions in Regional Integration*, edited by J. de Melo and A. Panagariya. Cambridge University Press, 1993.

Central Statistical Office (CSO). 2001. *Foreign direct investment in Hungary, 1998–1999*. Budapest: Cambridge: CSO.

Dethier, J. J., and W. Orlowski. 1998. The setting: Macroeconomic policy in Hungary in the 1990s. In L. Bokros and J. J. Dethier, *Public Finance Reform during the Transition*.

European Bank of Reconstruction and Development (EBRD). 2000. *Transition report*. London: EBRD.

Ferge, Zs. 1998. Szociálpolitika 1989–1997 (Social policy, 1989–1997). In *Magyarország Évtizedkönyve* (Decade book of Hungary). Budapest: Demokrácia Kutatások Magyar Központja.

Ferreira, F. H. G. 1999. Economic transition and the distributions of income and wealth. *Economics of Transition* (2).

Gács, J. 1993. Foreign trade liberalization (1986–90). In

Halpern, L., and C. Wyplos. 1977. Equilibrium real exchange rates in transition economies. IMF Staff Papers, no. 4. Washington, D.C.: World Bank.

Kolosi, J. et al. 1998. *Társadalmi Riport, 1998* (Social report, 1998). Budapest: TÁRKI.

———. 2000. *Társadalmi Riport, 2000* (Social report, 2000). Budapest: TÁRKI.

Kornai, J. 1986. The Hungarian reform process: Visions, hopes and reality. *Journal of Economic Literature* (3).

———. 1992. *The socialist system*. Princeton, N.J.: Princeton University Press.

Lipschitz, L., and D. McDonald. 1993. Real exchange rate and competitiveness: A clarification of concepts and some measurements for Europe. *Empirica* (1).

Milanovic, B. 1999. Explaining the increase in inequality during transition. *Economics of Transition* (2).

Oblath, G. 1991. Trade policy recommendations. In *Foreign economic liberalization*, edited by A. Köves and P. Marer. Boulder, Colo.: Westview Press.

———. 1992. The limits, successes and question marks of import liberalization in Hungary. *Russian and East European Finance and Trade* (Summer).

———. 1995. Economic growth and fiscal crisis in Central and Eastern Europe. The Vienna Institute for Comparative Economic Studies (WIIW), Research Report no. 218, May. Vienna: WIIW.

———. 1999. Capital inflows to Hungary and accompanying policy responses, 1995–1996. In *The mixed blessing of financial inflows*, edited by J. Gács, R. Holzman, and M. L. Wyzan. Cheltenham, UK, Luxembourg, and Austria: Edward Elgar and IIASA.

———. 2000. The liberalisation of imports in Hungary: Alternative proposals, conditions, consequences and the role of the World Bank. Paper prepared in the framework of the Hungarian SAPRI Project, Budapest, May.

Oblath, G., and A. Sebestyén. 1998. Interpreting and measuring seigniorage: Hungary's case. Kopint-Datorg Discussion Papers, no. 58, Budapest, August.

Samuelson, P. 1964. Theoretical notes on trade problems. *Review of Economics and Statistics* (May):

System of National Accounts (SNA). 1993. Eurostat, IMF, OECD, UN, World Bank.

Szamuelly, L. 1996. Establishment and erosion of the Soviet model of CPE as reflected in economic science in Hungary, 1995–1980. Frankfurt Institute for Transformation Studies Discussion Papers, no. 1/96.

Szapáry, Gy., and Z. Jakab. 1998. Hungary's experiences with the crawling peg. National Bank of Hungary

Working Paper, no. 98/6, August. Budapest: National Bank of Hungary.

Tanzi, V., M. I. Blejer, and M. O. Teijerio. 1987. Effects of inflation on measurement of fiscal deficits: Conventional versus operational measures. IMF Staff Papers, no. 4. Washington, D.C.: IMF.

Tóth, I. G. 2000. A század és rendszerváltás társadalma (The society of the century and that of systemic transformation). Budapest: MTA.

UN Economic Commission for Europe (ECE). 2000. *Economic survey of Europe*, no. 2/3. Washington, D.C.: World Bank.

———. 2001. *Economic survey of Europe*, no. 1. Washington, D.C.: World Bank.

World Bank. 1976. *Hungary: Structural change and sustainable growth*. Washington, D.C.: World Bank.

———. 2000. *World development indicators*. Washington, D.C.: World Bank.

5

A Decade of Reforms: The Indian Economy in the 1990s

J. Mohan Rao and Amitava Krishna Dutt

1. Introduction

Since mid-1991, India has undergone wide-ranging economic reforms that—in the words of its government—aim to liberalize and globalize its economy. Not unlike many other developing and transitional economies, the reforms were undertaken following a foreign exchange crisis that brought India on the verge of defaulting on its foreign loans. Besides a stabilization program, both internal and international economic activity have been deregulated and liberalized. Internal liberalization included the dismantling of a complex industrial licensing system, opening up a number of sectors previously reserved for the state to private investors, some divestment of stock in the public sector, decontrol of administered prices, and financial liberalization. External liberalization measures included the removal of non-tariff barriers to imports; the reduction in import tariffs; increased incentives for foreign direct investment and technology inflows, allowing Indian firms to borrow abroad; and the opening up of Indian stock markets to foreign investors.

As might be expected, the reform program has evoked a variety of responses, some based on a priori theoretical expectations and others relying on the trickle of empirical evidence. These responses range from euphoria about freeing a caged tiger from *dirigiste* shackles to fierce mistrust about free markets among those enamored with autarkic, state-led development. Others hold guardedly optimistic expectations for certain aspects of the reforms. Many are concerned with their "social" impact—which encompasses the effects on employment, poverty, income inequality, and the quality of life for the majority of people. Table 5.1 places some examples of these diverse views along two axes in terms of their potential longer-term impact: economic growth and social outcomes.[1]

Reform-minded economists such as Bhagwati and Srinivasan (1993) view globalization as not only accelerating growth but also promoting mass

TABLE 5.1 Alternative Views on the Effects of Economic Reforms

		Social Outcomes		
		Positive	Neutral	Negative
Growth Impact	Positive	Official view Bhagwati and Srinivasan (1993) Bhagwati (1994) Joshi and Little (1996) World Bank (1998)	Dreze and Sen (1995)	Kumar (2000a)
	Neutral			Bhaduri and Nayyar (1996)
	Negative			Patnaik (1997) Nagaraj (1997, 2000a)

well-being. Compared to India's *dirigiste* and autarkic policies, it is foreign competition and foreign direct investment, they argue, that will improve allocative and production efficiency. For them, trade liberalization increases the demand for semiskilled and unskilled workers, increases their wages, and thereby reduces poverty and improves income distribution. Higher growth also augments fiscal resources for health, education, and other social needs. Furthermore, reforms can release any foreign exchange or aggregate demand constraints on economic growth (although these effects are not typically emphasized in neoliberal eulogies of reform).

An alternative view is that the reforms, while desirable for promoting growth, are largely orthogonal to trajectories of social outcomes. Dreze and Sen (1995) argue that reforms that increase growth will not automatically expand opportunities to lead a normal span of life (and to live in good health, read and write, and not go hungry). Rather, their social impact depends on whether reform benefits are channeled toward improving the conditions of the poorest, breaking down caste and gender hierarchies, and generating employment. Therefore, they argue that the "removal of counterproductive government controls may indeed expand social opportunities for many people. However, to change the circumstances (such as illiteracy and ill health) that severely constrain the actual social opportunities of a large part of

the population, these permissive reforms have to be supplemented by a radical shift in public policy in education and health" (Dreze and Sen 1995, 16).

A third view, articulated by some economists (such as Kumar 2000a) and social activists, is that even if economic reforms have a positive or neutral effect on growth, they will have an adverse impact on social well-being. A primary concern here is that globalization will slow down employment growth if it succeeds in improving the rate of technological change, even if output growth increases. Slow employment growth, especially that of unskilled labor, will increase economic inequality. Even the sectoral changes that are supposed to ensue from the reforms are likely to cause employment losses for the many who are ill equipped to find employment in expanding sectors. Second, a shift in employment toward unprotected and low-paid informal or casual labor is feared as employers try to respond to the pressures of reforms by reducing labor costs. Third, if reforms shift the terms of trade toward agriculture, the rise in the price of food will reduce the real income of the poor. Lastly, cuts in social spending that accompany liberalization and globalization will also reduce the disposable income of the poor and the government services available to them.

A final view (see, for instance, Patnaik 1997) is that the reforms have a negative effect on both growth and mass well-being. First, increasing inequality along the lines just discussed will depress aggregate demand and slow down industrial growth. Second, trade liberalization will increase imports but not significantly affect exports, thus further reducing aggregate demand. Third, cuts in government spending that accompany the reforms (especially in infrastructure investment) will further reduce industrial demand and have adverse consequences on industrial and agricultural growth from the supply side. Fourth, agricultural investment and growth will not respond to price incentives, especially in the absence of land reforms that are not on the reformist agenda, and in view of declining infrastructure investment. Finally, the liberalization of capital inflows is unlikely to significantly increase direct foreign investment, given the low level of development, the low educational levels of unskilled workers, and political uncertainty. Portfolio flows, if they increase, are likely to exacerbate economic uncertainty and lead to intermittent foreign exchange crises. High interest rates for attracting such capital flows will also have an adverse effect on investment and growth.

This chapter examines the record and evaluates the diverse views (as mentioned above) about India's globalizing reforms. In section 2, we examine the content of reforms undertaken, clarify the meaning and significance of the term "globalization," and explain how we shall investigate the effects of globalization in the following sections. Section 3 looks at some macroeconomic dimensions of performance including the realized effects of openness on external transactions, on economic growth and other macroeconomic indicators, as well as on trends in the rural sector, which remains the mainstay of employment in India. Section 4 summarizes trends in employment and its distribution across sectors and the formal-informal divide. Section 5 assesses the evidence and discusses the controversial debates about changes in income distribution and poverty brought about by reforms. Section 6 turns to a discussion on government policy toward social safety nets. Section 7 concludes.

2. The Reforms, Openness, and Globalization

2.1. Reform Planks

India's post-colonial governments pursued determinedly interventionist and autarkic policies. Apart

from high walls of tariffs and quotas, the accumulation regime rested on the twin pillars of state-led investment and state-led coordination of economic activity. The public sector grew from small beginnings to acquire a gross domestic product (GDP) share of one-quarter and an investment share of one-half in the late 1980s. Significant parts of the private, especially formal, sector were controlled through an industrial licensing system, financial and credit controls, price and distribution controls, and labor laws. In addition to extensive quantitative limits on foreign trade, foreign direct investment (FDI) was heavily restricted, both in terms of sectors and in terms of the equity share of participation.

After the crisis of June 1991, the self-professed policy of the government has been liberalization and globalization. Although this policy change was not an altogether abrupt one—through the late 1970s and the 1980s, there were attempts at reducing state control and autarky by successive governments—the reform of 1991 was unprecedented in scope. In July 1991, immediately following the general elections, the balance of payments crisis, and the imposition of IMF conditions, the new government of Narasimha Rao announced a radical policy overhaul in its Industrial Policy Statement. Changes included the removal of most non-tariff restrictions on imports of capital and intermediate goods, the broadening and simplification of export incentives, and the elimination of state trading monopolies. A list of restricted imports was drawn up to include items of national sensitivity (chiefly defense and health care), and some capital goods and most consumer goods (the number of which has subsequently been reduced) for protectionist reasons. The import of all other goods was allowed except those still reserved for import through the government's agencies.

The percentage of products covered by non-tariff barriers, using the harmonized system of trade classification, came down from 90 percent in the pre-reform period to 44 percent by 1995 (Mehta 1997). These barriers are being phased out for all tradables other than consumer goods. Tariff rates have also fallen. According to the World Trade Organization, the (weighted) average nominal tariff fell from 87 percent in 1990–1991 to 20 percent in 1998–1999, the highest rates falling from 355 percent to 200 percent. The average economy-wide effective rate of protection has been estimated to have declined from 87 percent in 1989–1990 to 62 percent in 1993–1994

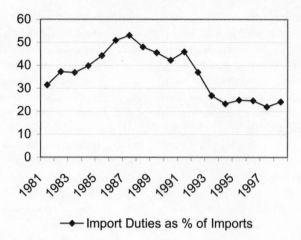

FIGURE 5.1 Import Duties as Percentage of Imports

and further, to about 30 percent in 1995–1996 (Mehta 1997). The ratio of import duties to the total value of imports fell from a peak of 53 percent in 1987 to 22 percent in 1997, although it was rising slightly in 1998 (see figure 5.1). But the dispersion in import tariffs remains high (Mehta 1997) and, very recently, there been some backpedaling on tariffs for products such as automobiles in response to industry pressures.

The rupee was devalued by 20 percent against the U.S. dollar in July 1991 and further in February 1992 when an official dual exchange market was created. Since the inflation rate was about 14 percent in 1991–1992, the real exchange rate depreciated by 7.89 percent. In August 1994, a unified floating exchange rate regime was adopted, with the rupee becoming fully convertible on the current account. Figure 5.2 shows movements in the rupee price of the dollar, which has increased steadily since 1994.

Restrictions on FDI inflows have been considerably reduced. Departing from the earlier restriction of 40 percent required by the Foreign Exchange Regulation Act (FERA), foreign equity holding of up to 51 percent was allowed in thirty-four high-priority industries requiring large investments and advanced technology. Foreign ownership of up to 74 percent was allowed in fourteen additional infrastructure and high-priority industries, and 100 percent foreign ownership on an automatic basis is allowed in ports

and roads. Full ownership status is also given to nonresident Indian (NRI) investors in priority industries. A Foreign Investment Promotion Board is allowed to approve up to 100 percent foreign ownership in cases involving transfer of high technology, export-oriented projects, energy and infrastructure projects, and consulting and trading companies; and the Board is required to pass approvals expeditiously and transparently. To encourage technology transfers, the government announced that it would provide automatic approval (within specified parameters) for technology agreements related to high-priority industries.

Portfolio capital inflows have also been deregulated. NRIs and foreign institutional investors (FIIs) such as pension funds and mutual funds were allowed to own stock in the corporate sector subject to some limits (which were gradually relaxed), with full repatriation rights, without restrictions on volume of trading or lock-in period, and with favorable tax rates. Subsequently, the markets for debt and for government securities were also opened up to FIIs. Larger Indian firms were allowed to obtain long-term low-cost financing from international capital markets, subject to government approval. But many types of capital account transactions are still banned or restricted (Nayyar 2000). Commercial borrowing on international capital markets is restricted to selective longer maturities. All other borrowing requires case-by-case approval. Commercial banks are not allowed

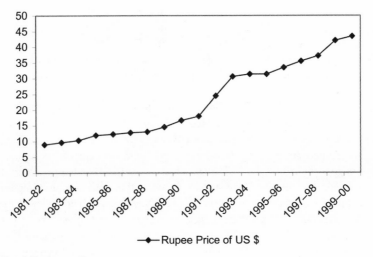

FIGURE 5.2 Official Exchange Rate

(with a few exceptions) to accept deposits or make loans denominated in foreign currencies. Apart from capital outflows associated with capital inflows, the regime of capital outflows has not been significantly liberalized.

Sweeping measures of internal deregulation, which complement the external liberalization measures, have also been implemented. India's byzantine licensing system was dismantled by abolishing the licensing requirement for industrial investment in all but fourteen specified industries (on grounds of environmental hazards, national security, or social well-being). Industries and services (including infrastructure such as telecommunication, roads, power generation, and petroleum refining) that were earlier reserved for the public sector were opened up to private (including foreign) investors. Restrictions on investments by large industrial houses (and foreign companies) under the Monopolies and Restrictive Trade Practices Act were abolished. A phased program of the privatization of public sector enterprises (PSEs) has been launched: shares in PSEs have been sold and a limited amount of actual privatization has occurred. The financial sector has also been drastically liberalized. Banking reform permitted the entry of new private sector banks including foreign joint ventures as well as private non-bank financial intermediates. The Capital Issues Control Act was repealed, and the regulation of a liberalized capital market has been entrusted to a newly created Securities and Exchange Board of Trade. Online and dematerialized trading have been introduced. Moreover, a program of economic stabilization has accompanied the above measures: in particular, the fiscal deficit was reduced by over a third.

Successive governments have expressed their intention of carrying these reforms further. It has been announced that import tariffs shall be reduced to international levels, quantitative controls removed ahead even of initial schedules, and the rupee made fully convertible by opening the capital account (though this last step seems to have lost support in the aftermath of the Asian financial crisis).

2.2. Globalization and Openness

Much of the literature and, even more so, common parlance in India use "openness" and "globalization" synonymously. But in this chapter we reserve the term "openness" to refer to policies that aim to bring about economic integration with international markets, and take "globalization" to be some measure of increased external integration actually achieved.[2] The reason for distinguishing between the two terms, despite the close relation between them, is that openness may not go hand in hand with globalization, as defined here.[3]

The importance of openness and globalization in India's economic reforms is obvious. As noted earlier, the official case for the reforms relies on both positive and negative arguments. The key positive arguments are (1) that trade liberalization will improve allocative efficiency by shifting resources from capital-intensive to labor-intensive sectors, (2) that reduced protection will raise technical efficiency by exposing Indian firms to foreign competition, and (3) that lowered barriers to foreign capital inflows will speed up capital accumulation and raise productivity levels through technology upgrading and spillovers. The official view also takes aggregate demand and foreign exchange constraints on growth to be the consequences of an autarkic policy orientation, the remedy for which lies in openness and globalization; this constitutes the negative case for the reforms. Each of these arguments makes external integration—or globalization—the engine of economic growth, and openness the centerpiece of policy. As described above, the reforms also involve internal deregulation and liberalization, and the adoption of other elements of domestic policy orthodoxy. However, these are viewed as economic prerequisites, or at least facilitators, of a successful policy of openness for increasing globalization and are, in turn, the likely political consequences of a policy of openness. Therefore, openness, as perceived by its architects, does indeed constitute the focal point of the new regime, and globalization its touchstone.

Since our purpose is to examine the consequences of globalization, for the most part, we will focus on import liberalization, the removal of restrictions to capital flows and technology imports—which are the main elements of greater openness. But we shall also take account of the domestic policy changes that are inextricably linked to and flow from these reforms.

2.3. Methodological Remarks

To assess the growth and social impacts of globalization, we will compare trends before and after the onset of the reforms in 1991. It is important to be forewarned of the problems of this method.

The "before/after" method is problematic because the year 1991 witnessed a harvest failure and a severe payments crisis that obliged the government to undertake stabilization measures that were not necessarily part of the structural reforms. Moreover, as we have seen, the government embarked not only on external liberalization but also on reforms liberalizing domestic activities, all of which may not be related to openness. Finally, the economy has been subjected to a number of shocks—such as the East Asian crisis and economic sanctions—which are, arguably, independent of the reform process. Given that the post-1991 outcomes are likely to be affected by all of these changes, it is impossible to attribute the differences solely to policy changes affecting external economic relations. We will guard against this problem by analyzing the causal links between aspects of the reform and economic performance, in addition to examining the general trends relating to growth and the social sector.

It may be considered preferable to examine the effects of reforms using a suitable computable general equilibrium model to consider the effects of changes in parameters that reflect foreign-sector reforms alone. This has the virtue of isolating the effects of external policy changes. However, such an analysis is problematic because it ignores the close relationship between external and domestic policy changes alluded to earlier: the requirements of consistency might force domestic policy changes to conform with external policy changes, and "domestic" policy changes, in turn, might affect the level of "globalization." For instance, the dismantling of the licensing apparatus, usually thought of as an internal liberalization measure, might make exports more competitive and the economy more attractive to foreign investors.

A second issue is whether 1991 is an appropriate date for our comparison. It is generally accepted that the most important policy discontinuity in India occurred in 1991. But some have argued that since liberalization started in the 1980s and even earlier, it is not appropriate to compare the period before and after 1991 to measure the effects of reforms. We view 1991 as the crucial divide for three reasons. First, despite some degree of liberalization during the 1980s, the process never gained real momentum. After Indira Gandhi's return to power in 1980, there were some cosmetic changes. When Rajiv Gandhi became the prime minister following his mother's assassination in 1984, there was some amount of reform. But by 1987, after some political setbacks, the push toward economic liberalization had slowed down (Kohli 1990, 305–24). Second, the most important policy reforms during the 1980s centered on reducing internal barriers to entry—that allowed large business houses to play a larger role in industrial development—rather than on external liberalization. With respect to the external sector, there was some liberalization of raw material and component imports (by shifting importable items from restricted lists to what was called the Open General License); the easing of technology imports; and some very limited liberalization of capital goods imports. But even in the middle of the decade, Indian nominal tariffs were among the highest in the world (Ahluwalia 1991, 27). As shown in figure 5.1, import duties as a percentage of imports increased through most of the 1980s, exceeding 50 percent in 1987 and 1988, before coming down especially after 1991 (though part of this increase reflects a shift from quantitative to tariff restrictions). Third, most observers attribute the higher growth of that period, especially in the industrial sector, to expansionary fiscal policies, infrastructure investment, and foreign borrowing. Even pro-reform observers like Ahluwalia (1991) and Bhagwati and Srinivasan (1993, 92), who argue that the microeconomic reforms of the 1980s may have made some contribution to the higher growth, agree with this conclusion. Therefore, it has become established practice, in recent discussions and appraisals of reforms, to consider 1991 as their real beginning (see, for instance, Ahluwalia 1995; Bhagwati 1998).

A third issue with the before/after method is that the beneficial effects of external integration take time to be felt, and too few years have passed (and fewer still for which relatively complete evidence is available) since 1991 to judge these longer-term effects. While there is some merit in this argument, especially in a large country like India, it can be overemphasized. More than a decade has already passed since the reforms were initiated. Moreover, we propose to examine both events immediately following 1991 and those occurring subsequently to distinguish the shorter and longer terms.

3. Openness and Economic Growth

To understand whether economic opening has had any identifiable effect on economic growth and related macroeconomic indicators, we first discuss the extent to which the Indian economy has become more globalized under the new regime. We also examine the mechanisms by which these changes have affected the economy. We then turn our attention to the overall macroeconomic indicators, and to the agricultural sector in particular, which is home to over three-fifths of the labor force and an even higher fraction of the poor.

3.1. Increased Openness and Globalization

3.1.1. Trade Flows

India's foreign trade as a fraction of its gross domestic product (GDP) has grown significantly, from around 15 percent in the 1980s and 17 percent in 1990–1991 to about 25 percent in the late 1990s. However, despite continued import liberalization there has been a marginal fall in the ratio since the peak of 1995–1996 (see figure 5.3). Whereas India's share of world exports fell consistently from about 2 percent in the 1950s to about 0.6 percent in the 1970s, and then stayed at around 0.5 percent from 1973 onwards through the 1980s, the share in the post-reform period has risen spiritedly to 0.8 percent. In growth terms, the dollar value of India's exports increased annually at 12 percent between 1990–1991 and 1995–1996, which is significantly higher than the 7.5 percent (annual) growth rate for world trade. By any standard, this must be reckoned as rapid globalization. But these trends conceal some problems.

1. The growth of exports does not appear to be sustained. After growing by about 20 percent annually (in dollar terms) in 1993–1994 and 1995–1996, exports only grew by 5.3 percent and 4.6 percent in 1996–1997 and 1997–1998 respectively, and growth actually declined by 3.9 percent in 1998–1999. The sharp acceleration has been attributed both to a rapid growth in world trade and to a marked real depreciation of the rupee in the early 1990s (see Srinivasan 1998), which may be a direct result of economic reforms. The subsequent sluggishness may be partially explained by the slowdown of world trade and the East Asian crisis (and the resulting sharp depreciation of East Asian currencies). The real exchange rate appreciation in the mid-1990s (at least in part the outcome of capital inflows resulting from reforms) also, arguably, had an impact (see below).

FIGURE 5.3 Foreign Trade as Percentage of GDP

2. The import-GDP ratio has increased even faster than the export/GDP ratio, attaining a level of about 14 percent in the second half of the 1990s (see figure 5.4). This implies that the trade deficit (as a percentage of GDP) has worsened for much of the 1990s, presumably due to liberalization (although there has been some recent improvement). Further reductions in import taxes and the removal of non-tariff barriers on consumer goods, as planned, are likely to further widen the trade deficit.

3. While there was a shift in the composition of imports between 1980–1981 to 1990–1991, no further shift occurred during the post-reform period (Mehta 1997). This is surprising considering the large changes in the structure of protection. It suggests that changes in trade policy that affected the relative competitiveness of import-competing sectors might have been neutralized by other policy shifts.

4. Econometric evidence does not support the conventional conjecture that changes in competitiveness have increased India's exports. Nor do the reforms appear to have had an appreciable impact on exports as measured by the post-reform dummy variable (Mehta 1997).

5. As with imports, the composition of India's exports has not changed significantly in the 1990s, while it did so between 1980–1981 and

1990–1991 (Mehta 1997). Kumar (2000a) has argued that India's export competitiveness has been adversely affected by the failure to diversify exports. India's export growth acceleration appears to have been caused by a shift in export composition toward relatively dynamic Asian markets.

3.1.2. Foreign Direct Investment Inflows

After stagnating since the 1970s, the inflow of FDI has recently increased. Following limited liberalization, the FDI stock nearly tripled in the 1980s. In the wake of the 1991 policy changes, approvals of FDI inflows increased spectacularly: compared to $200 million in 1991, about $17 billion worth of FDI proposals was approved in 1997. As figure 5.5 shows, *actual* inflows also increased rapidly, although they were considerably smaller than approvals. FDI as a percentage of gross domestic investment (GDI) and GDP has also grown rapidly between 1991–1992 and 1997–1998, as shown in figure 5.6, although it should be noted that all FDI does not represent capital formation (see below).

Despite this rapid expansion, however, FDI inflows to India remain low compared to inflows to other less developed countries (LDCs) in Asia (such as China, Malaysia, Thailand, and Indonesia) and also far below that of all LDCs in relation to their

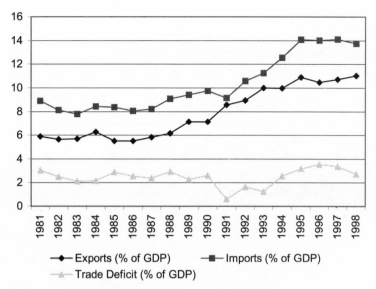

FIGURE 5.4 Exports, Imports, and Trade Deficit as Percentage of GDP

GDP. Compared to India's peak level of 0.85 percent in 1997–1998, the ratio of inflows to GDP for all LDCs increased from 0.8 percent in the early 1990s to 2 percent in 1997 according to World Bank estimates. Cumulative FDI into India in the 1990s has been around $15 billion. Compare that to China's inflow of $238 billion during 1994–1999. Moreover, it is unclear to what extent the increase in FDI will

be sustained. As figure 5.5 shows, FDI inflows fell in both years after 1997–1998, reversing the upward trend since 1991–1992.

There is also some doubt about whether the spurt in FDI was a result of liberalization. Kumar (1998) has pointed out that India's share of FDI inflows from Germany, France, and the United States does not show any significant change, which suggests that

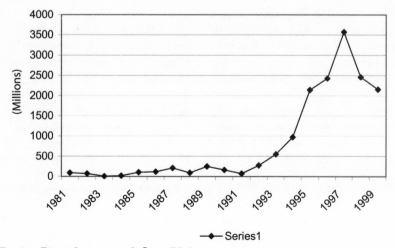

FIGURE 5.5 Foreign Direct Investment Inflows (Net)

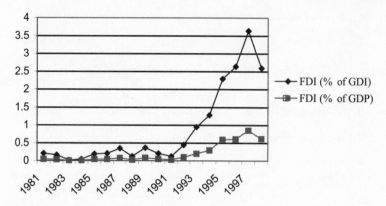

FIGURE 5.6 Foreign Direct Investment as Percentage of GDI and GDP

liberalization has not had a major impact. India seems to have merely benefited from the dramatic expansion in FDI flows from advanced countries to developing countries in the 1990s (these inflows can, to a large extent, be explained by conditions internal to advanced countries). However, to the extent that the increase in this FDI was the result of less restrictive policies in developing economies in general, it can also be argued that India's reforms at least enabled it to maintain its share in these higher flows.

Has the increase in FDI had (or is it likely to have) a positive effect on growth in India? FDI is supposed to foster growth by increasing capital accumulation, inducing technological change and greater efficiency, improving the balance of payments, and increasing exports. With respect to capital formation, we have seen that the FDI/GDI ratio has remained small (see figure 5.6). In fact, the state— through the financial institutions that it controls— remains the principal financier of local enterprises, in both the public and private sector. The share of foreign firms in fixed asset formation in the corporate sector remained unchanged at about 10 percent in the 1990s. Moreover, foreign firms used a smaller fraction of their investable resources in physical investment when compared to Indian firms. During the five years after 1991–1992, the ratio of gross fixed assets to total uses of funds for the foreign private sector was about 13 percent lower for foreign compared to indigenous private firms (Nagaraj 1997). It

appears that FDI largely represents the acquisition of managerial control of existing firms rather than representing new capital formation. During 1997–1999 nearly 40 percent of FDI inflows have taken the form of mergers and acquisitions of existing Indian enterprises, reversing the trend till 1990 when nearly all FDI inflow took the form of greenfield projects (Kumar 2000b).

With respect to technological change, the evidence provides little support for the widely held expectation that the new liberalization of FDI will help upgrade technology, enhance product innovation, and transfer management skills. The growth rate of productivity for industries with relatively high advanced foreign technology inflows is not significantly greater than that for other industries (Goldar 1993). Moreover, since a large portion of FDI takes the form of mergers and acquisitions, the extent of technological inflows and diffusion of knowledge within the economy is likely to be low. Kumar (2000b, 2855) points out that in many cases transnational corporations (TNCs) have bought up profitable enterprises to obtain distribution channels, where managerial and technological improvements have been negligible. In fact, efficiency in these enterprises may have declined because of inappropriate new management practices and technology (as suggested by a fall in the market share of firms taken over by TNCs). Since TNC acquisition has also largely taken the form of buying out joint ventures—previously important conduits for knowledge inflows—the effect on technological change is negligible, and that on the future of technological diffusion is arguably negative. While greenfield investment can increase competition, mergers and acquisitions by TNCs—mostly of a horizontal rather than a vertical nature—have tended to increase industrial concentration (Kumar 2000b), with possible adverse effects on efficiency, especially due to the recent relaxation of antitrust laws. Mani and Bhaskar (1998), Goldar and Ranganathan (1999), and Basant (2000) find that there has been a decline in the trend of in-house R & D in the corporate sector in the 1990s, arguably because of easier access to foreign technology.

To the extent that the effectiveness and speed of technology transfers depend on domestic technological capability, the effect of this trend on technological change is arguably negative. Domestic technological capability may be adversely affected by competition faced by domestic firms from foreign brand and trade names that put domestic competitors at a disadvantage (Kumar 2000a). Finally, there has been a shift in the sectoral composition of FDI flows—from high-technology manufactures to services, infrastructure, and low-technology manufacturing sectors.

Regarding the balance of payments, Kumar (2000b) points out that a significant portion of investment by TNCs does not involve net inflows of foreign capital. In about 27 percent of the deals associated with TNCs in India between April 1993 to February 2000, acquisitions have been made by Indian affiliates of TNCs, often with their internal fund accruals and domestic borrowings. Taking into account the repatriation of profits to foreign parent firms, the effect of this on the balance of payments is likely to be negative. The effect on exports is also likely to be negligible, given that the bulk of FDI in India is directed to the home market, with TNCs and their affiliates acquiring domestic firms to take over established domestic distribution networks (Kumar 2000a). Overall, there is little evidence that growth has been positively affected by FDI inflows. Measuring FDI as a ratio of GDP, we find that there is no evidence that either FDI or growth Granger-cause each other, even at the 10 percent level of significance.

3.1.3. Portfolio Investment and Foreign Currency Bank Deposits

Total foreign portfolio investment in India expanded rapidly, from $6 million in 1990–1991 to over $3 billion in 1999–2000 (see figure 5.7). Indeed, the growth was initially much more rapid than the growth of FDI, so that portfolio investment constituted the bulk of total foreign investment until 1996–1997. Foreign currency deposits in banks have also

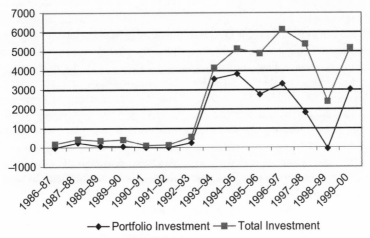

FIGURE 5.7 Total Foreign Investment and Portfolio Investment

increased rapidly, including NRI deposits. Despite these rapid increases, the magnitude of the flows has been small, both in relation to the size of the economy and in comparison to flows in many other Latin American and East and Southeast Asian economies.

The increased flows of foreign capital were expected to promote higher saving, investment, and capital formation, and thereby increase the rate of growth. However, the expected growth effects of portfolio flows and bank deposits do not appear to have been fulfilled.

The deregulation of the stock market and its opening up to international capital flows did produce enormous growth in the market (see Singh 1998), with market capitalization ratios increasing dramatically in the early 1990s. However, according to some estimates the volatility of stock prices also appears to have increased in the 1990s. This is, in part, because of the growing influence of foreign institutional investors and a direct consequence of deregulation (see Roy 2001). Kohli (2001a) finds that correlation measures between portfolio capital flows and stock price indices are strong and positive, as was the case during the capital market surge in the 1992–1995 period.

While market enthusiasts hoped that the stock market stimulation from foreign inflows would help bump up the saving rate, no such connection appears to have materialized. While the volume of household savings held in the form of shares and debentures and in units of the Unit Trust of India (a public sector mutual fund) has risen thirty-five-fold since 1980–1981, the overwhelming part of this reflects a shift from bank deposits to stocks. After the sharp fall in stock prices following the boom, the share of stocks went down again in favor of bank deposits (Pal 1998). Moreover, a large proportion of these inflows did not contribute to fixed capital formation in manufacturing since the ratio of gross fixed capital formation to the supply of long-term funds available to that sector fell significantly during 1992–1996 (Nagaraj 1997).

Nagaraj argues that the resources were more important for intercorporate investment, financing mergers and takeovers, and to fuel the real estate boom. Mumbai's real estate prices increased by between four and six times from 1991 to 1996. The cost of office space in Mumbai reached levels well beyond those in New York, London, Tokyo, or Hong Kong, but sharply declined after that to levels 60 percent lower than the peak prices of 2000. Though Mumbai's experience was extreme, it reflects trends in other

major cities in India (Nijman 2000). It is likely that a significant part of the demand surge was fueled by capital inflows, even if foreign inflows were not directly responsible for financing real estate purchases. To the extent that the stock market did supply funds for capital formation, this increase was compensated by a fall in internal corporate funding—possibly the result of lower profitability (Singh 1998). Pethe and Karnik (2000) find that there is weak causality running from the index of industrial production and stock prices, but not the other way around. Roy (2001), using a number of variables to measure economic activity, also reports that there is no stable long-run relationship between stock price and the macro economy. Thus, there is little evidence that a rise in stock prices (by reducing the cost of finance or improving business expectations) translated into higher industrial investment and growth.

The volatility of these hot money flows seen elsewhere in the world is also reflected in Indian experience since 1991. Portfolio flows, subject as they are to "sudden reversal," are more volatile than FDI. Kohli (2001a) reports that the standard deviation of portfolio investment between 1990 and 1999 is 5163.2, as compared with 4592.3 for FDI taken for annual figures, and the difference increases when measured at higher frequency, that is, quarterly and monthly. The fact is that the absence of full convertibility of the rupee on the capital account has partially shielded India from the crises that affected East and South Eastasia. Nevertheless, the volatility of portfolio flows is obvious from figure 5.7.

When inflows are high, the rupee tends to appreciate, eroding the competitiveness of Indian exports. Impulse response analysis shows that a one standard deviation positive shock to net inflows of foreign currency causes real exchange appreciation by 0.14 percent in the next quarter (Kohli 2001a). The Reserve Bank of India (RBI) has tried to contain the effects of capital inflows on exchange rate appreciation by intervening in foreign exchange markets. Following the heavy capital inflows in the 1993–1995 period, and again in 1997–1998, the RBI purchased dollars to prevent an appreciation of the rupee. Consequently, there has been a large increase in foreign exchange reserves: the stock of international reserves in 1999–2000 is 552 percent higher than its 1991 level. In periods of high capital inflows, the RBI has tried to lean against the wind by raising the discount rate and by increasing cash reserve

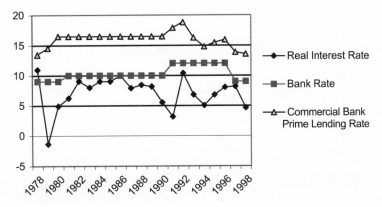

FIGURE 5.8 Interest Rates

requirements, with open market operations having a small role because of the limited ability of bond and equity markets to absorb government securities (Kohli 2001b). Thus, interest rates have occasionally been increased when capital inflows have increased, as in 1993–1994 and 1996–1997, when both nominal and real rates increased (see figure 5.8).

When capital flows are reversed, pressures are created on the balance of payments that require import compression and restrictive government policies. These policies, in turn, slow economic growth. Note that capital outflows may be the result of factors exogenous to the economy, such as political disturbances in India, or contagion effects due to problems elsewhere in the world, as occurred during the East Asian crisis.

3.2. Economic Growth and Other Macroeconomic Indicators

3.2.1. Growth

Leaving aside the high-growth year of 1988 and the crisis year of 1991, figure 5.9 shows that real GDP growth fluctuated between 3.5 percent and 8 percent during the 1980s and 1990s. As such, it is difficult to come to any clear conclusion about trends before and after 1991. On the one hand, the highest rate of growth for a single year occurred before the 1991 reforms. On the other hand, the economy grew consistently above the 7 percent level between 1994 and 1996, a feat not

achieved in the pre-reform years. This high rate of growth, however, has not been maintained thereafter: in 1997–1998, it fell to below 5 percent and was just above 6 percent in 1998–1999. As the recession continues, GDP growth was officially estimated at about 4 percent in 2000–2001.

Average and trend growth rates are more revealing. According to the new series of GDP that makes the comparison more favorable for the post-reform period, average GDP growth was 5.6 percent between 1991–1992 and 1998–1999 compared to 5.9 percent in the 1980s. However, if one leaves out the bad year of 1991–1992, the average for the post-reform period becomes 6.4 percent. Thus, the rate of growth for the post-reform period is higher than that of the previous decade if one leaves out 1991–1992, but lower if one includes it (both cases exclude the recent recession years). Nagaraj (2000a) examines GDP data for the 1980–1981 and 1999–2000 period using a dummy variable for the post-liberalization period. He finds that there is no statistically significant break in the trend growth rate of 5.7 percent after 1991–1992. This result holds even when the year 1991–1992 is excluded. It has been argued that the recent slowdown has been caused by exogenous factors such as the East Asian crisis, economic sanctions following the nuclear tests, and war in the region, and does not reflect long-run trends, which makes the comparison even more favorable for the later period. However, to the extent that the recent slowdown reflects an industrial recession triggered mainly by a slowdown in

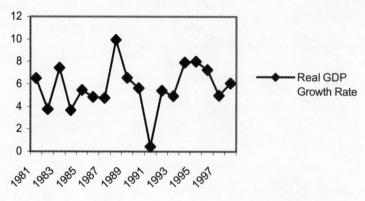

FIGURE 5.9 Real GDP Growth

public investment (see Kumar 2000a), it is arguably a consequence of reforms.

At the disaggregate level, there is some disagreement about rates of growth differences before and after reforms, depending on what series one examines. Table 5.2 provides data (from the Government of India's *Economic Survey* 2000–2001) on the annual average growth rates of several sectors in the pre-reform period (defined as 1980–1981 to 1991–1992) and the post-reform period (1992–1993 to 1999–2000). The data show a decline in the rate of growth of agriculture, not only in food grain production but also in all crop production. There is also a decline in industrial production as well as in total manufacturing. Of the manufacturing sectors shown in table 5.2, only the intermediate and consumer goods sectors reveal an the increase in the growth rate in the post-reform period, while there is a sharp decline in capital goods. In terms of GDP (value-added) in manufacturing, however, there is an increase in the rate of growth in the post-reform period. Turning to the trend rates of growth using National Account Statistics data, Nagaraj (2000a) finds no statistically significant change in the trend growth for the primary sector or the tertiary sector during this period, and a modest though statistically significant reduction in the growth rate for the secondary sector. The tertiary sector has grown no faster in the post-reform period, but given the slowdown in the growth rate of the secondary sector, it has emerged as the highest growing sector. At an even more disaggregate level, none of the industry groups (the one-digit level) has experienced an increase in the growth rate, while two sectors—manufacturing and public, social, and personal services, which constituted about 30 percent of GDP in the 1990s—have registered a statistically significant slowdown.

One consequence of the tertiary sector becoming the fastest growing sector of the economy is that its share in GDP has increased by virtually 1 percentage point every year from 41 percent in 1990–1991 to about 49 percent in 2000–2001, an issue to which we will return below.

TABLE 5.2 Sectoral Rates of Growth

	1980–1981 to 1991–1992	1992–1993 to 1999–2000
Agriculture and allied sectors	3.9	3.6
Agriculture (all crop)	4.2	3.7
Food grains	2.9	2.0
Industrial production	7.8	6.0
Manufacturing	7.6	6.3
Basic goods	7.4	6.1
Capital goods	9.4	5.9
Intermediate goods	4.9	9.1
Consumer goods	6.0	6.3
GDP—manufacturing	6.1	7.4

Source: Government of India, Ministry of Finance (2000–2001).

3.2.2. Saving and Investment

Figure 5.10 shows trends in domestic saving and investment rates. It reveals that domestic savings, investment, and fixed investment rates fell after the reforms—presumably due to the stabilization-induced economic contraction—but then increased steeply until 1995–1996. These increases, however, were reversed in 1995–1996. Though domestic saving and investment rates have somewhat recovered, fixed investment as a share of GDP has fallen consistently since 1995–1996. Gross fixed capital formation as a share of GDP in the private corporate sector has also fallen steadily since 1995–1996. Overall, however, gross fixed capital formation grew at a faster rate of 6.9 percent during the 1990s than in the 1980s when it grew at 4.2 percent. The average gross domestic fixed investment as a percentage of GDP was also higher in the 1990s than in the 1980s.

While this increase may be counted as a positive payoff of financial (internal and external) liberalization, it has not resulted in higher growth. The added accumulation appears to have contributed to increased capital intensity rather than to income growth. Actual capital/output ratios confirm this: the net fixed capital to output ratio for the economy, after

falling from 2.63 in 1980 to 2.38 in 1990, increased to 2.46 in 1994. The net capital/output ratio in industry, after showing a declining trend in the 1980s, has risen from 5.6 in 1990–1991 to 7.1 in 1998–1999. Whatever the relative influences of wage growth, technology upgrading, or exposure to foreign competition may be, this trend belies the expectation that external liberalization will reduce capital intensity.

3.2.3. Government Finance

As figure 5.11 shows, the gross fiscal deficit of the central and state governments increased in the 1980s, from 7.5 percent of GDP in 1981–1982 to over 11 percent in 1990–1991. Fiscal stability was the key feature of the stabilization program adopted after the 1991 crisis. This explains the deficit's declining trend (with a brief reversal in 1993–1994) until 1996–1997, when it fell around 7.5 percent. Since then, however, the deficit/GDP ratio has increased, going above the 10 percent mark by the end of the 1990s. This increase is attributed to the growth in the revenue or current account deficit of the central and state governments. The interest burden on the central budget has continued to rise throughout the 1990s, its share in current expenditure rising from 29 percent in 1990–1991

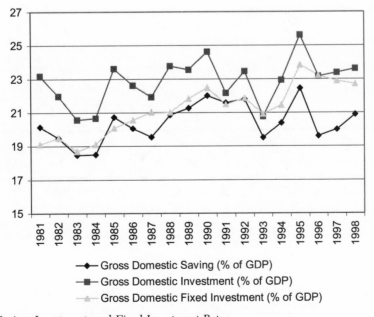

FIGURE 5.10 Saving, Investment, and Fixed Investment Rates

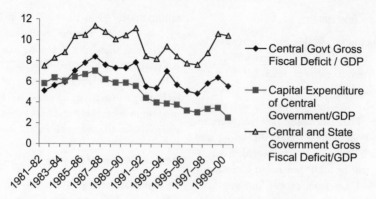

FIGURE 5.11 Government Deficit and Government Capital Expenditure Rates

to 36 percent in 1999–2000, with its level as a proportion of GDP increasing from 3.8 percent to 4.7 percent. While this is the primary source of the fiscal squeeze, another source of revenue squeeze (especially noticeable during the last half of the 1990s) is import tariff revenue. Customs revenue as a ratio of total central government revenues fell from above 33 percent in 1991 to below 27 percent in 1999–2000. The effect of this on tax revenues is clear from looking at the 1999–2000 gross tax revenues that declined by 0.9 percent of GDP (composed of a fall in indirect taxes by 1.6 percent and a rise in direct taxes by 0.7 percent). The impact on the government budget

deficit may be seen by comparing the actual central government deficit to GDP ratio to what it would have been had the 1991 ratio of customs to total revenue been maintained, as shown in figure 5.12.

One predictable consequence of this fiscal squeeze is that public capital formation has slowed down during the 1990s. As shown in figure 5.10, the central government's capital expenditure as a proportion of GDP has declined from 5.6 percent in 1990–1991 to 2.6 percent in 1999–2000. It is widely acknowledged that one of the major factors behind India's strong growth performance in the 1980s was increased infrastructure investment, especially in railways and

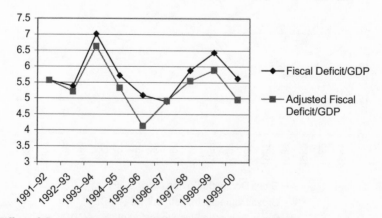

FIGURE 5.12 Effect of Custom Duties Loss on Central Government Deficit

power generation (Ahluwalia 1991, 85–87). Such investment not only has a positive supply-side effect; there is also evidence that there is a positive demand-led effect as government investment "crowds in" private investment, both in the industrial and agricultural sectors. There is consensus that between the declining fiscal capacity of the state and the unresolved regulatory complexities of privatization, the low level of infrastructure development is an increasingly important constraint on economic growth (World Bank 1996). Many argue that the industrial recession after 1995 is largely a consequence of the decline in government investment. Public sector capital formation slowed down to just 3.4 percent per annum (from 5.5 percent in the 1980s). In particular, gross fixed capital formation growth in electricity, gas, and water fell from 7.9 percent per annum in the 1980s to just 4.8 percent in the 1990s.

3.2.4. Prices

Figures 5.12 and 5.13 show trends in inflation and interest rates (the real rate of interest refers to the prime lending rate adjusted for inflation measured by the GDP deflator). The sharp spurt in prices in 1991 is the combined effect of drought, monetary restriction (associated with the stabilization program), increases in administered and issue prices of government-subsidized food grains, and the extraction of an export surplus from the economy. Bank rates were jacked up to curb inflation, to entice capital inflows, and as part of a program of financial liberalization. With the

cooling of inflation, interest rates have fallen 2–3 points below where they had been prior to liberalization, reflecting the massive growth of the primary issues market after 1994. The real interest rate, however, increased again, although it has recently fallen as the result of rate cuts attempting to overcome the recession.

The rate of inflation, measured by the GDP deflator or the consumer price index (CPI), has been somewhat lower than in the pre-reform period. Measured by the CPI, it fell from an annual average of 8.9 for the 1981–1982 to 1990–1991 period to 8.5 in the 1992–1993 to 1998–1999 period, while in terms of the GDP deflator it fell from 8.4 to 7.3 percent. However, the inflation rate has fluctuated in the recent period: in 1998–1999, it almost reached the high level of the crisis year of 1991–1992. Additionally, the trend of CPI inflation has been higher than that in terms of the GDP deflator (and also of wholesale prices). The main reason for this divergence is the higher weight of the food group in the CPI, though the costs of other items of mass consumption, such as housing and medical care, have also shown significant increases.

The growing relative price of food is also reflected in the relative price of agricultural products, which increased from 113 in 1992–1993 to 129 in 1999–2000, with 1981–1982 as the base, as shown in figure 5.14. Although the relative price shown refers to wholesale prices—and this price need not affect the market price of food grains, given India's subsidized public food distribution system—the market price of

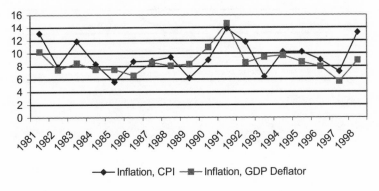

FIGURE 5.13 Inflation Rates

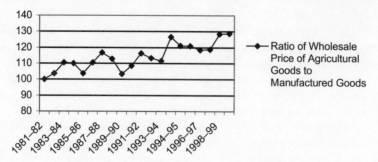

FIGURE 5.14 Relative Price of Agricultural Goods

food has generally followed procurement prices in the 1990s (see Balakrishnan 2000). This implies that the consumer price ratio has shown a trend similar to the wholesale relative price of food grains. There is some evidence that this trend in the relative price of agricultural products, although determined by policy, has been affected by the performance of agricultural growth relative to demand growth. Measuring the latter by the difference between the real rate of growth of agricultural value-added and the real rate of growth of GDP at market prices, we find a negative correlation between the relative price of agricultural products and the lagged relative performance of agriculture for the 1970–1998 period. There is also evidence of Granger causality from relative growth to the relative price at the 10 percent level of significance, so that slow agricultural growth may have caused a rise in the agricultural terms of trade. These changes in the relative price of agricultural products and food, in turn, have important implications for the debates concerning economic reforms on agricultural growth and poverty, to which we will turn later.

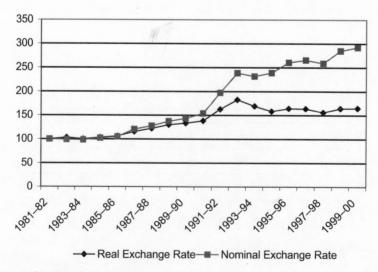

FIGURE 5.15 Nominal and Real Exchange Rates

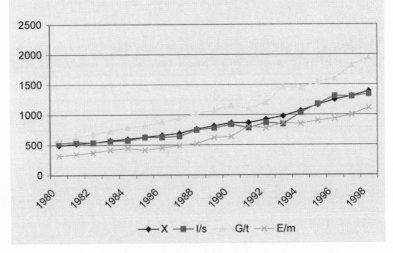

FIGURE 5.16 Contributions of Components of Aggregate Demand to GDP

Another price relevant for the discussion of India's reform is the relative price of traded goods to non-traded goods, which can be measured by the real exchange rate. As shown in figure 5.15, although the nominal trade-weighted exchange rate increased for most of the 1990s, the real exchange rate did not show a similar pattern. There was a significant real depreciation of more than 80 percent between the mid-1980s and 1993–1994, after which there was some appreciation, with fluctuations around the 160 mark (with 1981–1982 = 100).

3.3. Growth Constraints

We now turn to three sets of factors that can constrain the rate of growth of the economy, namely, aggregate demand, total factor productivity growth (TFPG), and foreign exchange constraints.

3.3.1. Aggregate Demand

Lately the concern with aggregate demand as a determinant of growth has been pushed aside by the focus on supply-side cures implicit in the reformist agenda. However, we believe that aggregate demand remains highly relevant in stimulating investment and in raising utilization in the oligopolistic non-agricultural sectors of the formal economy, and

thereby output and savings (see Dutt 1996). The role of different components of aggregate demand—private investment, government spending, and export—in stimulating growth is analyzed in figure 5.16. Following Godley and McCarthy (1997), we take I/s, G/t, and E/m to be the contributions of investment, government spending, and exports to GDP. X (total supply) is a weighted average of these three contributions. We find that government spending has, since the 1980s, been the major expansionary component of demand, since G/t consistently lies above the X line. The domestic private sector has more or less played a neutral role, since I/s has been close to X, while exports have consistently played a depressive role, since E/m is consistently below X. This pattern, strongest during the 1980s, confirms the importance of government fiscal policy in generating growth in the 1980s. The contraction of fiscal spending during the crisis of 1991 is reflected in the data, as is the contraction in the private domestic sector and the expansion in the role of exports. However, soon thereafter we find the fiscal factor recovering its role—though leveling off between 1993–1994 and 1996–1997 as the role of the private domestic sector and exports has grown. Despite these changes, the basic pattern—even after the reforms—remains that fiscal policy is the major expansionary component of aggregate demand. Given the recessionary tendencies

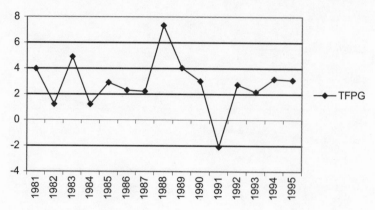

FIGURE 5.17 Total Factor Productivity Growth

since 1996–1997, this analysis finds further confirmation in the growing clamor for fiscal boosts to the sagging growth of industry and in the resultant increase in G/t.

3.3.2. Productivity Growth

Turning to the supply-based approach, we use the simple and popular method of calculating TFPG using Solow's residual, despite its well-known problems. Our estimates of the residual, using the equation

$$TFPG = g(Y/L) - _K\, g(K/L)$$

where $g\,(i)$ refers to the rate of growth of i, Y is real output, L is total employment, K is real net fixed capital stock, and $-_K$ is the share of capital in output,[4] are shown in figure 5.17. As expected, TFPG is negative in the crisis year of 1991. Leaving aside 1991 (when TFPG is negative), the average TFPG is 3.4 for 1980–1990 and 2.5 for 1991–1995, suggesting that there has been a decline in TFPG after the 1991 reforms.

Other available estimates of productivity growth performance—including those using more micro-level data—do not reveal an improvement in the post-reform period. Reviewing the evidence, Kumar (2000a) argues that the productivity performance of Indian industries actually deteriorated in the 1990s as compared to the 1980s, and that this holds true at both three-digit and two-digit levels. Balakrishnan, Pushpangadan, and Suresh Babu (2000), using data

from a panel of 2,300 firms spread over five industry groups at the two-digit level for the years 1988–1989 to 1997–1998, find evidence of a statistically significant fall in TFPG after 1991–1992. Krishna and Mitra (1998) report a statistically significant increase in productivity growth after 1991 in four select industries, but this study is criticized by Balakrishnan, Pushpangadan, and Suresh Babu (2000) on account of the method used for the construction of capital and labor input variables.

Given that productivity growth in services is usually lower than in other sectors, it may also be surmised that the relative growth of the service sector (as noted earlier), without an increase in its relative price, may have reduced overall TFPG. To examine this hypothesis and to examine the contributions of productivity change within sectors and the structural changes to overall productivity trends, we turn to labor productivity figures, since the data required for total factor productivity calculations by sectors are not available. For this purpose we use sectoral real GDP, workforce, and gross value-added per worker data from the most recent NSS rounds (see Sundaram 2001). Growth rates for these over the 1993–1994 to 1999–2000 period are shown in table 5.3. We find a contraction in employment in the agricultural sector, a rise in manufacturing and mining, and a relatively larger rise in construction and services. The workforce has grown annually at less than 1 percent, significantly below the rate of population growth. Labor productivity has grown most rapidly in mining

TABLE 5.3 Labor Productivity Change Decompositions, 1993–1994 to 1999–2000

	Growth Rate			% Contributions in Total		
	GDP	Workforce	GVA	Own	Reallocation	Sector Total
Agriculture	3.08377	−0.24541	3.337365	16.8082	2.020379	18.82858
Mining and manufacturing	7.334804	1.260611	5.998575	20.87087	0.602388	21.47326
Construction and services	8.993408	3.226636	5.586515	53.32946	6.368701	59.69816
Total	6.891888	0.840983	6.000442	91.00853	8.991468	100
Agriculture and allied activities	3.08377	−0.24541	3.337365	16.8082	2.020379	18.82858
Mining and quarrying	4.686208	−2.9436	7.861212	3.125213	−0.66949	2.455722
Manufacturing less repair services	7.738465	1.51368	6.131966	18.67442	0.343124	19.01754
Electricity, gas, and water	6.833561	−4.80335	12.22407	4.564322	−1.24889	3.31543
Construction	6.348739	6.22767	0.113971	0.129523	0.939297	1.068819
Trade, hotels, and restaurant	9.184884	6.22401	2.787387	8.289924	2.785044	11.07497
Transport, storage, and communications	8.728242	5.224443	3.329833	4.88077	2.432232	7.313003
Financing, insurance, and so on, less GDP in dwellings	12.64451	5.290468	6.984525	10.2628	4.266936	14.52974
Community and social services, including repair services	8.462587	−1.47759	10.08925	22.25536	0.140834	22.3962
Total	6.891888	0.840983	6.000442	88.99054	11.00946	100

Source: Authors' calculations, using data from Sundaram (2001).

and manufacturing, and only slightly more slowly in construction and services, and total labor productivity has grown at around 6 percent per annum. The last three columns of table 5.3 decompose the total change in labor productivity utilizing the method used by Pieper (2000). They show that over 90 percent of total productivity changes are the result of changes within sectors. Less than 10 percent of changes are due to intersectoral changes in employment, primarily because of a shift from agriculture to construction and services. The more detailed sectoral classification confirms these trends. But it also shows that the greatest employment growth was in construction—in which productivity growth was slowest—while the highest growing services sector (community and social services, including repair services) lost labor and made the largest single contribution to total productivity growth. There is little evidence that services have produced a drag on overall productivity growth, although some sectors, such as construction, seem to

have played some role. We also find no evidence of a significant sectoral shift toward traded-goods sectors, such as manufacturing, that could have boosted overall productivity growth by improving intersectoral efficiency in ways expected by proponents of reform.

3.3.3. Balance of Payments

Another potential constraint on growth is the balance of payments. If the economy is exchange constrained in that it is subject to periodic shocks due to foreign exchange shortages, the rate of growth of the economy on average will be determined by its balance of payments position.

We have seen that the trade deficit continues to be large. This problem, however, has been reduced by the invisibles account. Private transfers by Indians working abroad have increased from 1 percent of GDP in the late 1980s to 2.5 percent between 1993–1994 and 1998–1999. Invisible receipts have also increased thanks to booming software exports since 1993–1994, which are currently at about 0.6 percent of GDP. Indeed, the information technology sector has been acknowledged as one of the success stories of the globalization process, given the rapid growth of the industry worldwide (although recent troubles in the United States are likely to have a dampening effect). This sector has increased not only exports and remittances from Indians working abroad, but also promises to improve efficiency in the industrial and service sectors. These items remained buoyant in the late 1990s when, as mentioned earlier, export growth spluttered, helping to keep the current account deficit within manageable proportions.

Turning to the capital account, foreign capital inflows in terms of non-debt resources—FDI and portfolio—increased over the 1990s. This has reduced the relative reliance on external commercial borrowing, especially short-term debt. The total capital account surplus has been at an average of 2.5 percent of GDP during the period 1996–1997 to 1998–1999, which has been more than sufficient to offset the current account deficit.

The result of these trends—with the RBI intervening in the foreign exchange market to stabilize the rupee—has been a large increase in foreign exchange reserves, which stood at the $35 billion level in January 2000. The improvement in India's balance of payments is also apparent from the fall in the external debt/GDP ratio from 41 to 24 percent between 1991–1992 and 1998–1999 and a corresponding decline in the debt/service ratio from 30 to 18 percent.

Although the balance of payments situation appears to be comfortable, and growth has not been adversely affected by foreign exchange constraints in the post-reform period, a large proportion of capital inflows takes the form of volatile capital flows—that include portfolio flows and short-term debt, for instance, NRI deposits. Kumar (2000a) estimates that about 61 percent of foreign exchange reserves represent short-term debt and portfolio liabilities (such as FII stock market investment). In short, while growth in the post-reform period has not been constrained by foreign exchange availability, the economy remains vulnerable to shocks that reverse hot money flows.

3.4. Agriculture under the Reforms

During the two decades prior to the reforms, there had been a growing belief in some quarters that the agriculture sector had been discriminated against via policies of industrial protection and quantitative restrictions on international trade. Reformers understood the resulting "negative subsidy" to agriculture as the principal constraint on agricultural growth and higher rural living standards. It was expected that trade liberalization would confer large benefits on agriculture via reduced prices of inputs and increased prices of outputs. The Agreement on Agriculture under the WTO was also expected to be favorable because it would raise the world prices of agricultural commodities and expand trading opportunities for Indian agriculture.

Critics of liberalization maintain that it neglects agriculture. They fear that structural adjustment policies together with the falling trend (dating from the 1980s) in public investment in agriculture will undermine the basis for labor-absorbing and equitable growth. The defenders of reform argue that, at least during the early years of reform, agriculture is a prime if indirect beneficiary. This is because of reduced protection for industry and the (partial) removal of restrictions on agricultural exports. They maintain that further movement on the reform path—especially freeing up the food and agricultural markets and the relaxation of quantitative restrictions in conformity with the WTO agreement—can only further these benefits as India emerges as a major exporter in this sector.

But experience since the reforms appears to bear out the critics' argument. Despite the highly unusual succession of normal monsoons throughout the decade, there has been a substantial deceleration in the annual growth rate of the index of agricultural production from 3.4 percent in the 1980s to just 2.2 percent in the 1990s. Food grain output growth has also slowed from 3.5 percent in the 1980s to a mere 1.7 percent in the 1990s, implying a declining trend in per capita supply. The decline in the rate of growth of agricultural GDP between the same two periods was considerably less, from 3.9 percent to 3.3 percent. Part of this difference (some would argue the major part) may be accountable to data revisions, especially in value-added in horticulture. The GDP share of agriculture at 1980–1981 prices has fallen from 29.96 percent in 1991–1992 to less than 25 percent. While one might argue that this decline reflects a healthy process of structural change, this seems distinctly implausible not merely because trade reforms, in the liberal reckoning, greatly reduced "urban bias" but also because food consumption fell and poverty increased at least during the early years. How could it be that as a "pro-agriculture" policy took root, the share of agriculture fell so significantly? And how could continued low levels of food consumption be construed as structural progression? Perhaps the liberal diagnosis and prescription for agricultural development are flawed.

The disappointing effect of reforms on agricultural performance cannot be blamed on adverse developments on the price front. In the case of the dominant agricultural commodities whose prices continue to be domestically determined, the steady and steep increases in procurement prices have prevented an even greater decline in the growth of agricultural GDP. According to Sen (2001), the terms of trade for agriculture were far more favorable during the 1990s than during the 1980s, reaching their highest level in 1998–1999 since 1974–1975. Successive grants of generous minimum support prices for wheat and rice have made their market prices rise considerably faster than the prices of most other agricultural commodities (and produced a massive accumulation of unwanted stocks). Moreover, agriculture is now more protected from import competition in relation to industry since duties on most agricultural imports are significantly higher than the 35 percent maximum on industrial products. Therefore, whether assessed in terms of trends in domestic relative prices or in terms of a comparison of domestic and border prices, it is just not true anymore that agriculture has been discriminated against or suffers under the burden of "negative subsidy." While agricultural performance under the reforms has been decidedly disappointing, this is not because of the failure of the policy regime to conform to liberal strictures.

One intent of reforms was to prune agricultural input subsidies (for power, irrigation, and fertilizers) to make fiscal room for raising public investment in agricultural infrastructure (including research). On the whole, however, progress in this direction has been tardy so that, by default, supply-shifting public investment has continued to be well below the levels attained in the late 1960s and the 1970s. This situation has been aggravated by the worsening fiscal situation of the states. Although private investment has been higher during the 1990s, and this despite a slackening of bank lending to the rural sector following financial sector reforms, returns in terms

of output and income growth have been well below par.

While the poor record of agriculture under the reforms has disappointed reformers' expectations, informed observers had known all along that those expectations were founded on a poor understanding of Indian agriculture, especially the extravagant claim about the growth-augmenting power of prices. The restoration of fiscal allocations for agriculture and its infrastructure remains crucial, but this will require that policy makers shed their neoliberal penchant for downsizing government and their supply-side faith that lowering tax rates will enhance the fiscal take. In addition, private investment and complementary public investment will not yield higher returns if inertial elements in policy are not overcome. These elements include (1) a continuing reliance on a high-input and high-capital intensity strategy (that is evident in the heavy subsidization of inputs), the failure to mobilize surplus labor on farm or for infrastructure building off the farm; (2) capital-intensive and environment-degrading programs to augment the effective supply of land; and (3) the assumption of the immutability of the particular combination of agrarian inequalities and market failures together with government policies themselves that alone can account for the low rate of labor absorption in Indian agriculture.[5]

External liberalization, far from fulfilling the liberal hope that India would emerge as a successful exporter of food grains and many other agricultural commodities, has prompted growing concerns that a flood of cheap imports will undercut domestic production and the livelihood of millions. As many as 229 of the 714 items on the recently freed list of imports are agricultural commodities, and there have been steep declines in world market prices in recent years. In addition, even when pre-integration domestic supply prices may be below normal world prices, the volatility of world markets means added risks so that integration, rather than conferring an incentive, may impose a penalty on farmers. The unequal World Trade Organization (WTO) accords have imposed market access conditions on the developing world while allowing the developed countries to retain their subsidy regimes virtually intact.

The agriculture import bill is dominated by edible oils, oil cakes, and pulses (legumes). Domestic production of these items is concentrated in dryland regions, particularly in the hands of relatively poor farmers. Production and yield constraints derive from the continued failure of public investment and action, especially with respect to credit, irrigation, high-yield varieties, and drought proofing. Unfortunately, India's position at the WTO has been to defend quantitative restrictions solely in terms of balance of payments constraints when, in fact, considerations of livelihood, employment, and food security are at least as important. The expectation is that the government will be compelled to raise tariff rates on agricultural products to prevent erosion of the domestic production base. Import duties have already been doubled in 2001 with respect to coffee, tea, and edible oils. Since the WTO binding tariff rates are considerably higher for agricultural commodities than for industrial products, there is ample potential cushion against import competition, at least for the foreseeable future.

Paradoxically, these developments have rejuvenated the old debate about industry versus agriculture. Notwithstanding the declining trend in public investment in Indian agriculture, the government fears that WTO ceilings on the Aggregate Measure of Support (AMS) for agriculture may be found to be binding. The extent of AMS, however, remains a contentious issue. Even the Bank and the Fund hold irreconcilable positions. According to various World Bank estimates, AMS for Indian agriculture has been negative but the negative subsidy has declined over time, from 30 percent in the 1970s and early 1980s, to 9 percent in the early 1990s. The continued fall in global agricultural prices during the 1990s implies a further decline in the negative AMS (Alagh 2001). On the other hand, the IMF estimates government expenditure on agriculture at 29 percent of agricultural GDP in 1990–1993, most of this being interpreted to be a subsidy. This number is considerably larger than the WTO ceiling and compares unfavorably with, say, Indonesia (6.9 percent) or Thailand (12.9 percent). The presumption is that the IMF measure of agricultural support has risen further during the 1990s.

How far the government will have to go down the path of raising agricultural tariffs remains to be seen, but farmers' lobbies, including those in the agriculturally prosperous state of Punjab, are girding for a fight to reverse or stall the ongoing liberalization. An illiberal turn may be good for Indian agriculture, provided that the government returns to a sensible

program of public investment, agrarian and institutional reforms, and environmental sustainability. It also depends on whether the government can stave off challenges from the WTO while instituting its own employment and food security policies. More than the future of Indian agriculture may well depend on such a reversal.

4. Changes in the Employment Structure

Employment and wages are probably the major channels through which the social impact of increased openness and globalization is felt. In this section, besides presenting the evidence on overall employment and unemployment trends, we examine trends in formal and informal sector employment, as well as in the sectoral composition of the labor force.[6] One should be forewarned, however, that given the preponderance of household and tiny enterprises, high rates of underemployment, very high incidence of casual—frequently part-time—work, and widespread seasonal and gender gaps in employment opportunities in spatially dispersed—often localized—labor markets, our information base is not very reliable.

4.1. Trends in Formal Employment

Figure 5.18 shows the changes in employment levels through the mid-1990s in the "organized" sector, which includes all public sector employment (mostly in industry and services), and employment in private sector units that employ more than ten persons. It shows that organized sector employment grew sluggishly during the 1980s and through the mid-1990s, and that most of this was in the public sector while private sector employment stagnated. Figure 5.19 shows that the growth rate of organized sector employment fell steadily over the entire period, a trend dominated by the decline in the rate of growth of public sector employment. Private sector employment growth, throughout the 1980s, was slower than public sector employment growth. Only as late as 1992 did it equal the latter. Through the mid-1990s, it fluctuated at a level that did not counter the decline in the growth of public sector employment, so that total organized sector employment growth continued to fall.

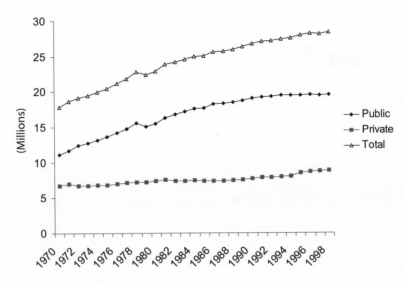

FIGURE 5.18 Formal Sector Employment

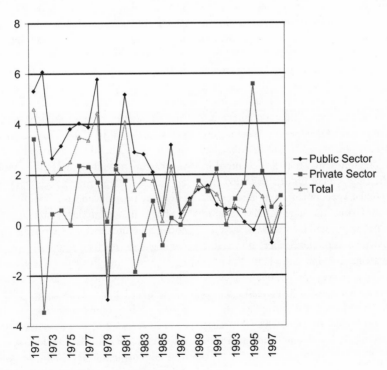

FIGURE 5.19 Growth Rates of Formal Sector Employment

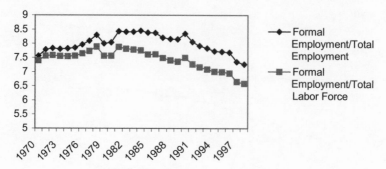

FIGURE 5.20 Formal Employment as Proportion of Total Employment

However, formal employment growth appears to have recovered after the mid-1990s. In particular, the faster growth of private sector employment in the 1990s attracted some attention, especially in the wake of the stagnation of the 1980s, and some have been quick to attribute the growth to the reforms. Goldar (2000) uses pooled time series cross-industry data to argue that faster employment growth in the 1990s is explained by slower wage growth and a faster growth in smaller factories in response to post-liberalization changes in trade and industrial policies. Nagaraj (2000b), however, questions this interpretation, pointing out that the trend decline in average factory size is not a recent phenomenon, but one that has occurred for a long time—and that also occurred in the 1980s when employment growth stagnated. He also questions Goldar's econometric specification for not appropriately taking into account the relation between wages per person and days worked, with the result that employment is primarily affected by value-added. Nagaraj argues that slow output growth in the 1970s resulted in excess labor. When output grew in the 1980s, it was accommodated by increasing hours per person rather than by increasing employment. As output growth continued in the 1990s, the labor overhang was exhausted, and employment growth recovered.

While the trend in organized sector employment is suggestive, this sector accounts for only around 10 percent of total employment. We therefore need to examine figures for total employment, to which we now turn.

4.2. Aggregate Employment and Employment Structure

One way of measuring total employment in India is to use available figures for the total workforce, applying officially available unemployment figures from the formal sector and assuming that there is no open unemployment in the informal sector. Following this approach, it appears that while in the 1980s employment generally grew at a rate below population growth, in the 1990s employment growth was somewhat higher, though much of the increase occurred in 1997. These employment figures are, however, highly dubious, since the unemployment figure actually refers to the number of persons on the live employment register and may include employed people who wish to move to a different job.

The dubious employment series can be used to obtain an estimate of the percentage of formal sector employment to total employment, as shown in figure 5.20. Since this series is seen as reflecting quite closely the series on the share of formal employment in the total labor force, which is also shown in the figure, we have some confidence in the direction of changes revealed by it. The series bears testimony to the decline in the share of formal employment in total employment in the 1990s, accentuating a trend that was present in the 1980s.

More reliable employment figures for the economy as a whole (including the unorganized sector) are available only from the decadal censuses and from the periodic surveys conducted by the national sample survey (NSS) organization. Census figures available for 1981 and 1991 cannot reveal any trend changes that may have been caused by the recent reforms. NSS estimates, however, are available for 1983, 1987–1988, 1993–1994, and 1999–2000, and for others years in the 1990s based on "thin" samples. NSS figures are disaggregated for urban and rural areas and for males and females.

Going by these estimates, the annual rate of employment growth between 1983 and 1991 averaged 2.39 percent, with organized sector employment growing more slowly than unorganized sector employment (1.73 percent compared to 2.41 percent). Subsequent thin survey results showed a considerable slackening of employment growth during 1990–1991 and 1997–1998 to a mere 1 percent per annum, with organized sector employment growing by a dismal 0.6 percent per annum (Datt 2001), as compared to an estimated labor force growth rate of about 2.5 percent for the decade.

The NSS 1999–2000 statistics on employment further confirm this decelerating trend in employment growth. In terms of long-term or usual status, the ratio of rural workers (as primary or subsidiary workers) to rural population fell from 44.4 percent in 1993–1994 to just 41.7 percent in 1999–2000. There was a drop, though smaller in magnitude, for urban India as well. These findings imply a workforce growth rate of just 0.81 percent per annum compared to a population growth rate of 1.75 percent per annum. This reduction is independent of shifts in the age structure and only partly due to increased school enrollment (Sundaram 2001). It is notable that this trend contrasts sharply with a rising trend in worker/employment ratios: between 1987–1988 and 1993–1994, these had risen marginally for urban males and females and for rural females but significantly for rural males (from 53.9 to 55.3 percent).

The sectoral distribution of the workforce also reveals some surprises. The share of agriculture and allied sectors in total employment declined sharply from 63.9 percent in 1993–1994 to 59.8 percent in 1999–2000, with absolute employment declining for the first time since independence. This trend in agriculture, which had also been observed during the 1980s, had been stalled between 1987–1988 and 1993–1994, mostly during the early years of the reforms (Kundu 1997). Community, social, and personal services also witnessed a substantial decline in their absolute workforce, while mining and utilities

suffered minor absolute declines. The decline in the former sectors is a reversal in the trend observed between 1987–1988 and 1993–1994.

Employment in manufacturing has risen only slightly from 10.7 percent of the workforce in 1993–1994 to 11.1 percent in 1999–2000, with practically all of the increase concentrated in urban areas. Even this slight gain is only a recovery from the decline in the percentage of workers in manufacturing in urban areas between 1987–1988 and 1993–1994. The biggest gains in workforce occurred in construction and in trade, hotels, and restaurants, the compound rate of growth in both sectors exceeding 6 percent per annum (see table 5.3). The latter sector now rivals manufacturing in the size of the labor force it employs. Kundu (1997) explained the loss of manufacturing employment during the early years of the 1990s in terms of jobs being subcontracted out by large manufacturing units to smaller ones that are often household units that classify themselves as service units. While such misclassification may well occur, some of it is undoubtedly real. The virtual stagnation in the share of manufacturing employment should be seen in light of our earlier conclusion that, for the economy as a whole, output growth has not kept pace with investment growth, both possibly manifestations of capital deepening.[7]

As for unemployment, for both rural men and women in the labor force, the rate of (current daily status) unemployment rose sharply. Urban male unemployment rose a little, while urban female unemployment actually fell. Overall, then, the employment situation has worsened during the 1990s especially in rural areas.

Post reforms, there has also been a rise in the casualization of the workforce and a decline in the share of self-employment. The share of casual labor in employment rose from 31.2 percent in 1988 to 37 percent in 1998. The quinquennial surveys show the change to have been from 33.8 percent in 1993–1994 to 36.2 percent in 1999–2000 (Sundaram 2001). It should be noted, however, that the declining trend in both regular employment and self-employment had also been observed during the prereform period from 1977–1978 to 1987–1988, and on through 1993–1994, although the trend seems to have intensified after 1987–1988. While growing casualization is certainly in keeping with services accounting for the major share of workforce increments, even in the sectors of regular employment, retrenchment, closures, and lockouts have risen as the price that unions must pay when they resist casualization (Datt 2001). The government is now seeking to boost private employers' bargaining position and increase labor market "flexibilization" by proposing that industrial establishments employing up to 1,000 workers will no longer be obliged to seek approval from the appropriate government to fire or lay off workers. Existing provisions in the Industrial Disputes Act require such approval for all units employing more than 100 workers. The proposal, billed as a key plank in the "second-generation reforms," is expected to encounter considerable political resistance.

Certainly, there is enough evidence in the employment trends to bolster the critics of the reform process. First, the decrease in participation rates for rural workers is worrisome. It may be symptomatic of slowed employment growth in an economy long accustomed to high rates of underemployment disguised as non-participation. Second, the decline in formal employment growth (both public and private) below the rate of growth of the labor force over nearly a decade, when formal sector output has grown at its fastest pace in history, suggests an unhealthy pattern of development. When this is coupled with the increasing incidence of casual labor and the decline in self-employment, it appears that *informalization* has become endemic to the Indian labor market. This has potentially serious consequences for wages, job security, inflation protection, workers' basic rights, and indeed the future of the Indian labor movement as a whole. It is undoubtedly a symptom of the further weakening of labor vis-à-vis capital. Third, the increasing feminization of the regular labor force may well be a further cause of concern for the working classes. At first, feminization appears to be a trend toward greater gender equality. But, as Kundu (1997) has argued, this is probably a continuation of a trend starting in the 1980s in which female regular employment has been in low-wage, low-productivity sectors. Indeed, female *regular* wages are often no higher, and are usually even less, than *casual* male wages. A final cause for concern is the stalled share of employment in manufacturing (along with a decline in agriculture) with much of the gain accounted for by service sectors. On the whole, these trends in employment structure run counter to reformers' expectations: tradable sectors (agriculture and manu-

facturing) have not become more labor intensive, while it is non-tradables that have enjoyed the biggest employment (and output) gains.

5. Income Distribution and Poverty

Growing income inequality under globalization has been a nearly ubiquitous concern both in rich and in poor countries. In India, absolute poverty has traditionally received overwhelming attention in both academic research and policy debate long before the "globalizing" reforms of 1991, and this tendency has continued after the reforms. The inattention to inequality may not be entirely, or perhaps even primarily, a matter of social priority; it may also be the result of the relative stability of expenditure distribution over several decades. But as with employment statistics, statistics on distribution also leave much to be desired. Of late, even the statistics on poverty have become muddled. Sophisticated but divergent arguments concerning what large-scale surveys "really" tell us, the challenge of reconciling gaps between national accounts statistics and the surveys, and a variety of often conflicting corroborative evidence have left us with a wide range of poverty "estimates" differing by a factor of 2 or more. In what follows, we will try to tease out some conclusions about trends in poverty and inequality from such numbers as are available, and attempt to link these with the reform process.

5.1. The Incidence of Poverty

The official all-India poverty line is defined by the per person expenditure required (given the pattern of actual consumption expenditures in the base-year sample) to assure a minimum food intake of 2,100 calories in urban areas and 2,400 calories in rural areas. The poverty line equaled an expenditure of Rs. 49 for rural areas and Rs. 57 for urban areas at 1973–1974 all-India prices. Between 1951 and 1975, the proportion of people below the poverty line (the headcount ratio) showed sharp fluctuations but no long-run trend. Table 5.4 shows trends in rural and urban poverty incidence from the mid-1970s. These numbers have been refined to correct for price level variations across states and survey period following the 1993 recommendations of the Planning Commission's Expert Group on Poverty Estimation

(World Bank 1998). As the table shows, the head-count ratio fell rapidly and fairly steadily from the mid-1970s to the late 1980s, the average annual rate of decline being 2.4 percent (World Bank 1998). After 1986–1987 the poverty measures started fluctuating again, and they registered increases after 1991, the headcount ratio rising from 36 percent in 1990–1991 to 41 percent in 1992. Note also that the headcount ratio fell back in 1993–1994.

In recent years, controversy has plagued India's poverty statistics. Poverty statistics have become something of a litmus test of the success of the reforms. Barring the balance of payments situation, there is no evidence of improvement in overall growth or employment during the 1990s relative to the 1980s (as argued in the preceding sections). Unfortunately, the latest round of the National Sample Survey (NSS) Organization has aggravated the statistical and interpretative muddle. The controversy had been incipient through most of the reform period. Based on results from the large survey of 1993–1994 and the succeeding "thin" surveys carried out annually by the NSS (shown in table 5.4), a rough consensus prevailed among researchers that rural poverty—unlike urban poverty—in India showed no trend reduction.[8] But proponents of the reforms dissented on the ground that without another large survey, firm conclusions could not be drawn about either the trend in poverty or its link to the reforms. In normal course, the NSS 55th round (July

TABLE 5.4 Poverty in India, 1973–1998 (Head Count, %)

Period	Rural	Urban
October 1973–June 1974	55.7	48.0
July 1977–June 1978	50.6	40.5
January 1983–December 1983	45.3	35.7
July 1986–June 1987	38.8	34.2
July 1987–June 1988	39.2	36.2
July 1988–June 1989	39.1	36.6
July 1989–June 1990	34.3	33.4
July 1990–June 1991	36.4	32.8
July 1991–December 1991	37.4	33.2
July 1992–December 1992	43.5	33.7
July 1993–June 1994	36.7	30.5
July 1994–June 1995	41.0	33.5
July 1995–June 1996	37.2	28.0
January 1997–December 1997	35.8	30.0

Source: Datta (1999).

1999 through June 2000) should have settled the matter, since the previous large survey was carried out in 1993–1994, allowing for a six-year period covering the key years when reforms would have taken effect. But this was not to be, owing to methodological changes incorporated in the 55th round.

Until the large survey of 1993–1994 (the 50th round; National Sample Survey Organization [NSSO] 1996), respondents' consumption levels were assessed for the previous thirty days. The suspicion that the thirty-day recall underestimated the true level of food consumption prompted experiments using both the seven-day recall and the thirty-day recall in separate samples during the years succeeding the 50th round. Between 1994 and 1998 poverty levels in India, based on the seven-day recall method, were lower by as much as 40–50 percent than estimates using the thirty-day recall (Visaria 2000).

The 50th round showed the rural and urban poverty ratios in 1993–1994 to be 36.7 and 30.5 percent respectively, whereas the 55th round in 1999–2000, based on a different survey methodology, showed steep declines in these ratios to 27.1 percent and 23.6 percent respectively. Taken at face value, therefore, the 55th round implies a compound annual rate of decline in rural poverty of 4.9 percent and in urban poverty of 4.2 percent. The rate of decline in national poverty is more than twice as large as that recorded in the 1980s.

But there is little doubt that the change in the reference period of the 1999–2000 survey from thirty days—the norm since the mid-1950s—to seven days in 1999–2000 and the simultaneous collection of information for both reference periods from the same respondents has "contaminated'" the 55th round estimates. The justification for the seventh-day recall is not only that this is the standard practice elsewhere in the world but also that recall errors would be lower than with the thirty-day recall. But critics allege that estimates using the thirty-day recall have lost their independent standing because they are tied to the seven-day estimates: respondents and surveyors alike would be under pressure to record consistent numbers (dividing the monthly numbers by four or multiplying the weekly numbers by four). Indeed, they have correctly noted that estimates based on the seven-day recall actually show a worsening of the poverty situation. Thus, going by Visaria's seven-day recall figures, rural poverty incidence increased from

19.1 percent in 1995–1996 to 24.8 percent in July–December 1999 and urban poverty ratios increased from 15.2 percent to 23.4 percent. The only thing that seems beyond reasonable doubt is that because the last quinquennial survey did not use a seven-day recall, the latest estimates cannot be compared to the previous estimates.

Corroborative evidence has also been adduced for both the conflicting views about poverty. Consider the evidence on real wage growth. Based on the latest quinquennial round of the NSS, Sundaram (2001) finds that real wages of casual agricultural labor rose 2.80 percent per annum for rural men and 2.94 percent for rural women between 1993–1994 and 1999–2000. For casual labor in non-agricultural activities, the rate of rise was higher still. Despite the decline in employment ratios, estimated real yearly wage earnings per worker and per capita have risen for all categories of labor. This seems to provide a possible basis of support for the claim that poverty ratios have declined during the last six years of the 1990s. On the other hand, observed declines in employment ratios and in per capita consumption of food grains both point to a worsening of poverty. Moreover, the growth in real wages during the 1990s was not any higher than in the 1980s and overall inequality seems to have definitely worsened (see below). Coupled with the observation that the rate of growth of per capita income is not significantly higher in the 1990s as compared to the 1980s, these facts simply cannot support the massive trend decline in poverty that some commentators have read into the data based on the 55th round.

The poverty line, defined as it is in terms of a base-year level of total expenditure sufficient to secure an exogenously given nutritional norm, implies a behavioral rather than a normative specification of non-food items of consumption. Updating such a poverty line by accounting for general price inflation in subsequent years does not guarantee that the resulting poverty lines will remain adequate to secure the nutritional norm. In the Indian case, in fact, the divergence between the updated poverty lines and the nutritional norm has increased since the base year 1973–1974 (Mehta and Venkatraman 2000). In 1993–1994, for example, the updated poverty lines were only 66 and 74 percent of the corresponding levels of expenditure "required" to secure the nutritional norm. Put differently, the updated rural and poverty lines implied actual caloric intake in the

respective expenditure groups of only 82 and 90 percent of the nutritional norms. With rough "corrections" for the divergence, the incidence of nutrition-based poverty is 75 and 54 percent respectively rather than the official poverty ratios of 37 and 32 percent respectively.

The divergence is primarily owing to a shift in consumption expenditure from food to non-food, from cereals to non-cereal foods, and from coarse to fine cereals. In a preference-based approach, these shifts would be interpreted as the revealed preferences of consumers. But this would render the nutrition "norm" quite irrelevant to the poverty measurement exercise. Another approach seeks to explain at least the greater decline in rural as compared to urban calorie consumption to increased agricultural mechanization that reduces the exogenously given calorie requirement (Rao 2000). But mechanization is known to reduce employment so that the decline in calorie intake may represent a decline in availability rather than in requirement (Saha 2000).

In fact, Mehta and Venkatraman provide evidence that while cereal intake has declined significantly, expenditure shifts to non-cereal foods have meant negligible increases in their quantities, and expenditure shifts to non-food (e.g., transport) also do not reveal unambiguous gains in the quality of life. They suggest that these expenditure shifts resulted from "the foreclosing of earlier choices and a compulsive interaction with markets" (Mehta and Venkatraman 2000, 2381).

Further support for this interpretation is provided by an analysis of the survey and valuation methods employed in the NSS against the backdrop of changes in rural institutions and production structures. One part of the argument is that the trend decline in measured poverty reflects an overestimation of poverty in the 1950s and 1960s. The overestimation is on two counts: (1) a significant part of wage payments, made in the form of cooked meals, was recorded in the NSS as consumption of the employer; and (2) while own production—a major source of consumption at the time—was valued at farm-harvest prices, the poverty lines were inflated because they were price-adjusted using market prices (including trade and transport margins). The first source of overestimation declined progressively with the shift to cash wages, while the second declined as market purchases grew at the expense of own production. The second part of the argument is that there has been an increasing

underestimation of poverty since the 1970s: the reduced availability of coarse cereals (driven by changing prices and technologies, and increasing reliance
on market access) compelled substitution by the
costlier fine cereals. Poverty lines adjusted with base-
year weighted deflators thus understate the cost of the
nutrition-based consumption norm. The decline in
access to cooked meals also forced expenditure on
necessary complements such as fuel and edible oils,
and on the overhead cost of acquiring the same level of
nutrition.

India's progress in the fields of education and
health has been similarly tardy. In the last census
(1990–1991), the literacy rate among females and
males aged seven and above was 39 and 64 percent
respectively, up from 30 and 56 percent in 1980–1981.
Life expectancy at birth was 59.2 years in 1990–1991
compared to 50.4 years in 1980–1981. Estimates for
these measures after 1990–1991 suggest that the upward trend is continuing. Although the improvements
compared to 1950–1951 (when the female and male
literacy rates were 9 and 27 percent, and life expectancy at birth was 32.1 years) are notable, India lags far
behind other developing countries, including some of
its Asian neighbors.

It is useful to examine the general determinants of
trends in poverty before we turn to a consideration of
the particular effects of globalizing reforms. One route
to reducing poverty is agricultural growth. Trends in
poverty may be explained mainly by agricultural
growth. The evidence across states, according to Datt
and Ravallion, shows that poverty reduction has occurred fastest in states that experienced rapid rural
growth with strong infrastructure development (such
as Punjab and Haryana) and in those that have relied
on human resource development (such as Kerala). In
contrast, Sen (1996) finds that for the period after the
Green Revolution, there is a rather weak link across
states between the rate of per capita agricultural
growth and reduction in rural poverty.

A second route to reducing poverty is through
labor-intensive industrial or non-agricultural growth
in urban or in rural areas. Sen (1996) reports that
increases in non-agricultural incomes tend to reduce
poverty in both rural and urban areas. Of particular
importance in this respect is the role of increases
in non-agricultural employment in rural areas not
merely because it may reduce unemployment and
underemployment but also because it is strongly associated with rising real wages in agriculture during

the 1980s. This rise in real wages seems to discredit the
view that increases in rural non-agricultural employment were due to the distress needs of those pushed
out of labor-shedding agriculture. It seems natural to
suppose that the association between rising wages and
rising non-farm employment must reflect the pull of
demand. Sen (1996) has argued that rising government expenditures in rural areas, on revenue and
capital account, have provided a major impetus for the
growth. This view is compatible with the further observation that non-farm employment growth is broadly
unrelated to the rate of agricultural growth across
states.[9] Since government expenditures in rural areas
have slowed under the reforms, the presumption must
be that this source of poverty alleviation has weakened
considerably.

A paradox of the 1980s experience is that the
sharp decline in rural poverty and a rise in rural real
wage rates occurred despite the very slow growth of
urban organized sector employment and the slower
growth of agricultural employment as compared to
the labor force. An alternative hypothesis, which de-
parts from the assumption of full employment and
relies on an exogenous rise in rural wage rates (due
perhaps to increased bargaining power of laborers)
helps to explain this paradox (see Rao 1998b). Such a
wage rise can explain both the fall in the employ-
ment/output ratio within agriculture and the
concomitant fall in poverty rates. A relative rise in
non-farm employment can still occur provided that
labor demand increases due to increased government
expenditure (as argued by Sen), but also because of a
rise in the wage share. Sen provides evidence that
real wages increased almost twice as fast as labor
productivity in agriculture. The resultant increase
in the wage share increases the demand for non-
agricultural rural products, given a higher marginal
propensity to consume (in general and for non-
agricultural goods in particular) out of rural wages
than out of non-wage income.

A third determinant of poverty, which has attracted much attention, is the price of food.[10] It has
been argued (and is consistent with all available
evidence) that an increase in the price of food increases poverty by reducing the real incomes of wage
earners whose wages do not keep up with food prices.
The fact that this holds for rural areas as well as urban
areas is not a puzzle, since most of India's rural poor
(and even some of the non-poor) are net purchasers
of food. Ravallion (1998), however, argues that the

correlation between the two variables is actually spurious. He finds that the movement in both the poverty rate and the relative price of food are the result of changes in a third variable, agricultural output: a bad harvest can be expected to increase the relative price of food and also increase rural (and total) poverty. Pooling time-series data for 1960–1961 to 1993–1994 across states, Sen (1996) finds, however, that a rise in the relative price of cereals increases poverty even if agricultural output per worker is included as a variable.

Ravallion's argument that a change in food price affects poverty via its impact on mean rural consumption but not on the distribution of rural consumption (or income) rests on erroneous inequality measures. His measures of inequality are premised on the incorrect assumption that the cost of living index is the same for the rural poor and non-poor. While his conclusion that price changes have statistically zero distributional effects applies to the nominal inequality of rural incomes, the same data nevertheless imply a worsening of real inequality (see Rao 1998a). This last conclusion leads us directly back to the established understanding that food price increases hurt the poor through the mechanism of (real) inequality increases. It also follows that price reforms incur the risk of both transitional and permanent reductions in real wages and corresponding increases in poverty. As we shall discuss in the following section, this is precisely what seems to have happened during the 1990s.

Critics of the reforms have attributed the rise in poverty in the initial years of the reforms to the Public Distribution System (PDS) issue price increases, the consequent open market price rise, and the curtailment in supplies. Suryanarayana shows that there were roughly symmetric declines in cereal availability in both rural and urban areas and that the reforms were responsible for the adverse effect on poverty. The part of food subsidies actually accruing to consumers has fallen since 1991 through a combination of price increases and quantity reductions. Indeed, both open market (wholesale) prices and issue prices through the PDS have more than doubled. That this has most likely had an adverse effect on poverty can be seen from Sen (1996), who adds a relative price of food term to what is essentially the Ravallion equation discussed above, and finds that this modified equation is able to explain the post-1991 increase in poverty.

5.2. Dimensions of Economic and Social Inequality

Income inequality as proxied by the Gini coefficient of consumption expenditure shows little change over the years. Table 5.5 shows that in both rural and urban areas, this coefficient has fluctuated without a clear trend. However, the mean Gini coefficients for the "pre-reform" years (1989–1991) are lower than their "post-reform" (1995–1997) counterparts: these are, respectively, 28.0 and 29.5 for rural expenditures and 34.8 and 36.0 for urban expenditures. Though modest, these increases do indicate a worsening of the nominal expenditure distributions in both sectors.

Let us leave aside the controversial and noncomparable numbers from the 1999–2000 NSS. The fact that NSS surveys for the 1990s show that poverty did not decline despite the similarity of GDP trend growth to that in the 1980s (when poverty did decline significantly) implies that "skepticism will continue unless it is established that there was an increase in inequality" (Sen 2000, 4501). Two points are pertinent to an informed assessment of this issue. First, the fact that growth in rural real consumption expenditure as estimated by the NSS fell well short of the growth in real income as per National Accounts Statistics (NAS) has been seized upon by defenders of the reform to discredit NSS poverty estimates (prior to the 55th round). How justified is this? Second, NSS consumption surveys are known to underenumerate the rich, leading to persistently lower

TABLE 5.5 Gini Coefficient of Nominal Consumption Expenditure Distribution

Period	Rural	Urban
October 1973–June 1974	28.5	30.8
July 1977–June 1978	30.9	34.7
January 1983–December 1983	30.1	34.1
July 1986–June 1987	30.2	36.8
July 1987–June 1988	29.4	34.6
July 1988–June 1989	29.5	34.8
July 1989–June 1990	28.2	35.6
July 1990–June 1991	27.7	34.0
July 1991–December 1991	29.9	38.0
July 1992–December 1992	29.9	35.1
July 1993–June 1994	28.6	34.3
July 1994–June 1995	30.2	37.2
July 1995–June 1996	28.4	35.5
January 1997–December 1997	30.6	36.5

Source: Datta (1999).

estimates of total non-food consumption as compared to the NAS. Hence, NSS-based point estimates of the inequality of consumption distribution understate income inequality both because savings are left out and because the rich are undercounted. Furthermore, if the rich had gained disproportionately from the income growth of the 1990s, then, NSS mean consumption estimate would be biased downward relative to the NAS estimate while, at the same time, the NSS consumption inequality estimate would be biased downward relative to true inequality (Sen 2000).

On the first of these points, Rao (1998a) argues that when the key food/non-food relative price is changing, Gini coefficients based on the nominal distribution of expenditure do not measure inequality in real expenditure. The latter can only be calculated after converting nominal expenditures into real ones by means of class-specific deflators. Not surprisingly, Sen (2000) finds that the difference in the NSS real consumption trend during the 1990s and the corresponding NAS trend arises not chiefly from differences in estimates of nominal magnitudes but from differences in the price deflators used to derive the real magnitudes. While the NAS magnitudes are deflated by the implicit consumption deflator, the NSS consumption data are deflated by price indices for agricultural laborers and industrial workers. Both these price indices have risen faster during the 1990s than the implicit NAS deflator primarily because prices of food items, especially cereals, have risen relative to all other items, which are mainly consumed by the rich. Hence, at least in an ex post statistical sense, the rise in the relative price of food is a principal factor explaining why poverty did not decline in the 1990s.

Even if one were to ignore the undernumeration of the rich, Sen (2000) concludes that (1) urban nominal expenditure inequality that had no trend in earlier periods trended up during the 1990s; (2) rural nominal inequality, which had been declining earlier, reversed course during the 1990s; and (3) there was also increased disparity between rural and urban areas. In conjunction with the preceding argument that given a trend increase in the relative price of food, the trend in nominal rural inequality understates the trend in real rural inequality, these conclusions (based on uncontaminated NSS data) indicate an unambiguous rise in real inequality during the 1990s.

Changes in the functional distribution of income may be gleaned from estimates of the growth in per worker gross value-added (GVA) and in "earnings per worker" per annum. Based on NAS, the annual compound rate of growth of GVA per worker over the period 1993–1994 to 1999–2000 was 3.3 percent in agriculture, 6.1 percent in manufacturing, and 6.1 percent for the economy as a whole (Sundaram 2001). With the GDP share of agriculture at about a quarter, the growth rate of GVA per worker in non-agriculture is approximately 7.04 percent. Real wages of casual agricultural labor rose 2.80 percent per annum for rural males and 2.94 percent for rural females, while the average number of days worked per rural worker fell at the rate of 0.2 percent per annum for rural males and rose at the rate of 0.34 percent for rural females. Assuming that the latter figures for rural India apply equally to agricultural workers and that there is no change in the relative wages of regular workers vis-à-vis casual workers, these trends in real wages and employment per worker imply that real labor earnings per worker rose at the rate of 2.6 percent per annum for male agricultural workers and 3.28 percent for females. The weighted average growth rate of earnings per agricultural worker is thus 2.83 percent per annum, which is significantly less than the rate of growth of GVA per agricultural worker (3.3 percent). Thus, assuming that the distribution of GVA between regular and casual workers remained unchanged, the share of "surplus" (profits, interest, and rents) in agriculture rose during the 1990s.

As for non-agriculture, real wages of casual non-agricultural labor rose 2.74 percent per annum for urban males and 4.18 percent for urban females. Meanwhile, the average number of days worked per worker fell at the rate of 0.09 percent per annum for urban males and rose at the rate of 0.53 percent for females (based on figures reported in Sundaram 2001). Assuming that these figures apply equally for all non-agricultural workers and, as before, that there is no change in the relative wages of regular workers vis-à-vis casual workers, real labor earnings per worker rose at the rate of 2.65 percent per annum for males and 4.71 percent for females. The weighted average growth rate of earnings per non-agricultural worker is thus 3.06 percent per annum, which is much smaller than the rate of growth of GVA per worker in non-agriculture (7.04 percent) or in the economy as a whole (6.1 percent). Once again, assuming that the distribution of GVA between regular and casual workers remained unchanged, the share of "surplus" (profits, interest, and rents) in non-agriculture rose during the 1990s.[11]

Given the significant excess of the growth rates of value-added over the wages bill in both agriculture and non-agriculture, these calculations strongly indicate that the income share of labor in both sectors, but especially in non-agriculture, has fallen over the years from 1993–1994 to 1999–2000. While the growth in real wage rates and annual wage earnings over the six-year period cannot be reconciled with the position that poverty failed to decline, the significant deterioration in the functional distribution of income and in the personal distribution of income (both within and between sectors) indicates that the rate of poverty reduction declined under the reforms.

For the period between 1970–1971 and 1995–1996, there is strong evidence of divergence in per capita real state domestic product (SDP) across Indian states based on the trend in the yearly coefficient of variation. The divergence was especially evident in the case of agriculture, whereas SDP in services was convergent (Dasgupta et al. 2000). Although the analysis suggests that there was convergence in the SDP from "infrastructure" (defined as transport, electricity, and banking), it is doubtful that this can be interpreted as showing that unequal development in infrastructure is not the primary cause of divergence. For one, convergence was evident only in the case of banking; in respect of both transport and electricity, there was divergence. For another, the constructed "infrastructure" variable does not include elements of public services (e.g., research and extension, education, and health) that may be highly productive especially in the case of agriculture, which is identified as the leading sector underlying overall income divergence.

During the post-independence era, agricultural growth has depended on central initiatives despite agriculture being a state subject. Over the past decade and more, interstate variation in agricultural performance has widened, in part due to the steep rise in current input subsidies overwhelming the growth of public investment. As a result, the share of public investment in agriculture has fallen to just 25 percent today. Whereas the coefficient of variations for rural and urban poverty ratios in the states fell during the 1970s and 1980s, they have risen during the 1990s. This seems to be a consequence of the devolution of resources and decentralization of policies and programs from the center to the states brought on by the reforms.

The poor in India are concentrated among the landless, among members of scheduled castes and tribes, and among households in which all members are illiterate (World Bank 1998). These are not disjoint groupings. The vast majority—74 percent—of the Indian poor make their living in the rural, still mainly agricultural, economy. A recent study of the incidence of poverty among socially disadvantaged groups such as scheduled castes (SC), scheduled tribes (ST), and female-headed (FH) households provides graphic evidence of the economic differentiation imposed by social disadvantage (Meenakshi, Ray, and Gupta 2000). Going by per capita total expenditure unadjusted for family size, poverty rates are higher among SC and ST households than among all households in virtually all states, the excess incidence varying typically between a quarter and a half. But surprisingly, unadjusted poverty incidence is significantly lower among FH households. However, when per capita expenditure is adjusted for family size (to reflect economies in consumption), the differential incidence of poverty among SC and ST households rises further while the apparent advantage of FH households is reversed.

6. Aspects of Social Policy

Past experience suggests that government "social sector" policy influences poverty, the distribution of income, and the social opportunities available to the population. Given India's low level of success in poverty alleviation and in increasing social opportunities, as well as the inequitable impact (unaccompanied by accelerated income growth) of the reforms, government policy plays a key role. In this section, we examine trends in public social spending and the robustness of existing social safety nets in the face of the reforms.

6.1. Trends in Government Expenditure

Several studies have argued that the reforms had adverse effects on government spending on the social sector (see Guhan 1995): for instance, expenditure on rural development and social services declined by 0.4 percent of GDP between 1990–1991 and 1992–1993. Considering a longer span of time and including both central and state governments, Nagaraj (1997) finds that government final consumption expenditure as a percentage of GDP (at factor cost) has declined from an annual average of 11 percent for 1986–1991 to 10.1 percent during 1992–1995. However, the expenditure on health, education, housing, and social services—which include, but are not confined to, spending on items that benefit the poor—stayed the same over the two periods at 2.9 percent of GDP, and was in fact higher than the 2.4 percent level for 1981–1985. Defense and economic services bore the brunt of the cuts. For the same two periods, government current expenditure as a percentage of GDP fell from 19.4 to 17.9 percent and government capital expenditure fell from 7.5 to 5.7 percent. Here, current expenditure on health, education, housing, and social services as a percentage of GDP fell slightly, from 6.1 to 6.0 percent, but capital expenditure stayed the same; the losers again were defense and economic services.

These budgetary figures show that government social spending did not decrease as a percentage of GDP except immediately after the crisis. However, this does not imply that the benefits the poor received did not decrease, since this depends on the effectiveness of the programs funded by these expenditures, the extent to which the poor actually benefited, and changes in relative prices affecting the real delivery of services (this is considered below). Nor does it imply that globalizing reforms had "no effect" if the counterfactual would have allowed increases in these expenditures from increased revenue mobilization rather than the fiscal compression that was actually pursued. The need for increased social expenditures and their potential for raising both living standards and economic growth may be judged rather from the evidently low levels of social opportunity both before and after the reforms. The tradeoff imposed by globalizing reforms arguably consists in the failure to cultivate this complementarity between growth and social opportunity.

6.2. Social Safety Nets

Recognizing social security as an obligation of provincial and central governments, the Indian Constitution calls upon the state, within the limits of its capacity, to make effective provision for "public assistance in the case of unemployment, old age, sickness, disability, in other cases of undeserved want," and for maternity relief. Since independence, social security legislation has been extended by acts relating to retirement funds, maternity benefits, family pension schemes, deposit-linked insurance schemes, and medical, disability, and employment injury benefits (Guhan 1992). Organized labor is covered under these various acts, and public and quasi-public employees are covered by non-legislated directed benefits. Social security expenditures are estimated to be less than 3 percent of GNP (Guhan 1992).

However, social security for over 90 percent of workers (those in the unorganized sector, or the self-employed) is extremely meager, being confined to some "means"-tested old-age pension and accident, group life, and hut insurance schemes for specific groups. Moreover, the legislation suffers from shortcomings that thwart the effectiveness of the programs, allowing evasion by employers in providing contributions. Areas in which benefits are provided by state governments show enormous differences in coverage. No Western-style unemployment relief is offered in India: this is a severe problem for self-employed and unorganized sector workers for whom no employment security exists. Some relief from unemployment, particularly in drought-affected regions, is offered in rural areas through schemes of employment creation, to which we now turn.

6.3. Employment Generation Schemes

The highly successful Maharashtra Employment Guarantee Scheme, which was established to provide relief during severe droughts in rural Maharashtra in 1970–1973, has become a country-wide model. The scheme had wide coverage (its daily attendance reaching a seventh of the total rural population at its peak), was well targeted (since the very cash wage allowed the program self-select the poorest), and had a clear objective (Joshi and Little 1996, 235). Given its success in reducing widespread misery, starvation, and death, the scheme continued beyond the droughts, but with the wage increasing steadily and with reduced funding, it became progressively less successful, and the amount of employment it generated declined.

All-India public employment generation schemes are similar to the Maharashtran one. The biggest of these schemes, the Jawahar Rozgar Yojna (JRY), was established in 1989 by merging two previous programs. Its primary aim was to create additional employment for the unemployed or underemployed below the poverty line who lived in rural areas, but its additional aim was to create rural assets, especially those that would benefit scheduled castes and tribes. Among the program's stipulations was that the wage could not be below prevailing legal minimum wage rates. Part of the JRY is confined to "backward" areas. The JRY and its various components take up as much as 60 percent of the central government's budget on rural development and social expenditures.

The JRY provides an average monthly employment of five person days per beneficiary family. However, the employment provided in the larger poorest states was much lower. Moreover, its ability to reach the poor within states is also limited. In 1992, 57 percent of participants were from families above the family poverty line and only 18 percent fell in the category of the very poor or worse (partly because the higher wage removed the self-selection advantage enjoyed by the Maharashtra program). The net transfer to the poor, taking into account the fact that other work is reduced, has been estimated at only about 14 percent of expenditure (Joshi and Little 1996, 238).

6.4. Education Policy

Despite the stated objected of providing free and compulsory education up to the age of fourteen (one of the directive principles of the Constitution urged the state to provide such education by 1960!), compulsory education has not been implemented anywhere in India. Indian literacy rates are low: lower than in China; lower than rates in many East and Southeast Asian countries more than thirty years ago; lower than the average for low-income countries other than China and India; and no higher than in sub-Saharan Africa. There are great disparities in literacy rates by regions and by sex. The student/teacher ratio for the 6–10 age group is 58, dropout rates are extremely high, and public expenditure on education remains low by international standards, with a strong bias against primary education. Some improvement in the 1980s seems to have focused on increasing enrollments, but not on increasing the number of teachers. Structural adjustment measures in the 1990s slowed education expenditure growth and even caused a decline in the number of primary and upper-primary school teachers between 1991–1992 and 1992–1993 (Dreze and Sen 1995, 111–23).

These trends, however, have subsequently been partially reversed.

6.5. Public Distribution System (PDS) for Food Grains

The PDS is a public safety-net program that buys agricultural products from farmers to protect them against excessive losses in periods of surplus production and sells them to consumers to protect them from high prices in and out of shortage years. The PDS distributes rice, wheat, edible oil, kerosene, and sugar at subsidized prices through a network of 400,000 shops in urban and rural areas all over the country. The implicit subsidy under the PDS has been stable at around 0.5 percent of GDP. Retail prices are fixed by each state government, taking into account local distribution costs and retailer margins, besides the issue price fixed by the Food Corporation of India, and some states provide additional subsidies.

The ability of the PDS to provide effective protection and help to the poor has been questioned. It has been found that states making the greatest use of the PDS are not necessarily the poorer ones. The poor are not more likely to consume basic food grains distributed through the PDS. It has been estimated that only about 40 percent of the total quantity of wheat and 47 percent of rice supplied through the PDS are consumed by the poorest 40 percent of the population (World Bank 1998: Joshi and Little 1996, 233). Moreover, the costs of administering the program are high for a number of reasons, including pilferage and inefficiency.

Public distribution of food grains at subsidized price remains the single most important instrument of direct poverty alleviation available. Yet, reforms through the 1990s have worked at cross purposes in deploying this key instrument. Per capita food grains availability has fallen successively over the closing years of the last century. At the beginning of the reform process, the issue price of rice was raised by 30 percent and that of wheat by 21 percent in December 1991. This narrowed the gap between the procurement and issue prices. Since procurement prices paid to farmers were repeatedly raised throughout the 1990s, issue prices (especially for the above-poverty households) were also raised periodically. Although increased procurement followed, the decision to raise issue prices for PDS recipients above the poverty line has reduced the total subsidized sales. The upshot has been a rapid buildup of stocks to over 40 million tons and a rise in government expenditure on the food subsidy even though consumer subsidy per se has fallen.

It has long been implicitly understood that the stabilization of cereal price dynamics is the most important form of "social safety net" available in India. It is also the closest thing to an "incomes policy" that a poor country can wield. While orthodox stabilization concerned itself with lowering the rate of inflation, orthodox structural adjustment in relation to agriculture and food was expected to lead to a rise in the relative price of food. In fact, however, the move toward trade liberalization has been accompanied by continuing high domestic support prices for the main food commodities. Consequently, domestic relative food prices have risen rather than declined in sync with recent world market trends. As previously noted, this is the principal reason for an adverse movement in real (as opposed to nominal) inequality in rural India.

The reforms have tended, in conformity with World Bank orthodoxy, to move the PDS toward greater targeting toward the below-poverty households. Although the targeted PDS introduced in 1997 lowered prices for the below-poverty households, it also reduced the ration for these households to 10 kilograms. Only later, in the budget for 2000–2001, was the ration was raised to 20 kilograms. Moreover, targeting fails to take note of the gap between the numbers who are vulnerable to being poor and the numbers who are actually poor at any given time. This gap provides strong justification for moving in the opposite direction toward greater universality. Errors of exclusion from the PDS are presumptively far more serious than errors of including those who are not vulnerable. Yet, the targeting principle has been upheld with consequent increases in issue prices and narrowing of the difference between the issue price and the open market price. While these moves have scarcely changed the food subsidy relative to GDP, the decline in PDS total subsidized sales even as open market relative prices of food commodities have been on the upswing is an indicator of increased distress among the vulnerable.

Swaminathan also notes that the primary reason for the failure of PDS to reach the intended beneficiaries has less to do with corruption and mismanagement and more to do with wide interstate disparities in the scale of distribution. Coverage of the relevant population is an increasing function of the overall scale of the program at the state level. The poorer states actually had a proportionately smaller share of the total subsidized sales as compared to the better-off states. Increasing coverage under the PDS, both among poorer states and to include the vulnerable, will necessarily raise fiscal expenditures and thus require confronting the ruling neoliberal orthodoxy at its root.

7. Conclusion

This chapter has attempted an overall assessment of the impact of the economic reforms undertaken in India since the crisis of 1991. It pays particular attention to the effects of reforms, both directly and via economic growth, on mass well-being. We have argued that openness—policies that aim to increase economic integration with international markets—has been the focal point of the reforms, whilst globalization—the *actual* increase in external integration—has been the touchstone of the new policy regime as perceived by its architects.

In the official view, supported by many Indian economists, policies of liberalization and globalization are justified as the best means to social ends such as poverty alleviation and human development. By accelerating growth, these policies can directly improve social opportunities and, by augmenting public expenditure and capability, indirectly enable government to take direct actions aimed at creating social opportunities. At the very least (even if it is supposed that neither of these linkages holds automatically), the pursuit of public action for enhancing social opportunities can proceed on a track parallel with integration. Thus, social progress and globalizing policies are at worst independent of each other and at best strongly complementary.

But it is increasingly apparent that these neoliberal tenets have not been vindicated by the decade-plus of experience since the reforms began. True, the balance of payments has been restored in terms of both current account deficits and foreign exchange reserves. But the promise of accelerated economic growth has not been fulfilled, while industrial growth has fallen from 7.8 percent in the 1980s to less than 6 percent in the 1990s and is no longer leading the economy. The expected increase in economy-wide labor intensity and a consequent decline in unemployment have failed to materialize. The hope that getting agricultural prices "right" will shift resources into the rural economy has been belied. The faith in increasing external integration as the singular goal of a strategy of development has been contradicted by growing internal disintegration, in the form of increasing economic disparities across states and across the urban-rural divide. The desire to strengthen the fiscal situation through supply-side policies has been frustrated by stagnant government revenues and a continued rise in public debt. The drive to curb the food subsidy bill through reduced coverage and higher consumer prices only served to raise that bill through a phenomenal increase in food stocks. Unless one willingly reposes faith in the non-comparable evidence on poverty yielded by the National Sample Survey for 1999–2000, there is little reason to celebrate continued, let alone accelerated, progress on the poverty front. On the whole, the evidence shows increased inequality in the personal and functional distribution of real income within the rural and urban sectors, and a rising rural-urban income gap. Thus, neither direct nor indirect channels of complementarity have been realized. And the record provides sufficient grounds to doubt even the weaker expectation that social ends and globalizing policies can be pursued simultaneously without tradeoff or conflict.

If the principal charge against earlier regimes is that they failed to set up or implement effective policies for expanding social opportunities, the new regime has not proved immune to the same charge. Without an account of this failure, the idea that meaningful development can be assured by the neoliberal strategy appears skeptical. Such an account must be found not just in the purely economic assumptions underlying the prevalent wisdom but also in the realities of India's political economy. This general point may be illustrated in relation to agriculture. If genuinely equitable agricultural growth and rapid rural poverty alleviation are to be achieved, this will require a substantial step-up in public investment in rural infrastructure, research, and thorough reforms in land relations and credit delivery. There is little room to believe, however, that such a program can be pursued without producing major contradictions within the fiscal, economic, and, ultimately, political priorities of the reform regime presently in place.

Notes

Portions of this chapter update and draw on an earlier paper by us (see Dutt and Rao 2001). We are grateful to the Center for Economic Policy Analysis and the Ford Foundation for financial support, and to participants of conferences at Beijing and Hanoi, and especially to Lance Taylor, for comments and suggestions. We are also grateful to Kajal Mukhopadhyay for help with the econometrics.

1. The exact placement of some of the contributions in the table may be a matter of debate given that the views expressed in them do not unambiguously lend themselves to easy classification in the 2×2 scheme adopted in the table. For instance, some of those finding positive growth effects warn about some longer-run growth problems.

2. For further discussion see Rao (1998c), a cross-country empirical attempt to separate openness from trade-related globalization.

3. To illustrate, openness with respect to FDI implies policies that reduce restrictions and controls on foreign direct investment, while globalization may be measured by increases in the FDI/GDP ratio. On the one hand, openness may not increase globalization, as the experience of a number of LDCs—including Bangladesh—shows, because of low growth, low levels of education of the labor force, and labor unrest. On the other hand, countries that have been quite restrictive in their policies toward TNCs, including Taiwan and Malaysia, have been able to increase FDI inflows, because of their high rates of growth (Dutt 1998).

4. Employment and real output data are taken from World Bank data, and net real fixed capital and the share of operating surplus in NDP from the Economic and Political Weekly Research Foundation (EPW; 1997). The employment data actually refer to labor force data, since no reliable annual time series data for the unemployment rate are available; the implicit assumption of a constant unemployment rate is made. Two adjustments were made for the operating surplus share. First, India has a large share of income (around 50 percent) that falls in the category of mixed income of the self-employed. We assume that the capital share for that income is the same as the share for the rest of the economy to find the share of capital stock (operating surplus) for the economy as a whole. Second, data on income shares were available for the years 1980–1981 to 1993–1994; we computed the figures for the next two years applying ordinary least squares on a time trend.

5. The New Agricultural Strategy's relative success in achieving food self-sufficiency in the three decades since the food crisis of the mid-1960s has masked the economic, social, and environmental costs of the strategy.

Low labor absorption is perhaps the chief of these costs. For elaboration of this thesis, see Rao and Storm (1997).

6. The growth of rural non-farm employment and the role of government employment programs will be discussed separately in connection with their effects on poverty in a later section.

7. Kambhampati, Krishna, and Mitra (1997) have taken annual estimates of the total and manufacturing labor force and found that the reforms have had little effect on employment at a macroeconomic level. The total labor force expanded steadily from 298 million in 1987 to 341 million workers in 1993. The number of workers in manufacturing increased steadily as well, though at a faster rate. But there were no significant changes in trends after 1991. Since the annual labor force figures are presumably no more than rough estimates, it is not clear how much credence to attach to these propositions.

8. NSS thin samples canvass questionnaires from about 20,000 respondents, while the large samples cover six times that number.

9. Sen (1996) rejects the view that agricultural growth provided an impetus to rural non-agricultural employment (as a result of an increase in the demand for non-agricultural goods). He also disagrees that evidence overwhelmingly supports the hypothesis that non-agricultural growth has occurred as a result of factors outside rural areas, including an expansion in government expenditure.

10. Dharm Narain made the pioneering contribution that spawned a large literature on this topic (see Mellor and Desai 1986).

11. There is anecdotal evidence on the rapid rates of increase in the incomes of highly skilled workers and managers in the 1990s, especially in transnational corporations. These increases are especially pronounced among graduates of leading management and technology institutes, suggesting increases in the skilled-unskilled wage differential. However, we know of no aggregate data confirming this trend.

References

Ahluwalia, Isher J. 1991. *Productivity and growth in Indian manufacturing*. New Delhi: Oxford University Press.

Ahluwalia, Montek S. 1995. India's economic reforms. In *India: The future of economic reform*, edited by Robert Cassen and Vijay Joshi. New Delhi: Oxford University Press.

Alagh, Yoginder. 2001. WTO and India: Getting facts right. *Business Line*, February 9.

Balakrishnan, Pulapre. 2000. Agriculture and economic reforms: Growth and welfare. *Economic and Political Weekly*, March 18, 999–1004.

Balakrishnan, Pulapre, K. Pushpangadan, and M. Suresh Babu. 2000. Trade liberalisation and productivity growth in manufacturing: Evidence from firm-level panel data. *Economic and Political Weekly*, October 7, 3679–82.

Basant, Rakesh. 2000. Corporate response to economic reforms. *Economic and Political Weekly*, March 4, 813–22.

Bhaduri, Amit, and D. Nayyar. 1996. *The intelligent person's guide to liberalization*. New Delhi: Penguin.

Bhagwati, Jagdish. 1994. *India in transition: Freeing the economy*. New Delhi: Oxford University Press.

———. 1998. The design of Indian development. In *India's economic reforms and development: Essays for Manmohan Singh*, edited by I. J. Ahluwalia and I. M. D. Little. New Delhi: Oxford University Press.

Bhagwati, Jagdish, and T. N. Srinivasan. 1993. *Indian economic reforms*. New Delhi: Government of India, Ministry of Finance.

Dasgupta, Dipankar, P. Maiti, R. Mukherjee, S. Sarkar, and S. Chakrabarti. 2000. Growth and interstate disparities in India: Statistical analysis. *Economic and Political Weekly* 35:2413–22.

Datt, Ruddar. 2001. Where are the jobs Mr. Sinha? *Business Line*, April 6, 2001.

Datta, Gaurav. 1999. Has poverty declined since economic reforms? Statistical data analysis. *Economic and Political Weekly*, 34:3516–18.

Deshpande, Sudha, and L. Deshpande. 1998. Impact of liberalisation on the labour market in India. What do facts from the NSSO's 50th round show? *Economic and Political Weekly*, May 30, L31–L39.

Dreze, Jean, and A. Sen. 1995. *India: Economic development and social opportunity*. Delhi: Oxford University Press.

Dutt, Amitava K. 1996. The role of Keynesian policies in semi-industrialized economies: Theory and evidence from India. *International Review of Applied Economics* 10(1): 127–40.

———. 1998. Globalization, foreign direct investment and southern growth: Evidence from selected Asian countries. *In Economic Effects of Globalization*, edited by J. R. Chen, 45–96. Aldershot, UK: Avebury.

Dutt, Amitava K., and J. M. Rao. 2001. Globalization and its social discontents: The case of India. In *External liberalization, economic performance, and social policy*, edited by Lance Taylor. New York: Oxford University Press.

Economic and Political Weekly Research Foundation. 1997. *National Accounts Statistics of India, 1950–51 to 1995–96*. Mumbai: EPW Research Foundation.

Godley, Wynne, and G. McCarthy. 1997. Fiscal policy will matter. Jerome Levy Institute, Bard College, New York.

Goldar, B. N. 1993. Impact of technology and productivity growth in Indian industry. *Productivity* 34 (1): 87–90.

——. 2000. Employment growth in organized manufacturing in India. *Economic and Political Weekly*, April 1–7.

Goldar, B. N., and V. S. Ranganathan. 1999. Economic reforms and R and D expenditure in industrial firms in India. *Indian Economic Journal* 46 (2): 60–75.

Government of India, Ministry of Finance. 2000–2001. *Economic Survey*. New Delhi: Government of India.

Guhan, S. 1992. Social security in India: Looking one step ahead. In *Poverty in India: Research and policy*, edited by B. Harriss, S. Guhan, and R. H. Cassen. Bombay: Oxford University Press.

——. 1995. Social expenditures in the union budget: 1991–96. *Economic and Political Weekly*, May 6.

Joshi, Vijay, and I.M.D. Little. 1996. *India's economic reforms, 1991–2001*. Oxford: Oxford University Press.

Kambhampati, Uma, P. Krishna, and D. Mitra. 1997. The effect of trade policy reforms on labor markets: Evidence from India. *Journal of International Trade and Economic Development* 6 (2): 287–97.

Kohli, Atul. 1990. *Democracy and discontent: India's growing crisis of governability*. Cambridge: Cambridge University Press.

Kohli, Renu. 2001a. Capital account liberalisation: Empirical evidence and policy issues—I. *Economic and Political Weekly*, April 14.

——. 2001b. Capital account liberalisation: Empirical evidence and policy issues—II. *Economic and Political Weekly*, April 21, 1345–48.

Krishna, Pravin, and D. Mitra. 1998. Trade liberalisation, market discipline and productivity growth: New evidence from India. *Journal of Development Economics* 56: 447–62.

Kumar, Nagesh. 1998. Liberalisation and changing patterns of foreign direct investments: Has India's relative attractiveness as a host of FDI improved? *Economic and Political Weekly*, May 30, 1321–29.

——. 2000a. Economic reforms and their macroeconomic impact. *Economic and Political Weekly*, March 4, 803–12.

——. 2000b. Mergers and acquisitions by MNEs: Patterns and implications. *Economic and Political Weekly*, August 5, 2851–58.

Kundu, Amitabh. 1997. Trends and structure of employment in the 1990s: Implications for urban growth. *Economic and Political Weekly*, June 14, 1399–405.

Mani, Sunil, and M. V. Bhaskar. 1998. A curmudgeon's guide to economic reforms in India's manufacturing sector. *Economic and Political Weekly*, December 19.

Marjit, Sugata, B. Dasgupta, and S. Mitra. 2000. Currency devaluation and exports: Separating actual from statistical. *Economic and Political Weekly*, April 29, 1553–58.

Meenakshi, J. V., R. Ray, and S. Gupta. 2000. Estimates of poverty for SC, ST and female-headed households. *Economic and Political Weekly* 35:2748–54.

Mehta, Jaya, and S. Venkatraman. 2000. Poverty statistics: Bermicide's feast. *Economic and Political Weekly* 35:2377–82.

Mehta, Rajesh. 1997. Trade policy reforms, 1991–92 to 1995–96: Their impact on external trade. *Economic and Political Weekly*, April 12, 779–84.

Mellor, John W., and G. M. Desai. 1986. *Agricultural change and rural poverty: Variations on a theme by Dharm Narain*. Oxford: Oxford University Press.

Nagaraj, R. 1997. What has happened since 1991? Assessment of India's economic reforms. *Economic and Political Weekly*, November 8, 2869–79.

——. 2000a. Indian economy since 1980: Virtuous growth or polarisation? *Economic and Political Weekly*, August 5, 2831–38.

——. 2000b. Organized manufacturing employment. *Economic and Political Weekly*, September 16, 3445–8.

National Sample Survey Organization. 1996. *Key results on employment and unemployment, 50th round*. New Delhi: Department of Statistics.

Nayyar, Deepak. 2000. Capital controls and the World Financial Authority: What can we learn from the Indian experience? Center for Economic Policy Analysis Working Paper Series III, no. 4. New York: New School University.

Nijman, Jan. 2000. Mumbai's real estate market in 1990s: De-regulation, global money and casino capitalism. *Economic and Political Weekly*, February 12, 575–82.

Pal, Parthapratim. 1998. Foreign portfolio investment in Indian equity markets: Has the economy benefited? *Economic and Political Weekly*, March 14, 589–98.

Patnaik, Prabhat. 1997. The context and consequences of economic liberalization in India. *Journal of International Trade and Economic Development* 6 (2): 165–78.

Pethe, Abhay, and K. Ajay. 2000. Do Indian stock markets matter? Stock market indices and macroeconomic variables. *Economic and Political Weekly*, January 29, 349–56.

Pieper, Ute. 2000. Deindustrialisation and the social and economic sustainability nexus in developing countries: Cross-country evidence on productivity and employment. *Journal of Development Studies* 36 (4): 66–99.

Rao, C.H.H. 2000. Declining demand for foodgrains in rural India: Causes and implications. *Economic and Political Weekly* 35:201–6.

Rao, J. Mohan. 1998a. Food prices and rural poverty: Liberalisation without pain? *Economic and Political Weekly* 33:799–800.

———. 1998b. Food, agriculture and reforms: Change and continuity. *Economic and Political Weekly* 33:1955–60.

———. 1998c. Openness, inequality and poverty. Background Paper prepared for the Human Development Report, 1999. New York: UNDP.

Rao, J. Mohan, and Servaas Storm. 1997. Distribution and growth in Indian agriculture. In *The Indian economy: Major debates since independence*, edited by T. J. Byres. Delhi: Oxford University Press.

Ravallion, Martin. 1998. Reform, food prices and poverty in India. *Economic and Political Weekly*, January 10, 29–36.

Roy, M. K. 2001. Stock markets in a liberalised economy: Indian experiences. *Economic and Political Weekly*, January 27, 367–76.

Saha, Anamitra. 2000. Puzzle of declining rural foodgrains consumption. *Economic and Political Weekly* 35:201–6.

Sen, Abhijit. 1996. Economic reforms, employment and poverty: Trends and options. *Economic and Political Weekly*, September, 2459–77.

———. 2000. Estimates of consumer expenditure and its distribution: Statistical priorities after NSS 55th round. *Economic and Political Weekly* 35: 4499–518.

———. 2001. A whole crop of uncertainties. *Frontline*, 18.

Singh, Ajit. 1998. Liberalization, the stock market, and the market for corporate control: A bridge too far for the Indian economy? In *India's economic reforms and development: Essays for Manmohan Singh*, edited by I. J. Ahluwalia and I. M. D. Little. Delhi: Oxford University Press.

Srinivasan, T. N. 1998. India's export performance: A comparative analysis. In *India's economic reforms and development: Essays for Manmohan Singh*, edited by I. J. Ahluwalia and I. M. D. Little. Delhi: Oxford University Press.

Sundaram, K. 1998. *Weakening welfare: The public distribution of food in India*. New Delhi: LeftWord Books.

———. 2000. How real is the secular decline in rural poverty? *Economic and Political Weekly* 35: 2129–40.

———. 2001. Employment-unemployment situation in the nineties: Some results from NSS 55th round survey. *Economic and Political Weekly* 36:931–40.

Visaria, Pravin. 2000. Alternative estimates of poverty in India. *Economic Times*, June 29.

World Bank. 1996. *India: Five years of stabilization and reform and the challenges ahead*. Washington, D.C.: World Bank.

———. 1998. *India: Achievements and challenges in reducing poverty*. Washington, D.C.: World Bank.

6

Indonesia's External Liberalization: Policy Dynamics and Socio-Economic Impact

Iwan J. Azis

1. Introduction

This chapter discusses Indonesia's experience with trade and external liberalization. With the exception of the capital account, most of the country's liberalization policies were promulgated during the 1980s. This discussion will emphasize the policy dynamics and the socio-economic effects of liberalization.

Section 2 analyzes the country's overall socio-economic performance before and after liberalization. I shall discuss the interactions between monetary and fiscal policies and the general trend of social development. The government's struggle to manage macroeconomic policy during liberalization is elaborated upon in Section 3. The tradeoff between maintaining a competitive exchange rate and controlling inflation is particularly stressed. More detailed discussions on the impact of liberalization on employment, income distribution, and poverty are presented in Section 4. The effect of the 1997 financial crisis on these variables is discussed in Section 5.

2. Economic Performance before and after Liberalization

When the price of oil fell in 1983, resulting in a swelling of the current account deficit (reaching US$6.4 billion), the Indonesian government devalued the currency by 28 percent. The strong growth of exports following the devaluation, however, was short-lived. In fact, in 1985, non-oil exports declined in value, before reviving slightly in 1986 only because of another major devaluation (by 31 percent) that year. While the 1983 devaluation was primarily based on the fear of a balance of payments crisis, the 1986 devaluation was related more to the major plunge in oil prices, that is, from over $30 to below $10 per barrel. That very year a major trade and investment liberalization was announced, aimed primarily at boosting non-oil exports.

Meanwhile, a new era of monetary policy began in 1983. The early signs of the government's intention to reform the financial sector had actually emerged in mid-1982, when the central bank (Bank Indonesia, or BI) cut back on the provision of credits that had been directed for several years toward low-priority activities. But it was the June 1983 package that produced a considerable impact on the financial sector. Practically all credit ceilings were eliminated, resulting in an increased flexibility of prices (interest rates) and quantities (credit). However, no provision to ease entry into financial markets was made. The dominance of state-owned banks—an important sign of the country's financial repression—continued.

Realizing the need for competition, in October 1988 the government promulgated another major policy change aimed at increasing bank competition by allowing the entry of new private banks, including foreign bank branches outside Jakarta. Such a policy route was deemed necessary given the high degree of financial repression at the time. Combined with the effects of the June 1983 reform, the 1988 package increased competition in the financial system. Despite an increase in market players, however, only a few commercial banks controlled a large share of an oligopolistic market structure, and their shareholders were large industrial groups (conglomerates). Indeed, the structure of banking and non-banking financial institutions corresponds very closely to the pattern of distribution of economic power.[1] As expected, these industrial groups, either in a quasi or direct way, were the largest borrowers. From this perspective, there seems to be a strong indication that the country's industrial organization structure—marked by a high degree of industrial concentration—determined the nature of its financial structure, not vice versa. It is in this context that most analysts claim that the 1988 bank deregulation was the embryo of the country's financial vulnerability that eventually led to the crisis in 1997.

It took less than a year after the promulgation of the 1988 reform for the economy to start overheating. By 1989, GDP growth accelerated by 7.5 percent, up from 5.8 percent in the previous year. Non-oil exports grew fairly fast, and private investment surged. An investment boom was clearly detectable. As reported in table 6.1, investment grew persistently at a double-digit rate, reaching 13.4 percent in 1989.

In an IS-LM framework, the investment increase is shown by a rightward shift of the IS curve to IS_1. To accommodate the increase in private demand, the government accelerated the pace of monetary expansion. By 1990, the growth of M2 reached an

TABLE 6.1 Basic Monetary Sector Indicators

	i	Credit	I	MS2	CA	CPI	GDP
1988	17.72	33.94	11.52	25.16	−1.86	5.47	5.78
1989	18.63	44.56	13.36	23.86	−1.60	5.97	7.46
1990	17.30	53.60	14.58	45.74	−3.74	9.53	7.24
1991	23.27	16.29	6.52	26.03	−4.35	9.52	6.95
1992	20.37	8.87	4.94	24.25	−2.56	4.94	6.46
1993	16.00	19.90	5.69	22.19	−2.94	9.77	6.50
1994	14.30	27.16	7.70	21.23	−3.60	9.24	7.34
1995	17.10	26.30	8.50	27.60	−7.90	8.64	7.50

Source: Azis (1997a).

i = Deposit rate (% p.a), midpoint of range: IFS-IMF (1995 figure is for three-month deposit rate). Credit = Growth rate (%) of credits outstanding in *Rp* and foreign exchange at end of period, include KIK and KMKP: Bank I = Growth rate (%) of gross fixed investment, at 1983 prices, except for 1994 and 1995 at 1993 prices: Central Bureau of Statistics (CBS; n.d). MS2 = Growth (%) of money supply in broad terms, March position: 1995–1996 Government Budget, 284. CA = Current account balance (US$ billion), fiscal year data: Bank Indonesia. CPI = Change in consumer price index (%), fiscal year, December 1995–1996: Government Budget document, 266. GDP = Growth rate (%) of GDP at 1983 prices, except for 1994 and 1995 at 1993 prices: CBS (n.d).

unprecedented level (44 percent), supported by heavy flows of credit allocation (54 percent). Such a relaxed monetary policy is depicted by a shift of the LM curve to the right, bringing the interest rate down to $i_2 = 17.30$ percent.

The first impact was on price levels. Inflation soared to 7.8 percent and continued increasing to 9.4 percent in 1991. Not surprisingly, exchange rate competitiveness was damaged (see the reverse direction of the real exchange rate [RER] from 1989–1990 to 1990–1991 in table 6.2). The second pressure came from the greater demand for imports to support the investment boom. While the growth of non-oil exports dipped to a one-digit rate, non-oil imports grew at an unprecedented rate, that is, by more than 31 percent. Consequently, the current account deficit swelled to US$3 billion and US$4.3 billion in 1990 and 1991 respectively. The end result was predictable: devaluation that led to a series of capital outflows.[2]

At any rate, the overall performance immediately following the liberalization policy in the mid-1980s was characterized by a classic case of high growth leading to overheating (Pangestu 1991). Strong growth continued in the 1990s, up to the 1997 financial crisis. The average annual growth rate reached 8 percent during 1987–1996 (post-liberalization), a marked increase from 6.2 percent during 1983–1986

TABLE 6.2 Changes in Exports and Financial Variables[a]

	Non-Oil Exchange	Exchange Rate		Interest Rate			NFA		Open Market Operations			
	Nominal	REER	Nominal	SBI	LIBOR	Spot	Swaps	Exchange	Credit	SBI/SBPU	Special[b]	Others[c]
1989–1990	17.2	2.3	5.01	13.1	8.4	−2.3	−4.1	4.1		0.4	0	3.7
1990–1991	7.7	−6.3	4.11	23.7	6.3	−5.6	7.3	5		1.8	−2.5	−1.8
1991–1992	22.1	1.3	5.83	18	4.3	7.2	−10	7.8		0.8	−5.2	3.2
1992–1993	31.9	1.8	4.08	12.5	3.2	−1.2	−0.4	12.2		−14.3	1	3.1
1993–1994	9.7	−0.8	2.82	8.5	3.1	−2.8	−0.1	7.6		1.9	1.5	1.4
1994–1995	16.5	−3.8	3.53	12.8	6	−6.3	2.6	2		8.1	−0.6	0.9

Source: Azis (1997b).

a. Except for exchange rate and interest rate changes (in %), all are in rupiah (Rp) trillion.

b. "Special" refers to special SBI/SBPU.

c. Others = Including BI's domestic credit.

(pre-liberalization). The peak years were 1989 and 1990, when the annual growth rate topped 9 percent.

Looking at aggregate demand and its composition, the investment boom during the late 1980s led to an almost doubling of real aggregate demand (from 4.9 to 8.4 percent). With increased incentives, exports surged, especially of the non-oil category, but imports (of capital goods, intermediate goods, and raw materials) also went up. The size of the trade surplus began to decline in the 1990s.

Unlike most other countries, Indonesia started with a fairly open capital account as early as 1970, way before the liberalization period of the 1980s. As the economy boomed, following liberalization, private capital inflows began to surge in the 1990s.

This led to a significant increase in domestic credit, supported by low real interest rates. Although the nominal rate tended to increase in the post-liberalization period, the real interest rate moved in the opposite direction, since the price level generally increased.

On the government sector side, strong economic growth did not produce a dramatic increase in tax revenues. In fact, the tax/output ratio declined, despite the implementation of tax reform in 1984–1985 (see table 6.3). While non-tax revenues and government spending increased, the country's prudent fiscal policy had been always supported by official foreign borrowings (see the government's expansionary position up to 1994 in figure 6.1). Hence, along with increased private capital inflows, the post-liberalization period was marked by rising foreign debts.

By 1995, the private sector took over the expansionary role in a major way. The sharp increase in Ip/sp, largely supported by rising private foreign debts, lasted until the 1997 crisis. Although it plunged during 1997–1999, private expenditures continued to be the main contributor to output, even when the latter collapsed in 1998 (see figure 6.1). Much of the contribution came from private consumption, suggesting that private savings dropped from 16 percent in 1996 to only 9 percent in 1999. The dramatic change in Indonesia's savings during the crisis is even more visible when one compares the figures with their peak in 1988 and 1999, when the private savings rate reached 24 percent immediately after the major banking reform was promulgated (more on the crisis period in section 5).

Despite strong economic performance, the employment increase was not as dramatic as expected, except that export growth stimulated more employment at the early stage of liberalization (Azis 1992; Pitt 1991). Prior to liberalization, the agricultural sector was the major absorber of the increased labor force, causing labor productivity to remain low and real wages to rise albeit slightly. With a growing population, this implies that the open unemployment rate was on the rise (see table 6.3). So was the rate of disguised unemployment.

The post-liberalization period did not produce dramatic changes in the labor market. Real wages increased, and the wage rate of urban laborers was approximately twice as much as that of rural workers. The wage ratio of skilled to unskilled workers increased from 1.87 to 2.33 (see table 6.3), less than

TABLE 6.3 The Trend before and after Liberalization

	1983–1986	1987–1996	1997–1999
Growth, Employment, and Inequality			
GDP growth rate (%)	6.21	8.00	–6.59
Real exchange rate (+ = real app.)	–2.88	4.03	–18.01
Wage share in GDP	0.44	0.49	0.53
Real wages growth (Using CPI 1993 = 100)	n.a	7.20	–8.20
Income inequality			
Gross domestic income per capita (constant 93, rupiah)	991.41	1441.41	1780.37
% change	2.91	6.27	–3.72
Primary incomes, wage (current, billion rupiah)			
Tradables/non-tradables			
employment	1.66	1.71	1.29
wage (83 – 86 = 100)	100.00	81.00	125.00
Skilled/unskilled (wage)	1.87	2.33	2.30
Urban/rural (wage)	NA	2.03	1.96
Aggregate Demand Decomposition (Growth Rate)			
Aggregate demand	4.51	8.40	–11.06
Direct multiplier effects			
Investment/saving rate (Ip/sp)	–1.02	12.48	–25.88
Government spending/tax rate (G/t)	7.48	4.83	–11.03
Exports/import propensity (E/m)	9.11	7.27	3.32
Effect of leakages			
Saving rates $sp = (Yp - Cp)/X$	12.43	–3.17	–17.26
Taxes ($t = T/X$), current	–5.90	–0.64	2.22
Imports propensity ($m = M/X$)	–3.86	1.22	–15.72
Productivity and Employment			
Overall productivity growth	8.43	5.67	–7.36
Overall growth in employment	–2.67	2.21	1.01
Labor supply			
Participation rate	0.42	0.43	0.46
Unemployment rate	0.02	0.04	0.05
Employment rate	0.98	0.96	0.95
Macroeconomic Variables (Yearly Average)			
Trade balance (million US$, current)	3737.50	6280.40	14252.00
% change	109.22	13.22	76.15
Domestic credit (billion rupiah, current)	15929.00	141613.30	389469.33
Changes in reserves (– = increase)	–167.75	–1431.50	5915.00
Real interest rate (money market rate/inflation)	0.12	0.09	0.02
Nominal interest rate	16.90	17.40	19.30
Interest rate spreads	0.11	0.12	0.14
Imports/GDP	0.28	0.25	0.29
Exports/GDP	0.25	0.26	0.29

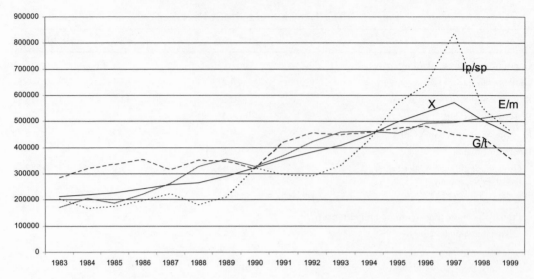

FIGURE 6.1 *Ip/sp, G/t, E/m,* and X (Using Total Government Revenue)

what other countries in East Asia have experienced.[3] The increase in real wages was more or less commensurate with productivity growth, the largest of which was in the manufacturing and services sector (Hill 1996).

The distinctive feature of the post-liberalization period was that the agricultural sector ceased to be the major absorber. Institutional changes (for example, minimum wage law and labor regulations) also emerged, albeit with limited effects on the labor market, at least until the 1997 crisis broke out. In general, the process of labor transformation, far from being dramatic, has been fairly slow, despite liberalization and major changes in the country's macroeconomic policies.

Given the above trend, the overall income distribution slightly improved in the early 1990s, but has worsened ever since. However, poverty, measured by the headcount index, improved persistently until 1996.[4] A more detailed analysis of the labor market, poverty, and income distribution is given in sections 4 and 5.

In the context of external liberalization, one needs to understand the political and economic background during the policy's implementation. As should be clear from the above discussions, external liberalization is not a stand-alone package. It is often promulgated along with other pro-market policies, ranging from

monetary to investment, banking, and exchange rate policies. The link between export-biased trade liberalization policy and financial sector policy is too critical to be overlooked. The following section is devoted to discussions on how the government managed macroeconomic policy during liberalization.

3. Macroeconomic Management during Liberalization

Since the promulgation of trade liberalization in 1986, Indonesia's exchange rate policy has been guided by the considerations of external competitiveness, albeit with occasional interruptions. The rupiah depreciated by approximately 3 to 5 percent annually (see table 6.2), and the real effective exchange rate (REER) remained relatively stable, despite the drastic change during the 1990–1991 to 1991–1992 period. Since 1987, the REER has depreciated by an average of about 1 percent per year.[5] Supported further by a series of trade and investment liberalization steps, non-oil exports surged dramatically, at double-digit rates, before dropping to around 8 percent in 1990.

In addition to the 1983 and 1986 devaluations, the government removed trade barriers in tariff and non-tariff categories. The first policy package, announced in May 1986, covered trade and investment deregulation. This marked the beginning of trade liberalization. A series of policy reforms have been launched since then, primarily—though not exclusively—aimed at removing structural rigidities in order to encourage exports and export-oriented foreign investment.[6]

Private investment increased significantly following the announcement of the package. In the case of foreign investment, the trend was also accelerated by a "push" factor emanating from the realignment of the yen, the Taiwanese dollar, and the Korean won. Investments from these countries came pouring forth.[7] The establishment of a "growth triangle," linking Singapore, Johor, and Batam Island, also helped increase foreign investment flows, albeit largely from Singapore.

There were two other important policy changes worth mentioning: one was announced in December 1987, allowing the greater flexibility of the interest rate and further liberalizing the capital market (e.g., the listing requirements on the Jakarta Stock Exchange were simplified). The second was the replacement of the "priority industry list" (DSP) with the "negative industry list" (constituting sixty-four sectors); any sector not on the list was open to foreign investment.[8] To be entitled for "national treatment," the Indonesian ownership share requirements in the establishment were reduced from 75 to 51 percent. In order to boost capital markets, the percentage was lowered further to 45 percent if some 20 percent of the company's shares were sold in the capital markets. No further obligation was made with respect to the 5 percent minimum requirement of the share of Indonesian ownership for export-oriented investment. Such a requirement was also applied to firms with only a 65 percent export requirement (not 85 percent),[9] as long as they were located in one of Indonesia's eastern provinces.[10]

Toward the end of the 1980s, monetary policy was loosened in order to accommodate increased private demand. As a result, the inflation rate soared to almost two digits in 1990. To counter inflation, a reversal in monetary policy was implemented in 1991. This marked the beginning of a tight money policy (TMP). It took almost a year before one could see the impact of such a policy on some major indicators, albeit not necessarily on the inflation rate. With interest rates hovering at more than 23 percent, the growth of credits was immediately contained,

dropping to 16.3 and 8.9 percent in 1991 and 1992 respectively. However, the target growth of money supply (i.e., 20 percent) could not be met although the actual rate (around 25 percent) was already half the rate in 1990. The LM curve moved back to the left, but not far enough to reduce the inflation rate (which remained high at 9.5 percent).

This brought up the question of policy effectiveness. With GDP growth at around 7 percent, and the income elasticity of demand for M2 at roughly 1.6, the M2 expansion of 20 percent seems inconsistent with the inflation target of 5 percent. Yet, the actual growth of M2 was greater than 25 percent. Another important question is "To what extent does M2 determine inflation behavior?" From the empirical data, M2 does not seem to explain (compared to M0) the inflation movement in Indonesia. But the question remains, "Why was the M2 growth target not met, despite the high interest rate?"

As discussed in Azis (1999a), the primary source of the growth of base money was the rapid increase in net foreign assets (NFA), the breakdown of which is reported in table 6.2. The high interest rate prompted many private sector and commercial banks to borrow from abroad, as partly indicated by a dramatic increase in the swap transaction (i.e., Rp7.3 trillion). While it is not possible to derive the exact amount of foreign private borrowing,[11] three factors support this prediction: first, lower world interest rates as shown, among other things, by a drop in the LIBOR from 8.4 to 6.3 percent; second, the swelling amount of "other sector" under the "other capital" item in the BOP capital account, reaching US$3.4 billion in 1991; and third, a record level of swap transactions reaching Rp7.3 trillion.

Even the money contraction resulting from open market operations—in other words, the selling of the central bank's (BI) certificate, known as SBI—could not offset such enormous inflows. In retrospect, this was the beginning of the vulnerability buildup in the country's financial sector that eventually led to the 1997 crisis. At the time, not much could be done, because an open capital account system had been in place since the early 1970s.[12]

Hence, it is clear that the experience of the early TMP in the 1990s was a failure, because control over NFA, particularly export credit, was ineffective. Frustrated by such a development, the government imposed a shock measure in March 1991. It began to redeem a significant part of BI promissory notes

(SBPUs) purchased from state-owned companies, particularly state banks.[13] As it turns out, this was capable of providing a Rp5.2 trillion monetary contraction. But the growth of export credits could not be restrained; they grew even faster (7.8 percent) during 1991–1992. Therefore, another move was needed. One such move was announced in November 1991: liquidating the swap mechanism.

In addition to a direct spot market intervention, until 1991 BI could use its swap mechanism to intervene in the forex market (this mechanism was introduced in 1979 to enhance foreign capital inflows by way of reducing exchange rate risk).[14] In response to the abolishment of the swap mechanism, there were huge spot foreign exchange purchases from the central bank by commercial banks throughout 1991–1992 (see table 6.2). This was countered by an even larger contraction through the last transaction of the BI's swap, such that, on a net basis, the swap-spot operations managed to reduce the NFA by some Rp2.8 trillion.

What led the government to abolish the swap mechanism—the enormous capital inflows, the risk of suppressing the growth of private forward markets, the inability of the monetary authority to constantly adjust the swap margin, or the high moral hazard involved in the mechanism—is not clear. What is clear is that the growth in NFA was reduced by swap elimination, even taking into account the expansion of the spot operation (see table 6.2).[15] The growth of M2 was dramatically cut to 26 percent—still high, but almost half of the rate in 1990. The effectiveness of swap elimination in restricting monetary expansion was further demonstrated when it was combined with reduced operations in the forex spot market. Another notable case was the dramatic size of liquidity absorption through open market operations that reached more than Rp14 trillion. Also, the growth of domestic credit sharply decelerated, dropping from 16 to less than 9 percent in 1991 and 1992 respectively.[16]

Such a tight monetary trend, however, was countered by the following two sources of monetary expansion. For the first time the fiscal sector raised, not reduced, the size of base money. The increase occurred while the government budget was still contracting. It was the *non-budget expenditures* that led to the increase. Non-budget expenditure is linked to the funding of several sectors considered "strategic," yet too sensitive to be discussed in parliament (off-budget expenditures). Clearly, in that year there

was no consistency between (tight) monetary policy and (expansionary) fiscal policy. Another source of concern was the continued—even larger—increase in export credit that reached an all-time high of Rp12.2 trillion. Once again, this shows that a pro-export (trade) bias policy had a significant impact on the financial sector.

It is obvious that the sharp drop in the growth of base money in 1992–1993 that contributed to low inflation (less than 5 percent in 1992) was primarily a result of the government's heavy open market operation. From the macroeconomic perspective the results were encouraging, but the micro impact on the central bank's profitability was devastating.[17]

The process of cooling down had practically ended by 1993. Having experienced a slower growth of credit, investment, and GDP in the preceding years, the government began loosening monetary policy, as indicated by an expansionary market operation (Rp3.4 trillion), and reduced the interest rate.[18] The growth of credit surged with the relaxation of prudential regulations. The monetary sector trend expectations during an election year held true in many instances. All these facts, however, did not contribute to an excessive growth in base money (its increase, by Rp3.3 trillion, was still lower than that in 1991–1992), primarily because economic policy makers succeeded in convincing political leaders to impose a limit on non-budgetary expenditures.[19] Furthermore, even though export credits increased by Rp7.6 trillion, the government finally decided to terminate these subsidized credits, despite increased pressures from potential and existing users.

Hence 1993–1994 was characterized by a monetary expansion but a fiscal contraction. The net result in terms of the growth of effective demand was neutral, that is, around 6.5 percent. Although in 1994–1995 some non-budgetary expenditures reappeared, and the loosening of monetary policy continued (credit growth expanded by 27 percent), the combination of a very contractionary fiscal policy and spot operations led to an even lower growth in base money (2.8 percent).

Yet inflation was persistently high (greater than 9 percent), current account deficits increased to $3.6 billion, credit grew by more than 27 percent, and GDP growth was a very strong 7.3 percent. Data on approved investment, including direct foreign investment, also show a more than 100 percent increase. Enormous flows of short-term capital toward the end of 1993 made the central bank face a classic dilemma of preventing exchange rate appreciation while attempting to stabilize prices at the same time.

In the end, the REER appreciated during the last few months of 1993. The growth of non-oil exports dropped sharply from 32 percent in 1992–1993 to less than 10 percent in 1993–1994. BI's attempt to defend the exchange rate was strengthened ever since. While the official rate continued depreciating at around 4 percent, both real and nominal effective rates also depreciated through 1994, the former at 3.8 percent (if measured in the fiscal year; see table 6.2), and the latter at 9 percent. Although the growth of non-oil exports started to pick up, bottlenecks in the real sector began to produce more formidable effects compared with the exchange rate movement.

Hence, while in general the government preferred to defend the exchange rate, a market-determined rate was occasionally allowed, as evidenced from the 1993 case. But as soon as concerns over the slowdown of the growth of non-oil exports arose, the trend was immediately halted by accelerating the depreciation of the rupiah (e.g., in January 1994).

This brings up the question of whether or not defending the exchange rate is a suitable task for the central bank. The influx of capital flows continued. The central bank was determined to reduce speculative movements, and at the same time wanted to encourage foreign exchange trading among market participants (the country's foreign exchange market was fairly thin). Therefore, in late 1993 BI widened the exchange rate band from Rp6 to Rp20 per U.S. dollar and then to Rp30 per U.S. dollar in 1994 (equivalent to 1.5 percent of the currency's value).[20] In December 1995, the band was further widened to 3 percent (i.e., Rp60 per U.S. dollar). When announcing the latter, it was explicitly stated that the move was meant to improve the effectiveness of monetary policy and exchange rate stability in order to deal with the anticipated future growth of capital flows.[21] Unfortunately, such a spread between BI's buying and selling rates was still too low to provide enough room for price adjustment in the foreign exchange market. As a result, potential instability from short-term capital flows remained high, and the forex market remained thin (less than US$5 billion a day in 1995, while transactions with BI only amounted to US$24 million a day).[22]

Concerns over the overheated economy mounted in 1995. While the inflation rate was still high,

between 8 and 9 percent, and the economy posted a strong 7.5 percent growth rate, the current account deficit increased, reaching more than US$7 billion (3 to 4 percent of GDP).[23] TMP was then implemented, albeit with limited effectiveness. In the wake of massive capital flows, BI had to intervene heavily in the currency markets. In so doing, additional liquidity was pumped into the money market, making the monetary target impossible to achieve.[24]

On June 13, 1996, BI decided to widen the band again, allowing the rupiah to fluctuate by 5 percent. The new range was set between Rp.2,315 and Rp.2,433.[25] Clearly, the major impetus for such a substantial increase was the continued flood of capital inflows, most of which came from Japan.[26] Although the rupiah surged, expectations remained low, since the current account deficit was large and on the rise.

Continued capital inflows did not make the management of monetary and exchange rate policy easier. While the inflation target was persistently set at 5 percent, more often than not such a target could not be met. As indicated earlier, in order to maintain the competitiveness of the exchange rate and simultaneously contain the growth of base money, a massive sterilization was needed. Enormous quantities of foreign exchange had to be bought if the exchange rate was to be defended.[27] The expansionary effects of NFA can be sterilized by an open market operation, that is, by the selling of SBIs. Such measures are almost "menu of the day" whenever short-term capital inflows increase. But the BI's own profitability may be severely reduced. As an illustration, in 1992–1993 when short-term capital continued to flow in, BI purchased more than US$14 billion in foreign exchange in order to defend the exchange rate. To sterilize the potential money growth, an open market operation was conducted, involving some US$11 billion in SBI sales. This contributed to the swelling of BI's foreign reserves. With the LIBOR stabilized at 3.2 percent, the SBI interest rate at 12.5 percent, and the nominal exchange rate depreciation at 5.3 percent, this would mean a 4 percent negative spread, or a US$0.4 to US$0.5 billion loss on BI's portfolio.

To summarize, following trade and investment liberalization in the mid-1980s, the Indonesian government struggled to manage the monetary and exchange rate repercussions of the policy. Coupled with a series of widening exchange rate bands, a managed floating system was maintained until August 1997. The country's exchange rate policy has been guided by the considerations of external competitiveness. Inflation has hardly been the target for the exchange rate policy, since a depreciating exchange rate is generally associated with a lower inflation rate. The sizable external debt and its implication for raising foreign exchange revenues (exports) seem to be among the most important motives for such a policy.[28] But the cost was also clear: the targeted inflation rate was hard to meet.

4. The Impact of External Liberalization on Employment, Income Distribution, and Poverty

Theoretically, trade liberalization can reduce prices in the tradable sector through competition, although the actual outcome depends on the speed and scope of liberalization. It may also increase (reduce) the ratio of wages (labor demand) in tradable and non-tradable sectors. In many cases, the non-tradable sector absorbs labor surplus or the lack of demand in the tradable sector. However, the absorption capacity depends on the effective demand generated by the economy.

As far as the Indonesian case is concerned, the price ratio of the tradable to non-tradable sector increased during the post-liberalization period (see figure 6.2).

The trend continued until the 1997 crisis broke out (see figure 6.3).[29] Such a pattern also holds when manufacturing is considered to be the only tradable sector. Many tradable goods were depressed and heavily subsidized during the pre-liberalization period. When some of them were liberalized in the mid-1980s, market price adjustments took place, despite more open competition from abroad. During the 1990s, the structure of Indonesia's non-oil exports did not change much and continued to rely upon labor-intensive and natural resource–based sectors (e.g., wood products and textiles). Although competition from other developing countries increased, the pressures on prices could not reverse the increasing trend in the price ratio of the tradable to non-tradable sectors. In general, the exchange rate is negatively correlated with non-tradable prices, a scenario similar to that of most Asian countries but unlike Latin American cases (Kamin 1997).

Productivity in the tradable sector also increased, and it was accompanied by rising nominal and real wages, except after the 1997 crisis. Based on wage data for manufacturing and services, the post-liberalization period was characterized by a fluctuation in the wage ratio of the tradable and non-tradable sector (see figure 6.4). For the agricultural sector, the fluctuation was less, but the trend of a rising ratio was more visible, especially since 1992 (see figure 6.5).

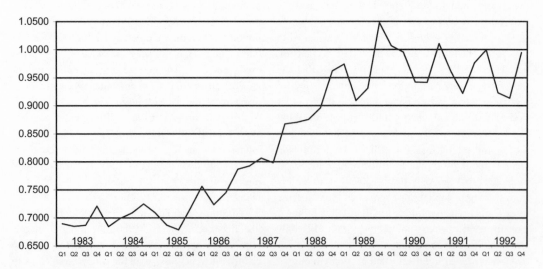

FIGURE 6.2 Ratio of Deflators of Tradable Manufacturing and Non-tradable Sector: 1983–1992

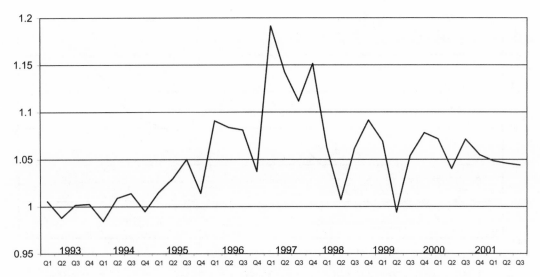

FIGURE 6.3 Ratio of Deflators of Tradable Manufacturing and Non-tradable Sector: 1993–2001

The absolute and relative increase of wages in the tradable sector did not only affect the unemployment figure, but it also altered the employment composition. As illustrated in figure 6.6, the open unemployment rate increased since the mid-1980s, peaked in 1995, and has fluctuated ever since. More interesting is the employment trend of the tradable and non-tradable sectors. Figure 6.7 shows that the employment

share in the tradable sector increased toward the end of the 1980s. Since then, the share dropped rather significantly up to the onset of the crisis.

The drop from 1996 to 1997 and the moderate rise of the ratio afterward reflect the dissociation between exports and the exchange rate, largely because of the rising difficulties in the export sector, for example, dried-up trade financing and institutional

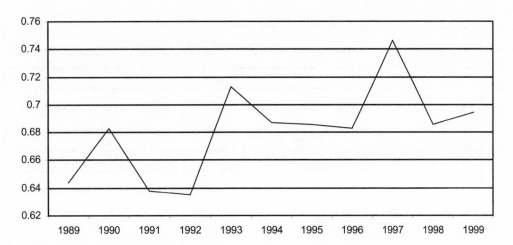

FIGURE 6.4 Wage Ratio of Tradable Manufacturing and Non-tradable Sector

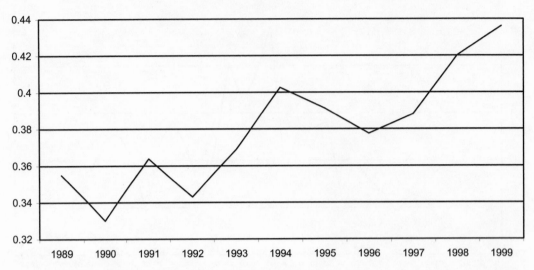

FIGURE 6.5 Wage Ratio of Tradable Agriculture and Non-tradable Sector

breakdown resulting from the multidimensional crisis. Indeed, despite the collapse of the exchange rate, export growth has been disappointing. The current account surplus has been driven mainly by the sharp fall in imports.

Rapid structural change along with high economic growth during the post-liberalization period resulted in a decline in the employment share of the agricultural sector. As depicted in table 6.4, the agricultural share dropped from 55 percent in the 1980s to 50 and 44 percent in 1990 and 1995, respectively. If the experience of many developing countries is any guide, with the agricultural share reaching 50 percent, the absolute number of people employed in the sector will also decline. This is indeed the case with the Indonesian experience, as shown in table 6.4.

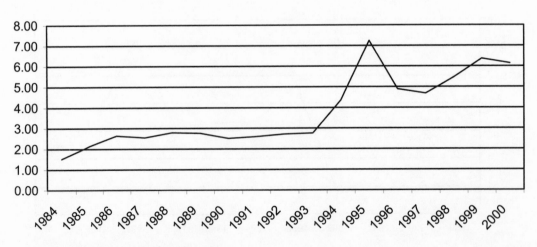

FIGURE 6.6 Open Unemployment Rate (%)

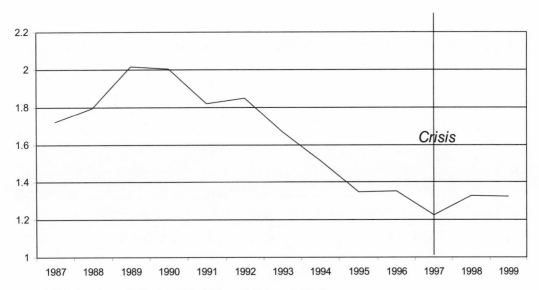

FIGURE 6.7 Employment Ratio of Tradable and Non-tradable Sector

The above structural changes, however, may have been caused by a set of domestic policies, and not necessarily as the result of trade liberalization. If the agricultural sector is excluded from the tradable component, figure 6.8 clearly indicates that the employment ratio of the tradable share rose during the immediate period after liberalization, remained stagnant in the 1990s (except for a single jump in 1994), and began to decline ever since. Following the crisis, the ratio dipped in 1998 as most manufacturing and urban-based activities were hard-hit. Only

when the economy began to show a sign of recovery, albeit a premature one, did the employment ratio increase once again (in 1999).

Data also support the hypothesis that the decline in the tradable share during the 1990s was partly a result of increased employment in the services sector. When effective demand grows slowly, such employment is likely to concentrate in the informal sector, but when economic growth is high, the formal sector is likely to absorb most of the employment. As discussed earlier, the Indonesian economy displayed

TABLE 6.4 Employment by Industry, 1971–1995

	1971		1980		1985		1990		1995	
	Million	%	Million	%	Million	%	Million	%	Million	%
Agriculture	26.5	64.0	28	54.7	34.1	54.5	35.5	50.1	35.2	43.9
Mining	0.1	0.2	0.4	0.8	0.4	0.6	0.7	1.0	0.6	0.7
Manufacturing	2.7	6.5	4.4	8.6	5.8	9.3	8.2	11.6	10.1	12.6
ElectGW	0	0.0	0.1	0.2	0.1	0.2	0.1	0.1	0.2	0.2
Construction	0.7	1.7	1.6	3.1	2.1	3.4	2.8	4.0	3.8	4.7
Trade	4.3	10.4	6.6	12.9	9.4	15.0	10.6	15.0	13.9	17.4
Trans-Com	1	2.4	1.5	2.9	2	3.2	2.7	3.8	3.5	4.4
Finance	0.1	0.2	0.2	0.4	0.3	0.5	0.5	0.7	0.7	0.9
Public Service	4.1	9.9	7.7	15.0	8.3	13.3	9.7	13.7	12.1	15.1
Others	1.9	4.6	0.7	1.4	0.1	0.2	0	0.0	0	0.0
Total	41.4	100.0	51.2	100.0	62.6	100.0	70.8	100.0	80.1	100.0

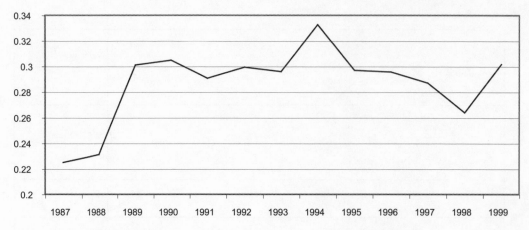

FIGURE 6.8 Employment Ratio of Tradable Manufacturing and Non-tradable Sector

robust growth following the liberalization policy all the way until the crisis broke out in 1997. With such a pattern, it is expected that most employment gains went to the (non-tradable) formal sector, since that sector also benefited from expanding manufacturing activities. Figure 6.9 confirms this expectation, showing a sharp increase in formal sector employment during the first half of the 1990s. The trend fluctuated during the second half of the 1990s and the period of crisis.

Based on the employment decomposition method employed by Berg and Taylor (2000), the growth rate of employment ratio may be expressed as a weighted average of differences between growth rates of per capita output (x_i) and labor productivity (ρ_i):

$$\lambda = \sum \lambda_i(\xi_i - \rho_i)$$

Figures 6.10 and 6.11 show the growth rates of output per capita and labor productivity upon which

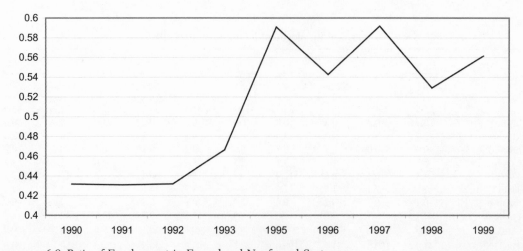

FIGURE 6.9 Ratio of Employment in Formal and Nonformal Sector

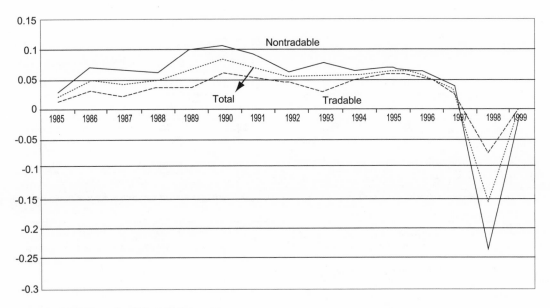

FIGURE 6.10 Growth of Output Per-capita

the above decomposition is based.[30] After accelerating in the 1980s, the growth in per capita output began to decline in the early 1990s, and stabilized thereafter until the financial crisis of 1997. Much of the decline was in the non-tradable sector, but the latter was persistently higher compared with the tradable sector. The growth of labor productivity, however, was relatively stable before collapsing during the crisis. From 1988 to 1995, the growth trend of the labor productivity of tradables was increasing, in contrast with the growth path of non-tradables. However, since the growth of tradables was slower than that of non-tradables during post-liberalization, the improved productivity of the former caused the growth trend of the employment ratio to decline (see figure 6.12). The opposite was true for non-tradables. Again, the absorption capacity of the agricultural and manufacturing sectors in the 1990s has been taken over by the services sector (see the declining ratio in figure 6.7).

The crisis led to a decline in the overall employment ratio, albeit a modest one. Although the fall in the growth rates of both labor productivity and per capita output in tradables was less than those in non-tradables at the beginning of the 1997 crisis, the latter

still managed to maintain positive—albeit small—growth while the tradable sector's employment ratio fell (see figure 6.13). The trend reversed itself in 1998. Again, the relatively flexible labor market helped prevent more devastating repercussions on employment from occurring, as indicated by a quick turnaround in the total employment ratio.

Depending on the income composition of different workers (households) in each sector, the above trend resulted in a slight worsening of income distribution, at least according to some measures based on standard consumption expenditure data. As depicted in table 6.5, while the percentage of income received by the bottom 40 percent had been relatively stagnant, and that of the middle 40 percent declined, the income share of the top 20 percent increased. The overall Gini index also shows an increasing trend during 1987–1996. As is often the case with emerging markets, Indonesia's worsening distribution was more visible in urban areas. In fact, during the period immediately after liberalization (1987–1990) the distribution within urban areas worsened, while that in rural areas improved.

Overall, however, the change in income distribution has been relatively insignificant. But some

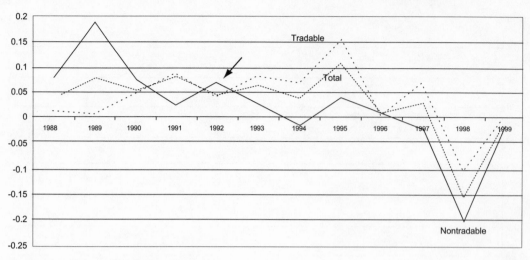

FIGURE 6.11 Growth of Labor Productivity

explanations are warranted. First of all, the data are based on consumption expenditure surveys that suffer from a serious exclusion of the very top income group. The data also conceal the socio-political dimensions of distribution, for example, between small and medium-sized business groups and conglomerates or other big business communities, especially the ethnic Chinese. This ethnic/class dimension proved

to be much more serious, as evidenced in a major riot in 1998. Another veiled yet important dimension, especially for a large archipelago such as Indonesia, is the spatial concentration in Java, the major island.

Two variables are critical in determining the incidence of poverty: household incomes (or consumption) and prices that affect the poverty line. After liberalization, the number of poor people continued

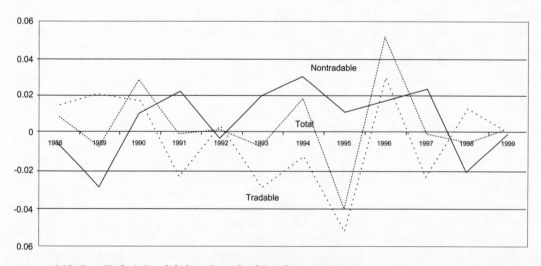

FIGURE 6.12 Berg-Taylor's Lambda-hat (Growth of Employment Ratio)

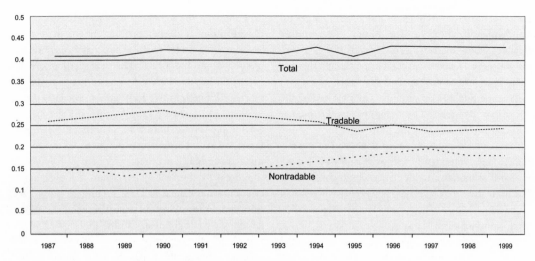

FIGURE 6.13 Employment Ratio (Employment/Population)

to decline, that is, from 35 (9.3 and 25.7) million in 1984 to 22.5 (7.2 and 15.3) million in 1996 (figures in parentheses are the urban and rural poverty figures). In terms of the headcount index, the number dropped from 21.6 (23.1 and 21.2) to 11.3 (9.7 and 12.3) percent. As poverty is reduced, the speed of poverty reduction cannot be maintained, that is, the poverty elasticity figures must decline. Indeed, the implicit poverty elasticity shows a declining trend, for example, from –0.76 during 1984–1987 to –0.52 for 1993–1996.

For the headcount index the elasticity dropped more sharply, that is, from –1.04 to –0.69. Hence, strong growth accompanied by price stability has contributed to a relatively rapid decline in the incidence of poverty.

The country's progress in poverty alleviation has been stimulated by a number of factors, ranging from the government's emphasis on education and health to its pricing policy for basic consumption goods (such as rice), its massive investment in infrastructure

TABLE 6.5 Income Shares of Various Expenditure Brackets and Gini Index prior to the Crisis

Area Type	Year	40% of Population with Lowest Expenditure	40% of Population with Moderate Expenditure	20% of Population with Highest Expenditure	Gini Index
Urban	1987	21.49	38.01	40.51	0.32
	1990	19.67	36.91	43.42	0.34
	1993	20.47	37.29	42.24	0.33
	1996	19.03	36.93	44.04	0.36
Rural	1987	24.29	39.26	36.44	0.26
	1990	24.41	39.22	36.36	0.25
	1993	25.13	38.42	36.45	0.26
	1996	23.18	38.99	37.83	0.27
Total	1987	20.87	37.48	41.65	0.32
	1990	21.31	36.75	41.94	0.32
	1993	20.34	36.90	42.76	0.34
	1996	20.25	35.05	44.70	0.36

and agricultural technologies, and a fairly successful family planning program. In addition, the country's flexible labor markets also helped mitigate unemployment and poverty problems, although this was more pronounced during the 1997 crisis.

Yet one ought to be cautious when evaluating the above poverty trend. The "fragility" of the picture comes from the fact that the number of those whose incomes or expenditures are just above the poverty line is large. Through a sensitivity analysis, it is revealed that the poverty incidence could simply double from the 1996 level (11.3 percent) with only a 25 percent increase in the poverty line (see figure 6.14). Hence, the relatively sharp decline in poverty during the post-liberalization period is highly sensitive to the poverty line, suggesting that the role and effectiveness of price policy, especially regarding prices of basic commodities such as rice (a conceptually tradable good), has been extremely crucial.

This explains why even today the control of a government agency (named BULOG) over this major staple remains significant, albeit less than before the crisis. In retrospect, this also elucidates why, despite various subsidy programs that prevented consumption from dropping sharply, poverty incidence still dramatically increased during the crisis. The surge in inflation, reaching almost 80 percent, is the reason (more on this in the next section).

Following the generally understood sequence of liberalization, a deeper opening up of the capital account after trade liberalization has been also implemented in Indonesia. This was particularly apparent during the 1990s. As a result, capital inflows surged. Although in size FDI remains the largest type of flow, in terms of growth net portfolio capital (including private borrowing) has been faster (see figure 6.15).[31] Current account deficits, the mirror image of capital flows, have widened. This has been supported by the real appreciation of the exchange rate following capital inflows.[32] Through a sterilized intervention (discussed in an earlier section), monetary policy was tightened, causing the interest rate to rise. Hence, the sequence of trade followed by capital account liberalization has brought about a bad combination of widening deficits and high interest rates immediately after the 1983 and 1988 financial sector deregulation, a situation predicted by Ocampo and Taylor (1998). By 1996, the deficits reached more than 4 percent of GDP, and the inflation rate was close to 10 percent.

The distributional impact of the capital inflow surge cannot be overlooked. As the data suggest, during the period of massive capital inflows, bank credits rose, as did imports, investment, and GDP growth. Since a considerable share of imported goods is consumed by urban-based medium- and

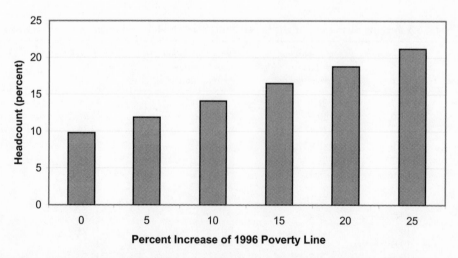

FIGURE 6.14 Sensitivity of Headcount Poverty to Poverty Line Based on 1996 Data

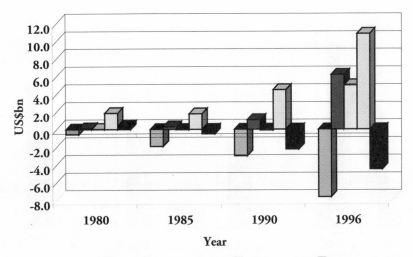

FIGURE 6.15 Balance of Payment: Indonesia

high-income groups, most private capital flows have greater linkages with urban-related activities. It is expected that income distribution tends to favor the urban household group. A simulation based on a dynamic CGE model confirms such a prognosis (see Azis 1999a).

5. Financial Crisis and Its Impacts

The question surrounding the financial crisis episode is "If the country's macroeconomic fundamentals were relatively good, why was there a crisis and what really caused it?" Despite widening current account deficits, the deficit level was less than 5 percent, the government budget remained under control, inflation was at a one-digit level, and the growth rate continued to be high. What, then, triggered the crisis? Some point to the real appreciation of the rupiah and the credit boom. However, elsewhere, I have explained that even these two are not sufficient enough to result in crisis (Azis 2001; Chinn 1998).

As far as the origins of the crisis are concerned, the reversed expectations of future investment profitability was pointed out by Krugman (1999a), McKibbin and Stoeckel (1999), and Corden (1999). But such a change in expectations, which led investors to pull

their money out of the country, was clearly not triggered by deteriorating macroeconomic fundamentals, except in Thailand (Azis 1999b). Another argument, along the Bernanke and Gertler (1989) line of reasoning, focuses on the deteriorating balance sheets of the corporate and banking sectors as the primary source of currency crisis (Krugman 1999b; Aghion, Bacchetta, and Banerjee 1999; Azis 2001). This is similar to Keynes's concept of "debt-bankruptcy" or Minsky's idea of the "financially fragile" system.[33]

While the debate continues, the explanation of the crisis surely must be financial in nature. I believe that the mismatch between private foreign debt maturity (largely short term) and the country's capacity to repay its debt obligations (as measured by the size of foreign reserves) holds the key to the story (Azis 2002).[34] Indonesia's private foreign borrowing increased dramatically during the 1990s. By mid-1997, the amount reached more than US$50 billion, most of which fell under the category of corporate (nonbank) borrowing, with Japanese banks having the largest exposure (see figure 6.16). More seriously, the proportion of short-term debts (STD) was considerably larger than long-term borrowings. At the onset of the crisis, STD already made up 170 percent of the foreign reserves.[35] This is obviously a strong case of *international illiquidity*.[36]

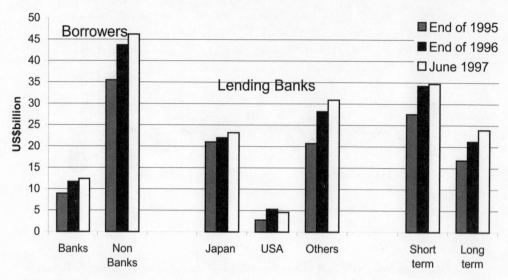

FIGURE 6.16 Indonesia's Private Foreign Debts

Banks' foreign borrowings were also on an upward—albeit relatively minor—trend. But given the quasi-fixed exchange rate system and the full convertibility of the capital account, domestic currency deposits should have been included in the asset/liability position of the financial system, as additional international currency obligations. A depositor could withdraw rupiah from banks to convert it into dollars at the announced parity. In this situation, unless there are sufficient foreign reserves to honor such a demand, a financial system can still suffer from international illiquidity if it holds excessive domestic liabilities. Notably, Indonesia's ratio of M2 to foreign reserves (6.3) before the onset of the crisis was indeed the highest among the crisis-affected Asian countries.

The main lesson is that in a more liberalized system (especially in terms of the capital account), bank deposits, currency mismatch, and short-term foreign debts are important indicators that require monitoring.[37] But the issue goes beyond a sovereign country's policy; Eatwell and Taylor (2000) stress the importance of the effective regulation of international finance to avoid a major shock and to maintain the economic health of each country.

The financial shock led to a major recession: the GDP growth dropped to minus 14 percent in 1998 (see figure 6.17).[38] Despite the high interest rate

policy, the exchange rate continued to collapse (see figure 6.18).

The devastating impact of the shock on poverty can be seen in figure 6.19. Note that the figure shows comparative trends of poverty in Indonesia using official numbers and welfare-consistent estimates.[39] Although the size of poverty incidence at any point in time is different for the two estimates, the trend is practically similar, that is, rising poverty from February 1997 (9.4 percent) to February 1998

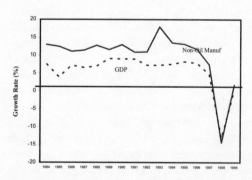

FIGURE 6.17 Growth of GDP & Non-Oil Manufacturing GVA, 1984–1999

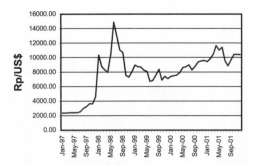

FIGURE 6.18 Exchange Rate

(14.8 percent), peaking in December 1998 (17.9 percent), before declining in February 1999 (16.6 percent).

A dramatic surge in inflation can lift up the poverty line significantly. This holds true even if there is no decline, or even if there is a nominal increase, in consumption expenditures. After enjoying a long period of a single-digit inflation rate, Indonesia's CPI jumped by 78 percent in 1998. The tragedy of May 1998 that led to the downfall of Suharto caused the prices of many basic goods to go up sharply. This hurt the poor severely, raising the poverty line (in current prices) significantly: its annual growth during 1993–1996 and 1996–1998 jumped from 16 to 41 percent in the urban areas, and from 13 to 39 percent in the

rural areas. Between 1998 and 1999, the overall poverty line changed very slightly (the increase is due to a small upward trend in rural areas).

The surge in inflation (78 percent) and in the number of people below the poverty line (over 40 percent) would have been enough to increase the incidence of poverty in 1998, even with rising nominal income and consumption. In terms of wage income, nominal wages increased by 17 percent during 1997–1998, but real wages in both tradable and nontradable sectors plummeted by 34 percent. The largest drop occurred in the manufacturing sector (over 38 percent: see figure 6.20). Along with the fact that the change in employment remained positive even after the crisis (employment grew by 2.7 percent during 1997–1998) and that the unemployment rate increased by "only" less than 1 percentage point (around 0.8 percent according to the Labor Force Survey), this suggests that there has been a fairly high degree of flexibility in labor markets. This was not entirely expected by most observers, given the country's stage of development and industrialization.[40]

In terms of consumption, the growth in the nominal consumption of the lowest two quintiles was as high as 115 to 120 percent, but in real terms it dropped to 6 to 9 percent. The increase in the nominal consumption of the middle- and upper-income groups

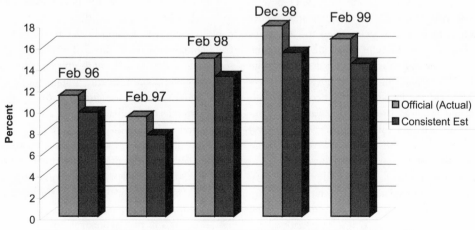

Notes: 1996 & 1999: CBS, Susenas; 1997 & Feb. 1998: Gardiner, Susenas Core; Dec. 1998: CBS, Mini Susenas

FIGURE 6.19 From Pre- to Post-crisis Poverty: Indonesia

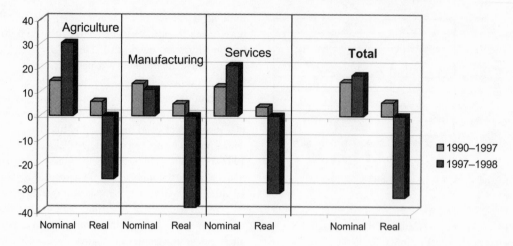

FIGURE 6.20 Annual Growth of Nominal and Real Wages

(the remaining three quintiles) was lower, ranging from 102 to 110 percent, and their real consumption also declined more sharply, that is, between 11 and 14 percent. In turn, the real consumption of the top quintile fell by an impressive 24 percent. This prompted the well-known conclusion that the hardest-hit group during the crisis was the country's urban middle class, most of whom are on the main island of Java (Azis 2000).

This is also consistent with the finding that, although all Foster-Greer-Thorbecke (FGT) poverty indicators (particularly P_2) were significantly higher in rural than in urban areas, these indicators increased significantly more in urban areas during the crisis.[41] The amount of resources needed to alleviate poverty, as estimated through the poverty gap measure P_1, would also be larger. This is consistent with the greater downward trend of real wages in essentially urban activities (manufacturing and services) compared with agriculture, as observed in figure 6.20, and the trend of reverse migration.

As already indicated in the earlier discussions, another important explanation for a rather sharp increase in poverty is the growing concentration of the population whose income is just marginally above the poverty line (the "near poor"). The fall in public expenditures (see figure 6.1), forced by the IMF at the early stage of the crisis, did not help either, even

after the government's new programs designed to help the poor were subsequently introduced (too little and rather too late).

But, as most analysts agree, things could have been much worse. It is clear that an important "built-in stabilizer" is the flexibility of labor markets, without which the poverty and unemployment story could have been worse. An important manifestation of labor mobility is the change in population size in rural and urban areas (reverse migration) during 1996–1999. The number of people in the urban areas (the last three categories in table 6.6) declined by more than 6 million between 1998 and 1999. On the other hand, the population size of the first two rural groups (*agricultural workers* and *small farmers*), which happen to be the poorest income groups, increased by 12 million. Even after the natural growth is accounted for, this trend suggests that there was a fairly massive urban-rural migration during this period.[42]

During the crisis, real wages in the rural non-farm sector declined less than wages in urban activities. This factor, combined with the reverse migration, partially mitigated the potential unemployment consequences of a 14 percent drop in real GDP in 1998. Based on the national labor force survey (Sakernas) data, the increase in unemployment was only less than 1 percentage point, much lower than the increase in Thailand and Korea, that is, from 2.3

TABLE 6.6 Number of Households and Populations, 1995–1999

	1995		1998		1999	
Household Category	# Household	# Pop	# Household	# Pop	# Household	# Pop
1. Agricultural Workers	5,064,667	20,794,316	5,893,304	24,196,504	7,099,082	30,608,337
2. Small Farmers (land < 0,5 ha	8,024,174	32,990,982	8,358,655	34,366,184	10,097,924	40,009,288
3. Medium Farmers (land 0,501–1 ha)	3,076,379	13,796,229	3,204,615	14,371,313	2,915,904	13,694,954
4. Large Farmers (land > 1 ha	2,190,677	10,697,076	2,281,994	11,142,975	2,379,946	10,618,552
5. Rural Low (non Farm)	6,843,656	28,701,887	7,180,472	30,114,475	7,309,818	29,933,080
6. Non Labor Force (Rural)	2,795,633	9,097,513	2,933,223	9,545,255	3,051,457	9,877,266
7. Rural High (non Farm)	3,263,466	15,267,947	2,909,464	13,611,768	3,201,555	13,805,324
8. Low Urban	7,708,983	33,835,022	8,418,047	36,947,134	7,386,730	30,856,354
9. Non Labor Force (Urban)	2,660,015	10,197,213	2,904,680	11,135,142	4,130,884	10,131,141
10. Urban High	4,025,435	19,376,621	3,623,575	17,442,250	2,930,900	17,902,804
Total	45,653,084	194,754,808	47,708,029	202,873,000	50,504,200	207,437,100

Source: Central Bureau of Statistics (CBS n.d.), based on SAM tables.

to 4.8 percent, and from 2.6 to 6.8 percent, respectively (World Bank 2000).[43]

The decline in the farm sector's real wages was largely the result of the excess supply of labor induced by urban-rural migration. It is revealing that owing to the agricultural sector's role in absorbing these reverse migrants, even during the crisis, the employment rate continued to increase, albeit at a slower pace.

While the relative income distribution between urban and rural areas could potentially improve (because of the greater impact of the crisis on urban areas), the high interest rate policy and the continued depreciation of the rupiah disrupted the process by generating a windfall to large (mostly urban) savers. Hence, distribution worsened. When a slow recovery began in 1999, albeit a premature one, the more

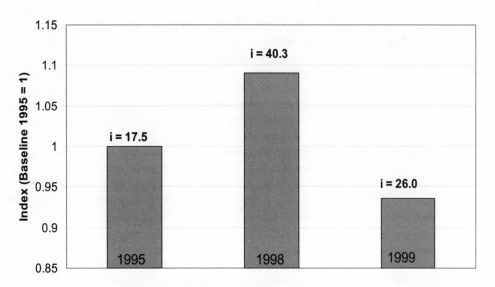

FIGURE 6.21 Gini Index (SAM Data) and 3-Mo Deposit Rate

devastating effects on the urban middle class started to set in and relative income distribution improved.

As revealed in figure 6.21, there is a close correlation between a worsening (improving) trend in income distribution and an increasing (lowering) interest rate (the latter is indicated by i on top of each bar in figure 6.21). Surely, the interest incomes and the windfall from foreign asset holdings (e.g., time deposit in foreign currency) in an environment of super-high interest rates and the severe collapse of the exchange rate have contributed to such a relation.

5. Conclusion

As was often the case with other countries, Indonesia's trade liberalization was not a stand-alone package. It was promulgated along with other policies such as those in the monetary, investment, banking, and exchange rate areas. An export- (trade-) biased policy and other types of external liberalization had significant effects on the monetary and financial sector. As shown in this paper, these links are intricately connected, suggesting that whatever benefits a particular liberalization policy provides, there are costs that must be incurred (e.g., unmet inflation targets, rising current account deficits and debts, and high interest rates).

The strong growth following the liberalization policy led to a classical overheating toward the end of the 1980s. While more liberalization and strong growth continued in the 1990s, capital inflows surged.

However, no dramatic changes in the labor market are observed. Real wages, along with the wage and employment ratio of skilled to unskilled workers, tradables to non-tradables, urban to rural, and formal to informal sectors, have all increased, but at a rate much less than what has been experienced by other East Asian countries. Open unemployment also rose since the mid-1980s. The increase in real wages was more or less commensurate with productivity growth, the largest of which was in the manufacturing and services sector. The distinctive feature of the post-liberalization period was that the agricultural sector ceased to be the major absorber (its labor-absorbing role returned during the crisis). Institutional changes, for example, minimum wage law and labor regulations, also emerged, albeit with limited effects on the labor market.

The resulting change in income distribution indicated a slight (albeit insignificant) worsening. The number of poor continued to fall, stimulated by a number of factors, ranging from the government's emphasis on education and health, its pricing policy for basic consumption goods, massive investment in infrastructure and agricultural technologies, and a fairly successful family planning program. In addition, the country's flexible labor markets also helped mitigate the unemployment and poverty problems. Therefore, one cannot really conclude that the improved social conditions were due to liberalization policy. Other policies played an important role.

The sequence of liberalization—that is, from current account to capital account—brought about a bad combination of widening deficits and high interest rates. Yet massive inflows of capital put pressures on the currency to appreciate. Credit lending also surged, contributing to high investment—and high imports as well—and strong growth. Seemingly, these developments resembled a classical trend prior to a crisis. But looking at the numbers more carefully, and comparing them with those in other crisis countries (e.g., Latin America in the 1980s and Mexico in 1994–1995), one cannot dismiss the fact that Indonesia's macroeconomic fundamentals prior to the 1997 crisis were relatively sound.

While the real cause of the crisis remains debatable, it is fairly clear that the mismatch between private foreign (primarily short-term) debt maturity and the country's capacity to repay (measured by the size of foreign reserves) holds the key to the story. It is argued in the paper that in a more liberalized system, bank deposits, currency mismatch, and short-term foreign debts are important indicators of financial fragility and require monitoring.

When the GDP growth dropped to minus 14 percent in 1998, and the exchange rate continued to collapse, despite the high interest rate policy, the shock had a devastating impact on poverty. A dramatic surge in inflation—and hence the poverty line—and a decline in real wages across all sectors caused the poverty headcount to double. Rather surprisingly, the increase in unemployment was relatively small. The relatively flexible labor market is one of the important reasons. The high interest rate policy and the continued depreciation of the rupiah created a windfall for large (mostly urban) savers, worsening income distribution. Only when a sign of recovery became apparent in 1999 did the relative income distribution improve.

Notes

1. To some extent, this is similar to the situation in Korea, where a few large industrial groups, the *chaebols*, dominate the industrial as well as the financial sector.

2. Actually, the phenomenon of capital outflows was detected in late 1989, but it became widespread in 1990.

3. See Manning (2000). The format of table 6.3 follows Berg and Taylor (2000).

4. Based on the Gini index, urban income distribution began to worsen in 1990. Rural distribution began worsening in 1993 (see Booth 2000). The impact of liberalization and structural adjustment on Indonesia's income distribution is analyzed in detail in Thorbecke et al. (1992) and Azis (1999a).

5. Using the CPI as the price index, the trade weights are the following: 37 percent for Japan, 25 percent for European countries, 13 percent for the United States, 12 percent for ASEAN countries, 7 percent for North Asia, and 2 percent each for China, Canada, and Australia. With such a high weight for Japan, movements in the dollar-yen rate would automatically translate into the real effective depreciation of the rupiah.

6. Policy changes were basically in tariff reduction, divestment and ownership requirement, and the reduction of sectoral restriction, and less so in the legal and tax system. While the importance of foreign investment in national development has been fully recognized, increased competition—primarily from China, Vietnam, and neighboring ASEAN countries—became an important factor prompting those policy changes. International pressures, for example, the formation of the ASEAN Free Trade Area (AFTA), also played a significant role (for further details, see Azis 1998).

7. Policy changes in some ANIEs were not negligible. For example, in 1986, the Korean government set up two important agencies: the Promotion Agency for Small Scale Companies and the foreign investment consulting centers for firms planning to invest in Southeast Asian countries. The establishment of the Export-Import Bank in 1987 was another important development. Strong push factors were also detected in Taiwan. The abolition of foreign exchange controls in August 1986 had promoted outflows of Taiwanese investments to various countries including Indonesia. Prior to that, the foreign exchange controls imposed by the government prevented Taiwanese investors from investing openly in other countries (Thee 1991). In addition, the number of trade and investment missions sent by Taiwan and Korea to Southeast Asian countries increased considerably during this period.

8. Many objectives were behind the December 1987 package. Pressures to further open up the economy in order to compete with neighboring countries were imminent. There was also a need to expand capital markets, to maximize foreign exchange earnings in the face of mounting debt services, and to safeguard income inequality, both between income groups (small- versus large-scale businesses) and between regions (western versus eastern region). Concern about income disparity was reflected in the new DSP list, in which small-scale industries remained closed to foreign investment.

9. After ten and fifteen years the phase-down requirements should be met, that is, 20 and 51 percent respectively.

10. There were other important signs of relaxed restrictions in the package. For example, foreign investors were allowed to diversify up to 30 percent of their existing capacity without requiring a new license; this will give them the opportunity to operate under a broad-banding situation. A more precise guideline was provided through the use of ISIC in the product definition. To help domestic investors secure additional funds and acquire foreign investment status, foreign investors can reinvest their profits in new or existing domestic companies. Soon after the 1987 package was announced, approved foreign investment figures increased dramatically.

11. It is very difficult to obtain accurate data in order to split the components of swap transactions into those that reflect foreign exchange sales and repurchases for protection against devaluation risk and those that are due to foreign (private) borrowing.

12. It turns out that the determining component is the provision of *subsidized export credits*, which amounted to Rp5 trillion in 1991 (see table 6.2). These subsidized credits were provided by the central bank to finance export transactions. Since their nature is similar to standard bank lending, except that they were issued in foreign currency (directly related to export activities), export credits added to money supply and were recorded under NFA. This type of subsidized credit distorted market resource allocations and also tended to reduce the effectiveness of the TMP.

13. SBPU (Surat Berharga Pasar Uang) is BI's promissory note. It is important to note that their purchase by the state was the second shock measure. The first, known as "Sumarlin shock," was promulgated in 1987. In that measure, a strong liquidity squeeze was imposed by repurchasing SBPUs before maturity and forcing a number of SOEs to purchase SBIs.

14. Through the system, BI buys foreign currencies at the spot rate, and sells them through a contract at a specified future point in time using the then-current spot exchange rate, with some margin. Since the inception of this mechanism, the swap margin has been raised several times, primarily to counter short-term speculative movements that are likely to occur during periods of high interest rates (wider interest rate differential). From

the original 2.5 percent per annum with the maturity ranging from thirty to eighty days, the swap margin settled at 9 percent in 1987. Obviously there is a risk of BI's financial loss if the interest rate differential falls. However, rather than making an announcement about the swap margin several times, in 1988 the government finally decided to follow "the market" by adopting the covered interest parity condition.

15. The spot operation was the result of foreign exchange purchases from BI by commercial banks.

16. Despite a declining trend in the interest rate of the SBI, many commercial banks preferred to hold SBI, primarily because of the enforcement of loan equity ratios and other prudential regulations.

17. The SBI rate was 13 percent, to be paid by BI as a "borrower," whereas the received rate from export credit was only roughly 3 percent (with BI as a "lender").

18. As expected, a stream of capital outflows was detected, in part because of lower interest rates but largely also because of the scandal involving one of the largest state-owned banks, BAPINDO.

19. The "cost" of such a move, however, was unexpectedly very high: a significant reduction in the number of economic technocrats in the new (1993–1994 to 1997–1998) cabinet.

20. Actually, September 1992 marked the beginning of the band-widening policy.

21. Later, BI also announced the use of two, not one, exchange rates: the conversion rate (CR) and the intervention rate (IR). The latter refers to the rate at which banks can purchase and sell rupiah for dollar, but only when interbank exchange rates reach the upper band of IR can they buy, and only at the lower band of IR can they sell.

22. In terms of BI's flexibility to set the interest rate, when the market exchange rate is in the middle of the band, short- and medium-term interest rates may be adjusted by only 1–2 percentage points above or below world interest rates.

23. The World Bank's figure is even higher, close to US$11 billion, or more than 5 percent of GDP.

24. A case in point was the experience during the first two weeks in June 1996. In that period alone, three interventions, involving some US$800 million, had to be conducted by BI. Unless sterilized, that would mean an inducement of a fresh rupiah supply in the market. Yet, the growth of money supply was already way beyond the 17–20 percent target, that is, 30.8 percent in May and 29.8 percent in June. As a result, there was high liquidity in the economy. Another liquidity injection came from US$1.2 billion worth of IPOs and rights issues in the stock market at the time.

25. "Increasing the spread" means shifting the risk to the market, such that BI will "purify" its role as a lender of last resort. The number of interventions needed in the forex market could also be reduced. The less frequently the BI has to intervene, the fewer rupiah should be pumped into the market, avoiding serious inflationary consequences.

26. Faced with near-zero returns at home, Japanese investors have poured money into overseas markets, particularly the so-called emerging markets, including Indonesia.

27. An interesting NBER study by Chinn and Michael Dooley (1995) indicates that, of the ten Asia-Pacific countries under study, only Indonesia and Malaysia show an inverse relation between capital flows and bank lending. The authors then contend that Indonesia and Malaysia sterilized capital inflows on a large scale. In other words, in response to capital inflows, some of the decline in bank credit was manifested as a reduction in private sector lending.

28. In the words of then–finance minister Mar'ie Muhammad, "We will maintain our exchange rate policy so that it is as realistic as possible. But personally I prefer the rupiah to be undervalued rather than overvalued in order to support Indonesian exports."

29. Note that the fluctuations apparent in figures 6.2 and 6.3 are largely due to quarterly-based data.

30. I wish to thank Per Gunnar Berglund for his help in doing the decomposition.

31. The historical trend of FDI and its impact on distribution is discussed in Azis (1998).

32. The high dependence of many exporting sectors on imported capital goods and raw materials reinforces the trend of widening current account deficits.

33. External factors also cannot be dismissed. As argued by Mundell (2000), "The appreciation of the dollar against the yen between 1995 and 1998, following the devaluation of the renmimbi, is to blame for the so-called Asian crisis."

34. In the aftermath of the Asian crisis, the ratio of short-term external debt to reserves has become the IMF's basic indicator of reserve adequacy. In Stanley Fischer's words, "the ratio of short-term external debt to reserves is the single best crisis indicator" (Fischer 2001).

35. While the crisis episodes in Latin America were often characterized by inappropriate government policies (weak fundamentals), Asian countries were inferior in terms of international illiquidity (e.g., in mid-1997, the STD/forex ratios were recorded at 170, 206, and 145 percent in Indonesia, Korea, and Thailand, respectively, compared with 120 percent in Mexico and less than 100 percent in Brazil, Peru, Colombia, and Chile).

36. The increasing trend in private foreign debts was a regional phenomenon. Thanks to widespread optimism about East Asia's future growth and the celebrated label of the "East Asian Miracle," many private investors—local and foreign alike—were poised to expand their activities throughout the region. This was the

second wave of foreign capital flows into ASEAN, coming mostly from the United States, Europe, and Japan (the first wave occurred during the second half of the 1980s, when Japanese FDI in the region surged, following the Yendaka phenomenon). The relatively high domestic interest rates failed to dampen investment growth, since foreign loans could be obtained easily at a relatively low rate. Furthermore, stable pegged exchange rates were perceived as a guarantee for earning stability. The label "miracle" swayed lenders and the international financial community, leading them to lend recklessly. The fast-growing number of banks and multifinance corporations, following the 1988 deregulation, also produced considerable effects. Many big companies set up new banks primarily to serve their own often-risky projects. Despite the regulatory measures formally imposed by the monetary authorities (e.g., legal lending limits and capital adequacy ratios), weak enforcement discouraged the development of a healthy financial sector.

37. In classifying the sources of Indonesia's vulnerabilities, Summers (2000) assigned a value of 1 (meaning "very serious") for short-term foreign indebtedness, along with the problem of general governance and banking weaknesses.

38. For detailed mechanisms of the transmissions from financial shock to real sector recession, see Azis (2001, 2002).

39. I do not include the methodologically consistent estimates in figure 6.6. It is important to note that while the welfare-consistent estimates may be preferred because the price index share being used represents the actual consumption pattern of (some of) the poor, as argued by Suryahadi et al. (2000), the fact that it ignores the substitution effects tends to result in an overestimation of poverty incidence.

40. The positive growth of employment is almost entirely due to the increase of employment in agricultural sector. For all other sectors, the employment has actually declined.

41. FGT is a poverty measure that can be used to estimate not only the incidence of poverty but also the severity of poverty (see Foster, Greer, and Thorbecke 1984). Incidentally, because of its advantageous features, FGT has been adopted as the standard poverty measure in a developing country like Mexico, as stipulated in Chapter V, Article 34, of the Mexican Constitution.

42. Most observers failed to notice this migration trend primarily because their post-crisis analyses were based on 1998 data, which, as indicated above, did not seem to show the presence of massive urban-rural migration. It is noteworthy that prior to the crisis, the rural-urban migration was affected more by perceived employment opportunity rather than by wage differential (Azis 1997b).

43. While the economy has not really fully recovered, beginning in 1999 the government vigorously pursued a minimum wage policy that could change (increase more significantly) the unemployment rate. During the last two years, the average wages have been very close to the minimum wage. Yet, the elasticity of total employment to minimum wage is roughly –0.11, suggesting that the already high unemployment rate could rise further with the continued increase in the minimum wage. Worse, the unskilled and less educated workers tend to be the first to go. Clearly, vigorous minimum wage policy implemented during difficult times tends to raise unemployment, forcing many into the informal sector. Such a policy is far from being helpful in reducing poverty.

References

Aghion, P., P. Bacchetta, and A. Banerjee. 1999. A simple model of monetary policy and currency crises. Mimeo.

Azis, Iwan J. 1992. Export performance and the employment effect. In *The future of Asia-Pacific economies: Emerging role of Asian NIEs and ASEAN*, edited by F. C. Lo and N. Akrasane. APDC: Allied Publishers Limited.

———. 1998. The impact of foreign investment in Indonesia: Historical trends and simulation analysis. In *Economic development and cooperation in the Pacific Basin: Trade, investment, and environment issues*, edited by H. Lee and D. Roland-Holst. Cambridge: Cambridge University Press.

———. 1999a. Exchange rate, capital flows and reform sequencing in Indonesia: Policy trend and CGE model application. In *Macroeconomic policy and the exchange rate*, edited by Julio de Brun and Rolf Lüders. San Francisco: International Center for Economic Growth (ICEG).

———. 1999b. Do we know the real causes of the Asian crisis? In *Global financial turmoil and reform: A United Nations perspective*, edited by Barry Herman. Tokyo, New York, Paris: United Nations University Press.

———. 2000. Simulating economy-wide models to capture the transition from financial crisis to social crisis. *The Annals of Regional Science* 34:1–28.

———. 2001. Modeling crisis evolution and counterfactual policy simulations: A country case study. ADB Institute Working Paper, no. 23. Tokyo: ADB Institute.

———. 2002. What would have happened in Indonesia if different economic policies had been implemented when the crisis started?" In *The Asian Economic Papers*, vol. 2. Cambridge, Mass.: MIT Press.

Berg, Janine, and Lance Taylor. 2000. External liberalization, economic performance, and social policy. CEPA Working Paper, no. 12, February. New York: Center for Economic Policy Analysis, New School University.

Bernanke, B., and M. Gertler. 1989. Agency costs, net worth, and economic fluctuations. *American Economic Review* 79:14–31.

Booth, Anne. 2000. Poverty and inequality in the Soeharto era: An assessment. *Bulletin of Indonesian Economic Studies* 36 (1).

Central Bureau of Statistics (CBS). 1998. *Survey on crisis impacts on cost of production and informal sector*. Jakarta: CBS.

———. n.d. *SUSENAS*, various volumes. Jakarta: CBS.

Chinn, Menzie D. 1998. Before the fall: Were East Asian currencies overvalued? NBER Working Paper no. W6491, April. Cambridge, Mass.: NBER.

Chinn, W., and Michael Dooley. 1995. Asia Pacific capital markets: Integration and implications for economic activity. NBER Working Paper 5280, September. Cambridge, Mass.: NBER.

Corden, M. 1999. *The Asian Crisis: Is there a way out?* Singapore: Institute of Southeast Asian Studies.

Eatwell, J., and Lance Taylor. 2000. *Global finance at risk: The case for international regulation*. New York: The New Press.

Fischer, Stanley. 2001. Asia and the IMF. Speech made at the Institute for Policy Studies, Singapore, June 1.

Foster, J., J. Greer, and E. Thorbecke. 1984. A class of decomposable poverty measures. *Econometrica* 52.

Hill, Hal. 1996. *The Indonesian economy since 1996*. Cambridge: Cambridge University Press.

Kamin, Steven B. 1997. A multi-country comparison of the linkages between inflation and exchange rate competitiveness. BIS Working Paper, no. 45. Basel: Bank for International Settlements.

Khan, M. S., and R. Zahler. 1989. Macroeconomic effects of changes in barriers to trade and capital flows: A simulation analysis. Washington D.C.: IMF.

Krugman, P. 1999a. Recovery? Don't bet on it. *Asia Magazine* (June).

———. 1999b. Analytical afterthoughts on the Asian crisis. Mimeo. Cambridge, Mass.: MIT.

Manning, Chris. 2000. Labor market adjustment to Indonesia's economic crisis: Context, trends and implications. *Bulletin of Indonesian Economic Studies* 36 (1).

McKibbin, Warwick, and Andrew Stoeckel. 1999. East Asia's response to the crisis: A quantitative analysis. Paper for ASEM Regional Economist's Workshop, Denpasar, September 15–17.

Mundell, Robert A. 2000. Exchange rates, currency areas and the international financial architecture. Remarks delivered at an IMF panel, September 22, Prague.

Ocampo, J. Antonio, and Lance Taylor. 1998. Trade liberalization in developing economies: Modest benefits, but problems with productivity growth, macro prices, and income distribution. CEPA Working Paper, no. 8, March. New York: Center for Economic Policy Analysis, New School University.

Pangestu, Mari. 1991. Managing economic policy reforms in Indonesia. In *Authority and Academic Scribblers: The Role of Research in East Asian Policy Reform*, edited by S. Ostry, 93–120. San Francisco: International Center for Economic Growth.

Pitt, Mark. 1991. Indonesia. In *Liberalizing Foreign Trade*, vol. 5, edited by D. Papageorgiou et al. Cambridge, Mass.: Basil Blackwell.

Summers, Lawrence H. 2000. International financial crises: Causes, prevention, and cures. *American Economic Review* 90 (2).

Suryahadi, A., S. Sumarto., Y. Suharso., and Lan Pritchett. 2000. The evolution of poverty during the crisis in Indonesia, 1996 to 1999. SMERU Working Paper. Jakarta: SMERU.

Thorbecke, Erik, et al. 1992. *Adjustment and equity in Indonesia*. Paris: OECD, Development Centre Studies.

World Bank. 2000. *East Asia brief: East Asia's recovery, gathering force*. East Asia and Pacific Region, World Bank, presented in Tokyo, September 18.

7

The Long and Winding Road to Liberalization: The South Korean Experience

Jong-Il You

South Korea (Korea, hereafter), one of the poorest countries in the world in the early 1960s, became a member of the OECD in 1996. Its average per capita income was comparable to that of Mozambique and Ghana in the early 1960s, but by 1996 it was greater than $10,000. This miraculous growth entailed a thorough societal transformation, not to mention changes in the industrial structure, technology, and employment patterns. Various quality of life indicators such as life expectancy, educational attainment, and political freedom also exhibited dramatic improvements. On top of this, Korea's income distribution remained relatively egalitarian.

This rosy picture changed abruptly toward the end of 1997 when the currency crisis forced the Korean government to resort to IMF rescue financing. The crisis came as a rude awakening. There have been debates on what exactly went wrong. On the surface, it seems obvious that financial liberalization, particularly the opening of the capital account, created vulnerabilities in the economy. Without disputing

this, I argue that there was also an underlying crisis of accumulation that helped convert the currency and liquidity crisis into a full-blown financial and economic crisis.

Korea has been pursuing economic liberalization, with varying emphases and speeds, for the last two decades since the early 1980s. It was hoped that the liberalization policy would cure the economic ills of the government-led rapid industrialization program. However, Korea has been less successful in liberalizing than in industrializing. The gradual and cautious approach to liberalization of the 1980s failed to arrest the development of an accumulation crisis, while the more rapid liberalization policy of the 1990s resulted in a severe economic crisis. Further liberalization and other reforms that have been implemented since the crisis have yet to forge a coherent and dynamic model of development.

This chapter reviews Korea's experience with economic liberalization since the early 1980s. Section 1 provides a brief history of the economic liberalization policy in the broader context of the rise and fall of the Korean model of development. Section 2 analyzes the major economic consequences of the liberalization policy, including its impact on growth and distribution, the currency crisis, and the financial crisis. Section 3 examines the macroeconomic adjustments since the crisis, including the impact on the labor market and income distribution. Section 4 reviews the economic and social policy reforms that the government has pursued since the crisis. Finally, the concluding section draws some lessons on liberalization policy from the Korean experience.

1. The Korean Model and Liberalization

1.1. The Emergence of the Korean Model of Development

The challenges of modern economic development require substantial institution building that only the state can provide. Particularly, at the early stages of development when the entrepreneurial class is underdeveloped, the state can play a pivotal role in mobilizing resources and coordinating expectations. In Korea, a developmental state emerged in the 1960s and a historically unprecedented growth miracle followed.

The economic and political chaos that followed the liberation from the Japanese colonial rule and the Korean War did not provide Korea with favorable conditions for development. Despite enormous aid inflow from the United States, the economy under the Rhee regime failed to show much progress other than some import-substitution industrialization in light industries and the implementation of compulsory primary education. Rampant cronyism, extremely distorted prices, high unemployment, and persistent poverty characterized the economy. This was the backdrop to the military coup led by General Park in 1961. The military junta set out to lead the country out of poverty with its own brand of "guided capitalism." While its initial predisposition toward populist policies was checked by U.S. demands for stabilization, exchange rate reform, and interest rate policies, it never wavered from its commitment to government-led industrialization.

The government provided the vision of economic development around which private investments were organized. By such direct coordination of investment,

the government initiated every major diversification into new branches of industry in the 1960s and the 1970s:

> The state masterminded the early import-substitution projects in cement, fertilizers, oil refining, and synthetic fibers, the last greatly improving the profitability of the overextended textiles industry. The government also kept alive some unprofitable factories... that eventually provided key personnel to the modern general machinery and shipbuilding industries, which the state also promoted. The transformation from light to heavy industry came at the state's behest, in the form of an integrated iron and steel mill.... [The government] was responsible for the Big Push into heavy machinery and chemicals in the late 1970s. (Amsden 1989, 80–81)

In order to realize its ambitious investment and industrial upgrading plans, the government employed various methods of resource mobilization. Having unsuccessfully tried a currency reform to mobilize hidden funds, the Park government resorted to more conventional measures such as raising the deposit rate at the urging of its U.S. advisors. It also used unconventional methods. First, it pursued a policy of consumption restriction, including severe restrictions on the imports of consumer goods, luxury consumption taxes, and even frequent state-sponsored campaigns against "unnecessary consumption." Indirectly, the policy of labor repression to contain wage hikes and various measures to raise profits served a similar purpose (You 1998). Second, the government maintained tight controls on capital flows and foreign exchange in order to prevent leakages of domestic savings to foreign countries. Third, it decided to complement domestic savings with massive amounts of foreign savings. Since Korean firms did not have access to the international capital market, the government stepped in by allowing state-owned banks to extend guarantees on private sector foreign borrowing.

The Korean government maintained tight control over the allocation of financial resources in order to make sure that investment activities would take place according to its own priorities and plans. This was possible because of three important factors. First, the government had a firm control over domestic finance after nationalizing the commercial banks in 1961.[1] Second, the government controlled the use of foreign savings by requiring all foreign loans to be authorized by it. Third, the government could control the direction of industrial development by maintaining tight regulations on FDI. Had foreign multinational companies had a big presence in Korea, it would not have been easy for the government to conduct its industrial policy.

While the Korean government projected its own development vision, planned investments, and raised and allocated financial resources, it generally refrained from establishing state-owned enterprises except in a few crucial cases such as the POSCO steel company. Instead, it encouraged the private sector to follow its lead and make profits along the way. In this process, large *chaebol* groups with proven track records became favored partners in the government-led development scheme. With their explosive growth fueled by state subsidies, *chaebol* firms began to dominate the industrial scene in Korea.

1.2. The Shifting Balance between the State and the Market

Interventionist policies often create huge distortions and even promote rampant rent-seeking activities. This was indeed the case under the Rhee government in the 1950s. The policy shift toward liberalization in the early 1960s, including the currency devaluation, the unification of the exchange rate, trade liberalization, and raising the interest rates, helped reduce the enormous distortions in the economy and generated rapid export growth. However, the extent of liberalization was rather limited, and the government control of investment was strengthened in the 1970s when it undertook the "Big Push" toward heavy and chemical industrialization.

Prominent features of the Korean model of development—state intervention, developmental banking, the prominence of big business, industrialization policy, and authoritarian politics—are quite typical of late industrialization in many developing countries. What put Korea apart from the less successful countries was the immense effectiveness with which these instruments were used to accelerate capital accumulation and carry out development plans. The debate on the sources of this effectiveness has focused on the discipline of the state, pointing to the use of performance standards (Amsden 1989) by a neutral and competent bureaucracy (World Bank 1993). Some have also noted that the discipline of the state was facilitated by initial structural conditions such as the

relatively egalitarian income distribution (Rodrik 1995) and the absence of a dominant social class (You 1995; Aoki, Murdock, and Okuno-Fujiwara 1997).

Performance standards contributed to maintaining bureaucratic discipline in spite of the state-controlled allocation of financial resources that inherently bore the risk of breeding moral hazard problems and corruption.[2] In particular, the choice of export market performance as the standard served to promote exports. It was also a relatively objective and transparent performance criterion and forced subsidized firms to compete vigorously in world markets rather than to relax in the protected domestic markets.

However, maintaining high-quality bureaucratic discipline in the context of a government-led investment drive proved difficult. The general bailout of corporations with the August 3rd Emergency Decree sent the wrong signal to businesses. The further decay of bureaucratic discipline was a result of the Heavy Chemical and Industrial Drive. Having encouraged or even forced some businessmen to enter into high-priority sectors, it was difficult for the government to back off when they faced adverse business conditions.[3] The restructuring and bailout operations of the HCI firms in the early 1980s (following the economic crisis of 1979–1980) reinforced the implicit government guarantees to firms cooperating with the government (Cho and Kim 1997). Furthermore, top *chaebol* groups became "too big to fail" in the sense that the negative fallout in the event of their bankruptcy would be too devastating to the economy. Moral hazard in lending was exacerbated, and the erosion of bureaucratic discipline accelerated as political connections became increasingly important in lending decisions.[4]

A growing awareness of these problems concurrent with severe macroeconomic imbalances that developed in the late 1970s[5] led to a stabilization-cum-liberalization program in the early 1980s. Trade liberalization was pursued as part of a disinflation policy package. The government also started a program of financial liberalization in an attempt to introduce greater reliance on market forces in the allocation of financial resources.

1.3. The Dangers of Financial Liberalization: The 1980s Experience

It is conventional wisdom that the sequence of liberalization should run from trade liberalization to domestic financial liberalization and eventually to capital account liberalization. Korea followed such a sequence since the 1980s. Korea's experience shows, however, that following the correct sequence by no means guarantees success.

Trade liberalization that began in the early 1980s was not a drastic one-shot occurrence but a gradual multistage process. The strategic protection of selected industries such as agriculture and automobiles continued. One estimate of the degree of import liberalization incorporating both tariff protection and quantitative restrictions indicates that it steadily rose from about 66 percent in 1980 to about 88 percent in 1990 (Kim 1994). It is commonly argued, however, that the actual effects of liberalization were less than these numbers indicate owing to various nontransparent regulations.

In the 1980s the government also began to liberalize the tightly controlled financial system. The announcement of the financial liberalization plan in 1980 was followed by its gradual implementation. Important measures included the privatization of commercial banks, permitting the entry of new commercial banks and non-bank financial institutions (NBFIs), the partial deregulation of interest rates, and a gradual opening of the financial market. However, financial liberalization measures were taken in such a piecemeal and gradual fashion that government controls over commercial banks remained firm (Amsden and Euh 1990).[6] The meaningful opening of the financial market and the liberalization of capital flows had to wait until the 1990s.

Nonetheless, the financial liberalization of the 1980s produced an important change in the financial structure—that is, an explosive growth of NBFIs such as securities companies, insurance companies, and investment trust companies. While commercial banks were still effectively under government control, the NBFIs benefited from liberalization by offering higher interest rates and thereby attracting deposits away from banks. The NBFIs accounted for 29.1 percent of total deposits and 36.7 percent of total loans in 1980. By 1995, they accounted for 72.2 percent of total deposits and 63.5 percent of total loans. This meant that the allocation of financial resources was increasingly beyond the control of the government. Instead, financial resources came increasingly under the control of the *chaebol* groups that owned the NBFIs.[7]

Financial liberalization sought to replace the increasingly problematic bureaucratic discipline with market discipline.[8] What actually happened, however, was the weakening of bureaucratic discipline without the strengthening of market discipline. Mindful of the market power that *chaebol* groups possessed, the liberalization policy package of the 1980s included the legislation of fair competition law. Since then, regulatory measures to curb the concentration of economic power in the hands of the *chaebol* went through cycles of tightening and relaxation. However, the control of NBFIs bestowed upon *chaebol* groups independent power to raise financial resources without the approval of the government. This meant a fundamental change in the Korean model of development, with the government control of finance slipping into the hands of the *chaebol*.

1.4. Capital Account Liberalization in the 1990s

As a consequence of the financial liberalization of the 1980s, the probability of unscrupulous investment drives by *chaebol* groups increased. Checks on *chaebol* management by creditors and institutional investors were lacking, and government regulations were retreating. With the pace of liberalization gathering speed in the 1990s, the problem worsened.

In the 1990s the overriding theme of economic policy in Korea was "responding to globalization." Korea faced increasing pressures from its trading partners to open its markets in the early 1990s. The advent of the WTO regime and Korea's entrance into the OECD in the mid-1990s posed big challenges to the Korean economy. The course of action chosen by policy makers was to "accelerate liberalization and deregulation." First, trade liberalization proceeded to dismantle the last pockets of protected industries such as rice, financial services, retailing, and strategic manufacturing like automobiles. Second, industrial policy was wound down, with policy loans phased out and entry restrictions deregulated by the mid-1990s. Third, substantial financial liberalization measures were taken, including interest rate deregulation and the relaxation of entry barriers to financial activities. Finally and most importantly, capital account liberalization measures, mostly the deregulation of various forms of capital inflows, were taken (see You and Lee 2001).

These measures proved disastrous. With *chaebol* groups controlling most of the NBFIs, the intensification of competition with liberalization and deregulation did not necessarily result in enhanced market discipline. The corporate governance system of *chaebol* groups, the affiliates of which are interlinked through a nexus of cross-investment and cross-debt guarantees, imputed a bias toward overexpansion. With the dismantling of the regulations of the developmental state, the *chaebol* engaged in expansion and diversification races as exemplified by Samsung's entry into automobiles and Hyundai's entry into steel making. Capital account liberalization and the relaxation of entry barriers to the financial industry created much better access to financial resources for *chaebol* groups, and contributed to much greater risk in the financial system. Meanwhile, the government failed to apply prudential regulations and supervision that became all the more important as a result of liberalization. NBFIs were especially poorly supervised. In short, liberalization policies led to a rapid buildup of bad assets in the financial system and foreign debt in the country that culminated in the catastrophic exchange crisis of 1997.

Many have correctly argued that the foreign exchange and financial crisis was a result of mismanaged financial liberalization (Radelet and Sachs 1998; Chang, Park, and Yoo 1998). The problem was much more than some technical mistakes in implementing financial liberalization. The conception and execution of the whole series of liberalization policies were at fault. The champions of liberalization apparently failed to consider the importance of the distortions that could be caused by *chaebol*

power, especially their control of finance. They also failed to realize that a transition from bureaucratic to market discipline, and from a developmental to a liberal state, involves careful institution building as well as liberalization and the redesign of regulations rather than simple deregulation. Their most fatal mistake was, arguably, discounting the risks inherent in capital account liberalization.[9]

Liberalization in Korea took a radical step in the wake of the IMF bailout in December 1997. The IMF-mandated reforms included a full-fledged opening of the financial markets and the capital account. Inward foreign investment, both portfolio and direct, has been radically liberalized. The government implemented standard neoliberal policies such as labor market reforms, privatization, and deregulation with a zeal previously unseen in Korea.

2. The Economic Consequences of Liberalization

2.1. Growth and Distribution in the Liberalization Era

It is hard to detect if liberalization had any long-term effect on growth. Since liberalization began in the early 1980s, growth performance remained strong until the outbreak of the financial crisis in 1997. Figure 7.1 shows that the average growth rate in the

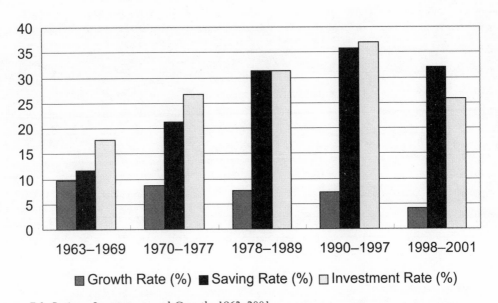

FIGURE 7.1 Savings, Investment, and Growth; 1963–2001

1980s and 1990s (before the financial crisis) was somewhat below that of the 1960s and 1970s, but this was a gradual and natural decline in the course of development. In fact, during the liberalization period, the growth rate never fell below 5 percent except in 1998 when the economy went into a free fall in the wake of the financial crisis. While there have been cyclical fluctuations, macroeconomic imbalances stayed within bounds and inflation remained modest until the financial crisis.

However, we cannot easily conclude that liberalization has had no effect on growth. First, it led to the catastrophic financial crisis of 1997–1998 that resulted in a substantial decline of growth (see figure 7.1). Even though growth recovered quickly during 1999–2000, there was a permanent loss of output, as clearly shown in figure 7.2. Second, it is possible that growth performance would have been worse without liberalization. In other words, liberalization may have improved microeconomic efficiency as its proponents claim. However, whatever such efficiency gains are likely to have been, they were offset by the inefficiencies stemming from *chaebol* dominance.

Proponents of capital account liberalization argue that it helps growth by inducing capital inflows and thereby augmenting financial resources for investment. The Korean experience does not lend support to this claim. As we can see from figure 7.1, it was

during the 1960s and 1970s, when capital flows were strictly controlled by the government, that Korea financed large gaps between investment and domestic savings with capital inflows. In the liberalization period, while the investment rate continued to rise, the savings rate rose sufficiently to reduce the gap to minimal levels. This observation applies not only to the 1980s but also to the 1990s, when there was serious capital account liberalization.

Prior to the 1990s, Korea managed its capital account in ways that supported the balance of payments, given the developments in the current account. In the first half of the 1980s, when the current account was chronically in deficit, the government used various liberalization measures in order to induce capital inflows and guided domestic banks to borrow from abroad. In the late 1980s, when the current account showed a large surplus, the government resorted to direct capital controls—for instance, banning commercial loans by domestic firms—in order to manage the external balance. However, in the 1990s, capital account liberalization was sought for its own sake in the context of the financial liberalization policy, and this led to a rapid increase in capital inflows, as we can see in table 7.1. Capital inflows amounted to only 2.8 percent of the GDP in 1993 when serious capital account liberalization started, but rose to 9.25 percent by 1996. However,

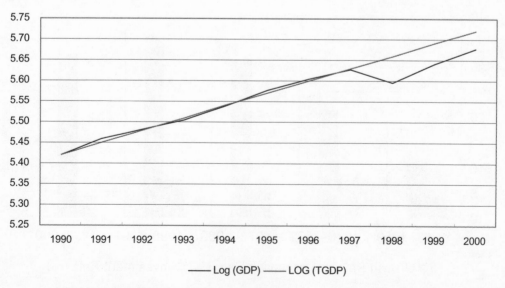

FIGURE 7.2 GDP and Trend GDP at 1995 Prices; 1990–2000

TABLE 7.1 Balance of Payments; 1981–2000

| | | Capital Account | | | | % Share of GDP |
Year	Current Account	Overall	Inflow	Outflow	Reserve Accumulation	Errors and Omissions
1981	−6.62	7.63	7.78	−0.15	−0.43	−0.59
1982	−3.43	5.29	6.70	−1.41	−0.12	−1.74
1983	−1.85	2.91	3.83	−0.93	0.09	−1.14
1984	−1.43	3.38	3.21	0.17	−0.97	−0.98
1985	−0.85	1.75	3.68	−1.93	0.04	−0.94
1986	4.38	−3.92	−2.05	−1.87	0.04	−0.50
1987	7.44	−7.67	−7.05	−0.62	−0.66	0.89
1988	8.02	−2.80	−1.18	−1.62	−4.90	−0.32
1989	2.43	−1.31	−0.13	−1.18	−1.45	0.32
1990	−0.79	1.02	2.58	−1.56	0.47	−0.69
1991	−2.82	2.17	3.57	−1.39	0.39	0.26
1992	−1.25	2.09	3.37	−1.28	−1.18	0.34
1993	0.29	0.79	2.80	−2.01	−0.87	−0.21
1994	−0.96	2.56	5.62	−3.06	−1.15	−0.44
1995	−1.74	3.43	7.58	−4.15	−1.44	−0.25
1996	−4.42	4.49	9.25	−4.76	−0.27	0.21
1997	−1.71	0.28	3.77	−3.49	2.50	−1.06
1998	12.71	−1.01	−1.17	0.03	−9.75	−1.95
1999	6.03	0.50	1.88	−1.37	−5.66	−0.87
2000	2.65	2.62	4.35	−1.73	−5.15	−0.13

Source: Bank of Korea

capital outflows increased as well, and the overall capital account balance registered surpluses that were less than those of the early 1980s.

The picture of income distribution in the liberalization period is similar to that of growth. There seems to have been no major impact on income distribution until the financial crisis. In terms of the functional distribution of income, the wage share exhibited no long-term trend since the 1980s. Household income distribution as well as wage distribution showed a modest improvement until the early 1990s, and then both stagnated (see You and Lee 2001). However, the financial crisis dramatically worsened income distribution. Figure 7.3, which compares the trends of labor productivity in manufacturing and the real wage rate, clearly shows a dramatic rise in the gap between the two after the crisis of 1997–1998.

2.2. Capital Account Liberalization and the Currency Crisis

The change in the policy stance toward the capital account brought about an important change in macroeconomic developments in Korea. Capital flows began to act as an independent external force that impinged upon other macroeconomic variables. First, capital flows became an important determinant of the exchange rate. The surge of capital inflows during 1993–1996 resulted in the real appreciation of the exchange rate. Real depreciation followed the reversal of capital flows in 1997 and 1998. The real exchange rate began to appreciate again in 1999 as capital inflows resumed. Second, capital account liberalization and the increase in capital inflows resulted in the expansion of consumption (a decline in the domestic savings rate) and domestic investment. Table 7.2 shows that, between 1993 and 1996, the gross domestic savings rate declined from 36.2 to 33.8 percent, while gross domestic investment increased from 35.4 percent of GDP to 38.1 percent.

However, the macroeconomic fundamentals remained relatively sound until just before the onset of the crisis. In fact, the most striking feature of the Korean currency crisis of 1997 is that it took place despite good macroeconomic fundamentals. It can be seen from table 7.2 that by any conventional macroeconomic indicator, the Korean economy was doing

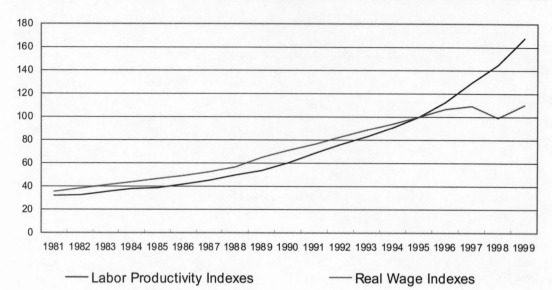

—— Labor Productivity Indexes   ——— Real Wage Indexes

FIGURE 7.3 Labor Productivity and Real Wage; 1981–1999

well until 1996. Growth was strong, though decelerating: inflation was modest at around 5 percent: and the unemployment rate was below 3 percent. The fiscal balance was showing a surplus. The only issue of concern was the large current account deficit but this was, to a large extent, the result of a severe adverse shock in the terms of trade, particularly the collapse of semiconductor prices. Moreover, the current account was rapidly improving in 1997: after recording a deficit of 7.4 percent of GDP in the first quarter, it was reduced to 2.7 percent in the second quarter and down to 2.1 percent in the third quarter before the exchange crisis erupted. There was a real appreciation of the exchange rate; however, its extent was rather modest, and correction started in early 1997. Table 7.2 also shows that domestic savings remained high and that there was no large-scale lending or investment boom in the years prior to the crisis. Deterioration in macroeconomic fundamentals, therefore, cannot be the reason for the currency crisis of 1997.

TABLE 7.2 Macroeconomic Fundamentals (Unit: %)

	1991	1992	1993	1994	1995	1996	1997	1998
Fiscal surplus[a]/GDP	−1.9	−0.7	0.3	0.5	0.4	0.3	−1.5	−4.2
Current account/GDP	−2.82	−1.25	0.29	−0.96	−1.74	−4.42	−1.71	12.46
Real effective exchange rate[b]	93.5	98.8	100.9	98.3	98.0	96.0	104.6	131.1
CPI inflation	9.3	6.3	4.8	6.2	4.5	4.9	4.5	7.5
Real GDP growth	9.2	5.4	5.5	8.3	8.9	6.8	5.0	−6.7
Unemployment rate	2.2	2.4	2.8	2.4	2.0	2.0	2.6	6.8
Gross savings ratio	37.3	36.4	36.2	35.5	35.5	33.8	33.4	33.2
Gross investment ratio	39.8	37.3	35.4	36.5	37.3	38.1	34.4	21.3
Real money growth[c]	15.2	12.6	14.9	18.8	11.8	15.2	16.2	—
Real credit growth[d]	16.0	12.5	13.4	18.8	13.7	13.7	14.3	−3.4

Source: National Statistical Office, Bank of Korea, Ministry of Finance and Economy, and KDI.

a. Consolidated public sector.

b. Trade volume weighted: numbers below 100 means overvaluation.

c. New M2 growth rate minus inflation rate.

d. Domestic credit growth rate minus inflation rate.

Another important perspective on the currency crisis is that it was caused by an international bank run rather than a speculative attack on the currency (Dooley and Shin 2000). Table 7.3 shows that the capital flows in 1997 were not unidirectional and that the extent of capital outflow was modest until October. Then, in November, there was a dramatic outflow of capital, and the usable reserves were slashed from about $22 billion to about $7 billion. Most of this is accounted for by the decrease in external debt and the increase in the Bank of Korea's deposit at overseas branches, which was to cover the withdrawal of foreign debt; the portfolio investment outflow was very small. Since, from the creditor's point of view, foreign debt is immune to exchange rate risks as it is denominated in foreign currency, it was not anticipated currency depreciation that triggered the abrupt reversal of capital flows and the currency crisis. It was, rather, an international bank run triggered by a perception of bankruptcy risks of the major Korean banks.

How Korea became vulnerable to a bank run can be seen in the balance sheet of the economy. Table 7.4 shows a steep increase in the external debt in the years preceding the crisis. At the end of 1996, gross external liabilities amounted to $164 billion, up two and a half times from the end of 1993 and five times from the end of 1990. However, the level of foreign debt itself was not a problem. Gross external liabilities at the end of 1996 represented only slightly more than 30 percent of the GDP. The real source of vulnerability was that too large a proportion of the external debt was short term. As a result, the short-term debt was much greater than foreign exchange reserves. At the end of 1996, the short-term external debt was 2.8 times greater than foreign exchange reserves, leaving the economy highly vulnerable to a bank run.

The rise in foreign indebtedness is closely tied to capital account liberalization measures and the ensuing rise in capital inflows. As restrictions on financial institutions in making foreign exchange loans to domestic firms were significantly relaxed since

TABLE 7.3 Trends of the Balance of Payment Components in 1997 (Unit: Billion US$)

| | 1997 | | | | | | |
	1st Quarter	2nd Quarter	3rd Quarter	4th Quarter	October	November	December
Foreign reserve decrease[a]	8.28	−4.17	2.89	13.55	0.12	15.04	−1.61
Private foreign asset decrease[a]	−1.88	−1.44	−1.76	−10.00	−1.14	2.37	−11.23
Total	6.40	−5.61	1.13	3.55	−1.02	17.41	−12.84
Decrease in external debt[b]	−5.59	−6.47	−2.94	−1.10	−2.95	6.55	−4.70
(public)	0.07	0.17	0.06	−15.92	0.04	0.05	−16.01
(private)	−5.66	−6.64	−3.00	14.82	−2.99	6.5	11.31
Increase in deposit at overseas branches[b]	4.20	0.00	0.00	3.33	0.00	8.91	−5.58
Net direct investment outflow[a]	0.51	0.23	0.66	0.21	0.10	−0.05	0.16
Net equity securities outflow[a]	−0.54	−2.54	−0.50	1.38	0.76	1.07	−0.46
Errors and omission	0.02	−0.15	1.17	4.03	0.50	2.35	1.18
Current account deficit[a]	7.35	2.72	2.05	−3.96	0.49	−0.86	−3.59

Source: *The Balance of Payments*, Bank of Korea (various issues). Data for external debt are from the Ministry of Finance and Economy.

a. "−" denotes increase, inflows, or surplus.

b. External debt is reckoned based on IBRD standards, and deposit at overseas branches denotes the deposit of the Bank of Korea at the overseas branches of the domestic banks.

TABLE 7.4 External Liabilities: 1992–1998 (Unit: US $ Billion, %)

	1992	1993	1994	1995	1996	1997	1998
Gross external liability[a]	62.9	67.0	88.7	119.7	164.3	158.1	149.4
(y-o-y growth rate)		(6.52)	(32.39)	(34.95)	(37.29)	(–3.82)	(–5.51)
Financial institutions[b]	43.6	47.5	65.1	90.5	116.5	89.6	71.9
Corporations	13.7	15.6	20.0	26.1	41.8	46.2	41.0
External liability/GDP	19.99	19.38	22.04	24.46	31.60	33.16	46.48
FX Reserves	16.64	19.70	21.03	31.93	32.40	19.71	51.96
Short-term external liability/ Total external liability	58.82	60.15	65.84	65.75	56.58	40.00	20.64
Short-term external liability/ FX reserves[c]	215.69	198.89	227.48	240.58	279.75	309.82	59.24

Source: Ministry of Finance and Economy.

a. External liabilities include external debts as defined by the IBRD, plus the offshore borrowings of Korean banks and overseas borrowings of Korean banks' overseas branches.

b. Including foreign bank branches operating in Korea.

c. External liabilities and foreign exchange reserves are year-end values.

1993, financial institutions went on borrowing from abroad at a dizzying speed.[10] From the end of 1992 to the end of 1996, the foreign exchange liabilities of commercial banks rose from about $62 billion to about $140 billion, and those of merchant banks increased from less than $5 billion to about $19 billion. In the process, there was a dangerous deterioration in the balance sheet of the economy, as a large part of short-term capital inflows were used to finance long-term projects and risky investments abroad. Domestic firms rapidly increased overseas investment, much of which proved costly. The outflow of portfolio investment was also dramatic, as financial institutions expanded their business in international finance, including in extremely risky derivatives and junk bond markets. Foreign portfolio assets rose from only $0.5 billion in 1993 to almost $6 billion in 1996.

These developments meant that financial institutions were taking on more risks. As financial liberalization exposed the weak banking system to competitive pressures, banks began to seek higher returns at the expense of higher risks. It goes without saying that financial deregulation must be accompanied with stricter prudential regulations and improved supervisory systems.[11] However, the government neglected to do this. In particular, there were no guidelines on foreign exchange liquidity and risk management, and virtually no supervision of the foreign exchange dealings of merchant banks and the foreign branches of commercial banks.

2.3. Financial Crisis as a Manifestation of a Crisis of the Accumulation Regime

Without denying the decisive role of mismanaged financial liberalization and capital flows in provoking the currency crisis, we must note that there was an underlying crisis of accumulation that contributed to converting the currency crisis into a full-blown financial crisis. Even before the currency crisis, the balance sheets of financial institutions seriously deteriorated as a result of the weakening profitability and deteriorating financial structure of firms.

Corporate profitability exhibited a declining trend in Korea since the early 1970s (Jang 1999). Figure 7.4 depicts the profit rate and the output/capital ratio in the manufacturing sector. It shows that the decline in the profit rate was largely driven by the decline in the output/capital ratio, although at times declines in the profit share also played a role. The decline in the output/capital ratio was particularly pronounced in the two periods 1976–1980 and 1988–1996. The first period was one of overinvestment in the heavy and chemical industrialization drive. The second period was one of overinvestment associated with the mismanaged liberalization.

Despite falling profitability, firms continued to invest heavily. As a consequence, corporate indebtedness rose. The historical trend of declining debt/equity ratio reversed itself from 1988. The ratio of corporate debt to the GDP continuously increased

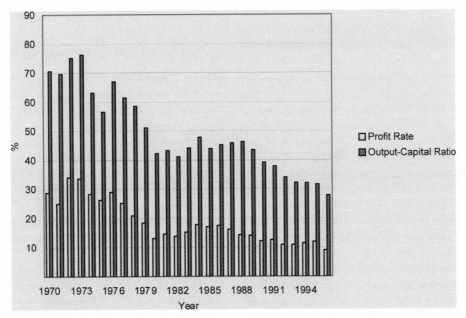

FIGURE 7.4 Manufacturing Gross Profit Rate and Output/Capital Ratio
Source: Jang (1999).

from 1.09 in 1988 to 1.63 in 1996. The debt/equity ratio of Korean companies also increased from around 2.5 in 1989 to above 3.0 in the first half of the 1990s to over 4.0 in 1997. For the top thirty *chaebol* groups, the debt/equity ratio was even higher, at about 3.5 in 1995 and 5.2 in 1997.[12] Given the decline in profitability and deteriorating financial structure of firms, the downturn in the economy since 1996 caused serious financial troubles for many firms. Starting with the collapse of the Hanbo Group at the beginning of 1997, *chaebol* groups such as Sammi, Jinro, and Kia successively went under.

These developments translated into deteriorating balance sheets for financial institutions. According to Hahm and Mishkin (2000), who estimate latent non-performing loans based on hypothetical asset classification criteria,[13] the ratio of non-performing loans to total loans increased from around 15 percent during 1988–1990 to 26 percent in 1997. For merchant banks, the deterioration in asset quality—for which the supervisory authority applied a much more lenient regulatory standard—was even more dramatic. At the end of 1996, the ratio of non-performing loans to capital was as high as 31.9 percent while the ratio was 12.2 percent in the commercial banking sector.

Falling profits, rising corporate indebtedness, *chaebol* bankruptcies, and deteriorating bank balance sheets are surface manifestations of a crisis in the accumulation regime. The rapid industrialization and growth since the early 1960s were based on a symbiotic combination of authoritarian politics, industrial policy based on the government control of finance, and the *chaebol* system. Having produced a miraculous growth, by the late 1980s, this system was running into inherent limits.

First, as we saw in figure 7.1, growth in Korea was based on ever-increasing capital accumulation until the crisis. The rate of investment increased over time from about 18 percent during 1963–1969 to about 27 percent during 1970–1977, 31 percent during 1978–1989, and 37 percent during 1990–1997. Nonetheless, as the output/capital ratio continuously fell, the growth rate declined steadily over the same period. With the share of output going into investment already at very high levels, growth based on capital accumulation was reaching its limits. Maintaining the growth momentum required a transformation of the input-driven growth regime into a more productivity-driven growth regime.

In a sense, liberalization policy was an attempt to meet such a challenge. More market-oriented allocation was expected to generate greater efficiency. However, liberalization only served to enhance *chaebol* power, and the misallocation problem became even more severe.[14] Furthermore, the *chaebol* responded to the steep increases in wages and unionization in the late 1980s not so much by productivity enhancement as by resorting to subcontracting and outsourcing, taking advantage of the large wage differential between *chaebol* firms and smaller subcontracting firms. With most subcontracting firms' survival dependent on orders from the *chaebol* firms, they fought to survive on the margin and failed to develop into a technically progressive and innovative sector. The productivity gap between the *chaebol* firms and smaller firms kept increasing in the 1990s.

Second, the very success of the authoritarian regime in delivering rapid growth undermined the social basis of authoritarian politics by strengthening various social groups (You 1995). As democratic transition began in 1987, the politics of finance also changed. Under the authoritarian regime, the government used discretionary powers to allocate financial resources to favored industries and to help out favored firms. Such powers were greatly diminished as a result of the winding down of industrial policy and financial liberalization. While cast as economic liberalization measures, these policy reforms were as political as they were economic in nature. Democratization made it increasingly difficult for the government to control resource allocation, while external pressures were also very instrumental in bringing about external liberalization policies.

When the problem of massive *chaebol* bankruptcies surfaced in 1997, the politics of finance was paralyzing the economy. The authoritarian governments of the past had utilized such forceful measures as the August 3rd Emergency Decree in 1972 or the government-dictated restructuring in the early 1980s of the heavy and chemical industries. Such blatant violation of property rights was not an option after democratization and liberalization. On the other hand, the market or institutional mechanisms to handle large bankruptcies were highly inadequate. In the end, the government chose to postpone (and thereby worsen) the problems by a measure called "suspension of default." The Korean economy in 1997 was severely lacking a correction mechanism for overinvestment.

3. Macroeconomic Adjustments since the Crisis

3.1. Overcoming the Liquidity Crisis

The rapid depletion of reserves in November 1997 sent the Korean government begging to the IMF. The announcement of the IMF rescue-financing package totaling $57 billion in early December, however, did not stop the panic. In fact, the crisis got much worse. The exchange rate continued to skyrocket and the rollover rate of commercial loans declined rapidly. It was only after the announcement of the emergency injection of $10 billion by the IMF and the G-7 countries on Christmas Eve and a move toward debt rescheduling by the creditor banks that the panic began to subside.

Given the bank run that started in November 1997, what was needed was massive up-front funding or an orderly debt workout under debt standstill rather than the IMF's phased funding with heavy conditionalities. The successful conclusion of debt rescheduling negotiations with creditor banks played a pivotal role in overcoming the liquidity crisis. It reduced the weight of the short-term debt in total foreign debt from almost 60 percent before the crisis to 26 percent in May 1998. The resumption of capital inflows, starting with the issuance of $4 billion of sovereign bonds in May, also contributed to ameliorating the foreign exchange liquidity crisis. It also helped that FDI inflows dramatically increased in 1998, with the fire sales of distressed firms. Furthermore, with the current account surplus running at more than $3 billion every month during 1998, the foreign exchange situation improved rapidly.

Even as the external debt was substantially reduced through debt repayment, the net capital inflow resumed thanks to the strong FDI and equity investment inflow since the crisis (see table 7.1). After recording a net outflow of $3.4 billion in 1998, the capital account recorded net inflows of $2.4 billion in 1999 and $12.3 billion in 2000. The current account also improved dramatically, recording a surplus of $40.4 billion in 1998, $24.5 billion in 1999, and $11.0 billion in 2000. Therefore, the foreign exchange reserves of the Bank of Korea increased enormously from their lowest amount of $3.9 billion during the crisis to $52.0 billion at the end of 1998 and further to $95.9 billion at the end of 2000. The ratio of short-term external liabilities to foreign exchange reserves that reached over 300 percent in 1997 dropped to only

46 percent by the end of 2000, putting the foreign exchange liquidity crisis firmly to a close.

A closer look at the capital account reveals significant changes between the before-crisis capital inflows and the after-crisis capital inflows (see figure 7.5). The most notable change is that other investment inflows (mostly banks' external debt) recorded large negative numbers since 1998 as debt repayment occurred, reversing the heavy accumulation of banks' external debt before the crisis. This was a temporary phenomenon associated with post-crisis adjustments. But there have been structural changes that are likely to stay.

First, the inflows of FDI rose dramatically. The annual inflow was only around $0.8 billion during 1990–1994 and between $1.8 and $2.8 billion during 1995–1997, but it rose to $5.4 billion in 1998, $9.3 billion in 1999, and $8.7 billion in 2000. As shown in figure 7.5, the net FDI inflow became positive in 1998 for the first time since 1990 and

remained so until 2000. Although the magnitude of FDI inflows is not huge compared to that of countries like China and Brazil, there is no question that the FDI regime has fundamentally changed from a restrictive to a very open one.

Second, there was a radical change in the composition of the portfolio investment inflow since the crisis. The portfolio investment in equity securities was a minor part of the total portfolio inflow, with investment in debt securities dominating the portfolio inflow, before the crisis. Since 1998, however, investment in equity securities increased substantially and dominated the portfolio inflow. In contrast, investment in debt securities became negative as debt was repaid.

3.2. A Deep Recession and a Steep Recovery

In the wake of the exchange crisis, the Korean economy suffered from the deepest recession ever

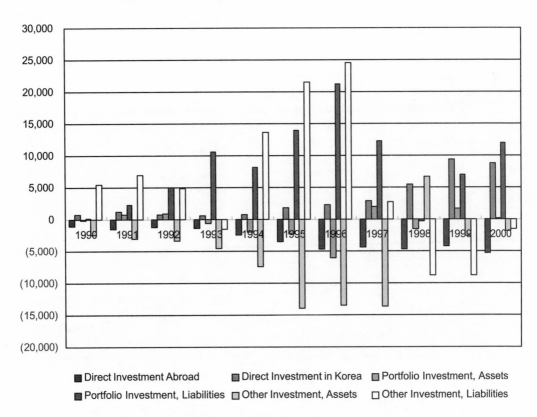

FIGURE 7.5 Decomposition of Capital Flows; 1990–2000
Source: Bank of Korea.

since the Korean War. The collapse of domestic demand pushed the economy into a 6.7 percent contraction in 1998. The unemployment rate, which remained below 3 percent before the crisis, shot up to about 7 percent. However, the economy rebounded and recorded an annual growth rate of 10.7 percent in 1999. This remarkable recovery continued into 2000, but growth began to decelerate from the fourth quarter of 2000.

The initial IMF program dictated that the short-term interest rate be raised from 12.5 to 21 percent, that money supply be tightened to contain inflation at 5 percent, and that the government budget be balanced or slightly in surplus. Requiring inflation to remain unchanged after the enormous depreciation of the currency was a definite call for a steep recession. As many have pointed out, Korea has not exhibited significant budget deficits, unlike a typical recipient of IMF rescue financing in Latin America or Africa. Furthermore, Korea's current account deficit was relatively small and declining in 1997. With the steep depreciation and the sagging domestic demand, it was clear that the deficit would improve further without any IMF-engineered hyperrecession. The appropriateness of the high interest rate policy as a temporary measure to prevent capital flight remains controversial, but tightening the budget at a time of extraordinary contraction in a country with a proven track record of fiscal responsibility was clearly out of line. But it was the high interest rate policy coupled with the demand for BIS capital adequacy

requirements that severely disabled the economy by producing a vicious circle of credit crunches and corporate bankruptcies.

The economy went into a free fall after the IMF involvement, with the growth rate plunging to minus 5 percent in the first quarter and to below minus 8 percent in the second and third quarters of 1998. As the depth and severity of the recession began to emerge, the IMF eased some of its conditions at several stages.[15] By the middle of 1998, interest rates were left to the discretion of the Korean authorities and the fiscal deficit was allowed to reach 4 percent of the GDP. Figure 7.6 shows that the yield on three-year corporate bonds came down to pre-crisis levels in the third quarter of 1998 and below pre-crisis levels after the fourth quarter of 1998. The budget deficit reached 4.2 percent of the GDP in 1998 and 5.1 percent of the GDP in 1999.

Defying dismal predictions, this macroeconomic policy shift succeeded in generating a very rapid recovery that started in the fall of 1998 and gathered force in early 1999. As a result, the GDP growth rate showed a remarkable turnaround from –6.7 percent in 1998 to 10.7 percent in 1999. The recovery also owed a great deal to the massive financial restructuring and other reform efforts by the government. Of critical importance were the bank restructuring in the fall of 1998, for which 40 trillion won were spent, and the quick buildup of the social safety net that cost more than 10 trillion won in 1998.[16] The bank restructuring made it possible to

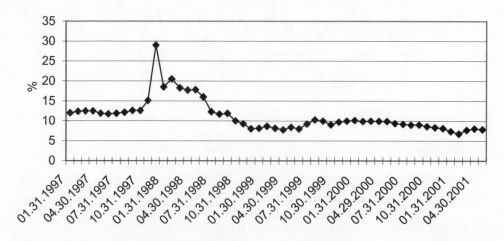

FIGURE 7.6 Market Interest Rate: Yields on Three-Year Corporate Bonds

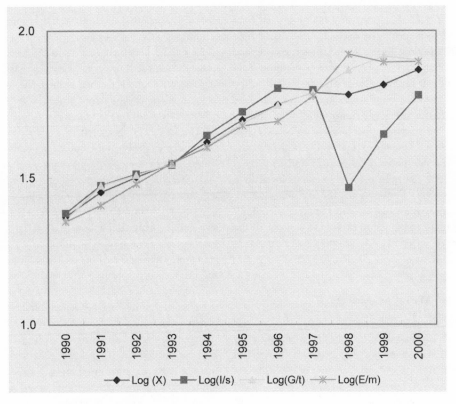

FIGURE 7.7 Decomposition of GDP Growth; 1990–2000

ease the credit crunch and put a stop to the vicious circle of corporate bankruptcy and financial crisis. The social safety net made it possible to keep the labor peace and social stability in the midst of mass unemployment and rising poverty. Finally, the recovery was helped by favorable external conditions, chiefly the strong growth and low interest rates in the United States.

For a closer examination of the growth recovery, figure 7.7 shows a decomposition of demand growth in the 1990s into private demand, government demand, and external demand in relation to leakages in the respective sectors.[17] It shows that private demand consistently led the overall demand growth before the crisis, but this changed dramatically due to the collapse of private demand after the crisis. Exactly the opposite can be said about external demand, while the government sector was generally neutral before the crisis but turned into a source for demand boosting after the crisis.

As for the recovery process, two observations can be made. First, even though the recovery of private

investment demand played an important role in output recovery, investment demand continued to be outweighed by the savings leakage through the recovery process. Second, both the external sector and the government sector helped contain recession and boost recovery. Particularly notable was the role of the government sector. While the external sector injected net demand, its contribution to the recovery was limited. Although not shown in the figure, the positive net foreign demand resulted not from an unusually strong export growth but from a collapse of import demand with the breakdown of investment. Exports grew at the annual rate of 19.1 percent during 1995–1997 and at 19.6 percent during 1998–2000.

The quick recovery of output growth does not mean that Korea is back to the favorable growth conditions of the past. Most seriously, there seems to have been a permanent decline in the savings and investment rates, reversing the continuously rising trend of the previous periods (see figure 7.1). Compared to the 1990–1997 period, the savings rate declined from 35.7 percent of the GDP to 32.1 percent during 1998–2001, and the investment rate fell from 37.0 to 25.8 percent. The decline in the savings rate has much to do with the financial restructuring and liberalization that led banks to expand household loans and cut business loans. The drastic fall in the investment rate is quite worrisome. Given the need for the restructuring and unwinding of overinvestment of the past, some decline was to be expected. But even excluding the exceptional year of 1998, the investment rate hovered between 27 and 28 percent during 1999–2001, 10 percentage points lower than in 1990–1997. Furthermore, the efficiency of investment, as measured by the incremental output/capital ratio, continued to decline in spite of all the rationalization efforts.[18] Raising the efficiency of investment remains a big challenge.

3.3. Labor Market Adjustments and Income Distribution

The deep recession following the financial crisis produced massive joblessness. Korea had enjoyed full employment for about ten years up to 1997, with the unemployment rate staying in the ~2–3 percent range. As shown in table 7.5, the number of unemployed jumped from about half a million in 1997 to about 1.5 million in 1998. The unemployment rate jumped from 2.6 percent in 1997 to 6.8 percent in 1998 and stayed at 6.3 percent in 1999.[19] There was

also a substantial decline in the labor force participation rate. It was lower by 1.3 percentage points in 1998 and 1.5 percentage points in 1999 than the average during the three years before the crisis. If this represents discouraged worker effect, the unemployment problem was about four times as severe in 1998–1999 as it was during the three years before the crisis.

The impact of increased joblessness was uneven across sectors, occupations, and demographic groups. Table 7.6 reports employment changes between 1996 and 1999 that reveal large variations in employment adjustment across industries, occupations, and the educational attainment of workers. Most of the massive employment contraction in 1998 is accounted for by the job losses in manufacturing and construction, although the job loss as a proportion of the previous year's employment was the heaviest in mining and public utilities.

It is interesting that the agricultural sector employment increased by 6.7 percent in 1998, defying the consistently declining trend of the past. This is because the job losers in cities went back to their home villages or other rural areas. Similarly, many job losers went into taxi driving or other services.

In terms of occupation, table 7.6 shows that the greatest job losses in 1998 occurred among craftsmen and simple laborers, while professional jobs increased by more than 10 percent. Consistent with this pattern, table 7.6 also reveals that workers with less than

TABLE 7.5 Employment and Unemployment: 1995–2000 (Unit: 1,000 Persons, %)

Year	Population (Above 15)	Economically Active Population	Employed	Unemployed	Economical Active Population Rate	Unemployment Rate
1995	33,664	20,853	20,432	420	61.9	2.0
1996	34,285	21,243	20,817	426	62.0	2.0
1997	34,842	21,662	21,106	556	62.2	2.6
1998	35,362	21,456	19,994	1,461	60.7	6.8
1999	35,765	21,634	20,281	1,353	60.5	6.3
1998 1/4	35,184	20,941	19,761	1,179	59.5	5.6
1998 2/4	35,304	21,725	20,243	1,481	61.5	6.8
1998 3/4	35,424	21,646	20,049	1,597	61.1	7.4
1998 4/4	35,537	21,511	19,924	1,588	60.5	7.4
1999 1/4	35,615	20,854	19,105	1,748	58.6	8.4
1999 2/4	35,715	21,797	20,362	1,435	61.0	6.6
1999 3/4	35,820	21,914	20,695	1,220	61.2	5.6
1999 4/4	35,910	21,972	20,962	1,011	61.2	4.6
2000 1/4	35,986	21,405	20,313	1,092	59.5	5.1
2000 2/4	36,081	22,108	21,268	840	61.3	3.8

Source: National Statistical Office (each year).

TABLE 7.6 Patterns of Employment Changes; 1996–1999

	1996–1997		1997–1998		1998–1999	
By Industry						
Agriculture and fishery	−81	−3.4%	156	6.7%	−131	−5.3%
Mining	3	12.5	−6	−22.2	−1	−4.8
Manufacturing	−202	−4.3	−577	−12.9	108	2.8
Gas and water	2	2.7	−15	−19.7	0	0.0
Construction	36	1.8	−426	−21.3	−102	−6.5
Retail and wholesale	51	1.3	−100	−2.6	86	2.3
Restaurants and hotels	119	6.8	−127	−6.8	67	3.8
Trans. Comm	54	4.9	4	0.3	33	2.8
Finance, Insurance, and Real Estate	136	7.7	−52	−2.7	69	3.7
Public administration and services	166	5.3	87	2.7	157	4.7
By Occupation						
Legislator, senior officials, managers	−18	−3.3%	−20	−3.8%	−31	−6.1%
Professionals	−17	−1.7	106	10.6	−42	−3.8
Technicians and associate professionals	208	10.5	−63	−2.9	201	9.5
Clerks	10	0.4	−156	−6.1	−199	−8.2
Service workers and shop and sales workers	185	4.0	−121	−2.5	83	1.8
Skilled agriculture and fishery workers	−82	−3.6	151	6.8	−147	−6.2
Craft and related trade workers	−66	−2.0	−623	−19.7	60	2.4
Plant and machine operators and assemblers	3	0.1	−80	−3.7	23	1.1
Elementary occupations	60	2.6	−247	−10.5	338	16.0
By Education						
Under primary school	−12	−0.3%	−468	−11.1%	−16	−0.4%
Middle school	151	4.5	−585	−16.6	62	2.1
High school	−56	−0.6	−427	−4.7	126	1.5
College and university	200	4.9	427	10.0	114	2.4
Total Employment Changes	284	1.4%	−1054	−5.0%	287	1.4%

Source: Annual Report on the Economically Active Population Survey (1996–1999).

Note: All entries are measured in 1,000 persons.

a high school education were the hardest hit, while the employment of those with college or university degrees increased by 10 percent. In sum, job losses were greater for non-skilled workers than for skilled workers.

The employment status of workers has also deteriorated. The proportion of regular employees declined, while that of temporary and daily workers increased after the crisis. The ratio of regular to nonregular employees, as a result, declined from 1.34 in 1996 to 0.96 in 1999. A recent study finds that some of the employees classified as regular employees in the official survey are in fact non-regular; taking this into account, the ratio went down to 0.71 in August 2000 (Y. Kim 2001). The rise in non-regular employment has become an important social issue, as non-regular employees suffer not only from job insecurity but also from low wages and benefits. The

above study claims that the average wage of nonregular workers was only 53.7 percent of that of regular workers, while working hours were slightly longer for non-regular workers.

The changes in wages are reported in table 7.7. Four observations can be made. First, nominal wages exhibited a remarkable degree of flexibility. Between 1997 and 1998, nominal wages fell by 5.9 percent, which meant a fall of 12.5 percent in real wages after taking the inflation rate of 7.5 percent in 1998 into account. The recovery of nominal and real wages in 1999 was also remarkable. Second, the wage changes were not sector neutral. In 1998, industries that incurred the greatest job losses such as manufacturing and construction experienced the largest wage declines. Interestingly, the wage change between 1998 and 1999 is a mirror image of the change between 1997 and 1998. That is, industries that experienced the largest wage declines in 1998 gained the most in 1999, while industries that experienced relatively small wage declines or even increases in 1998 suffered wage declines in 1999. Third, by 1999, the finance, insurance, and real estate (FIRE) sector became the highest wage sector, replacing the public utilities sector where wages were cut severely as a result of the public sector reform. Fourth, in terms of firm size, the wages of the smallest and the largest firms declined the most in 1998, but they also recovered the best in 1999.

There have also been profound institutional changes in the labor market brought about by the crisis. In the name of enhancing labor market flexibility, the government took measures such as legally sanctioning redundancy layoffs, establishing temporary work agencies, and hiring replacement workers. At the same time, the compensation system is rapidly moving away from the traditional seniority wage system toward a performance-based system.[20]

These labor market adjustments brought about a rise in wage inequality. The wage differential by education, the single most important factor in wage inequality, had been narrowing until 1993, but ceased to narrow in spite of the continuous quantitative expansion in higher education ever since. This is most likely attributable to a structural shift in labor demand in favor of the more highly educated; and is an outcome of the liberalization and globalization of the economy (You and Lee 2001).[21] The uneven impact of the economic crisis, which fell most heavily on unskilled workers, produced a jump in the college wage premium by 5 percent between 1997 and 1998 (D. Kim 2001).

The rise in unemployment and wage inequality, coupled with a sharp increase in financial rent owing to the high interest rate in the first half of 1998, resulted in substantial deterioration in income inequality. Table 7.8 reports changes in urban working household income distribution based on government surveys. There is a remarkable correlation between income levels and their changes in 1997–1998, producing a highly regressive change in income distribution. The average income of the top decile income earners rose by 4 percent, whereas that of lower income earners decreased, with the rate of decrease increasing with the fall in the income level. The bottom decile income earners' average income

TABLE 7.7 Nominal Wages and Growth Rates[a]

	1996	1997	1998	1999
All	1,401.4	1,491.8 (6.4)	1,403.6 (–5.9)	1,572.6 (12.0)
Men	1,563.8	1,659.7 (6.1)	1,549.7 (–6.6)	1,747.1 (12.7)
Women	985.1	1,055.5 (7.1)	997.3 (–5.5)	1,133.2 (13.6)
Manufacturing	1,322.1	1,357.5 (2.7)	1,233.4 (–9.1)	1,408.4 (14.1)
Public utility	1,892.0	2,124.0 (12.3)	2,288.1 (7.7)	1,736.1 (–24.1)
Construction	1,424.6	1,548.1 (8.7)	1,444.5 (–6.7)	1,736.2 (20.2)
Retail/wholesale	1,274.9	1,427.0 (11.9)	1,292.9 (–9.4)	1,472.0 (13.9)
Trans. Comm.	1,264.5	1,456.7 (15.2)	1,429.9 (–1.8)	1,372.4 (–4.0)
Finance, Insurance, and Real Estate (FIRE)	1,630.5	1,695.2 (4.0)	1,578.7 (–6.9)	1,958.9 (24.1)
Services	1,677.7	1,818.8 (4.4)	1,796.5 (–1.2)	1,777.5 (–1.1)
Firm size				
10–29	1,205.2	1,328.1 (10.2)	1,236.6 (–6.9)	1,401.3 (13.3)
30–99	1,270.4	1,380.8 (8.7)	1,321.9 (–4.3)	1,477.4 (11.8)
100–299	1,336.8	1,430.6 (7.0)	1,398.6 (–2.2)	1,536.6 (9.9)
300–499	1,544.3	1,686.6 (9.2)	1,589.1 (–5.8)	1,709.1 (7.6)
500+	1,755.6	1,777.0 (1.2)	1,637.7 (–7.8)	1,869.6 (14.2)

Source: *Monthly Labor Statistics* (July issues in 1996–1999).

a. The sample is firms with no fewer than ten employees. July wages are reported in each year.

TABLE 7.8 Urban Worker Households' Average Monthly Income Distribution (Unit: Won)

Decile	1997	1998	1999	2000	1997–1998	1998–1999	1999–2000	1997–2000
1	729,243	562,741	602,235	683,505	−22.83%	7.02%	13.49%	−6.27%
2	1,164,951	1,005,431	1,028,866	1,114,861	−13.69	2.33	8.36	−4.30
3	1,435,441	1,255,177	1,293,411	1,389,602	−12.56	3.05	7.44	−3.19
4	1,667,593	1,481,475	1,514,806	1,636,005	−11.16	2.25	8.00	−1.89
5	1,900,159	1,703,445	1,747,536	1,886,139	−10.35	2.59	7.93	−0.74
6	2,155,964	1,951,006	2,022,731	2,172,344	−9.51	3.68	7.40	0.76
7	2,460,398	2,252,089	2,341,707	2,502,552	−8.47	3.98	6.87	1.71
8	2,847,124	2,628,348	2,742,260	2,907,269	−7.68	4.33	6.02	2.11
9	3,419,821	3,193,028	3,327,581	3,519,498	−6.63	4.21	5.77	2.91
10	5,089,836	5,294,871	5,622,517	6,053,059	4.03	6.19	7.66	18.92

Source: National Statistical Office's Korean Statistical Information System (KOSIS;) Household Income, Consumption, Assets.

Note: 1997–2000: The rate of increase from 1997 to 2000.

declined by 22.8 percent. While all income groups experienced rising incomes in 1999 and 2000, there is no consistent pattern across income classes except that both the bottom and the top classes gained more than the middle. If we compare the average incomes of 1997 and 2000, the correlation between income levels and their changes is still perfectly preserved. The actual rise in income inequality is probably significantly greater than table 7.8 indicates, since it covers only those households with labor incomes.

The combination of worsening income distribution and a severe recession resulted in a sharp rise in poverty. One estimate, using the poverty line of about $800 per month for a four-person household, shows that the poverty rate increased from 4.2 percent in 1997 to 9.1 percent in 1998 (Yoo 2000). Other institutions such as the National Statistical Office and the World Bank reported different estimates based on different definitions of poverty, but they all agree that the proportion of households below the poverty line increased by more than twice after the crisis.

4. A Liberal Market Economy at Last?

4.1. Policy Reform after the Currency Crisis

The Kim Dae-jung government, elected two weeks after the signing of the agreement with the IMF in December 1997, committed itself to a vigorous reform program. This was done in order to gain the confidence of the international financial community, on the one hand, and to reorient development strategy toward the "parallel development of democracy and market economy" on the other. Recognizing the need for a fundamental reform of the political economy, the government sought comprehensive reforms both in the economic arena, including both external liberalization and domestic structural reforms, and in the field of social policy.

In terms of external liberalization, the government faithfully carried out the IMF-mandated reforms including a full-fledged opening of financial markets, selling off troubled financial institutions to foreign investors, lifting foreign exchange regulations, and radically liberalizing inward foreign investment— both portfolio and direct. Domestic structural reforms were launched in four sectors: the financial, corporate, labor, and public. The reforms included both restructuring in order to restore financial viability and increase efficiency and institutional changes aimed at enhancing market discipline.

The reforms pursued after the financial crisis are somewhat different in nature as well as much more comprehensive than the earlier liberalization policies. First, liberalization measures were accompanied by domestic institutional reforms intended to discipline agents that had the power to distort the market. At the center of the reform program was *chaebol* reform that sought to enhance transparency and accountability in corporate management and to promote fair competition and speedy restructuring.[22]

Second, the recent reforms included not only liberalization measures but also measures to address market failures. For instance, as a part of the financial sector reform, the government strengthened the financial safety net. It instituted deposit insurance, consolidated financial supervisory functions, and toughened asset management criteria for financial institutions in line with international standards.[23] This contrasts sharply with the past financial liberalization that was accompanied by the weakening, rather than the strengthening, of prudential regulations.

Third, the new government attempted to support its policy reform by constructing new policy networks and processes. In particular, the Tripartite Commission composed of representatives from labor, employers, and the government was formed in early 1998 in order to build social consensus for reform. The Commission became a forum for the discussion and negotiation of all matters that affected employment conditions, including labor, industrial policies, and social policies.

In fact, social security programs have emerged as a crucial means of maintaining social cohesion in the context of comprehensive economic restructuring. The government acted quickly to expand the social safety net in response to the sudden increase in joblessness and poverty in the aftermath of the financial crisis. In return for allowing greater employment flexibility, the government expanded unemployment and other social insurance coverage, executed public works programs and training programs for the unemployed, and increased public support for the poor. The expansion of social insurance programs proceeded with the following measures: the extension of the Unemployment Insurance Scheme to all workplaces in October 1998, the extension of the National Pension Scheme to cover the self-employed in urban areas in April 1999, the integration of medical insurance societies into a unified national health system, and the extension of the Industrial Accident Compensation Insurance Scheme to all workplaces in July 2000. Social policy took on a more redistributive nature as a result of the implementation of the National Minimum Livelihood Security Scheme, under which the government provides living allowances for all those whose monthly income falls below the minimum living costs, regardless of their ability to work, since October 2000.

Consequently, social security expenditures under the Kim government rapidly increased. The ratio of social security expenditures to the GDP increased from 5.1 percent in 1997 to 7.5 percent in 1999.[24] While it is true that the IMF urged expanding the social safety net, the Korean government went beyond the IMF recommendation toward developing a universal social security system. It is interesting that this occurred as the Korean economy was being fully integrated into the world markets. Domestic politics rather than external constraints determined the direction of social policy reform in Korea (Shin and You 2001).

4.2. Unresolved Questions

While the recent reforms are meant to dismantle the vestiges of the past authoritarian government-led development regime and to create a democratic market economy, there are still uncertainties about exactly where Korea's political economy is headed. The influence of the IMF and the local U.S.-trained economists has imparted a certain degree of neoliberal bias in the post-crisis reform process, with the U.S. model being touted implicitly or explicitly as the ideal model. However, there are reasons to doubt that the Korean economy is on its way toward a smaller version of the American economy across the Pacific.

First, despite serious efforts and much progress, *chaebol* reform remains a difficult challenge. The politics and rules of finance have indeed changed dramatically. As foreign capital has been injected into the banking sector, banks enjoy a great deal of autonomy and largely operate on commercial principles. As large *chaebol* groups have gone under, the myth of "too big to fail" is no more. However, the problematic management structure and practices of the *chaebol* are still present. As the weakened government of Kim Dae-jung retreated with respect to *chaebol* reform since 2000, the monolithic control of the affiliated firms by group heads, market expansion and control through circular investment among the *chaebol* affiliates, and market distortion by insider trading among the affiliates are on the rise. In particular, the *chaebol*'s control over the NBFIs has greatly increased, raising concerns about the concentration of economic power and the integrity of the financial system. Meanwhile, market discipline still appears too weak to tame the power of the *chaebol*. Precisely what the future holds for the *chaebol* in the new political economy of Korea remains to be seen.

Second, there remains confusion over the role of the state. While the reform ostensibly sought to reduce the role of the state, the reform process itself revealed that the role of the state is still of utmost importance. At a fundamental level, the state's role in establishing market institutions and enforcing market discipline is crucial. At a functional level, the government has relinquished some of its past roles and functions, especially in the areas of resource mobilization and allocation. But its roles and functions have been expanded in other new areas in order to deal with various market failures.[25] In this context, there have been controversies about what functions legitimately belong to the state.

While financial and corporate restructuring inevitably became an exercise led by the government, there has been constant criticism that it should be left to the market. Strengthening regulations in areas such as corporate governance and fair trade also met with resistance and was criticized as excessive government intervention. On the other hand, the government was prodded into implementing an active industrial policy, even by advocates of "small government." The Kim Dae-jung government, in fact, has not abandoned its entrepreneurial role, although the mode of industrial policy has radically changed.[26]

Third, a social consensus on how income and power should be distributed among different groups has yet to emerge. In the context of economic restructuring and worsening income distribution, the expansion of social welfare has generally been regarded as necessary, although not immune from criticisms from conservative forces. More controversial and problematic has been the experiment in social corporatism through the Tripartite Commission. The attempt to include labor in the policy decision process has faltered not only because of inertia in the behavior of the related parties but also because of unfavorable institutional conditions such as low unionization rates and fragmented union organization. Issues of labor market flexibility and the substantial increase in non-regular workers have also generated intense controversy.

Korea is still in search of a new, economically viable, and socially acceptable constellation of economic and social policies. Legacies of the past development regime such as the dominating presence of the *chaebol* and the expectation of activist government coexist with elements of American-style economic liberalism and European-style welfare capitalism. The search will continue until the problem of reinvigorating growth dynamism and reconstructing a social consensus on the distribution of income and power is solved.

5. Conclusion

After two decades of liberalization policy since the early 1980s, Korea has not yet succeeded in forging a new viable political economy that is capable of generating sustained growth and social cohesion. Liberalization policy was more or less neutral in its effect on growth and income distribution until the financial crisis of 1997–1998. The crisis then dealt a severe blow on both fronts. In spite of the relatively quick recovery of growth, the crisis resulted in a permanent loss of output and a long-lasting deterioration in income distribution. Furthermore, post-crisis reforms have brought about very substantial declines in both savings and investment without any signs of increasing investment efficiency, casting a shadow on future prospects for growth. Despite the long and painstaking efforts to liberalize the economy, there are still uncertainties regarding the basic parameters of the political economy, such as the role of the *chaebol*, the function of the state, and class relations. Economic liberalism has yet to be fully embedded in the Korean political economy.

This is not to say that the liberalization policy has been a total failure in Korea. There has been a drastic change in the way in which financial resources are allocated, and both the product and factor markets are much more open and competitive than they have been in the past. There is greater transparency and accountability in the economic system. It is quite conceivable that the accumulation crisis might have been worse had it not been for the admittedly imperfect liberalization policy. Nonetheless, the Korean experience with economic liberalization shows that liberalization is not a simple matter of implementing textbook policies but involves complex multivariable transformation. In particular, the Korean experience illustrates several pitfalls.

First, liberalization could lead to the strengthening of the entrenched power hierarchies in the private sector, as was the case with financial liberalization in the 1980s that ended up giving greater control over financial resources to the *chaebol*. As a result, liberalization could exacerbate market distortions. Privatization can also lead to the same perverse outcome. But it is not enough to simply address the technical aspects of designing a second-best policy. Liberalization policy, like any other policy, does not take place in a political vacuum. In the Korean case, it was very much shaped by the influence of the *chaebol*, and it is no surprise that liberalization led to strengthening of their position. This problem must given serious attention when liberalization policy is implemented.

Second, liberalization could compound the problems of market failure. As the economic activities under government control become liberalized, new problems may occur. For example, when industrial policy was dismantled in Korea, there were few mechanisms to check the *chaebol*'s appetite for excessive expansion. Financial liberalization increased systemic risks in the financial system. Labor market deregulation brought about an unwelcome deterioration of income distribution. Liberalization, therefore, should not be conceived as a simple matter of deregulation, decontrol, and disengagement. It has to be accompanied by complementary policies to establish market discipline and contain market failures.

Third, the Korean experience once again shows that financial liberalization, especially the liberalization of capital account transactions, is likely to be followed by a financial crisis. This has both a micro and macro dimension. According to the macroeconomic logic, increased capital inflows lead to currency appreciation, lower savings, and current account deficits. In terms of the microeconomic logic, greater competition in the financial sector squeezes the profits of financial firms and thereby induces riskier behavior. Despite its gradual and relatively cautious approach, Korea was unable to avoid a punishing crisis. Prudence in macroeconomic management and financial policy cannot be overemphasized.

Notes

I wish to thank Lance Taylor for encouragement and helpful comments. I also benefited from comments and suggestions by Amitava Dutt and many others who participated in the meetings in Delhi, Beijing, and Hanoi.

1. However, since official interest rates were set far below market rates, a large and active curb market for loans developed. The curb market provided a channel for the diversion of credit from its intended uses (Cole and Park 1983).

2. The history of capitalist development demonstrates that some degree of socialization of risk is absolutely critical in promoting investment and that inevitable moral hazard problems should be checked by bureaucratic discipline (Chang 2000).

3. Hyundai's shipyard was such a case. The shipyard, built at the personal exhortation of President Park, was confronted with the worldwide collapse of the

shipping industry in 1975. The government responded by forcing all Korean refineries to ship oil in Korean-owned tankers, creating a captive demand for Hyundai (Jones and SaKong 1980).

4. Chang et al. (1998) argue that there were no serious moral hazard problems in financial resource allocation in Korea, citing many cases of bankruptcies of *chaebol* firms and the fact that rescue operations usually involved government-mediated takeovers. However, this is not entirely accurate as there are many more instances of *chaebol* firms receiving financial support in times of difficulty until drastic restructuring became unavoidable. Political connections also played an increasingly important role in the bankruptcy and takeover decisions. For example, politically well-connected Daewoo was able to retain its management rights when its shipyard was rescued in the late 1980s. Also see Schopf (2001) for how the industry rationalization program of the early 1980s was closely connected with political corruption.

5. The macro imbalances were a result of overinvestment in heavy and chemical industrialization. They were exacerbated by external shocks, that is, the steep rise in world real interest rates and oil prices.

6. Most significantly, the government retained the power to appoint the top managers of commercial banks even after they were privatized (Jung 1991).

7. By 1990 the top five *chaebol* groups owned 36.5 percent of the total shares of life insurance companies, 26.3 percent of the total shares of the securities companies, and 12.8 percent of the total shares of merchant banking companies (Yoo 1995).

8. See Lim (2000) and You and Jang (2001) for analyses of the decay of bureaucratic discipline.

9. I have argued elsewhere that these problems in the liberalization policy were not just unfortunate mistakes but also a consequence of the increasing influence of *chaebol* groups on economic policy (You and Lee 2001). The *chaebol* pushed for liberalization to gain greater freedom of business, but they also wanted to maintain their unfair advantages. Maintaining restrictive regulations on inward FDI while permitting cross-border borrowing and outward FDI, for instance, reflected the interests of the *chaebol*.

10. Despite important capital account liberalization measures such as deregulating the overseas issuance of foreign currency–denominated bonds by domestic firms in 1991, opening the stock market to foreign investors in 1992, and allowing domestic firms to obtain commercial loans overseas, the Korean government remained cautious and maintained explicit or implicit quantity controls on capital flows led by firms or through the stock market. However, it allowed banks to enjoy relatively greater freedom in borrowing from foreign creditors.

11. See Diaz-Alejandro (1985) for a classic argument of this position. Dooley and Shin (2000) argue that the Korean government failed to detect the increasing vulnerability of the economy, since about half of the foreign currency operations of the banking sector were handled by overseas branches and therefore not reflected in domestic monetary indicators.

12. In 1997 six groups among the top thirty had a debt/equity ratio of over 10, even after the collapsed *chaebol* groups such as Kia and Sammi are excluded (Joh 1999).

13. The official numbers are quite misleading owing to various loopholes in asset classification and loan loss provision.

14. Rather than replacing financial resource allocation based on government policy with one based on market criteria, liberalization enabled gross distortions by the politically influential *chaebol*. The infamous case of Hanbo Steel Co. is a good example. Offering generous sums of political contributions to the nation's most powerful politicians, Hanbo's founder-chairman, Chung Tae-soo, managed to secure a total of 5.7 trillion won (about $7 billion) in bank loans before his empire crumbled under the weight of snowballing debts.This was not an exceptional case, as many *chaebol* groups accumulated unmanageable amounts of debt in similar ways. Another notorious instance of the politicization of economic decisions is the Samsung Motor case. The government had been denying Samsung entry into the auto industry for fear of overcapacity and excessive competition, but suddenly granted it entry in 1995 after Samsung's successful manipulation of the public opinion in Pusan, the political hometown of President Kim Young Sam. The Samsung auto project, even without the industry-level overcapacity problem, was nonsensical, as its plant was to be built on reclaimed land that needed massive fortifying as a move to give political benefits to the president in return for granting permission to Samsung.

15. "Recognizing that the downturn in economic activity is proving to be more severe and protracted than anticipated," the IMF's July 1998 Memorandum says that "economic policies aim to support a recovery of domestic demand and strengthen the social safety net so as to mitigate the hardship of the unemployed."

16. In comparison, the sum of banking deposits was 22 trillion won. Initially, 60 trillion won in public funds were raised for the purpose of financial restructuring in 1998. However, the government tried to minimize the liquidation of financially troubled companies. It continued to support many financially non-viable firms in order to avoid massive layoffs. When some of these firms collapsed in 1999, notably the Daewoo group, the bad assets of financial institutions once again increased. This led to the second round of raising of public funds, this time in the amount of 40 trillion won in 2000. Including the funds that were once recouped and reused, a total of about 155 trillion won were used for financial restructuring by the end of 2001. This amounts to 28.4 percent of the GDP in 2001 (or 34.9 percent of GDP in 1998).

17. Considering an economy that imports only inputs and no finished products, the output, X, can be expressed as injections divided by leakages as follows:

$$X = C + I + G + E = (I + G + E)/(s + t + m)$$

where s, t, and m are private savings, taxes, and imports scaled by output. Expressing this in terms of the "own" multiplier effects, we have

$$X = a_1(I/s) + a_2(G/t) + a_3(E/m)$$

where $a_1 = s/(s + t + m)$, $a_2 = t/(s + t + m)$, and $a_3 = m/(s + t + m)$.

18. Note that the incremental output/capital ratio $= \Delta Y/\Delta K = (\Delta Y/Y)/(\Delta K/Y) =$ growth rate/investment rate. This ratio was 0.55 during 1963–1969, 0.33 during 1970–1977, 0.24 during 1978–1989, 0.20 during 1990–1997, and only 0.16 during the post-crisis period of 1998–2001.

19. The unemployment rate peaked at 8.4 percent in the first quarter of 1999 and began to decline since then thanks to the strong growth recovery. By the second quarter of 2000, the unemployment rate fell to below 4 percent.

20. This is a case of globalization putting pressure on domestic institutions and norms that have been put into place to ameliorate income inequality and social conflict (Rodrik 1995).

21. Given the steady increase in the ratio of college graduates among the labor force (from 6.7 percent in 1980 to 12.5 percent in 1988, 17.5 percent in 1993, and 23.4 percent in 1998), the sudden pause in the decreasing trend in the college wage premium is likely to have been caused by a demand shock in favor of the highly educated. There are some indications of such an increase in the demand for the highly educated since 1992. During the period from 1992 to 1996, the increase in the employment in finance, insurance, and real estate (FIRE) and business services amounted to 30.2 percent of the total employment increase. This compares with only 18.4 percent during the period from 1988 to 1992.

22. The five principles of *chaebol* reform agreed upon between the government and the *chaebol* in early 1998 were (1) enhancing transparency by requiring *chaebol* groups to disclose combined financial statements and by raising corporate accounting standards;

(2) enhancing accountability by requiring listed companies to establish audit committees and appoint outside directors, improve minority shareholder rights, and relax restrictions on M&As; (3) prohibiting cross-debt guarantees among *chaebol* affiliates; (4) improving the financial standing of *chaebol* affiliates by requiring them to reduce their debt/equity ratio to 200 percent by the end of 1999; and (5) inducing *chaebol* groups to focus on areas of core competence. In the summer of 1999, when it became clear that the *chaebol* reform was not making sufficient progress, the government declared three additional principles: (1) the prohibition of undue intragroup transactions and "circular investments" among *chaebol* affiliates, (2) stricter regulations on the inheritance of wealth and management rights, and (3) the separation of industrial and finance capital.

23. For instance, all banks are required to meet the BIS capital adequacy ratio, and NBFIs are also required to recapitalize non-performing loans. Financial institutions that do not meet the criteria have been closed. In 1998 alone, 217 out of a total of 2,077 financial institutions were closed.

24. This increase by 2.4 percentage points in just two years during the middle of the crisis compares with an increase by 1.4 percentage point over the five years during the Kim Young Sam government that expanded social welfare in its own way. The central government budget for social security increased even more dramatically since the crisis. It rose by 33.4 percent between 1998 and 1999 and by 32.3 percent between 1999 and 2000, while the total central government budget increased by 10.7 percent and 6.0 percent, respectively.

25. For example, as the government liberalized foreign exchange and capital account transactions, it created new regulations on foreign borrowing by firms and new monitoring institutions like the International Finance Center and the Financial Information Unit.

26. While reforming and restructuring the *chaebol*, the government promoted the venture industry as a new source of growth dynamism. The old industrial policy imposed restrictions on inward FDI, but now the government actively seeks FDI. It has been promoting a knowledge-based economy by assisting human capital formation and R&D in high-tech sectors like the information technology industry (Woo 1999).

References

Amsden, Alice. 1989. *Asia's next giant*. Oxford: Oxford University Press.

Amsden, Alice, and Y. Euh. 1990. Republic of Korea's financial reform: What are the lessons? Discussion Paper, no. 30. Geneva: United Nations Conference on Trade and Development (UNCTAD).

Aoki, Masahiko, Kevin Murdock, and Masahiro Okuno-Fujiwara. 1997. Beyond the East Asian miracle: Introducing the market-enhancing view. In *The role of the government in East Asian economic development*, edited by Masahiko Aoki, et al. Oxford: Clarendon Press.

Chang, Ha-Joon. 2000. The hazard of moral hazard: Untangling the Asian crisis. *World Development* 28: 775–88.

Chang, Ha-Joon, Hong-Jae Park, and Chul Gyue Yoo. 1998. Interpreting the Korean crisis: Financial liberalization, industrial policy and corporate governance. *Cambridge Journal of Economics* 22: 735–46.

Cho, Yoon Je, and Joon Kyung Kim. 1997. *Credit policies and the industrialization of Korea*. Seoul: Korea Development Institute.

Cole, David C., and Yung Chul Park. 1983. *Financial development in Korea, 1945–1978*. Cambridge, Mass.: Harvard University Press.

Diaz-Alejandro, Carlos. 1985. Good-bye financial repression, hello financial crash. *Journal of Development Economics* 19: 1–24.

Dooley, Michael, and Inseok Shin. 2000. Private inflows when crises are anticipated: A case study of Korea. in *The Korean crisis: before and after*, edited by Inseok Shin, 145–82. Seoul: Korea Development Institute.

Hahm, Joon-Ho, and Frederic S. Mishkin. 2000. Causes of the Korean financial crisis: Lessons for policy. In *The Korean crisis: before and after*, edited by Inseok Shin, 55–144. Seoul: Korean Development Institute.

Jang, Ha-Won. 1999. The undercurrent of the crisis in Korea. ICSEAD Working Paper, no. 99–21. Kitakyushu: International Center for the Study of East Asian Development.

Joh, Sung Wook. 1999. The Korean corporate sector: Crisis and reform. KDI Working Paper 9912. Seoul: Korea Development Institute.

Jones, Leroy, and Il SaKong. 1980. *Government, business and entrepreneurship in economic development: The Korean case*. Cambridge, Mass.: Harvard University Press.

Jung, Un-Chan. 1991. *Keumyung Gaehyeoknon (A tract on financial reform)*. Seoul: Beobmunsa.

Kim, Dae-Il. 2001. Recent labor market developments in Korea. Mimeograph. Seoul: Seoul National University.

Kim, Kwang Suk. 1994. Trade and industrialization policies in Korea: An overview. In *Trade Policy and Industrialization in Turbulent Times*, edited by G. K. Helleiner, 317–63. London: Routledge.

Kim, Yu-Seon. 2001. Non-regular employment in Korea (in Korean). *Labor and Society* (May).

Lim, Wonhyuk. 2000. The rise and fall of the Korean model of development. Mimeograph. Seoul: Korea Development Institute.

Radelet, Steven, and Jeffrey Sachs. 1998. The East Asian financial crisis: Diagnosis, remedies, prospects. *Brookings Papers on Economic Activity*, no. 1, 1–74.

Rodrik, Dani. 1995. Getting interventions right: How South Korea and Taiwan grew rich. *Economic Policy* 20:55.

Schopf, James. 2001. An explanation for the end of political bank robbery in the Republic of Korea: The T+T model. *Asian Survey* 41 (5).

Shin, Dong-Myeon, and Jong-Il You. 2001. Changing definition of the social good in South Korea: From welfare society to welfare state. Mimeograph. Seoul: Korea Development Institute, School of Public Policy and Management.

Woo, Cheonsik. 1999. Inbound FDI and industrial upgrading of Korea: Prospect and challenges. KDI Working Paper 9914. Seoul: Korea Development Institute.

World Bank. 1993. *The East Asian miracle*. New York: Oxford University Press.

Yoo, Kyung Joon. 2000. Changes in income distribution and poverty since the IMF crisis. Mimeograph. Seoul: Korea Development Institute.

Yoo, Seongmin. 1995. Chaebol in Korea: Misconceptions, realities, and policies. KDI Working Paper, no. 9507. Seoul: Korea Development Institute.

You, Jong-Il. 1995. Changing capital-labor relations in South Korea. In *Capital, the state and labour*, edited by Juliet Schor and Jong-Il You. Aldershot, UK: Edward Elgar.

———. 1998. Income distribution and growth in East Asia. *Journal of Development Studies* 37–65.

You, Jong-Il, and Hawon Jang. 2001. Changing role of the state in Korea: From leading to supporting the market. *International Journal of Economic Planning Literature* 16 (3/4).

You, Jong-Il, and Ju-Ho Lee. 2001. Economic and social consequences of globalization: The case of South Korea. In *External liberalization, economic performance and social policy*, edited by Lance Taylor. New York: Oxford University Press.

8

External Liberalization, Economic Performance, and Distribution in Malaysia

Jomo K. S. and Tan Eu Chye

This chapter examines the growth and distributional impacts of Malaysia's policy of maintaining open current and capital accounts. Malaysia was the true jewel in the crown of the British Empire, contributing more export earnings than any other part of the empire for many years after World War II. While exports were encouraged from the nineteenth century, if not earlier, imports from outside the empire were discouraged to maximize the colony's net economic contribution. Malaysia's relatively open current account continued after its independence in 1957 with the exception of selective tariff protection for two rounds of import-substituting industrialization—for consumer goods in the 1960s and for heavy industries in the early and mid-1980s.

Unlike other developing countries, tariffs have not been important for revenue purposes. Malaysia's current account liberalization initiatives[1] have mainly involved the reduction and consolidation of tariff rates. Except for automotive imports, quantitative trade restrictions have been limited. There have been reductions in average tariff rates since the 1970s and especially since the mid-1980s. At the same time, Malaysia has been giving fiscal and other investment incentives to promote high value-added, export-oriented, and other desired industries (Jomo and Felker 1999).

Since 1957, Malaysia has maintained a relatively liberal capital account regime, which became more pronounced after the changes in the international monetary system in the early 1970s. Significant new efforts to attract capital inflows occurred in 1987 and 1994 (although the second occasion mainly reversed temporary capital control measures introduced earlier in the year). Countries liberalize capital flows for various reasons: to respond to external political pressures, to finance a growing fiscal deficit, or to secure foreign exchange financing for imports. In Malaysia, these measures were intended to attract foreign capital for import-substituting and then export-oriented industrialization and, more recently, in an attempt to become an international financial center. However, temporary short-term exchange control measures were introduced to discourage destabilizing capital inflows in early 1994 and to stem capital outflows in 1998.

The rest of the chapter is organized as follows. The following section describes Malaysia's external liberalization policy initiatives. Next, we provide a broadbrush assessment of Malaysia's external liberalization experience. This is followed by an assessment of the macroeconomic impact of external liberalization à la Berg and Taylor (2000). The socio-economic impacts of external liberalization are dealt with in the following section. The penultimate section provides a more detailed discussion of certain aspects of external liberalization, centering on international trade, foreign direct investment, international finance, intellectual property rights, and international economic governance, before concluding.

External Liberalization Initiatives

Current Account

Malaysia has long been an open economy with a relatively liberal trade regime, though it has employed selective protectionism to advance import-substituting industrialization in the early 1960s and heavy industrialization in the mid-1980s.[2] Tariffs have been primarily used to protect infant industries, rather than for revenue. Except for the early 1980s when import protection measures were used to promote heavy industries (automobiles, steel, and cement), Malaysia has reduced import protection since its move to export-oriented industrialization in the late 1960s and has committed to trade liberalization and regional economic integration since the 1990s. In general, Malaysian tariff rates have been quite moderate by international standards. The average unweighted tariff rate with respect to imports was about 26 percent in the early 1960s, and declined to about 14 percent by 1990 (see table 8.1).

Malaysia's trade liberalization has kept pace with trends led by the General Agreement on Tariffs and Trade (GATT) Uruguay Round and its successor, the World Trade Organization (WTO). The advent of the ASEAN Free Trade Area (AFTA) in 1992 and the Asia Pacific Economic Cooperation (APEC) forum have also lowered import barriers. GATT and WTO commitments are more comprehensive, with

TABLE 8.1 Malaysia: Average Unweighted Tariff Rates, 1960–1990 (%)

Period	Imports	Exports[a]
1960	20.93	8.11[b]
1962	25.37	7.50[b]
1964	25.95	7.31[b]
1966	25.08	8.67[b]
1969	23.59	8.89[b]
1973	19.50	8.16[b]
1978	20.29	9.89[b]
1984	16.45	19.00
1988	15.61	15.96
1990	13.81	15.97

Source: Aslam (1993).

a. Export duties are primarily levies or royalties on petroleum.

b. Does not include rates of duty for rubber, tin, and palm oil.

far-reaching implications. Under its GATT commitment, Malaysia has offered to reduce and bind tariffs for about 6,000 products. By binding these tariff lines, Malaysia will not be allowed to raise tariff levels for these products. Almost all imported items have been offered for tariff reductions ranging from 5 to 30 percent. The biggest tariff reductions have been in the agricultural sector as tariff rates for industrial products were already quite low (Ariff, Mahani, and Tan 1997). These tariff reductions have lowered the overall average Malaysian tariff rate. The post–Uruguay Round trade-weighted average nominal tariff rate for Malaysia was only 9 percent and is still declining.

Some primary commodity exports (e.g., palm oil) continue to be constrained by tariff and non-tariff barriers. The government has successfully used trade policy instruments to encourage investments in palm oil refining. This has resulted in the most efficient palm oil refining capacity in the world, all within the span of less than a decade (Gopal 1999). The Malaysian authorities also intervened to overcome collective action and other problems to sell palm oil in new markets in India, Russia, Pakistan, China, and elsewhere. In other words, export promotion also involves pro-active selective industrial promotion rather than simply liberalizing trade.

The original AFTA schedule called for tariffs to be reduced to 0.5 percent within fifteen years and for non-tariff barriers to be dismantled within eight years from January 1, 1993. To prepare for the full implementation of AFTA, the Malaysian government has been liberalizing its tariffs unilaterally on a most favored nation (MFN) basis, so that preferential treatment is not given to any trading partner. Since 1993, the Malaysian government has reduced or abolished import duties on over 4,000 items. However, to protect its automotive industry, Malaysia has successfully lobbied its ASEAN partners to delay automotive import liberalization. Trade liberalization under APEC auspices has been more ambivalent, with future progress unclear.

Trade liberalization has led to an increased propensity to import, though this has mainly been the result of greater imports of intermediate and capital goods. Malaysia's trade to GDP ratios have been exaggerated by the high import content of Malaysia's principal manufactured exports in the electric and electronic sector.

Capital Account

Exchange controls administered by the Central Bank of Malaysia have been based on provisions of the Exchange Control Act of 1953 (Bank Negara Malaysia 1994). Malaysia had long maintained relatively liberal exchange controls until September 1998. Generally, both residents and non-residents were allowed to freely remit funds abroad, but there have been restrictions on private borrowing from abroad. This exchange control policy is uniformly applicable to transactions with most countries.[3]

Malaysia has had three episodes of exchange controls liberalization—in 1973, 1987, and 1994–1996 (Bank Negara Malaysia 1999). However, as noted earlier, there have also been temporary moves to tighten exchange controls from time to time to curb destabilizing capital outflows—first, after massive speculative inflows in 1992–1993, and again, from September 1998, in response to the East Asian financial crisis. The first step toward maintaining a liberal exchange control regime, after the collapse of the Bretton Woods system in 1971, was taken in 1973 with the flotation of the ringgit as regulations on foreign exchange transactions with all countries were substantially relaxed.[4]

To lower export business operation costs in the country, exchange controls were further loosened on January 1, 1987 (Ariff, Mahani, and Tan 1997). Formalities that businesses have to comply with when exporting goods were simplified. The move also allowed investors greater access to credit facilities to enable them to expand their domestic productive capacities. The main changes included the following:

1. Raising the threshold for completion of the export exchange control declaration form from RM5,000 to RM20,000 free on board (f.o.b.) per shipment
2. Increasing the limit on residents obtaining offshore loans without prior approval from the controller of foreign exchange from RM100,000 per loan to RM1 million
3. Increasing the limit for a non-resident-controlled company to obtain domestic loans without prior approval from RM500,000 to RM10 million
4. Allowing the public to deal freely in physical gold

As the Malaysian economy continued rapid growth, an even more liberal regime emerged to further ease foreign exchange transactions by residents. Accordingly, exchange control rules were further relaxed from December 1, 1994, with the following objectives (Ariff, Mahani, and Tan 1997):

1. Reducing the cost of compliance
2. Allowing greater access to foreign credit facilities for small- and medium-scale industries
3. Enhancing efficiency in cross-border transactions by residents
4. Encouraging multinational corporations to relocate their operational headquarters to Malaysia

The liberalized rules included the following:

1. Permitting exporters to retain part of their foreign exchange proceeds without requiring conversion into ringgit
2. Raising the threshold for exchange control export declarations from RM20,000 to RM100,000 f.o.b. per shipment
3. Raising the limit for procuring funds from abroad without prior approval from the aggregate limit equivalent to US$2 million (or RM5 million equivalent)
4. Allowing non-resident-controlled companies to obtain any amount for a maximum period of twelve months for forward exchange contracts, guarantee facilities, and short-term trade financing facilities from domestic banking institutions on top of the RM10 million credit limit already allowed
5. Exempting approved operational headquarters from certain exchange control rules

6. Giving greater flexibility to the central bank in determining requests made by Malaysian companies to invest abroad using funds raised domestically. Approval would be readily granted if the overseas investment projects satisfied the following criteria:

   a. Enhancement of Malaysia's overseas market access and use of Malaysian inputs,
   b. Transfer of technological know-how to Malaysia, or
   c. Supply resident companies with required inputs.

Against this long-term trend toward greater liberalization, exchange control rules were temporarily tightened in early 1994 and again in September 1998. In early 1994, the central bank sought to stem volatile inflows after the economy experienced sudden massive inflows from late 1993. The central bank tried the following measures (Bank Negara Malaysia 1999):

- Subjecting funds deposited with banking institutions to statutory reserve and liquidity requirements;
- Imposing limits on net outstanding external non-trade-related liabilities of banking institutions;
- Restricting sales of short-term monetary instruments to non-residents;
- Compelling commercial banks to place the ringgit funds of foreign banking institutions in non-interest-bearing vostro accounts with the central bank; and
- Forbidding commercial banks from undertaking non-trade-related swaps and outright forward transactions on the bid side with foreign clients to prevent offshore parties from taking speculative long ringgit positions. (The ringgit was perceived to be undervalued owing to its managed peg against the U.S. dollar until the reversal of the yen-dollar relationship in mid-1995.)

These measures were subsequently repealed around August 1994. One explanation is that the pressure from short-term capital inflows had eased by that time. Another view is that the controls had so effectively discouraged speculative portfolio inflows that Malaysia was no longer attractive to foreign portfolio investors, unlike the heady days of 1992–1993.

The controls were probably lifted to encourage foreign—and hence, domestic—investments in the stock market that had languished after the imposition of the controls.

Restrictive measures on outflows were introduced again in September 1998 following the massive exodus of funds from the country during the East Asian financial turmoil. These targeted measures did not apply to current account and long-term capital flows. Apart from pegging the ringgit to the U.S. dollar at RM3.80 on September 2, 1998, the restrictive measures undertaken included the following (Bank Negara Malaysia 1999):

1. Placing a limit of US$2 million per foreign customer on non-commercially related swap transactions in effect from August 4, 1997. The objective was to deny the swap market as a source of ringgit funds for speculators.
2. In September 1998, the Malaysian government "deinternationalized" the ringgit by banning offshore ringgit trading from October 1998. The amount of ringgit that could be imported or exported and the quantity of foreign exchange that could be exported were restricted. Ringgit loans to non-residents were also limited.
3. Compelling non-residents to retain their portfolio investments in Malaysia for at least twelve months. As regional financial market conditions stabilized and the likelihood of massive capital flight receded after the economic and political crises of September 1998, this rule was amended on February 15, 1999, with the introduction of an exit levy option. Under the new system, foreign portfolio investors were permitted to repatriate the principal sum of their portfolio funds subject to an exit levy that declined over time—in other words, the longer the wait, the lower the levy—from September 1998 to zero in September 1999. This system was modified on September 21, 1999, when a flat 10 percent exit levy was imposed on repatriated profits from portfolio investments. With the 2001 budget placed on the agenda in Parliament on October 27, 2000, only profits from investments of less than a year would be subject to the levy. The levy was later abolished altogether.

Malaysia has long been keen on attracting long-term capital inflows, particularly in the form of greenfield foreign direct investment. To maintain investor confidence, the Malaysian government has reached investment guarantee agreements with more than forty countries (Ariff, Mahani, and Tan 1997). The agreements provide for protection against nationalization and expropriation; compensation in the event of nationalization or expropriation; unlimited repatriation of profits, capital, and other fees and payments; as well as the settlement of investment disputes in accordance with the Convention on Settlement of Investment Disputes. It has also granted generous fiscal incentives to foreign-owned companies such as tax holidays, investment tax allowances, reinvestment allowances, and export allowances to encourage them to establish operations in Malaysia.[5]

The 1959 Pioneer Investment Ordinance sought to attract import-substituting industrial investments while the Investment Incentives Act (1968) sought export-oriented industrial investments; the latter was replaced with the Promotion of Investment Act (1986). A major revision to the 1968 act liberalized the guidelines on foreign direct investment (FDI) to allow foreigners greater equity participation in companies, rising with the degree of export orientation. Full foreign ownership is permitted for projects that export at least 80 percent of their products. Projects that export less than 80 percent are allowed less foreign equity participation, with the maximum permissible level rising with the degree of export orientation, the level of technological sophistication, the greater the positive spin-off effects, as well as the bigger the capital outlay and value-added.

In the 1990s, prior to the East Asian financial crisis, the government also promoted outward direct investment especially in other Third World countries, in line with South Commission recommendations (Jomo 2002). Overseas investments were expected to enhance international market shares for Malaysian products and to utilize Malaysian expertise and experience (especially for resource extraction, agricultural development, and property as well as infrastructure development).

Malaysia seems committed to further financial sector liberalization under the late 1997 Financial Services Agreement of the General Agreement on Trade in Services (GATS) of the World Trade Organization (WTO). The Malaysian authorities appear resigned to such new international conventions and regulations requiring greater exposure of the domestic financial sector to foreign competition. They have prepared for this eventuality by trying to develop a more efficient, competitive, and market-driven financial sector. They adopted a pro-active approach toward imminent international financial liberalization, ostensibly to ensure the survival of domestic financial institutions. However, there remains considerable suspicion that the financial consolidation process announced in 1999 was mooted by powerful interests in order to enhance their own interests. This policy has resulted in increased foreign participation in the Malaysian financial sector, where there are now thirteen wholly foreign-owned commercial banks.

External Liberalization: Broad Assessment

By and large, there have been net inflows of long-term private capital into Malaysia. In the early decades, these comprised official development assistance (ODA) and greenfield foreign direct investment. ODA inflows peaked in the early and mid-1980s as Malaysia borrowed heavily from the Japanese government to finance new heavy industry joint ventures with Japanese firms until the 1985 Plaza Accord resulted in a ballooning of the yen-dominated debt as the Malaysian ringgit fell against the falling U.S. dollar.

Labor shortages and the 1988 withdrawal of privileges under the Generalized System of Preferences (GSP) from the first-tier East Asian newly industrialized economies (NIEs) of South Korea, Taiwan, Hong Kong, and Singapore encouraged the relocation abroad of production facilities from these NIEs to Malaysia and other countries in the region. From the late 1980s, greenfield FDI has been supplemented by surges of portfolio inflows in 1992–1993 and again in 1995–1996. Unlike the other East Asian economies badly affected by the 1997–1998 currency and financial crises, the Malaysian central bank limited foreign bank borrowings to firms expecting significant foreign exchange earnings. Despite its more open economy, Malaysia had the smallest share of short-term loans.

The success of Malaysian investment promotion efforts in attracting greenfield investments is reflected in the official data on approved investments in the manufacturing sector. The foreign share of total approved investments rose from 35 percent in 1980 to 46 percent in 1993 (Ariff, Mahani, and Tan 1997). In fact, there were surges in such inflows after the 1987 liberalization measures, partly intended to attract portfolio investments into the stock market. Net inflows increased dramatically from RM1,065 million in 1987 to RM13,204 million in 1992. The rise did not, however, cause the Malaysian ringgit to appreciate, owing to effective—if expensive—central bank "sterilization" measures. Instead, the ringgit depreciated in value against the US$ most years after 1987 (see table 8.2). An alternative set of figures that may also reflect the success of Malaysia's investment promotion efforts in attracting greenfield investments is reflected in the official data on approved investments in the manufacturing sector. The FDI share of total approved investments rose from 35 percent in 1980 to 46 percent in 1993 (Ariff, Mahani, and Tan 1997).

Indeed, FDI has been very important for Malaysian manufacturing, especially for exports. Malaysia's export-oriented industrialization has been spearheaded by FDI since the early 1970s. As table 8.2 shows, since the early 1970s, there has been a net inflow of private long-term capital. This helped break Malaysia's dependence on primary commodity exports. For instance, during 1991 to 1995, the foreign share of all approved investments in resource- as well as non-resource-based industries was never less than 23 percent (see table 8.3).

While manufactured exports accounted for only 11.9 percent of total exports in 1970, they accounted for 84.5 percent by 1999 (see table 8.4). The share of the manufacturing sector in total employment also expanded from 9.4 percent in 1971 to 27.2 percent in 1999, while its share of total national output increased from 11.2 percent to 30.8 percent over the same period (see table 8.5). However, there is considerable evidence that manufactured exports from developing countries have involved little domestic value-added, and have thus not contributed much to foreign exchange earnings.[6]

TABLE 8.2 Malaysia: Net Long-Term Capital Flows, Economic Growth, and Exchange Rate (RM/US$) Movements, 1971–1999

Year	Net Long-Term Capital Flows		Economic Growth (%)	Exchange Rate Changes (%)
	Official (RM Million)	Private (RM Million)		
1971	411	306	10.0	−2.0
1972	857	320	9.4	−7.1
1973	185	420	11.7	−12.8
1974	234	1,374	8.3	−1.6
1975	884	839	0.8	−0.2
1976	597	969	11.6	5.8
1977	618	999	7.8	−3.2
1978	418	1,158	6.7	−5.9
1979	800	1,255	9.4	−5.5
1980	180	2,033	7.4	−0.5
1981	3,017	2,914	6.9	5.8
1982	5,169	3,263	6.0	1.4
1983	6,284	2,926	6.2	−0.6
1984	4,691	1,869	7.8	1.0
1985	2,504	1,725	−1.1	5.9
1986	2,124	1,262	1.2	4.0
1987	−2,470	1,065	5.4	−2.4
1988	−5,100	1,884	9.9	3.9
1989	−2,458	4,518	9.1	3.4
1990	−2,836	6,309	9.0	−0.1
1991	−665	10,996	9.6	1.7
1992	−2,876	13,204	8.9	−7.4
1993	979	12,885	9.9	1.1
1994	861	10,798	9.2	1.9
1995	6,147	10,464	9.8	−4.4
1996	748	12,777	10.0	0.3
1997	4,645	14,450	7.6	11.8
1998	2,137	8,490	−7.5	39.5
1999	6,697	5,901	5.7	−3.1

TABLE 8.3 Malaysia: Foreign Shares of Investments in Approved Manufacturing Projects, 1991–1995 (%)

Resource-Based	50.4	Non-Resource-Based	56.7
Food manufacturing	39.4	Textiles and textile products	79.5
Beverages and tobacco	66.1	Leather and leather products	42.5
Wood and wood products	43.1	Basic metal products	33.9
Furniture and fixtures	43.8	Fabricated metal products	67.2
Paper, printing, and publishing	23.1	Machinery manufacturing	68.0
Chemicals and chemical products	59.0	Electrical and electronic products	77.0
Petroleum refineries/products	80.2	Transport equipment	30.6
Natural gas	22.6	Scientific and measuring equipment	84.8
Rubber products	42.4	Miscellaneous	48.4
Plastic products	42.9		
Non-metallic mineral products	33.4		

Source: Computed from *Seventh Malaysia Plan, 1996–2000*

While the Malaysian economy seems to have benefited from FDI, this is only true of the greenfield FDI Malaysia received until the mid-1990s. Greenfield FDI adds new economic capacities, quite unlike much recent post-crisis FDI, which has included much more investment for mergers and acquisitions (M&As). Ironically, Britain—which had ceased to be the largest foreign investor in Malaysia in the 1970s—became the largest source of FDI in Malaysia again in 1998, when British firms acquired a couple of cement plants, an independent power producer, and a telecommunications firm.[7]

With its high domestic savings rate, Malaysia has not been desperately in need of foreign inflows. In spite of the issues associated with greenfield versus M&A investment, foreign capital has brought

TABLE 8.4 Malaysia: Manufactured and Non–Manufactured Exports, 1970–2000

Year	Total Exports (RM Million)	Manufactured Exports (% Share)	Non-manufactured Exports (% Share)
1970	5,163	11.9	88.1
1975	9,231	21.9	78.1
1980	28,172	22.4	77.6
1985	38,017	32.8	67.2
1987	45,225	45.0	55.0
1990	79,646	58.8	41.2
1995	184,987	79.6	20.4
1997	220,890	81.0	19.0
1999	321,560	84.5	15.5
2000	373,307	85.2	14.8

Source: Computed from Bank Negara Malaysia, *Quarterly Economic Bulletin* (various issues).

technology and marketing know-how, with some positive spillover effects—via technology transfer and learning by doing—for the economy. Though these may not have significantly contributed much to value-added,[8] they have helped develop new "comparative advantages" for the Malaysian economy. Malaysia's ability to produce manufactured exports has thus been enhanced. For example, American and Japanese investments have made Malaysia one of the world's leading sites for producing electronic components. The share of manufactures in total exports expanded considerably from 18 percent in 1970–1980 to 29 percent in 1981–1985 and 60 percent in 1986–1999. Both foreign- and locally owned companies contributed to this spectacular performance (spearheaded by foreign companies) as part of Malaysia's export-oriented industrialization program, dating back to the early 1970s.

Table 8.6 shows that over twenty-nine years (1971–1999), Malaysia experienced fifteen years of net capital outflows. During these three decades, Malaysia experienced recessions in 1975, 1985, and 1998, but it is difficult to establish any clear relationship from annually aggregated data. The table suggests that there is no correlation between nominal exchange rate movements and the volume and direction of short-term capital flows, but annual aggregation is unlikely to capture such short-term movements anyway. Large outflows did not necessarily result in the depreciation of the domestic currency, while large inflows did not inevitably result in currency appreciation owing to central bank interventions. In fact, the 7.5 percent contraction in 1998 cannot be ascribed to the massive outflows of short-term

TABLE 8.5 Malaysia: Shares of Employment and GDP[a] by Sector, 1971–1999 (%)

Year	Agriculture	Mining and Quarrying	Manufacturing	Construction	Services
1971	52.0 (27.2)	2.5 (12.4)	9.4 (11.2)	2.9 (4.5)	33.2 (44.7)
1975	47.6 (25.1)	2.2 (10.3)	11.1 (15.4)	4.0 (3.8)	35.1 (45.5)
1980	39.7 (21.0)	1.7 (10.5)	15.6 (17.9)	5.6 (4.7)	37.4 (45.9)
1985	31.3 (18.9)	0.8 (10.8)	15.2 (17.9)	7.6 (4.9)	45.1 (47.6)
1990	28.3 (17.0)	0.4 (10.1)	19.9 (24.3)	6.3 (3.6)	45.1 (45.0)
1993	22.4 (13.4)	0.5 (7.9)	23.2 (27.3)	7.3 (4.0)	46.6 (47.5)
1997	16.7 (9.5)	0.5 (7.6)	26.9 (31.1)	9.9 (5.0)	46.0 (46.8)
1999	15.9 (9.6)	0.5 (7.5)	27.2 (30.8)	9.2 (3.7)	47.2 (48.4)

Source: Bank Negara Malaysia, *Quarterly Economic Bulletin* (various issues).

a. Figures in parentheses refer to sectoral shares of GDP.

TABLE 8.6 Malaysia: Net Private Short-Term Capital Inflows, Economic Growth, and Exchange Rate (RM/US$) Movements, 1971–1999

Year	Net Private Short-Term Capital Inflows (RM Million)	Economic Growth (%)	Exchange Rate Changes (%)
1971	68	10.0	–2.0
1972	–15	9.4	–7.1
1973	258	11.7	–12.8
1974	366	8.3	–1.6
1975	–158	0.8	–0.2
1976	–242	11.6	5.8
1977	–982	7.8	–3.2
1978	–145	6.7	–5.9
1979	–1,584	9.4	–5.5
1980	902	7.4	–0.5
1981	97	6.9	5.8
1982	326	6.0	1.4
1983	–263	6.2	–0.6
1984	–288	7.8	1.0
1985	870	–1.1	5.9
1986	–47	1.2	4.0
1987	–2,491	5.4	–2.4
1988	–2,914	9.9	3.9
1989	1,562	9.1	3.4
1990	1,356	9.0	–0.1
1991	5,135	9.6	1.7
1992	11,957	8.9	–7.4
1993	13,931	9.9	1.1
1994	–8,484	9.2	1.9
1995	2,529	9.8	–4.4
1996	10,317	10.0	0.3
1997	–12,913	7.6	11.8
1998	–20,633	–7.5	39.5
1999	–37,750	5.7	–3.1

Sources: Department of Statistics, Malaysia; and Bank Negara Malaysia, *Quarterly Economic Bulletin*

portfolio capital alone. The deflationary policies undertaken by the government from late 1997—under IMF influence, in response to the regional financial turmoil—are principally responsible for the sharp downturn.

Malaysian measures have sought to attract particular types of capital flows from abroad, initially of FDI and ODA, and more recently—in the early and mid-1990s—of portfolio investments. Since the late 1980s, such efforts switched from ODA to portfolio investments until the 1997–1998 debacle.

The generally liberal external trade regime has not resulted in an unfavorable merchandise trade balance for Malaysia, though it has suffered from persistent current account deficits, mostly because of its large services account deficit. From 1970 to 1999, Malaysia only managed to record a current account surplus in eleven years. Deficits in the merchandise trade balance only occurred twice after 1970, in 1981 and 1982 (see table 8.7). Meanwhile, large invisibles (services) trade deficits have been sustained due to continued heavy reliance on foreign services—such as shipping, finance, insurance, and education—and foreign investment income repatriation.[9] Foreign participation is strong in both resource-based and non-resource-based industries, especially beverages, tobacco, chemicals and chemical products, petroleum refineries and products, textiles and textile products, fabricated metal products, machinery manufacturing, electrical and electronic products, and scientific and measuring equipment. Consequently, profits and other payments repatriated from the country have been very substantial.

Table 8.8 shows current and capital account flows since 1970, and suggests that the bulk of existing

TABLE 8.7 Malaysia: Merchandise Trade, Current Account Balances, and Net Investment Income Flows, 1971–1999 (RM Million)

	Merchandise	Current Account	Net Investment Income
1971	686	−329 (−2.5)	−363
1972	365	−698 (−4.9)	−378
1973	1,594	246 (1.3)	−659
1974	540	−1,307 (−5.7)	−997
1975	614	−1,187 (−5.3)	−727
1976	3,722	1,474 (5.3)	−1,097
1977	3,738	1,074 (3.3)	−1,276
1978	3,690	249 (0.7)	−1,716
1979	6,908	2,033 (4.4)	−1,991
1980	5,238	−620 (−1.2)	−1,820
1981	−243	−5,633 (−9.8)	−1,836
1982	−1,758	−8,409 (−13.4)	−2,679
1983	1,002	−8,117 (−11.5)	−4,208
1984	6,986	−3,917 (−4.9)	−5,255
1985	8,883	−1,522 (−2.0)	−5,434
1986	8,378	−316 (−0.4)	−4,597
1987	14,703	6,642 (8.2)	−4,824
1988	14,524	4,739 (5.1)	−5,019
1989	11,871	698 (0.7)	−5,935
1990	7,093	−2,483 (−2.1)	−5,072
1991	1,449	−11,644 (−8.6)	−6,735
1992	8,609	−5,622 (−3.7)	−7,920
1993	8,231	−7,926 (−4.6)	−8,174
1994	4,460	−14,770 (−7.6)	−9,448
1995	97	−21,647 (−9.7)	−10,338
1996	10,088	−11,226 (−4.4)	−11,629
1997	10,274	−16,697 (−5.9)	−14,639
1998	69,216	37,394 (13.2)	−14,817
1999	86,535	47,902 (16.0)	−20,275

Note: Figures in parentheses are percentages of nominal GDP.

TABLE 8.8 Malaysia: Cumulative Current Account and Capital Account Flows, 1970–1999 (RM Million)

	Current Account	Official Long-Term Capital	Private Long-Term Capital	Private Short-Term Capital
1970–1999	−106,890	25,980	123,269	19,132
1978–1987	−19,610	22,717	19,470	−2,623
1988–1997	−86,578	−555	98,285	22,476
1988–1999	−1,282	8,279	112,676	−35,907

Macroeconomic Assessment

For analytical purposes, in this section, Malaysia's tradable sector is defined as encompassing export-oriented and import-competing industries, while services and construction are considered non-tradable. Agriculture and mining have been declining relatively if not absolutely. Although Malaysia has long had a relatively open economy, there was some further external liberalization from the second half of the 1980s. Thus, in order to assess the macroeconomic impact of liberalization in this section, the period under study is divided into two—namely, 1970–1987 and 1988–1999—with the former considered less liberal than the latter. However, one should not exaggerate the significance of these changes, especially in long-term comparative perspective. Also, causality should not be ascribed to statistical correlations.

Decomposition of Effective Demand

In general, the liberalization of the current and capital accounts would bring significant changes in aggregate demand-side parameters like import coefficients, savings rates, and various demand components and, hence, to the behavior of macroeconomic variables in general. Thus, it is worthwhile to examine the output response to these shifts by decomposing demand injections (investment, government spending, and exports) and leakages (savings, taxes, and imports) following Berg and Taylor (2000).

The leakage parameters (s_p, t, m) derived from the decomposition exercise are plotted in figure 8.1. The figure suggests that external liberalization did not necessarily result in a persistent decline in the private savings rate. While external liberalization increased during 1987–1997, the private savings rate declined

international reserves came from inflows of long-term and short-term private capital, rather than from current account surpluses. The table also suggests that capital account liberalization increased after the mid-1980s. Meanwhile, official long-term capital inflows—mainly official development assistance—declined, as short-term capital inflows, primarily in the form of portfolio investments, contributed more to Malaysia's capital account surplus—and current account deficit—until the 1997 financial crisis. From a macroeconomic perspective, net capital inflows prior to the crisis enabled foreign savings to supplement domestic savings. However, it seems that such capital inflows increased investments that contributed little to growth, but instead caused asset price bubbles as well as other poor investments (Palma 2000).

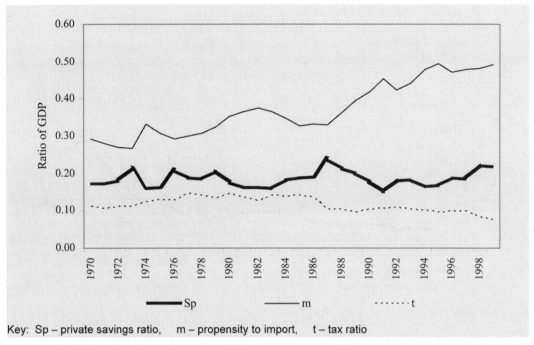

Key: Sp – private savings ratio,   m – propensity to import,   t – tax ratio

FIGURE 8.1 Malaysia: Leakage Parameters, 1970–1999
Key: Sp, private savings ratio; m, propensity to import; and t, tax ratio.

during 1987–1991, after which it rose again. However, as expected, external liberalization has increased the propensity to import, which grew sharply after 1987. This steep increase was largely due to the surge in imports of intermediate and capital goods for industrialization that also increased exports.

The direct "own" multiplier effects of private investment (I_p/S_p), government expenditure (G/t), and exports (E/m) on output in figure 8.2 suggest a sharp increase in the multiplier effect of private investment during 1987–1995. This phenomenon was not observed before 1987, as one would expect due to the heavy industrialization drive of the early and mid-1980s. The sharp reduction in the multiplier effect after 1997 can be attributed to the contractionary consequences of the 1997–1998 financial crisis. Steeper positive trends in the multiplier effects of government expenditure and exports were also evident during 1987–1999, compared to the earlier period. It is therefore difficult to deduce a clear relationship between a more liberal regime and multiplier effects.

Malaysia's external trade (merchandise and invisibles), private investment-savings, and government expenditure-revenue gaps—plotted in figure 8.3—suggest a weakening external trade balance with

greater liberalization, as one would expect a priori. The abrupt improvement in the trade balance after 1997 can be attributed to the precipitous depreciation of the ringgit and its various consequences, including the sharp recession of 1998, as well as deliberate government efforts to strengthen Malaysia's external reserves position. The figure also shows investments growing faster than savings after 1987, narrowing the excess of savings over investments. The economic contraction caused by the 1997–1998 financial crisis subsequently led to a drastic decline in private investment and significantly increased the surplus of savings over investments.

The government expenditure-revenue gap also rose steeply after 1987, mainly because of increases in government development—rather than operating—expenditure as it invested heavily in infrastructure to meet the needs of a rapidly expanding economy. The revenue shortfall was met by domestic—rather than external—borrowing due to the government's desire to maintain low external debt after its debt burden ballooned with the yen's appreciation in the mid-1980s (Jomo 1990). At the end of 1997, domestic debt constituted about 85 percent of total federal government debt. Government policy favoring

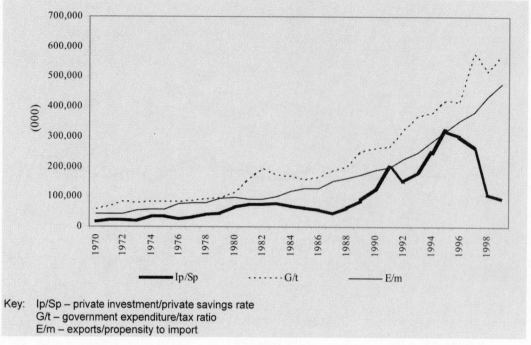

FIGURE 8.2 Malaysia: Multiplier Effects on Output, 1970–1999

Key: *Ip/Sp*, private investment/private savings rate; *G/t*, government expenditure/tax ratio; and *E/m*, exports/propensity to import.

domestic—against external—financing has helped keep domestic inflation low at below 4 percent.

However, in the mid-1990s, as government revenue increased more rapidly than public expenditure, the government ran modest fiscal surpluses. After a disastrous further contraction of government spending in late 1997, following IMF advice, the Malaysian authorities increased public spending from mid-1998. It seems likely that countercyclical fiscal policy had a greater effect in reviving the economy compared to the September 1998 monetary measures.

Employment Decomposition and Labor Productivity

This section will identify sectors that have experienced significant employment changes following the further liberalization of Malaysia's current and capital accounts after the mid-1980s. Following Berg and Taylor (2000), the growth of the overall employment ratio is the weighted average of differences between the per capita output growth rate and the labor productivity growth rate in various sectors of the economy.

In general, liberalization may result in fairly slow overall productivity growth if it leads to slow output growth (despite positive productivity growth) in the traded-goods sector, and to low—or even negative—productivity growth despite faster output growth in the non-tradable sector. Figure 8.4 presents the results of the employment decomposition exercise based on Berg and Taylor's decomposition. It shows no appreciable difference in the overall employment ratio growth rate before and after 1987. The more liberal external regime since 1987 did not undermine employment growth in the tradable sectors as the manufacturing sector managed to record generally larger positive contributions to the growth of the overall employment ratio after that year until the crisis of 1997–1998.

The declining contribution of agriculture and the negligible contribution of mining and quarrying to employment may be attributed to the government's policy of promoting manufacturing and modern services, the collapse of tin mining (Jomo 1990), as well as the leveling off of petroleum and gas output increases in the 1980s. Meanwhile, the government

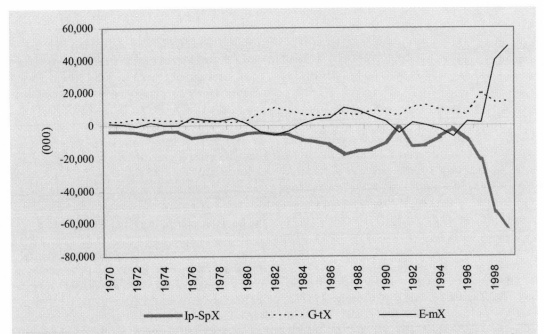

FIGURE 8.3 Malaysia: External Trade, Private Investment Savings, and Government Expenditure-Revenue Gaps, 1970–1999

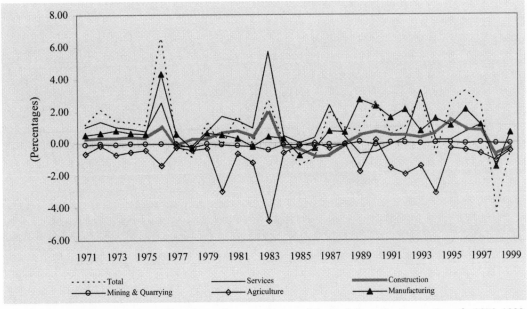

FIGURE 8.4 Malaysia: Growth of Overall Employment Ratio and Sectoral Contributions to Growth, 1970–1999

also recognized that poverty had declined, primarily because of outmigration from low-income peasant agriculture. Meanwhile, the non-tradable sectors—construction and services—still contributed to overall employment growth, even with further external liberalization after 1987.

Figure 8.5 presents the labor productivity decomposition results. Growth of overall labor productivity appears to be more stable and sustained after 1987. There also seems to be an increase in the labor productivity trend in the tradable manufacturing sector after that year. However, this was also true of non-tradable services. Hence, while greater external liberalization did not lower labor productivity, it is not possible to attribute the increased labor productivity to external liberalization since the trend was also true of non-tradable services.

Other tradable sectors—namely, agriculture as well as mining and quarrying—also registered modest increases in labor productivity after 1987. The construction sector—which experienced a tremendous increase in (often illegal) immigrant labor—was the only sector to experience a persistent decline. Generally, the more liberal post-1987 regime did not undermine growth in either the tradable or the non-tradable sectors. Figure 8.6 shows that the

manufacturing sector recorded faster per capita output growth after the mid-1980s, while per capita output growth in the services and construction sectors remained largely positive.

Interestingly, all these favorable developments occurred despite an appreciation of the real exchange rate from 1.1351 in 1973–1987 to 1.0336 in 1988–1997,[10] casting doubt on the popular explanation of the post-1987 Malaysian export-led manufacturing boom as having been facilitated by an undervalued exchange rate.

The Socio-economic Impact of Liberalization

There is no clear trend in terms of income inequality after 1987. In any case, trends cannot be simply attributed to external economic liberalization as much else was going on at the same time. Also, the relationship between external economic liberalization and domestic inequality is hardly straightforward. Export-oriented industrialization with foreign capital has generated direct employment (as the main motive for such foreign investment has been to reduce labor costs). However, the limited linkages of such industries to the rest of the national economy have

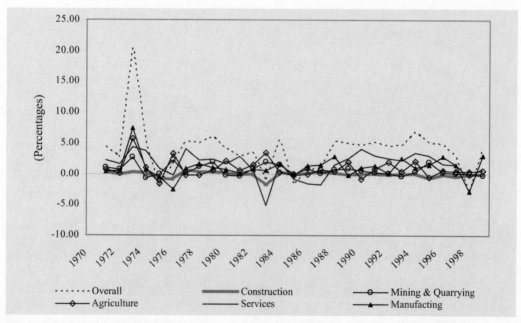

FIGURE 8.5 Malaysia: Growth of Overall Labor Productivity and Weighted Growth of Labor Productivity by Sector, 1970–1999

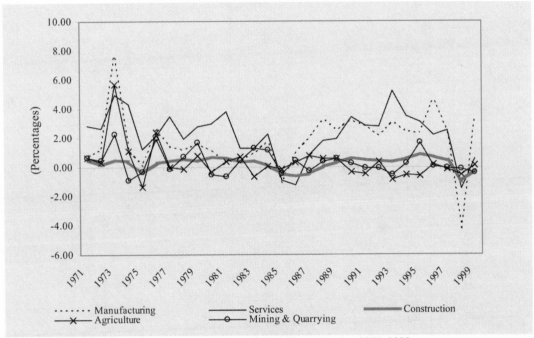

FIGURE 8.6 Malaysia: Weighted Growth of Sectoral Output per Capita, 1971–1999

limited indirect employment generation from such investments.

Industrialization led by FDI has significantly transformed employment distribution in various sectors of the economy. The proportions of the workforce in agriculture, forestry, fishing, mining, and quarrying have declined in favor of manufacturing (a tradable sector) and services (a non-tradable sector), sectors that offer generally higher and more stable earnings. The unemployment rate declined—though not steadily—from 7.5 percent in 1970 to 2.4 percent in 1997, before increasing marginally to 3.2 percent in 1998, following the East Asian financial debacle (see table 8.9).

All this has raised per capita incomes and reduced poverty, though the consequences for income inequality have been more ambiguous. As table 8.10 shows, poverty incidence dropped significantly from 39.6 percent in 1976 to 6.8 percent in 1997, before rising moderately to 7.6 percent in 1998 in the wake of the financial crisis. Meanwhile, the number of poor households declined from 764,000 in 1976 to 346,000 in 1997. The incidence of hard-core poverty (defined as half the official poverty line) also fell correspondingly from 6.9 percent in 1984 to 1.5 percent in 1998,

TABLE 8.9 Malaysia: Unemployment Rate, 1970–1999 (%)

1970	7.5	1983	5.6	1992	3.7
1975	6.9	1984	5.8	1993	3.0
1976	6.4	1985	6.9	1994	2.9
1977	6.3	1986	8.8	1995	3.1
1978	5.4	1987	7.3	1996	2.5
1979	5.2	1988	7.2	1997	2.4
1980	5.7	1989	6.3	1998	3.2
1981	5.0	1990	5.1	1999	3.0
1982	4.7	1991	4.3		

Source: Treasury, *Economic Report* various issues.

with an absolute drop in the number of hard-core poor households from 216,000 to 70,000 over the same period. As table 8.11 indicates, poverty was reduced in all sectors and regions of the economy. As shown in table 8.12, not only the more advanced states—Penang, Perak, Selangor (including the Federal Territory of Kuala Lumpur), and Johore—but other states as well have lowered poverty levels.

The reduction in poverty was achieved with the help of rising real per capita incomes—and mean monthly household incomes—and falling unemployment rates. Real GDP per capita in 1999 was RM8,493 against

TABLE 8.10 Malaysia: Incidence of Poverty and Number of Poor Households, 1976–1998

	1976			*1984*			*1985*			*1989*			*1990*		
	Total	*Urban*	*Rural*	*Total*	*Urban*	*Rural*	*Total*	*Urban*	*Rural*	*Total*	*Urban*	*Rural*	*Total*	*Urban*	*Rural*
Incidence of poverty (%)	39.6	17.9	47.8	20.7	8.5	27.3	20.7	8.5	27.3	17.1	7.5	21.8	17.1	7.5	21.8
Number of poor households ('000)	764.4	94.9	669.6	649.4	93.0	556.4				619.4	89.1	530.3			
Incidence of hard-core poverty (%)	—	—	—	6.9	2.4	9.3	6.9	2.4	9.3	4.0	1.4	5.2	4.0	1.4	5.2
Number of hard-core poor households ('000)	—	—	—	216.1	26.2	189.9				143.1	16.3	126.8			
Total households ('000)	1,931.4	530.6	1,400.8	3,133.3	1,095.3	2,038.0				3,614.6	1,182.7	2,431.9			

	1993			*1995*			*1997*			*1998*		
	Total	*Urban*	*Rural*	*Total*	*Urban*	*Rural*	*Total*	*Urban*	*Rural*	*Total*	*Urban*	*Rural*
Incidence of poverty (%)	13.5	5.3	18.6	9.6	4.1	16.1	6.8	2.4	11.8	7.6	—	—
Number of poor households ('000)	517.2	77.9	439.3	417.2	95.9	321.3	346.0	67.4	278.6			
Incidence of hard-core poverty (%)	3.0	1.1	4.3	2.2	0.9	3.7	1.4	0.5	2.4	1.5	—	—
Number of hard-core poor households ('000)	116.4	15.7	100.7	93.5	20.5	73.0	70.3	13.8	56.5			
Total households ('000)	3,826.9	1,464.7	2,362.2	4,347.8	2,357.0	1,990.8	5,117.1	2,764.3	2,352.8			

Sources: *Sixth Malaysia Plan, 1991–1995; Mid-Term Review of the Sixth Malaysia Plan, 1991–1995; Seventh Malaysia Plan, 1996–2000; and Mid-Term Review of the Seventh Malaysia Plan, 1996–2000.*

Notes: "Hard-core poverty" is estimated using half the poverty line income. In 1997, poverty estimation is based on the following poverty line incomes: RM460 per month for a household size of 4.6 in Peninsular Malaysia, RM633 for a household size of 4.9 in Sabah, and RM543 for a household size of 4.8 in Sarawak.

TABLE 8.11 Peninsular Malaysia: Incidence of Poverty by Sector, 1970, 1975, 1976, 1980, 1984, and 1987 (%)

	1970[a]	1975	1976[b]	1980	1984[c]	1987[d]
Rural						
Rubber smallholders	64.7	59.0	58.2	41.3	43.4	40.0
Oil palm smallholders	30.3	9.1	—	7.8	—	—
Coconut smallholders	52.8	50.9	64.0	38.9	46.9	39.2
Estate workers[e]	40.1	—	—	—	19.7	15.0
Padi farmers	88.1	77.0	80.3	55.1	57.7	50.2
Other agriculture[f]	91.8	78.8	52.1	64.1	34.2	—
Fishermen	40.0	47.0	62.7	35.2	27.7	24.5
Other industries[g]	35.2	35.4	27.3	22.8	10.0	—
Urban						
Mining	34.3	31.8	10.1	34.0	3.4	—
Manufacturing	32.3	28.8	17.1	18.4	8.5	—
Construction	26.6	30.5	17.7	21.3	6.1	—
Transport and utilities	36.6	26.8	17.1	23.0	3.6	—
Trade and services	23.8	24.6	13.9	14.2	4.6	—
Rural subtotal	58.7	54.1	47.8	37.7	24.7	17.3
Urban subtotal	21.3	19.0	17.9	12.6	8.2	8.1
Total	49.3	43.9	39.6	29.2	18.4	17.3

Sources: *Third Malaysia Plan, 1976–1980; Fourth Malaysia Plan, 1981–1985; Mid-Term Review of the Fifth Malaysia Plan, 1986–1990; and Sixth Malaysia Plan, 1991–1995.*

Notes: (1) The incidence of poverty for 1970 was based on the per capita poverty line income, while those for 1976, 1984, and 1987 were based on the respective gross poverty line incomes; (2) the calculations took into consideration the effects of programs implemented during 1971–1980, as well as changes in other factors, such as prices and other costs; and (3) data from studies conducted by the Economic Planning Unit and the Socio-economic Research Unit in the Prime Minister's Department, Ministry of Agriculture, Department of Statistics, and other agencies were used in the computations.

a. The *Post-Enumeration Survey (PES)* covered 25,000 households in Peninsular Malaysia.

b. The *Agricultural Census, 1977* (for reference year 1976) covered 188,000 households in Malaysia.

c. The *Household Income Survey, 1984* is a sample survey covering 60,250 households in Malaysia.

d. *Household Income Survey, 1987*, as reported in the *Mid-term Review of the Fifth Malaysia Plan.*

e. Statistics on estate workers for 1970 were derived from indirect sources and, therefore, not comparable with 1984. The *PES* did not make any distinction between estate workers and laborers on smallholdings. The *Agricultural Census, 1977* did not cover estates, and, therefore, estimates on estate workers are not available for 1976.

f. Includes other agricultural farmers such as oil palm smallholders, pepper smallholders, pineapple and tobacco farmers, and livestock and poultry farmers.

g. Includes households engaged in mining, manufacturing, construction, transport and utilities, and trade and services sectors.

RM2,460 in 1970 in 1987 prices. Over this thirty-year period, Malaysia only experienced four years of declining per capita income (i.e., in 1975, 1985, 1986, and 1998), with contractions of 1.7 percent, 3.6 percent, 1.3 percent, and 9.6 percent respectively. The 1998 decline precipitated by the East Asian financial turmoil lowered per capita income to RM8,213, still higher than the RM8,050 attained in 1995. Table 8.13 shows that mean monthly household income rose from RM423 in 1970 to RM827 in 1989, and to RM2,453 in 1997.

Though rising household incomes were observed in both urban and rural areas, earlier reductions in rural-urban and interethnic income disparities have been reversed in the 1990s. Though the urban-rural

income ratio declined from 2.1 in 1970 to 1.7 in 1993, it rose to 2.0 in 1997. However, actual rural-urban disparities in economic welfare may not be as severe since the cost of living in urban areas is higher than in rural areas.

Table 8.14 shows that professionals, on average, commanded 1.62 times more income than non-professionals in 1996, while directly employed skilled workers commanded 1.33 times and 1.60 times more than the semiskilled and the unskilled in direct employment respectively. For those employed indirectly via labor contractors, the skilled earned 1.85 times more than the semiskilled and 2.51 times more than the unskilled in the same year.

TABLE 8.12 Malaysia: Incidence of Poverty by State, 1970, 1976, 1984, 1987, 1989, 1995, and 1997

State	1970 Total Households (000)	1970 Total Poor Households (000)	1970 Incidence of Poverty (%)	1976 Total Households (000)	1976 Total Poor Households (000)	1976 Incidence of Poverty (%)	1984 Total Households (000)	1984 Total Poor Households (000)	1984 Incidence of Poverty (%)	1987 Total Poor Households (000)	1987 Incidence of Poverty (%)	1989 Incidence of Poverty (%)	1995 Incidence of Poverty (%)	1997 Incidence of Poverty (%)
Johor	1,158	520	45.7	268.1	77.8	29.0	365.8	44.5	12.2	44.7	11.1	10.1	3.2	1.6
Kedah	1,550	966	61.0	216.3	131.9	61.0	253.9	93.0	36.6	82.1	31.3	30.0	12.1	11.5
Kelantan	1,383	1,044	74.1	167.8	112.7	67.1	206.7	81.0	39.2	70.4	31.6	29.9	23.4	9.5
Melaka	291	131	34.7	85.8	27.8	32.4	95.1	15.1	15.8	12.1	11.7	12.4	5.2	3.6
Negeri Sembilan	494	241	50.5	106.0	35.0	33.0	132.8	17.3	13.0	30.1	21.5	9.5	4.8	4.5
Pahang	584	325	56.1	115.4	44.5	38.9	190.9	30.0	15.7	23.8	12.3	10.3	6.8	4.1
Penang	405	209	52.7	150.1	48.6	32.4	204.2	27.4	13.4	28.2	12.9	8.9	4.1	1.6
Perak	1,501	833	52.2	340.7	146.4	43.0	400.2	81.1	20.3	79.7	19.9	19.3	9.1	4.5
Perlis	292	187	63.2	29.7	17.8	59.8	40.1	13.5	33.7	12.1	29.1	17.2	12.7	10.6
Selangor	672	287	42.7	211.4	48.3	22.9	359.2	31.0	8.6	40.8	8.9	1.8	2.5	1.3
Terengganu	558	380	65.1	100.6	60.7	60.3	129.9	37.6	28.9	49.6	36.1	31.2	23.4	17.3
Kuala Lumpur	—	—	—	139.4	12.5	9.0	242.1	11.8	4.9	12.2	5.2	3.8	0.7	0.1
Peninsular Malaysia	8,888	5,123	56.7	1,931.4	764.4	39.6	2,621.1	483.3	18.4	485.8	17.3	15.0	—	—
Sabah[a]	—	—	—	163.9	95.5	58.3	229.8	76.0	33.1	89.0	35.3	34.3	26.2	22.1
Sarawak	—	—	—	205.1	115.9	56.5	282.2	90.1	31.9	74.3	24.7	21.0	10.0	7.5

Sources: Sudhir Anand (1983) table 5.3; *Fifth Malaysia Plan, 1986–1990; Mid-Term Review of the Fifth Malaysia Plan, 1986–1990; The Second Outline Perspective Plan, 1993–2000; and Mid-Term Review of the Seventh Malaysia Plan, 1996–2000*, table 3.2.

a. Includes Federal Territory of Labuan.

TABLE 8.13 Peninsular Malaysia: Mean Monthly Income by Location, 1970–1997 (in Constant 1978 Prices)

	Overall	Urban (U)	Rural (R)	Disparity Ratio (U/R)
1970	423	687	321	2.14
1973	502	789	374	2.11
1976	566	913	431	2.12
1979	669	942	531	1.77
1984	792	1114	596	1.87
1987	760	1039	604	1.72
1989	827	—	—	1.72
1993[a]	1167	1617	957	1.70
1995[b]	1617	2092	1040	2.01
1997	2453	3205	1570	2.00

Sources: *Fourth Malaysia Plan, 1981–1985; Mid-Term Review of the Fifth Malaysia Plan, 1986–1990; Sixth Malaysia Plan, 1991–1995; Seventh Malaysia Plan, 1996–2000;* and *Mid-term Review of the Seventh Malaysia Plan, 1996–2000.*

a. Constant 1990 prices.

b. Constant 1995 prices.

There is sketchy evidence that the economic welfare of wage and salary earners has not been severely undermined by inflation. Table 8.15 compares consumer price inflation against the growth of average wages and salaries paid in the manufacturing, construction, and mining and quarrying sectors. The evidence suggests that the growth of wages and salaries has outpaced inflation.

Globalization and Income Inequality

At least four aspects of economic globalization have probably exacerbated international inequalities, to the detriment of developing countries such as Malaysia. Many now think of external liberalization as inimical to, or at least as problematic for, development rather than as an unqualified boon, as claimed by proponents of globalization. It is therefore useful to disaggregate globalization to consider the impact of various specific aspects—including international trade, foreign direct investment (FDI), international finance, and strengthened intellectual property rights—on Malaysia.[11]

International Trade Liberalization

Malaysia's terms of trade have declined sharply in the 1980s. The import price index increased substantially while the export price index significantly declined, affecting the country's terms of trade (see table 8.16). As table 8.17 shows, for the period between 1960 and 1997, the volume of exports rose about 50 percent more than the increase in import volume. However, import prices rose almost four times more than export prices, resulting in a 52 percent fall in the terms of trade. Thus, while export income rose sixtyfold, the import bill rose almost eightyfold. The value of exports rose far less than the value of imports. Owing to

TABLE 8.14 Malaysia: Average Monthly Nominal Wage of Paid Full-Time Employees by Major Occupation Category in the Manufacturing Sector, 1994–1996

		1994	1995	1996
Professional and Managerial				
i	Professional (P)	5,163	5,220	5,749
ii	Non-professional (NP)	3,409	3,415	3,552
Disparity Ratio: (P) / (NP)		1.52	1.53	1.62
Directly Employed Workers				
i	Skilled (S)	846	903	1,001
ii	Semiskilled (SS)	626	675	755
iii	Unskilled (US)	521	560	624
Disparity Ratio: (S) / (SS)		1.35	1.34	1.33
Disparity Ratio: (S) / (US)		1.62	1.61	1.60
Workers Employed through Labour Contractors				
i	Skilled (S)	1,063	1,233	1,389
ii	Semiskilled (SS)	677	688	750
iii	Unskilled (US)	503	544	553
Disparity Ratio: (S) / (SS)		1.57	1.79	1.85
Disparity Ratio: (S) / (US)		2.11	2.27	2.51

Source: Ministry of Human Resources, Malaysia (1994–1998).

TABLE 8.15 Malaysia: Consumer Price Index and Periodic Average Wages and Salaries by Sector (%)

	Consumer Price Index Growth	Wages and Salaries
Manufacturing Sector		
1971–79	5.9	8.0
1982–90	2.6	5.7
1991–97	3.7	9.1
Construction Sector		
1971–79	5.9	7.9
1986–90	2.0	3.7
1991–94	4.1	11.2
Mining		
1971–79	5.9	8.2
1984–90	2.0	11.1
1991–93	4.2	23.3

Source: Department of Statistics, Malaysia.

the decline in the terms of trade, Malaysia suffered severe losses (see table 8.18). These developments seem to have been exacerbated by the secular decline in the primary commodity terms of trade, especially in the early and mid-1980s, and possibly by a similar decline in the terms of trade for Malaysia's manufactured exports as well.

For a long time, Malaysia's merchandise trade surpluses were undermined by its growing services account deficits (see table 8.19). The country's rapid economic expansion in the mid-1980s involved further deterioration in the services account of the balance of payments. Net investment income payments abroad continued to be the largest cause of the services deficit in 1998. Malaysia has also experienced rising freight costs. As table 8.20 shows, net payments for freight and insurance services during 1970–1998 rose rapidly. This was partly due to the rising volume and value of trade, but was also attributable to rising freight and insurance rates. Opening up services to greater foreign participation—as required by the various WTO agreements under the GATS, such as the Financial Services Agreement—will almost certainly adversely affect Malaysia's current account position.[12]

Foreign Direct Investment (FDI)

Foreign direct investment (FDI) has been relatively more important in Malaysia than in most other countries.[13] The impact of foreign direct investment on income outflows in terms of profit and dividends

TABLE 8.16 Malaysia: Terms of Trade, 1960–1997 (1960 = 1.00)

Year	Export Price Index	Import Price Index	Terms of Trade
1960	1.00	1.00	1.00
1961	0.80	1.00	0.80
1962	0.80	0.98	0.82
1963	0.78	1.00	0.78
1964	0.80	1.01	0.79
1965	0.84	1.00	0.84
1966	0.80	1.02	0.78
1967	0.73	1.00	0.73
1968	0.70	1.04	0.67
1969	0.80	1.05	0.76
1970	0.77	1.05	0.73
1971	0.71	1.13	0.63
1972	0.67	1.17	0.57
1973	0.88	1.36	0.65
1974	1.17	1.93	0.61
1975	1.02	2.05	0.50
1976	1.23	2.08	0.59
1977	1.44	2.13	0.68
1978	1.54	2.18	0.71
1979	1.78	2.34	0.76
1980	1.96	2.81	0.70
1981	1.84	3.21	0.57
1982	1.65	3.19	0.52
1983	1.74	3.06	0.57
1984	1.75	2.97	0.59
1985	1.63	2.94	0.55
1986	1.34	2.83	0.47
1987	1.53	2.84	0.54
1988	1.63	3.04	0.54
1989	1.80	3.23	0.56
1990	1.60	3.31	0.48
1991	1.66	3.40	0.49
1992	1.71	3.42	0.50
1993	1.77	3.49	0.51
1994	1.83	3.62	0.51
1995	1.94	3.69	0.53
1996	1.94	3.67	0.53
1997	1.97	3.78	0.52

Sources: Bank Negara Malaysia, *Quarterly Economic Bulletin* (various issues); Bank Negara Malaysia, *Annual Report 1992, 1994, 1996, and 1997*; and International Monetary Fund, *International Financial Statistics* (various years).

is reflected in tables 8.21 and 8.22. Total FDI rose elevenfold during 1981–1998, whereas total investment income outflows abroad in the same period increased more than tenfold. Net declared profits of foreign firms increased almost sixfold (see table 8.23), while the average profit rate decreased from 48 percent to 29 percent (see table 8.23). In contrast, net fixed assets of foreign firms increased from

TABLE 8.17 Malaysia: Terms of Trade Effects on Imports and Exports, 1960–1997

	Exports	Imports
(a) Changes between 1960 and 1997		
1960: Current value	RM3,632.6 million	RM2,786.0 million
Volume increase	2,986.7%	1,997.9%
Price increase	97.0%	378.0%
Value increase	5,980.8%	7,830.2%
1997: Current value	RM220,890.5 million	RM220,935.5 million
(b) Changes between 1960 and 1975		
1960: Current value	RM3,632.6 million	RM2,786.4 million
Volume increase	149.4%	49.4%
Price increase	44.0%	205.0%
Value increase	154.1%	206.1%
1975: Current value	RM9,230.9 million	RM8,530.4 million
(c) Changes between 1975 and 1994		
1975: Current value	RM9,230.9 million	RM8,530.4 million
Volume increase	1,137.9%	1,304.6%
Price increase	36.8%	84.4%
Value increase	2,292.9%	2,490.0%
1997: Current value	RM220,890.5 million	RM220,935.5 million

Sources: Bank Negara Malaysia, *Quarterly Economic Bulletin* (various issues); Bank Negara Malaysia, *Annual Report 1997*; and International Monetary Fund, *International Financial Statistics* (various years).

36 percent to 47 percent in the same period, while the average reinvestment rate increased from 46 to 54 percent. Recent developments, especially from the mid-1980s, differ from the longer term trends for FDI inflows and investment income outflows.

In the 1980s, the share of profits accruing to foreign-controlled companies was reduced to about 30 percent. However, this was still proportionately larger than their share of equity capital in limited companies in the country, which was 25 percent in 1990. The foreign share of corporate assets continued to decline until the late 1980s, when the government liberalized equity conditions for foreign direct investment, particularly for export-oriented manufacturing investments.

In the aftermath of the 1997–1998 Southeast Asian economic crises, it is now generally acknowledged that, like the rest of Southeast Asia, Malaysia's own industrial capabilities have been much weaker than previously thought because of greater reliance on and domination by FDI. Malaysia's success in attracting FDI has been partly due to generous investment incentives offered by the government over the years. Some studies have suggested that the incentives have been overly generous and more than necessary to attract the investments desired. In other words, the generosity of these incentives has meant that the net gains for Malaysia have been limited. Foreign industrial domination has also meant that

public policy became increasingly influenced by domestic rentier interests, which contributed to Malaysia's greater financial vulnerability to contagion and the crisis of 1997–1998.

International Financial Liberalization

Thanks to increased petroleum production from the mid-1970s, Malaysian borrowings from abroad declined during the latter half of the 1970s despite increased government borrowing and public spending (Jomo 1990). In the face of international recession in the early 1980s, the Mahathir regime began to borrow heavily for countercyclical spending and to fund the then-new prime minister's pet heavy industrialization program. The problems faced by these projects, political rivalries, and the mounting debt burden (despite low interest loans from Japan) resulted in a U-turn in economic policy in the mid-1980s in favor of more balanced budgets, economic liberalization, and privatization. The Malaysian decision to depreciate against the U.S. dollar, as the "greenback" fell against the yen and other major currencies, resulted in a ballooning of Malaysia's recent low-interest, yen-dominated debt. Since then, the Malaysian authorities have been much more circumspect of foreign borrowings, especially by the government, but also by the private sector.

TABLE 8.18 Malaysia: Trading Losses, 1960–1997

Year	Gross Exports at Current Prices (RM Million) (1)	Export Price Index (1960 = 1.00)(2)	Import Price Index (1960 = 1.00) (3)	Export Purchasing Power (RM Million) (1)/(3) (4)	Real Exports at Constant 1960 Prices (1)/(2) (5)	Trading Gain or Loss at 1960 Prices (4) − (5)	Trading Gain or Loss (% of GDP)
1960	3,632.6	1.00	1.00	3,632.6	3,632.6	0.0	0.0
1961	3,238.3	0.80	1.00	3,238.3	4,047.5	−809.2	11.8
1962	3,259.6	0.80	0.98	3,324.0	4,074.1	−750.1	10.4
1963	3,330.0	0.78	1.00	3,330.0	4,263.5	−933.5	12.2
1964	3,381.9	0.80	1.01	3,349.0	4,227.0	−878.0	10.7
1965	3,782.5	0.84	1.00	3,782.5	4,513.0	−730.5	8.1
1966	3,845.8	0.80	1.02	3,772.8	4,806.8	−1,034.0	10.7
1967	3,723.7	0.73	1.00	3,723.7	5,077.5	−1,353.8	13.8
1968	4,122.6	0.70	1.04	3,968.9	5,929.1	−1,960.2	19.0
1969	5,063.1	0.80	1.05	4,820.7	6,317.8	−1,497.1	12.9
1970	5,163.1	0.77	1.05	4,924.1	6,692.9	−1,768.8	14.1
1971	5,016.8	0.71	1.13	4,454.4	7,023.0	−2,568.6	20.0
1972	4,854.0	0.67	1.17	4,131.8	7,177.5	−3,045.7	21.7
1973	7,372.1	0.88	1.36	5,424.1	8,413.7	−2,989.6	16.5
1974	10,194.7	1.17	1.93	5,276.5	8,702.5	−3,426.0	15.7
1975	9,230.9	1.02	2.05	4,506.1	9,058.5	−4,552.4	20.5
1976	13,442.0	1.23	2.08	6,469.6	10,941.2	−4,471.6	15.9
1977	14,959.2	1.44	2.13	7,035.4	10,402.1	−3,366.7	10.4
1978	17,073.9	1.54	2.18	7,816.5	11,066.3	−3,249.8	9.0
1979	24,222.0	1.78	2.34	10,352.2	13,599.7	−3,247.5	7.2
1980	28,171.6	1.96	2.81	10,040.4	14,359.1	−4,318.7	8.1
1981	27,109.4	1.84	3.21	8,436.0	14,748.3	−6,312.2	11.0
1982	28,108.2	1.65	3.19	8,799.9	17,059.7	−8,259.8	13.2
1983	32,771.2	1.74	3.06	10,715.3	18,803.9	−8,088.6	11.6
1984	38,646.9	1.75	2.97	13,008.8	22,130.5	−9,121.7	11.5
1985	38,016.7	1.63	2.94	12,923.7	23,343.1	−10,419.4	13.4
1986	35,318.6	1.34	2.83	12,501.3	26,299.3	−13,798.0	19.2
1987	45,224.9	1.53	2.84	15,898.8	29,492.2	−13,593.4	17.2
1988	55,260.0	1.63	3.04	18,185.3	33,930.9	−15,745.6	17.3
1989	67,824.5	1.80	3.23	20,983.2	37,723.9	−16,740.7	16.5
1990	79,646.4	1.60	3.31	24,035.6	49,902.6	−25,867.0	22.6
1991	94,496.6	1.66	3.40	27,794.5	57,428.1	−29,633.6	22.9
1992	103,656.7	1.71	3.42	30,276.4	60,575.3	−30,298.9	20.5
1993	121,237.5	1.77	3.49	34,717.2	68,516.2	−33,799.0	20.7
1994	153,921.2	1.83	3.62	42,545.0	84,286.3	−41,741.3	23.0
1995	184,986.5	1.94	3.69	50,128.6	95,297.8	−45,169.2	22.2
1996	197,026.1	1.94	3.67	53,685.6	101,559.8	−47,874.2	19.2
1997	220,890.5	1.97	3.78	58,436.6	112,127.2	−53,690.6	19.5

Sources: Bank Negara Malaysia, *Quarterly Economic Bulletin* (December 1996); and Bank Negara Malaysia, *Annual Report 1992, 1994, 1996, and 1997*.

Unlike most other developing and transitional economies, there were massive net flows of funds into Malaysia and East Asia during the early and mid-1990s. These net inflows served to finance the current account deficits that became a feature of Malaysia's balance of payments during the 1990s before the advent of the 1997–1998 crisis. However, despite the massive increase in capital inflows, there was some—but not a corresponding—increase in gross domestic capital formation. The excess of the investment rate over the savings rate can be explained by FDI rather than by other capital inflows.

The Malaysian regulatory authorities—unlike those in Thailand, Indonesia, and South Korea—did not allow easy Malaysian access to foreign bank borrowings. Intending borrowers were generally

TABLE 8.19 Malaysia: Net Services Balance, 1965–1998 (RM million)

Year	Freight and Insurance	Other Transportation	Travel	Investment Income	Government Transactions	Other Services	Services Balance
1965	−162	−16	−80	−255	225	−53	−341
1966	−165	−11	−78	−268	189	−74	−407
1967	−170	−9	−69	−144	132	−91	−351
1968	−186	−12	−73	−154	125	−100	−400
1969	−247	−14	−96	−334	105	−116	−702
1970	−304	−21	−105	−355	68	−145	−862
1971	−322	−34	−106	−363	52	−105	−878
1972	−309	−35	−101	−378	25	−108	−906
1973	−420	49	−94	−659	29	−102	−1,197
1974	−714	82	−39	−997	43	−94	−1,719
1975	−621	98	−105	−727	47	−402	−1,710
1976	−726	94	−151	−985	36	−288	−2,020
1977	−883	158	−196	−1,272	22	−344	−2,515
1978	−1,072	110	−308	−1,571	27	−372	−3,186
1979	−1,362	70	−455	−1,797	25	−656	−4,175
1980	−1,934	−11	−521	−1,954	36	−792	−5,176
1981	−2,008	7	−672	−1,836	7	−810	−5,312
1982	−2,158	154	−775	−2,679	29	−1,151	−6,576
1983	−2,132	53	−1,104	−4,208	35	−1,742	−9,098
1984	−2,120	−99	−1,249	−5,255	23	−2,113	−10,813
1985	−1,852	64	−1,332	−5,434	−31	−1,806	−10,391
1986	−1,306	149	−1,368	−4,597	−190	−1,478	−8,790
1987	−1,185	45	−1,327	−4,824	−193	−925	−8,409
1988	−2,072	−44	−1,403	−5,019	−217	−1,425	−10,180
1989	−3,027	−5	−891	−5,935	−261	−1,273	−11,392
1990	−3,837	−25	632	−5,072	−3	−1,418	−9,723
1991	−4,847	−10	547	−6,735	−55	−2,095	−13,195
1992	−4,265	−355	657	−7,920	54	−2,739	−14,568
1993	−4,890	−196	906	−8,174	−72	−4,244	−16,670
1994	−7,367	441	3,603	−9,448	−36	−4,198	−17,005
1995	−9,028	737	4,143	−10,338	−23	−4,720	−19,227
1996	−8,203	1,725	4,801	−11,629	−27	−5,038	−18,371
1997	−9,162	1,747	3,252	−14,639	−150	−3,796	−22,748
1998	−8,435	2,268	3,070	−14,817	−215	−4,209	−22,338

Sources: Bank Negara Malaysia, *Quarterly Economic Bulletin* (various issues).

required to demonstrate evidence of likely foreign exchange earnings to pay off the foreign debt. One estimate is that total private foreign bank borrowings came to about US$35 billion when the crisis broke out, with three-quarters accounted for by three partially privatized state-owned enterprises, namely Malaysia Airlines; the national power utility, Tenaga Nasional; and the telecommunications company, Telekom Malaysia.

As a consequence, Malaysian bank borrowings from abroad were limited, with a lower share accounted for by short-term loans, despite Malaysia's more open economy in terms of trade and the consequently greater need for short-term trade credit. Hence, as noted earlier, Malaysia was not compelled

to seek much emergency credit from abroad, and did not have to go to the IMF for such facilities. However, although Malaysia was less vulnerable to the regional crisis on account of limited bank borrowings from abroad, its stock market was much harder hit, due to a greater share of foreign portfolio investments in the bourse.[14]

The greater policy influence of financial interests was reflected in the prime minister's desire to achieve "zero inflation" before the 1997–1998 crisis and the central bank's recent preference for inflation targeting. However, this more deflationary macroeconomic policy bias did not prevent Malaysia from achieving rapid economic growth averaging over 8 percent during the 1988–1997 decade.[15] Nevertheless, it is

TABLE 8.20 Malaysia: Freight and Insurance Payments, 1970–1998 (RM Million)

Year	Net Payments for Freight and Insurance	Exports of Goods (FOB)	Freight and Insurance as % of Exports
1970	304	5,020	6.1
1971	322	4,884	6.6
1972	309	4,736	6.5
1973	420	7,263	5.8
1974	714	10,022	7.1
1975	621	9,057	6.9
1976	726	13,330	5.4
1977	883	14,861	5.9
1978	1,072	16,925	6.3
1979	1,362	23,977	5.7
1980	1,781	28,013	6.4
1981	2,008	26,900	7.5
1982	2,154	27,946	7.7
1983	2,132	31,762	6.7
1984	2,120	38,452	5.5
1985	1,852	37,576	4.9
1986	1,306	34,970	3.7
1987	1,185	44,733	2.6
1988	2,072	54,607	3.8
1989	3,027	66,727	4.5
1990	3,837	77,458	4.9
1991	4,847	92,220	5.2
1992	4,265	100,910	4.5
1993	4,890	118,383	4.1
1994	7,367	148,506	5.0
1995	9,028	179,491	5.0
1996	8,203	193,363	4.2
1997	9,162	217,712	4.2
1998	8,435	281,947	3.0

Sources: Bank Negara Malaysia, *Quarterly Economic Bulletin* (various issues).

Note: F.O.B., free on board.

likely that its even greater growth potential was not fully realized due to "sterilization" and other anti-inflationary policy efforts.

Financial liberalization has also undermined financial policy instruments to accelerate development, which even the World Bank's 1993 *East Asian Miracle* study acknowledged had been successful in promoting growth and structural change in the region. Instruments of "financial restraint" were far more developed and extensively deployed in Northeast Asia compared to Southeast Asia. Financial policy instruments for development have been limited and modest, though prudential regulation had limited Malaysian vulnerability to the 1997–1998 currency and financial crises due to foreign bank borrowings.

For a brief period in the mid-1970s, the Malaysian authorities required commercial banks to lend at least 20 percent each to manufacturing as well as to the economically disadvantaged Bumiputera community. However, the former lending requirement was abandoned in the late 1970s, though the latter was retained. By the mid-1990s, before the crisis, lending to the manufacturing sector was barely over 20 percent, while lending to Bumiputeras exceeded 40 percent. With only 2 percent of lending going to agriculture and another 1 percent to mining, only a quarter of total bank lending was directed toward productive purposes. Instead, bank lending for property and share purchases was high, and ironically became even higher since the crisis. Thus, bank intermediation in Malaysia probably served to finance asset price bubbles including overinvestment in the construction and property sector.

Technology Transfer

While the pace of technological change and innovation has undoubtedly accelerated in recent years, strengthened intellectual property rights (IPR) — especially since the mid-1980s — have raised the costs of acquiring technology, reduced the likelihood of technology transfers, and strengthened transnational corporations' monopoly powers and abuses. These changes have adverse consequences for development and industrialization in developing countries. However, it is difficult to estimate the likely developmental consequences of a different intellectual property rights regime favoring developing countries rather than transnational corporations.

It has already been noted above that manufactured exports from developing countries have experienced declining terms of trade against manufactured imports. This is probably due to the weaker intellectual property rights asserted over the former, allowing for relatively easier entry into and consequently greater competition in some industries and markets. This has been compared to a "race to the bottom" in terms of product prices and incomes accruing to producers, quite unlike the monopolistic rents enjoyed by those holding intellectual property rights.

Payments accruing to patent holders from technology transfer agreements hardly capture the complexities and significance of the developmental impact of the strengthened international IPR regime. The problem is

TABLE 8.21 Malaysia: Foreign Capital Inflows and Outflows, 1966–1998 (RM Million)

Year	Foreign[a] Capital Inflow	% of Private Capital Formation	Gross[b] Revenue	Net Profit[b]	Investment Income Outflow
1966	170	18.8	4,669.4	n.a.	268
1967	130	12.9	5,331.0	251	144
1968	93	9.5	6,280.9	250	154
1969	245	25.8	7,730.7	380	334
1970	287	19.7	8,207.1	414	355
1971	306	18.3	8,168.6	449	363
1972	320	15.6	9,115.8	616	378
1973	420	14.4	11,561.2	1,095	659
1974	1,374	33.1	15,989.0	1,216	997
1975	839	24.0	14,806.5	787	727
1976	969	26.2	19,425.3	1,241	931
1977	999	23.0	19,767.6	1,423	1,276
1978	1,158	17.7	22,351.4	1,875	1,716
1979	1,255	18.5	25,782.2	2,353	1,991
1980	2,033	22.4	32,717.9	2,316	1,820
1981	2,914	28.3	36,368.1	2,317	1,836
1982	3,263	29.4	36,257.4	2,382	1,679
1983	2,926	23.1	39,302.2	3,007	4,208
1984	1,869	14.0	41,329.7	3,121	5,255
1985	1,725	14.1	38,403.0	2,586	5,434
1986	1,262	12.3	32,415.0	1,837	4,597
1987	1,065	9.7	36,931.1	2,597	4,824
1988	1,884	13.5	45,110.0	3,505	5,019
1989	4,518	23.8	57,219.6	4,675	5,935
1990	6,309	26.1	72,473.3	5,733	5,072
1991	10,996	35.0	88,850.2	6,811	6,735
1992	13,204	41.3	101,532.0	7,439	7,920
1993	12,885	32.8	116,716.7	8,354	8,174
1994	10,798	20.9	144,201.3	11,045	9,449
1995	10,464	15.7	175,382.4	15,342	10,338
1996	12,777	16.6	n.a.	n.a.	11,629
1997	14,450	16.8	n.a.	n.a.	14,639
1998	8,490	21.1	n.a.	n.a.	14,817

Sources: Bank Negara Malaysia, *Quarterly Economic Bulletin* (various issues); and Ministry of Finance, *Economic Report* (various years).

a. Approved foreign direct investment.

b. From *Financial Survey of Limited Companies*, Department of Statistics.

further complicated by widespread transfer pricing, which may have confusing effects depending on the various tax regimes faced by the transnational corporation in question. Such a firm may be induced to underreport the transfer value of assets in the face of onerous taxes, or to do the opposite in the face of lower taxes or tax exemptions.

Implications of Economic Liberalization for Equity

Although the World Bank's 1993 *East Asian Miracle* volume suggests that Malaysia was the only exception to the regional trend of declining income inequality,[16] government efforts to reduce interethnic inequality during the 1970s and 1980s apparently reduced overall inequality in Malaysia as well. Overall inequality in the 1980s (Hashim 1997) declined slightly more than in the 1970s (Ikemoto 1985, 358). It is also likely that the mid-1980s' recession reduced inequality by reducing the incomes of the higher income groups. Partial economic liberalization and reduced government interventions for redistribution since the late 1980s appear to have contributed to increased interethnic as well as overall inequality since the early 1990s (Jomo 2001a).

Poverty alleviation in Malaysia has been facilitated by rapid growth and structural change. Malaysia has also relied heavily on resource rents[17] to finance

TABLE 8.22 Malaysia: Inflows and Outflows of Capital, 1970–1998

	1970	1975	1978	1979	1980	1981	1982	1983	1984	1985	1986	1987	1988	1989	1990	1991	1992	1993	1994	1995	1996	1997	1998
1. Investment income to abroad	-355	-727	-1,571	-1,797	-1,820	-1,836	-2,679	-4,208	-5,255	-5,434	-4,597	-4,824	-5,019	-5,935	-5,072	-6,109	-6,419	-8,174	-9,448	-10,338	-11,629	-14,639	-14,817
2. Net transfers	-180	-79	-82	-119	-45	-78	-75	-21	-90	-14	-96	+348	+395	+219	+147	+102	+337	+513	-2,225	-2,515	-2,943	-3,345	-9,876
3. Current account movements (1 + 2)	-535	-806	-1,653	-1,916	-1,865	-1,914	-2,754	-4,229	-5,345	-5,448	-4,693	-4,476	-4,624	-5,716	-4,925	-6,007	-6,082	-7,661	-11,673	-12,853	-14,572	-17,984	-24,693
4. Private financial capital (short term)	-10	-83	-349	-1,579	902	97	+326	-263	-288	+870	-47	-2,491	-2,914	1,562	1,356	5,135	11,957	13,931	-8,484	-2,529	10,317	-12,913	-20,633
5. Errors and omissions	-260	-397	-1,034	2,247	-1,493	-1,488	-963	-885	-2,043	-368	1,322	147	287	-988	3,019	-395	81	9,370	3,333	-1,896	-6,371	-1,254	13,513
6. Inflows of long-term capital	294	1,780	1,718	2,238	2,245	5,856	8,740	9,357	7,421	4,026	2,893	-1,366	-3,192	1,849	3,458	10,362	10,423	14,028	11,795	16,599	13,442	19,133	10,670
(a) Publicsector borrowing	2	936	542	703	352	2,942	5,477	6,431	5,552	2,301	1,631	-2,431	-5,076	-2,669	-2,851	-634	-2,781	1,143	997	6,135	665	4,683	2,180
(b) Private capital	287	862	1,258	1,448	2,033	2,914	3,263	2,926	1,869	1,725	1,262	1,065	1,884	4,518	6,309	10,996	13,204	12,885	10,798	10,464	12,777	14,450	8,490
7. Capital account movement (4 + 5 + 6)	24	1,300	335	2,906	1,654	4,465	8,103	8,209	5,090	4,528	4,168	-3,710	-5,819	2,423	7,833	15,102	22,461	37,329	6,644	17,232	17,388	4,966	3,550
8. Total movement of funds (3 + 7)	-511	494	-1,318	990	-211	2,551	5,349	3,980	-255	-920	-525	-8,186	-10,443	-3,293	2,908	9,095	16,379	29,668	-5,029	4,379	2,816	-13,018	21,143
9. Total outflows (1 + 2 + 4 + 5)	-805	-1,286	-3,036	-4,660	-2,456	-3,305	-3,391	-5,377	-7,676	-4,946	-3,418	-6,820	-7,251	-5,142	-550	-1,267	5,956	15,640	-16,824	-12,220	-10,626	-32,151	-31,813
10. Total inflows (6)	294	1,780	1,718	2,238	2,245	5,856	8,740	9,357	7,421	4,026	2,893	-1,366	-3,192	1,849	3,458	10,362	10,423	14,028	11,795	16,599	13,442	19,133	10,670

Sources: Bank Negara Malaysia, *Quarterly Economic Bulletin* (various issues); and Khor Kok Peng (1983, 196–97).

Note: Errors and omissions are mainly unrecorded short-term capital outflows.

TABLE 8.23 Malaysia: Rates of Reinvestment, Local and Foreign Companies, 1970–1995

	1970	1975	1977	1978	1979	1980	1981	1982	1983	1984	1985	1986	1987	1988	1989	1990	1991	1992	1993	1994	1995
1. Net profits	590	1,458	3,091	4,021	6,293	6,948	6,957	7,337	7,973	10,696	7,558	4,457	7,471	9,377	15,509	20,246	24,262	27,793	35,983	45,681	51,735
Local (RM million)	176	670	1,668	2,147	3,941	4,632	4,637	4,955	4,966	7,575	4,971	2,619	4,874	5,872	10,835	14,513	17,451	20,354	27,629	34,656	40,201
Foreign subsidiary (RM million)	164	574	683	800	957	1,186	1,241	1,127	1,298	1,315	876	934	1,304	1,960	2,539	2,965	4,122	4,443	4,496	6,780	7,932
Foreign branch (RM million)	250	313	740	1,075	1,396	1,130	1,076	1,255	1,709	1,806	1,710	903	1,293	1,545	2,136	2,768	2,689	2,996	3,858	4,245	3,602
Foreign share (%)	70	54	46	47	37	33	33	32	38	29	34	41	35	37	30	28	28	27	23	24	22
2. Increase in net fixed assets	407	1,512	1,574	2,258	2,553	3,053	4,582	5,650	2,958	4,172	3,176	848	284	1,945	5,024	8,587	17,291	19,101	22,109	26,504	28,483
Local (RM million)	236	877	1,165	1,565	1,672	2,237	2,756	2,820	1,882	3,412	2,896	443	−356	819	2,952	4,612	11,328	13,609	15,364	21,432	22,284
Foreign subsidiary (RM million)	120	469	108	331	309	487	1,022	924	583	676	96	412	533	956	1,752	3,364	5,208	4,614	6,240	4,861	5,992
Foreign branch (RM million)	51	167	301	362	572	329	804	1,906	492	83	183	−7	107	170	320	611	755	878	505	211	206
Foreign share (%)	42	53	26	31	35	27	40	50	36	18	9	48	225	58	41	46	34	29	31	19	22
3. Reinvestment rate (%)																					
Local	134	131	70	73	42	48	59	57	38	45	58	17	−7	14	27	32	65	67	56	62	55
Foreign subsidiary	73	99	16	41	32	41	82	82	45	51	11	44	41	49	69	113	126	104	139	76	72
Foreign branch	20	53	41	34	41	29	75	152	29	5	11	−1	8	11	15	22	28	20	13	6	5
All foreign companies	41	81	29	37	37	35	79	119	36	24	11	22	25	32	44	69	88	74	81	54	46

Source: Malaysia, Department of Statistics, *Financial Survey of Limited Companies* (various issues).

public spending, which generated considerable employment, especially in the 1970s, and has included efforts to alleviate poverty.

New policies toward trade and capital flows since the early 1970s do not seem to have dramatically exacerbated or improved income inequalities. Various investment incentives induced foreign capital inflows, thus facilitating structural change and industrialization. New, more lucrative and stable employment opportunities were generated, encouraging rural-urban migration and uplifting living standards. The notion that poverty reduction is positively related to growth is borne out by the Malaysian experience, where growth has been experienced in both tradable and non-tradable sectors. Capital and (both skilled as well as unskilled) labor moved from tradable agriculture to tradable manufacturing and also to non-tradable services. Decreasing returns to unskilled labor in the services sector do not seem to have occurred.

There was no appreciable labor productivity decline in either the tradable or non-tradable sector that may be attributed to economic liberalization (specifically because of heavy reliance on FDI). Although average real wages in manufacturing increased with the switch from import substitution to export orientation in industrialization from the late 1960s, this temporary decline was probably due to labor's weaker bargaining position rather than lower labor productivity. Instead of an unskilled labor surplus, with rapid employment growth, scarcity has actually set in, attracting labor from neighboring countries in both the tradable and non-tradable sectors.

Export-oriented industrialization, driven primarily by foreign capital, helped reduce unemployment, and thus raised household incomes. Before the currency and financial crises of 1997 induced a regional recession in 1998, international economic liberalization had not significantly increased poverty, but seems to have been accompanied by worsening inequality in Malaysia. In other words, although poverty continued to fall with rapid growth, productivity gains, and declining unemployment, income inequality has been worsening in Malaysia from the 1990s, after declining modestly and unevenly in the two preceding decades.

Clearly, different aspects of liberalization—including globalization—have had rather different consequences for equity at the national level. It is also likely that international economic liberalization

has exacerbated international inequalities, rather than inequality at the national level, whereas domestic economic liberalization has been primarily responsible for increasing domestic inequalities. This is not to suggest that various aspects of external economic liberalization have had no consequences for domestic inequalities, but this is difficult to establish conclusively.

Liberalization since the mid-1980s in general—rather than external liberalization in particular—seems to have adversely affected income distribution. Income inequality, which had a more ambiguous trend since independence, seems to have increased once again since liberalization and worsened over the last decade. Deregulation, reduced government intervention, and declining commitments to earlier redistribution policies, as well as greater government efforts to meet investor expectations, have probably all contributed to slightly increased overall household income inequality and interethnic as well as rural-urban income disparities since the early 1990s. After falling from 0.50 in 1970 to 0.446 in 1989, the Gini index rose again to 0.462 in 1995 and 0.47 in 1997 (see table 8.24). Recent and current trends suggest the likelihood of worsening inequality in the future.

In light of these developments, it is important to consider possible measures to try to sustain poverty decline and to reduce inequality—at both national and international levels—in the face of continued pressures for trade, financial, and investment liberalization. This is especially important after the unprecedented regional recession in the aftermath of the 1997–1998 currency and financial crises. More targeted poverty alleviation[18] and redistribution policies are needed in Malaysia.

Since one size does not necessarily fit all, there is no universal formula for desirable national-level reforms to cope with globalization. Appropriate policies need to take into account specific national conditions, feasible options available, and so on, but the challenges outlined earlier will all need to be addressed. The big challenge for economic policy and regulation is really at the international level. The governance of international organizations—such as the Bretton Woods institutions and the WTO—has to be fundamentally reformed in favor of equitable and sustained development, rather than assuming that liberalization and globalization will somehow miraculously achieve this objective.

TABLE 8.24 Peninsular Malaysia: Household Income Shares by Income Group, 1970–1997

	1970		1973		1976	1979	1984	1987	1989	1995	1997
Total											
Top 20%	(55.9)	(54.8)	(53.7)	(55.2)	61.9	54.7	53.2	51.2		51.9	53.5
Middle 40%	(32.5)	(32.9)	(34.0)	(32.2)	27.8	34.4	34.0	35.0		34.7	33.7
Bottom 40%	(11.6)	(12.3)	(12.3)	(12.6)	10.3	10.9	12.8	13.8	14.5	13.4	12.8
Urban											
Top 20%	55.0		(55.2)		—	—	52.1	50.8			
Middle 40%	32.8		(31.4)		—	—	34.5	35.0			
Bottom 40%	12.2		(13.4)				13.4	14.3			
Rural											
Top 20%	51.0		(50.7)		—	—	49.5	48.3			
Middle 40%	35.9		(34.9)		—	—	36.4	36.7			
Bottom 40%	13.1		(14.4)				14.1	15.0			
Gini index	0.50		0.50		0.57	0.49	0.480	—	0.446	0.462	0.470
Theil index	0.48		0.43		0.71	0.42	—	—	—		

Sources: Ikemoto (1985), 350, table 1; Jomo and Ishak (1986, 5, table 1); percentages in parentheses on a per capita basis are from Kharas and Bhalla (1991, table 1), and their figures for 1984 and 1987 are not used as they are from a 30 percent sample; *Mid-Term Review of the Fifth Malaysia Plan, 1986–90; Sixth Malaysia Plan, 1991–1995; and Mid-Term Review of the Seventh Malaysia Plan, 1996–2000.*

Macroeconomic and Social Redistribution Policies

Malaysia has had a long history of social and redistribution policy interventions. Many of the major social reforms during the late colonial period, that is, the early and mid-1950s, were meant to win hearts and minds in the face of a communist-led insurgency, one of only two in the British Empire at the time, the other being the Mau-Mau revolt in Kenya. Agrarian reforms short of redistributive land reforms sought to deter the predominantly Malay peasantry from joining the insurrection.

There were also very important labor and social reforms initiated to check communist recruitment from among the working class. After the insurgency weakened from the mid-1950s and Malaya gained political independence in 1957, social policy considerations ensured rural development and other efforts to capture the rural Malay "vote bank" in the gerrymandered electoral system. The late colonial period also saw the establishment of the Rural Industrial Development Authority (RIDA, since renamed MARA) to develop a Malay business community. These efforts were lukewarm at best and gained some momentum after independence, especially after the first two Bumiputera Economic Congresses in 1965 and 1968 (Jomo 1986).

Both labor and social reforms were increased with the redistributive New Economic Policy to create the conditions for achieving "national unity" after the post-election race riots of May 1969. The NEP sought to create the socio-economic conditions for "national unity" by reducing poverty as well as interethnic economic disparities. The two NEP objectives of "poverty eradication" and "restructuring society" are the principal official social policies for the country. "Poverty eradication" has meant increased rural development efforts, including agrarian reforms short of land redistribution. "Restructuring society" has primarily involved affirmative action in favor of the predominantly Muslim Malay Bumiputera—or indigenous—community, especially in terms of tertiary education, business, employment, promotion, and other opportunities (e.g. preferential credit, low-cost housing allocations, and special discounts), and especially in areas where the government has discretionary powers.

Although the tradable agricultural and mining sectors have ceased to grow, if not actually shrunk, since the 1980s, this is principally because of land and mineral resource limitations and rising labor costs in the case of agriculture, besides the declining terms of trade. In the last three decades, the government has introduced and maintained politically important income support programs for the agricultural sector. However, most of these social policies were not designed or implemented primarily to address economic distress resulting from liberalization. Such subsidies have probably helped reduce poverty among those remaining in the agrarian sector, although education and structural employment changes have been far more important for reducing poverty.

The earlier discussion suggested how international economic liberalization has adversely affected economic inequality in Malaysia. However, many of the adverse consequences of trade, investment, and financial liberalization are not clearly captured and demonstrated by the methodology employed in the preceding exercises. The effects of recent changes in international economic governance—and strengthened intellectual property rights—are also difficult to capture except by advancing moot counterfactual propositions.

Not surprisingly, then, Malaysian public discourse about globalization—long dominated by official concerns—was rather uncritical before the 1997–1998 crisis. For many, Malaysian economic growth has greatly benefited from international trade and foreign direct investment. However, Malaysia has not exactly simply been an open laissez-faire economy. Exports—including manufactures—have been promoted, rather than simply left to the market, although the Malaysian industrial policy track record leaves a lot to be desired (Jomo et al. 1997; Jomo and Felker 1999; Jomo, Felker, and Rasiah 1999; Jomo and Tan 1999; Jomo 2001b). Meanwhile, investment regulations have changed significantly over time to attract desired investments.

The 1997–1998 economic crises in the region led to considerable discussion of "social safety nets." The Malaysian government did set up special funds to increase food production on "idle land" and for small businesses. However, most of the public policy effort has been oriented toward saving the financial system and major corporate debtors, as well as containing the impact of crisis through expansionary monetary and fiscal policies. To minimize public objections to this policy bias, the government has sought justification in terms of saving jobs for workers in the affected banks and corporations.

Table 8.25 suggests that Malaysia has benefited from foreign exchange earnings due to manufactured exports over the long run.[19] The growth of overall manufacturing capacity has been enhanced by FDI, both directly and indirectly, through learning by doing, technology diffusion, and other positive spillover effects. The indirect effects probably explain some (modest) gains in total factor productivity. The table provides a rather crude but conservative estimate of some benefits that Malaysia has reaped from exporting manufactures. The estimate seems to support the hypothesis that manufactured exports do not significantly augment foreign exchange generation capacity, and it rests on the following crucial assumptions:

1. All investment income repatriations are attributable to FDI in the export-oriented manufacturing sector.
2. There are no investment income earnings from abroad, which may be a reasonable assumption as Malaysian investment abroad is recent and still modest (Jomo 2002).
3. All imports of intermediate goods are only meant for manufacturing goods for exports.

TABLE 8.25 Malaysia: Estimates of Net Benefits from Manufactured Exports (RM Million)

Year	(A) Gross Manufactured Exports	(B) Net Investment Income	(C) Imports of Intermediate Goods	$D = (A) - (B) - (C)$ "Net Foreign Exchange Benefits"
1970	614.2	−355	1,515.1	−1,255.9
1975	2,020.4	−726	3,527	−2,232.6
1980	6,319.2	−1,954	11,752	−7,386.8
1985	12,470.8	−5,434	14,519	−7,482.2
1987	20,343.8	−4,824	16,029	−509.2
1990	46,840.5	−5,072	35,904	5,864.5
1995	147,253	−10,338	86,917	49,998
1997	178,945.1	−14,639	94,303	70,003.1
1998	237,648.9	−14,817	108,285	114,546.9
1999	271,730.2	−20,275	n.a.	n.a.
2000	317,908.3	−27,934	n.a.	n.a.

Source: Bank Negara Malaysia, *Quarterly Economic Bulletin* (various issues).

While export-oriented production facilitated by foreign participation in the Malaysian industrial sector might have been necessary to sustain long-term growth by overcoming the limitations of national markets, equity may not improve without effective mechanisms for redistribution, usually achieved through government intervention.

The 1997–1998 Financial Crisis

Not unlike other currencies in the region, the Malaysian ringgit had long been trading within a limited band against the greenback. Capital inflows had been encouraged by the de facto pegging of regional currencies to the U.S. dollar as well as by reduced regulations desired by speculators and other financial investors. Massive short-term inflows into the country encouraged investments in the country's stock and real estate markets. According to Palma (2000), the East Asian currency, financial, and subsequent economic crises of 1997–1998 were due to foreign capital inflows financing asset price bubbles, poor investments, and consumption binges.[20]

Massive portfolio investment inflows into Malaysia largely involved the stock market. There was some imprudent lending and excessive risk taking owing to relaxed government regulation, supervision, and oversight, especially just before the mid-1997 crisis. Many banks were happy to accept borrower assets—including stock and property—as collateral without evaluating project risks properly. Partial liberalization of the domestic financial system had encouraged risk taking, prompting banks to expand operations by opening new branches wherever possible and by lending more aggressively.

After the Thai baht was floated on July 2, 1997, like other currencies in the region, the Malaysian ringgit was under strong pressure due to contagion. After an aborted currency defense, which is believed to have cost over RM9 billion (US$3.6 billion at the time), the ringgit was also floated, following the Thai baht, the Indonesian rupiah, and the Filipino peso. This ringgit devaluation lowered the foreign exchange value of Malaysian assets, for example share prices. This, in turn, triggered a vicious cycle of asset price deflation, precipitating the flight of foreign as well as domestic portfolio capital. Lower asset prices also caused lending institutions to make margin calls, requiring additional collateral, which their suddenly distressed borrowers were in no position to come up with.

Declines in the Malaysian stock market index also had repercussions for the banking system. In fact, the Kuala Lumpur Stock Exchange collapsed to a greater extent than other regional bourses as foreign portfolio investors had a much higher stake in the Malaysian capital market.[21] The proportionately higher capitalization of Malaysia's share market meant that the adverse wealth effect of this collapse was greater than elsewhere in the region.[22] Besides the stock market, the property sector was also adversely affected by asset price deflation, again with significant consequences for the banking sector, due to the declining value of loan collateral.

There is also evidence of imprudent borrowing and excessive risk taking owing to implicit or even explicit government guarantees and poor corporate governance. Many banks practiced relationship banking without having sufficiently competent staff to evaluate project risks well, preferring to rely on collateral availability in making lending decisions. Liberalization of the domestic financial system encouraged banks to expand operations by competing to open more branches and lending more aggressively. Bank lending for property and share purchases was high, contributing to asset price bubbles.

The de facto pegs had encouraged banks and others to borrow from abroad without hedging for exchange rate changes. Those borrowing from abroad were confident that the monetary authorities would defend the exchange rate stability of their domestic currencies. Thus, a problem of currency mismatch arose; while banks were borrowing in foreign currencies, they lent to projects that would not generate foreign exchange in the domestic currency. With easier access to cheap foreign funds, a borrowers' market for loans developed. Interest rates also rose for a variety of reasons, including efforts to reverse the capital flight, exacerbating the effects of reduced liquidity in the financial system.

The Malaysian economy experienced a severe downturn from late 1997, with economic contraction through 1998 as the currency crisis developed into a financial crisis and then economic recession. Tighter monetary policy from late 1997 exacerbated deflationary pressures due to government spending cuts from around the same time. Thus, macroeconomic policy responses to the currency and financial crises worsened the situation. The crisis contributed to new macroeconomic problems, besides disrupting and undermining the rapid economic growth and structural transformation of the previous decade in various ways, including the following:

1. With the massive ringgit devaluation, imported inflation was inevitable, especially given Malaysia's very open economy. Prices of domestically produced goods increased markedly from 1997 to 1998, with inflation rising from 2.7 to 10.7 percent, before falling again in 1999.
2. Official efforts to reverse capital flight and check inflation in these circumstances—recommended by market analysts as well as the IMF—exacerbated deflationary tendencies.
3. Public spending cuts and credit restraint policies adopted by the government from December 1977 further dampened economic activity.
4. Business failures, growing unemployment, reduced incomes, and tighter liquidity exacerbated contractionary tendencies.
5. The precipitous stock market collapse adversely affected private consumption as well as investment via its wealth effects.
6. The flight of foreign capital could not be replaced by domestic capital, which also joined in the rush to exit the Malaysian economy.
7. Suddenly increased collateral requirements as well as the sudden economic contraction made loan recovery more difficult, raising the proportion of non-performing loans, constraining the banking system, and thus reducing liquidity as well as economic activity.
8. The depreciated ringgit increased the relative magnitude of the mainly privately held foreign debt as well as the related external debt-servicing burden.
9. Technological progress and structural change slowed down with the greater ringgit costs of foreign technology acquisition. This probably discouraged greater industrial mechanization and automation while encouraging continued dependence on cheap labor, particularly foreign labor.

However, it is now generally agreed that the Malaysian economy was not as adversely affected as the Thai, South Korean, and Indonesian economies, with the financial crisis less severe in Malaysia compared to these countries. Differences in the gravity of the crisis may be explained by the following. First, owing to the severe banking crisis in the late 1980s, when the ratio of non-performing loans rose to 30 percent of all commercial bank loans, Malaysia

later developed tighter prudential regulations—including the 1989 Banking and Financial Institutions Act (BAFIA)—and supervision. This prudential regulatory system was not completely undermined by the pressures for liberalization in the early and mid-1990s.

Second, although the private sector was allowed to borrow from abroad, the Malaysian authorities did not allow easy access to foreign borrowings, by generally insisting on the prospect of foreign exchange earnings from the project to be financed. However, there were exceptions[23] that seemed to grow in the year and a half before the crisis began in mid-1997. Most importantly, although foreign bank borrowings rose rapidly during 1996 and the first half of 1997, exposure to foreign loans was still relatively lower in Malaysia compared to the three other regional economies that had to seek IMF emergency credit.

Critically, unlike the other three, Malaysia's external liabilities did not exceed its foreign exchange reserves. Malaysia had the smallest share of short-term debt amongst the four crisis-afflicted countries, though the pre-crisis level of indebtedness (from foreign and domestic sources) of Malaysia was very high. The level of foreign debt exposure was far less as a share of GDP and especially as a share of export earnings since Malaysian exports constitute a far higher share of its GDP.

Third, since Malaysia had borrowed proportionately less, and a lower share of Malaysian borrowings was short term in nature, it did not need to seek IMF emergency credit and, hence, was not obliged to accept IMF policy conditionalities. Fourth, Thailand, South Korea, and Indonesia had much more bank-based financial systems compared with Malaysia's capital market–oriented system. Hence, Malaysia was less vulnerable as it was less reliant on its banking system, which was in far less trouble anyway.

Although it is not clear that Malaysia's heterodox monetary policy responses were crucial to its subsequent strong recovery in 1999 and 2000, Malaysia clearly did not suffer the doom predicted by orthodox critics of its September 1998 policies (Jomo 2001a). It has been suggested that the fixed exchange rate and lower interest rates associated with the introduction of capital controls from September 1998 helped Malaysia rebound from the crisis. However, this is difficult to confirm as exchange rates became more stable and interest rates declined in the region generally from around the same time after the international responses to the Russian crisis and its aftermath on Wall Street in August 1998.

Also, all the crisis-hit economies in the region recovered from the beginning of 1999, whereas the Malaysian recovery dates back only to the second quarter. And although the Malaysian recovery since has been stronger than that of Thailand and Indonesia, Korea has performed more impressively. Moreover, Malaysia had not been as badly affected by the crisis compared to the three other regional economies in the first place; hence, meaningful comparisons remain problematic. But it is generally agreed that the Malaysian approach has probably limited the reforms and restructuring that might otherwise have proven necessary if recovery was far more subject to international pressures and expectations.[24]

Conclusion

Export-led growth has been important for the Malaysian economy, from the tin boom in the mid-nineteenth century and the rubber boom of the early twentieth, to the electronics boom of the late twentieth century. But this has also meant that Malaysian economic growth has been very much affected by the vicissitudes of external demand, with growth slowing down sharply with declines in foreign demand, especially from the United States. The principal methodology employed in this study does not fully capture the negative consequences of adverse terms of trade trends that have been emphasized here.

Trade liberalization since the late 1960s has led to an increased propensity to import, though this has been mainly due to greater imports of intermediate and capital goods. This trend was interrupted by a second round of import substitution in the early and mid-1980s in order to promote heavy industries. Protection of these heavy industries caused Malaysia to delay liberalization of the automotive trade within the ASEAN Free Trade Area (AFTA) and encouraged Malaysia to impose 50 percent tariffs on a range of steel imports in response to U.S. President Bush's early 2002 imposition of steel tariffs.

Foreign reserves have mainly been accumulated from capital inflows, rather than current account surpluses. Malaysian growth has probably benefited from official development assistance (ODA) and greenfield foreign direct investment since the 1960s. However, gains have been offset by investment payments abroad,

negative externalities, and the crowding-out effect of officially favored FDI. FDI inflows are correctly associated with various foreign investor guarantees, rights, and privileges, rather than simply maintaining an open capital account regime. Before the 1990s, such capital flows had been relatively stable, consisting primarily of ODA and greenfield FDI. Such flows ebbed and flowed over time, but they were never as volatile as the portfolio investments and short-term borrowings that precipitated the 1997–1998 crises and derailed Malaysian economic development.

New measures to attract portfolio investments from the late 1980s succeeded in attracting such inflows in the early and mid-1990s. However, these flows have been highly volatile, with much more dubious, if not adverse, effects on economic growth and development. Thus, Malaysia became vulnerable to sudden reversals of such capital inflow surges. Moreover, these short-term capital inflows contributed to stock market (and real estate) asset price bubbles in the 1990s, involving irrational euphoria, growing financial fragility, and, eventually, economic collapse.

In Malaysia, unlike the rest of the region, access to cheaper foreign funds was limited by strict central bank regulation. Despite restricted access to foreign credit, nominal and real interest rates remained lower than in Thailand or Indonesia. Hence, in several important respects, Malaysia was different from the three other crisis-hit economies in the region. First, owing to a severe banking crisis in the late 1980s, when the ratio of non-performing loans rose to 30 percent of all commercial bank loans, Malaysia had implemented tighter prudential regulations—including the 1989 Banking and Financial Institutions Act (BAFIA)—and supervision.

Second, the Malaysian authorities did not allow easy private sector access to foreign borrowings, generally insisting on the prospect of foreign exchange earnings from the projects to be so financed. Hence, despite having the most open economy of the four, with exports exceeding GDP in value, Malaysia had the smallest share of short-term debt. Third, although Malaysia was less vulnerable to foreign bankers refusing to roll over short-term loans, it was much more vulnerable to the reversal of portfolio investments, mainly into the relatively highly capitalized Kuala Lumpur Stock Exchange (KLSE).

Fourth, Malaysia's different circumstances and lower vulnerability to capital account openness did not require it to seek IMF emergency credit and subject itself to accompanying conditionalities. Fifth, although it is not clear that Malaysia's heterodox monetary policy responses were crucial to its subsequent strong recovery in 1999 and 2000, Malaysia clearly did not suffer the doom predicted by orthodox critics of its September 1998 policies (Jomo 2001a). Malaysia's countercyclical fiscal response from mid-1998 and more favorable external demand conditions, especially for electronics, undoubtedly helped.[25]

The policy measures considered and implemented by the Malaysian government in response to the 1997–1998 crisis also offer important lessons. The Malaysian government strongly supported the Japanese government initiative to set up an Asian monetary facility during the third quarter of 1997. Although the effort failed, owing to Western objections, the establishment of regional monetary arrangements is an important option to consider and encourage. Such arrangements would allow countries more options in both crisis prevention and management, besides developing regional capacities and capabilities more sensitive to regional and national conditions than those offered by the IMF. The existence of choice would also undermine the monopoly powers currently enjoyed by the IMF in disbursing emergency credit with adverse policy conditionalities unrelated to the sources or causes of the crisis.

While the Malaysian experiment with currency and capital controls from September 1998—fourteen months after the crisis began—may have been too late to stem massive capital flight, it did provide breathing space for countercyclical macroeconomic policies. However, it is not clear how crucial these policies were for subsequent recovery, which also happened elsewhere in the region, especially in South Korea (Jomo 2001a). This underscores the importance of retaining national autonomy in economic policy making, not only for macroeconomic policy, but also for development and redistribution.

Most importantly, national macroeconomic policy autonomy is critical in order to be effectively countercyclical, especially during downturns. While social and redistribution policies should be an integral part of economic policy generally, progressive countercyclical policies not only serve as a safety net, but also contribute to economic recovery. Especially given Malaysia's very open economy, sustaining incomes for—and hence spending by—poorer groups is more likely to have more multiplier effects at the national level, thus contributing more to economic recovery than additional disposable income for the better off, who have a lower propensity to consume.

We are grateful to Foo Ah Hiang and Liew San Yee for their help in the preparation of this paper. They are not responsible for any errors that we might have made.

Notes

1. Current account liberalization may involve replacing import quotas or other non-tariff barriers with tariff levies, reducing and consolidating tariff rates into a fairly narrow band (e.g., between 0 and 20 percent), and removing export subsidies.

2. Unlike the 1960s' promotion of (consumer goods) import substitution, the early 1980s' second round of import substitution focused on heavy industries such as automotive and steel industries. With the advent of the (first) national car, the Proton, imports of completely assembled cars have been limited to a number requiring import permits while import duties on the completely knocked-down parts of imported car assembly kits were raised. The (two) national cars enjoy lower duties for similar imports.

3. Except for Israel and, more recently, the Federal Republic of Yugoslavia (i.e., Serbia and Montenegro), with special restrictions imposed on transactions with these two countries.

4. Until 1971, the Malaysian ringgit (RM) was pegged to the U.S. dollar at RM3 = US$1. The ringgit strengthened afterward; before the 1985 Plaza Hotel Agreement, it fluctuated around RM2.4 = US$1. The exchange rate weakened to RM2.7 = US$1 from around 1987, before strengthening slightly as the U.S. dollar continued to decline against the yen to RM2.5 = US$1 during the 1990s until July 1997. From September 2, 1998, the ringgit was pegged at RM3.8 = US$1. Despite the open economy, consumer prices have risen modestly, except after the oil price shock in 1974, and after the collapse of the ringgit in 1994.

5. One of the first steps taken to attract FDI in export-oriented industries was the creation of free trade zones for factories to manufacture products for export. To date, there are twelve such zones all over the country. Companies located in the zones are subjected to very minimal customs control formalities for their imports of raw materials, parts, machinery, and equipment as well as for exports of their finished products. Licensed manufacturing warehouses (LMWs) have also been established when it is neither practical nor desirable to establish a free trade zone. This facility was first introduced in 1975 and is offered to companies that export at least 80 percent of their products and import almost all their raw materials.

A number of other export incentives appeal to both foreign and domestic investors. These include export credit refinancing; double tax deduction for expenses incurred for export promotion and export credit insurance; industrial building allowance for warehousing export goods; import duty exemption and drawback of excise and sales taxes paid for imported intermediate goods; sales tax exemption for imports of machinery and equipment; and other tax incentives for R&D, training, and industrial upgrading to promote efficiency.

6. Manufactured goods exported by Malaysia include electronic components, electrical appliances and machinery, transport equipment, food, beverages and tobacco, textiles, clothing and footwear, wood and rubber products, paper and paper products, petroleum products, chemicals and chemical products, non-metallic mineral products, manufactures of metal, optical and scientific equipment, and toys and sporting goods.

7. The 1999 UNCTAD *World Investment Report* shows that most FDI in the 1990s was for mergers and acquisitions (M&As), rather than greenfield FDI. In developing countries, M&As have mainly involved acquisitions, particularly during periods of distress, especially after the ever more frequent currency and financial crises of recent times. "Fire-sale FDI" has further undermined the likelihood of superior management due to M&As, already considered dubious in business management theory.

8. There are no reliable statistics on value-added for export-oriented manufacturing alone. Official data show value-added for all manufacturing as well as for specific subsectors by industrial group, some of which are more export oriented than others, although there is no subsector that is purely export oriented. Some studies from the 1980s suggested that only 7 percent of the value of electronic exports from Malaysia consisted of value-added in Malaysia, in other words, the rest consisted of imported intermediate and capital goods.

9. Profit repatriation is not, however, only due to foreign direct investment, but is also due to foreign portfolio investment, though the latter is typically interested in capital appreciation, reflected in stock prices, rather than dividends, and so on.

10. The real exchange rate is defined as the ratio of the price of tradable goods to the price of non-tradable goods. In computing the rate, the price of tradable goods is approximated by the producer price index (PPI), while the consumer price index (CPI) is used as a proxy for the price of non-tradable goods.

11. Assistance from Mohd. Aslam, Foo Ah Hiang, and Lee Hwok Aun is gratefully acknowledged. The usual caveats apply.

12. Malaysia has offered to bind nearly all financial services to underscore its commitment to the WTO's Financial Services Agreement under the GATS.

13. The role of FDI in the Northeast Asian miracle was modest. FDI accounted for less than 2 percent of gross domestic capital formation during the high-growth periods in Japan, South Korea, and Taiwan compared to the developing country average of around 5 percent and Malaysia's average of 10 to 15 percent from the 1960s (Jomo et al. 1997).

14. These inflows could be more easily reversed then even short-term bank borrowings that are not rolled over.

15. The post-war record suggests that moderate inflation—of less than 20 percent—has been good for growth.

16. The World Bank recommends that other developing countries try to emulate the second-tier Southeast Asian NICs, especially since the mid-1980s, when they liberalized. Contrary to the claims of the World Bank and others, the East Asian economies do not demonstrate any clear relationship between export-oriented industrialization and better income distribution. While export-oriented production probably helped sustain long-term growth by overcoming the limitations of national markets, there is little reason for equity to improve without effective mechanisms for redistribution, usually achieved through government intervention. There is little evidence that distribution determined by market mechanisms is necessarily more equitable in effect than the distributional consequences of progressive government regulations and interventions.

The simplistic picture of East Asian "growth with redistribution" or "egalitarian growth" does not stand up to careful empirical scrutiny. Interestingly, those economies with more elaborate, effective, and successful industrial policies have also been more egalitarian, although available data do not allow meaningful testing for causality. Northeast Asia has been distinctly more egalitarian than Southeast Asia, though recent economic liberalization has exacerbated inequality in that region as well.

17. Mainly from petroleum and natural gas owned by the federal government's national petroleum company, Petronas, reputedly one of the best run in the world.

18. Regional efforts targeting poor groups—for example, land reform, subsidized housing, and subsidized access to education—have been successful and should be emulated with greater transparency and accountability in Malaysia.

19. There are no reliable statistics on value-added for export-oriented manufacturing alone. Official data show value-added for all manufacturing as well as for specific subsectors by industrial group, some of which are more export oriented than others.

20. Although there was no major consumption binge in the case of Malaysia.

21. Before the crisis, the Malaysian government was probably the most pro-active in organizing "road shows"

and other efforts to induce foreign portfolio investments in its stock market.

22. Likewise, the recovery of the stock market since September 1998 has also probably had a significant positive wealth effect, reflected in increased domestic consumer demand.

23. It seems that three-quarters of corporate foreign borrowings were accounted for by three partially privatized state-owned enterprises.

24. A regional monetary facility, as advocated by the Japanese government at the height of the 1997 crisis, might allow countries more options in both crisis prevention and management, besides developing regional capacities and capabilities more responsive to regional and national conditions.

25. Conventional growth accounting exercises suggest that Malaysian GDP growth has been input rather than productivity driven. In one such exercise, 75 to 85 percent of Malaysia's GDP growth over the past three decades has been explained by inputs of labor and capital, with less than 25 percent attributable to total factor productivity increases (Wee 2001). There has been a lot of investment in physical capital that has precipitated a high incremental capitaloutput ratio (ICOR). This pales in comparison with Ireland, Japan, and Hong Kong, where productivity apparently explains 45 to 55 percent of growth. Hence, the new conventional wisdom is that Malaysia needs to become more competitive by stressing productivity-driven growth, especially as countries such as China, India, and others compete increasingly effectively with Malaysia.

References

Ariff, Mohamed, Z. A. Mahani, and E. C. Tan. 1997. *Trade and investment policies in developing countries: Malaysia case study*. Economic Development Research Department Monograph, March. Tokyo: Institute of Developing Economies.

Bank Negara Malaysia. 1994. *Money and banking in Malaysia, 1959–94*. Kuala Lumpur: Bank Negara Malaysia.

———. 1999. *The central bank and the financial system in Malaysia: A decade of change*. Kuala Lumpur: Bank Negara Malaysia.

Berg, Janine, and Lance Taylor. 2000. *External liberalization, economic performance and social policy*. CEPA Working Paper, no. 12, February. New York: New School University.

Gopal, Jaya. 1999. Malaysia as palm oil refining industry: Policy, growth, technological change and competitiveness. In *Industrial technology development in Malaysia*, edited by K. S. Jomo, Greg Felker, and R. Rasiah. London: Routledge.

Hashim, Shireen M. 1997. *Income inequality and poverty in Malaysia*. Boulder, Colo.: Rowman & Littlefield.

Ikemoto Yukio. 1985. Income distribution in Malaysia, 1957–80. *The developing Economies* 23 (4).

Jomo K. S. 1986. *A question of class*. Oxford University Press, Singapore.

———. 1990. *Growth and structural transformation in the Malaysian economy*. London: Macmillan.

———. 1997. *Southeast Asia's misunderstood miracle: Industrial policy and economic development in Thailand, Malaysia and Indonesia*. Boulder, Colo.: Westview.

———. ed. 1998. *Tigers in trouble: Financial governance, liberalisation and crises in East Asia*. London: Zed Books.

———. ed. 2001a. *Malaysian eclipse: Economic crisis and recovery*. London: Zed Books.

———. ed. 2001b. *Southeast Asia's industrialization*. Houndmills, UK: Palgrave.

———. ed. 2002. *Ugly Malaysians? South-South Investments Abused*. Durban, South Africa: Institute for Black Research.

Jomo K. S., and Greg Felker, eds. 1999. *Technology, competitiveness and the state*. London: Routledge.

Jomo K. S., Greg Felker, and R. Rasiah, eds. 1999. *Industrial technology development in Malaysia*. London: Routledge.

Jomo K. S., and S. Nagaraj, eds. 2001. *Globalization versus development: Heterodox perspectives*. Houndmills, UK: Palgrave.

Jomo K. S., and Ishak Shari. 1986. *Development policies and income inequality in Peninsular Malaysia*. Kuala Lumpur: Institute for Advanced Studies, University of Malaya.

Jomo K. S., and Tan Kock Wah, eds. 1999. *Industrial policy in East Asia: Lessons for Malaysia*. Kuala Lumpur: University of Malaya Press.

Kharas, Homi, and Surjit Bhalla. 1991. Growth and equity in Malaysia: Policies and consequences. Paper presented at the Eleventh Malaysian Economic Convention, "The Sixth Malaysia Plan: The way forward to a developed Nation," Kuala Lumpur, 24–26 September.

Palma, Gabriel. 2000. The three routes to financial crises: The need for capital controls. CEPA Working Paper no. 18, November. New York: New School University.

Wee, Victor. 2001. Higher productivity key to economic growth. *The Star*, August 28.

9

External Liberalization, Growth, and Distribution in the Philippines

Joseph Y. Lim and Carlos C. Bautista

1. Introduction

The worldwide trend toward financial openness that began in the early 1990s undoubtedly led to the growth of financial asset markets in less developed economies. Foreign funds found their way into domestic capital markets, which were then labeled "emerging markets." In the beginning, several developing economies appeared to benefit from the free flow of foreign capital, which augmented their domestic savings and allowed higher growth paths. Jubilation over these developments was short-lived, however. Emerging market economies suffered severe recessions during the Asian financial crisis of 1997 as foreign capital moved out as fast as it arrived.

Years before capital account liberalization, in the 1980s, several countries, including the Philippines, initiated trade liberalization schemes as part of structural adjustment efforts under IMF–World Bank guidance. These programs were supposed to trigger changes in the industrial structure from import dependency to export-oriented competitiveness. While external liberalization in the real and the financial side of the economy was believed to foster sustained economic growth, proponents of the programs were never explicit about their distributional effects.

This study attempts to examine the effects of external liberalization efforts in the Philippines on growth and distribution. This requires that several complex issues be sorted out—how the timing, length, and depth of trade and capital account reforms interacted with macro conditions and how macroeconomic policy, as part of these reforms, was directed and coordinated during the period these were instituted. To accomplish this task, the important political and economic events that took place during the period these reforms were undertaken are analyzed in relation to the movements of relevant variables. This is supported by simple quantitative decomposition techniques of key macroeconomic relationships. The decomposition techniques owe their origins to the structuralist writings of Taylor (1983) and Berg and Taylor (2000).

The second section gives a description of Philippine economic performance. For completeness, the narrative begins from the time the Philippines acquired its independence. The focus of the study, however, will be from 1980 to the present because this is when the reforms were put in place. The discussion highlights the presence of stronger and more frequent bust-recovery cycles since the 1980s that have been detected by various researchers (see Fabella 1995; De Dios 1998, 2000: Bautista 2000). A decomposition of aggregate demand offers a quantitative perspective into historical events and also shows how aggregate demand components reflect the policy stance at particular periods under study. The third section analyzes distribution effects through a decomposition of employment. By this, it is hoped that the distributional effects of liberalization and deregulation may be better understood. The final section discusses areas for further research and concludes.

2. Philippine Macroeconomic History and Analysis

2.1. Background: 1949 to 1979

The infusion of foreign resources (mainly U.S. reparation money) allowed the Philippine economy to recover from damages suffered during the Second World War. This was short-lived, as a significant part of the aid was squandered in importing final goods. The first balance of payments (BOP) crisis in 1949 brought about import and exchange controls that led to a full decade of strong import-substituting industrialization. This resulted in the economic prosperity of the 1950s. One of the key elements of the import-substituting industrialization strategy was the erection of strong import quota restrictions supplemented by high tariffs to protect industries at their infancy.

However, the expected structural transformation under this industrialization strategy—the maturity of industries using domestic inputs to produce goods that were previously imported—did not materialize. Import-substituting firms remained dependent on imported raw materials, intermediate inputs, and capital equipment as the strategy failed to achieve backward linkaging. The domestic market remained

small because of the lack of redistributive efforts (especially a lack of genuine agrarian reform), the absence of a cohesive industrial strategy, and corrupt practices in the issuance of import licensing as alternating governments in the 1950s used their monopoly power to expand their rent-seeking activities. Import dependence, corrupt politics, a war-devastated agricultural sector, and an overvalued peso (determined by exchange controls) assured that trade and current account deficits became the rule.

Reasonable growth rates were recorded in the 1950s. However, toward the end of the decade, another balance of payments crisis loomed and pressures to devalue the peso increased. Multiple exchange rates systems were implemented to stave off a de facto devaluation. Inflation rose, and in 1960 the GDP growth rate fell to 1.2 percent.

A regime defending the import-substitution strategy was replaced in 1962 by a new government that promoted some trade and foreign exchange liberalization.[1] The peso was allowed to succumb to exchange market pressure as the exchange rate moved from 2.02 to 3.85 pesos per dollar. IMF help was sought (Montes 1987). The IMF would be instrumental in designing economic policies for the Philippines starting in this period. It is ironic that the Philippines, the most abiding follower of the conservative economic policies of the multilateral institutions compared with other countries in the region, would become the basket case for the non-socialist countries in the region.

While the 1962 devaluation eased the pressure on the balance of payments for a while, import growth consistently outstripped export growth in the remaining years of this decade. This was because the export promotion strategy adopted to replace the import-substituting strategy was difficult to implement. Reliance on volatile agricultural export markets (coconut and sugar, which met stiff competition either from substitutes or from exports of other countries) and the lack of a manufacturing base for exports (with the garments and textile sector far from being competitive) did not bring about the necessary export spurt. The sluggishness of the foreign trade sector throughout the decade (despite the investment incentives to export firms) contributed to another balance of payments crisis in 1970 (see Jurado 1976). This was the country's first foreign debt crisis and was directly triggered by an inability to pay multilateral loans used to finance an infrastructure building spree by the Marcos government.[2]

To cushion the impact of the 1970 crisis, the Philippines entered another IMF-sponsored structural adjustment program that aimed to correct the structural defects of the economy. The World Bank and the Asian Development Bank pushed for an even more outward-oriented strategy. The structural adjustment program and new development strategy included a radical devaluation of the peso, the promotion of manufactured exports (centered on garments and electronics), and incentive schemes to attract export-oriented multinationals.[3]

The move toward a centralized government with the imposition of martial law in 1972 made it easier for the government to spend on capital outlays using foreign money. During this period, foreign borrowing was the primary mode of financing public investment. Because of this, the 1970s are known as the decade of "debt-driven growth." The debts were derived not only from multilateral sources but also, starting in the middle of the decade, from foreign banks awash with "petrodollars" incurred by the central government as well as by the public and private corporations run by people close to Marcos.

Also during this decade, a series of exogenous shocks led to large swings in domestic business activity. The highest growth rate for the decade (8.5 percent in 1973), attributable to the export and commodities market boom, was followed by 3.5 percent growth in 1974 after the first oil shock. Because available foreign resources were directed toward low-productivity investment and "white elephants," little genuine economic transformation took place. In this decade, one sees an inconsistent implementation of an outward-looking strategy, combining export promotion with the protection of economic sectors run by close Marcos allies. Unlike in South Korea, in the Philippines there were no performance-based incentive schemes for either the export-oriented or the domestic-oriented firms. Cronies close to the Marcos regime were not subject to any sort of discipline and threat of punishment.

Table 9.1 summarizes the important events that occurred in each decade. As a further guide, figure 9.1 shows the graph of annual per capita GDP growth from 1960 onwards. This diagram gives a visual perspective of Philippine boom-bust cycles. From the historical account, one will notice a pattern of moderate growth for several years, followed by deterioration. After a slowdown, an inflow of foreign resources lift the foreign exchange constraint and the economy is back on track on the normal growth path. One can see this pattern in the early growth years of the 1950s that were fueled by import substitution. This was followed by a bust period in 1960, when binding foreign exchange constraints resulted in exchange market pressure. Another cycle began in the 1960s when recovery was made possible with IMF assistance. Growth continued until the balance of payments crisis in 1970 and the first oil shock of the mid-1970s hit the economy.

TABLE 9.1 Important Events by Decade

Decade	Highlights
1950–1959	Reconstruction financing based on war reparations dries up; import-substituting industrialization strategy implemented to stave off BOP crisis; high growth in manufacturing and the economy; BOP crisis toward end of the decade
1960–1969	1962 devaluation; abandonment of import-substituting industrialization strategy; initial IMF help; infrastructure spending spree in second half of decade; foreign debt crisis toward the end of the decade
1970–1979	1970 devaluation to solve BOP crisis; centralized government under martial law; first oil shock; foreign debt-driven growth with IMF assistance and support
1980–1989	Second oil shock; high interest rate policies by developed countries; Latin American foreign debt crisis begins in 1982; 1983 Aquino assassination and BOP crisis; debt default and moratorium; capital flight; political instability; economic collapse in 1984–1985; end of martial law; trade and financial liberalization in second half of decade; recovery with IMF assistance; series of coups against the Aquino government
1990–2000	Slowdown in 1990 and recession in 1991 (owing to another crisis brought on by the debt overhang, monetarist policies, and loss of confidence); power crisis in 1992–1993; tariff reduction and capital account liberalization; locking into AFTA, WTO, and APEC[a] in the early and mid-1990s; bullish growth in 1994–1997; Asian currency crisis in 1997–1999; weak and uncertain recovery afterwards

a. The ASEAN Free Trade Area, the World Trade Organization, and the Asia-Pacific Economic Cooperation, respectively.

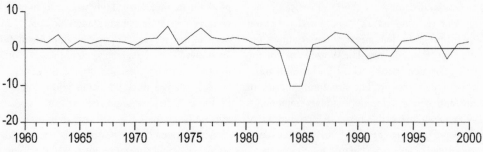

FIGURE 9.1 Per Capita GDP Growth, 1960–2000

2.2. 1980 to 2000

The period 1980 to 2000 is an interesting episode for several reasons. First, the increasing frequency and depth of bust-recovery cycles experienced by the Philippines point to the important issue of the sustainability of growth (see Fabella 1995). An examination of the GDP growth path in figure 9.1 shows a more volatile movement and a seemingly shorter cycle length beginning in 1980 as compared to the previous periods. Only in this episode did the Philippines experience negative growth. Secondly, this is the period when reforms in trade and the capital account were undertaken. To aid in the analysis, a decomposition of aggregate demand and employment along structuralist lines is utilized. The analysis using aggregate demand decomposition techniques is strikingly different from traditional analyses of liberalization, which rely on supply-side arguments. Traditional macro indicators as well as national income and balance of payment tables will also be referred to in the discussion.

2.2.1. Aggregate Demand Decomposition

Following Berg and Taylor (2000), the aggregate supply and demand balance can be written as[4]

$$X = Y + T + M = C + I + G + E \qquad (1)$$

The leakage parameters[5] can be used to rewrite equation (1) as

$$X = \frac{s}{s+t+m}\left(\frac{I}{s}\right) + \frac{t}{s+t+m}\left(\frac{G}{t}\right)$$
$$+ \frac{m}{s+t+m}\left(\frac{E}{m}\right) \qquad (2)$$

The ratios in parentheses are the direct multiplier effects of investment, government, and export demand on output, appropriately scaled by the respective leakage parameters. The simple decomposition above can be used in many ways.

From equation (2), it is easy to see sectoral account imbalances using the direct multipliers or "stances" of aggregate demand components against output. For example, $G/t > X$ implies that the government is incurring a deficit. The reworked identities are used in Philippine national accounts data and are shown in table 9.2. In figures 9.2, 9.3, and 9.4, these direct multipliers are graphed along with output, X. These diagrams conveniently reveal at what periods an account is in deficit or in surplus or, equivalently, which sectoral accounts are contributing to increases or decreases in demand. This study more or less follows the periodization in Lim and Montes's (2000) discussion, and makes extensive use of data *of different frequencies in graphical form* whenever necessary.

2.2.2. 1981–1983: Economic Slowdown; 1984–1985: Economic Collapse

The Philippine economy deteriorated in the late 1970s up to the early 1980s. The slowdown had its roots in the inefficient allocation of foreign debt-financed public investment, the second oil price shock and world recession, and the increasing dependence on commercial foreign debt. Rising incremental capital/output ratios and deteriorating external terms of trade reflected these inefficiencies and difficulties. The previous decade's "hybrid" industrialization strategy (export promotion under a fixed exchange rate regime and protection of key economic sectors) made the economy vulnerable to external shocks. A widening

TABLE 9.2 Aggregate Demand Decomposition (All Values in Constant 1985 Prices)

	$Y=GDP-T$	$X=GDP+M$	$S=Y-C$	$s=(Y-C)/X$	$t=T/X$	$m=M/X$	I/s	G/t	E/m
1981	569,674	836,342	161,716	0.193	0.073	0.246	608,741	1,325,153	700,100
1982	590,704	874,022	168,637	0.193	0.072	0.252	735,315	1,253,742	639,197
1983	600,138	882,591	175,504	0.199	0.074	0.246	733,196	1,280,263	733,192
1984	553,253	795,487	127,486	0.160	0.080	0.224	602,991	845,729	784,668
1985	511,310	727,933	90,478	0.124	0.083	0.214	520,112	732,103	686,440
1986	533,476	759,793	98,661	0.130	0.076	0.222	551,793	817,109	799,770
1987	549,457	824,902	97,071	0.118	0.082	0.252	753,408	797,429	705,470
1988	598,747	905,137	118,185	0.131	0.066	0.272	785,275	1,079,623	716,324
1989	628,326	979,204	123,707	0.126	0.073	0.286	956,320	1,127,982	778,905
1990	646,066	1,020,654	114,294	0.112	0.073	0.294	1,193,772	1,317,301	796,345
1991	634,785	1,006,994	90,997	0.090	0.081	0.288	1,191,619	1,123,484	862,136
1992	630,517	1,020,674	69,008	0.068	0.087	0.296	1,763,800	1,042,769	906,440
1993	643,349	1,073,765	64,760	0.060	0.085	0.316	2,054,759	1,196,874	903,833
1994	673,185	1,164,396	73,079	0.063	0.080	0.342	2,280,589	1,249,667	988,567
1995	704,085	1,275,846	81,100	0.064	0.077	0.371	2,359,208	1,338,731	1,099,792
1996	750,613	1,389,678	98,823	0.071	0.071	0.389	2,410,039	1,517,711	1,204,327
1997	797,145	1,528,931	112,829	0.074	0.063	0.416	2,555,265	1,882,168	1,369,973
1998	802,835	1,424,420	94,931	0.067	0.060	0.377	2,251,448	1,959,904	1,245,532
1999	832,117	1,423,919	105,539	0.074	0.060	0.356	2,067,124	1,908,325	1,319,040
2000	869,006	1,428,095	117,080	0.082	0.059	0.332	1,910,255	1,899,025	1,334,731

Source of basic data: National Statistical Coordinating Board; NEDA planning and policy staff.

crisis in the financial sector, which began with the near-collapse of the commercial papers market in 1981,[6] and a worsening external debt profile in which short-term debt amounted to 25 percent of total external debt were clear indications of further deterioration. This was especially alarming as world interest rates were rising rapidly due to tight monetary policies in the United States and Europe. Deficits on the fiscal side and the current account rose to critically dangerous levels. This can be seen in figures 9.3 and 9.4 for the years 1980 to 1983, when government demand financed by foreign resources increased (also see figure 9.5 for a view of public investment to GDP ratio). Apparently the government was undertaking countercyclical policies to artificially stir up domestic demand to offset the adverse effects of the worsening

international environment. The foreign debt crisis that started in Mexico and Brazil in 1982 took its toll in the Philippines as long- and medium-term debt access was virtually cut off and short-term debt instruments were obtained at exceedingly high interest rates. In July 1983 the peso was allowed to depreciate by 10 percent to ease the foreign exchange pressures.

These developments set the stage for the Philippines' worst balance of payments and economic crisis. This occurred in the third quarter of 1983, two years after the start of the world recession and about a year after the eruption of the Latin American foreign debt crisis. The assassination of an opposition leader led to capital flight, a large discrete devaluation, and a spike in the price level. In October 1983, a moratorium on external debt payments was declared, which

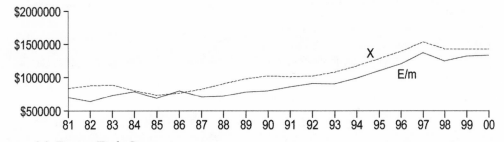

FIGURE 9.2 Foreign Trade Stance

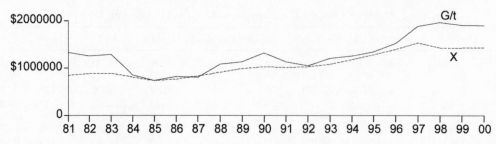

FIGURE 9.3 Government Stance

effectively meant that no new inflows from abroad would be forthcoming. The policy makers followed the typical monetarist response prescribed by IMF programs. A draconian tightening of liquidity and credit was effected to stem capital outflows and to control rising prices (see table 9.3, M3/GDP, growth of M3/CPI, and lending rates). The side effect of very tight money was a discrete rise in the interest rates that, because of portfolio-substitution effects, eventually led to a halt in the upward trend of the nominal currency depreciation (see figure 9.6). Working capital cost-push effects led to closures of firms and work stoppages in key industries. The total collapse of the Philippine economy was manifested by negative annual growth rates of –7.6 percent for both 1984 and 1985. The effect of this depression was perhaps more than what Indonesia experienced in 1998. Gross domestic savings and gross capital formation fell precipitously, never to recover the rates achieved in the early 1980s (see table 9.3). Decapitalization occurred as investments fell short of the amount needed to meet depreciation needs. Table 9.3 shows that the GNP per capita contracted by almost 20 percent from 1983 to 1985. This brought the economy back one full decade, and the country's chances of becoming an East Asian success vanished. Even with the sharp contractions in 1984–1985, inflation rates rose to enormous heights,

fueled partly by the devaluation processes, partly by the sharp cut in supply via the working capital cost-push effect brought about by the extreme monetarist policy. It was only in 1986, when the economy hit rock bottom, that inflation fell to zero and negative levels (but only briefly). External deficits also improved—to be expected during very harsh depressions—as can be seen by the movements of the current account and trade balances in table 9.3.

Deteriorating financial conditions, very similar to what happened to hard-hit countries in the Asian crisis, brought non-performing assets into the lap of the Central Bank and state-owned banks. It would take a long while to finally dispose of these assets, rehabilitate the financial sector and government financial institutions, and create a new Central Bank that was not seriously debt strapped.

2.2.3. 1986–1989: Recovery Period; 1990–1993: Slowdown, Recession, and Power Shortages

It is important to note that the crisis prompted policy makers under the new government led by Corazon Aquino (1986–1992) to seriously institute structural adjustments as per the dictates of the IMF and World Bank. The disastrous Marcosian interventions (with their share of corrupt administrators) were seen as

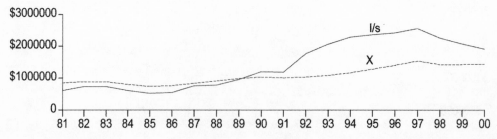

FIGURE 9.4 Private Stance

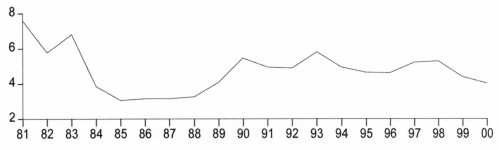

FIGURE 9.5 Government Investment/GDP

proof that market liberalization, deregulation, and privatization would be the appropriate economic policies. The new policy measures included the lifting of import restrictions in May 1986, tax reforms, and the large-scale privatization of state-owned enterprises (Lim and Montes 2000).[7] The economy slowly and partially recovered toward the end of the 1980s with IMF assistance, but not without a lot of difficulty, what with the debt overhang and political instabilities. This was reflected in an average growth rate of 5.6 percent from 1987 to 1989 under the new government.

In the 1986–1989 recovery period, replacement investments and consumption were the primary sources of growth, followed by significant increases in public investment financed by domestic borrowing (see figure 9.10 and table 9.3—the movements of public investment and M3). Private investment also began to rise starting in 1986 until 1991, when another recession occurred.

In the later part of the 1980s, increases in investment rates and the government's pump-priming program allowed capacities and demand to grow. However, the growing fiscal and external deficits became unsustainable in 1989 and 1990 (see table 9.3), especially since the debt overhang of the foreign debt crisis continued with the government assuming most of the private debts. The Baker Plan as well as other debt restructuring attempts, which only rescheduled payments and required continuing interest payments, doomed the possibility of long-run recovery and growth. The debt overhang accompanied by import-intensive growth (caused partly by the lifting of import restrictions and an overvalued currency; see a rising m in figure 9.7) also led to growing and large trade and current account deficits (see figure 9.2 and table 9.3). To steer the economy away from the external and fiscal crisis (accompanied by rising double-digit inflation rates; see table 9.3), the government adopted a tight monetary policy, cut spending, and raised indirect taxes. Monetary cutbacks were undertaken and interest rates climbed back to more than 20 percent in 1990 to 1991, while fiscal spending was also cut to trim the budget deficit (see table 9.3). Monetarist policies once again assured that domestic credit would fall amidst outgoing external debt flows due to the overhang. A recessionary situation was created.

A series of right-wing military coup attempts against the Aquino government, culminating in a nearly successful one in December 1989, further eroded business confidence. This and the uncertainties in the international environment with the impending Gulf War aggravated demand cutbacks and led to a slowdown beginning in 1990. In 1991 economic recession occurred with the gross domestic product contracting by 0.6 percent (see figure 9.1 and table 9.3). Recovery was not in the near horizon as power shortages, culminating in 1992, forced firms to cut production. The effects of the power crisis lasted until the first half of 1993. The fiscal and balance of payment crisis and the response by policy makers can be observed in figures 9.2 and 9.3.

2.2.4. 1993–1996: Tariff Reduction and Capital Account Liberalization; 1997 Onward: The Asian Crisis and Aftermath

A new administration under Fidel Ramos[8] (1992–1998), the second since the lifting of martial law, vigorously pursued trade liberalization, moving from lifting import restrictions to genuine tariff reduction. This was facilitated by locking the country into international agreements in which the Philippines committed to international trade and international trade regulation; these agreements included the

TABLE 9.3 Some Macro Indicators of the Philippines, 1981–2000

Year	GDP Growth Rate	GNP Growth Rate	GNP per Capita (1985 Prices)	Unemployment Rate (%)	Labor productivity ('000 Pesos; 1985 Prices)	Inflation Rate	Exchange Rate (Average)	Growth of Exchange Rate	Fiscal Balance (% of GDP)	Gross Domestic Savings (% of GDP)	Gross Capital Formation (% of GDP)	I-S Gap (% of GDP)	Lending Rate (%)	M3/ GDP	Growth of M3/CPI (%)	Current Account Balance (% of GDP)	Trade Balance (% of GDP)
1981	3.4	3.2	12.643	8.7	36.1	17.3	7.9	5.2	-4.3	26.8	27.7	1.0	15.3	0.293	13.3	-5.9	-6.2
1982	3.6	2.8	12.633	9.4	37.6	8.6	8.5	8.1	-4.5	25.3	27.5	2.2	18.1	0.303	7.2	-8.6	-7.1
1983	1.9	0.9	12.526	7.9	34.7	5.3	11.1	30.1	-2.0	27.4	29.9	2.5	19.2	0.309	12.8	-8.3	-7.5
1984	-7.3	-9.1	11.110	10.6	31.4	47.1	16.7	50.3	-1.9	22.9	23.1	0.1	28.2	0.233	-27.1	-4.1	-2.2
1985	-7.3	-7.0	10.086	11.1	28.9	23.4	18.6	11.4	-2.0	18.8	16.5	-2.3	28.6	0.235	-11.2	-0.1	-1.6
1986	3.4	3.6	10.205	11.1	28.7	-0.4	20.4	9.6	-5.0	19.1	16.0	-3.0	17.5	0.237	8.1	3.2	-0.7
1987	4.3	5.1	10.476	9.1	29.7	3.0	20.6	0.9	-2.4	21.0	16.5	-4.5	13.3	0.237	8.8	-1.3	-3.1
1988	6.8	7.2	10.971	8.3	30.6	8.9	21.1	2.6	-2.9	21.0	17.8	-3.3	15.9	0.248	12.6	-1.0	-2.9
1989	6.2	6.2	11.385	8.4	32.0	12.2	21.7	3.0	-2.1	20.3	20.8	0.5	19.3	0.274	14.1	-3.4	-6.1
1990	3.0	4.8	11.661	8.1	32.0	13.2	24.3	11.8	-3.5	18.7	23.1	4.4	24.1	0.279	3.7	-6.1	-9.1
1991	-0.6	0.5	11.456	9.0	31.2	18.5	27.5	13.0	-2.1	16.6	20.0	3.4	23.1	0.278	-2.7	-2.3	-7.1
1992	0.3	1.6	11.382	8.6	30.1	8.6	25.5	-7.2	-1.2	14.9	20.9	6.0	19.5	0.285	1.9	-1.9	-8.9
1993	2.1	2.1	11.151	8.9	30.0	7.0	27.1	6.3	-1.5	13.8	23.8	10.0	14.7	0.326	15.8	-5.5	-11.4
1994	4.4	5.2	11.456	8.4	30.5	8.3	26.4	-2.6	1.1	14.8	23.6	8.8	15.1	0.359	16.0	-4.6	-12.2
1995	4.7	4.9	11.743	8.4	31.2	8.0	25.7	-2.7	0.6	14.5	22.2	7.7	14.7	0.400	15.9	-2.7	-12.1
1996	5.8	7.2	12.298	7.4	30.9	9.1	26.2	2.0	0.3	14.6	23.4	8.8	14.8	0.406	6.8	-4.8	-13.7
1997	5.2	5.3	12.657	7.9	32.0	5.9	29.5	12.4	0.1	14.2	24.4	10.2	16.3	0.440	15.1	-5.3	-13.5
1998	-0.6	0.4	12.432	9.6	31.4	9.8	40.9	38.8	-1.9	12.8	21.0	8.2	16.8	0.429	-2.4	2.4	0.0
1999	3.4	3.7	12.615	9.4	31.7	6.6	39.1	-4.4	-3.7	14.9	19.0	4.0	11.8	0.457	12.7	10.0	6.5
2000	4.0	4.5	12.871	10.1	34.4	4.4	44.2	13.1	-4.1	17.0	17.8	0.8	10.9	0.430	0.2	12.4	9.2

Sources: National Statistics Coordination Board (NSCB), Bangko Sentral ng Pilipinas (BSP; various years); and International Financial Statistics, ADB Key Indicators of Asia-Pacific Countries (various years).

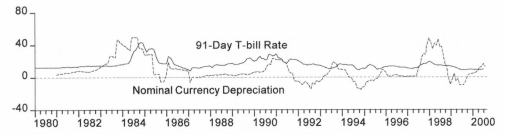

FIGURE 9.6 Interest Rate and Exchange Rate

ASEAN Free Trade Area (AFTA), the World Trade Organization (WTO), and the Asia-Pacific Economic Cooperation (APEC).

Full capital account liberalization was achieved in the last quarter of 1993 but was initiated in 1991. It is also important to point out that trade and capital account liberalization were initiated independently of each other, as trade liberalization started early on in 1986. The passage of the Foreign Investments Act in 1991 marked the beginning of the liberalization of the capital account. This law provided for the gradual removal of restrictions on foreign investment over a three-year period. The relaxation of rules on foreign exchange transactions by the Central Bank followed in the first quarter of 1992. In the third quarter of the same year, all the remaining restrictions on foreign exchange transactions that prevented foreign investors from freely repatriating their capital were removed (see Bekaert and Harvey 1998). By the start of the second quarter of 1993, the government permitted the repatriation of cash dividends without Central Bank approval. In the middle of 1993, the stock price index climbed rapidly because of foreign demand and the easier entry and exit of foreign capital. The stock market boom continued until the middle of 1994, when the market corrected itself and growth in the market indices slowed down (see figure 9.8). The

"emerging market" syndrome continued until the Asian crisis, with the stock market index peaking in early 1997, a few months before the outbreak of the crisis.

The liberalization moves of the Ramos government produced much economic confidence and bullishness, as indicated by the stock market. The high optimism seemed to be justified by what was perceived as better economic management. The power shortages ended with the fast tracking of hydroelectric plants.[9] The foreign debt overhang was reduced by the Brady Plan, which converted the debt into long-term guaranteed bonds. The plan also included some interest reduction schemes. The debt-strapped Central Bank was revamped into a new institution with the national government effectively taking over its debts.

As the economy recovered from a slowdown during this liberalization period, policy makers opted to loosen credit partly by reacting passively to private foreign inflows, that is, they did not conduct extensive sterilization operations to offset the capital flows[10] (see table 9.3). The impact on some macro prices is seen in figures 9.9 and 9.10. During this period, interest rate spreads declined. The real exchange rate also appreciated until the second quarter of 1997. It is interesting to note that the government account was

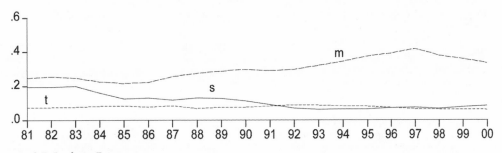

FIGURE 9.7 Leakage Parameters

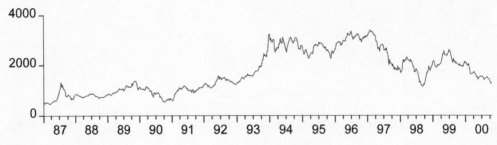

FIGURE 9.8 Stock Price Index

kept in balance by the Ramos administration before the outbreak of the Asian crisis (see figure 9.4). The fiscal balance, falling inflation rates (see table 9.3), and continuing foreign inflows fueled even more optimism for the Ramos growth strategy. But the last two years of the Ramos term, concurrent with the Asian crisis, brought fiscal deficits back. The following Estrada and Arroyo administrations would have even more trouble with high fiscal deficits. Periods of fiscal balance followed by those of fiscal deficits (see figure 9.3) also marked the previous Aquino government, and fiscal aggressiveness (see discussion in the previous subsection) appeared toward the end of Aquino's term. De Dios (2000) relates this to the pattern of business fluctuations and offers a "political business cycle" hypothesis to complement the "real structural" hypothesis of the bust-recovery cycle.

With the capital account liberalization, foreign capital inflows reached their highest level at approximately 5 percent of GDP in 1996. The economy's average GDP growth rate for the years 1994 to 1997 was 5 percent, while GNP growth rate averaged 5.7 percent.

But not all indicators were bright.[11] First, the external sector continued to register current account deficits during this period (see figure 9.2). More

seriously, the investment-savings gap widened in the mid-1990s (the size of which was unprecedented), as can be seen in figure 9.4 and table 9.3. The gap can be explained by growing private investments accompanied by declining private savings rates, as shown in figure 9.7, and is consistent with the historically high trade balance deficits (reaching more than 13 percent of GDP) right before the crisis (see table 9.3). The continuing external deficits and rising investment-savings gap are offshoots of rising import intensity and falling private savings rates, as shown in figure 9.6. Again, the sharp rise of m and the sharp fall of s in the mid-1990s were unprecedented. The sharp rise in m was obviously a natural response to the quick pace of tariff reduction combined with a sharply appreciating currency (in real terms) that made imports and tradables particularly cheap. The sharp fall in s even during a time of growth reflects the increasing dependence on foreign funds and foreign savings to finance the external deficits and investment-savings gap.

As is well known by those acquainted with the Asian crisis, the foreign inflows that came in were largely in the form of short-term debts and portfolio investments that poured in after the capital account liberalization. These unhedged dollar borrowings

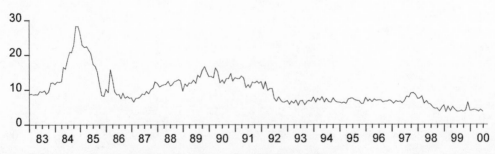

FIGURE 9.9 Interest Spread: Bank Lending Rate – Savings Deposit Rate

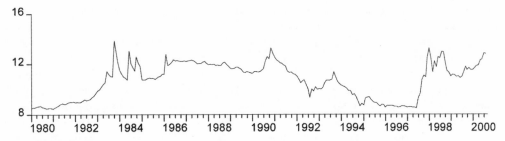

FIGURE 9.10 Real Exchange Rate

(used to finance real estate, construction, speculation, and manufacturing activities) as well as "hot money" provided the classic key ingredients for the Philippine variant of the Asian crisis. This included the rise of speculative bubbles in the financial and real estate sectors and their bursting once the Thai devaluation and financial outflows infected the region.

The crisis, in addition to the El Niño weather phenomenon that had detrimental effects on agriculture, halted the growth episode, and GDP growth stood at –0.54 percent in 1998. In 2000, the nominal consolidated public sector deficit to GDP ratio stood at more than 4 percent and was expected to grow further in 2001 and beyond (the real government deficit account was almost balanced in 1996).[12] In 1998, the Philippines experienced a positive nominal current account surplus but was in deficit in real terms, as shown in figure 9.2. Meanwhile, the savings rate did not really improve and the tax effort remained the same. Economic confidence remains very weak as political corruption during the Estrada administration and political upheavals during the early days of the Arroyo government stifled and continue to stifle "animal spirits."

2.3. A Synthesis and Analysis of the Philippine Macroeconomic History

Ever since bust-recovery cycles became systemic from the 1980s onward, most of the growth during 1980 to 2000 was the result of either filling up excess capacity or using more imports for production rather than the outcome of more efficient and productive use of existing domestic resources. (We shall tackle this more at length in the employment section.) Typically, at the start of a growth cycle, the economy was awash with dollars, allowing it to raise import levels. Initial high confidence allowed foreign funds to pour in to

finance the increasing import needs. Bust periods were characterized by foreign exchange shortages that curtailed the imports of raw materials and capital goods (see De Dios 1998). These shortages occurred as rising import needs and/or foreign debt payments outpaced foreign financial inflows, or as net foreign inflows fell due to losses of confidence caused by internal or external factors.

Paradoxically, the economic decline improved the external position of the country during the recession period. Economic crises and recoveries in the Philippines, therefore, ran along the lines of the traditional, old-fashioned, two-gap analysis.

Growth interruption is a consequence of continuing and growing dependence on imports and unsustainable inflow of foreign capital (which ends up in capital flight during crisis periods). This was the case in the balance of payment crises in 1949, in the late 1950s and early 1960s, in 1970, in 1983–1985, in 1991, and in 1998. It must be pointed out that recessions themselves are the temporary solution to this dependence on foreign capital and the periodic shortage of foreign funds (usually a combination of increased dollar needs during growth periods and capital flights after the "good days" are over). Investment-savings gaps as well as current account and trade deficits are reduced as a result of the recession (see figures 9.2 and 9.4 as well as table 9.3). No doubt belt-tightening and output contraction (with a very distinct monetarist-IMF flavor) have been prescribed for the Philippines as periodic solutions to its "profligate" use and need for foreign currency, but these increasingly frequent recessions are the main manifestations of the Philippines' lack of economic development. As table 9.3 shows, the level of GNP per capita in 2000 is just about the same as in 1981. In terms of this indicator the Philippines has, on the whole, remained stagnant for two decades.

In modern Philippine economic history, growth interruptions were caused by crisis events—external and fiscal crises aggravated by power crises, or political crises and externally imported crises such as the Latin American foreign debt crisis and the Asian financial crisis. The change in the growth pattern, cycle length, and depth of the bust phase after 1980 may be attributed to structural adjustments and external liberalization made after the 1983 crisis. Ironically, the more frequent bust periods occurred during the heyday of the external liberalization, from 1980 to 2000. The structural adjustments and external liberalization, though extensive, seemed insufficient, at best, at addressing structural problems. These problems, which proved to be the barriers to sustained growth (see De Dios 1998), included high trade and current account deficits incurred during growth periods, low domestic savings rates, and weak tax collection efforts (see figure 9.7 for the trends in the private savings rate and tax rate).

The link between external liberalization and the frequent bust periods of the last two decades may be viewed in two lights. First, external liberalization exposes the country to more volatile financial risks. This is exactly what the Philippines experienced in the early 1980s, when economic collapse began with the country's embroilment in the Latin American foreign debt crisis, and again in 1997–1998 when "contagion" from Thailand, Indonesia, and Korea wreaked havoc on the economy. Furthermore, the growing import dependence of the country in the 1980s and 1990s no doubt had a lot to do with import liberalization and an appreciating currency (during the good times), the latter aggravated by capital account liberalization. The two-gap edge has become sharper and more dangerous.

Second, whatever merits external liberalization (plus domestic liberalization, privatization, and deregulation) bestows in terms of efficiency and productivity gains are, of course, controversial and can be argued either way. But one outcome that the Philippines shared with many other liberalizing economies (from Russia to Argentina to Turkey to South Africa) was that the liberalization, privatization, and deregulation processes did not automatically effect changes in the institutional and governance structures of the country.

This brings us directly to the internal and domestic causes of the crisis-recovery cycles. One can see in the case of the Philippines that periodic political and governance crises have contributed to the collapse of the economy and business confidence in the 1980s, the 1990s, and the present. One also has to add that the lack of infrastructure, human capital development, technology improvements, and practical industrial policy—not to mention the lack of social cohesion—has inhibited the rise of competitiveness and efficiency gains. The Philippines has already lost a big share of the world garment export market with the reduction of quotas as well as the rise of cheap garment exports from South Asia, China, and Eastern Europe. The rise of free market ideology (as epitomized by IMF policies) has been detrimental to encouraging dynamic and constructive interventions on the part of the state to effect a technologically sound and performance-based private and public sector. It is not surprising that the Philippines has been the most obedient disciple of the IMF- and World Bank–sponsored market liberalization processes in East Asia. Ironically, the country has also been the weakest among the non-transition economies in terms of dynamic sectoral development, confidence building, and human and technological capital innovations. Indeed, the ideology still pursued by the Philippines is anachronistic in a world where even theoretical economics has admitted that externalities, market failures, and asymmetric information are more the rule than the exception. Indeed, markets, on one hand, and institutional and state structures, on the other, are no longer dichotomous and mutually exclusive but should be viewed as complementary and mutually reinforcing.

Finally, we should not forget the perennial role of the IMF and monetarist ideology in instilling severe contractionary and recessionary measures throughout all the balance of payment crises. One sometimes wonders which is the disease and which the cure in the stabilization prescriptions for the Philippines and similar countries. We pose that one factor contributing to the difference in the Philippine path from that of its more successful East Asian neighbors is its long internship with the IMF.

The enmeshing of the above factors explains the laggard condition of the Philippines. Figure 9.11 shows the GNP per capita picture for the Philippines, Thailand, and South Korea, translating their gross national products into 1960 U.S. dollar prices for the period 1960 to 2000. One can see that in 1960, the Philippine GNP per capita was above that of the other two countries. South Korea overtook the Philippines

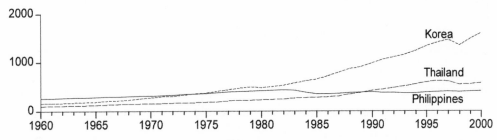

FIGURE 9.11 GDP per Capita (in 1960 U.S. Dollars)

in the mid-1970s because of its tremendously high growth in the 1950s and 1960s. More importantly, Thailand was able to overtake the Philippines in the late 1980s and increased the gap in the 1990s because of the series of bust-recovery cycles experienced by the Philippines in those two decades. Thailand never experienced a serious bust before 1997–1998, and Korea experienced it only once before 1998 (in 1980). One can see the Philippines' stagnation throughout the 1980s and 1990s, as the other two countries grew at a tremendously fast pace (except in the 1998–1999 period), very clearly in the graph.

3. Employment and Labor Productivity Effects of External Liberalization

3.1. Employment and Productivity at the Aggregate Level

This subsection describes the general trend in employment, productivity, and real wages. Figure 9.12 shows the composition of GDP by origin. It can be seen that during crisis periods, the trend of the industry

share declines whenever a crisis hits the economy, while the opposite is true of the service sector. It should also be pointed out that industry had the highest share until 1984 but was overtaken by the services sector and has since never regained its position.

Labor productivity, defined as the ratio of GDP to total employment, plunged during the crisis years of 1983–1985 but increased slightly when the economy recovered. The trend in overall labor productivity seems to follow the changes in economic activity (see figure 9.13). Productivity declines if the economy is in a crisis period. After the 1983–1985 crisis, real wages were on an increasing trend up to 1990 but declined gradually as the economy entered the 1990s (see figure 9.14). The unemployment rate, however, declined in the recovery years but started rising during economic slowdown, as can be observed in figure 9.15. The next section presents a more detailed discussion of these variables at a disaggregated level.

3.2. Employment and Labor Productivity Decomposition: Methodology

As in Berg and Taylor (2000), the economically active population is the sum of the employed and the

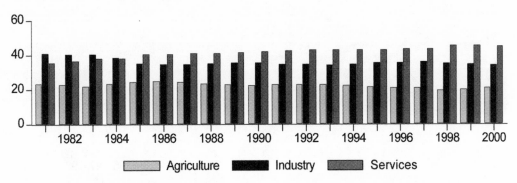

FIGURE 9.12 Share of Major Sectors in GDP

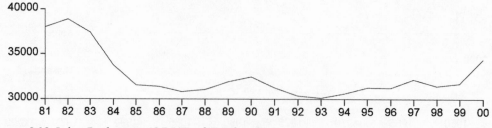

FIGURE 9.13 Labor Productivity (GDP/Total Employed)

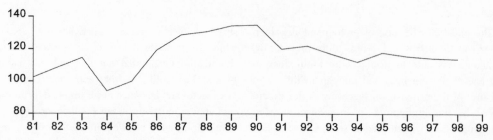

FIGURE 9.14 Real Wage (1985 = 100)

unemployed: $E = L + U$. The participation rate and the unemployment rate are $\varepsilon = \frac{E}{P}$ and $u = \frac{U}{E}$ respectively.[13] $\lambda = \frac{L}{P}$ refers to the percent of employed in the population. From this, one can derive an expression for the participation rate: $\varepsilon = \lambda + \varepsilon u$. Log-differentiating this yields

$$(1 - u)\hat{\lambda} - (1 - u)\hat{\varepsilon} = -u\hat{u} \qquad (3)$$

where variables with "^" denote percent change (e.g., $\hat{q} = dq/q$).

The decomposition can also be done at the sectoral level. Let i be the index for the sectors. Let the labor/output ratio, the sectoral output per (working) capita, and the sectoral employment share of the working population be, respectively, $b_i = \frac{L_i}{X_i}$, $x_i = \frac{X_i}{P}$, and $\lambda_i = \frac{L_i}{P}$.

These ratios can be used to write the aggregate employment share as $\lambda = \sum_i \lambda_i = \sum_i \frac{L_i}{X_i} \frac{X_i}{P} = \sum_i b_i x_i$. Log-differentiating this yields

$$\hat{\lambda} = \frac{1}{\lambda} \sum_i \lambda_i(\hat{x}_i + \hat{b}_i) = \frac{1}{\lambda} \sum_i \lambda_i(\hat{x}_i - \hat{\rho}_i) \qquad (4)$$

where $\hat{\rho}_i = -\hat{b}_i = \hat{X}_i - \hat{L}_i$ is the sectoral productivity growth. Thus, the growth of total employment as a percent of the working population is the sum of sectoral per capita output growth less sectoral productivity growth weighted by the share of sectoral employment to total employment. Overall labor productivity, $\rho = \frac{X}{L} = \frac{\Sigma_i X_i}{\Sigma_i L_i}$, is also decomposed in terms of percentage rates of change: $\hat{\rho} = \sum_i \frac{X_i}{X} \hat{\rho}_i + \sum_i \left(\frac{X_i}{X} - \frac{L_i}{L}\right)\hat{L}_i$

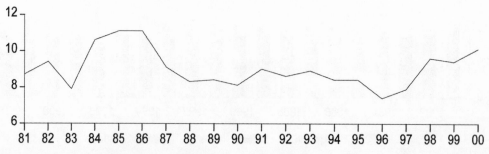

FIGURE 9.15 Unemployment Rate, 1981–2000

3.3. Description of the Data and Categories

We classified the economic sectors into non-tradables, exportables, and importables.[14] Using the 1994 Input-Output Table, we calculated the export and import shares of total output for each sector. Arbitrarily, we set 20 percent as the cutoff point. Sectors with more than 20 percent export and import shares are classified as exportables and importables, respectively. Those sectors whose export and import shares fall below 20 percent are considered non-tradables. Table 9.4 shows that with reasonable aggregation, the non-tradable sectors are agriculture, fishery,[15] livestock, and forestry (henceforth to be called simply "agriculture"); food, beverages, and tobacco (henceforth to be called "food"); construction; electricity, gas, and water (henceforth to be called "EGW"); transportation, storage, and communications (henceforth to be called simply "transportation"); wholesale and retail trade (henceforth to be called "trade"); finance,[16] insurance, real estate, and business services (henceforth to be called "FIRE"); and government and private services excluding recreational and cultural services and hotels and restaurants (henceforth to be called "services" [but different from the service sector]).

Exportables, which are not importables, consist of mining and quarrying (henceforth to be called "mining") and recreational and cultural services and hotels and restaurants (henceforth to be called "tourist-related services"). Importables, which are not exportables, are the manufacturing sectors of paper and paper products, chemicals and chemical products, and non-metallic mineral products (including coal, petroleum, and rubber). They are lumped into one sector called "importable manufacturing." Sectors that are both exportables and importables consist of textiles (including garments); leather and wood products (henceforth to be called "traditional exportables"); and basic metal industries, fabricated metal products, electronics, and other manufacturing industries (henceforth to be called "non-traditional exportables"). It must be pointed out that garments dominate the traditional exportables while electronic products dominate the non-traditional exportables.

The table shows that the manufacturing sector is clearly the core of the tradable sectors. The 1994 IO underestimates the export role of electronics, since by 1998–2000 this category comprised around 70 percent of the merchandise exports of the Philippines. It must also be pointed out that the biggest exportable sectors (electronics or non-traditional exportables and garments or traditional exportables) are also importables since their inputs (electronic parts and textile fabric) are also included in their respective sectors. This means that the bulk of Philippine exports are import intensive. Especially in the case of garments, these products also compete fiercely with foreign products even in the domestic market. Because of their high import intensity, these two sectors combined have very low value-added and employment impact in the economy. In 2000 the import-intensive export sectors combined only made up 6.9 percent of total gross value-added (see table 9.6) and 5.7 percent of total employment (see table 9.8).

Tables 9.5 and 9.6 give us a more detailed look at the gross value-added of the various economic sectors from 1980 to 2000, based on our sectoral classification above. We will refer to these tables when discussing the decomposition exercises, especially when analyzing output movements.

The labor force and employment statistics employ data from 1988 to 2000. Starting the third quarter of 1987, the Labor Force Statistics (LFS) of the Philippines changed the reference period for determining employment and labor force statistics from one month to one week. By definition, this effectively increased levels of unemployment rates and reduced levels of labor force participation rates. Thus, data before 1988 would not be comparable with the data from 1988 onward. Because of this limitation, we ran the decomposition exercises only from 1988 and beyond. This correlates with the period of intense liberalization and deregulation in the Philippines, as 1988 marked the almost complete lifting of all quantitative restrictions on imports.

The labor force and employment data we used are averages of the January, July, and October surveys of each year. The April data were not used because of their high volatility and uncharacteristically high seasonal unemployment because of the lack of agricultural activities (it is between planting and harvesting seasons) and the entry of new graduates to the labor market during this period (since March is graduation time).

Tables 9.7 and 9.8 show the employment data for the various sectors in terms of growth rates and percentage share of employment in each sector to the labor force (we term these percentages "employment rates"). We again refer to these tables to facilitate our discussion of the decomposition exercises, especially when analyzing employment and labor force movements.

Major Categories	Economic Sector	% of Total Output	% of Total Exports	% of Total Imports	Total Exports/ Total Output (Export Share)	Total Imports/ Total Output (Import Share)
Agriculture	Agriculture, livestock fishery, and forestry	14.16	6.46	3.83	7.33	3.36 Non-tradable
	Agricultural products and agricultural services	7.39	3.08	2.48	6.69	4.16
	Livestock, poultry, and other animals	3.92	0.03	1.11	0.11	3.51
	Fishery	2.65	3.36	0.23	20.32	1.06
	Forestry and hunting, trapping, and game propagation	0.19	0.00	0.02	0.00	1.04
Industry		46.61	59.71	78.88	20.56	21.00
Mining	Mining and quarrying	0.94	2.45	0.80	41.85	10.49 Exportable
	Metallic ore mining	0.63	2.39	0.62	60.76	12.20
	Non-metallic mining and quarrying	0.31	0.07	0.18	3.42	7.02
Manufacturing		37.70	56.80	69.72	24.18	22.95
Manufacturing 1	Food, beverages, and tobacco	14.87	8.59	5.22	9.27	4.35 Non-tradable
Manufacturing 2	Importable manufacturing	9.04	6.35	26.47	11.27	36.34 Importable
	Paper and paper products	0.95	0.80	2.09	13.51	27.44
	Chemicals and chemical products	7.04	4.87	22.91	11.09	40.37
	Non-metallic mineral products	1.05	0.68	1.47	10.44	17.35
Manufacturing 3	Traditional exportable (Wearing apparel, footwear, and wood products)	5.19	14.62	9.91	45.23	23.71 Exportable/ importable
	Textiles and leather	4.03	11.86	9.19	47.31	28.32
	Wood and wood products	1.16	2.76	0.73	38.04	7.74
Manufacturing 4	Non-traditional exportable	8.60	27.24	28.11	50.85	40.57 Exportable/ importable
	Basic metal industries	1.54	4.90	1.79	51.04	14.42
	Fabricated metal products	0.66	0.93	1.74	22.61	32.55
	Electronics and other manufacturing industries	6.40	21.41	24.59	53.73	47.70
Construction	Construction	5.28	0.27	4.31	0.81	10.13 Non-tradable
EGW	Electricity, gas, and water	2.69	0.19	4.06	1.16	18.73 Non-tradable
	Electricity and gas	2.49	0.17	3.97	1.10	19.77
	Waterworks and supply	0.19	0.02	0.08	1.91	5.24
Services		39.23	33.83	17.29	13.84	5.47
	Transportation, storage, and communication	5.71	5.32	4.75	14.97	10.32 Non-tradable
	Transportation services and storage/warehousing	4.65	4.44	4.27	15.34	11.40

(continued)

TABLE 9.4 (continued)

Major Categories	Economic Sector	% of Total Output	% of Total Exports	% of Total Imports	Total Exports/ Total Output (Export Share)	Total Imports/ Total Output (Import Share)
	Communication	1.06	0.89	0.48	13.37	5.59
	Wholesale trade and retail trade (trade)	11.52	14.31	4.33	19.94	4.66 Non-tradable
	Finance, insurance, and real estate (FIRE)	9.69	6.56	2.52	10.87	3.22 Non-tradable
	Banking institution	2.00	4.43	0.97	35.48	5.98
	Non-bank financial intermediaries	0.99	0.85	0.52	13.81	6.53
	Insurance	1.01	0.45	0.32	7.23	3.95
	Real estate	4.38	0.29	0.28	1.07	0.79
	Business services	1.31	0.54	0.43	6.54	4.09
	Gov't and private services (except recreation, cultural services, restaurants, and hotels)	9.05	0.69	4.30	1.22	5.90 Non-tradable
	Public administration, defense, public education, and health services	5.50	0.00	1.58	0.00	3.56
	Personal and household services	1.84	0.55	1.65	4.79	11.13
	Other private services	1.71	0.14	1.07	1.32	7.80
	Recreation, cultural services, and hotels and restaurants	3.26	6.94	1.39	34.21	5.30 exportable
	Recreational and cultural services	0.91	2.33	0.38	41.04	5.13
	Restaurant and hotels	2.35	4.61	1.01	31.55	5.36
	Total	100.00	100.00	100.00	16.05	12.41

Source: 1994 I-O tables.

3.4. The Decomposition Results

Tables 9.9 to 9.14 give us the decomposition of the labor productivities of the various sectors, while Tables 9.15 to 9.20 give us the decomposition of the employment of the sectors and the aggregate movements. The notation p_i denotes the labor productivity of sector i, X_i / L_i. v refers to the unemployment rate, and e refers to the labor force participation rate. gr denotes the growth rate of the variable. We subdivide the 1988–2000 period (slightly different from the discussion above) into (1) 1988–1990: the growth period of the Aquino government; (2) 1990–1991: recession; (3) 1991–1993: the stagnant period (power crisis) and transition from the Aquino to the Ramos governments; (4) 1993–1997: the bullish growth period of the Ramos government; (5) 1997–1998: the Asian financial crisis; and (6) 1998–2000: slow growth and lack of confidence in the Estrada administration.

3.4.1. Jobless Growth: 1988–1990

Tables 9.9 and 9.15 show that between 1988 and 1990, there was output per capita growth in all sectors except for mining, food manufacturing, and agriculture.[17] These output increases, however, were not translated into high absorption of labor. In fact, there was a slight decline in total employment per working population (L/P)—which we call the "employment ratio"—during this period. The main reasons for this

TABLE 9.5 Growth Rates of GVA by Industry of Origin, 1980–2000

Growth Rates	1980	1981	1982	1983	1984	1985	1986	1987	1988	1989	1990	1991	1992	1993	1994	1995	1996	1997	1998	1999	2000
1. Agriculture, fishery, forestry	4.04	3.62	0.78	-3.38	-0.93	-1.88	3.68	3.22	3.24	3.01	0.48	1.37	0.39	2.13	2.60	0.85	3.82	3.09	-6.43	5.95	3.42
2. Industry	4.96	4.65	2.48	1.52	-11.51	-15.75	2.30	4.01	8.75	7.38	2.56	-2.67	-0.54	1.65	5.77	6.97	6.19	6.14	-2.12	0.88	3.63
a. Mining and quarrying	10.67	2.43	-1.98	0.86	-3.08	32.75	3.53	-8.78	4.20	-2.69	-2.62	-2.89	6.73	0.66	-6.98	-0.76	-4.82	1.69	2.77	-8.36	8.67
b. Manufacturing	4.18	1.95	1.60	-0.32	-10.11	-7.90	1.81	5.57	9.52	5.81	2.66	-0.44	-1.73	0.75	5.01	6.77	5.58	4.22	-1.13	1.59	5.59
Food, Beverage, and Tobacco (nt)	6.43	4.58	3.38	-0.89	-9.93	-6.66	3.79	0.07	1.92	2.03	0.29	-1.33	-2.55	-2.16	5.41	2.85	6.78	1.79	2.45	4.65	2.07
Importable manufacturing	0.76	-6.37	7.02	1.07	-9.86	-1.35	-4.30	11.78	21.69	5.95	8.28	0.02	3.00	-0.17	4.18	8.90	6.63	3.17	-5.75	-2.05	4.31
Traditional Exportable/importable	2.37	5.23	-5.60	-6.89	-15.60	-17.25	2.75	16.83	10.55	13.12	0.68	0.98	-7.19	3.86	-1.39	7.35	-5.39	2.82	-0.10	-11.29	4.95
Non-traditional exportable/importable	4.20	3.60	-7.04	7.75	-5.39	-16.40	5.23	7.71	15.37	12.64	1.03	0.13	-4.14	9.86	11.37	13.25	8.71	13.40	-1.87	8.19	16.00
c. Construction	5.62	10.78	1.09	9.51	-20.19	-48.17	-1.69	11.19	4.70	19.99	4.97	-15.70	2.77	5.74	8.95	6.51	10.89	16.18	-9.65	-1.55	-5.96
d. Electricity, Gas, and Water	8.73	14.66	22.26	-9.12	6.80	-6.47	13.22	-11.43	12.56	5.39	-0.44	4.70	0.66	2.92	13.85	13.00	7.48	4.82	3.26	3.11	3.65
3. Service sector	6.11	1.92	6.82	5.56	-6.53	-2.08	4.23	5.23	7.16	7.03	4.86	0.15	1.02	2.49	4.23	5.02	6.37	5.42	3.47	4.09	4.42
a. Transportation, Communication, and Storage	4.26	4.98	2.57	3.84	-1.72	-1.23	4.45	6.08	8.01	6.19	2.15	0.45	1.40	2.56	4.25	5.81	7.41	8.23	6.49	5.26	9.94
b. Trade	6.07	0.22	8.59	3.94	-6.80	-0.96	4.93	3.59	5.71	7.93	4.57	0.53	1.65	2.46	3.95	5.57	5.52	3.90	2.45	4.88	5.61
c. FIRE (including business services)	7.84	-4.59	7.58	6.78	-13.02	-7.05	4.66	7.32	7.28	8.86	5.54	-0.83	0.44	1.87	4.14	4.92	8.12	7.87	3.09	1.59	1.06
d. Services (excluding recreation, hotels, restaurants)	5.12	11.02	4.24	4.16	-0.23	1.17	2.62	4.00	7.92	4.82	7.26	0.67	0.57	2.76	4.44	3.75	5.36	3.39	3.60	4.49	2.79
f. Recreational, hotels, and restaurants	5.32	10.98	13.64	23.07	-6.84	-1.01	3.44	9.99	11.06	3.85	1.30	-0.66	0.40	4.32	5.74	4.87	5.40	4.73	3.49	6.11	3.01
Gross domestic product	5.15	3.42	3.62	1.87	-7.32	-7.31	3.42	4.31	6.75	6.21	3.04	-0.58	0.34	2.12	4.39	4.76	5.76	5.19	-0.59	3.32	3.95
Net factor income from abroad	1,125.53	5.88	176.72	13.91	78.18	-15.71	-2.56	-19.64	-10.39	6.03	-75.28	-198.27	236.99	2.49	54.86	12.80	57.44	6.84	23.93	10.10	8.98
Gross national product	4.51	3.41	2.43	1.65	-9.11	-6.96	3.64	5.15	7.21	6.21	4.78	0.46	1.55	2.12	5.25	4.96	7.16	5.25	0.40	3.66	4.21

Source: National Statistics Coordination Board.

TABLE 9.6 GVA by Industry of Origin, as Percentage of GDP, 1980–2000

GVA by Industry Origin as % of GDP	1980	1981	1982	1983	1984	1985	1986	1987	1988	1989	1990	1991	1992	1993	1994	1995	1996	1997	1998	1999	2000
1. Agriculture, fishery, forestry	23.75	23.50	23.54	22.90	21.72	23.22	24.58	24.64	24.38	23.58	22.87	22.30	22.74	22.75	22.75	22.36	21.53	21.13	20.71	19.50	19.99
2. Industry	40.59	40.52	41.00	40.55	40.41	38.58	35.07	34.69	34.59	35.24	35.62	35.46	34.71	34.41	34.25	34.71	35.44	35.58	35.91	35.35	34.52
a. Mining and quarrying	1.42	1.50	1.48	1.40	1.39	1.45	2.08	2.08	1.82	1.78	1.63	1.54	1.50	1.60	1.58	1.40	1.33	1.20	1.16	1.20	1.06
b. Manufacturing	27.86	27.60	27.21	26.68	26.10	25.32	25.15	24.76	25.06	25.71	25.61	25.52	25.56	25.03	24.69	24.84	25.32	25.27	25.04	24.91	24.49
Food, Beverage, and Tobacco (nt)	13.64	13.80	13.96	13.92	13.55	13.17	13.26	13.31	12.77	12.19	11.71	11.40	11.31	10.99	10.53	10.63	10.44	10.54	10.20	10.51	10.64
Importable manufacturing	6.87	6.58	5.96	6.16	6.11	5.94	6.32	5.85	6.27	7.15	7.13	7.49	7.54	7.74	7.56	7.55	7.85	7.91	7.76	7.36	6.98
Traditional exportable/importable	4.08	3.97	4.04	3.68	3.36	3.06	2.73	2.72	3.04	3.15	3.36	3.28	3.33	3.08	3.13	2.96	3.03	2.71	2.65	2.66	2.29
Non-traditional exportable/importable	3.27	3.24	3.25	2.92	3.08	3.15	2.84	2.89	2.98	3.22	3.42	3.35	3.38	3.23	3.47	3.70	4.00	4.11	4.44	4.38	4.59
c. Construction	9.35	9.39	10.06	9.81	10.55	9.08	5.08	4.83	5.15	5.05	5.70	5.81	4.92	5.04	5.22	5.45	5.54	5.81	6.42	5.83	5.56
d. Electricity, gas, and water	1.96	2.03	2.25	2.66	2.37	2.73	2.76	3.02	2.56	2.70	2.68	2.59	2.73	2.74	2.76	3.01	3.25	3.30	3.29	3.41	3.41
3. Service sector	35.66	35.98	35.46	36.55	37.88	38.20	40.35	40.67	41.03	41.19	41.51	42.24	42.55	42.84	42.99	42.93	43.04	43.29	43.38	45.15	45.49
a. Transportation, Communication, and Storage	4.83	4.78	4.86	4.81	4.90	5.20	5.54	5.59	5.69	5.75	5.75	5.70	5.76	5.82	5.85	5.84	5.90	5.99	6.17	6.60	6.73
b. Trade	12.90	13.01	12.61	13.21	13.48	13.56	14.48	14.70	14.59	14.45	14.69	14.91	15.07	15.27	15.32	15.26	15.37	15.34	15.15	15.61	15.85
c. FIRE (including business services)	9.88	10.13	9.35	9.70	10.17	9.54	9.57	9.69	9.96	10.01	10.26	10.51	10.49	10.50	10.47	10.45	10.46	10.70	10.97	11.38	11.19
d. Services (excluding recreation, hotels, and restaurants)	6.71	6.70	7.20	7.24	7.40	7.97	8.70	8.63	8.60	8.70	8.58	8.94	9.05	9.07	9.13	9.13	9.04	9.01	8.86	9.23	9.33
f. Recreational, hotels, restaurants	1.35	1.35	1.45	1.59	1.92	1.93	2.07	2.07	2.18	2.27	2.22	2.18	2.18	2.18	2.23	2.25	2.26	2.25	2.24	2.33	2.39
Gross domestic product	100.00	100.00	100.00	100.00	100.00	100.00	100.00	100.00	100.00	100.00	100.00	100.00	100.00	100.00	100.00	100.00	100.00	100.00	100.00	100.00	100.00
Net factor income from abroad	−0.06	−0.67	−0.69	−1.83	−2.05	−3.93	−3.58	−3.37	−2.60	−2.18	−2.18	−0.52	0.52	1.73	1.74	2.58	2.78	4.13	4.20	5.23	5.58
Gross national product	99.94	99.33	99.31	98.17	97.95	96.07	96.42	96.63	97.40	97.82	97.82	99.48	100.52	101.73	101.74	102.58	102.78	104.13	104.20	105.23	105.58

Source: National Statistics Coordination Board.

285

TABLE 9.7 Growth Rates in Employed Persons by Industry

Growth Rates	1988	1989	1990	1991	1992	1993	1994	1995	1996	1997	1998	1999	2000
1. Agriculture, fishery, forestry		-1.45	2.00	2.27	1.54	7.20	0.06	0.58	3.16	-2.75	-1.06	3.32	-5.87
2. Industry		6.64	-1.63	5.31	4.73	0.25	3.61	4.22	9.53	2.68	-1.82	-0.25	-1.37
a. Mining and quarrying		5.12	-20.85	6.35	-2.34	0.25	-18.17	-3.88	3.31	17.26	-9.73	-16.20	11.20
b. Manufacturing		5.22	-3.02	5.28	6.14	-2.28	3.46	2.73	4.78	-0.26	-1.19	2.02	-0.01
Food, beverage, and tobacco (nt)		4.62	-0.60	4.83	6.41	-2.34	0.13	7.59	2.38	0.12	1.04	1.69	-3.28
Importable manufacturing		19.05	-0.80	10.92	6.60	-4.44	8.50	6.56	14.35	-2.86	-3.19	-2.82	-4.84
Traditional exportable/importable		2.08	-6.07	-0.28	6.50	-3.53	2.29	-1.17	-0.16	-6.29	-3.53	5.45	-0.37
Non-traditional exportable/importable		9.11	3.01	21.30	4.39	3.08	7.78	4.38	13.63	14.35	1.94	-0.77	6.65
c. Construction		11.52	4.71	4.70	3.74	4.90	6.29	8.67	19.59	6.64	-3.12	-2.85	-3.29
d. Electricity, gas, and water		-1.49	4.14	11.26	-8.87	16.17	7.03	-0.57	11.00	5.43	9.29	-1.21	-15.64
3. Service sector		5.57	3.73	0.99	1.80	4.05	4.30	5.87	6.99	5.86	4.70	4.18	1.62
a. Transport		7.04	1.35	3.93	4.17	9.50	6.56	7.12	10.08	6.12	6.49	5.96	3.12
b. Trade		5.28	3.39	-0.02	2.36	4.34	4.35	6.69	6.22	3.71	3.30	5.04	1.99
c. FIRE (including businesss services)		2.62	10.23	6.69	-3.05	11.75	-2.25	10.29	14.01	10.81	-1.06	7.25	-2.62
d. Services (excluding recreation, hotels, and restaurants)		5.21	4.36	0.19	0.64	0.98	4.08	3.75	6.45	6.25	4.89	1.80	1.63
f. Recreational, hotels, and restaurants		9.52	1.30	1.72	5.81	4.72	6.09	8.27	1.64	11.26	12.81	7.05	-0.15
Total employed		2.45	2.09	2.23	2.15	4.84	2.25	3.24	5.72	1.68	1.27	3.13	-1.83
Unemployment rate	8.78	8.35	8.42	9.21	8.85	8.60	8.93	8.64	7.74	8.10	9.01	8.91	10.16
Labor force participation rate	65.51	64.90	64.42	64.74	63.78	64.75	64.58	65.15	65.86	65.51	65.31	66.56	65.21

TABLE 9.8 Employed Persons as % of Labor Force, by Industry

As % of Labor Force	1988	1989	1990	1991	1992	1993	1994	1995	1996	1997	1998	1999	2000
1. Agriculture, fishery, forestry	42.67	41.24	41.17	40.83	40.75	41.78	40.73	39.81	39.23	37.37	36.15	36.26	34.29
2. Industry	14.01	14.66	14.11	14.41	14.83	14.22	14.36	14.54	15.21	15.30	14.69	14.22	14.09
a. Mining and quarrying	0.67	0.69	0.53	0.55	0.53	0.51	0.40	0.38	0.37	0.43	0.38	0.31	0.34
b. Manufacturing	9.42	9.72	9.22	9.41	9.82	9.18	9.25	9.24	9.24	9.03	8.73	8.64	8.68
Food, beverage, and tobacco (nt)	2.14	2.20	2.14	2.17	2.27	2.12	2.07	2.16	2.12	2.08	2.05	2.02	1.97
Importable manufacturing	0.91	1.06	1.03	1.11	1.16	1.06	1.12	1.16	1.27	1.21	1.14	1.08	1.03
Traditional exportable/importable	5.13	5.14	4.72	4.57	4.78	4.41	4.40	4.22	4.03	3.70	3.49	3.57	3.57
Non-traditional exportable/importable	1.24	1.32	1.33	1.57	1.61	1.59	1.67	1.69	1.83	2.06	2.05	1.97	2.11
c. Construction	3.56	3.89	3.99	4.05	4.13	4.15	4.29	4.53	5.18	5.41	5.12	4.83	4.69
d. Electricity, gas, and water	0.37	0.36	0.36	0.39	0.35	0.39	0.41	0.39	0.42	0.43	0.46	0.44	0.38
3. Service sector	34.54	35.76	36.30	35.55	35.57	35.40	35.97	37.01	37.82	39.22	40.15	40.60	41.45
a. Transport	4.34	4.56	4.52	4.56	4.67	4.89	5.07	5.28	5.55	5.77	6.01	6.18	6.41
b. Trade	12.46	12.86	13.02	12.62	12.70	12.67	12.88	13.36	13.55	13.77	13.90	14.18	14.53
c. FIRE (including business services)	1.65	1.66	1.79	1.86	1.77	1.89	1.80	1.93	2.10	2.28	2.21	2.30	2.25
d. Services (excluding recreation, hotels, and restaurants)	14.20	14.65	14.96	14.54	14.38	13.89	14.09	14.20	14.44	15.03	15.41	15.23	15.55
f. Recreational, hotels, and restaurants	1.88	2.02	2.00	1.98	2.06	2.06	2.13	2.24	2.17	2.37	2.61	2.72	2.72
Total employed	91.22	91.65	91.58	90.79	91.15	91.40	91.07	91.36	92.26	91.90	90.99	91.09	89.84
Unemployed	8.78	8.35	8.42	9.21	8.85	8.60	8.93	8.64	7.74	8.10	9.01	8.91	10.16
Total labor force	100.0	100.0	100.0	100.0	100.0	100.0	100.0	100.0	100.0	100.0	100.0	100.0	100.0

TABLE 9.9 Decomposition of Labor Productivity, 1988–1990

	1 Xi/X	2 Li/L	3 gr(pi)	4 Li/L* gr(pi)	5 Xi/X − Li/L	6 gr(Xi)	7 (Xi/X − Li/L)* gr(Xi)	sum(4) + sum(7)
1. Agriculture, fishery, forestry	0.2327	0.4584	0.0292	0.0134	−0.2257	0.0344	−0.0078	0.0056
2. Industry	0.3590	0.1539	0.0486		0.2052	0.0964		
a. Mining and quarrying	0.0168	0.0066	0.1298	0.0009	0.0102	−0.0538	−0.0006	0.0003
b. Manufacturing	0.2601	0.1019	0.0625		0.1582	0.0827		
Food, beverage, and Tobacco (nt)	0.1196	0.0234	−0.0161	−0.0004	0.0962	0.0230	0.0022	0.0018
Importable manufacturing	0.0744	0.0106	−0.0290	−0.0003	0.0638	0.1371	0.0088	0.0084
Traditional exportable/importable	0.0327	0.0538	0.1716	0.0092	−0.0212	0.1299	−0.0027	0.0065
Non-traditional exportable/importable	0.0334	0.0141	0.0124	0.0002	0.0194	0.1291	0.0025	0.0027
c. Construction	0.0553	0.0414	0.0755	0.0031	0.0139	0.2297	0.0032	0.0063
d. Electricity, gas and water	0.0269	0.0040	0.0226	0.0001	0.0228	0.0481	0.0011	0.0012
3. Service Sector	0.4239	0.3877	0.0245		0.0362	0.1152		
a. Transportation, communication, and storage	0.0582	0.0485	−0.0001	0.0000	0.0097	0.0813	0.0008	0.0008
b. Trade	0.1492	0.1394	0.0362	0.0051	0.0098	0.1209	0.0012	0.0062
c. FIRE (including business services)	0.1044	0.0189	0.0155	0.0003	0.0855	0.1385	0.0118	0.0121
d. Services (excluding recreation, hotels, and restaurants)	0.0896	0.1596	0.0238	0.0038	−0.0700	0.1170	−0.0082	−0.0044
f. Recreational, hotels, and restaurants	0.0226	0.0213	−0.0532	−0.0011	0.0013	0.0506	0.0001	−0.0011
All sectors			0.0451	0.0342			0.0124	0.0466

TABLE 9.10 Decomposition of Labor Productivity, 1990–1991

	1 Xi/X	2 Li/L	3 gr(pi)	4 Li/L* gr(pi)	5 Xi/X − Li/L	6 gr(Xi)	7 (Xi/X − Li/L)* gr(Xi)	sum(4) + sum(7)
1. Agriculture, fishery, forestry	0.1858	0.4496	−0.0088	−0.0040	−0.2639	0.0136	−0.0036	−0.0076
2. Industry	0.2894	0.1564	−0.0788		0.1330	−0.0271		
a. Mining and quarrying	0.0125	0.0059	−0.0908	−0.0005	0.0066	−0.0294	−0.0002	−0.0007
b. Manufacturing	0.2107	0.1022	−0.0558		0.1085	−0.0044		
Food, beverage, and tobacco (nt)	0.0937	0.0236	−0.0605	−0.0014	0.0700	−0.0133	−0.0009	−0.0024
Importable manufacturing	0.0620	0.0117	−0.1034	−0.0012	0.0503	0.0002	0.0000	−0.0012
Traditional exportable/importable	0.0273	0.0509	0.0125	0.0006	−0.0237	0.0098	−0.0002	0.0004
Non-traditional exportable/importable	0.0278	0.0159	−0.1912	−0.0030	0.0118	0.0013	0.0000	−0.0030
c. Construction	0.0443	0.0441	−0.2159	−0.0095	0.0002	−0.1704	0.0000	−0.0096
d. Electricity, gas, and water	0.0219	0.0042	−0.0607	−0.0003	0.0178	0.0459	0.0008	0.0006
3. Service sector	0.3497	0.3939	−0.0083		−0.0442	0.0015		
a. Transportation, communication, and storage	0.0473	0.0498	−0.0341	−0.0017	−0.0025	0.0044	0.0000	−0.0017
b. Trade	0.1236	0.1406	0.0056	0.0008	−0.0169	0.0053	−0.0001	0.0007
c. FIRE (including business services)	0.0866	0.0200	−0.0730	−0.0015	0.0666	−0.0083	−0.0006	−0.0020
d. Services (excluding recreation, hotels, and restaurants)	0.0742	0.1618	0.0047	0.0008	−0.0876	0.0067	−0.0006	0.0002
f. Recreational, hotels, and restaurants	0.0180	0.0218	−0.0236	−0.0005	−0.0039	−0.0066	0.0000	−0.0005
All sectors			−0.0278	−0.0215			−0.0054	−0.0268

TABLE 9.11 Decomposition of Labor Productivity, 1991–1993

	1 Xi/X	2 Li/L	3 gr(pi)	4 Li/L* gr(pi)	5 Xi/X – Li/L	6 gr(Xi)	7 (Xi/X – Li/L)* gr(Xi)	sum(4) + sum(7)
1. Agriculture, fishery, forestry	0.2275	0.4535	−0.0599	−0.0271	−0.2261	0.0249	−0.0056	−0.0328
2. Industry	0.3448	0.1571	−0.0378		0.1877	0.0110		
a. Mining and quarrying	0.0154	0.0058	0.0929	0.0005	0.0096	0.0717	0.0007	0.0012
b. Manufacturing	0.2512	0.1020	−0.0465		0.1492	−0.0100		
Food, beverage and tobacco (nt)	0.1091	0.0236	−0.0860	−0.0020	0.0856	−0.0476	−0.0041	−0.0061
Importable manufacturing	0.0755	0.0119	0.0093	0.0001	0.0636	0.0278	0.0018	0.0019
Traditional exportable/importable	0.0323	0.0492	−0.0638	−0.0031	−0.0169	−0.0368	0.0006	−0.0025
Non-traditional exportable/importable	0.0342	0.0173	−0.0215	−0.0004	0.0169	0.0518	0.0009	0.0005
c. Construction	0.0508	0.0450	−0.0014	−0.0001	0.0058	0.0831	0.0005	0.0004
d. Electricity, gas and water	0.0274	0.0043	−0.0217	−0.0001	0.0231	0.0353	0.0008	0.0007
3. Service sector	0.4277	0.3893	−0.0227		0.0384	0.0347		
a. Transportation, communication, and storage	0.0581	0.0519	−0.0924	−0.0048	0.0062	0.0392	0.0002	−0.0046
b. Trade	0.1520	0.1388	−0.0252	−0.0035	0.0132	0.0406	0.0005	−0.0030
c. FIRE (including business services)	0.1048	0.0206	−0.0572	−0.0012	0.0842	0.0230	0.0019	0.0008
d. Services (excluding recreation, hotels, and restaurants)	0.0909	0.1559	0.0167	0.0026	−0.0650	0.0328	−0.0021	0.0005
f. Recreational, hotels, and restaurants	0.0220	0.0222	−0.0562	−0.0012	−0.0001	0.0463	0.0000	−0.0013
All sectors			−0.0442	−0.0403			−0.0039	−0.0442

TABLE 9.12 Decomposition of Labor Productivity, 1993–1997

	1 X_i/X	2 L_i/L	3 $gr(p_i)$	4 $L_i/L *$ $gr(p_i)$	5 $X_i/X - L_i/L$	6 $gr(X_i)$	7 $(X_i/X - L_i/L)*$ $gr(X_i)$	$sum(4) +$ $sum(7)$
1. Agriculture, fishery, forestry	0.2163	0.4303	0.0924	0.0398	-0.2140	0.1020	-0.0218	0.0179
2. Industry	0.3516	0.1614	0.0489		0.1902	0.2420		
a. Mining and quarrying	0.0135	0.0051	-0.0643	-0.0003	0.0084	-0.1126	-0.0009	-0.0013
b. Manufacturing	0.2489	0.0993	0.1050		0.1496	0.2093		
Food, beverage, and tobacco (nt)	0.1034	0.0229	0.0650	0.0015	0.0806	0.1637	0.0132	0.0147
Importable manufacturing	0.0767	0.0124	-0.0286	-0.0004	0.0643	0.2208	0.0142	0.0138
Traditional exportable/importable	0.0287	0.0440	0.0849	0.0037	-0.0153	0.0293	-0.0004	0.0033
Non-traditional exportable/importable	0.0400	0.0200	0.0617	0.0012	0.0200	0.4344	0.0087	0.0099
c. Construction	0.0588	0.0525	0.0148	0.0008	0.0063	0.3968	0.0025	0.0033
d. Electricity, gas, and water	0.0305	0.0045	0.1514	0.0007	0.0260	0.3669	0.0095	0.0102
3. Service sector	0.4321	0.4083	-0.0187		0.0238	0.2043		
a. Transportation, communication, and storage	0.0602	0.0584	-0.0391	-0.0023	0.0018	0.2474	0.0004	-0.0018
b. Trade	0.1523	0.1446	-0.0192	-0.0028	0.0077	0.1844	0.0014	-0.0014
c. FIRE (including business services)	0.1075	0.0229	-0.0665	-0.0015	0.0846	0.2412	0.0204	0.0189
d. Services (excluding recreation, hotels, and restaurants)	0.0898	0.1581	-0.0341	-0.0054	-0.0684	0.1655	-0.0113	-0.0167
f. Recreational, hotels, and restaurants	0.0223	0.0243	-0.0593	-0.0014	-0.0019	0.2016	-0.0004	-0.0018
All sectors			0.0695	0.0336			0.0354	0.0690

TABLE 9.13 Decomposition of Labor Productivity, 1997–1998

	1 Xi/X	2 Li/L	3 gr(pi)	4 Li/L* gr(pi)	5 Xi/X − Li/L	6 gr(Xi)	7 (Xi/X − Li/L)* gr (Xi)	sum(4) + sum(7)
1. Agriculture, fishery, forestry	0.2011	0.4020	−0.0558	−0.0224	−0.2009	−0.0664	0.0134	−0.0091
2. Industry	0.3563	0.1640	−0.0031		0.1923	−0.0215		
a. Mining and quarrying	0.0118	0.0044	0.1295	0.0006	0.0074	0.0273	0.0002	0.0008
b. Manufacturing	0.2498	0.0971	0.0007		0.1527	−0.0113		
Food, beverage, and tobacco (nt)	0.1035	0.0226	0.0138	0.0003	0.0809	0.0242	0.0020	0.0023
Importable manufacturing	0.0756	0.0128	−0.0267	−0.0003	0.0628	−0.0592	−0.0037	−0.0041
Traditional exportable/importable	0.0266	0.0393	0.0350	0.0014	−0.0127	−0.0010	0.0000	0.0014
Non-traditional exportable/ importable	0.0441	0.0224	−0.0381	−0.0009	0.0216	−0.0189	−0.0004	−0.0013
c. Construction	0.0613	0.0576	−0.0697	−0.0040	0.0037	−0.1014	−0.0004	−0.0044
d. Electricity, gas, and water	0.0335	0.0049	−0.0568	−0.0003	0.0286	0.0321	0.0009	0.0006
3. Service sector	0.4426	0.4341	−0.0118		0.0086	0.0341		
a. Transportation, communication, and storage	0.0638	0.0645	0.0000	0.0000	−0.0006	0.0628	0.0000	0.0000
b. Trade	0.1538	0.1513	−0.0083	−0.0013	0.0025	0.0242	0.0001	−0.0012
c. FIRE (including business services)	0.1117	0.0245	0.0410	0.0010	0.0872	0.0304	0.0027	0.0037
d. Services (excluding recreation, hotels, and restaurants)	0.0904	0.1665	−0.0124	−0.0021	−0.0761	0.0354	−0.0027	−0.0048
f. Recreational, hotels, and restaurants	0.0228	0.0273	−0.0862	−0.0023	−0.0044	0.0343	−0.0002	−0.0025
All sectors			−0.0185	−0.0303			0.0118	−0.0186

TABLE 9.14 Decomposition of Labor Productivity, 1998–2000

	1 Xi/X	2 Li/L	3 gr(pi)	4 Li/L* gr(pi)	5 Xi/X − Li/L	6 gr(Xi)	7 (Xi/X − Li/L)* gr(Xi)	sum(4) + sum(7)
1. Agriculture, fishery, forestry	0.1970	0.3895	0.1191	0.0464	−0.1924	0.0914	−0.0176	0.0288
2. Industry	0.3486	0.1592	0.0607		0.1895	0.0445		
a. Mining and quarrying	0.0115	0.0040	0.0664	0.0003	0.0075	−0.0042	0.0000	0.0002
b. Manufacturing	0.2489	0.0963	0.0502		0.1526	0.0701		
Food, beverage, and tobacco (nt)	0.1048	0.0222	0.0825	0.0018	0.0826	0.0660	0.0054	0.0073
Importable manufacturing	0.0717	0.0120	0.0998	0.0012	0.0597	0.0216	0.0013	0.0025
Traditional exportable/importable	0.0248	0.0390	−0.1207	−0.0047	−0.0142	−0.0715	0.0010	−0.0037
Non-traditional exportable/ importable	0.0476	0.0230	0.1701	0.0039	0.0246	0.2262	0.0056	0.0095
c. Construction	0.0542	0.0543	−0.0147	−0.0008	−0.0001	−0.0771	0.0000	−0.0008
d. Electricity, gas, and water	0.0341	0.0046	0.2476	0.0011	0.0294	0.0665	0.0020	0.0031
3. Service sector	0.4543	0.4514	0.0262		0.0029	0.0833		
a. Transportation, communication, and storage	0.0687	0.0687	0.0574	0.0039	0.0000	0.1458	0.0000	0.0039
b. Trade	0.1587	0.1573	0.0334	0.0052	0.0014	0.1021	0.0001	0.0054
c. FIRE (including business services)	0.1112	0.0246	−0.0170	−0.0004	0.0865	0.0264	0.0023	0.0019
d. Services (excluding recreation, hotels, and restaurants)	0.0923	0.1713	0.0375	0.0064	−0.0790	0.0715	−0.0056	0.0008
f. Recreational, hotels, and restaurants	0.0235	0.0295	0.0222	0.0007	−0.0060	0.0888	−0.0005	0.0001
All sectors			0.0590	0.0651			−0.0061	0.0590

293

TABLE 9.15 Decomposition of Employment by Sectors, 1988–1990

	dpi/pi	dxi/xi	$dxi/xi - dpi/pi$	Li/L	Li/L $(dxi/xi - dpi/pi)$	$gr(L/P)$
1. Agriculture, fishery, forestry	0.0292	−0.0234	−0.0526	0.4584	−0.0241	
2. Industry	0.0486	0.0386	−0.0100	0.1539	−0.0015	
a. Mining and quarrying	0.1298	−0.1115	−0.2414	0.0066	−0.0016	
b. Manufacturing	0.0625	0.0249	−0.0376	0.1019	−0.0038	
Food, beverage, and tobacco (nt)	−0.0161	−0.0348	−0.0187	0.0234	−0.0004	
Importable manufacturing	−0.0290	0.0795	0.1085	0.0106	0.0012	
Traditional exportable/importable	0.1716	0.0722	−0.0994	0.0538	−0.0054	
Non-traditional exportable/ importable	0.0124	0.0714	0.0591	0.0141	0.0008	
c. Construction	0.0755	0.1724	0.0969	0.0414	0.0040	
d. Electricity, gas, and water	0.0226	−0.0097	−0.0323	0.0040	−0.0001	
3. Service sector	0.0245	0.0575	0.0330	0.3877	0.0128	
a. Transportation, communication, and storage	−0.0001	0.0235	0.0236	0.0485	0.0011	
b. Trade	0.0362	0.0632	0.0270	0.1394	0.0038	
c. FIRE (including business services)	0.0155	0.0809	0.0654	0.0189	0.0012	
d. Services (excluding recreation, hotels, and restaurants)	0.0238	0.0593	0.0355	0.1596	0.0057	
f. Recreational, hotels, and restaurants	−0.0532	−0.0072	0.0460	0.0213	0.0010	
All sectors					−0.0128	−0.0129

	1988	1990	average	growth rate		
Unemployment rate (v)	0.0878	0.0842	0.0860	−0.0417		
LFPR (e)	0.6551	0.6442	0.6496	−0.0168		
$(1 - v)$	0.9140					
$(1 - v)$ gr(L/P)	−0.0117					
$(1 - v)$ gr(e)	−0.0153					
v gr(v)	−0.0036					
$(1 - v)$gr(L/P) − $(1 - v)$gr(e) + $v$gr(v)	0.0000					

were the increases in labor productivities in the majority of sectors,[18] especially agriculture and traditional exportables (see tables 9.9 and 9.15), which simply reflected a jobless growth condition.

There was, however, positive growth in the employment ratio in services, which meant that output per capita increases were stronger than productivity increases in the service sector in general. This reinforces a general trend—that the service sector is the one that absorbs the most labor. In a boom-bust context, this means that its labor productivity must be lagging or declining.

There was also a significant contribution of intersectoral productivity improvement (column 7) comprising 1.24 percent compared to the total productivity improvement of 4.6 percent. This is accounted for by the movement from low-productivity agriculture to the higher-productivity service sector.

Part of the reason for the lack of labor-absorptive capacity during this period of growth may be attributed to the lack of confidence brought about by political and economic instabilities during this period (the series of coups, the debt overhang, and the contractionary policies of 1989–1990, as discussed

TABLE 9.16 Decomposition of Employment by Sectors, 1990–1991

	dpi/pi	dxi/xi	$dxi/xi - dpi/pi$	Li/L	Li/L $(dxi/xi - dpi/pi)$	$gr(L/P)$
1. Agriculture, fishery, forestry	−0.0088	−0.0121	−0.0032	0.4496	−0.0015	
2. Industry	−0.0788	−0.0527	0.0260	0.1564	0.0041	
a. Mining and quarrying	−0.0908	−0.0550	0.0358	0.0059	0.0002	
b. Manufacturing	−0.0558	−0.0301	0.0257	0.1022	0.0026	
Food, beverage, and tobacco (nt)	−0.0605	−0.0390	0.0215	0.0236	0.0005	
Importable manufacturing	−0.1034	−0.0254	0.0779	0.0117	0.0009	
Traditional exportable/importable	0.0125	−0.0159	−0.0284	0.0509	−0.0014	
Non-traditional exportable/ importable	−0.1912	−0.0244	0.1668	0.0159	0.0027	
c. Construction	−0.2159	−0.1959	0.0200	0.0441	0.0009	
d. Electricity, gas, and water	−0.0607	0.0203	0.0810	0.0042	0.0003	
3. Service sector	−0.0083	−0.0242	−0.0159	0.3939	−0.0062	
a. Transportation, communication, and storage	−0.0341	−0.0212	0.0129	0.0498	0.0006	
b. Trade	0.0056	−0.0203	−0.0259	0.1406	−0.0036	
c. FIRE (including business services)	−0.0730	−0.0340	0.0391	0.0200	0.0008	
d. Services (excluding recreation, hotels, and restaurants)	0.0047	−0.0190	−0.0237	0.1618	−0.0038	
f. Recreational, hotels, and restaurants	−0.0236	−0.0323	−0.0087	0.0218	−0.0002	
All sectors					−0.0036	−0.0036
	1990	1991	average	growth rate		
Unemployment rate (v)	0.0842	0.0921	0.0882	0.0898		
LFPR (e)	0.6442	0.6474	0.6458	0.0050		
$(1-v)$	0.9118					
$(1-v)$ gr(L/P)	−0.0033					
$(1-v)$ gr(e)	0.0046					
v gr(v)	0.0079					
$(1-v)$gr(L/P) − $(1-v)$gr(e) + $v$gr(v)	0.0000					

earlier). In bearish times, firms increase output through existing resources and will not hire new labor to expand output. This hypothesis will be partly confirmed in another period of lackluster growth a decade later.

Table 9.15 shows that overall the unemployment rate declined marginally since the labor force participation rate also fell slightly, offsetting the fall in the employment ratio. Table 9.21 clearly shows that the employment elasticity (with respect to output or GDP, or the reciprocal of Okun's elasticity)[19] was practically nil for the period (–0.02, which means that a 1 percent

growth in GDP in this period reduced the unemployment rate by only 0.02 percentage points).

3.4.2. Recession and Productivity Declines in 1991

Between 1990 and 1991, as table 9.10 shows, there was a virtual standstill in output in manufacturing and the service sector (with a slight fall in output in manufacturing and a slight increase in the service sector). Although there was some increase in agricultural output, this was completely offset by the sharp fall in construction (by 17 percent), which

TABLE 9.17 Decomposition of Employment by Sectors, 1991–1993

	dpi/pi	dxi/xi	$dxi/xi - dpi/pi$	Li/L	Li/L $(dxi/xi - dpi/pi)$	$gr(L/P)$
1. Agriculture, fishery, forestry	−0.0599	−0.0366	0.0232	0.4535	0.0105	
2. Industry	−0.0378	−0.0506	−0.0129	0.1571	−0.0020	
a. Mining and quarrying	0.0929	0.0101	−0.0827	0.0058	−0.0005	
b. Manufacturing	−0.0465	−0.0716	−0.0250	0.1020	−0.0026	
Food, beverage, and tobacco (nt)	−0.0860	−0.1091	−0.0231	0.0236	−0.0005	
Importable manufacturing	0.0093	−0.0338	−0.0431	0.0119	−0.0005	
Traditional exportable/importable	−0.0638	−0.0983	−0.0345	0.0492	−0.0017	
Non-traditional exportable/ importable	−0.0215	−0.0098	0.0117	0.0173	0.0002	
c. Construction	−0.0014	0.0215	0.0230	0.0450	0.0010	
d. Electricity, gas, and water	−0.0217	−0.0263	−0.0046	0.0043	0.0000	
3. Service sector	−0.0227	−0.0269	−0.0041	0.3893	−0.0016	
a. Transportation, communication, and storage	−0.0924	−0.0224	0.0700	0.0519	0.0036	
b. Trade	−0.0252	−0.0210	0.0042	0.1388	0.0006	
c. FIRE (including business services)	−0.0572	−0.0386	0.0185	0.0206	0.0004	
d. Services (excluding recreation, hotels, and restaurants)	0.0167	−0.0287	−0.0455	0.1559	−0.0071	
f. Recreational, hotels, and restaurants	−0.0562	−0.0152	0.0410	0.0222	0.0009	
All sectors					0.0069	0.0069

	1991	1993	average	growth rate		
Unemployment rate (v)	0.0921	0.0860	0.0890	−0.0692		
LFPR (e)	0.6474	0.6475	0.6475	0.0001		
$(1-v)$	0.9110					
$(1-v)\, gr(L/P)$	0.0063					
$(1-v)\, gr(e)$	0.0001					
$v\, gr(v)$	−0.0062					
$(1-v)gr(L/P) - (1-v)gr(e) + vgr(v)$	0.0000					

made up the bulk of the contraction in industry and in the economy. The stagnant outputs converted into an overall decline in output per capita in all sectors except EGW, as shown in table 9.16.

However, the fall in output per capita was offset by a general decline in labor productivity, especially in the industrial and manufacturing sector.[20] This cushioned the adverse impact on the employment ratios. The sharp fall in productivity in industry and manufacturing even allowed some labor absorption in industry and manufacturing. The significant fall in employment ratios occurred mainly in the service

sector and agriculture. Another modest contribution to unemployment was the small increase in the labor force participation rate.

Table 9.10 shows that the fall in labor productivity came mainly from construction (whose output fell drastically but was still able to absorb some labor), manufacturing, and agriculture. Table 9.21 shows that employment elasticity during this recession year was−1.54, which means that the 0.58 percent decline in GDP translated into a rise in the unemployment rate by 0.9 percentage points. On the one hand, the previous period's positive growth brought no

TABLE 9.18 Decomposition of Employment by Sectors, 1993–1997

	dpi/pi	dxi/xi	$dxi/xi - dpi/pi$	Li/L	Li/L $(dxi/xi - dpi/pi)$	$gr(L/P)$
1. Agriculture, fishery, forestry	0.0924	−0.0074	−0.0998	0.4303	−0.0429	
2. Industry	0.0489	0.1335	0.0846	0.1614	0.0137	
a. Mining and quarrying	−0.0643	−0.2212	−0.1569	0.0051	−0.0008	
b. Manufacturing	0.1050	0.1005	−0.0044	0.0993	−0.0004	
Food, beverage, and tobacco (nt)	0.0650	0.0546	−0.0104	0.0229	−0.0002	
Importable manufacturing	−0.0286	0.1121	0.1406	0.0124	0.0017	
Traditional exportable/ importable	0.0849	−0.0801	−0.1650	0.0440	−0.0073	
Non-traditional exportable/ importable	0.0617	0.3289	0.2673	0.0200	0.0054	
c. Construction	0.0148	0.2905	0.2758	0.0525	0.0145	
d. Electricity, gas, and water	0.1514	0.2602	0.1088	0.0045	0.0005	
3. Service sector	−0.0187	0.0954	0.1141	0.4083	0.0466	
a. Transportation, communication, and storage	−0.0391	0.1390	0.1781	0.0584	0.0104	
b. Trade	−0.0192	0.0754	0.0946	0.1446	0.0137	
c. FIRE (including business services)	−0.0665	0.1327	0.1993	0.0229	0.0046	
d. Services (excluding recreation, hotels, and restaurants)	−0.0341	0.0564	0.0904	0.1581	0.0143	
f. Recreational, hotels, and restaurants	−0.0593	0.0927	0.1520	0.0243	0.0037	
All sectors					0.0175	0.0170
	1993	1997	average	growth rate		
Unemployment rate (v)	0.0860	0.0810	0.0835	−0.0591		
LFPR (e)	0.6475	0.6551	0.6513	0.0117		
$(1-v)$	0.9165					
$(1-v) gr(L/P)$	0.0160					
$(1-v) gr(e)$	0.0107					
$v gr(v)$	−0.0049					
$(1-v)gr(L/P) - (1-v)gr(e) + vgr(v)$	0.0004					

improvement in employment. On the other hand, the current recession brought about a significant fall in employment.

3.4.3. 1991–1993: Stagnancy and Continuing Productivity Declines during the Power Crisis

The period of stagnation from 1991 to 1993 saw output per capita declining in all sectors except construction and mining. More so than in the previous period, labor productivity fell across the board in agriculture, manufacturing, industry, and the service sector (see table 9.17). The declines in output per capita were offset by the fall in labor productivity so that labor absorption in general improved and the unemployment rate fell. Labor absorption took place mostly in agriculture as the industrial and service sectors contributed negatively to the employment ratio.

The general decline in labor productivity affected all sectors, unlike in 1991 when only construction and the manufacturing sector suffered heavy declines.

TABLE 9.19 Decomposition of Employment by Sectors, 1997–1998

	dpi/pi	dxi/xi	$dxi/xi - dpi/pi$	Li/L	Li/L $(dxi/xi - dpi/pi)$	$gr(L/P)$
1. Agriculture, fishery, forestry	−0.0558	−0.0921	−0.0363	0.4020	−0.0146	
2. Industry	−0.0031	−0.0472	−0.0441	0.1640	−0.0072	
a. Mining and quarrying	0.1295	0.0016	−0.1280	0.0044	−0.0006	
b. Manufacturing	0.0007	−0.0371	−0.0377	0.0971	−0.0037	
Food, beverage, and tobacco (nt)	0.0138	−0.0016	−0.0154	0.0226	−0.0003	
Importable manufacturing	−0.0267	−0.0849	−0.0581	0.0128	−0.0007	
Traditional exportable/ importable	0.0350	−0.0267	−0.0617	0.0393	−0.0024	
Non-traditional exportable/ importable	−0.0381	−0.0446	−0.0065	0.0224	−0.0001	
c. Construction	−0.0697	−0.1270	−0.0573	0.0576	−0.0033	
d. Electricity, gas, and water	−0.0568	0.0064	0.0631	0.0049	0.0003	
3. Service sector	−0.0118	0.0084	0.0202	0.4341	0.0088	
a. Transportation, communication, and storage	0.0000	0.0371	0.0371	0.0645	0.0024	
b. Trade	−0.0083	−0.0015	0.0067	0.1513	0.0010	
c. FIRE (including business services)	0.0410	0.0047	−0.0363	0.0245	−0.0009	
d. Services (excluding recreation, hotels, and restaurants)	−0.0124	0.0096	0.0220	0.1665	0.0037	
f. Recreational, hotels, and restaurants	−0.0862	0.0086	0.0948	0.0273	0.0026	
All sectors					−0.0130	−0.0131

	1997	1998	average	growth rate
Unemployment rate (v)	0.0810	0.0901	0.0856	0.1066
LFPR (e)	0.6551	0.6531	0.6541	−0.0031
$(1-v)$	0.9144			
$(1-v)\,gr(L/P)$	−0.0119			
$(1-v)\,gr(e)$	−0.0028			
$v\,gr(v)$	0.0091			
$(1-v)gr(L/P) - (1-v)gr(e) + vgr(v)$	0.0000			

The decline was strongest in agriculture, manufacturing, and the service sector, respectively.

The labor-absorbing capacity, despite the stagnancy, might have indicated increased optimism and confidence with the entry of the Ramos government—with the confidence increasing tremendously in 1993, when the power shortages ended and the stock market started to skyrocket.

Table 9.21 shows that the employment elasticity for this period is again almost zero (−0.04). This is not

surprising, since although GDP growth rates were positive during this period, they were smaller than the population growth rate. We cannot expect such low growth to have significant employment absorption.

3.4.4. 1993–1997: Bullish Growth; The Service Sector as Labor Absorber

Table 9.18 shows that the bullish Ramos period (1993 to 1997) brought about sharp increases in output per

TABLE 9.20 Decomposition of Employment by Sectors, 1998–2000

	dpi/pi	dxi/xi	dxi/xi − dpi/pi	Li/L	Li/L (dxi/xi − dpi/pi)	gr(L/P)
1. Agriculture, fishery, forestry	0.1191	0.0649	−0.0542	0.3895	−0.0211	
2. Industry	0.0607	0.0180	−0.0427	0.1592	−0.0068	
a. Mining and quarrying	0.0664	−0.0306	−0.0970	0.0040	−0.0004	
b. Manufacturing	0.0502	0.0437	−0.0065	0.0963	−0.0006	
Food, beverage, and tobacco (nt)	0.0825	0.0395	−0.0430	0.0222	−0.0010	
Importable manufacturing	0.0998	−0.0049	−0.1047	0.0120	−0.0013	
Traditional exportable/importable	−0.1207	−0.0979	0.0227	0.0390	0.0009	
Non-traditional exportable/ importable	0.1701	0.2000	0.0299	0.0230	0.0007	
c. Construction	−0.0147	−0.1035	−0.0888	0.0543	−0.0048	
d. Electricity, gas, and water	0.2476	0.0400	−0.2075	0.0046	−0.0010	
3. Service sector	0.0262	0.0568	0.0306	0.4514	0.0138	
a. Transportation, communication, storage	0.0574	0.1194	0.0621	0.0687	0.0043	
b. Trade	0.0334	0.0757	0.0423	0.1573	0.0067	
c. FIRE (including business services)	−0.0170	−0.0001	0.0169	0.0246	0.0004	
d. Services (excluding recreation, hotels, and restaurants)	0.0375	0.0450	0.0075	0.1713	0.0013	
f. Recreational, hotels, and restaurants	0.0222	0.0624	0.0401	0.0295	0.0012	
All sectors					−0.0141	−0.0142

	1998	2000	average	growth rate		
Unemployment rate (v)	0.0901	0.1016	0.0959	0.1196		
LFPR (e)	0.6531	0.6521	0.6526	−0.0015		
$(1 − v)$	0.9041					
$(1 − v)$ gr(L/P)	−0.0128					
$(1 − v)$ gr(e)	−0.0013					
v gr(v)	0.0115					
$(1 − v)$gr(L/P) − $(1 − v)$gr(e) + $v$gr(v)	0.0000					

TABLE 9.21 Employment Elasticity and Okun's Elasticity for the Relevant Periods

Period	(1) Change in Unemployment Rate	(2) % Change in GDP	(1)/(2) Employment Elasticity	(2)/(1) Okun's Elasticity
1988–1990	−0.20	9.43	−0.02	−47.15
1990–1991	0.90	−0.58	−1.54	−0.65
1991–1993	−0.10	2.47	−0.04	−24.70
1993–1997	−1.00	21.66	−0.05	−21.66
1997–1998	1.70	−0.58	−2.92	−0.34
1998–2000	0.50	7.55	0.07	15.09
1988–2000	1.80	45.00	0.04	25.00

capita in most sectors, except for traditional exportables, agriculture, and mining. The sharpest increase in output per capita came from the non-traditional exportable sector (the mid- to late 1990s saw a big boom in electronic exports and production unaffected by the Asian crisis), construction, EGW, transportation, FIRE, tourist-related services, and trade.

There was a notable decline in garment exports (the traditional exportable sector) in the 1990s as many newly liberalized trade markets (especially China and South Asian countries) trounced the Philippines in the world market. The Philippines' previously favored position was also adversely affected

TABLE 9.22 Factor Shares by Institution, 1980 to 1999 (% of GDP)

	1980	1981	1982	1983	1984	1985	1986	1987	1988	1989	1990	1991	1992	1993	1994	1995	1996	1997	1998	1999
Total household income	77.27	79.19	80.28	78.39	76.40	79.48	78.27	73.81	74.30	73.67	73.36	73.02	71.34	68.75	67.49	67.88	66.40	65.97	67.44	66.85
Compensation of employees	25.68	25.89	25.98	24.49	22.32	22.85	23.62	24.25	23.50	26.67	26.02	25.23	24.93	25.19	25.28	25.32	25.95	27.20	27.47	27.14
Household and Non-corporate net operating surplus	51.59	53.30	54.30	53.90	54.08	56.63	54.65	49.56	50.80	47.00	47.34	47.79	46.42	43.56	42.21	42.57	40.45	38.76	39.97	39.71
Total corporate income	15.49	14.07	12.31	13.77	16.15	14.27	14.95	18.20	19.69	19.24	19.27	18.71	19.54	21.48	21.84	21.26	23.49	23.67	23.18	24.11
Depreciation	7.02	7.10	7.17	7.88	9.22	9.91	9.86	9.37	8.40	7.82	7.65	7.88	8.07	8.92	8.95	9.02	8.77	8.58	8.84	9.09
Corporate net operating surplus[a]	8.47	6.97	5.14	5.89	6.92	4.36	5.09	8.83	11.29	11.42	11.61	10.83	11.47	12.56	12.88	12.24	14.72	15.09	14.34	15.02
Government income	7.24	6.73	7.41	7.85	7.45	6.26	6.78	7.99	6.01	7.09	7.37	8.27	9.11	9.77	10.68	10.86	10.11	10.36	9.38	9.04
Indirect taxes excluding import duties and taxes	5.44	5.31	4.09	3.73	4.07	4.41	4.73	5.26	4.29	4.76	5.17	4.58	4.94	5.11	6.07	5.97	5.93	6.90	6.99	6.29
Import duties and taxes	3.07	2.56	3.83	4.43	3.30	2.90	2.79	3.81	3.15	4.17	4.22	5.23	5.28	5.48	5.06	5.37	4.75	3.99	2.83	2.84
Less: subsidies	0.25	0.19	0.18	0.16	0.06	0.16	0.38	0.34	0.34	0.67	1.23	0.66	0.35	0.39	0.43	0.44	0.55	0.45	0.38	0.17
Government net operating surplus	−1.02	−0.95	−0.34	−0.15	0.14	−0.89	−0.36	−0.74	−1.09	−1.18	−0.79	−0.88	−0.77	−0.43	−0.02	−0.04	−0.03	−0.07	−0.07	0.08
Gross domestic product	100.00	100.00	100.00	100.00	100.00	100.00	100.00	100.00	100.00	100.00	100.00	100.00	100.00	100.00	100.00	100.00	100.00	100.00	100.00	100.00

Source: National Statistics Coordination Board.

a. Includes government corporations.

300

TABLE 9.23 Employment in Each Economic Sector by Skill (in %)

	1998			1990			1991			1992			1997			1998			2000		
	A[a]	B	C	A	B	C	A	B	C	A	B	C	A	B	C	A	B	C	A	B	C
Agriculture, fishery, and forestry	0.11	0.89	99.00	0.30	1.02	98.69	0.25	1.12	98.64	0.18	0.89	98.93	0.17	0.91	98.92	0.20	0.85	98.96	0.23	0.93	98.84
Mining and quarrying	5.87	14.77	79.37	4.07	16.66	79.27	4.59	9.10	86.32	6.11	12.52	81.38	8.30	16.93	74.77	8.81	14.47	76.73	8.57	19.46	71.97
Food, beverage, and tobacco	6.00	11.95	82.05	6.63	14.91	78.46	6.93	14.11	78.96	7.29	14.48	78.23	6.75	14.08	79.17	6.67	12.71	80.62	7.43	11.71	80.86
Importable manufacturing	14.73	38.95	46.31	15.64	38.38	45.98	13.87	36.90	49.23	15.25	36.56	48.20	13.82	33.69	52.49	12.86	34.27	52.86	15.32	34.23	50.45
Traditional exportable/importable	3.44	5.61	90.96	4.33	5.79	89.88	3.76	5.51	90.73	4.13	6.52	89.35	3.72	5.69	90.58	4.67	5.42	89.91	3.98	5.47	90.55
Non-traditional exportable/ importable	8.66	50.73	40.62	10.36	45.48	44.15	10.46	45.80	43.74	9.81	50.76	39.42	9.50	56.42	34.09	9.27	54.01	36.72	8.43	52.74	38.83
Construction	6.97	7.30	85.73	6.97	6.58	86.45	6.85	6.05	87.09	5.76	6.56	87.68	6.14	8.19	85.66	6.31	7.24	86.45	5.85	7.04	87.12
Electricity, gas, and water	20.90	65.74	13.36	20.47	56.49	23.04	18.47	56.80	24.73	17.04	59.40	23.56	19.58	60.88	19.54	21.24	59.10	19.65	18.66	59.87	21.47
Transport, storage, and communications	5.09	10.68	84.23	5.40	9.66	84.94	5.78	9.47	84.75	5.65	9.18	85.16	7.69	8.94	83.37	7.43	8.35	84.21	7.30	7.94	84.77
Trade	1.16	3.43	95.42	1.76	4.70	93.54	1.69	4.42	93.89	1.77	4.95	93.28	2.29	6.37	91.35	2.33	6.10	91.57	2.22	6.28	91.50
FIRE	31.35	60.56	8.09	31.25	58.97	9.79	31.25	57.40	11.35	29.58	58.81	11.61	32.59	54.34	13.07	33.37	54.25	12.39	32.02	55.01	12.97
Private government services	9.92	42.56	47.52	10.66	43.57	45.76	10.97	42.04	46.99	10.93	44.17	44.90	11.24	42.45	46.32	10.75	41.91	47.35	10.77	42.69	46.53
Recreational and hotels	8.79	27.32	63.89	9.95	30.65	59.40	9.23	28.02	62.74	9.74	29.63	60.63	9.59	26.89	63.52	8.74	25.94	65.33	10.30	24.46	65.25
Total	3.75	12.01	84.24	4.33	12.88	82.79	4.35	12.54	83.11	4.20	12.76	83.04	4.98	13.97	81.06	5.00	13.89	81.11	5.06	14.24	80.70

a. A: professionals and managers; B: skilled and mid-level managers; and C: low-skilled workers.

when its garment export quotas were cut following WTO rules.

The increase in output was accompanied by sharp increases in labor productivity in the agricultural, industrial, and manufacturing sectors, thus offsetting the potential labor absorption from the output increases. Table 9.18 shows that there was a fall in the employment ratio of agriculture. The only labor absorbers in industry were construction, non-traditional exportables, and importable manufacturing,[21] and construction virtually dominated labor absorption in this sector.

Interestingly, the biggest labor absorber in the economy during this period was the service sector, whose output per capita increased and whose labor productivity declined (especially in FIRE, transportation, and tourist-related services). Thus, the improvement in the employment ratio and in the unemployment rate was primarily the result of the increase in output and the fall in labor productivity in the service sector, and secondarily because of the sharp rise of output in construction and (to a lesser extent) electronics.

The increased productivity in industry and manufacturing may be explained by the rise of strong competition among tradables, given the strong tariff reduction and real appreciation of the currency. Manufacturing could not absorb much labor. The largely non-tradable service sector and construction became the main labor absorbers, but their labor productivity fell. Table 9.12, however, shows that the rise in labor productivity in the economy was mainly caused by increases in productivity in the agricultural sector, and only secondarily in the industrial and manufacturing sectors. This indicates a movement away from low-productivity agriculture to the more attractive and higher-productivity sectors of service and industry. Table 9.12 shows that, unlike in other periods, the productivity improvements caused by intersectoral movements (column 7) are stronger than the weighted average of the productivity changes of the various sectors (column 3). Because of the strong labor productivity in industry and the strong movement out of agriculture during this period, the employment elasticity of this period is again practically nil (−0.05; see table 9.21). This should put into question the employment-absorption capacity of the liberalizing growth periods in the Philippines. We will address this at length in the summary section.

3.4.5. 1997–1998: The Asian Financial Crisis and El Niño Effects

Tables 9.13 and 9.19 show that the recession in 1998 due to the Asian financial crisis and El Niño led to sharp falls in the output of construction, agriculture, and importable manufacturing, and moderate falls in traditional and non-traditional exportables. However, all areas in the service sector, except for the trade sector, increased their output.

The fall in agricultural, manufacturing, and construction outputs was partly offset by declines in labor productivity in these areas (except traditional exportables) and declines in labor productivity in the service sectors (except FIRE) as shown in table 9.19. Decreases in the employment ratios in agriculture, manufacturing, and industry were partly offset by increases in the employment ratios of the service sector (except in FIRE). The service sector continues to be the labor absorber even in this period of crisis.

What is the main difference between the recession in 1998 and the recession in 1991? The recession in 1991 was met by large declines in labor productivity in industry and manufacturing, so that labor was not displaced from manufacturing and industry, but was instead displaced from agriculture and service (see table 9.16 and section 3.3.2). In 1998 the labor productivity declines in manufacturing and industry were much smaller than in 1991, so that there was some displacement in the two sectors, especially in construction, traditional exportables, and importable manufacturing. The El Niño weather disturbance also meant that the biggest displacement would be from agriculture. This time, a partial cushion was provided for by the service sector, which meant that its employment increases outpaced its output increases (except in FIRE), leading to productivity declines in the sector.

Table 9.13 also shows that there was a 1.18 percent intersectoral productivity improvement offsetting the general decline in productivity in almost all sectors. This was again due to the shift from agriculture to the higher-productivity service sector.

The smaller productivity declines in industry and manufacturing in 1998 compared to 1991 may be a result of the increased competition provided by foreign products as a result of intense trade liberalization and tariff reduction in the 1990s. In a way, this was a continuation of the trend of the earlier period when labor was absorbed in the service sectors much more so than in the industrial sector. As labor productivity in the industrial and manufacturing sector increased (or fell relatively less), it decreased (or declined relatively more) in the service sectors. An important implication is that in 1998 the adjustment to the bust portion of the cycles was borne more by industrial workers, as many of them had to switch to lower-productivity employment in the service sectors or be unemployed. With the displacement of workers from the manufacturing and industrial sectors and the strong outflow of employment from agriculture, one can see (comparing Table 9.19 with Table 9.16) that the rise in unemployment was stronger in 1998 than in 1991. Thus, even if GDP declined by an equal amount during both periods, the 1998 crisis was much more painful in terms of employment losses.

Table 9.21 shows that employment elasticity for this period hit a high of –2.92 as a 0.58 percent decline in GDP caused a 1.7 percent increase in unemployment. Again, as previous growth periods failed to effect significant employment absorption, bust periods were effectively and increasingly churning unemployment.

The switch to the service sectors also had a gendered impact, as the service sector has a greater female workforce than the industrial sector. Thus, the latest 1998 crisis saw a bigger displacement of male workers (especially young male workers) relative to female workers, especially in the urban areas (see Lim 2000).

3.4.6. 1998–2000: Continued Low Confidence— Jobless Growth Revisited

As tables 9.14 and 9.20 show, there was some recovery between 1998 and 2000 as the agriculture, service, and manufacturing sectors registered reasonably adequate growth. The high growth in agriculture signaled the return of normal weather after the unusually bad year of 1998. Industry posted positive but lower growth as construction still remained in a depressed state, registering a strong output contraction.

This period was very similar to the situation a decade earlier in 1988–1990, when output growth was accompanied by large productivity increases in most sectors and led to a jobless growth condition. This time, however, the effect was stronger and led to an increase in the unemployment rate between 1998 and 2000 (unlike in 1988–1990).

The biggest labor productivity increases were in agriculture, non-traditional exportables, importable manufacturing, and food manufacturing.[22] Even the service sector posted gains in productivity (with the notable exception of FIRE), although the productivity gains were much lower than that in agriculture, industry, and manufacturing (continuing the trend of lagging productivity in the service sector during the 1990s).

The net result was a large displacement of labor from agriculture (despite its high growth), a continued displacement from industry (mainly from construction), and stagnancy in employment per capita in manufacturing. The partial cushion was, once again, provided by the service sector, which absorbed labor in trade, transportation, private services, and tourist-related services because of the reasonable economic growth in these sectors.

But the labor absorption in the service sector was not enough to stem the strong rise in unemployment during this period since labor productivity increased. The unemployment in 2000 was 10.1 percent, the highest registered since the new labor force data set was constructed in 1987.

As mentioned earlier, the exceedingly bad confidence during this period may have contributed to the reluctance of firms to rehire labor, just as in the 1988–1990 period. This time, the loss in confidence was a result of bad governance and a widespread perception of wanton corruption in the Estrada government. As table 9.21 shows, the employment elasticity sign in 2000 was positive, meaning that increases in output coincided with increases in unemployment.

3.4.7. A Short Summary

Table 9.21 shows the alarming employment problem faced by the Philippines. For the whole period 1988 to 2000, the employment elasticity (or Okun's elasticity) was perverse and became positive. This meant that for the entire period as a whole, output increased by 45 percent but unemployment increased by 1.8 percent as well. We have seen how this happened. The growth periods had very low—almost nil—employment elasticities. During busts, these elasticities were quite significant, as recessions worsened the unemployment problem. The result should not have been unexpected.

Thus, the problem of Philippine unemployment is not only the bust-recovery cycles that have left the economy stagnant but also the distinct anti-employment bias to these cycles. Let us recall some of the reasons for the lack of employment absorption during growth periods. They are (1) the lack of confidence in some of these periods and (2) the required increases in labor productivity in the tradable sectors owing to increased competition with external liberalization. We can also add a third reason, which we already touched upon in the macro section of the paper. The exceedingly high import dependence and structural BOP crises manifest a lack of integration and backward linkaging in the development process, and a lack of domestic resource use and innovation. The high dependence on foreign intermediate goods can only lead to a lack of domestic resource usage—including the most important resource, which is labor. Furthermore, the bust cycles have become more vicious, displacing more labor than before.

In the 1990s, we also detect the stronger labor-absorption capacities of the service as well as the construction sectors (for the latter, only in boom times). The manufacturing (which is the most tradable) sector requires stronger adjustments in terms of labor productivities because of its increasing exposure to competition. On the output side, inasmuch as manufacturing, construction, and the industrial sector as a whole strongly contract during slowdowns, and agriculture experiences a long downward trend, output also becomes more and more weighted toward the service sector.

This increasing share of the service sector in terms of output and employment is shown in tables 9.6 and 9.8. One can also see a slight decrease in the share of manufacturing in terms of both output and employment after the Asian crisis.

4. Distribution Effects of External Liberalization

4.1. Factor Income Shares

Table 9.22 gives us the distribution of factor shares by institutions. Looking at household incomes, one can see that, starting in the late 1980s when external liberalization began to intensify, the share of net operating surplus of households and non-corporate entities began to fall, and this trend continued until 2000.[23] The other side of this story is the concurrent rise in the share of corporate income. The corporate income share grew rapidly in the late 1980s and

mid-1990s, while declining temporarily (a tendency opposite that of the household operating surplus) during recessions (1985, 1991, and 1998). It must be emphasized that the corporate income share increased significantly in every turn of recession to recovery—in 1987, in 1993, and in 1999. This is most likely because recoveries allow firms to use excess capacity without much new labor absorption, and therefore income shares shift to them.

Thus, on the whole, the household income share fell over time from 80 percent in 1982 to 66.9 percent in 1999, while the corporate income share increased from 12.3 percent in 1982 to 24.1 percent in 1999.[24] The government income share increased notably in the pre–Asian crisis period of the 1990s as tax reforms improved both indirect tax and import duties revenue collection. But the lowering of tariffs began to have negative revenue effects on import duties starting in 1996, and government revenues started to decline and fell drastically during and after the Asian crisis (1998–1999), giving rise to the growing fiscal deficit problems of the country in the post-crisis period.

The fall in the share of the household operating surplus indicates the shrinking of income derived from the informal, self-employed sector—especially in agriculture—and in the manufacturing and service sectors as well, in a time of external liberalization. The consistent and significant move out of agriculture and its decline in both the value-added and employment share account for a significant portion of the large drop in the share of household operating surplus over time (from 54.3 percent in 1982 to 39.7 percent in 2000). The lack of a corresponding increase in compensation for employees as peasants moved out of agriculture simply reflects the lack of labor absorption in the Philippine setting.

Employee compensation had a rather steady share during the period, with a notable increase during the Asian crisis period and beyond (1997–1999). This reflects an increase in the income shares of the formal sectors (corporate and formal labor income) and a decrease in the income shares of the informal sectors over time—a reverse trend from the employment shift from formal manufacturing and agriculture to more informal services. As service (and much of it is informal sector) becomes the employment sink for a non-labor-absorptive economy, its low productivity and declining real wages offset the increasing number of persons entering the sector, making the total informal wage bill decline in relation to the formal economy. This can occur because of a labor surplus condition.

The improvement in government income throughout much of the 1990s shows the emphasis on macro stability and the need to reduce fiscal deficits as a prerequisite to confidence-building liberalization (which the Aquino and Ramos governments strove for). But the fall in the share of government income right before, during, and after the Asian crisis shows how dependent the Philippines is on import duties, and how tax revenues are very elastic in relation to incomes during recessions. Recessions, sharp currency devaluations, and tariff reduction without compensating gains from other revenue sources will have an adverse impact on the fiscal sector and macro stability, as is now the case in the Philippines.

4.2. Income Distribution between Low-Skilled and Skilled Labor

There are questions about how the incomes of skilled and unskilled labor are affected by external liberalization. The problem with Philippine labor statistics is that wage data are very scarce and generally not regularly available except from the establishment sources. The latest set of wages corresponding to labor force statistics dates back to 1995. Thus, the succeeding discussion simply discusses the employment figures of various categories of labor, and derives implications without giving any time-series wage data across different types of labor.

Appendix 1 shows the mean quarterly earnings data of various occupations for the third quarter of 1995 (the latest wage data set available). We categorize the various occupations into three classes: professionals and managers, skilled and middle-level workers, and low-skilled workers. Arbitrarily, those with mean quarterly earnings of P15,000 are considered professionals and managers, those with mean quarterly earnings of P10,000 to P15,000 are considered skilled and middle-level workers, and those with mean quarterly earnings of below P10,000 are considered low-skilled workers.

Table 9.23 gives us employment figures for the three categories for selected years between 1988 and 2000,[25] in terms of percentages of the total employed in a sector. One can see that there were not very major changes in the skill composition of the sectors over time.[26] On the whole, there is a noticeable decline in the percentage of low-skilled workers (from 84.2 percent in 1988 to 80.7 percent in 2000). Simultaneously, there are increases in the percentages of both middle-level workers (from 12.0 percent in 1988 to 14.24 percent in 2000) and professionals and managers (from 3.8 percent in 1988 to 5.1 percent in 2000).

The moderate shift from low- to higher-skilled workers is most likely a result of employment shifts across sectors rather than changes in the composition of skilled and unskilled workers within sectors. A cursory look at tables 9.9 to 9.14 or 9.15 to 9.20 shows that the shares in sectoral employment (L_i/L) have changed significantly between 1988 to 2000. Specifically, the movement out of agriculture and the traditional exportable sector reduced the composition weights of low-skilled workers, since table 9.22 shows that these two sectors are the most heavily dependent on low-skilled workers. Of course, there are movements toward sectors that are also dependent on low-skilled workers (such as transportation, construction, and trade). But these are more than offset by movements to sectors that are more weighted toward middle-level, professional, and managerial workers—areas such as government and private services, the non-traditional exportable sector, and FIRE (look at table 9.22 to see their greater dependence on higher-skilled workers).

This modest shift from low-skilled workers to middle-level workers, managers, and professionals may imply a deteriorating trend in the income distribution within labor. This surely needs more verification since we need to know (1) the trend of wage differentials between the categories of workers and (2) whether labor skills have been upgraded from low skilled to middle level over time. The general fall in real wages in the 1990s (see figure 9.14) might imply a fall in wages for the majority of low-skilled labor (who comprise more than 80 percent of the employed labor force). This reinforces our claim that there would have, most likely, been a deterioration of income within labor income.

5. Conclusion

This chapter has dwelled on the following issues:

1. Because of its dependency on imports and unsustainable foreign capital flows, the

Philippines has suffered through many bust-boom cycles, which are the main cause of its lack of macroeconomic development.

2. Since the second half of the 1980s, the strong external liberalization program has been accompanied with an increased volatility and frequency of recession-recovery cycles.

3. This study shows that from 1988 to 2000, the bust periods displaced labor but the growth periods had very little employment absorption. This led to a long-run increase in the unemployment rate trend. The lack of employment absorption in the growth periods has to do with a lack of business confidence in some of the periods, the need to improve labor productivity in the tradable (manufacturing) sector, and a high import dependence that is biased against the use of domestic resources and inputs. Thus, the employment problem has to do not only with more frequent and intense bust-recovery cycles, but also with the lack of employment generation during the growth periods and the more intense displacement of labor during the bust periods.

4. Labor productivity in most sectors has fallen during recessions and increased during booms. The series of growth and recessions, corresponding increases and decreases in labor productivity, as well as periods of confidence and non-confidence have resulted not only in the lack of long-run output growth but also in the lack of improved labor productivity as well as unemployment rates.

5. In the 1990s, we also detected stronger labor-absorption capacities in the service sector relative to the manufacturing (the more tradable) sector, which requires stronger adjustments in terms of labor productivity because of its increased exposure to competition. Agriculture also declined in terms of output and employment. The increasing share of service, (since the late 1980s) the relatively constant share of industry and manufacturing, and the falling share of agri-culture in both output and employment can be partly explained by the labor productivity and employment movements during the recession-recovery cycles.

6. Another factor contributing to the attractiveness of the service sector was its relative insulation from competitive forces unleashed in the process of external liberalization.

7. These tendencies also imply falling and/or lagging labor productivities in the service sector, which contributes to the lack of improvement in overall labor productivity as the service sector increases its share in output and employment.

8. The paper also presented evidence of the increasing share that goes to corporate income after every bust-recovery transition, and the squeeze in the informal household sector's operating surplus with external liberalization and as labor moved out of agriculture.

9. Government income inevitably improved during the growth periods and with painful tax reforms. However, during recessions and sharp currency devaluations the contraction in imports and incomes significantly reduced tax revenues and resulted in the deterioration of the fiscal position. The general trend of tariff reductions aggravated this problem, affecting the fiscal sector during currency devaluations and recessions.

10. There is evidence of moderate but discernable shifts in labor employment from low-skilled workers to middle-level as well as managerial and professional workers. Together with the fall in real wages in the 1990s, this points to some deterioration in income distribution within households and the labor sectors.

11. Overall, therefore, the combination of boom-bust or recession-recovery cycles with external liberalization has not improved labor productivity, employment generation, and factor income distribution in the last two decades.

Appendix 1: Categorization of Labor Occupations into Three Classes, Using Mean Quarterly Earnings, July–September 1995

Occupation	Mean (Quarterly Earnings) July to September 1995		
Professionals and Managers	*Both*	*Male*	*Female*
Managers—wholesale and retail trade	42,314	60,530	23,927
Justices, judges, and lawyers	32,899	33,051	31,643
Managers	30,790	33,321	25,057
Aircraft and ship's officers	30,326	31,987	10,875
Managers—catering and lodging services	22,030	19,676	23,456
Architects, engineers, and related technicians	20,647	20,966	17,394
Accountants and auditors	20,413	20,376	20,442
Social scientists and related workers	20,012	23,379	17,263
Composers and performing artists	19,375	21,253	14,906
Clerical supervisors	19,174	17,890	22,115
Physical scientists and related technicians	19,148	21,559	18,592
Production supervisors and general foremen	18,668	18,442	19,615
Insurance, real estate, securities, and business service			
Salesmen and auctioneers	17,709	16,967	18,506
Mathematicians, statisticians, and system and related workers	17,512	21,920	15,120
Professional, technical, and related workers	16,581	20,785	13,928
Transport and communications supervisors	16,379	16,431	15,665
Medical, dental, veterinary, and related workers	15,743	23,239	13,480
Authors, journalists, and related workers	15,625	17,950	13,651
Tanners and pelt dressers	15,000	15,000	—
Skilled and Middle-Level Workers			
Teachers, including supervisors and principals	14,693	16,110	14,330
Computing machine operators	14,190	14,876	13,604
Life scientists and related technicians	13,677	12,239	18,158
Working proprietors—catering and lodging	13,441	16,741	12,014
Technical salesmen, traveling salesmen, and manufacturer's agents	12,858	15,184	8,959
Stationary engine and related equipment operators	12,818	13,196	10,744
Housekeeping and related services	12,650	13,898	11,245
Printers and related workers	12,637	13,167	10,132
Legislative officials, government administrators, and government executives	12,423	13,261	10,981
Telephone and telegraph operators	12,332	10,989	13,400
Bookkeepers, cashiers, and related workers	12,311	14,274	11,462
Athletes, sportsmen, and related workers	12,301	13,986	7,075
Protective service workers	12,211	12,262	10,078
Chemical processors and related workers	12,144	12,491	10,745
Machinery fitters, machine assemblers, and precision-instrument makers	12,066	12,129	8,112
Clerical and related workers not elsewhere classified	11,601	11,931	11,356

(continued)

Appendix 1: (continued)

Occupation	Mean (Quarterly Earnings) July to September 1995		
Professionals and Managers	Both	Male	Female
Secretaries, stenographers, typists, and card- and tape-punching machine operators	11,539	13,044	11,264
Electrical fitters and related electrical and electronics workers	11,467	11,383	11,755
Metal processors	11,271	12,236	5,682
Mail distribution clerks and messengers	11,129	10,968	12,716
Farm managers and overseers	11,087	11,947	5,005
Blacksmiths, toolmakers, and machine-tool operators	10,818	10,614	11,873
Sculptors, painters, photographers, and related workers	10,367	9,765	13,596
Plumbers, welders, and sheet metal and structural metal preparers and erectors	10,169	10,142	13,594
Low-Skilled Workers			
Sales supervisors and buyers	9,942	12,631	7,468
Working proprietors—wholesale and retail trade	9,895	15,412	7,974
Transport equipment operators	9,365	9,383	6,923
Painters	9,342	9,371	8,505
Jewelry and precious workers	9,041	9,958	5,902
Tobacco preparers and tobacco product makers	8,971	13,247	6,944
Building caretakers, cleaners, and related workers	8,794	9,135	7,364
Service workers not elsewhere classified	8,151	8,810	6,563
Bricklayers, carpenters, and other construction workers	8,004	7,980	12,394
Glass formers, potters, and related workers	7,926	9,256	5,507
Miners, quarrymen, well drillers, and related workers	7,763	8,145	3,199
Rubber and plastics products makers	7,581	7,870	6,623
Wood preparation workers and paper makers	7,554	7,705	6,106
Broadcasting station and sound equipment operators, and cinema projectionists	7,551	6,779	12,191
Material handling and related equipment operators	7,478	7,528	6,701
Cooks, waiters, bartenders, and related workers	7,392	8,676	5,971
Furniture makers and related workers	7,180	7,594	4,676
Footwear and leather goods makers	7,040	7,521	6,296
Tailors, dressmakers, sewers, and upholsterers	7,040	9,816	6,445
Food and beverage processors	6,858	7,676	5,288
Hairdressers, barbers, beauticians, and related workers	6,438	7,163	6,117
Farmers	6,370	6,989	3,225
Transport conductors	6,283	6,322	5,005
Workers in religion	6,270	7,299	4,112
Production and related workers not elsewhere classified	6,099	8,022	4,668
Paper and paperboard products makers	6,082	7,742	5,074
Laborers not elsewhere classified	5,913	6,089	3,342
Stone cutters and carvers	5,847	5,533	7,890

(continued)

Appendix 1: (continued)

Occupation	Mean (Quarterly Earnings) July to September 1995		
Professionals and Managers	Both	Male	Female
Spinners, weavers, knitters, dryers, and related workers	4,915	7,962	4,106
Salesmen, shop assistants, and related workers	4,859	6,157	4,261
Fishermen, hunters, and related workers	4,852	5,043	1,551
Forestry workers	4,614	5,080	2,152
Sales workers not elsewhere classified	4,453	5,439	3,714
Helpers and related housekeeping service	3,956	4,042	3,942
Launderers, dry cleaners, and pressers	3,137	5,359	3,096
Agricultural and animal husbandry worker	1,356	1,867	679

Notes

This chapter was written for the international conference on "External Liberalization, Growth, Development and Social Policy" from January 18 to 20, 2002, Hanoi, Vietnam. Comments on an earlier draft by Lance Taylor, Erinç Yeldan, and Jong-Il You are gratefully acknowledged. The usual disclaimer applies.

1. The Garcia administration championed the import-substitution strategy, but was weakened by corruption charges in dispensing with the import franchises. The balance of payment crisis helped defeat Garcia in the presidential elections and brought the Macapagal administration to power. Macapagal campaigned publicly for the liberalization of the economy and the seeking of assistance from the IMF.

2. In 1965 Marcos defeated Macapagal and from the start of his term embarked on high public spending.

3. Foreign direct investments had been dominated by multinationals catering to the domestic market, mainly in the chemical and manufacturing sectors of a still import-dependent economy.

4. Where X is aggregate supply, Y is private income, T is net taxes, and M is imports. Aggregate demand components are consumption (C), investment (I), government demand (G), and exports (E).

5. Some notations: private savings rate is s, the import propensity is m, and the tax rate is t.

6. One of Marcos's business allies (Dewey Dee) escaped the country, leaving millions of pesos' worth of unpaid debts in the financial institutions, which had an adverse domino-like effect in the financial sector.

7. See Beckaert and Harvey's (1998) appendix for a listing of major political and economic events in several countries including the Philippines.

8. The Ramos presidential term ran from 1992 to 1998. During the previous six years, Corazon Aquino was in power (immediately after the dismantling of the Marcos dictatorship).

9. The fast tracking, however, may have led to higher electricity costs for the Philippines compared to its neighbors.

10. This is a controversial point since some economists blame the Central Bank for some sterilization in order to maintain a fixed exchange rate.

11. These indicators may also explain why Philippine growth has rarely gone beyond 6 percent, in a sort of two-gap analysis.

12. The data used in the decomposition are the national deficit in real terms. The CPSD is the nominal national deficit plus the deficits of government entities not under the national government. The CPSD/GDP ratio is the parameter often used by policy makers to gauge performance.

13. Where P is the population.

14. As will be explained later, some economic sectors include both exportables and importables.

15. The fishery sector actually qualifies as an exportable sector, but the authors decided to keep it in the agricultural sector (since it is too small to separate out).

16. Banking institutions also qualify as an exportable sector, but we decided to keep the financial and FIRE sector intact rather than break it up.

17. Furthermore, in EGW and tourist-related services, outputs per capita virtually remained unchanged.

18. All sectors improved their productivities except for tourist-related services, importable manufacturing, food manufacturing, and transportation.

19. Employment elasticity in table 9.21 refers to the ratio of the change in the unemployment rate to the percentage change in GDP from the starting year to the ending year of that period.

20. The only sector whose labor productivity slightly improved was the traditional exportable sector.

21. This last sector was virtually the only sector in industry whose labor productivity fell, except for mining, which is a very small sector.

22. Only traditional exportables registered a fall in productivity (and a very sharp one at that) in the manufacturing sector. Another sector in the industrial sector whose productivity registered a decline was construction.

23. Although there was a tendency for this item to register small temporary increases during recessions (1984–1985, 1991, and 1998).

24. These very sharp changes may be exaggerated by data and statistical errors, but the trends are not counterintuitive.

25. The years correspond to the period categorization we used in the decomposition exercises for employment and labor productivity.

26. Perhaps the biggest changes are in EGW, FIRE, and importable manufacturing, which over the years increased their share of low-skilled workers at the expense of middle-level workers. But these sectors have very low employment-generating capacity, as shown by their L_i/L.

References

Bautista, C. 2000. Boom-bust cycles and crisis periods in the Philippines: A regime-switching analysis. UP School of Economics Discussion Paper no. 0009. Diliman: University of the Philippines.

Bekaert, G., and C. Harvey. 1998. Capital flows and the behavior of emerging market equity returns. NBER Working Paper no. 6669. Cambridge, Mass.: NBER.

Berg, J., and L. Taylor. 2000. External liberalization, economic performance and social policy. CEPA Working Paper no. 12. New York: Center for Economic Policy Analysis, New School University.

De Dios, E. 1998. Philippine economic growth: Can it last? In *The Philippines, new directions in domestic policy and foreign relations*, edited by D. Timberman. New York: The Asia Society.

———. 2000. The boom-bust cycle (Will it ever end?). In *The Philippine economy: Alternatives for the 21st century*, edited by D. Canlas and S. Fujisaki. Tokyo: Institute of Developing Economies.

Fabella, R. 1995. Sustainability of the 1994 economic recovery: Portents from the past. In *Towards sustained growth*, edited by R. Fabella, and H. Sakai. Tokyo: Institute of Developing Economies.

Jurado, G. 1976. Industrialization and trade. In *Philippine economic problems in perspective*, edited by J. Encarnación. Institute of Economic Development and Research, UP School of Economics.

Lim, J. 2000. The effects of the East Asian Crisis on the employment of women and men: The Philippine Case. *World Development* 28 (7): 1285–1306.

Lim, J., and M. Montes. 2000. The structure of employment and structural adjustment in the Philippines. *Journal of Development Studies* 36 (4): 149–81.

Montes, M. 1987. Macroeconomic adjustment in the Philippines, 1983–85. Philippine Institute for Development Studies, Working Paper Series no. 8701. Makati City, Philippines: PIDS.

Taylor, L. 1983. *Structuralist macroeconomics: Applicable models for the Third World*. New York: Basic Books.

10

External Liberalization, Growth, and Distribution: The Polish Experience

Leon Podkaminer

1. A General (Macro)Economic History

1.1. The Years 1988–1989: Repressed Inflation

Up to the end of 1988, Poland had *not* been a market economy. It had not been a centrally planned economy either. The central authorities attempted to administratively control—with varying degrees of success—wages, prices, (multiple) exchange rates, (multiple) interest rates, credit, and real "quantities" such as production, use of inputs, consumption, employment, investment, and foreign trade. A sizeable private sector (75 percent of agriculture and unidentifiable quantities of informal activities outside farming) was tolerated and somehow managed to function quite well within the system, although it was also affected by interference from the state.

The bureaucratic controls were not about aggregate items, but involved detailed instructions and commands passed down the bureaucratic hierarchies in charge of specific branches or specific aspects of production and exchange. Not only was the whole system vastly inefficient but also, because state directives were not consistent (and often contradicted one another), the attempts at their execution created chaotic conditions. This demoralized everyone (including the bureaucracy) and strengthened anarchic attitudes among both the managers of state-owned firms and other economic organizations as well as labor.

Structurally, the priorities of the development policy were grossly mistaken, as they stipulated the preferential treatment of agriculture, mining, and "heavy" branches of manufacturing (metallurgy, shipbuilding, heavy armaments such as tanks, and basic chemicals such as fertilizers) at the expense of services and technologically advanced high-skill branches. The policy strongly supported farmers' incomes. This preserved small-scale farming and prevented the outflow of labor from farming to other branches that suffered from chronic and acute labor shortages. The whole system was highly egalitarian, and public consumption was quite high—with free access to education, health services, and recreation. A part of the generous social policy was conducted at the firm level (with state-owned firms also providing some benefits, funding, recreation, etc.).

From the macroeconomic point of view, the Polish economy was in a state of "repressed inflation" (borrowing the term from E. Malinvaud). There was an acute shortage of both goods and labor. From 1988 to 1989, practically all consumer items were in short supply—with most of them subject to formal or informal rationing. At the same time, the acute shortage of labor manifested itself in huge vacancies and zero unemployment. The economy was insulated from the world market—through the state monopoly on foreign trade (and of course through foreign exchange transactions). But significant amounts of forex remittances flowed in (private possession of U.S. dollars was permitted, and state-owned banks administered dollar-denominated personal deposit accounts). Foreign trade was "planned" and also "coordinated" within the COMECON (by far Poland's most significant collective partner). Global market conditions did not matter much to the planning bureaucracy—and even less so to state-owned firms. From 1980 onwards, Poland was technically in default to the West. By 1989 its (long non-serviced) debt was about $40 billion.[1] Growth was disappointing. As a result of the deep economic and social crisis in 1979–1982—national income fell by some 20–25 percent there was high open inflation and no unemployment, and martial law was introduced—output remained virtually stagnant throughout the 1980s.

1.2. Enter Shock Therapy (and the Keynesian Recession)

Through 1989, the system disintegrated politically and economically. Amidst high and rising inflation, successive segments of the market freed themselves of price (and other) controls. Private activities emerged from the shadows and were quickly legalized—as was private foreign trade. The spontaneous liberalization of foreign trade assumed unprecedented proportions, and large private fortunes were made on foreign trade (both imports and exports). The trick was to exploit inconsistencies among various types of exchange rates, customs/tax, and subsidy arrangements. Domestically, state-owned firms and

other organizations (e.g., banks) were liberating themselves from bureaucratic tutelage even though property conditions were to remain fuzzy for some time. Weak governance resulted in the loss of state control of just about everything. The state's activities were reduced to printing money and distributing subsidies to firms that, suddenly confronted with the (somewhat chaotic) market conditions, found themselves without cash (but also to firms and population groups that were able to extract money on other grounds).

The year 1990 started with the shock therapy imposed by the new government (supported by the politically victorious "Solidarity" movement). Shock therapy introduced some disciplining principles— providing clear rules for the managers of state-owned firms, banks, and other organizations. These entities were "commercialized"—that is, made to conform to market rules—with a view to being privatized as soon as possible. The systemic aspects of shock therapy, progressively developed in the following years, allowed a relatively successful transformation of the Polish economy into a functioning market economy, with many of its typical advantages (and most of its imperfections).

The macroeconomics of shock therapy involved quite excessive measures. It stipulated a very restrictive fiscal position: huge cuts in spending, not subsidizing (most) losers, exorbitant increases in indirect taxation, astronomical interest rates, and an effective freeze on wages and pensions. Within a few weeks, the economy left the repressed inflation regime for good. Everything became available, most crucially, labor. Within one year, the unemployment rate went from zero to 6.5 percent. Though not expected by the authorities (and their IMF tutors), inflation (which had been falling at the end of 1989) surged ahead. Inflation, together with other measures, cut into real wages (average wages went down by 24 percent). All in all, the economy was pushed into a deep recession combined with ever-rising unemployment and high (though gradually decreasing) inflation. Though statistical data for 1989–1990 leave much to be desired, we can gather from tables 10.1 and 10.2[2] that the share of consumption was very low at 67 percent[3] and that net exports $(E - M)$ were very high (7 percent). Overall, the changes in the volumes of exports and imports in 1990 (unknown) moderated the GDP growth decline (of 11.6 percent)[4] by 3.8 percentage points.

TABLE 10.1 Real Growth Rates, GDP Components

	1990	1991	1992	1993	1994	1995	1996	1997	1998	1999	2000	Estimate 2001	Average per Annum 1992–1995	Average per Annum 1995–2000	Average per Annum 1995–2001
GDP	-11.6	-6.3	2.3	3.8	5.2	6.5	6.0	6.8	4.8	4.1	3.9	1.1	5.2	5.1	
NT=CG+SG			12.9	14.6	0.5	7.9	7.6	6.4	3.9	-2	0.9		7.5	3.3	
YD=GDP−NT			13.1	14.1	0.5	7.4	7.6	6.5	3.8	-1.9	0.6			5.5	
C	-11.7	8.5	3.4	4.9	3.9	3.3	7.1	6.1	4.1	4.4	2.4		4	4.8	
CP	-15.3	6.3	2.3	5.2	4.3	3.2	8.6	6.9	4.8	5.2	2.6	2.1	4.2	5.6	
CG	-0.5	14	6.4	3.8	2.8	3.8	2.1	3.2	1.6	1.3	1.4		3.4	2	
I	-24.8	-20.1	-13	12.8	9.1	24.1	19.5	20.8	13.8	6.1	3.9	-10.2	15.1	12.6	
I$_p$			-21	10.6	9.9	31.4	15.6	23.2	15.5	12.2	6.9		14.5	15.0	
IG			33.5	20.4	6.3	0.2	36.6	12.1	6.8	-20.5	-14.6				
G=IG+CG				0.13	-2.73	2.50	12.52	10.94	4.08	-7.18	-3.10				
M	29.6		1.7	13.2	11.3	24.3	28	21.4	18.5	1	15.6		16.1	16.5	
E	-1.7		10.8	3.2	13.1	22.8	12	12.2	14.3	-2.6	23.2		12.8	11.5	

Decomposition of GDP Growth Rates into Final Demand Components

Contribution of:	1990	1991	1992	1993	1994	1995	1996	1997	1998	1999	2000	Estimate 2001	Average per Annum 1992–1995	Average per Annum 1995–2000	
C	-7.9	5.7	2.8	4.1	3.3	2.8	5.6	4.9	3.3	3.5	1.9		3.4	3.8	
C$_p$		3	1.3	3.2	2.7	2.1	5.2	4.3	3	3.3	1.7		2.7	3.5	
CG		2.7	1.4	0.8	0.6	0.7	0.4	0.6	0.3	0.2	0.2		0.7	0.3	
I	-7.5	-5.2	-2.6	1.9	1.4	3.8	3.8	4.6	3.4	1.6	1		2.4	2.9	
I$_p$			-3.6	1.3	1.2	3.8	2.5	4	3.1	2.6	1.6		2.1	2.7	
IG			1	0.7	0.2	0	1.4	0.6	0.3	-1	-0.6		0.3	0.1	
E		-0.5	2.5	0.8	3	5.5	3	3	3.7	-0.7	6.1		3.1	3	
M		-6.4	0.4	2.9	2.5	5.6	6.5	5.5	5.5	0.3	5.1		3.7	4.6	
E−M	3.8	-6.9	2.1	-2.2	0.5	-0.1	-3.4	-2.6	-1.9	-1.1	1		-0.6	-1.6	
TOTAL. GDP	-11.6	-6.3	2.3	3.8	5.2	6.5	6	6.8	4.8	4.1	3.9		5.2	5.1	

Memorandum Items	1990	1991	1992	1993	1994	1995	1996	1997	1998	1999	2000	Estimate 2001	Average per Annum 1991–1994	Average per Annum 1994–1998	Average per Annum 1995–2001
Nominal exchange rate	.	11.4	29	33	27.4	16.1	7.7	9.9	5.7	7.8	-5.1	-8	29.8	9.8	2.8
PPI—manufacturing	630	39.6	26.8	29.3	24.2	25.9	10.7	8.5	6.5	5	7.5	1	26.7	12.7	6.5
Import prices (excluding oil and gas)	634	20.1	18.2	17.1	28.2	19.8	8.5	13.4	3.6	5.6	-1		21.1	11.2	4.9
Export prices	514	18.7	27.6	25.6	28.8	21.2	8.1	12.9	6.8	8.1	1.2		27.3	12.1	6.1

Ratios (%)	1990	1991	1992	1993	1994	1995	1996	1997	1998	1999	2000	Estimate 2001			
E/M[a]	133	92	107	104	105	110	94	86	84	80	65	0.65			
Customs/M[a]	7.3	13	18.4	20.6	17.5	14.6	11.3	6.7	4.7	4.6					
(CA/GDP)[b]	1.2	-3.4	-1.8	-3.3	0.7	4.2	-1.0	-3.0	-4.3	-7.5	-6.3	-4.2			

a. E and M as in customs statistics on merchandise trade.

b. At current prices, %.

313

TABLE 10.2 Structure of Final Demand

	1990	1991	1992	1993	1994	1995	1996	1997	1998	1999	2000
At Constant Prices											
GDP = Y	100	100	100	100	100	100	100	100	100	100	100
NT (net taxes)		16.2	17.9	19.6	18.8	18.9	19.2	19.2	19	17.9	17.3
YD = GDP − NT		83.8	82.1	80.4	81.2	81.1	80.8	80.8	81	82.1	82.7
C	72.3	80.4	81.3	81.8	80.7	77.9	78.8	78.3	77.7	78.1	76.7
C_p		62.4	62.5	63	62.4	60.2	61.7	61.8	61.8	62.5	61.6
CG		18.1	18.8	18.7	18.3	17.7	17.1	16.5	16	15.6	15.2
I	21.7	17.8	15.2	16.4	17	19.7	22.2	25.1	27.3	27.9	27.8
I_p		15.2	11.8	12.5	13	16	17.4	20.1	22.2	23.9	24.6
IG		2.6	3.4	3.9	4	3.7	4.8	5	5.1	3.9	3.2
G = IG + CG		20.7	22.2	22.6	22.2	21.4	21.8	21.5	21.1	19.5	18.4
M	13.1	17.3	17.3	18.7	19.8	23	27.8	31.6	35.7	34.7	38.5
E	19	19.2	20.8	20.6	22.1	25.4	26.8	28.2	30.7	28.8	34
E − M	6	1.8	3.5	1.8	2.3	2.3	−1	−3.4	−5	−5.9	−4.5
Savings											
S_p		21.4	29.7	17.3	18.8	20.9	19.1	19.1	19.3	19.6	21.1
SG		−1.9	−0.9	0.9	0.5	1.2	2.1	2.7	3	2.3	2.2
Deficit = IG − SG		4.5	4.3	3	3.5	2.5	2.6	2.4	2.1	1.6	1
Memo: At Current Prices											
E − M	7.1	−1.9	1.5	1.0	2.2	2.4	−1.6	−4.3	−5.2	−6.4	−6.9
S_p		24.5	20.4	17.3	16.9	20.9	18.4	18.0	18.4	18.6	18.4
SG		−6.5	−3.7	−0.8	0	1.2	1.9	2.2	2.6	1.4	0.8
Deficit = IG − SG		9.4	7.1	4.5	3.7	2.5	2.8	2.7	2.3	2.3	2.2

1.3. The Recession Years, 1990–1991: Liberalization Aspects

That foreign trade helped reduce the damage wrought by the shock therapy was a matter of luck, rather than design. In fact the shock therapy blueprint envisioned rather high trade and current account deficits—but neither of these materialized. The essential factor behind the high trade surplus was the very strong devaluation of the zloty (the Polish currency) at the beginning of 1990. The precise rate of devaluation is hard to determine because throughout 1989 there were several exchange rates—with varying degrees of operational significance—and the free market rates moved too chaotically (generally much faster than inflation) to be captured by any statistics. The initial devaluation of 1990 went far (30–50 percent) beyond the observed free market rates because the authorities did not want to be forced to devalue again in a matter of weeks. As it turned out, they devalued again only after some eighteen months—and that, too, rather moderately. With import prices rising suddenly (well in excess of domestic prices)—and, of course, falling incomes—

an overall trade surplus was made possible. Notice also that this outcome was not preventable by a very low tariff level. (Very few non-tariff barriers were actually in force at that time.)

1991 was characterized by constant change. Though investment continued its free fall, consumption rebounded. Although the private saving rate was rather high (and the excess of private savings, $s_p X$, over private investment, I_p, was correspondingly large), the authorities found themselves forced to allow budget deficits to rise (to over 9 percent of the GDP—see table 10.2). The deficit "automatically" moderated further decline. But with continuing real appreciation (the initial exchange rate remained stable despite very high inflation), exports stagnated and imports boomed. This eventually forced devaluation, an introduction of non-tariff protections, and a steep rise in tariff rates. Nonetheless, the continuation of a liberal attitude toward imports (under too strong real appreciation) turned out to be rather costly in GDP terms. The trade developments cost Poland close to 7 percent in GDP decline—more than the level recorded (see table 10.1).

1.4. Liberalization Controlled: The Recovery Years, 1992–1995

Recovery started in 1992 and lasted four years. The GDP losses from 1990 to 1991 were recovered in 1995. Overall, the cumulative growth of 16.4 percent (1995/1992) was driven primarily by private consumption (contributing over 8 percentage points) and investment (over 6 percentage points in contribution). Net exports did not affect the GDP growth very much. Throughout the period the share of the government deficit $(G - tX)$ kept falling rather strongly, and there was always a trade surplus $(E > mX)$.[5] Over the period there was some real appreciation—although the spread between domestic (CPI) prices and the devaluation rates was not large.[6] This was a consequence of the exchange rate regime of the period, which was a pre-announced crawling peg, with the devaluation factor periodically adjusted to the falling inflation rate. (The factor was always somewhat lower than inflation: "to keep firms under some competitive import pressure.")

Most probably, the real appreciation could have had much more harmful effects had it not been accompanied by a rather illiberal approach to imports and exports. The "illiberality" of the period was reflected in very high tariff rates (see table 10.1, memo items). The reported tariff ratios only tell part of the story. Apart from high tariffs, the authorities of the period excelled in obstructing imports by other means (and they also clandestinely subsidized selected export items such as hard coal, steel, and some agricultural products).

The change of attitudes was possible for both external and internal reasons. Internally there was a political change: the Solidarity-sponsored parties (firm believers in laissez-faire and "sound macroeconomic policy" à la IMF) were voted out of power in 1993. Until 1997 Poland had been ruled by a coalition of the Social Democrats and the Peasant Party (both strongly rooted in the pre-1989 political establishment). Their governments had no inclination to return to any type of "planned economy" but did not reject the principle of interfering with foreign trade whenever they considered it useful.[7] Externally, Poland could get away with protectionism because the agreement on association with the European Union (enforced in 1993–1994) allowed the possibility of the asymmetric liberalization of mutual trade.[8] The asymmetry principle was at that time to

Poland's advantage: the EU lowered its tariffs and other barriers more (and earlier) than Poland was obliged to do. But there was a potential problem: eventually the protection levels were to be the same (or zero) on both sides. The time horizons for the unification of protection levels were product-specific but on the whole rather short, except for some "sensitive" commodities. The negative aspects of the association agreement became more evident in the second half of 1990s, as I will discuss later.

1.5. Year 1995: The Turning Point

From the macroeconomic point of view, the year 1995 fits well into the recovery period that began in 1992. The year 1996, together with the consecutive ones, is entirely different. The change in basic tendencies was a result of several major events that occurred over the course of 1995. Before I describe these events in some detail, it is worth discussing the results of the decomposition of aggregate demand along the lines used throughout this volume. See table 10.3[9] and figure 10.1.

The main conclusions from the decomposition findings are as follows:

1. Until 1996 I_p/s_p was substantially lower than X. Later on, it was increasingly larger than X. Until 1996 the private sector did not "pump" demand into the system, as it has been doing ever since.
2. Until 1995 E/m has been higher than X, meaning that high exports pumped demand into the system. Since 1996, excessive imports sucked demand out of the system.
3. G/t has always been higher than X, meaning that government spending pumped demand into the system all along. However, until 1996 G/t was falling. After 1996, G/t was rising.
4. The private savings rate, s_p, was high until 1995 and diminishing afterwards. The import propensity, m, was low until 1995 and rising strongly afterwards. Leakages to I_p/s_p and G/t have been declining throughout the whole period, indicating an "erosion" of the importance of these "stances." In contrast, the leakages to E/m have been rising—very strongly after 1995.
5. The government has been running a substantial debt[10] all along.
6. Quite large trade surpluses prior to 1996 indicate the reduction of foreign liabilities.

Since 1996, there has been a rapid accumulation of new foreign liabilities.

7. Until 1996 the private sector was the net creditor of the government (and the foreign sector). Since 1997 the private sector (together with the government) has been a net debtor of the foreign sector. The decomposition indicates that there was a "structural break" in 1995. Indeed, much happened in that year. By 1995 Poland was essentially the only success case among the "transition countries." As such, it was the darling of international financial institutions, Western governments, and the foreign business community. Consequently, Poland was richly rewarded with (1) fairly generous treaties reducing/rescheduling old foreign debt, (2) admittance into the WTO and OECD, and (3) rapidly increasing FDI inflows. Poland's very strong foreign position (high surpluses on both current and trade balances) was therefore reinforced.

As befitting an OECD member, in 1995, Poland substantially increased the scope of free capital flows (current account transactions were fully liberalized at the end of 1989, and capital flows had also been progressively liberalized prior to 1995). Foreign portfolio investment was now welcome. At the same time, limitations regarding access to shorter-term Treasury debt were eased. These developments set in motion several mutually reinforcing processes. High

and growing foreign reserves increased Poland's creditworthiness, and that translated into growing inflows and reserves themselves. But growing inflows instantly triggered the Central Bank's (hereafter, CB) sterilization operations (on the principle that "too much money prevents disinflation"), thereby pushing up already high nominal interest rates and yields on the Treasury debt. Rising interest rates also induced more inflows. In the end the CB saw no other way out but to revalue the zloty and then to allow a float within some bounds[11] around a "central parity." (The central parity continued to be determined as in the pre-announced sliding peg regime but with the devaluation factor now much lower than the inflation rate.) Revaluation and a slower pace of devaluation turned out to be insufficient in the sense that the free market rate had been consistently on the "stronger side" of the central parity. That created an additional incentive for short-term capital inflows.

The year 1995 ended with more than doubled foreign reserves (from $6.5 to $15 billion). The trend continued (despite crises in Latin America, Asia, and Russia) until 1999, bringing reserves to over $28 billion at the end of 1998 (reserves have been roughly constant afterwards—that is, so far). Other associated trends continued into the future as well:

1. There has been a steady evolution of the exchange rate regime. The devaluation factor

TABLE 10.3 Decomposition of Aggregate Demand (*All Items at Constant Prices*)

	1990	1991	1992	1993	1994	1995	1996	1997	1998	1999	2000
GDP	85.4	83.3	85.1	88.8	93.5	100	106.0	113.1	118.6	123.3	128.5
X (aggregate demand)	96.5	97.8	99.8	105.4	112	123	135.5	148.9	161	166.1	178
Rates											
s_p		0.183	0.168	0.148	0.157	0.169	0.149	0.145	0.142	0.145	0.152
T		0.138	0.152	0.165	0.157	0.154	0.15	0.146	0.14	0.133	0.125
M	0.115	0.148	0.147	0.158	0.165	0.187	0.218	0.24	0.263	0.258	0.278
Leakages											
to I_p/s_p		0.39	0.356	0.311	0.328	0.332	0.289	0.273	0.26	0.271	0.274
to G/t		0.294	0.326	0.353	0.327	0.301	0.291	0.274	0.256	0.248	0.225
to E/m		0.316	0.315	0.336	0.345	0.367	0.421	0.453	0.483	0.481	0.501
Stances											
I_p/s_p		69.4	59.7	75.9	77.6	94.4	123.9	157.4	185.3	203.1	207.3
G/t		125	124	121.9	132.7	139.3	153.9	167.2	179	180.8	188.5
E/m		108.1	120.3	115.8	124.9	135.6	130.6	132.7	138.4	137.7	157.2
Financial Balance											
$I_p - s_p X$		−5.2	−6.7	−4.3	−5.4	−4.9	−1.7	1.2	3.4	5.4	4.5
G − tX		3.7	3.7	2.7	3.2	2.5	2.8	2.7	2.5	2	1.2
E − mX		1.5	3	1.6	2.1	2.3	−1.1	−3.9	−6	−7.3	−5.8

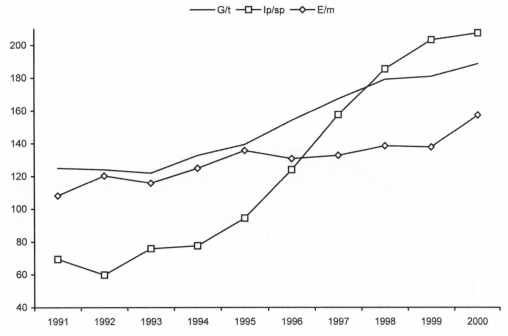

FIGURE 10.1 Decomposition of Aggregate Demand

for the central parity rate was progressively lowered (with a rising differential versus domestic inflation). The bands around the central parity widened over time. The CB progressively reduced, by law, the degree of its allowable involvement in forex market operations. All this culminated, in early 2000, in the formal introduction of the pure free float.

2. The reliance on the interest rate for monetary policy has been strengthening, culminating in a formal introduction of inflation targeting with the interest rate as the sole CB instrument. In practical terms, monetary policy alternates between the application of excessive and exorbitant interest rates, with real commercial interest rates never falling below 10 percent.[12]

3. There has been a persistent and rather strong real appreciation of the zloty, culminating in the strong nominal appreciation of the Polish currency against both the dollar and the euro (see table 10.2, memo items, and figure 10.2).

1.6. The Years 1996–1999: Growing Foreign Deficits

The momentum gained by consumption over the years 1992–1995 and investment (1993–1995) did not dissipate by 1996–1997: both items (and particularly their private components) contributed decisively to high GDP growth in both years. However, in both years, net exports reduced the GDP growth rate by 3.4 and 2.6 percentage points respectively (see tables 10.2 and 10.3). First, exports sagged while imports pressed forward, then exports performed quite well, only to be dwarfed by rising imports. Within two years the share of trade deficit in GDP moved from +2.35 percent to −4.3 percent. The trade deficit share rose consecutively in the following years (1998–1999), further diminishing the realized GDP growth rates by 1.9 and 1.1 percentage points respectively. Private consumption and investment carried the day—though the magnitudes of their contributions to the GDP growth have been diminishing. Since 1996 there has been a steady growth in the excess of private investment over private saving (see table 10.1). Finally, note the infinitesimal contribution of government consumption to the GDP growth rates in 1998–2000 and the *negative* contributions of government investment (1999–2000).[13]

The disturbing trade performance in the post-1995 period is directly related to the advances in external liberalization:

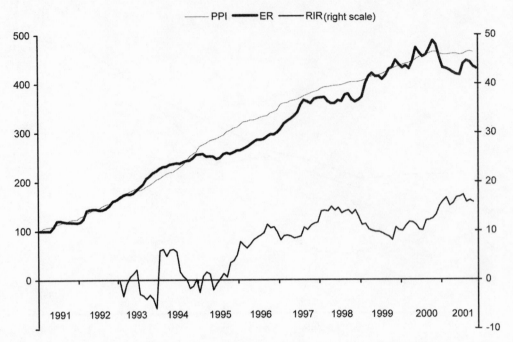

FIGURE 10.2 Industrial Producer Price Index (PPI), Nominal Exchange Rate (PLN/USD) Index (ER), and the PPI-Deflated National Bank Discount Rate (RIR), 1991–2000

1. Excessive real appreciation, affecting both exports and imports, is the direct outcome of the premature liberalization of the capital account.
2. There has been a rapid decline in tariff rates and other import barriers. This was because the EU association agreement turned out to require, as early as 1996–1997, the removal or reduction of barriers on many items protected by the asymmetry clauses. The irony of this situation is that, for the second half of the 1990s, the "asymmetry" has clearly been to the advantage of the EU. The "sensitive" products for which the liberalization of mutual trade was to be postponed for much longer periods of time (or, apparently indefinitely, as seems to be the case with food and farm products) are all potentially competitive exports for Poland. No product "sensitive" to Poland is exempted from mutual liberalization.[14]

1.7. Policy Mishaps after 1997

In the fall of 1997, the conservative Solidarity-sponsored parties returned to power. They initiated, and for the most part executed, a kind of supply-side economic policy. Apart from dismantling most of the surviving public services, they also radically changed the tax system. The tax rate on corporate profits has been progressively lowered from 38 percent in 1997 to 24 percent at present. The highest personal income tax (44 percent in 1997) was lowered to 40 percent. The flat tax rate of about 18 percent proved too controversial—but the effective tax rate on high personal incomes was reduced by other means (e.g., generous tax allowances on real estate purchases, tax-free interest income, and capital gains). In addition, the rich hugely benefited from the reform of health and pension systems because these reforms introduced upper limits to compulsory health and pension contributions. The reduced direct tax burden (primarily benefiting high-income households) was, in part, compensated by higher indirect tax rates (VAT, excises), which, of course, primarily burdened low-income households. The declared intentions behind these changes were to (1) speed up growth, (2) lower trade and current account deficits, and (3) reduce fiscal deficits. The basic "philosophy" behind all this was clear enough. Besides alluding to the "Laffer-curve effects," the official justification of the tax reforms pointed out the deplorably high consumption propensity among low-income families. With higher disposable incomes of the wealthy, the overall national savings would be higher—so the argument went. Therefore, there would be higher capital formation and lower demand for foreign savings (and foreign deficits would also fall). With much greater capital formation, employment, output, as well as tax revenue would be much higher.

However, reality has proved very different:

1. There has been a steady deceleration in GDP growth (see table 10.1).
2. There has been a steady deceleration in investment growth (which actually declined in 2001).
3. Since 1997, the unemployment rate has been rebounding—from 10 percent to about 18 percent at present (breaking the record level of 1993). The rate is rising perceptibly every month. Improvement is not expected anytime soon because the current policy response has in fact been to demand cuts in wages—this is the gist of the postulate of further "flexibilization of the labor market." That this will, in the first place, create room for cuts in wages and hence further depress consumer demand, sales, and employment has not been acknowledged.
4. There has been very little progress made in reducing fiscal deficits. Cuts in spending have not followed cuts in tax revenue.[15] Until 2001 the truth about the state of public finances was successfully covered up (e.g., through creative budget accounting and high privatization revenue).[16] In 2001 the day of truth came as many hidden liabilities accumulated in recent years were revealed and expected privatization revenues failed to materialize. The actual deficit (PSBR) in 2001 may be close to 6 percent of the GDP (rather than to 3.2 percent, initially planned). The estimates for 2002 forecast a deficit in excess of 8 percent of the GDP. Certainly, the negative developments since 1997 cannot be attributed solely to the changes in fiscal policy. High interest rate policy has also played a role in slowing down the pace of investment and restricting consumer demand. That policy also had an impact on the growing indebtedness of the business sector (and of small-scale firms, including farms), thereby reducing their growth potential. Besides, there has been a steady erosion of the position of domestic producers caused by the surge of imports and the falling profitability of exports (both related to the real appreciation of the Polish currency and the former also related to the ongoing lowering of tariffs and non-tariff barriers).

On only one account has there been some recent improvement. The current account deficit—which peaked in the first quarter of 1999 at 8.3 percent of the GDP—has been narrowing in 2000 and 2001 (see table 10.1, memo items). This has been achieved primarily because of sagging incomes, consumption, and investment. Strangely enough, throughout much of 2001, there was a strong expansion in exports—and that, too, despite a new fit of real appreciation. Firms may have been trying to keep afloat by exporting even at a loss. (Export sales at least bring, with a fair amount of certainty, badly needed liquidity. Domestic sales, at nominally better prices, carry a growing risk of payments for deliveries never being made.)

1.8. Prospects: Further Painful Adjustments Unavoidable

The Social Democrats (allied with the Farmers' Party) returned to power in September 2001, and the conservatives ruling since 1997 were wiped off the political landscape. The new government faces Herculean tasks in almost every aspect of economic and social life. Even with the most skillful policies, it cannot expect very satisfactory results anytime soon. Worse still, the policies it seems to have embraced differ rather radically from those successfully pursued in 1993–1997. First, it resists the reintroduction of some barriers to imports—though this could also directly raise fiscal revenue (through income from an import surcharge or higher customs revenue). Second, it rejects the reintroduction of higher effective taxation of high personal incomes—though this would fairly easily avert the public finances crisis without having adverse effects on investment and consumer demand (at least for domestically produced goods and services). Third, it extends the scope of indirect taxation. Fourth, reductions in fiscal deficits are to be achieved primarily by further cuts in spending. Quite certainly, all this spells trouble. If carried through, such a fiscal policy will only deepen the approaching recession—without really reducing the fiscal deficit. If anything, deficits will be higher because of the contraction of taxable incomes and sales. Sooner or later, the policy will have to be changed.

Whatever fiscal policy is followed, Poland will have to cope with other macro problems. First, it defies any logic to continue, for the seventh consecutive year, with a monetary policy resulting in double-digit real interest rates. The Central Bank has dragged its feet in terms of reducing interest rates. There may be a rational reason behind this. A radical reduction of the interest rate is likely to trigger a possibly excessive fall of the Polish currency. Perhaps a "salami tactic"—a slow and gradual reduction of the interest rate—will secure a gradual and moderate devaluation. Whether or not the tactic will succeed is anybody's guess. In any case, the reversal of the appreciation trend will occur sooner or later, even if high interest rates are maintained.[17]

If the reversal is rather abrupt (and excessive), it will have grave consequences for firms (and banks) that have accumulated large foreign debts (and also for their domestic partners). Even if relatively moderate, devaluation may—in the short run—strengthen the recession rather than initialize an export boom. In the course of several years, the economy must have adapted to cheap imports of intermediate goods (which account for about 65–70 percent of all imports). The import intensity of exports is particularly high. Firms relying on imports of intermediate goods will be heavily hit. Their losses may well be higher than the possible gains to exporters. All in all, it may take painful adjustments—with requisite losses in output and employment—before a sustained depreciation tendency may create some room for the development of proper import-substitution and/or export-expansion specialization.

Whether or not the depreciation of the currency is excessive or just "optimal," Poland will have to cope with foreign debt, which has snowballed during the years of high foreign deficits. Gross external debt rose from $47.5 billion (end of 1996) to $69 billion (June 2001). Private sector debt rose particularly strongly, from $11 billion to $30 billion respectively. These numbers ought to be considered together with some other facts such as (1) *officially*, the stock of short-term capital is about $16 billion;[18] (2) much of the approximately $45 billion in foreign direct investment has gone into "speculative" rather than "productive" uses; (3) the grace periods on servicing the "old" pre-1980 debt (which were agreed upon in deals with the London and Paris Clubs) are about to end; each year, the payments on that debt will be rising steeply to a climax of about $7 billion in 2008; and (4) the bulk of the Polish "family silver" (i.e., the largest and most profitable domestic firms, banks, insurance companies, etc.) has already been

privatized—and sold to foreign parties (often for a song).

1.9. Concluding Remarks on Macroeconomic Aspects of Liberalization in Poland

There are two periods in recent Polish history that differ as far as the levels of external liberalization are concerned. The first may be dated as 1992–1995. The second started in 1995–1996 and has not yet ended.

1. During the first period, imports were controlled through tariffs and other instruments, and exports were (clandestinely and selectively) promoted through subsidies. Currency appreciation was controlled via a managed nominal exchange rate and a relatively illiberal approach to capital movements. Real interest rates were moderate. There was a fast acceleration in capital formation. Foreign trade did not affect GDP growth significantly. The economy pulled itself out of a deep recession without incurring any new foreign debt—and without selling its assets to foreigners. Public sector deficits declined without reductions in spending.

2. During the second period, there has been a rapid and steady liberalization of imports along with significantly reduced levels of export support. Capital inflows were liberalized all along during this period, which paradoxically failed to bring down the domestic interest rates—in fact, the inflows have been responsible (via sterilization operations) for the persistence of very high interest rates. The determination of the exchange rate has increasingly been left to the (still shallow) forex market. There has been a tendency for a strong real appreciation. Foreign trade performance has been disappointing all along and has reduced the GDP growth rates significantly. Although initially investment and consumption continued to expand strongly (following the momentum gained in the previous period), in the second phase of the period they have been weakening—lately entering the threshold of a contraction. After initial declines, unemployment has strongly rebounded. In contrast with the first period, huge foreign debt has accumulated and most domestic assets have been dissipated. An attempt to strengthen growth and reduce foreign deficits through a "supply-side" fiscal policy misfired, resulting in

TABLE 10.4 Average per Capita Expenditure by Type of Household in 1993, 1996, and 1999
(Average per Capita Expenditure = 1)

	Farmers	Employees	Blue Collar	White Collar	Part-Time Farmers	Self-employed	Retirees	Unemployed etc.
1993	0.89	0.99	0.84	1.27	0.83	1.28	1.12	0.63
1996	1.10	1.12	0.99	1.33	1.21	1.51	0.74	0.62
1999	0.71	1.04	0.83	1.39	0.74	1.28	1.10	0.60

Source: HBS (1993, 1996, 1999).

huge public deficits. A high potential for a currency crisis has been created.

2. Distribution and Inequality

2.1. The Evidence from the Household Budget Surveys

There are obvious and well-known problems with the results derived from the Household Budget Surveys (HBS). Generalizations of these results are, for various reasons, likely to be misleading. First, it is virtually impossible to mirror the genuine social structure of incomes and expenditures, even in large samples of household surveys. Thus, even with 30,000 households (with 100,000 persons)[19] surveyed in Poland, the likelihood of a proper representation of units with very high and very low incomes is rather low. The homeless, residents of asylums for the poor and "pathological" individuals and families (most of whom are extremely poor), are excluded from HBS. "True" social inequality is therefore not really reflected in the inequality measures. Second, there are some problems with the way in which households report income and expenditure. Some systematic "errors" in reporting are quite common.[20] Nonetheless, for the purpose of cross-country comparisons, it makes some sense to calculate the income/expenditure

inequality indicators based on the HBS. Also, such indicators shed some light on the development of inequality over time. Before the evolution of specific inequality indicators is discussed, it may be worthwhile to take a look at the changing relative position of average representatives of various household groups.

Table 10.4 suggests that farmers' position versus that of other social groups improved strongly between 1993 and 1996 (i.e., during the "illiberal" period) and then deteriorated very strongly in the "liberal" years of 1996–1999.[21] The first and relatively unproblematic set of proper inequality measures is about expenditure inequality for the years 1993, 1996, and 1999.[22]

As can be seen in table 10.5, expenditure inequality decreased in the first period and increased, rather strongly, in the second.

It is not quite possible to follow the developments of income inequality indicators, because in 1997 the definition of income was, for some reason, changed (capital gains were excluded from household income). However, for 1997 there are two parallel sets of HBS results. Assuming (somewhat heroically) that the ratios of income inequality indicators derived from the two alternative HBS 1997 sets also apply to 1999, one can produce a table with income inequality indicators (see table 10.6).

Table 10.6 suggests that income inequality rose rather slowly in the first period. It accelerated in the second period.

TABLE 10.5 Equivalent Expenditures Inequality Indicators

	Gini	Theil	90/10	75/25
1993	0.288	0.165	3.34	1.86
1996	0.286	0.159	3.32	1.85
1999	0.318	0.192	3.93	2.02

Note: All indicators are calculated using the commonly applied OECD (70/50) demographic equivalence scale. The columns 90/10 and 75/25 are the conventional percentile ratios.

TABLE 10.6 Equivalent Income Inequality Indicators

	Gini	Theil	90/10	75/25
1993	0.290	0.176	3.34	1.83
1996	0.301	0.189	3.42	1.83
1999[a]	0.316	0.216	3.79	1.90

a. Estimated.

The decomposition of Theil expenditure inequality indices for 1993, 1996, and 1999 sheds some light on the evolution of the within-group and the between-group inequality—with various criteria for distinguishing groups of households. Table 10.7 indicates that in the first period, within-group inequality was generally falling (rather strongly for part-time farmers, farmers, retirees, and the "unemployed etc."). There was a quite significant increase in between-group inequality—primarily on account of the improving position of employees. In the second period, there was a strong increase in both components of overall inequality. Inequality also rose strongly in all social groups (except farmers).

Also the decomposition based on type of residence (see table 10.8) indicates that in the "liberal" years, there was a strong rise in both components of inequality—with inequality rising relatively weakly in the rural areas. Finally, while in the "illiberal" period, the education level did not have a very strong impact on changes in inequality, in the liberal period that impact became very strong (see table 10.9).

2.1.1. Poverty

The *World Development Report 1999/2000* of the World Bank (2000, 237) put 23.8 percent of Poland's population in 1993 below the national poverty line (with 15.1 percent living on less than $2 [at PPP] a day, and 6.8 percent on less than $1). Available Polish statistics (HBS-based) indicate that poverty fell in the years 1993–1995. Since 1995—that is, during the "liberal" period—poverty has been expanding, especially in 1999 and 2000 (see table 10.10).

Unemployment is the major determinant of poverty. In 2000 some 20 percent of households with one

or more unemployed member lived on income below the official poverty line (and "only" 5 percent of households with no unemployed member).

2.2. Functional Distribution of Income

Available national account statistics allow an examination of the changing patterns of the functional distribution of income. The summary data for 1992, 1995, and 1999, contained in table 10.11 require some explanatory comments.

1. Within the household sector, four "classes" of population are distinguished: (a) farmers, (b) employers and self-employed, (c) employees, and (d) recipients of non-earned income. Class (d) includes retirees, the unemployed receiving unemployment benefits, and so on. Class (b) is a heterogeneous "class" with small-scale vendors lumped together with lawyers and owners of businesses employing hundreds of workers. Prior to 1995, classes (c) and (d) were also lumped together.[23]

2. The actual gross primary income of employers and the self-employed is, in all probability,

TABLE 10.8 Decomposition of Theil Expenditure Inequality Index into Indices for Groups Distinguished by Residence

	1993	1996	1999
Cities and towns[a]	0.147	0.161	0.202
Small towns	0.155	0.142	0.156
Rural areas	0.180	0.143	0.166
Within group	0.1592	0.1499	0.1775
Between group	0.0059	0.0094	0.0146
Overall inequality	0.1652	0.1593	0.1921

a. With 50,000 or more inhabitants.

TABLE 10.7 Decomposition of Theil Expenditures Inequality Index into Indices for Professional Groups

	1993	1996	1999
Employees	0.156	0.169	0.196
Part-time farmers	0.125	0.114	0.147
Farmers	0.173	0.163	0.158
Retirees	0.154	0.115	0.146
Self-employed	0.218	0.223	0.292
Unemployed etc.	0.175	0.149	0.215
Within group	0.1594	0.1516	0.1824
Between group	0.0058	0.0077	0.0097
Overall inequality	0.1652	0.1593	0.1921

TABLE 10.9 Decomposition of Theil Expenditure Inequality Index into Indices for Groups Distinguished by Education Level

	1993	1996	1999
University	0.162	0.172	0.188
Secondary	0.137	0.142	0.175
Elementary or below	0.170	0.119	0.136
Within group	0.1497	0.1416	0.1691
Between group	0.0155	0.0177	0.0231
Overall inequality	0.1652	0.1593	0.1921

TABLE 10.10 Poverty

	% of Persons in Households with Expenditure Less than 50% of the Average	% of Persons below Official Poverty Line ("Existential Minimum")	Official Poverty Line in PPP $ per Day (per Person in Households with Two Adults)	% of Households below Leyden Poverty Line (Subjective)
1993	12	n.a.	2.60	40
1994	13.5	6.4	3.00	33
1995	12.8	n.a.	3.68	30.8
1996	14	4.3	3.20	30.5
1997	15.3	5.4	3.94	30.8
1998	15.8	5.6	4.18	30.8
1999	15.5	6.9	4.40	34.8
2000	17.1	8.1	4.70	34.4

Source: CSO, IPiSS, and own calculations.

much higher. Employers and the self-employed have quite unlimited possibilities of adding the costs of many consumption goods and services (purchase, maintenance, and operation of personal cars; travel and telecommunication services; many durables; etc.) to the costs of operating their businesses.[24] Actual gross operating surpluses and/or net property incomes of class (b) are therefore (much) higher than table 10.11 indicates.

3. Net property income (which includes rental income, dividends, distributed profits, interest income, etc.) has been negative for farmers on account of high (and rising) indebtedness and interest cost burdens for that class.

Now, taking the data of table 10.11 at face value, one observes the following:

1. In the first period, the share of taxes in gross primary income declined for farmers and increased for employers and the self-employed. In the second period, the burden of taxation fell strongly for employees, and even more so for the employers and the self-employed. (In 1999, gross primary incomes of both classes were effectively taxed at the same rate.) Taxes charged on farmers' incomes rose very strongly.
2. The share of farmers' gross disposable income in the total did not change in the first period but was halved in the second. The gross disposable income share of employers and the self-employed rose strongly in the first period, and then, rather moderately, in the second period. The share of employees' gross disposable income rose in the second period,

while the income share of pensioners and the like declined in the second period.

3. In the first period, the real[25] gross disposable income of farmers strongly improved. In the second period, they fell rather dramatically. Moderate improvements in the real value of gross disposable incomes of the remaining classes in the first period were followed by much stronger improvements in the second period.
4. The disparities between the gross disposable income per income-earning member of individual classes have changed. In the second period, the gap between employees and employers and the self-employed narrowed somewhat. Farmers have suffered enormous losses relative to employers and self-employed (and also to employees) in both periods.

The most important conclusion from table 10.11 is that during the illiberal period, farmers managed to maintain—and even improve—their living standards. But under liberalization, they suffered heavy losses. Not only did their *relative* standing compared with other social classes deteriorate, but also their real incomes collapsed in absolute terms. Bearing in mind that farmers account for one-fourth of the professionally active population, one concludes that in the "liberal" period there has been a dramatic rise in the overall income inequality. Why have farmers fared so badly? Arithmetically speaking, the rising taxation and debt burden have not played a major role. Even if farmers' incomes had not been taxed at all in the second period, and the interest charged had been waived, their real incomes would still have been

TABLE 10.11 Income of the Household Sector by Class and Type of Income; 1992, 1995, and 1999

(Current PLN Billion)		Total	Farmers	Employers and Self-employed	Employees	Pensioners and Unemployed
Gross Operating Surplus						
	1992	25.5	5.4	20.1		
	1995	81.4	14	67.4		
	1999	144.4	14.2	130.2		
Wages						
	1992	39			39	
	1995	94.4			94.4	
	1999	190.5			190.5	
Net Property Income						
	1992	6.3	−0.1	1	5.4	
	1995	21.4	−0.4	13.6	5.4	2.8
	1999	37.5	−0.9	28.5	6.3	3.6
Gross Primary Income						
	1992	70.8	5.3	21.1	44.4	
	1995	197.2	13.6	81	99.8	2.8
	1999	372.4	13.3	158.7	196.8	3.6
Taxes on Income and Wealth minus Transfers						
	1992	−12.7	0.7	2.5	−15.9	
	1995	−23.7	1.5	10.8	10.6	−46.6
	1999	−67.6	2	10.5	13	−93.1
Gross Disposable Income						
	1992	83.5	4.6	18.6	60.3	
	1995	220.9	12.1	70.2	89.2	49.4
	1999	440	11.3	148.2	183.8	96.7
Share of Net Taxes in Gross Primary Income						
	1992		0.132	0.118		
	1995		0.110	0.133	0.106	
	1999		0.150	0.066	0.066	
Shares in Total Gross Disposable Income						
	1992	1.0	0.055	0.223	0.722	
	1995	1.0	0.055	0.318	0.404	0.224
	1999	1.0	0.026	0.337	0.418	0.220
Indices of Real Disposable Income						
	1995	1.1	1.226	1.1	1.09	
	(1992 = 1)					
	1999	1.205	0.575	1.273	1.241	1.195
	(1995 = 1)					
Indices of Real Disposable Income per Capita (Total) and per Income-Earning Member of the Class						
	1995	1.096	1.169	1.482		
	(1992 = 1)					
	1999	1.204	0.549	1.131	1.217	
	(1995 = 1)					
Gross Disposable Income per Income-Earning Member of the Class (Gross Domestic Income per Farmer = 1)						
	1992		1.0	7.0		
	1995		1.0	16.5	2.9	
	1999		1.0	34.5	6.7	

Source: CSO Yearbooks.

Note: For 1992, "employees" and "pensioners and unemployed" are lumped together. Numbers in italics (the last two items) are my own estimates.

TABLE 10.12 Price Indices for Agriculture

	Sold Farm Output	Consumer Items Purchased by Farmers	Inputs for Farm Production Purchased	All Items Purchased by Farmers	"Price Scissors"
1995 (1992 = 1)	2.31	2.20	2.12	2.14	1.08
1999 (1995 = 1)	1.29	1.63	1.62	1.62	0.77

Source: Central State Office.

some 33 percent lower (in 1999, compared with 1995). A direct reason for the farmers' misfortunes must be seen in the classical "price scissors" operating against them in the second period (see table 10.12).

Foreign trade in agricultural products (this does not include products of the food processing industry) may have had some impact on prices and farmers' incomes. In 1992 there was a rather large surplus on agricultural trade, equivalent to 4.6 percent of the agricultural output sold. By 1995 there was a deficit of 1.5 percent, followed by a 2.7 percent deficit in 1999. In both periods, farm produce imports were price competitive relative to domestic products. In the first period the index of import prices was about 2.2, and in the second it was 1.22. There was a major change in the profitability of farm produce exports. The index of export prices was 2.05 for the first period and 1.01 for the second. Clearly, the exchange rate appreciation must have had a significantly negative effect on output, the trade deficit, prices, and incomes. These developments have certainly been reinforced by import liberalization and the reduction of support to exports. All in all, farmers' losses (perhaps otherwise inevitable because of world-market developments, the low elasticity of demand for farm produce, and the atomistic structure of farming) may have been magnified under liberalization.

2.3. Inequality in Wages across Sectors

Table 10.13 contains data on average wages—relative to the national averages—for various sectors over the 1992–1999 period.[26] The data suggest the following tentative conclusions:

1. Some service sectors pay consistently low wages, irrespective of the liberalization regime. Some other service sectors pay consistently high wages, correspondingly. In either case, there is no sustained tendency for moving up or down the wage ladder.

2. There are two losing groups: in construction and the health services. Health service employees may be losing out primarily because of the ongoing reforms ("downsizing") of the public health system, and construction sector workers are certainly the indirect victims of high interest rates that have been depressing the demand for credit and housing all along.

3. Manufacturing employees had some gains under both regimes. Miners gained quite a lot prior to liberalization—and lost a lot under liberalization. Factors other than liberalization may be at work here (for instance, the long-overdue downscaling of coal mining).

The last two columns of table 10.13 report Gini coefficients for wages in individual sectors in 1995 and 1997[27] (and the Gini coefficients for wages in the entire economy in 1992, 1995, and 1999).

As can be seen, between 1995 and 1997 there was a strong increase in wage inequality in the entire economy and in most individual sectors. Only in hotels and restaurants did the Gini coefficient strongly decline (the Gini declined a little in health and social work). Perhaps this has something to do with very low (as compared with other sectors) average wages in both sectors. The ongoing privatization of the economy may have also been an important factor inducing a rise in inequality.[28]

The bottom part of table 10.13 reports data on some other non-wage incomes. Here the message is crystal clear: in recent years, social policy has been undergoing a radical change.[29] In relation to the average wage, average pension and unemployment benefits are becoming very low. There has been a drastic reduction in the number of unemployment benefits recipients since 1997. Certainly, the link between these developments and liberalization is not direct. Indirectly, though, these developments reflect a change in social and fiscal policies that, to some extent, attempt to overcome the negative effects of

TABLE 10.13 Wages And Social Benefits

	1990	1991	1992	1993	1994	1995	1996	1997	1998	1999	2000	2001	Gini Coefficients		
													1992	1995	1997
Average Monthly Gross Wage	Zloty														
Total economy[a]	103.0	175.6	289.7	390.4	525.0	690.9	874.3	1,065.8	1,232.7	1,697.1	1,923.8				
Real growth rate in %, net average wage	−24.4	−0.3	−2.7	−2.9	0.5	3.0	5.7	7.3	4.5	4.7	2.6	1.5			
As Share of the Average Gross Wage															
Agriculture and forestry	—	—	0.83	0.83	0.82	0.90	0.92	0.91	0.93	0.92	0.91			0.235	0.309
Mining and quarrying	—	—	1.64	1.75	1.99	1.93	1.92	1.84	1.83	1.74	1.68			0.253	0.291
Manufacturing	—	—	0.92	0.93	0.94	0.95	0.95	0.95	0.94	0.96	0.94			0.276	0.293
Electricity, gas, and water supply	—	—	1.30	1.42	1.50	1.46	1.44	1.39	1.37	1.35	1.34			0.248	0.257
Construction	—	—	1.02	0.94	0.88	0.87	0.87	0.90	0.92	0.92	0.93			0.277	0.296
Wholesale, retail trade, and repair motor vehicles	—	—	0.89	0.83	0.83	0.83	0.82	0.84	0.84	0.87	0.87			0.320	0.337
Hotels and restaurants	—	—	0.73	0.67	0.70	0.71	0.69	0.72	0.73	0.73	0.73			0.338	0.310
Transport, storage, and telecommunications	—	—	1.05	1.06	1.06	1.05	1.05	1.06	1.09	1.11	1.12			0.196	0.224
Financial intermediation	—	—	1.50	1.50	1.46	1.45	1.50	1.54	1.60	1.58	1.73			0.307	0.320
Real estate, renting, and business activities	—	—	1.12	1.09	1.08	1.07	1.09	1.10	1.09	1.09	1.09			0.305	0.332

(continued)

	1990	1991	1992	1993	1994	1995	1996	1997	1998	1999	2000	2001	Gini Coefficients		
													1992	1995	1997
Public administration, defense, and compulsory social security	—	—	1.27	1.26	1.21	1.24	1.29	1.28	1.30	1.28	1.26			0.325	0.328
Education	—	—	0.89	0.90	0.87	0.89	0.90	0.92	0.91	0.90	0.95			0.197	0.209
Health and social work	—	—	0.88	0.85	0.82	0.83	0.82	0.82	0.81	0.79	0.77			0.196	0.195
Other community, social, and personal services	—	—	0.90	0.93	0.94	0.93	0.91	0.92	0.92	1.00	1.00			0.293	0.292
TOTAL													0.247	0.285	0.329
Social benefits															
Monthly pension, average[a]															
Employees, old-age	0.65	0.76	0.73	0.72	0.74	0.74	0.71	0.70	0.68	0.55	0.52				
Individual farmers	0.46	0.45	0.38	0.39	0.43	0.43	0.42	0.42	0.41	0.33	0.31				
Unemployment benefits[a]															
Recipients, 1,000 persons, December	892	1,703	1,312	1,396	1,422	1,548	1,225	557	420	554	592	620			
Benefits per person per month, December			0.41	0.32	0.33	0.31	0.31	0.33	0.26	0.21	0.19				
Share of unemployed receiving benefits	0.79	0.79	0.52	0.48	0.50	0.59	0.49	0.31	0.23	0.24	0.20	0.20			

a. Up to 1991 net, from 1992 gross. From 1999, increased by mandatory security premium.

327

TABLE 10.14 Average Wages Across Branches of Manufacturing

	1992	1995	1999	Nominal Index 1995/1992	Wage Index 1999/1995	Labor Productivity Index 1995/1992	Labor Productivity Index 1999/1995
Manufacturing total	1	1	1	2.51	1.98	1.405	1.435
Food products, beverages, and tobacco	1.039	0.944	0.934	2.28	1.96	1.402	1.327
Textiles and textile products	0.818	0.730	0.667	2.24	1.81	1.331	1.155
Leather and leather products	0.778	0.730	0.680	2.35	1.85	1.556	1.336
Wood and wood products	0.888	0.851	0.767	2.40	1.79	0.953	1.264
Pulp, paper, and paper products; publishing and printing	1.207	1.251	1.302	2.60	2.06	1.686	1.524
Coke, refined petroleum products, and nuclear fuel	1.734	2.056	1.915	2.97	1.85	1.867	0.470
Chemicals, chemical products, and manmade fibers	1.125	1.330	1.431	2.97	2.13	1.171	1.448
Rubber and plastic products	1.050	1.107	1.029	2.64	1.84	1.217	1.784
Other non-metallic mineral products	0.957	1.005	1.024	2.63	2.02	1.418	1.523
Basic metals and fabricated metal products	1.105	1.135	1.093	2.58	1.91	1.394	1.321
Machinery and equipment n.e.c.	0.992	1.009	1.050	2.55	2.06	1.664	2.082
Electrical and optical equipment	1.009	1.102	1.198	2.74	2.15	2.213	1.814
Transport equipment	1.039	1.088	1.193	2.63	2.17	1.224	1.747
Manufacturing n.e.c.	0.917	0.842	0.799	2.30	1.88	1.336	1.255
Coefficient of variation (weighted)	0.191	0.191	0.22				
Gini coefficient		0.276	0.293				

liberalization (e.g., growing foreign imbalances and a slowdown of growth).

2.4. Inequality in Wages across Manufacturing

Overall, the dispersion in average wages across branches of manufacturing (measured by the weighted coefficient of variation) did not change between 1992 and 1995. By 1999 the dispersion increased (see table 10.14). Also, the overall inequality (Gini) in wages in the entire manufacturing sector rose in the second period. Average wages in the "light industries" (food processing, textiles, and leather and wood products) have been losing out during both periods.

Chemicals, paper and printing, and coke and petroleum refining further improved their already high standing. Employees of electrical, optical equipment, and transport equipment firms have been moving up the wage ladder.

Clearly, there are various factors behind the observed changes in wages paid in different branches (changes in technologies with effects on the demand for skilled versus unskilled labor, unionization levels, concentration of production, etc.). The very uneven spatial agglomeration of industries (with most dynamic industries located in a few highly industrialized areas with relatively low levels of unemployment) may be of some importance, too, especially in view of rather low labor mobility (owing to the un-availability of affordable housing). The light industries, on the other hand, tend to be dispersed throughout the country, and are often located in areas with extremely high unemployment. It certainly makes sense to search for some statistically sound determinants of the movements in wages across branches. Generally, the correlation coefficients between average wage indices and most other economically meaningful variables are too weak to deserve attention. There is certainly no association between wage rate indices and employment changes. (Hence, one does not observe "workers pricing themselves out of their jobs" or "saving their jobs by moderating wage claims.") There is no association between the wage rate indices and producer price indices (hence no "wage-price-spirals" seem to operate). Changes in wages are not correlated with changes in (real) sales.[30] There is some still rather weak association between wage rate indices and the indices of labor productivity. In the first period, the correlation between labor productivity growth rate (real GVA per employee) and the rate of growth of the average wage was 0.31. In the second period, this rose to 0.59.[31] This seems to support the idea that there is a tendency to adjust the growth of wages to the growth of productivity. Apparently, this tendency has become stronger under external liberalization.[32] Whether there is a causal effect between liberalization and the tendency asserting itself is hard to say. Many other factors have been at work too. Most importantly, there has been a profound change in ownership structures and management practices in Poland.[33]

2.5. Concluding Remarks on Distribution and Inequality

Overall, inequality, which did not increase perceptibly in the "illiberal" period, rose significantly under liberalization. Farmers have been the main losers—not only in relative but also in absolute terms—and their losses have been very heavy. Heavy relative losses have also been suffered by retirees and especially by the unemployed. Generally, the position of wage earners has improved. Wages in most service sectors did not change much in relation to the overall average wage. The wages of miners, construction workers, and health service employees have been declining. In manufacturing, a tendency has come to the fore for wages to be increasingly correlated with

advances in labor productivity. All the same, wage inequality has increased strongly in the "liberal" period. Employers and the self-employed have fared quite well in either period, but certainly better under liberalization. This, however, may at least in part be attributed to the changes in fiscal policy implemented in later years. Cuts in public spending, which have been part and parcel of these changes, have had a minor impact on the living standards of medium- and low-income social groups. The quality of public services (education, health, and safety) has been deteriorating strongly.[34]

3. The Dynamics of Unemployment

Table 10.15 presents the data on participation, and unemployment and employment rates, as defined in Berg and Taylor (2000). The data for 1989–1991 are incomplete. Nonetheless, many interesting observations can be made from the decomposition of unemployment rate changes into participation and employment effects for the period 1993–2000.[35]

There are four observations to be made:

1. Participation effects were negative (i.e., the unemployment growth rate was diminishing) throughout 1993–2000. The highest levels of withdrawals from "active life" occurred in the "illiberal" years 1994–1995.
2. The employment rate change contributed positively (i.e., unfavorably) to the unemployment rate in 1993 and 1994 (during the relatively "illiberal" period), and then again in 1998–2000 (during the second phase of the liberalized period).
3. The effects of employment change were insignificant in 1995 and negative (i.e., favorable) in 1996–1997.

All this seems to indicate that it takes time for the employment effect to have the expected impact on the unemployment rate. Increases in the employment rate followed the "illiberal" period with some delay in the first phase of the "liberal" period. Then, when things turned "normal," employment started to fall. All this might not be trivial. Not only are some prices and wages "sticky," but employment is—under Polish conditions—"sticky" as well.

The decline in employment in recent years, to some extent, reflects the overall growth slowdown.

TABLE 10.15 Decomposition of Changes in the Unemployment Rate into Employment and Participation Effects

	1989	1990	1991	1992	1993	1994	1995	1996	1997	1998	1999	2000	2001
Participation rate	0.75			0.617	0.612	0.592	0.584	0.579	0.574	0.571	0.566	0.564	
Unemployment rate	0	0.065	0.122	0.143	0.164	0.16	0.149	0.133	0.103	0.104	0.131	0.15	0.17
Employment rate	0.75			0.529	0.512	0.497	0.497	0.502	0.515	0.512	0.492	0.479	
Increase in													
Participation rate				−0.133	−0.005	−0.02	−0.008	−0.005	−0.005	−0.003	−0.005	−0.002	
Employment rate				−0.221	−0.017	−0.014	0.000	0.005	0.013	−0.003	−0.020	−0.013	
Unemployment rate				0.143	0.021	−0.004	−0.011	−0.016	−0.03	0.001	0.027	0.019	0.02
Decomposition of Unemployment Rate Change													
Employment effect				0.259	0.028	0.023	0.000	−0.009	−0.022	0.006	0.035	0.022	
Participation effect				−0.156	−0.007	−0.027	−0.011	−0.007	−0.007	−0.005	−0.008	−0.003	
Unemployment rate change (sum of employment and participation effects)				0.103	0.021	−0.004	−0.011	−0.016	−0.030	0.001	0.027	0.019	

330

With the ongoing labor productivity improvements (that have been the consequence of high capital formation in previous years and the overall evolution of ownership structure[36] and management practices, etc.), the insufficient expansion of demand must result in employment losses. Liberalization has been contributing to this directly and indirectly: directly, via diminishing protection (and expanding competitive imports) and less support to exports (I will return to this theme in section 4.5); and indirectly, trade expansion and current account deficits prompted macro policy adjustments (both fiscal and monetary) that magnified the tendency for domestic demand to slow down.

4. Labor Productivity, Employment, and Output

4.1. Labor Productivity: A Sectoral Analysis

On an aggregate level, labor productivity (gross value added per employee)[37] rose faster (5.6 percent per annum) during the "illiberal" (1992–1995) period than during the "liberal" years 1995–1999 (4.4 percent per annum; see table 10.16). At the aggregate level, the gains in labor productivity in the first period were primarily due to rising output (5.7 percent), which was corrected by rising employment (0.1 percent). In the second period, rising output (5.1 percent) was corrected by rising employment (0.8 percent).[38]

With a few exceptions, labor productivity in individual sectors also rose faster in the first period than in the second—generally following the aggregate patterns (GVA rising much faster than employment in the first period, less fast in the second). But it may be of interest to take a look at sectors where this pattern did not hold in one, or both, periods. In agriculture and forestry, there was a decline in labor productivity in the first period (rise in employment, stagnant output). In the second period, things returned to "normal." This may have something to do with a protective attitude toward farming during 1992–1995.[39] Labor productivity also declined (in the first period) in hotels and restaurants (employment rose faster than output). Both sectors thus acted as "absorbers" of employment. Again, in the second period, things returned to "normal" for either sector. In the second period, the role of such a "protected" sector was assigned, perhaps not by chance, to real estate, renting, and business services.

In the first period, there was a strong shedding of labor in construction and transport, storage, and communication, with high gains in both output and productivity. In the second period, things returned to "normal" (rising output, employment, *and* productivity). Possibly, the "abnormal" behavior in the first period had something to do with the ongoing privatization (which was particularly intense in these sectors in the first period) and technological change. Manufacturing and electricity, gas, and water supply underwent similar treatment only in the second period.

In both periods, mining shed labor *and* reduced output (with labor productivity rising in both periods, particularly under the "liberal" regime. This makes sense: Polish mining had been overdeveloped and overmanned. The demand for its output (primarily hard coal) has been declining partly because of the technological change in energy generation and use, and partly due to reduction in subsidies. Rising labor productivity under contracting output reflects its ongoing restructuring, with the closure of the oldest and most inefficient pits.[40] In the second period, health and social work reduced output, employment, and labor productivity. This also makes sense: given cuts in health expenditure, output and employment in that sector will fall—and given the economies of scale characterizing the operations, for instance, of hospitals, that translates into falling labor productivity as well.

4.2. Decomposition of Aggregate Labor Productivity Growth Rates into Sectoral "Net" Productivity and Reallocation Effects

Following Pieper (2000) and Boratav and Yeldan (2001), we decompose aggregate labor productivity growth rates into sectoral "net" productivity and reallocation effects (see table 10.16). Overall, it turns out that the sum of sectoral "net" productivity effects (0.184, or 5.8 percent per annum) in the first period was higher than the aggregate growth rate of labor productivity (0.177, or 5.6 percent per annum). A negative value of the sum of sectoral reallocation (−0.06, or −0.2 percent per annum) indicates that labor reallocation during the period actually reduced, even if insignificantly, the overall labor productivity gain. Reallocation effects from individual sectors were very small to be of importance—it is rather

TABLE 10.16 Decomposition of Aggregate Labor Productivity Growth Rate into Sectoral Net Productivity and Reallocation Effects

Part A: 1992–1995	L Growth Rate	GVA Growth Rate	L Shares 1992	GVA Shares 1992	LP Growth Rate	Net Productivity	Reallocation Effect	Weight	Per Annum		
									LP Growth Rate	Net Productivity	Real Effect
Total	0.004	0.182	1.00	1.00	0.177	0.184	-0.006	-0.233	0.056	0.058	-0.002
Agriculture and forestry	0.02	0.00	0.26	0.07	-0.019	-0.001	-0.005	-0.002	-0.006	0.000	-0.002
Mining and quarrying	-0.18	-0.10	0.03	0.04	0.099	0.003	0.000	-0.002	0.032	0.001	0.000
Manufacturing	0.01	0.42	0.21	0.28	0.406	0.115	0.000	0.033	0.120	0.037	0.000
Electricity, gas, and water supply	0.14	0.20	0.02	0.04	0.055	0.002	0.003	0.020	0.018	0.001	0.001
Construction	-0.18	0.10	0.07	0.08	0.341	0.023	0.000	-0.001	0.103	0.007	0.000
Wholesale, retail trade, and repair motor vehicles	0.03	0.11	0.12	0.14	0.075	0.011	0.000	-0.008	0.024	0.003	0.000
Hotels and restaurants	0.26	0.12	0.01	0.00	-0.107	-0.001	-0.002	-0.008	-0.037	0.000	-0.001
Transport, storage, and telecommunications	-0.07	0.14	0.06	0.06	0.221	0.013	0.001	-0.008	0.069	0.004	0.000
Financial intermediation	0.33	2.17	0.01	0.01	1.384	0.010	-0.003	-0.010	0.336	0.003	-0.001
Real estate, renting, and business activities	0.08	0.13	0.04	0.07	0.044	0.003	0.002	0.025	0.014	0.001	0.001
Public administration, defense, and compulsory social security	0.17	0.18	0.02	0.06	0.007	0.000	0.006	0.037	0.002	0.000	0.002
Education	0.07	0.12	0.05	0.04	0.050	0.002	-0.002	-0.025	0.017	0.001	-0.001
Health and social work	0.02	0.06	0.07	0.04	0.038	0.002	-0.001	-0.036	0.013	0.001	0.000
Other community, social, and personal services	-0.17	-0.14	0.03	0.07	0.035	0.002	-0.006	0.036	0.012	0.001	-0.002

(continued)

	L Growth Rate	GVA Growth Rate	L Shares 1995	GVA Shares 1995	LP Growth Rate	Net Productivity	Reallocation Effect	Weight	Per Annum		
Part B: 1995–1999									LP Growth Rate	Net Productivity	Real Effect
Total	0.031	0.222	1.00	1.00	0.186	0.163	0.022		0.044	0.038	0.005
Agriculture and forestry	-0.02	0.08	0.26	0.07	0.093	0.006	0.004	-0.250	0.023	0.002	0.001
Mining and quarrying	-0.30	-0.13	0.03	0.04	0.244	0.007	-0.003	0.010	0.056	0.002	-0.001
Manufacturing	-0.07	0.39	0.21	0.24	0.489	0.108	0.001	-0.022	0.105	0.026	0.000
Electricity, gas, and water supply	-0.12	0.04	0.02	0.04	0.178	0.006	-0.002	0.016	0.042	0.002	0.000
Construction	0.10	0.32	0.06	0.07	0.204	0.016	0.000	0.003	0.048	0.004	0.000
Wholesale, retail trade, and repair motor vehicles	0.15	0.29	0.13	0.20	0.123	0.028	0.007	0.045	0.030	0.007	0.002
Hotels and restaurants	0.09	0.63	0.01	0.01	0.490	0.005	-0.001	-0.007	0.105	0.001	0.000
Transport, storage, and telecommunications	0.02	0.29	0.06	0.07	0.267	0.018	0.000	-0.005	0.061	0.004	0.000
Financial intermediation	0.24	0.59	0.02	0.01	0.284	0.003	-0.003	-0.011	0.065	0.001	-0.001
Real estate, renting, and business activities	0.37	0.03	0.04	0.08	-0.248	-0.028	0.013	0.035	-0.069	-0.007	0.003
Public administration, defense, compulsory social security	0.20	0.19	0.03	0.06	-0.005	0.000	0.005	0.023	-0.001	0.000	0.001
Education	0.07	0.11	0.06	0.04	0.032	0.001	-0.002	-0.030	0.008	0.000	-0.001
Health and social work	-0.01	-0.09	0.07	0.04	-0.087	-0.004	0.000	-0.043	-0.022	-0.001	0.000
Other community, social, and personal services	0.19	0.05	0.02	0.04	-0.115	-0.005	0.002	0.012	-0.030	-0.001	0.001

difficult to identify the leading sectors. However, agriculture was certainly a lagging sector (with negative reallocation effects roughly equal to the overall reallocation effect and a large negative reallocation weight). The highest sectoral net productivity contribution (to the total of 5.8 percent per annum) was from manufacturing (3.7 percent).

Things are different in the second period. There, the sum of sectoral reallocation effects is positive and quite significant (0.5 percent per annum versus the sum of "net" sectoral effects of 3.8 percent per annum). However, the bulk of gain from reallocation came from two sectors: (1) wholesale, retail trade, repair motor vehicles; and (2) public administration, defense, and so on. Because of relatively high reallocation weights for both sectors, they acted as leading sectors during the period. Reallocation effects from all other sectors are too small to be of any importance (or, as in the case of real estate, renting, and business services, are fully offset by that sector's negative "net" effect contribution). The highest sectoral net productivity contribution (to the total of 3.8 percent per annum) was from manufacturing (2.6 percent). However, with a negative reallocation weight, manufacturing was not a leading sector in the second period. As in the first period, agriculture was a lagging sector (with a large negative reallocation weight).

4.3. Labor Productivity: "Tradables" versus "Non-tradables" and "Skill" versus "Low-Skill" Sectors

We define the sector producing "tradables" as consisting of manufacturing, mining, and agriculture. All remaining sectors are lumped together into the sector producing "non-tradables." It turns out (see table 10.17) that in the first period, labor productivity in either sector rose very fast—with labor productivity rising much faster in the tradable sector. Employment rose in either sector. The reallocation effect was nil—overall productivity growth was explained by net productivity effects (that were almost twice as large in tradables compared with non-tradables). In the second period, productivity growth rates were lower for either sector—and the differential between them was much higher. Employment in tradables fell quite strongly—and rose steeply in the non-tradables. The effects from reallocation were quite significant (0.4 percent per annum). Non-tradables were the leading sector, and tradables were the lagging sector.

This perhaps is not surprising as tradables include agriculture and mining—and neither of them could provide productivity leadership. Non-tradables acted as an employment "sink" in the second period (while tradables reduced employment rather strongly). Overall, the strong reallocation effects and sectoral employment/productivity trends prevailing under liberalization were to be expected.

I define the "low-skill" sector as consisting of agriculture, construction, retail trade, and hotels and restaurants. All other sectors are lumped together into the "skill" sector. In the first period, employment in the low-skill sector declined. Labor productivity rose much faster in the skill sector. Reallocation effects were very low—with the skill sector acting as the leading sector and the low-skill sector as the lagging sector. In the second period, employment rose steeply in the low-skill sector. Also, labor productivity in that sector increased significantly (more than in the skill sector). The overall reallocation effect was negative. The low-skill sector acted as the lagging sector, with its reallocation effect reducing the overall productivity gain. It would be difficult to term the skill sector as leading in that period, either—its reallocation weight was negative.

4.4. Labor Productivity in the Corporate Sector: Domestic Owned versus Foreign Owned

Foreign direct investment has been welcomed all along. However, prior to 1995, inflows of FDI were low (by the end of 1994, the FDI stock was $3.8 billion). From 1995 onwards, the inflows accelerated—by the end of 1999, the stock of FDI reached $26 billion. In the second half of the 1990s, privatization policy was much more keen on seeking foreign ("strategic") investors who were offered pieces of the "family silver," usually at very good terms. In addition, foreign investors have enjoyed many privileges (such as tax holidays or hidden subsidies). One of the reasons for the openness to foreign investment has been the conviction that foreign owners will boost productivity. Table 10.17 (the bottom part) sheds some light on the actual (as revealed by analyzing officially available data) contribution of the foreign-owned subsector to the overall labor productivity growth in the corporate sector.[41]

It turns out that despite a very high (19.5 percent per annum) rate of growth of labor productivity in foreign-owned corporations, the ongoing reallocation

TABLE 10.17 Decomposition of Aggregate Labor Productivity Growth Rate into Sectoral Net Productivity and Reallocation Effects (Tradables versus Non-tradables and "Unskilled" versus "Skilled" Sectors) Decomposition of Labor Productivity Growth Rate for the Corporate Sector (Foreign-Owned versus Domestic-Owned Subsectors)

	Labor Growth Rate	GVA Growth Rate	L Shares	GVA Shares	Labor Prod Growth Rate	Net Productivity	Reallocation Effect	Weight	Per Annum		
									Labor Prod Growth Rate	Net Productivity	Reall. Effect
Total											
1992–1995	0.004	0.182	1.000	1.000	0.177				0.56		
1995–1999	0.031	0.222	1.000	1.000	0.186				0.44		
1992–1995											
Tradables	0.002	0.294	0.498	0.385	0.292	0.113	0.000	−0.204	0.089	0.036	0.000
Non-tradables	0.006	0.112	0.502	0.615	0.105	0.065	0.000	0.022	0.034	0.021	0.000
						0.178	0.000	−0.182		0.056	0.000
1995–1999											
Tradables	−0.051	0.267	0.497	0.346	0.335	0.110	0.013	−0.261	0.075	0.026	0.003
Non-tradables	0.112	0.198	0.503	0.654	0.077	0.056	0.004	0.039	0.019	0.014	0.001
						0.167	0.018			0.039	0.004
1992–1995											
Unskilled	−0.003	0.080	0.460	0.292	0.082	0.024	0.001	−0.252	0.027	0.008	0.000
Skilled	0.010	0.224	0.540	0.708	0.213	0.152	0.001	0.070	0.066	0.048	0.000
						0.176	0.001			0.056	0.000
1995–1999											
Unskilled	0.048	0.266	0.457	0.350	0.208	0.076	−0.010	−0.208	0.048	0.019	−0.003
Skilled	0.016	0.199	0.543	0.650	0.180	0.119	0.000	−0.014	0.042	0.028	0.000
						0.195	−0.010			0.046	−0.003
Corporate Sector (Non-financial and Financial Corporations)											
1995–1999											
Total		0.010	0.330	1.000	1.000	0.316	−0.072		0.071	0.021	−0.018
Foreign-owned	0.822	2.71	0.1	0.046	1.0362	0.087	0.019	−0.087	0.195	0.064	0.005
Domestic-owned	−0.08	0.215	0.9	0.954	0.3207	0.281	−0.052	−0.243	0.072	0.082	−0.011
						0.368					

of labor from domestic- to foreign-owned firms has actually reduced labor productivity growth rate for the whole corporate sector. The foreign-owned sub-sector has been lagging behind the domestic-owned subsector in the sense that labor productivity in the domestic-owned sector is still much higher compared with that of the foreign-owned sector. Certainly, this is a surprising conclusion—also because foreign investors quite rationally pick up the best, most profitable, available projects (with the worst ones—such as coal mines and steel plants—left in the custody of the Polish state). There are two possible explanations for this anomaly: (1) foreign-owned firms are still in the running-in phase—hence, they will exhibit their full potential only after some delay; and (2) foreign firms are superior to domestic firms in underreporting taxable income. There are good grounds to believe that both explanations apply. The former seems to apply primarily to foreign firms that have taken over existing production capacities (together with their labor force); the latter primarily to greenfield projects (also to service activities, and particularly to retail trade).[42]

4.5. Labor Productivity in Manufacturing: A Branch Analysis

On the aggregate level, labor productivity in manufacturing rose faster (12 percent per annum) during the "illiberal" (1992–1995) period than during the "liberal" years 1995–1999 (10.5 percent per annum)—see table 10.18. The gains in labor productivity in the first period were primarily the result of rising output (12.3 percent per annum) that was corrected by rising employment (0.3 percent per annum). In the second period, rising output (8.6 percent per annum) was supplemented by falling employment (–1.7 percent per annum).

In only five out of fourteen branches, labor productivity gains in the second period were larger than in the first period. (In four out of these five branches, there was labor shedding.) Labor shedding was generally more widespread in the second period: ten branches shed labor (versus six in the first period). One branch registered a loss in labor productivity in either period (wood and wood products in the first, coke and petroleum in the second).[43] Interestingly, in the first period, no branch experienced a decline in output. In the second period, there was a very strong decline in coke and petroleum output and in the

output of two "light" industry branches: textiles and leather. The latter two branches may well have been the victims of the secular weakness of demand (falling income elasticity of demand for apparel) and the loss of export markets with increased import competition. In the case of coke and petroleum, the reasons are more complex. As far as the production of coke is concerned, it was affected by the reduction in foreign demand (and the discontinuation of the hidden subsidization of coal extraction, the main input in coke production). Gross value-added in petroleum products must have also been reduced with the dramatic strengthening of foreign competition in the retail market for motor fuels[44] and with the movements in the world market price of crude oil. An analysis of "net" productivity and reallocation effects for manufacturing leads to the following conclusions:

1. In the first period, the contribution of reallocation effects (0.3 percent per annum) to the overall manufacturing labor productivity growth (12 percent per annum) was negligible. No branch provided a clear leadership, and the textile branch was a laggard.
2. In the second period, the contribution of reallocation effects (1.4 percent) was sizable because the overall productivity growth was 10.5 percent. Only one branch (pulp, paper, and printing) acted as a clear leader during the period.

4.6. Employment and Output in Manufacturing: The Role of Foreign Trade

The growth rates of employment across manufacturing turn out to be uncorrelated with output growth rates (correlation coefficient of 0.06 in the first period, and 0.13 in the second), growth rates in the share of wages in gross value-added (0.16 and 0.27 respectively), or growth rates in labor productivity (–0.45 and 0.04 respectively). There was no correlation between the rates of growth of employment and the rates of growth of wages. A somewhat stronger link seems to have existed between rates of growth of employment and rates of growth of (real) sales: the correlation coefficient between both items for the first period was 0.60, and 0.66 for the second period. These results should not be surprising. Under high unemployment and generally insufficient demand, firms may have been adjusting employment to sales—and the latter may have been important for keeping (or extending)

TABLE 10.18 Decomposition of Aggregate Labor Productivity Growth in Manufacturing into Branch Net Productivity and Reallocation Effects

Part A: 1992–1995	Labor Growth Rate	Labor Share 1992	GVA Growth Rate	GVA Share 1992	GVA/Labor Growth Rate	Net Productivity Growth Rate	Reallocation		Growth Rates		Per Annum
							Effect Growth Rate	Weight Growth Rate	GVA/Labor	Net Productivity	Reallocation Effect
Manufacturing total	0.008	1.000	0.416	1.000	**0.405**				**0.120**		
Food products, beverages, and tobacco	0.044	0.171	0.463	0.182	0.402	0.076	−0.003	−0.057	0.119	0.025	−0.001
Textiles and textile products	0.095	0.143	0.457	0.089	0.331	0.032	−0.011	−0.112	0.100	0.011	−0.004
Leather and leather products	−0.147	0.032	0.327	0.017	0.556	0.008	0.004	−0.027	0.159	0.003	0.001
Wood and wood products	0.123	0.035	0.069	0.048	−0.047	−0.003	0.000	−0.001	−0.016	−0.001	0.000
Pulp, paper, and paper products; publishing and printing	0.073	0.035	0.809	0.059	0.686	0.043	0.001	0.010	0.190	0.014	0.000
Coke, refined petroleum products, and nuclear fuel	0.001	0.008	0.869	0.022	0.867	0.019	0.000	0.010	0.231	0.006	0.000
Chemicals, chemical products, and manmade fibers	0.004	0.050	0.176	0.106	0.171	0.018	0.000	0.036	0.054	0.006	0.000
Rubber and plastic products	0.239	0.026	0.508	0.045	0.217	0.012	0.002	0.009	0.068	0.004	0.001
Other non-metallic mineral products	−0.043	0.062	0.357	0.061	0.418	0.024	0.001	−0.026	0.123	0.008	0.000
Basic metals and fabricated metal products	−0.026	0.115	0.357	0.136	0.394	0.052	0.001	−0.025	0.117	0.017	0.000
Machinery and equipment n.e.c.	−0.094	0.119	0.508	0.086	0.664	0.051	0.008	−0.081	0.185	0.017	0.003
Electrical and optical equipment	−0.092	0.072	1.010	0.024	1.213	0.027	0.007	−0.077	0.303	0.009	0.002
Transport equipment	−0.097	0.085	0.106	0.081	0.224	0.016	0.004	−0.037	0.070	0.005	0.001
Manufacturing n.e.c.	0.211	0.047	0.618	0.044	0.336	0.018	−0.005	−0.023	0.101	0.006	−0.002
					Totals	**0.396**	**0.009**		Totals	**0.118**	**0.003**

(continued)

TABLE 10.18 (continued)

Part A: 1992–1995	Labor Growth Rate	Labor Share 1992	GVA Growth Rate	GVA Share 1992	GVA/Labor Growth Rate	Net Productivity Growth Rate	Reallocation Effect Growth Rate	Reallocation Weight Growth Rate	Growth Rates Per Annum GVA/Labor	Growth Rates Per Annum Net Productivity	Growth Rates Per Annum Reallocation Effect
Manufacturing total	-0.065	1.000	0.392	1.000	**0.489**				**0.105**		
Food products; beverages and tobacco	-0.019	0.177	0.338	0.189	0.364	0.067	0.001	-0.075	0.081	0.016	0.000
Textiles and textile products	-0.220	0.156	-0.115	0.092	0.136	0.010	0.031	-0.140	0.032	0.002	0.008
Leather and leather products	-0.222	0.027	-0.075	0.016	0.188	0.002	0.005	-0.024	0.044	0.001	0.001
Wood and wood products	0.248	0.039	0.393	0.036	0.117	0.005	-0.005	-0.022	0.028	0.001	-0.001
Pulp, paper, and paper products; publishing and printing	0.285	0.037	0.771	0.075	0.378	0.037	0.006	0.020	0.083	0.009	0.001
Coke, refined petroleum products, and nuclear fuel	-0.171	0.008	-0.561	0.028	-0.471	-0.011	-0.003	0.017	-0.147	-0.003	-0.001
Chemicals, chemical products, and manmade fibers	-0.204	0.050	0.272	0.088	0.598	0.042	-0.003	0.014	0.124	0.010	-0.001
Rubber and plastic products	0.244	0.032	1.188	0.048	0.759	0.046	0.000	0.001	0.152	0.011	0.000
Other non-metallic mineral products	-0.044	0.059	0.472	0.058	0.540	0.030	0.001	-0.030	0.114	0.007	0.000
Basic metals and fabricated metal products	-0.024	0.111	0.279	0.130	0.310	0.039	0.001	-0.035	0.070	0.010	0.000
Machinery and equipment n.e.c.	-0.215	0.107	0.672	0.091	1.129	0.081	0.015	-0.068	0.208	0.020	0.004
Electrical and optical equipment	-0.064	0.065	0.722	0.034	0.840	0.027	0.004	-0.063	0.165	0.007	0.001
Transport equipment	-0.185	0.076	0.525	0.064	0.871	0.045	0.009	-0.049	0.170	0.011	0.002
Manufacturing n.e.c.	0.145	0.057	0.358	0.050	0.186	0.011	-0.005	-0.035	0.044	0.003	-0.001
					Totals	0.430	0.057		Totals	0.094	0.014

market shares and earning liquidity. Certainly, the advances in labor productivity must have also played a role (especially in the first period, as evidenced by the quite high negative correlation between employment changes and labor productivity).

Foreign trade in manufacturing must have played a role in determining actual sales in the first period. Its importance was by far greater in the second period—with the advancing liberalization of imports, the lowering of tariffs, and strong real appreciation. Its impact was, on the whole, rather negligible in the first period and hugely detrimental in the second. Between 1992 and 1995, the foreign trade deficit in industrial goods[45] rose from 4.4 percent of production (sales) to 5.6 percent. Had the deficit in 1995 been unchanged (i.e., remained at 4.4 percent of domestic sales), then (ignoring the terms of trade effects) sales would have grown by as much as 3.5 percent—on account of much stronger real growth of imports compared with exports. Between 1995 and 1999, the deficit rose from 5.6 percent to a stunning 16.5 percent, implying a loss of over

9 percent of potential domestic sales. This corresponds to the actual 9 percent loss of industrial employment (see table 10.19).[46] As can be seen, there was some correspondence between employment indices and market loss indices[47] at the branch level in the first period. That correspondence seems to have become even stronger in the second period.

For data on trade, sales, and employment in the second period (see table 10.20), the correspondence between market loss indices and employment losses becomes much more pronounced. The largest losses in employment (in the textiles, leather, and chemical and machinery and equipment branches) tend to be associated with heavy market losses. Most branches that retained or expanded employment suffered rather moderate market losses. There are some "irregularities," however. Transport equipment suffered heavy losses in employment without suffering any loss of markets. This may be related to exceptionally high levels of foreign direct investment in the branch and the strong ongoing trend toward labor-saving technologies.

TABLE 10.19 Employment, Sales, and Foreign Trade in Industrial Products, 1992–1995 and 1995–1999

1992–1995	Employment Index	Real Sales Index	Balance of Trade Domestic[a] 1992	% Production 1995	Potential Sales Index	Market Loss Index	Market Loss Index[b]
Industry products total	0.998	1.308	−4.4	−5.6	1.355	−0.035	−0.012
Food products	1.050	1.339	−0.5	−0.1	1.326	0.010	0.004
Light industry products	1.058	1.232	7.5	5.4	1.351	−0.088	−0.023
Wood and paper industry	1.162	1.448	9.8	14.8	1.477	−0.020	0.058
Chemicals	1.092	1.471	−20.6	−29.6	1.585	−0.072	−0.069
Mineral industry products	0.963	1.319	1.9	−0.6	1.370	−0.038	−0.025
Products of metallurgy	0.981	1.393	21.3	10.6	1.583	−0.120	−0.120
Electro-engineering products	0.912	1.547	−24.9	−23.4	1.663	−0.069	0.012

1995–1999	Employment Index	Real Sales Index	Balance of Trade Domestic[a] 1995	% Production 1999	Potential Sales Index	Market Loss Index	Market Loss Index[b]
Industry products total	0.907	1.31	−5.6	−16.5	1.447	−0.095	−0.093
Food products	1.009	1.281	−0.1	−0.4	1.252	0.023	−0.003
Light industry products	0.750	1.088	5.4	−2.3	1.139	−0.045	−0.075
Wood and paper products	1.084	1.609	14.8	14.0	1.674	−0.039	−0.010
Chemicals	1.006	1.36	−29.6	−56.1	1.648	−0.175	−0.170
Mineral industry products	0.956	1.523	−0.6	−7.2	1.667	−0.086	−0.062
Products of metallurgy	0.968	1.279	10.6	−0.1	1.449	−0.117	−0.107
Electro-engineering products	0.863	1.626	−23.4	−48.2	1.991	−0.183	−0.167

a. At current prices.

b. Not corrected for the terms of trade effects.

TABLE 10.20 Employment, Sales, and Poland's Trade with the EU in Products of Manufacturing, 1995–1999

| | Employment Index | Real Sales Index | Balance of with the Trade EU | | Potential Sales Index | Market Loss Index[b] |
			Domestic[a] 1995	% Production 1999		
Manufacturing total	0.935	1.388	−4.72	−11.98	1.484	−0.065
Food products, beverages, and tobacco	0.981	1.274	−1.74	−0.48	1.258	0.013
Textiles and textile products	0.780	1.254	4.76	−0.54	1.324	−0.053
Leather and leather products	0.778	0.916	3.12	−17.57	1.112	−0.176
Wood and wood products	1.248	1.854	28.72	22.01	2.029	−0.086
Pulp, paper, and paper products; publishing and printing	1.285	1.731	−14.59	−14.81	1.734	−0.002
Coke, refined petroleum products, and nuclear fuel	0.829	0.941	2.91	−6.02	1.028	−0.084
Chemicals, chemical products, and manmade fibers	0.796	1.132	−19.58	−47.70	1.399	−0.190
Rubber and plastic products	1.244	1.889	−20.65	−23.79	1.938	−0.025
Other non-metallic mineral products	0.956	1.540	1.99	−5.47	1.657	−0.071
Basic metals and fabricated metal products	0.976	1.274	12.85	−1.45	1.483	−0.141
Machinery and equipment n.e.c.	0.785	1.160	−39.64	−68.61	1.401	−0.172
Electrical and optical equipment	0.936	1.755	−27.47	−39.46	1.920	−0.086
Transport equipment	0.815	1.956	−12.25	−11.12	1.936	0.010
Manufacturing n.e.c.	1.145	1.585	24.50	27.09	1.531	0.036

a. Not corrected for the terms of trade effects.

b. At current prices.

Conclusion

There are two distinct periods in recent Polish history with different degrees of liberalization. During the first period (1992–1995), imports were controlled and exports were promoted. Currency appreciation was controlled and capital movements were relatively restricted. Real interest rates were moderate and there was a rapid acceleration in capital formation. Foreign trade did not significantly affect GDP growth. The economy pulled itself out of a deep recession without incurring any new foreign debt—and without selling its assets to foreigners. Public sector deficits were declining without spending reductions.

The second period (1995–present) has witnessed rapid import liberalization and greatly reduced levels of export support. Capital inflows were liberalized—paradoxically, this failed to reduce domestic interest rates; in fact, they have been responsible for the persistence of very high interest rates. The determination of the exchange rate has been increasingly left to the (still shallow) forex market. There has been a tendency for a strong real appreciation, fed by capital inflows. Foreign trade performance has been disappointing and has reduced GDP growth rates significantly. Although initially investment and consumption vigorously expanded (following the momentum gained in the previous period), in the second phase of this period they have weakened—lately entering the threshold of contraction. After initial declines, unemployment has strongly rebounded. In contrast with the first period, huge foreign debt has accumulated and most productive domestic assets have been dissipated. An attempt to strengthen growth and reduce foreign deficits through a "supply-side" fiscal policy misfired, resulting in huge public deficits. A very high likelihood for currency crisis has been created.

Poland: Summary Table

Growth, Employment, and Inequality	1992–1995	1995–2000	2001
Growth rate (per annum)	5.2	5.1	1
Real exchange rate (+ = real appreciation)	0	++	++
Employment rate (+ = fall in unemployment)	−/+	++/−−	−−
Wage share in GDP	−	+	
Real wage (per annum)	0.5	4.2	1
Income Inequality			
Per capita household income	−	++	
Primary incomes (labor force)	−	++	
Skilled/unskilled	−	++	
Formal/informal	na	na	
Employment Structure			
Traded/non-traded	−	−−	
Skilled/unskilled	0	+	
Formal/informal	na	na	
Aggregate Demand Decomposition	*1991–1995*	*1995–2000*	
Aggregate demand (per annum)	7.2	7.7	
Direct Multiplier Effects			
Investment/savings	−	++	
Government/tax	+/0	++	
Exports/imports	+	−−	
Effect of Leakages			
Savings	+	+	
Taxes	0	+	
Imports	−	−−	
Productivity and Employment	*1992–1995*	*1995–1999*	*2000–2001*
Productivity Growth (per annum)			
Overall	5.6	4.4	
Traded	8.9	7.5	
Non-traded	3.4	1.9	
Overall growth in employment (per annum)	0	0.6	−1
Employment sector reallocation effects	0	0.5	
Labor Supply Changes			
Participation rate	−	−	−
Unemployment rate	+/−	−/+	++
Employment rate	−	−	−−
Macroeconomic Variables	*1992–1995*	*1996–1999*	*2000–2001*
Trade deficit	−	++	−
Domestic credit	+	+/0	−
Changes in reserves	0	++/0	0
Real interest rate	0	++	++
Interest rate spreads	0	0	+
Imports/GDP	+	++	0
Exports/GDP	+	+	+
Imposition of export incentives	+	−−	−−

Key: ++ = strong increase, + = increase, +/0 = slight increase, −− = strong decrease, − = decrease, 0/− = slight decrease, +/−+ = fluctuating trend, +/− = up then down (or vice versa), 0 = no changes, n.a. = not available.

Overall, inequality, which did not increase perceptibly in the "illiberal" period, rose significantly under liberalization. Farmers have been the main losers. Generally, the position of wage earners has improved. Wages in most service sectors did not change much in relation to the overall average wage. All the same, wage inequality has increased strongly in the second period. Employers and the self-employed have fared quite well in either period but certainly better under liberalization. This, however, may at least in part be attributed to the changes in fiscal policy implemented in later years. The quality of public services (education, health, and safety) has been deteriorating strongly. In the second phase of the "liberal" period, there has been a massive rise in poverty, whose main determinant is rising unemployment.

Throughout the 1990s, there has been a reduction in labor participation rates. The rapidly growing unemployment in recent years, to some extent, reflects the overall growth slowdown. With the ongoing improvements in labor productivity, the insufficient expansion of demand must result in employment losses. Liberalization has contributed to this directly and indirectly. Total labor productivity rose faster during the "illiberal" years (1992–1995) than the "liberal" years (1995–1999). In short, liberalization did not coincide with faster productivity improvements. In either period, the productivity in tradables improved faster than in non-tradables. But the productivity growth differential between tradables and non-tradables widened in the "liberal" period. The share of the tradable sector in employment did not change much in the first period and declined significantly in the second. The non-tradable sector increased employment in the "liberal" period and the tradable sector shed labor on a large scale. Reallocation effects were negligible during the "illiberal" period and quite significant in the "liberal" period. While it is difficult to single out any clear productivity leader, in either period, agriculture was certainly the lagging sector. The reallocation of labor from the domestic- to foreign-owned corporation has reduced the overall productivity gain.

In manufacturing, the productivity improvement was faster during the "illiberal" period. Moreover, during that period, there was generally no labor shedding, and productivity improvements were achieved through a very strong rise in output. But also in that period, the total effect from the reallocation of labor among individual branches was insignificant.

In the "liberal" period, the reallocation effect was quite high (with the pulp, paper, and printing branch acting as a productivity leader). However, despite the positive reallocation contribution, the overall productivity gain was lower. Moreover, it was achieved with large-scale labor shedding and with much less impressive output growth than under the "illiberal" regime.

Losses in manufacturing employment during the "liberal" period have been associated with the foreign trade developments. In contrast with the "illiberal" period, there has been a dramatic deterioration of trade balances for almost all branches. This implies a massive loss of potential sales and actual employment for the whole of manufacturing. Contrary to popular beliefs, the foreign-owned sector lags in terms of productivity. The reallocation of labor from domestic- to foreign-owned corporations has reduced the overall productivity gain.

Notes

1. The debt was accumulated in the early 1970s by borrowing heavily to import huge quantities of modern capital goods and technology.

2. The national account reporting was changed in 1995. For 1994 I have two sets of accounts, which allow (with some qualifications) the analysis of trends over the entire post-1990 period.

3. An apparently high share (26 percent) of gross capital formation does not tell the whole story—which is that about one-fifth of it was an increase in stocks.

4. See table 10.1.

5. See table 10.3.

6. The spread was even lower with producer prices (PPI has been lagging behind—often remarkably so—the CPI). Nominal devaluation was generally stronger than the PPI in manufacturing. For manufacturing there was a real depreciation—with exports (as captured by the customs statistics) well above imports (see table 10.2, memo items).

7. Following the same principle, they attempted to conduct a kind of selective—but rather limited—industrial policy, also through a rather discriminating approach to privatization and foreign direct investment.

8. Since 1990 the EU has been Poland's major trading partner, capturing 60–70 percent of its exports and imports shares. For Poland, liberalization, or even globalization, should be seen primarily in the context of relations with the EU.

9. In 1995 there was a change in the GDP accounting practice. (The major innovation was regarding the treatment of some part of indirect taxation, earlier included in the valuation of gross output.) For 1994 there are two parallel sets of accounts—with somewhat different data. Tables 10.1 and 10.2 are derived by the author from the basic GDP data recalculated against 1995. This was not without some problems. Suggestions by Professor K. Laski were essential in tackling these problems.

10. In the early 1990s, the debt was financed by "money-printing"—that is, credit from the National Bank and state-owned banks. Since 1994 considerable

parts of deficit spending have been financed by privatization revenues and, later on, by private sector borrowing. The interest burden has been rising accordingly, especially since 1998. At present it represents about 3 percent of the GDP.

11. Free movements of the exchange rate (within the bounds) were to somewhat deter short-term currency speculation by making it more risky. In fact, the forex market quickly developed instruments allowing speculation all the same (first futures, then more sophisticated exchange rate and interest rate derivatives). The major players on the (still rather shallow) Polish forex market are the London-based traders, gambling against the Polish parties, including banks. Generally, the short-term speculation has *not* been against the Polish currency—in view of very high Polish interest rates, such speculation may be too costly. In effect, the short-term speculations—based on agents "following the trend"— have been inflating a kind of a long-term rational (so far) bubble.

12. In real (PPI-deflated) terms, the Central Bank's discount rate was about 4 percent throughout 1994 and the first half of 1995. By the end of 1995, it was 8 percent, then it was around 10 percent in 1996 and 1997, 14 percent in 1998, around 10 percent in 1999 and the first half of 2000, and about 15 percent afterwards. The ambitious medium-term goal of the monetary authority has been to bring down inflation to the EU level (thereby allowing the speedy adoption of the euro as legal tender).

13. This reflected the "conservative-values" policies of the Solidarity-sponsored parties that returned to power in late 1997 and passed a number of painful reforms aimed at dismantling most of what had been left of any meaningful social policy (health, education, and pension systems were all "downscaled"). Of course, they won the 1997 elections on an entirely different mandate that promised precisely the opposite of what they did.

14. To put it differently, the initial asymmetry notwithstanding, the association agreement turned out to have stipulated a net gain for the EU—and a net loss for Poland. This impression is also reinforced by the trade practice in the field of "sensitive" products. As it happens, the EU exports of food and farm products to Poland, though subject to the (Polish) tariffs, are heavily subsidized by the EU. Poland is too poor to reciprocate in kind. In effect, the EU runs huge trade surpluses on *most* groups of products—including the "sensitive" ones.

15. Public (general government) current revenues were over 43 percent of the GDP in 1996. Since then they have been declining—to about 39 percent in 2000. Current expenditures fell from over 39 to 37 percent

respectively. The share of personal income tax revenue in GDP fell from 6.7 to 3.4 percent. The share of social security contributions fell from about 16 to 12 percent.

16. There has been a frantic acceleration of sales of state-owned banks, insurance companies, manufacturing firms, and even public utilities to foreign parties in recent years. Ironically, "privatization" also involves the sale of lucrative businesses owned by the Polish state (e.g., telecommunication and power stations) to firms owned exclusively by foreign (French, Swedish, etc.) states. The basic reason for the acceleration of sales was the necessity to earn revenue to narrow the fiscal gaps. Undoubtedly, prices and other conditions at which such fire sales were carried out imply huge short- and long-term losses to the Polish economy. It goes without saying that under such conditions, corruption has become rampant.

17. As long as there are reserves (or "solid" capital inflows, or sellable national assets), the currency may stay strong. If the reserves are depleted by CA deficits ("solid" inflows stop, and assets are dissipated), high interest rates will sooner or later fail to attract even "hot" money. Currently, the CA deficit is over 4 percent of the (stagnant) GDP. Clearly there is a "structural" problem here, which, sooner or later, will be solved (or will solve itself) only through a sustained depreciation.

18. Of course, the potential "hot" capital outflows are much higher because, as the exchange rate will be nearing an "adjustment," residents will also seek to convert their domestic currency stocks into dollars or euros.

19. This amounts to 0.26 percent of the total population.

20. Can one really believe that per capita consumption of alcoholic beverages in the households surveyed is only 50 percent of the national average?

21. During the 1980s, farmers enjoyed many economic privileges. Per capita expenditure in farmers' households was 10 percent higher than that of the average household.

22. Tables 10.5–9 were calculated by Dr. A. Szulc, Warsaw School of Economics.

23. Nonetheless, the share of wages in GDP in 1992 can be estimated at 47 percent. For 1995 and 1999, the official numbers are 43 and 45 percent respectively.

24. Thereby, lowering their taxable personal income and corporate taxes. Moreover, purchases of items classified as "production inputs" are free of the value-added tax (VAT).

25. Real gross disposable incomes are calculated using class-specific cost-of-living indices.

26. The wages under discussion are paid to persons employed on a regular "contractual" basis (incomes

earned by casual workers, working owners, farmers, etc., are not counted here).

27. These coefficients are taken from Borkowska (1999).

28. In 1992 the average wage in the private sector was some 3 percent lower than the average wage in the public sector. In 1995 that differential increased to 10 percent, in 1999 to 13.3 percent. At the same time, the inequality in private sector wages is higher and rising faster than in the public sector. In 1992 the Gini coefficient for wages in the private sector was 0.286; in the public sector it was 0.237. In 1995, the respective coefficients were 0.32 and 0.27; in 1997, these coefficients were 0.344 and 0.271.

29. Very generous unemployment benefits and pension systems in the early 1990s had a political and an economic purpose. Politically, they "sweetened" the transition to capitalism. Economically they pacified workers' opposition to privatization (which usually implied massive cuts in employment, sending them into either unemployment or early retirement), thus nipping in the bud the idea that workers had ownership rights to their factories. As privatization progressed, such generosity lost its economic usefulness.

30. The strength of product demand does not transmit itself into wages.

31. The correlation between labor productivity growth rate (real sales per employee) and the growth rate of average wages was 0.39 in the first period and 0.42 in the second.

32. However, the correlation between the wage level and labor productivity has been weakening from 0.925 in 1992 to 0.8 in 1995 and 0.51 in 1999.

33. In 1992 the private sector share in industrial sales was 30 percent (2 percent of which was contributed by foreign-owned firms). In 1995 these shares were 45 and 5.5 percent and in 1999, 72 and 15 percent respectively.

34. The total number of crimes reported rose from 883,000 in 1990, to 975,000 in 1995, and 1,267,000 in 2000.

35. Observe that the decomposition for 1992 is against the year 1989. Because the formula used here (a "finite differences" version of the formula suggested in Berg and Taylor 2000) is approximately right only for "small changes" of the variables in question, it is not informative in this case. For 1992 the total of the participation and employment effects equals 0.103—when the actual unemployment rate increased (from 1989 to 1992) by 0.143.

36. Large privatization contracts often contain "employment clauses" whereby the new owners pledge to keep cuts in employment limited—for definite periods. The clauses are to soften the employees' opposition to privatization. In recent years the clauses on very many large privatization deals have been expiring—a wave of labor shedding follows. This may have aggravated the macro problem (weakening of wage incomes and domestic demand).

37. GVA is of course in real terms. Employment includes both salaried (hired) workers and working owners, farmers, casual workers, and so on.

38. Statements about the components of labor productivity growth (output and employment) can be rephrased into statements about the components of employment growth. Thus, it can be said that in the first period, growth of employment was restricted to 0.1 percent by labor productivity rising almost as fast as output, while 1.5 percent growth in employment in the second period was due to output rising by 1.5 percentage points faster than productivity.

39. The "dual" statements on employment in agriculture (and in other sectors with high levels of self-employment) rising (or falling) because of falling (or rising) labor productivity sound a bit odd. Employment in farming does not respond, under high overall unemployment, to productivity changes. It is largely determined by the demography of farmers' families and is exogenous to changes in productivity, at least in the short term.

40. Alternatively, employment in mining can be said to have been falling because of simultaneous increases in labor productivity and falling production.

41. The corporate sector considered now includes both non-financial and financial corporations. Its domestic part includes private, state-owned, and communal corporations. The entire sector's share in the total economy's gross value-added was 52 percent in 1995, falling to 48 percent in 1999.

42. Transfer pricing in foreign trade is one vehicle of tax evasion. (Foreign-owned firms engage overproportionately in foreign trade. In 1999, they accounted for 56 percent of Poland's imports and 52 percent of exports—and 62 percent of the trade deficit.) Another popular trick involves payments for expensive "consulting services" from foreign firms' own headquarters located abroad.

43. The coke and petroleum branch could well afford losses in labor productivity because in 1995 its labor productivity was about 3.5 times the average.

44. A lucrative part of domestic petroleum processing is the retail trade in motor fuels. In this business, domestic refineries have lost (since 1995) about 20 percent of the market to major foreign distributors (Shell, Amoco, BP, etc.) who have invested approximately $1.5 billion in the development of their own retail networks.

45. Traded industrial goods include manufacturing, mining, as well as electrical products.

46. Industrial branches specified in table 10.19 do not match groups of the NACE branches of manufacturing (see table 10.18). For instance, tobacco is excluded from the food industry; furniture production (the major item of the NACE manufacturing n.e.c branch) is added to the wood and paper branch (which excludes printing). The underlying classification scheme (called SWW) is an old Polish system, surviving in some industrial and trade statistics. Because it often lumps together subbranches with definitely diverse features, the analysis cannot yield too sharp conclusions. There are no trade statistics for the NACE branches prior to 1995, and only partial NACE statistics (for trade with the European Union) from 1995 onwards (see table 10.20).

47. The market loss indices relate actual and potential sales.

References

Berg, J., and L. Taylor. 2000. External liberalization, distribution, and growth. CEPA Working Paper no. 12. New York: Center for Economic Policy Analysis, New School University.

Boratav, K., and E. Yeldan. 2001. Turkey, 1980–2000: Financial liberalization, macroeconomic (in)stability and patterns of distribution.

Borkowska, S. 1999. *Placa godziwa* (in Polish). Warsaw: IPiSS.

Pieper, U. 1998. Openness and structural dynamics of productivity and employment in developing countries: A case of deindustrialization? *Journal of Development Studies*.

World Bank, 2000. *World development indicators*. Washington, D.C.: World Bank.

11

The Russian Way of Adjustment: Mechanisms of Economic Growth in 1999–2001 and Patterns of Poverty and Income Distribution

Alexander Yu. Vorobyov and Stanislav V. Zhukov

Within the last decade, Russia has undergone several episodes of tumultuous macroeconomic adjustment. These episodes have determined the transformation of the economy's development regimes and the configuration of the macroeconomic environment.

Schematically, the first episode was adjustment to the orthodox liberalization shock of 1992. Its main outcomes were the tremendous fall in production, the contraction of final demand, an investment squeeze against the backdrop of forced savings increases, deindustrialization, an extremely high inflation rate, chaos in state finances, the distortion of monetary transactions, and the accumulation of enterprise debt. All these processes constituted the macro environment for an unprecedented redistribution of property rights, resources, as well as political commitments.

In 1996, Russia made its way from the post-liberalization abyss to the regime of depressive stabilization (Belousov 1996). Since then, the economy recovered from its negative growth trend, inflation rates fell significantly (pointing to the gradual exhaustion of the forced savings effect), and the enforcement of a hard currency exchange rate corridor set up the principal "nominal anchor" to decrease inflationary expectations. The budget deficit remained sizable while monetary expansion was constrained by the floating of short-term government securities to finance deficits. Overvalued in its corridor, the ruble hampered the growth of exports and spurred imports, deteriorating the balance of trade and the current account balance. The failure of investment continued to predetermine the structural weakness of the Russian economy.

The financial crisis of August 1998 undermined the two foundations of the depressive stabilization regime—the government short-term borrowing market (GKO market) as an instrument to finance current budget deficits, and the hard currency corridor. As a result, the Russian economy experienced dramatic shock associated with a large and uncontrolled ruble devaluation, the collapse of the financial system, aggravated inflation expectations, and demand constraints (both in the consumer and investment goods market). The adjustment to the shock produced a radical turn in the economy's growth regime.

1. Basic Indicators of the Russian Growth Regime (1999–2001)

Statistically, the development of the Russian economy in 1999–2001 differs significantly from the liberalization and depressive stabilization periods. The basic differences may be summarized as follows (see table 11.1):

- For the first time in the 1990s, Russia experienced significantly positive GDP growth rates. Starting from 5.4 percent in 1999 after a decade of unprecedented slowdown, GDP growth rates climbed to a fairly high 9.0 percent in 2000.
- After a decade of deindustrialization, industrial production during the last three years demonstrates pretty high growth rates (even if they are unevenly distributed across industrial sectors).
- Investment started to revive after a deep and long-term contraction: its contribution to final demand formation steadily increases.
- Significantly improved positive current account and trade balances reduced, at least temporarily, foreign gap constraints.
- In 1999, the budget deficit was reduced to almost zero while in 2000, for the first time since the 1990s, budget revenues exceeded expenditures by more than 5 percent of GDP. This tendency gained strength in 2001.
- Despite a revival of final demand and production as well as large increases in the monetary aggregates primarily caused by a significant inflow in the country of hard currency assets (owing to the considerable improvement of the trade balance), inflation rates stayed under control. This means that to a large degree, the growth of money supply was successfully sterilized by means of budgetary and monetary policies.

Thus, statistical data indicate positive shifts in the development of the Russian economy within the last three years. As we know, however, sometimes statistics can hide the truth. Especially in societies subject to structural distortions and external shocks, a proper understanding of the consequences of the 1999–2001 adjustment episode needs to answer the following fundamental questions:

- Will economic growth in Russia be sustainable, and to what degree?

- Will the current economic growth spurt lead to structural adjustment of the Russian economy, including the qualitative renewal of production, increased investment in technologically advanced sectors (triggered by efficient resource reallocation), the formation of a modern market environment, industrial organization, and institutions for economic policy management?
- Finally, will Russia be able to change its model of integration into the world economy by using still-available comparative advantages in the high-tech sectors of the economy?

To answer these questions, we first need to explain all the mechanisms and driving forces of growth in 1999–2001.

2. Driving Forces of Economic Growth (1999–2001)

The post-crisis period of economic revival is very clearly subdivided into two phases:

- "Devaluation" episode: October 1998–November 1999
- "Expansion of oil exports" episode: December 1999–October 2001

During the "devaluation" episode, growth was driven primarily by the following factors:

- Import substitution triggered primarily by massive ruble devaluation. Additional effects that contributed to the exclusion of imports from the market were decreases in the relative prices of production of natural monopolies (see table 11.2) and reductions in real wages. These effects favorably affected the price competitiveness of Russian manufacturing products.
- Increased investment by enterprises in working assets as well as the growth of gross fixed capital formation. Fixed capital investment was targeted to increase the capacity to produce a range of products.

The first stage of economic growth in 1999 was not supported by the expansion of final demand. Just the opposite occurred: both external and domestic (excluding investment) final demand stagnated (see table 11.1). The most serious decrease among demand components was that of private consumption,

TABLE 11.1 Basic Macroeconomic Indicators

Indicator	1991	1992	1993	1994	1995	1996	1997	1998	1999	2000	2001
GDP (% growth rate)	-5	-14.5	-8.7	-12.4	-4.1	-3.5	0.8	-4.6	5.4	9.0	5.1
Private consumption (% growth rate)	-6.1	-5.2	-1	-3.1	-2.7	-2.1	1.8	-5	-5.3	6.3	4.8
Government consumption (% growth rate)					-20.6	0	-2	0.1	0.9	2.3	3.4
Gross fixed capital formation (% growth rate)	-15	-40	-12	-24	-10	-18	-5	-6.7	5.3	17.4	8.7
Industrial production (% growth rate)	-8	-18	-14	-20.9	-3.3	-4	2	-5.2	11.0	11.9	4.9
Unemployment rate (% of economically active population)		4.8	5.6	7.4	8.5	9.6	10.8	11.9	12.4		8
Consumer prices (% growth rate)	160.4	2509	839.9	215.1	131.3	21.8	11	84.4	36.5	20.2	18.6
Producer prices (% growth rate)			987	235	180	25.6	7.5	23.2	67.3	31.6	10.7
Exchange rate (rubles per US$1, end of period)		0.415	1.247	3.55	4.64	5.56	5.96	20.65	24.6	28.2	30.4
Exchange rate (% growth rate)			200.5	184.7	30.7	19.8	7.2	246.5	19.1	14.6	7.8
Monetary base (% growth rate)		1179	645	178	115	26.7	25	27.9	54.1	69.4	
M2 aggregate (% growth rate)		696	407	192	127	34.2	29.9	20.8	57.2	62.4	40.1
Deficit of consolidated budget (% of GDP)			4.6	10.7	3.2	4.4	5.2	5.7	1.2	-5.3	-5.3
Exports (USD billions)				67.5	81.1	88.6	88.2	74.2	75.7	105.6	103.0
Exports (growth rate in %)				20	20	9.3	-0.4	-15.9	2.0	39.5	-2.5
Imports (USD billions)				50.6	60.9	68.8	73.7	59.1	39.5	44.9	53.4
Imports (% growth rate)				13	21	12.9	7	-19.8	-33.2	13.7	18.9
Balance of trade				16.9	20.2	19.8	14.5	15.1	36.2	60.7	49.6
Current account balance (USD billions)					7.9	12	3.3	1.6	27.5	48.2	39.2
Hard currency reserves (end of year, USD billions)				14.4	14.4	11.3	12.5	7.7	12.5	28.0	36.6

Source: Goskomstat data; data of Analytical Laboratory "VEDI"; Center for Macroeconomic Analysis and Short-Term Forecasts; Bureau of Economic Analysis; and Center of Development.

TABLE 11.2 Indices of Industrial Production

Industrial Sector	1994	1995	1996	1997	1998		1999		2000	2001
					Index of Industrial Production	Growth of Producer Prices (in % of Previous Year)	Index of Industrial Production	Growth of Producer Prices (in % to the Previous Year)		
Industry—total	79.1	96.7	96.0	102.0	94.8	23.0	108.1	67.3	111.9	104.9
Electricity sector	91.0	97.0	98.0	98.0	97.5	3.0	100.2	14.4	102.0	101.6
Fuel industry—total	90.0	99.2	99.0	100.3	97.5	0.8	102.4	135.0	105.1	106.1
Oil-extracting industry					99.0	−10.0	100.4	149.2		107.7
Oil-processing industry					92.6	12.4	102.5	242.3		102.7
Gas industry					100.8	10.5	104.1	22.1		100.4
Coal industry					95.0	6.1	108.8	32.2		105.4
Ferrous metals	83.0	110.0	98.0	101.0	91.9	11.0	114.4	89.0	116.2	99.8
Non-ferrous metals	91.0	103.0	96.0	106.0	95.0	76.0	108.5	116.0	111.0	104.9
Chemistry and petrochemistry	76.0	108.0	93.0	104.0	92.5	22.7	121.7	51.1	114.4	106.5
Machinery and metal working	69.0	91.0	95.0	104.0	92.5	29.0	115.9	50.0	115.5	107.2
Wood, wood processing, and pulp and paper industry	70.0	99.3	83.0	100.9	99.6	43.0	117.2	68.0	112.2	102.6
Building materials	73.0	92.0	83.0	96.0	94.2	13.0	107.7	37.0	108.6	105.5
Light industry	54.0	70.0	78.0	98.0	88.5	44.0	120.1	56.0	125.0	105.0
Food industry	83.0	92.0	96.0	99.2	98.1	53.0	107.6	63.0	108.8	108.4

Source: Goskomstat Data; and Center of Economic Conjuncture at the Government of Russian Federation.

which significantly contributed to the shrinking of imports.

The performance of different industrial sectors in 1999 was not necessarily closely correlated with price dynamics (see table 11.2). So, the greatest contribution to growth was machinery (46 percent), while price-leading export-oriented raw materials sectors (fuels, metallurgy, chemistry, pulp and paper, and wood processing) contributed 29 percent of industrial growth.

- In contrast with 1999, in 2000–2001 economic growth was triggered by a combination of factors associated with final demand expansion: a sharp increase in exports caused by a favorable state of international markets for Russian raw material exports, for example, oil.
- A huge rise in investment demand of enterprises backed by increased revenues from the first devaluation episode of the economic upsurge.
- A revival of private consumption spurred by the growth of real wages. The important fact is that because producer prices in 2000 grew a lot faster than consumer prices, the increase in real wages did not provoke growth in the marginal production costs of enterprises. In 2001, both consumer and producer price growth rates slowed down, indicating weak inflationary effects of real wage increases.

Growth rates in 2000–2001 were unevenly distributed in time. Accelerated growth was observed in the first half of the year, while beginning from September the potential of an upsurge was considerably reduced. Several shifts in relative prices constrained the augmentation of final demand:

- Increases of prices of intermediate inputs (fuels, transport) that started at the end of 1999 raised enterprise costs and dampened their propensity to invest.
- Steady growth of the real exchange rate that, according to some estimates, reached 15.3 percent for the year 2000.

3. Fundamental Characteristics of Economic Growth

3.1. Unsustainable Economic Growth

At present, the cycles of economic activity in Russia appear unsustainable. For all of 1999–2001, growth

accelerated as a rule at the beginning of the year, and stagnated in the second half of the year. Table 11.3 contains data on industrial intensity indices for 2000–2001 that, in general, reflect annual activity cycles.

In 1999, the growth potential of import substitution was practically exhausted by August. From August until the end of the year, average monthly growth rates of GDP fell to 0.3 percent as compared with 0.9 percent in the first half of the year. In the same time span, the average monthly growth rate of industrial production declined from 2.1 to 0.4 percent and the growth rate of gross fixed capital formation fell from 1.4 percent to (–1.2 percent).

The same story was observed in 2000. The growth slowdown in the second half of the year is explained by the impact of the above-mentioned shifts on relative prices (increases in the prices of primary inputs and the real exchange rate). Since September 2000 until the end of that year, the average monthly GDP growth rate equaled 0.2 percent as compared with 0.9 percent in the December 1999–August 2000 period, the average monthly growth rate of industrial production contracted from 1 percent to –0.3 percent, the growth of gross fixed capital formation fell from 2.8 percent to –1.9 percent, and the growth of exports declined from 1.8 to –1.9 percent.

In 2001, after moderate growth in the first three quarters (average monthly growth calculated on a quarterly basis varied from 0.6 to 0.8 percent), both GDP and industrial production stagnated in October (the GDP growth rate was 0.1 percent, and the industrial production growth rate was –0.8 percent).

3.2. Extreme Dependence on Foreign Markets for Raw Material Exports

The favorable state of international oil markets was the principal factor that pushed the Russian economy into a growth regime in 2000. In fact, Russia's dependence on exports (see table 11.4) is extremely high for a country that has experienced large-scale deindustrialization. As the bulk (more than 80 percent) of Russian exports consists of raw materials (primarily fuels and metals), the performance of the Russian economy is highly sensitive to foreign trade in raw materials.

Practically all sectors producing exportable raw materials depend on foreign trade, to an increasing extent since the collapse of the Soviet Union (see table 11.5). The economy's diminished size (with the

TABLE 11.3 Changes of Indices of Industrial Production Intensity[a]

Industry	2000			2001								
	October	November	December	January	February	March	April	May	June	July	August	September
Industry—total	0.0	−0.2	−0.1	0.3	0.6	0.5	0.2	0.1	0.3	0.7	1.4	2.3
Fuel industry—total	0.4	0.5	0.6	0.8	0.6	0.1	−0.2	−0.2	0.0	0.2	0.3	0.3
—Electricity sector	−0.1	0.2	0.9	1.2	0.5	−0.8	−1.6	−1.4	−0.7	−0.1	−0.2	−1.1
—Oil-extracting industry	0.5	0.3	0.3	0.4	0.5	0.7	0.9	1.0	1.1	1.0	0.8	0.6
—Oil-processing industry	0.9	1.1	1.2	1.2	0.9	0.2	−0.7	−1.3	−1.5	−1.0	0.0	1.5
—Gas industry	−0.4	−0.5	−0.2	0.2	0.4	0.3	0.1	−0.1	−0.4	−0.6	−0.8	−1.1
—Coal industry	0.5	0.6	0.3	−0.2	−0.4	0.0	1.2	2.2	2.6	2.3	1.5	0.5
Ferrous metals	−0.7	−1.2	−1.1	−0.6	0.0	0.5	0.9	1.0	0.7	0.3	−0.3	−0.5
Non-ferrous metals	0.5	0.0	−0.3	0.0	0.6	0.8	0.8	0.5	0.4	0.5	0.3	−0.6
Machinery	−1.3	−1.9	−1.2	0.1	0.7	0.2	−0.8	−0.9	0.0	1.8	4.5	8.4
Chemistry and petrochemistry	0.9	1.2	1.1	0.9	0.4	−0.1	−0.4	−0.2	0.1	0.3	0.5	1.0
Wood, wood processing, and pulp and paper industry	0.3	−0.6	−1.1	−1.0	−0.4	0.3	0.9	1.0	1.0	0.8	0.9	1.4
Building materials	−0.9	−1.1	−0.5	0.4	1.1	1.5	1.8	2.2	2.4	2.3	1.8	1.0
Food industry	0.8	0.4	0.0	0.4	1.3	1.8	1.4	0.8	0.5	1.0	2.0	3.1
Light industry	1.0	−0.1	−1.3	−2.2	−2.3	−1.0	1.2	2.8	3.3	2.7	2.1	2.7

Source: Center of Economic Conjuncture at the Government of Russian Federation (2001).

a. Industrial intensity indices represent composite growth rates of daily output volumes across industrial sectors. Sectoral intensity indices aggregate output changes across 127 most important commodity groups.

splitting off of former republics) increased the role of exports among the demand-side factors of economic growth. The openness of the Russian economy and its dependence on foreign markets rose overnight.

3.3. Income Concentration in Export-Oriented Raw Materials Sectors

One of the important symptoms of the Russian-style Dutch disease is an extremely unequal distribution of revenues across export-oriented and domestic market–oriented sectors. The lack of efficient mechanisms (either market or administrative) to ensure the reallocation of resources among sectors results in an unproductive overconcentration of revenues in export-oriented raw materials sectors. At the same time, domestic market–oriented manufacturing experiences shortages of working capital and problems with solvency that hamper innovation and the

investment activity of enterprises. The principal outcome is a tremendous gap in the finances of the export-oriented and the domestic market–oriented sectors of the economy (see table 11.6).

3.4. Stagnation of Government Consumption

Table 11.7 contains data on federal budget execution. Analyzing budget statistics, we find the following:

- The oil shock of 2000 triggered a drastic increase in the ratio of budget revenues to GDP. The major factor contributing to this growth was tax revenues.
- At the same time, the ratio of non-interest expenditures to GDP sharply decreased (as compared with the depressive stabilization period), provoking the decrease of budget expenditure ratios in general. Thus, in relative terms, the role of government consumption as a demand-side

TABLE 11.4 The Structure of GDP by Demand Aggregates (% of Spent GDP)

Demand Aggregate	2000[a]	2001[b]
Expenditures on final consumption, including the following:	63.4	65.2
Households	46.9	49.7
Government	14.4	14.3
Non-commercial organizations serving households	2.1	1.2
Gross investments, including the following:	17.2	22.1
Gross fixed capital formation	18.3	17.8
Increase in stocks	–1.0	4.3
Net exports	19.4	13.0
Exports	43.9	36.9
Imports	24.5	24.0
GDP	100	100

a. Goskomstat data.

b. Estimates of the Center of Development (2002).

economic growth factor becomes negligible, despite the significant expansion in government purchasing power.
• For the first time in modern Russian history, in 2000–2001 authorities executed the budget with a fairly large volume of excess revenues.
• Also unprecedented, the amount of Russian payments to the rest of the world (debt service) exceeded the scale of new foreign loans. In 2000–2001, the Russian government became a net creditor to the rest of the world.

In principle, under conditions of massive inflow of oil export revenues, the government has several policy options:

• Interventionism: the expansion of government demand to spur economic growth
• Maintenance of monetary equilibrium threatened by the huge inflow of petrodollars
• Repayment of foreign debt to mitigate the debt service load in the future

The policy priorities of the government became foreign debt servicing and monetary supply regulation, while demand interventions were abandoned.

The regulation of money supply was of special importance, given the large-scale inflow of petrodollars as well as the acute threat of the rapid real

appreciation of the ruble. The buying up of dollars led to the tremendous augmentation of the Central Bank's hard currency reserves (almost by four times; see table 11.1) at the expense of the fast growth of money supply (reserve money grew by 91 percent in 2000) that far outstripped increases in money demand (aggregate M2 grew by 60 percent that year; see table 11.1).

In this situation, the primary task of monetary policy was tying up excess liquidity. Two basic instruments were implemented:

• Increases in the financial balances of government institutions in their Central Bank accounts (by almost three times in 2000). The growth of government balances in the Central Bank equaled 25 percent of the total increase in reserve money that year.
• The maintenance of high rates of mandatory reserves at commercial bank deposits in the Central Bank.

Both of these instruments had a depressive impact on the real sector: excess government revenues did not transform into final demand increments, while banking credits to the real sector contracted.

3.5. Low Elasticity of Consumer Goods Production with Respect to Demand Signals and a High Probability of Consumer Import Recovery

Since the transition of the Russian economy, the share of household consumption in GDP is steadily declining. Meanwhile, the contribution of consumer demand to the growth in aggregate final demand remains significant.

Given the scale of consumer demand, the multiplier effect induced by the expansion of this final demand component is critical to the sustainability of growth. Meanwhile, as estimates show, the response of industrial output is disproportionate to the size of consumer demand increases (see table 11.8). The fundamental reason for such low elasticity of consumer goods output is associated with technological factors such as the depreciation of equipment, the obsoleteness of production assets and industrial organization models, and underinvestment in innovation.

In this situation, domestic production has a limited chance to sustain itself in the face of import competition. In 2000–2001, the real appreciation of

TABLE 11.5 Indicators of the Openness of the Russian Economy: Shares of Gross Output Across Sectors Induced by Separate Components of Final Demand (%)

| Sector | Soviet Union, 1990 | | Russia, 1999 |
	Deliveries to Former Republics	Exports to the Rest of the World	Exports
Energy and power	15.7	5.8	21.97
Oil and gas	27.8	16.0	42.0
Coal	15.1	12.7	29.9
Ferrous metals	26.2	8.4	38.4
Non-ferrous metals	28.3	12.6	38.5
Chemistry and oil refining	23.7	6.6	31.5
Machinery and metal working	15.4	6.5	25.0
Wood, wood processing, and pulp and paper industry	17.0	12.0	20.4
Building materials	7.3	1.5	6.2
Light industry	11.4	2.2	17.4
Food industry	2.6	1.5	6.3
Total industry	14.9	6.2	
Agriculture and forestry	3.0	1.6	5.5
Transportation and communication	18.9	7.9	26.3

Source: Own calculations based on 1990 (Soviet Union) and 1999 (Russia) input-output tables. Gross output induced by final demand components is calculated using the formula:

$$V = (I - A)^{-1} * F^6$$

the ruble as well as the growth in primary input costs contributed to a recovery in consumer imports. The growth of imports in this period (see table 11.1) was ensured mainly by the inflow of consumer goods from CIS countries. Unfortunately, the imports of high-tech equipment and investment goods crucial for the modernization of production are still insignificant.

3.6. The Shift toward a Wholly Monetary Economy

The gradual reduction of non-payments from interenterprise settlements (see table 11.9) is one of the most positive outcomes of the 1999–2001 growth period. The basic effects of monetization are as follows:

- Greater transparency of tax payments and the elimination of an environment conducive to tax evasion
- Availability of efficient tools to suppress cost inflation, and the elimination of conditions leading to the artificial overestimates of costs

(and, hence, increasing prices beyond reasonable levels)

Several factors are responsible for the progress in removing barter transactions and curtailing interenterprise arrears:

- Tougher demands on natural monopolies (RAO EES, and Gazprom) for payment for products and services in cash.
- Tougher demands by tax authorities on natural monopolies to pay their taxes on time and in full.
- Considerable increases in the money supply—associated with massive increases in hard currency reserves in 2000—met the growing demand for cash.

3.7. The Savings-Investment Gap

The savings-investment gap (or S-I gap: see table 11.10) is one of the fundamental structural imbalances of the Russian economy. As world experience

TABLE 11.6 Indicators of the Financial Solvency of Export-Oriented and Domestic Market–Oriented Industrial Sectors

Indicator	1999	2000
The Ratio of Profit-Loss Balances to the Value of Output across Industrial Sectors (in %)		
Total Industry	13.9	15.8
Export-Oriented Sectors, Including the Following:		
Oil industry	36.2	46.0
Oil refining	20.7	26.7
Gas industry	18.9	24.6
Ferrous metals	16.1	20.2
Non-ferrous metals	34.2	34.2
Chemistry and oil chemistry	13.0	12.6
Wood, pulp, and paper industry	15.7	11.2
Domestic Market–Oriented Industries, Including the Following:		
Energy and power	8.6	8.5
Machinery and metal working	8.9	8.9
Building materials	4.16	4.23
Light industry	4.9	4.4
Food industry	7.0	6.8
The share of sectoral net profits (balance profit—losses) in total value of industrial net profit (in %)	100	100
Export-oriented sectors	71.8	79.1
Domestic market–oriented industries	28.2	20.9
The volume of own circulating capital (days of production)	−20.4	6.7
Export-oriented sectors	−22.1	26.0
Domestic market–oriented industries	−19.0	−12.1
Credit indebtedness (months of production)	6.4	4.9
Export-oriented sectors	5.3	3.7
Domestic market–oriented industries	7.3	6.1

Source: The Center of Economic Conjuncture under the Government of Russian Federation and The Center for Macroeconomic Analysis and Short-Term Forecasts.

shows, an economy facing significant investment demand constraints that prevent the efficient absorption of saving resources has little chance of achieving sustainable growth. Table 11.10 shows that the S-I gap has been a structural obstacle to growth for a fairly long time. However, under the new economic regime of the last decade, the causal determination of the gap differs significantly.

The liberalization regime (especially in 1992) involved a strong inflation-driven inertia from the cost side, combined with relatively weak effects of demand-side shocks. On the one hand, in almost all industries, producers had sufficient market power to compensate for higher costs by higher prices (markup rates—measured as ratios of prices to marginal costs—strongly exceeded unity). On the other hand, market power has not been translated into productivity increases. At the macro level, the outcome of these factors was a forced savings effect that induced an extra-large S-I gap as well as massive leakages of resources from the domestic real sector.

Under the depressive stabilization regime, the forced savings effect was exhausted; savings and investment ratios stabilized while the magnitude of the gap was determined by investment demand constraints and investable resource leakages. The fall in

TABLE 11.7 Federal Budget Statistics (% of GDP)

Indicator	1997	1998	1999	2000	2001
Total revenues	13.6	12.1	13.5	16.2	17.0
Tax revenues	10.4	9.4	11.1	14.0	15.9
Total expenditures	20.6	17.6	14.6	13.7	15.3
Non-interest expenditures	14.7	11.1	9.8	9.7	12.1
Interest expenditures, including the following:	4.7	5.5	3.6	2.7	3.0
Servicing of internal debt	3.8	4.0	1.6	0.9	0.6
Servicing of external debt	0.9	1.5	2.0	1.8	2.4
Expenditures of target budget funds	1.2	1.0	1.2	1.3	0.2
Deficit (surplus − [−])	7.0	5.5	1.2	−2.5	−1.7
Internal financing	4.6	1.0	1.2	0.1	0.8
External financing, including the following:	2.0	3.4	1.0	−1.7	−2.2
New loans	2.5	5.3	4.1	0.4	0.3
Debt repayment	−0.4	−2.0	−3.0	−2.1	−2.5
Emission and other sources	0.4	1.1	−1.1	−0.9	−0.3

Source: Russian Ministry of Finance, Goskomstat data; and 2001 data are estimates of Center of Development.

the savings ratio in the crisis year of 1998 was provoked by a tremendous decrease of revenues in both the household and enterprise sectors.

Economic growth in 1999–2001 led to a radical upswing in the savings ratio. The main factor behind this structural shift was the redistribution of incomes from households in favour of enterprises that caused a serious decline in the share of final consumption in GDP (see table 11.8). The growth in investment (see table 11.1) couldn't exhaust large-scale hard currency inflows that—given demand constraints—transformed into savings.

There are two groups of reasons explaining the misuse of excess savings:

- Factors associated with the poor investment environment in Russia as well as the uncertain prospect of the Russian high-tech sector's integration into the world economy.
- The lack of efficient resource reallocation mechanisms in favor of investments: the Russian banking system suffered heavily from the financial crisis of 1998 and during the following two years was in the process of rehabilitation (see table 11.11). Despite the observed increase in banking assets in 2000 (at the end of the year, banking assets exceeded the pre-crisis level by 10 percent), the contribution of the Russian

banking system to economic growth in 1999–2001 was negligible. In fact, just the opposite occurred: economic growth and the upsurge of export revenues helped the banking system to survive.

The growth in exporters' revenues reduced their demand for banking credits. As a result, during the first three quarters of 2000, credit arrears to the banks of export-oriented industries decreased considerably: the oil industry cut its arrears by 8 percent, the refining industry by 18 percent, and the chemistry and ferrous metals industry by 7 percent.

Excess savings generated by the extra revenues of raw materials exporters provoked massive leakages of resources from the domestic real sector. These leakages were primarily absorbed by capital flight (very often in the form of illegal capital transactions).

3.8. Capital Flight

There are no precise statistics of capital flight. Based on balance of payments data, a rough estimate can be made by taking the following aggregates into account:

- Net errors and omissions
- Trade credits and advanced payments to foreign partners

TABLE 11.8 Household Consumption as a Demand-Side Factor of Economic Growth

The Share of Final Consumption Components in GDP (in %)	1997	1998	1999	2000
Total final consumption	76.3	76.6	69.3	63.8
Households	51.1	54.5	52.4	47.3
Government	21.8	18.8	14.6	14.5
Non-commercial organizations serving households	3.5	3.3	2.3	2.1
Contribution of households' consumption of goods to the growth of total final demand (%)[a]				24.7
The contribution of industrial sectors producing consumer goods[b] to the growth of GDP (%)[a]				7.2
Structure of imports across commodity groups (in %)				100
Consumer goods				52.6
Investment goods				22.5
Other goods				24.9

Source: Goskomstat data except indicators marked by "a."

a. Estimates of the Center for Macroeconomic Analysis and Short-Term Forecasts.

b. Car construction, light, and food industry.

- Increases in export hard currency arrears and ruble earnings from exports not transferred promptly to the country
- Increases in arrears for advanced payments on imports not cleared by commodity transactions to the country

The sum of these aggregates gives the upper-level estimate of capital flight; the aggregate "net errors and omissions" alone provide the lower-level estimate.

It can be seen from table 11.12 that the scale of capital flight was stable during the second half of the 1990s. It varied (if the upper-level estimate is applied) in the range of US$25–28 billion per year, or over 30 percent of export volume.

The financial crisis of 1998 did not lead to the upsurge of capital flight. However, the sources of its

TABLE 11.9 Transition toward a Monetary Economy

Indicator	1998	1999	2000	2001
The share of barter deals in sales across industry, end of the period (in %)	49	36	19	15
Ratio of ruble assets of non-financial enterprises to GDP, end of the period (in %)	3.0	3.9	4.7	
Real increase of ruble assets held by non-financial enterprises, for the period (in %)	−35.6	44.4	48.6	

Source: Russian Economic Barometer poll data; 2001 data from Center for Macroeconomic Analysis and Short-Term Forecasts.

counterbalancing changed substantially. Before the crisis, capital flight was balanced to a large extent by private portfolio imports and increases in government debt. Currently, the only source is the positive current account balance.

Data for the first two quarters of the last two years may be interpreted as evidence of some decline in the volume of capital flight. However, such a conclusion should be drawn very carefully, taking into account the fact that the bulk of exposed capital outflows occurs in the last quarters of the year (see table 11.12).

Large-scale resource leakages in the form of capital flight provide cheap financing for the world economy. In fact, Russia uses the favorable situation in foreign raw material markets to transfer excess revenues as credits to the rest of the world. It is clear that such dissipation is not a sound basis for sustainable economic growth.

4. Decomposition of the Sources of Effective Demand

The decomposition of effective demand helps to systematize the driving forces and basic characteristics of Russian economic development within the last decade.

In the following decomposition exercises, we employ methodology proposed by Lance Taylor. For analytical purposes, it would be useful to disaggregate the multiplier effects of demand injections by distinguishing real multiplier effects and effects associated with dynamic shifts in the system of relative

TABLE 11.10 Trends in Russian Savings: Investment Balance

Year	Gross Savings Ratio (% of GDP)	Gross Fixed Capital Formation Ratio (% of GDP)	S-I Gap (% of GDP)
1988	31.3	24.7	6.6
1989	32.7	23.8	8.9
1990	29.7	22.4	7.3
1992	59.5	14.0	45.5
1993	26.5	15.8	10.7
1994	28.2	17.8	10.4
1995	22.2	16.8	5.4
1996	22.3	17.1	5.2
1997	22.1	15.8	6.3
1998	19.8	16.2	3.6
1999	25.5	15.9	9.6
2000	35.3	18.1	17.2
2001	33.2	22.1	11.1

Sources: Goskomstat data; own calculations based on Social Accounting Matrices (SAMs) integrated by the Center for Macroeconomic Analysis and Short-Term Forecasts (Belousov 1996); 1998 and 2001 data are estimates of the Center for Macroeconomic Analysis and Short-Term Forecasts; and 1999–2000 data are estimates of the Bureau for Economic Analysis.

prices. To get this result, we should perform decompositions in both constant and current prices.

Unfortunately, Russian statistics do not allow us to perform the exercise for constant prices without a loss of credibility. The main reasons are as follows:

- The structure of income sources of GDP is given only in current prices. That means that T and Y_p, and thus S_p parameters, cannot be calculated in comparable prices.
- Statistics on E and I are given only in current prices.

- Constant price growth rates of demand components of GDP (excluding exports) and net exports are available. However, all demand components have distinct deflators. One can reconstruct export and import data in comparable prices using the net export deflator. However, it is very problematic to determine the proper deflator for taxes and private sector incomes.

Bearing this situation in mind, we have performed decomposition exercises only in current prices. The results are presented in table 11.13. Because of the divergence of data sources, decomposition results may sometimes differ from the data in other tables. However, in terms of macroeconomic tendencies, one can reach some common conclusions.

The analysis of decomposition data highlights the following demand injections and leakages interrelations:

1. The impact and interaction of different multipliers fairly accurately reflects the transition of the Russian economy from one economic development regime to another.
2. During liberalization (1993 and 1994 in table 11.13), exports and government spending multipliers were strongly expansionary while the effect of investment injections was contractionary. The economy has been driven into a forced savings regime. The ratio of demand leakages (savings, taxes, and imports) remains high.
3. Under depressive stabilization, the impact direction of demand multipliers did not change. However, the scale of effects moderated. All injections/leakages ratios moved toward unity (especially in 1997), while demand leakages to output ratio decreased considerably.

TABLE 11.11 Main Aggregates of the Banking System (% of GDP)

Indicator (End of the Period)	1997	1998	1999	2000	2001
Assets	30.3	39.0	34.9	34.1	34.2
Credits to the real sector	9.6	12.5	11.3	11.3	12.8
Investments in securities	8.4	9.3	6.7	6.5	4.2
Liquidity	4.1	6.4	7.7	7.1	8.8
Capital	5.6	4.8	5.0	5.0	5.0
Deposits of enterprises	5.8	9.4	9.9	10.5	10.2
Deposits of individuals	6.8	7.8	6.6	6.6	6.9
Credits of non-residents	3.1	5.0	2.4	1.2	

Source: Data of the Central Bank; and 2001 data are estimates of the Center for Macroeconomic Analysis and Short-Term Forecasts.

TABLE 11.12 Estimates of Capital Flight from Russia (USD Billions)

Time Period	Trade Credits and Advanced Payments to Foreigners	Increase in Arrears of Non-transferred Export Earnings and Non-cleared Import Advanced Payments	Net Errors and Omissions	Upper-Level Estimate of Capital Flight	Net Inflow of Direct and Portfolio Foreign Investments	Current Account Balance	Export Volume (Estimate of the Central Bank of Russia)	Ratio of Capital Flight to the Exports (in %)
1996	**−9.39**	**−9.77**	**−9.78**	**−28.94**	**11.41**	**12.18**	**90.6**	**31.9**
1 quarter	−1.63	−1.94	−2.48	−6.04	1.36	3.88		
2 quarter	−1.72	−1.83	−3.24	−6.78	2.00	1.76		
3 quarter	−1.70	−2.85	−1.91	−6.46	0.68	2.20		
4 quarter	−4.35	−3.16	−2.16	−9.67	7.37	4.35		
1997	**−6.79**	**−11.46**	**−8.95**	**−27.19**	**52.23**	**3.98**	**89.0**	**30.6**
1 quarter	−0.86	−2.82	−2.26	−5.94	6.41	4.17		
2 quarter	−0.89	−3.03	−1.97	−5.88	10.12	0.09		
3 quarter	−1.65	−2.78	−1.49	−5.92	4.25	−0.68		
4 quarter	−3.39	−2.84	−3.23	−9.46	31.45*	0.41		
1998	**−6.82**	**−8.66**	**−9.47**	**−24.95**	**11.21**	**2.3**	**74.8**	**33.3**
1 quarter	−0.09	−3.40	−2.39	−5.87	4.28	−1.57		
2 quarter	−1.16	−1.65	−2.91	−5.72	5.36	−3.67		
3 quarter	−1.19	−1.51	−3.58	−6.27	0.18	0.90		
4 quarter	−4.39	−2.11	−0.59	−7.09	1.39	6.64		
1999 (January–September)	**−2.02**	**−4.15**	**−6.41**	**−12.58**	**1.49**	**14.58**	**50.6**	**24.9**
1 quarter	−1.82	−1.01	−1.55	−4.38	0.27	5.37		
2 quarter	1.84	−2.07	−1.96	−2.19	0.80	3.46		
3 quarter	−2.04	−1.07	−2.90	−6.01	0.41	5.75		
2000 (January–June)	**−0.9**	**−2.9**	**−2.8**	**−6.6**		**22.8**	**49.4**	**13.3**
2001 (January–June)	**0.3**	**−2.9**	**−3.1**	**−5.7**		**21.2**	**51.6**	**11.0**

Source: Data of the Central Bank of Russia; and estimates and calculations of Bureau for Economic Analysis.

TABLE 11.13 Decomposition of Sources of Effective Demand[a]

Year	(I/S)	(G/T)	(E/M)	$(s+t+m)$	(s)	Ratio of Taxes Leakages to the Output (t)	Ratio of Imports Leakages to the Output (m)
1993	0.703	1.038	1.253	0.656	0.294	0.128	0.234
1994	0.649	1.607	1.197	0.620	0.319	0.113	0.188
1995	0.798	1.182	1.142	0.583	0.256	0.132	0.195
1996	0.805	1.147	1.202	0.572	0.254	0.147	
1997	0.863	1.143	1.142	0.548	0.218		
1998	0.702	0.985	1.305	0.531	0.187		
1999	0.572	0.797	1.632	0.568	0.211		
2000	0.555	0.767	1.835	0.758	0.318		
2001	0.655	0.927	1.541	0.588	0.271		
							0.171
						0.157	
							0.173
						0.154	0.190
						0.145	0.212
						0.191	0.249
						0.124	0.193

Source: National Accounts of Russia (2001).

a. Where I/S: effect of investment injections; G/T: effect of government spending injections; E/M: effect of exports injections; $(s+t+m)$: ratio of savings leakages to the output; and s: ratio of savings, taxes, and imports leakages to the output.

4. The transition to a growth regime dramatically modified the impact of demand multipliers. The government spending effect became contractionary (especially so in 1999–2000), as did the investment effect. The situation was balanced by an extraexpansionary trade multiplier. Simultaneously, the ratio of demand leakages to output increased significantly (especially in 1999–2000) owing, first of all, to the rise of savings and import ratios.

5. Short- and Medium-Run Prospects

To sum up factors that will determine Russian economic development in the short and medium run, we apply the technique of SWOT analysis[1] (see table 11.14).

The SWOT analysis reveals that serious fragility is emerging in Russia's economic system:

1. Economic growth heavily depends on factors and variables that are either completely or partially out of the control of the economic authorities (the state of foreign markets, inconclusive talks with the Paris Club countries on Russian debt restructuring, etc.).
2. The absorption of huge excess savings both of raw material exporters and of the government

requires radical changes in the Russian market investment climate. That is a difficult task, even in the medium run. The removal of investment demand constraints must meet the following targets:

- Rapid and steady growth in gross fixed capital formation
- Radical modernization of Russian production and technology systems, and the support of innovation activity
- Efficient integration into the world economy by using competitive advantages embedded in high technologies
- Reinforcement of economic security by ensuring modernization and the sufficient development of basic system-supporting industries, such as the energy and power sector

3. There are some contradictions in the short- and medium-term policy targets. By upholding a competitive real exchange rate in the short run, authorities restrain the imports of equipment and other investment goods that are crucial for production system modernization in the medium run.

By evaluating the macroeconomic effects of declining oil prices, we can gauge the sensitivity of current economic growth to external factors. According to different estimates, a decrease in world market oil prices by $1 per barrel will induce different outcomes (see table 11.15).

The direct effects associated with a decline in oil prices (estimates of the Center of Development) will be strengthened by a fall in oil refinery product prices as well as natural gas prices, another principal Russian export commodity (with the time lag of approximately six months). The sensitivity of Russian economic performance to the state of the world oil market calls the sustainability of current economic growth in Russia into question.

The basic problem underlying Russia's economic prospects is the efficient absorption of huge excess savings and revenues. If these resources are invested in

the modernization of manufacturing production systems and the renewal of the public sector, economic growth will be able to overcome the current fragility. However, if all investments remain in export-oriented raw materials sectors and Russia continues to lend to the rest of the world through capital flight, economic recovery shall, once again, be delayed.

6. Social Adjustment: Incomes and Income Inequality

In an unprecedented short period of time, Russia was transformed from a highly egalitarian republic into a country with a highly uneven income distribution. The shocking deterioration in income distribution

TABLE 11.14 Swot Analysis of Economic Growth Prospects

Strengths	Weaknesses
• Resource potential: huge excess savings that can and should be transformed into investments	• Strong dependence of the economy on the situation in world markets for principal raw material exports
• Still existing innovation potential: opportunity to supply competitive goods to match investment demand and to access foreign markets	• Overaccumulation of resources in export-oriented sectors and a lack of efficient reallocation mechanisms to transform them into investments
• Reduction of barter and money substitutes; transition toward a wholly monetized economy	• A weak banking system
• Shifts in Russian industrial organization: appearance of competitive vertically integrated corporations with business activity in domestic and foreign markets	• Primarily raw materials composition of Russian exports • Investment demand constraints prevent the sustainable expansion of gross fixed capital formation and the radical modernization of the production and technological basis of the economy
• Administrative resources: signs of sensible and responsible economic policy, significant increase in tax revenues	• A low elasticity of consumer goods production that currently cannot efficiently compete with imports • A low contribution of government consumption demand to economic growth • Large-scale capital flight
Opportunities	*Threats*
• Favorable situation in world raw materials markets (prices for "Urals" crude oil are not lower than $22 per barrel)	• Unfavorable situation in world raw materials markets (prices for "Urals" crude are not higher than $18 per barrel)
• Restructuring of Russian foreign debt that helps mitigate the pressure of debt service in 2003 (peak debt servicing period: Russia must pay off up to $20 billion)	• Russia fails to restructure its foreign debt and makes repayments according to principal schedule
• Radical contraction in capital flight	• Russia fails to radically contract capital flight
• Absorption of excess savings and strong increases in gross fixed capital formation	• S-I gap does not improve; investment demand stagnates; investments in modernizing production as well as innovation activity are constrained
• Efficient tying up of money supply that curbs inflation and real appreciation of the ruble	• Prices for products and services of natural monopolies (especially in the energy and power sector) increase to compensate for the underinvestment in these sectors
• Revival of Russian banking system, growth of credits to the real sector	• Diminishing revenues aggravate the balancing of the budget; the inflation rate strongly increases • Strong real ruble appreciation impairs the competitiveness of Russian exports and contributes to imports growth

TABLE 11.15 Effects of Oil Price Changes

	Estimates of the Center for Macroeconomic Analysis and Short-Term Forecasts	Estimates of the Center of Development (Direct Effects)	Own Calculations
Fall of GDP growth rates (by percentage points)	0.4–0.6		0.35–0.5
Fall of investment growth rates (by percentage points)	0.7–0.9		0.6–0.7
Contraction of exports (in USD billions)	2.0–2.1	1	1.3–1.5
Decrease of federal budget revenues (in USD billions)	0.8–0.9	0.6–0.7	

took place parallel to a rapid fall in output and the absolute level of income—powerful redistributive processes were at work. The overall redistribution was launched at the beginning of market transition and multiplied by the internal but especially by the external liberalization of the national economy.

In this section, we trace the dynamics of the absolute level of income and income inequality in relation to the general course of economic developments in 1992–2001, specifically in relation to economic policies followed by the changing government teams.

We use two main data sources: first, national statistics regularly published by official statistical services and, second, field household studies regularly conducted by Russian and Western research institutions since 1992. There are wide disagreements between the two data sets. However, household surveys contain rich information that usefully supplement official statistics.

6.1. Dynamics of Income Level

The evolution of the income level in the 1990s can be subdivided into five short episodes:

1. The initial liberalization shock of January 1992
2. 1993–1994: overall inflationary redistribution amidst internal liberalization and privatization
3. 1995–1996: bursting of the first financial bubble combined with the start of external liberalization
4. 1997–August 1998: a national financial catastrophe caused by all-out external liberalization
5. 1999–2000: the gradual restoration of incomes to pre–August 1998 levels fueled by the windfall of petrodollars

Given the extremely chaotic economic, social, and institutional settings of the 1990s, the proposed periodization is very schematic. Some periods overlap. Nonetheless, it allows us to link changes in the income level with crucial shifts in economic policies and the macro environment.

In January 1992, after the initial dosage of shock therapy, real personal disposable income collapsed. About 70 percent of personal disposable income fell below the ex-Soviet "minimal consumption basket." Only a very small group, namely, former Soviet *nomenklatura* and criminal groups, gained (and tremendously so) from the dismantling of the remnants of centralized control and partial price liberalization. Average wages in 1992 dropped by 33 percent and pensions fell by 48 percent (see table 11.16). The average pension shrunk to below the official subsistence level.

During the first round of overall inflationary redistribution in 1992–1994 after the initial shock, household income on average remained stable (see table 11.17, and table 11.20 in appendix 1 at the end of this chapter). Real wages fell by 8 percent, while average pensions increased by 27 percent (calculated from table 11.16). In general, these tendencies are supported by household income data, summarized in table 11.17. The latter gives a more disaggregate picture of the losses/gains of various types of income. New sources of wage income from private and mixed sectors largely compensated for the income loss in the state sector. Besides, the loss of income from state sector employment was compensated for by the spread of cash-generating informal activities and increasing income from the non-cash self-subsistence sector.

The largest income losses are associated with the internal and external liberalization of the national

TABLE 11.16 Dynamics of Various Types of Income, 1990–2000

	1990	1991	1992	1993	1994	1995	1996	1997	1998	1999	2000
Real disposable income (1995 = 100)						100	101	108	91	78	88
Real wage due[a] (1991 = 100)	89.3	100	67.0	67.3	61.9	44.6	47.5	49.7	43.0	33.5	40.5
Real pension due[a] (1991 = 100)			52.2	68.4	66.3	53.7	58.6	55.6	52.8	32.0	41.0
Average wage due as % of official subsistence level						179	213	231	231	146	184
Average pension due as % of official subsistence level						71	82	80	81	43	57
Average monthly wage due, US$						103	153	164	110	64	79
Average monthly pension due, US$						41	59	57	40	18	25

Sources: Calculated from Institute of Socio-economic Problems of Population (1998, 187); UNDP (2000), 174; and "Russian Economic Trends" (2001–2002).

a. On a monthly basis.

economy. In 1995 real wages dropped by 28 percent and pensions by 19 percent. The respective declines in 1999 were 22 and 39 percent. In sum, for the 1995–1999 period, average wages shrunk by 46 percent and average pensions by 52 percent. At the end of this period, both wages and pensions were only one-third of their pre-transition levels. In 1999 the average wage was only 46 percent above the official subsistence level, while the average pension was 57 percent below that level.

The negative shock caused by external liberalization strongly affected all types of wage and salary earners without exception. In 1997–1998, household income from private sector employment fell by 36 percent, and by 44 percent in the mixed sector. The share of non-cash income from the self-subsistence sector increased to 15.2 percent of total household income. In 1998 cash and non-cash income from home production and informal activities provided 23.7 percent of cumulative household income.

The restoration of economic growth—driven by petrodollars—in 1999 did not immediately translate into income increases. Real personal income per capita that year fell by 14 percent. Real wages and average pensions decreased by 22 and 39 percent respectively. The ratios of wages and pensions to the official subsistence level declined to their lowest levels during the transition period.

Incomes recovered in 2000 mostly because of the continued inflow of petrodollars. Real wages recovered to their pre–August 1998 level by the autumn of 2001, and pensions recovered by the spring of 2002.

However, the average wage was still 46 percent and the average pension 42 percent short of their pre-transition levels. In the middle of 2002, both wages and salaries (in dollar terms) were still below their pre-transition levels. The total average household income in October 2001 was 17 percent less than that in September 1992 and only 7 percent above that in October 1996.

6.2. Dynamics of Inequality and Poverty

The dynamics of inequality and poverty generally corresponded with changes in income levels. In 1991–1994, the inequality in income distribution sharply increased, reversing the former socialist agenda toward the formation of an egalitarian income structure. By 1996, the official Gini coefficient rose to 0.409 from less than 0.3 before the transition period (see table 11.18).

The adjusted Gini coefficient, which better captures the income of the poorest and richest income earners, increased to above 0.45 since 1994. The ratio of the income of the richest decile of the population to the poorest decile grew by more than thirteenfold. Some authors (Aivazian 1997) claim that actual inequality in income distribution was even higher. Sophisticated econometric techniques show that in 1996, the Gini coefficient reached 0.531 and the ratio of the income of the richest 10 percent to the poorest 10 percent exceeded twenty-two-fold.

Judging from the official Gini, income distribution in 1996–1998 remained relatively stable. This is

TABLE 11.17 Dynamics of Household Income in 1992–2001 (%)

	Overall Inflationary Redistribution after Gaidar's Shock 1992–1994		Blow Up of First Financial Bubble and Start of External Liberalization, 1995–1996		Climax of External Liberalization, Blowup of State Short-Term Debt Bubble, 1997–1998		Partial Internal and External Deliberalization and Oil Bonanza Years, 1999–2001	
	Loss/Gain of Income	Income Level 1992 = 100	Loss/Gain of Income	Income Level 1992 = 100	Loss/Gain of Income	Income Level 1992 = 100	Loss/Gain of Income	Income Level 1992 = 100
Wage and salary								
Total	–11	89	–19	72	–35	47	68	79
State sector	–39	61	–25	46	–30	32	52	48
Private sector	300	400	–5	382	–36	243	104	496
Mixed sector	58	158	–18	130	–44	72	62	116
State transfers[a]	19	119	–29	84	–14	72	39	100
Cash income from home production and informal sector	16	116	–17	97	–19	79	79	141
Non-cash income from home production and informal sector	38	138	–9	125	8	135	70	94
Family and charity transfers	–31	69	–13	60	–38	37	27	47
Other	–	–	–58	–	–28	–	3	65
Total cash income[b]	–4	96	–23	74	–30	52	58	82
Total income	–1	99	–22	77	–26	57	44	83

Sources: Calculated from table 11.20 (appendix).

a. State transfers include pensions (about 90% of total transfers), stipends, unemployment benefits, and various state allowances.

b. Excludes non-cash income from home production and informal sector. 1992 excludes other income.

TABLE 11.18 Income Inequality and Poverty, 1990–2001[a]

	1990	1991	1992	1993	1994	1995	1996	1996[b]	1997	1998	1999	2000	2001 IQ
Share of quintile in total money income													
Lowest 20%	9.8	11.9	6.0	5.8	5.3	5.5	6.2	4.7	6.0	6.1	6.1	6.1	—
Second 20%	14.9	15.8	11.6	11.1	10.2	10.2	10.7	6.6	10.2	10.4	10.5	10.6	
Third 20%	18.8	18.8	17.6	16.7	15.2	15.0	15.2	11.7	14.8	14.8	14.8	14.9	
Fourth 20%	23.8	22.8	26.5	24.8	23.0	22.4	21.5	16.9	21.6	21.1	20.8	21.2	
Fifth 20%	32.7	30.7	38.3	41.6	46.3	46.9	46.4	62.1	47.4	47.6	47.8	47.2	
Gini coefficient	0.23	0.260	0.289	0.398	0.409	0.381	0.375	0.556	0.381	0.398	0.399	0.394	
Adjusted Gini		0.341	0.370	0.439	0.465	0.450	0.481		0.470				
Income of the richest 10% to the poorest 10%	—	4.5	8.0	11.2	15.1	13.5	13.0	22.8	13.5	13.8	14.0	13.7	
Population with income below the minimal subsistence level, as % of total population										24.6	39.1	33.7	29.8
nationwide data		11.7	33.5	31.5	22.4	26.2	21.4		21.2	39.0	—	28.8	
household surveys	—	—	11.1	13.1	17.2	29.5	36.3		—				
Extreme poverty (household surveys)	—	—	3.0	5.6	6.9	11.5	20.0		—	16.6	—	9.0	—

Sources: UNDP (2000), 175; Mroz, Henderson, and Popkin (2001); and Vorobyov and Zhukov (2001).

a. Data in the table are not fully consistent. Since 1994, the Russian State Statistical Committee estimates personal income on the basis of expenditures, while previously income was estimated on the basis of budgetary statistics. The methodology of minimal subsistence level calculation was changed twice—in November 1992 and in the fist quarter of 2000. The first revision adjusted former Soviet "minimal consumption basket" heavily downward. The second revision adjusted Russian "minimal subsistence level" 15–20% upward.

b. Data reconstructed by S. Aivazian (1997).

TABLE 11.19 Inequality and Poverty Before and After the Collapse of August 1998

Inequality	1996				1998			
	Russia	Moscow and St. Petersburg	Other Cities	Rural Areas	Russia	Moscow and St. Petersburg	Other Cities	Rural Areas
Gini index	0.404	0.367	0.393	0.420	0.399	0.256	0.401	0.397 48.8
Poverty[a]	32.6	14.7	28.4	44.1	43.3	47.4	39.6	48.8
Extreme poverty[b]	8.3	0.0	5.9	14.5	12.8	10.3	12.3	14.8

Source: *Review of Russian Economy* (1999), 28–29.

a. Share of population with income below the official poverty line.

b. Share of population with income less than one-quarter of the official poverty line.

also confirmed by the behavior of poverty indicators.[2] However, the financial crash of August 1998 reversed the tendency toward increasing income inequality. Since 1999, the official Gini coefficient has stabilized at about 0.39.

Disaggregated data on household income explain the underlying mechanism at work. After the crash, inequality declined in conjunction with a surge in the number of the poor (the population with income below that of the official subsistence level; see table 11.19).[3] The situation in already impoverished rural areas did not change significantly. The new poor are mostly concentrated in urban settlements and especially in the largest and most (relatively) prosperous cities.

In Moscow and St. Petersburg, the Gini coefficient decreased from 0.367 to 0.256, while poverty jumped from 14.7 to 47.4 percent of the total population. Before the crash, the two capital cities did not experience extreme poverty; after the crisis, the number of the severely poor rose to 10.3 percent of the population. Generally, the decrease in inequality resulted from a massive spread in poverty.

The restoration of economic growth in 1999–2000 worked in favor of the highest and the lowest income groups to the relative disadvantage of the middle ones. Real income increased in every percentile of income distribution, with the largest relative income increases registered at the lower end of distribution. From November 1998 to October 2000 the lowest two deciles gained the most, while the relative income of the lowest five percentiles went up by above 1.5-fold. Income earners in the highest deciles also gained more compared with the middle deciles, but less compared with the lowest deciles (Mroz, Henderson, and Popkin 2001, 8).

In the three successive years of high economic growth, poverty improved only to its previous 1993 standard. In 2001, the share of the poor was 29.8 percent compared with 33.7 percent in 2000 and 39.1 percent in 1999.

6.3. Emergence of a Bipolar Income and Social Structure

A general tendency toward sharp income polarization emerges from the five short-term episodes described above. Schematically, the story is the following: immediately after the start of market transition, a shaky bipolar income distribution with a large buffer zone between the two poles has crystallized. About 40 percent of the bottom strata fell into the category of poor, while 10 percent of the highest income earners formed the pole of relative richness. The third and the fourth quintiles, combined with the lowest 10 percent from the fifth quintile, comprised a buffer zone between the two poles.

Through some intermediate stages, by the middle of the 1990s, the large part of the third quintile migrated from the buffer zone to the poverty pole. In turn, the buffer zone received migrants from the rich pole. Since then, we witnessed a progressive shrinkage of the buffer and the rich zone as well as a swallowing of the poor zone. The process was temporarily interrupted in late 1999–2000 owing to the large inflow of petrodollars.

Given the highly probable drop in world oil prices and the anticipated liberalization of communal, education, and health services, it is easy to predict the further compressing of the buffer zone because of the massive migration of income earners toward the poor pole. In the short run, official indicators of income distribution may improve for two reasons. First, the highest income earners have developed a sophisticated technique to avoid reporting (hard currency) income. Second, the government has recently tried to narrow income gaps between and within the lowest quintiles. In fact, the official Gini improved in both 2000 and 2001. However, this insignificant improvement is just a statistical reflection of the shrinkage of the middle-income strata or an increase in downward mobility. As only a minor part of Russia's population cannot afford a minimal food basket (Ovcharova, Turuntsev, and Korchagina 1998, 4–5), Russian poverty differs considerably from poverty in populous Asian countries and in the least developed African countries. The most striking feature of Russian poverty is a large number of people with special and/or high education among the poor.

The emergence of a bipolar social structure with a diminishing middle class reflects a specific globalization of the Russian economy. Economic growth and (more generally) the social structure in contemporary Russia depend on natural resource rents. The bulk of natural resources were privatized during the 1990s with massive involvement of foreign and quasi-foreign (off-shore) capital. Value-added and income-generating sectors are owned by the very few.

In 1999–2002, the authorities succeeded in collecting more tax revenues from the natural resource sector. Through various channels, these revenues trickled down to the bottom income strata, making income distribution look more equal. At the same time, owing to relatively high world energy prices, increased taxation of the export sector has only marginally affected the profits of private owners. Only profits above some "normal" level were appropriated by the state and redistributed economy-wide. The "normal" or basic profits of exporters remained intact. With a possible fall in world energy prices, total export profits will fall to a "normal" level and, in order to ensure the redistribution of natural resource rents across the economy, authorities will have to increase pressure upon the most powerful social groups. Otherwise income inequality, which is presently softened by the large inflow of export earnings from abroad, is bound to deteriorate rapidly. More generally, the sharp income polarization mirrors the very uneven distribution of assets (and property structure) and is bound to remain a long-term structural problem.

Appendix 1

TABLE 11.20 Breakdown of Household Income (in June 1992 Rubles)

	September/ 1992	November/ 1993	December/ 1994	October/ 1995	October/ 1996	November/ 1998	October/ 2000
Wages and salaries							
Total	4,341	3,480	3,875	3,104	3,145	2,052	2,688
State sector	3,645	2,162	2,218	1,718	1,663	1,159	1,503
Private sector	230	364	921	833	878	558	723
Mixed sector	466	954	736	553	604	335	462
State transfers[a]	1,207	1,482	1,430	1,085	1,018	870	978
Cash income from home production and informal sector	485	488	563	474	469	381	620
Non-cash income from home production and informal sector	503	897	694	481	628	681	543
Family and charity transfers	927	537	639	459	558	344	406
Other	341	278	511	352	215	154	234
Total cash income[b]	7,301	6,265	7,018	5,774	5,405	3,800	4,926
Total income	7,804	7,162	7,712	5,955	6,033	4,481	5,469

Source: Adapted from Mroz, Henderson, and Popkin (2001).

a. Pensions (about 90 percent of total transfers, stipends, unemployment benefits, and various state allowances).

b. Excludes non-cash income from home production and informal sector.

Notes

1. Strengths, weaknesses, opportunities, and threats analysis, a standard analytical tool for strategic management decision-making processes.

2. There is a very wide discrepancy of poverty measurements between the official nationwide statistics and household surveys. The latter demonstrate only a slight increase in poverty in 1996–1998 and a large decrease in the number of the poor in 2000. The discrepancy is explained by different poverty line measurements in the two sets of data.

3. Some authors using sophisticated econometrics show that the actual Gini coefficient in November 1998 stayed within the range of 0.55–0.57 and the fund ratio (the ratio of the income of the top decile to the income of the bottom decile) was 36–39 fold. Thus, given the earlier findings of one of the authors for 1996 (Aivazian 1997), the economic and social shocks of the second half of the 1990s had only a minor effect on income distribution.

References

Aivazian, S. 1997. Model for the mechanism generating distribution of Russian population by per capita income (in Russian). *Ekonomica i Matematicheskie Metody* 33 (4): 74–86.

Belousov, A. 1996. Russia's economy in the situation of depressive stabilization (in Russian). *Alternativy* (Moscow) (3): 43–56.

Institute of Socio-economic Problems of Population. 1998. "Russia (1997): Social and Demographic Situation" (in Russian). VII Annual Report. Moscow: Russian Academy of Sciences.

Mroz, T. A., L. Henderson, and B. M. Popkin. 2001. Monitoring economic conditions in the Russian Federation: The Russia longitudinal monitoring survey 1992–2000. Report submitted to the U.S. Agency for International Development, Carolina Population Center, University of North Carolina, March.

Ovcharova, L., E. Turuntsev, and I. Korchagina. 1998. Indicators of poverty in transitional Russia. Economic Education and Research Consortium Working Paper N98/04.

Russian-European Centre of Economic Policy. 1999. Review of Russian Economy (1999) (in Russian), vol. 3. Moscow: Russian-European Centre of Economic Policy.

———. (2001, November 15, and 2002, June 18). *Russian economic trends.* Moscow: Russian-European Center for Economic Policy.

UNDP. 2000. *Russia human development report 2000* (in Russian).

Vorobyov, A., and S. Zhukov. 2001. Russia: Globalization, structural shifts and inequality. In *External liberalization, economic performance and social policy*, edited by Lance Taylor, 251–82. New York: Oxford University Press.

12

External Liberalization and Economic Growth: The Case of Singapore

Mun-Heng Toh

Introduction

Neoclassical economists contend that the sluggish growth of developing economies can be attributed to poor resource allocation as a result of non-market prices and excessive state intervention. They argue that growth and increased efficiency lies in promoting competitive free markets, privatizing public enterprises, supporting exports and free international trade, liberalizing trade, and allowing market-clearing exchange rates. Concurrently, they argue for removing barriers to foreign investment, rewarding domestic savings, reducing government spending and monetary expansion, and removing regulations and price distortions in financial, resource, and commodity markets. Neoclassical economists generally favor comprehensive change to liberalization, an immediate "big bang" or "shock therapy" rather than a gradual adjustment in price decontrol, market creation and reduced government spending, monetary restriction, deregulation, legal changes, and privatization. Neoclassical policies

are reflected in the Washington Consensus, a term coined by Washington's Institute of International Economics' economist John Williamson.

Of course, not all economists agree with the neoclassical prescription for stability and economic growth. There are those who identify structural barriers in both a country's internal system and in the international environment that impede the development of the LDCs.[1] While few would dispute the advantage of a single country striving for competitive exchange rates to expand exports, a given LDC may face an export trap, in which its export growth faces competition from other LDCs under pressure to expand exports. Moreover, critics charge that the neoclassical model for liberalization and adjustment hurts disadvantaged portions of the population without providing safety nets for the poor (Taylor 1993).

The historical experiences of nineteenth- and twentieth-century Western countries and Japan indicate that economic liberalization requires changes in economic institutions. A society's institutions—its civil service, banks, educational institutions, and professional organizations—and its cultural values (for example, the emphasis placed on honesty in business and personal relations) matter profoundly. As economic historian Douglass C. North argued in his Nobel lecture,

> Neoclassical theory is simply an inappropriate tool to analyze and prescribe policies that will induce development. It is concerned with the operation of markets, not with how markets develop. How can one prescribe policies when one doesn't understand how economies develop? North (1994, 359)

Many recent studies have revealed that the East Asian economies, namely, Japan, South Korea, Taiwan, and Singapore, did not succeed on the basis of free market policies. In the opinion of some specialists, including Wade (1990), von Alten (1994), and Amsden (1989), government intervention in East Asian countries played a crucial role in economic development. Wade terms the East Asian development strategy as one of "governing the market" through a variety of practices, such as preferential loans and incentive schemes for targeted industries. Such practices have allowed the East Asian economies to improve upon what even a perfectly functioning competitive economy would have achieved by allocating productive resources in even more dynamic directions than would have been achieved by the market alone. By governing the market, it may be possible to outperform what a perfectly functioning market would achieve.

Although the idea that the rapid growth of the East Asian economies has been the consequence of success in foreign trade is by now conventional wisdom, it is important to keep in mind that a growing domestic economy can generate economies of scale in industry and that a viable export capability typically follows from and builds upon successful performance in the domestic economy. Actually, causality runs both ways: exports can stimulate the growth of a local economy, and the growth of the domestic economy can strengthen a nation's capability to export via higher levels of investment, technology and research, training, education, and so on, which improve productivity and increase competitiveness on the international market. Domestic and international forces complement one another.

Economic Development of Singapore since 1960

The remarkable performance of the Singapore economy during the last forty years is certainly more complicated than that stylized in table 12.1. Behind the snapshots presented at the end of each decade are the many efforts and policies made to steer the economy from a simple trading port to a relatively advanced open economy based on manufacturing as well as financial and business services. GDP valued at constant prices was, at the end of the century, more than twenty-four times that in 1960. This represents an average compound growth rate of 8 percent per annum.

Since its founding in 1819, Singapore had been a trading outpost of the old British Empire until World War II. It was briefly occupied by Japan before returning to British administration in 1945. Heightened political awareness and nationalist fervor led indigenous political activists to fight for independence and self-determination. In 1959, Singapore was granted self-governance and autonomy in domestic affairs.

As indicated in table 12.2, the development experience of the Singapore economy in the last forty years may be divided into four phases. During the first phase, economic issues and social unrest were daily headlines in the media. Unemployment was rising as more graduates poured into the labor market amidst shrinking global commodity demand and threats of more direct trade among countries that would diminish the role of Singapore as an entrepôt port. The political environment was less than settled as political parties fought for supremacy: worker unions were

TABLE 12.1 Economic Performance Indicators

	1960	1970	1980	1990	2000
GDP at 1990 prices (S$billion)	5.8	13.9	32.9	66.5	139.8
Growth rate of GDP (% per annum)		9.3	9.0	7.4	7.8
Unemployment rate (%)	4.9	6.1	3.5	1.7	3.1
Inflation rate	0.4	5.3	3.4	1.6	1.8
Current account (S$billion)	−1.8	−1.8	−3.4	5.7	37.6
National saving rates (% of GNP)	n.a.	19.3	34.3	43.9	51.5

TABLE 12.2 Phases of Singapore's Economic Development

(I) 1959–1965 Inward-Looking Development Policy
• Import substitution
• EDB set up in 1961
• Independence: sovereign state in 1965
• Basic tax incentives for investments
• Economic Expansion Incentives Act
• Labor intensive activities preferred

(II) 1965–1978 Outward-Oriented Development Policy
• Employment Act, 1968
• Industrial Relation Act, 1968
• Transition to more capital intensive activities
• Export promotion

(III) 1979–1985 Restructuring Policy
• Intensification of export promotion
• Corrective wage policy
• Skill development policy
• Priority list of industries for foreign investments: capital technology intensive

(IV) 1986–Post-Recession Development Policy
• Service sector promotion
• Introduction of investment allowance
• Wage reform: variable bonus component
• Development of local SMEs as supporting industries: the LIUP program
• Overseas Headquarters Incentives
• Regionalization
• Further liberalization of financial sector
• Liberalization of telecomunication sector
• R&D, technopreneurship promotion

called upon to go on strikes, and students were mobilized for demonstrations fuelling civil disorder.

Economic growth was at best stuttering and modest. The need to expand the economy was not neglected despite the turbulence. As a solution, import-substituting industrialization (ISI) was opted for and technical assistance to plan, finance, and implement it was obtained from the United Nations[2] and the International Labour Organisation (ILO). A governmental investment promotion agency, the Economic Development Board (EDB), was set up in 1961 to plan and promote industrial development in the manufacturing and services sectors in Singapore. Right from the start of the industrialization program to restructure the economy from entrepôt to manufacturing activities, the government favored foreign direct investment (FDI) and transnational corporations (TNCs) as the conduit or package for capital, managerial expertise,

technology, markets, and other link-ups. Both local capital and entrepreneurship were lacking. Beginning in 1960, tariffs and quotas on manufactured goods were introduced for the first time. The objective was to encourage the development of import-substituting firms. The import-substitution policy was intensified when Singapore integrated with Malaysia in 1963. By the end of 1965, import duties had been imposed on 157 items, including steel bars, sugar, cement, chocolates, and a range of plastic and chemical products; and 230 commodities were subjected to import quotas. It was believed that a Pan-Malaysian market would ensure policy success. However, the policy of import substitution was ineffective because it tended to develop inefficient domestic manufacturing industries, especially when the domestic market was so limited. The inflow of foreign capital was unimpressive despite the various fiscal incentives and concessions provided by the government through the EDB. The separation of Singapore from Malaysia in 1965 spelled the end of the import-substitution phase.

Singapore became an independent nation on August 9, 1965. This marked the start of the second phase: the switch from an import-substitution strategy to an export-oriented development strategy. The need to develop, expand, and provide jobs became even more urgent. Economic survival became synonymous with national survival. The government was confronted with the need to industrialize quickly to solve the serious unemployment problem (unemployment rate recorded 13.5 percent in 1966). Constrained by a small domestic market and few natural resources, and lacking indigenous entrepreneurs who had the expertise and networks for industrial start-up and expansion, the government embarked on an intensive drive to attract foreign investors, especially transnational companies from the West. The Economic Expansion Incentive Act, introduced in 1967, offered new incentives to foster export activities, facilitate foreign borrowing, and encourage foreign technology inflows. These included the reduction of tax rates on export profits from 40 percent to 4 percent, the exemption of taxes on interest earnings on approved foreign loans, and the reduction of tax rates on royalties and fees paid to foreigners.

To improve industrial relations, the Employment and the Industrial Relations (Amendment) Acts passed in 1968, giving employers further power over their employees. The Industrial Relations Act mandated that all industrial disputes would be decided in an arbitration court under the charge of the Ministry of Labor. The number of national holidays was fixed at eleven and guidelines were given for a standard forty-four-hour workweek, remuneration for overtime work, and hygiene and health in working places.

Note that a symbiotic relationship existed between the government and the National Trades Union Congress (NTUC) dating back to the colonial struggle. This helped to hem in workers' demands at a time when belt tightening was called for to induce FDI flows. In return for this support, when the economy's performance improved, the National Wages Council (NWC) was formed in 1972 to ensure an orderly wage increase in tandem with Singapore's international competitiveness. By and large, healthy industrial relations and favorable labor market conditions formed a virtuous circle and created an environment conducive for FDI.

Complementing these fiscal incentives were physical infrastructure—as in communication, telecommunication, and transportation—that contributed directly to efficiency and competitiveness. Human resource development in both education and skills training was also vital for Singapore, as its labor force is its only renewable resource.

On the external front, active measures were taken to promote the export of labor-intensive goods and to remove barriers to trade in the domestic economy. Import quotas were gradually replaced with tariffs between 1965 and 1973 (Pang and Tan 1981). Tariff and excise rates were later reduced. Since 1981, the import duties have been lowered to a maximum ad valorem rate of 5 percent. Also, under the agreement of the ASEAN Preferential Trading Arrangements, since 1978 preferential rates of custom duty have been accorded to over 8,000 selected products of ASEAN origin.[3]

Singapore has been an ardent supporter of greater trade liberalization. Efforts by the WTO to start new rounds of multilateral negotiation and by the APEC to have an Asia Pacific–wide free trade area, as well as the implementing of the ASEAN Free Trade Area, are in sync with Singapore's development vision. The economy is on the path of ever-greater liberalization since the beginning of the second phase in 1965.

A brief statistical summary of the country's performance during the first two phases is shown in table 12.3. The economy was successful in attracting foreign investments. Cumulative investments in the manufacturing sector registered S$5.2 billion in 1978 compared to a meager S$156 million in 1965. Concurrently, employment in the manufacturing sector expanded by five times during the same period. The real wage increased moderately despite the 1973 oil crisis.

Compared with the GDP in 1965, the real GDP expanded by almost four times at the end of the second phase. The number of man days lost due to industrial stoppages declined from more than 410,000 in 1961 to virtually zero by 1978. Income inequality, as measured by the Gini coefficient, also improved during this period.

The third phase of Singapore's development experience covers the period from 1979 to 1985. During this phase, a deliberate effort was made by the government to restructure the economy from its low value-added, labor-intensive industrial structure to one that was capital and technology intensive, and yielded high value-added. Singapore began to be more selective about the type of foreign investment it desired. A wage-correction policy was instituted whereby wages were raised by 20 percent each year, starting in 1979, for three consecutive years. The intention was to give industries a strong signal to upgrade and convert their production processes to more labor-saving techniques. At the same time, the Skill Development Fund (SDF) was set up. Companies were made to contribute 2 percent of the payroll of those workers earning less than S$750 per month into the fund. The fund was used to finance training programs for the workers. Meanwhile, the EDB was also actively collaborating with TNCs in setting up industry skill–related courses to train more technicians as well as to upgrade the skills of the existing workforce.

In 1985–1986, the city-state was hit by a severe recession. For the first time in twenty years, the growth rate of Singapore's real GDP was negative (–1.8 percent). Unemployment reached 6.5 percent, and industrial output decreased by 8 percent. An Economic Committee was formed to help identify the causes of the recession. Both internal and external factors were identified. In particular, rising business costs engendered by accumulated increases in wages, social security contributions, and statutory charges were singled out as a major cause of losses in competitiveness. The services sector was singled out as a source of growth.

The Economic Committee report had a profound influence on subsequent investment policies in Singapore. In 1986, the EDB set up the Services

TABLE 12.3 Economic Performance of Singapore, 1961–1978

	Taking Stock of Performance, 1961 to 1978					
	1961	1965	1970	1973	1975	1978
Population (000)	1,702.4	1,886.9	2,074.5	2,193.0	2,262.6	2,353.6
GDP90 (S$million)	6,261.5	7,557.4	13,881.8	19,699.2	21,863.4	27,421.5
Index(1965 = 1)	0.83	1.00	1.84	2.61	2.89	3.63
GDP90 per capita (S$)	3,678	4,005	6,692	8,983	9,663	11,651
Index(1965 = 1)	0.92	1.00	1.67	2.24	2.41	2.91
Industrial stoppages (number of workers)	43,584	3,374	1,749	1,312	1,865	0
Man days lost	410,889	45,800	2,514	2,295	4,853	0
Trade disputes	1,225	801	486	997	709	577
Unemployment rate	4.9	9.2	6.1	4.5	4.6	3.6
Inflation rate (%)	0.36	0.35	0.33	19.53	2.56	4.84
Gini coefficent (LFS)	n.a.	0.498	n.a.	0.4845	0.469	0.4346
	Manufacturing Sector					
Manufacturing value-added as % of GDP	15.4	18.7	23.7	27.1	24.9	27
Cumulative foreign investment (S$million)	n.a.	156	995	2,659	3,380	5,242
Index (1965 = 1)	n.a.	1.00	6.38	17.04	21.67	33.60
Real wage rate (Manufacturing)	0.98	1.00	1.13	1.21	1.36	1.48
Employment (Manufacturing)	0.65	1.00	2.56	4.13	3.97	5.02

Promotion Division (SPD) that focused on the development of financial and engineering services, telecommunications, information technology, as well as educational and medical services. The SPD performs the following functions:

- Formulation of investment promotion plans, promotional incentives, and marketing strategies to attract services to Singapore
- Identification of desirable service industries overseas, and the promotion of Singapore as an international operational headquarters to these companies
- Developing an appropriate infrastructure to foster the growth of the services sector in Singapore

The Pioneer Incentives Act and the Economic Expansion Act were extended to include the promotion of investments in services. Between April 1985 and April 1986 alone, the EDB awarded pioneer status to fourteen companies in the services sector. The importance of local entrepreneurs was recognized, and concerted efforts were made to promote local small and medium enterprises (SMEs).

Programs such as the local industrial upgrading program (LIUP) were devised to foster closer cooperation and partnership between TNCs and local enterprises. The SMEs were also encouraged by such programs to become supporting industries; indeed, some of them have grown to become TNCs.

To help industries regain their international competitiveness, substantial reduction (15 percent) in the social security contribution (CPF) by employers was implemented. As a more long-term solution, workers' remuneration structure was reformed to take into consideration the variability in economic performance due to external demand shocks. Furthermore, rising business and production costs could only be ameliorated if land-and labor-intensive activities could be strategically guided to relocate to neighboring countries that were better endowed with land and labor. This marked the beginning of the concept of the "growth triangle," whereby industrial sites, with the approval and cooperation of the private sector and governments of neighboring countries, were developed to enable the incumbent TNCs to expand and upgrade their regional production activities.

That Singapore's regional and global role was fully taken advantage of was reflected in many incentives, such as the following:

- Overseas headquarters launched in 1987 (OHQs)
- Business headquarters (BHQs, 1994)
- International purchasing office (IPO, 1992)
- Approved Oil Trader (AOT, 1989)
- Approved International Trader (AIT, 1990)
- Approved International Shipping Enterprise (AIS, 1991)
- Approved Aircraft Licensing Leasing Incentive (AAI, 1995)
- Approved Cyber Trader Scheme (ACT, 1999)

These incentive schemes for manufacturing and service activities were over and above the pioneer and export incentives offered by the EDB and the Trade Development Board (TDB).[4] The first three schemes are administered by the EDB, and the rest by the TDB.

Under the overseas headquarters scheme, a company that sets up a regional office in Singapore providing management and other headquarters-related services—which include business development, research and development, and human resource training to its affiliated companies outside of Singapore—enjoys a concessionary tax rate of 10 percent. Companies participating in this scheme included several American-based companies like Eastman Chemical, Whirlpool, Unisys Asia Pacific, and Digital Equipment Corporation, as well as the French-based Danone Asia, and Groupe Schneider, Carnaud Metal Box Asia, and Datacraft Asia. Sony was the first Japanese TNC to be awarded this perk, as early as in 1987.

Launched in 1994, the business headquarters scheme helps local service-oriented companies and TNCs expand in the region. Because production can be easily shifted based on cost considerations, core business support capabilities—like product development, logistics operations and management, merchandising, and data management—give manufacturers a critical competitive advantage and broadens Singapore's standing along the value-added chain.

As of 2001, there were are more than 110 companies under the AOT/AIT schemes. Many of them are prominent traders in a wide range of commodities and products including oil, agri-commodities, paper, pulp, and metals. The other schemes mentioned above have also helped promote Singapore as a regional transport hub and provided alternative business opportunities in the area of electronic commerce.

To tap into the high-growth markets in the region, the Singapore government started encouraging local companies to invest in other growth areas. The Committee to Promote Enterprise Overseas (CPEO) was formed to make recommendations to remove impediments to overseas ventures and to facilitate the repatriation of their foreign earned income. Besides starting the Specific Assistance Program, the EDB has also come up with loan, grant, and tax incentives schemes to help firms expand abroad. The TDB also has various schemes to provide investment information and to develop overseas markets.

As the economy enters the next millennium, the EDB, which has already taken a client-based strategy in promoting FDI, has become more proactive with a number of initiatives, including the following:

1. Manufacturing 2000 to develop and strengthen Singapore's industry clusters
2. International Business Hub 2000 to make Singapore an international node, adding value with the flow of skills, capital, knowledge, and information between Asia and the rest of the world
3. Regionalisation 2000, where the EDB becomes the business architect to identify opportunities and bring together partners to invest in Asia Pacific in mutually beneficial ways
4. Local Enterprise 2000 to build promising Singapore enterprises into TNCs and industry leaders of tomorrow

The Strategic Economic Plan (SEP; Ministry of Trade and Industry 1991) recognized that an industrial policy that accounts for the relative strengths of Singapore in specific areas and intelligently supports those with the best chances of becoming world-class would overcome the limitations of small size. However, the identified sectors must still be subject to the tests of market efficiency and competitiveness. The EDB has identified fourteen clusters of industries that are potential growth generators for the economy—commodity trading, shipping, precision engineering, electronics, information technology, petroleum and petrochemical, construction, heavy engineering, finance, insurance, general supporting industries, tourism, international hub, and domestic industries. These clusters will have some common features or core capabilities in the form of natural advantages, created competitive advantages, or industry structure and attributes. The government is prepared to invest in these core capabilities or provide special incentives to accelerate their development.

Managing the Transition

The export-promotion strategy involves exploiting comparative advantage and importing goods too costly to produce domestically. Industrialization is a natural outcome of development rather than a goal pursued by import-substitution policy. The transition from an import-substitution mindset to an export-promotion strategy is not easy. Several structural adjustments have had to be made. New institutions and codes of practice have had to be put into place.

In the previous section, I indicated that several changes in the economic system were required in order to facilitate a smooth transition from one developmental phase to another. The education system was adapted to provide the necessary skilled manpower; legislations were altered to make the environment more conducive for cooperative industrial relations. In general, resources were tactfully mobilized for the purpose of generating value-added and employment. The success of the development strategy may be assessed in terms of what it has tangibly delivered in terms of jobs and steady income for workers. Home ownership is a very rough estimate of employment stability. By 1986, 85 percent of the population resided in the public housing estate and 90 percent of households owned their own home.

Several policies and governmental actions helped harness the necessary resources for economic development. The powerful Land Acquisition Act provided the government the means to acquire ownership of the limited land space for economic and social development at a historically low cost. The government is currently the largest landowner, owning 75 percent of the land space in Singapore. This has enabled the government to subsidize the provision of residential public housing and industrial sites for investors. As alluded to earlier, the government was able to muster the cooperation of the once-militant trade unions. A cabinet minister heads the National Trade Union Congress. The symbiotic relationship between the union and the government enabled the successful implementation of economy-wide wage-reduction measures during the 1985 and 1997 economic

downturns. Inviting FDI into Singapore may be interpreted as a measure to supplement the dearth of capital and entrepreneurship in the domestic economy. The government, from time to time, has had to co-invest in activities considered high risk.[5] More importantly, the government has had to play the role of a countervailing force to ensure that the benefits of FDI raise general economic well-being. The negative side effects of FDI include the stifling of local entrepreneurship and inventiveness, and these have to be managed to obtain a net positive outcome.

The policy that gave Singapore a headstart in attracting foreign capital was the government's highly liberal stance on ownership at a time when foreign investment was viewed with suspicion—TNCs were both footloose and exploitative—by other developing countries, following the experiences of Latin American economies. Since 1965, the government has consistently maintained an open policy toward foreign ownership and operations. There are no restrictions on equity ownership or foreign exchange controls and no limits placed on the repatriation of capital, dividends, interest, and royalties. There are also no restrictions on foreign borrowings from domestic capital markets and no regulations governing the transfer of technology. Furthermore, the government is willing to co-invest with foreign companies if there is a need for risk sharing and the nurturing of business confidence.

The government actively ensures there is sufficient infrastructure—as in telecommunication, transport, and logistic supports—to ensure an environment conducive to both foreign and local enterprises. At the same time, measures are taken to ensure that the working and social conditions of the workforce are maintained at a high level. Over the years, the government has through the CPF channeled household savings to the purchasing of housing/flats built by the state and to investments, besides providing reserves for retirement and medical needs.[6] The erosion of the purchasing power of workers' incomes is checked by prudent macroeconomic policies. In general, the government believes in balanced budgets; and in practice, there has always been a budget surplus. This has certainly helped Singapore avoid the need to resort to printing money and raising the money supply, which will in turn stoke inflation. Furthermore, the exchange rate has been actively managed to ensure that imported inflation is subdued. A strong and stable currency, primarily determined by market forces, is deemed critical for maintaining investor confidence. Put simply, Singapore's example of economic management is one that adheres to the precepts of capitalist production without abandoning the virtues of being socialist in distribution.

Decomposition Analysis

Decomposition analysis helps us identify the structural breaks associated with major economic changes. In the case of capital liberalization, opening the economy to foreign investment flows will certainly have an impact on standard socio-economic variables such as the gross domestic product, employment, inflation, the external trade balance, productivity, savings, income distribution, and the business environment. Decomposition analysis will often enable us to distinguish the resulting changes in these variables into effects that occurred within different sectors of the economy, and effects that occurred between different sectors.

Effective Demand

As noted in standard structural analysis, liberalization will entail substantial changes in demand-side parameters such as import coefficients and saving rates along with jumps in flows such as exports, investment, and government expenditure. It will be illuminating to see how output has responded to these shifts by decomposing effective demand.

Note the identity[7]

$$Y = C + I_P + G + I_G + X - M \qquad (1)$$

Disposable income is given as $Y - T - CPF$, where T is the transfer payment (mainly taxes and fees) made by the private sector to the government and CPF is the contribution made by employees and employers to the social security fund. Expressing private consumption, C, as a proportion of the disposable income $(Y - T - CPF)$, the identity is rewritten as

$$Y = c(Y - T - CPF) + I_P + G + I_G + X - M \qquad (2)$$

Defining the parameters—$c = C/(Y - T - CPF)$, $s = 1 - c$, $t = T/Y$, $f = CPF/Y$, and $m = M/Y$, $\Delta = [s + c(t + f) + m]$—the identity may be expressed in a Keynesian multiplier form:

$$Y = (s/\Delta)(I_P/s) + [c(t + f)/\Delta] \cdot$$
$$[(G + I_G)/c(t + f)] + (m/\Delta)(X/m) \qquad (3)$$
$$= S1(I_P/s) + S2[(G + I_G)/c(t + f)] + S3(X/m)$$
$$\qquad (3a)$$
$$= \quad P1 \quad + \qquad P2 \qquad + \quad P3 \quad (3b)$$

The expressions (I_P/s), $(G + I_G)/c(t + f)$, and (X/m) can be interpreted as the direct "own" multiplier effects on output of private investment, government spending, and export injections with their overall impact scaled by the corresponding "leakages," $S1$, $S2$, and $S3$ (respectively, savings, tax, and import propensities).

The time path of these leakages is shown in figure 12.1. A declining $S2$ indicates a declining

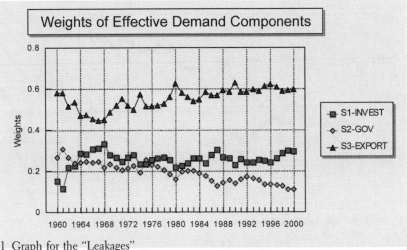

FIGURE 12.1 Graph for the "Leakages"

influence of the government expenditure in affecting the aggregate demand of the economy.

The import propensity (S3) is always higher than the other two propensities, S1 and S2, throughout the period 1960 to 2000. Up to 1968, the import propensity[8] declined, while the saving propensity increased. Since then, the import propensity rose steadily to stabilize at about 60 percent.

In figure 12.2, the components in equation (3b), expressed as percentages of Y, are plotted for the period 1960 to 2000. P3, the component pertaining to exports, does not exhibit its dominance until after 1973. Since then, the contribution of this component increases steadily to reach 70 percent by 2000. Meanwhile, the government expenditure component was contributing as much as 30 percent in 1965, but showing an obvious trend of diminishing contribution over the years. In 2000, the contribution of the government expenditure component is only 12 percent.

Another representation involves the identity in terms of the resource gaps:

$$0 = (I_P - sY) + [G + I_G - c(t + f)Y] + (X - mY) \quad (4)$$

The gaps are useful in identifying the expansionary and contractive factors in effective demand. The graphical presentation of the resource gaps for Singapore is shown in figures 12.3 and 12.4.

As figure 12.3 (which covers the period from 1960 to 1985) indicates, the current account was in deficit throughout the period. This deficit was particularly pronounced between 1970 and 1976 and was mirrored by the excess of investment over private savings. Private sector investment was largely funded by foreign savings. Government expenditure was in excess of disposable revenue from 1963 to 1972. However, this deficit was hardly as large as that of private investment. Countercyclical government spending was noted, especially in 1985 when the government deficit was used to pump-prime the economy during the first post-independence recession.

The picture changed dramatically after 1985. As figure 12.4 shows, trade deficits turned into trade surpluses from 1986. Meanwhile, private savings exceeded private investments. Foreign capital inflows did not cease. In fact, as a result of the Louvre Accord, the realignment (and relative appreciation) of international currencies such as the Japanese yen and the German mark triggered a new round of foreign capital into developing economies, especially those in Southeast Asia. At the same time, Asian NIEs had accumulated sufficient trade surpluses with their export-expansion drives and had begun to move into a new phase of encouraging their indigenous companies to invest abroad. Singapore had joined this outward foreign investment promotion drive. While

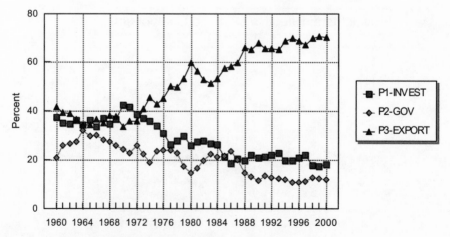

FIGURE 12.2 Contribution of Effective Demand Components

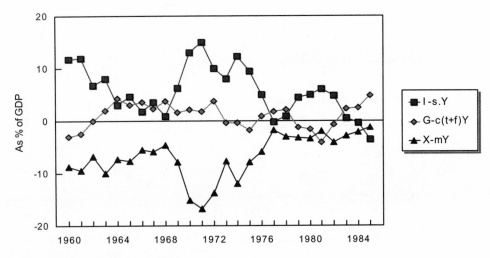

FIGURE 12.3 Resource Gaps, 1960–1985

the EDB continues to promote inward FDI, it also encourages local companies to partner with existing multinational corporations (MNC) to explore and invest in neighboring countries as well as emerging economies such as China, Vietnam, and countries in Eastern Europe.

Employment Decompositions

Starting with the identity[9]

$$E = L + U \qquad (5)$$

we define the labor participation rate as $\varepsilon = E/POP$, the unemployment rate as $v = U/E$, and the employed share of the population, $\lambda = L/POP$, where POP refers to population. We obtain the expression

$$\varepsilon = \lambda + \varepsilon v \qquad (6)$$

The change in the labor participation rate (ε_t) is a weighted sum of the change in the share of employed population (λ_t) and the unemployment rate (v_t).

$$\varepsilon_t - \varepsilon_{t-1} = [1/(1 - v_{t-1})](\lambda_t - \lambda_{t-1}) \\ + [\varepsilon_t/(1 - v_{t-1})](v_t - v_{t-1}) \qquad (7)$$

The employment ratio, $\lambda = L/POP$, provides a useful tool to analyze job growth across sectors. With

L_i as the employment in sector i, and Y_i as the real output in sector i, we define $x_i = Y_i/POP$, $b_i = L_i/Y_I$, and $\lambda_i = L_i/POP$. The sectoral labor productivity is given by $\rho_i = 1/b_i = Y_i/L_i$. We can write the identity of the employment ratio as

$$\lambda = L/POP = \Sigma L_i/POP = \Sigma(L_i/Y_i) \cdot (Y_i/POP) \\ = \Sigma b_i x_i \qquad (8)$$

Taking the first differences, and denoting the growth of a variable X_t as $g(X_t)$, we can show that the growth of λ_t is

$$[(\lambda_t - \lambda_{t-1})/\lambda_{t-1}] = g(\lambda_t) = \Sigma\phi_{it-1}[g(x_{it}) \\ + g(b_{it}) + g(x_{it}) \cdot g(b_{it})] \qquad (9)$$

where $\phi_i = \lambda_i/\lambda$

Furthermore, the growth in the labor productivity can be decomposed as

$$g(\rho_t) = g(Y/L)_t = \Sigma(Y_i/Y)_{t-1}g(\rho_{it}) \\ + \Sigma[(Y_i/Y)_{t-1}g(L_i/L)_t \qquad (10) \\ + \Sigma[(Y_i/Y)_{t-1}g(\rho_{it}) \cdot g(L_i/L)_t$$

The first term on the right-hand side of the equal sign is the weighted average of the labor productivity of sectors. The second and third terms provide measures of the resource reallocation effect reflected in changing employment shares, and the interaction

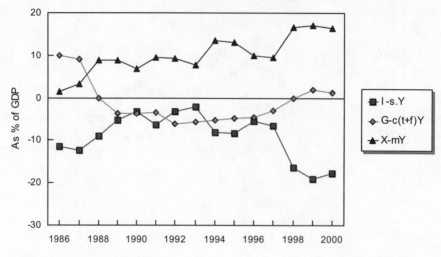

FIGURE 12.4 Resource Gaps, 1986–2000

between labor productivity growth and changing employment shares respectively.

Empirical Results for Singapore

The decomposition according to equation (8) is provided in table 12.4. More detailed exposition is given in figure 12.5.

The figures in table 12.5 represent the average percentage point increase. In 1995, the participation rate (ε) is 58.6 percent. The last row of table 12.5 indicates that the participation rate increases by an average of 1.72 percentage points each year, reaching 67.2 percent in 2000. Of this 1.72 percentage point increment, 1.50 percentage points are attributed to the increased share of the employed population, and the remaining 0.22 percentage points are owing to an enlarged unemployment rate.

As the unemployment rate is already relatively low in Singapore, the growth in the proportion of the economically active population is primarily determined by the increase in the proportion of the employed. More jobs have been created and filled. The rising share of the employed population also reflects the increase in foreign workers in the country's labor force. In 2000, the proportion of foreign workers

in the employed workforce was estimated to be 30 percent. The imported workers mainly came from the neighboring countries of Malaysia, Thailand, Philippines, and Indonesia. In recent years, the sources extended further north and west to China, Myanmar, and India. Furthermore, there are also skilled workers and professionals from developed countries such as Japan, Australia, and United Kingdom working in Singapore. The latter group of foreign workers are regarded as important contributors to Singapore's international competitiveness.

As table 12.5 shows, in the earlier period, 1973 to 1980, increased employment was primarily owing to increases in the manufacturing sector. The second major wave of FDI to Southeast Asia in the second half of the 1980s contributed substantially to the

TABLE 12.4 Decomposition of the Change in the Labor Participation Rate

	Participation Rate	Employed Share of Population	Unemployment Rate
1974–1975	0.20	0.19	0.01
1976–1985	1.29	1.30	−0.01
1986–1995	0.67	0.75	−0.08
1996–2000	1.72	1.50	0.22

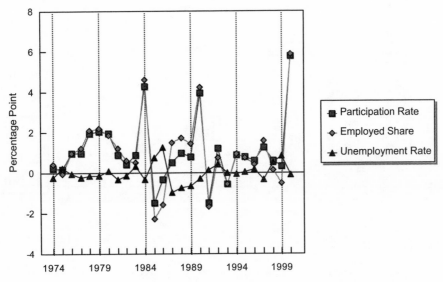

FIGURE 12.5 Decomposition of the Labor Participation Rate (%)

growth in employment. Of the total 2.76 percent growth in the employment ratio, the manufacturing sector contributed 1.54 percent. In the first half of the 1990s, the overall employment ratio increased marginally, and the negative contribution by the manufacturing, construction, and commerce sectors was offset by positive expansion in the finance and business services, transportation and communications, and community services (see figure 12.6).

Labor Productivity

Using equation (10), the overall labor productivity growth is decomposed into three components: the productivity growth within sectors, resource reallocation associated with changes in the employment share, and the interaction effects (see table 12.6 and figure 12.7).

Labor productivity growth is dominated by intrasectoral changes. Except for the brief period between 1973 and 1975, the resource reallocation effect is rather insignificant. This indicates that the labor market remains relatively segmented and the movement of labor from low-productivity sectors to those that have high productivity is not as smooth as neoclassical economists assert. The decomposition of the economy-wide labor productivity growth by sectors is shown in table 12.7 and figure 12.8.

TABLE 12.5 Decomposing Change in Employment Ratio (%) :: (Equation 9)

Period	Total	Manufacturing	Construction	Commerce	Transport and communications	Finance and Business	Community Services	Others
1973–1975	1.824	1.451	−0.486	0.046	0.177	0.862	−0.079	−0.147
1976–1980	3.984	1.918	0.619	0.581	0.335	0.532	0.140	−0.141
1981–1985	2.013	−0.344	0.585	0.876	0.023	0.434	0.205	−0.165
1986–1990	2.761	1.540	0.006	0.313	0.148	0.715	0.205	−0.165
1991–1995	0.075	−0.969	−0.244	−0.293	0.251	0.763	0.486	0.082
1996–2000	2.474	−0.170	1.566	0.236	−0.027	0.538	0.436	−0.106

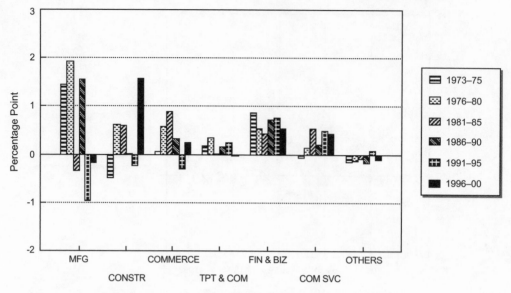

FIGURE 12.6 Decomposition of the Change in Employment Ratio

The manufacturing sector significantly contributes to national productivity growth, though the
contribution is not uniform throughout the period.
The commerce (wholesale and retail trade) sector
and the finance and business service sectors made
steady contributions to national labor productivity
growth in the period prior to 1996. The Asian financial crisis in 1997 dealt a severe blow to these
sectors, and their productivity contributions dwindled
significantly. In the second half of the 1990s, overall
productivity growth was a meager 2.0 percent compared with the average of 4.0 percent before 1996.

recent years than the coefficients for Taiwan
and Korea.
2. Changes in the Gini coefficients do not follow
   the Kuznets pattern,[10] although initially inequality seems to have fallen in all the economies
   during the period of rapid growth.
3. The Gini coeffcient for Singapore fell quite
   dramatically between 1966 and 1975, with a
   further fall between 1975 and 1979. Since
   then, inequality has fluctuated but trending
   upward. In Hong Kong, the Gini fell between
   1966 and 1971 but exhibited a fluctuating
   pattern after that and was higher in 1981 than
   in 1971.

Income Distribution in Singapore

Has income distribution worsened since Independence? Does continual liberalization imply a continual deterioration in income distribution? Studies of
the four East Asian economies have shown that income
inequality has not severely worsened as a result of rapid
growth. Various estimates of the Gini coefficient have
been computed for the four economies.

1. Gini coefficients for the city-states of Hong
   Kong and Singapore are noticeably higher in

TABLE   12.6 Decomposing Labor Productivity
Growth (%)

	Labor Productivity Growth	Within Sectors	Resource Reallocation	Interaction Effects
1973–1975	4.18	2.84	3.51	−2.17
1976–1980	3.01	2.32	0.93	−0.24
1981–1985	2.94	2.37	0.73	−0.15
1986–1990	3.79	3.48	0.48	−0.17
1991–1995	6.96	6.43	1.00	−0.46
1996–2000	2.06	3.00	0.29	−1.23

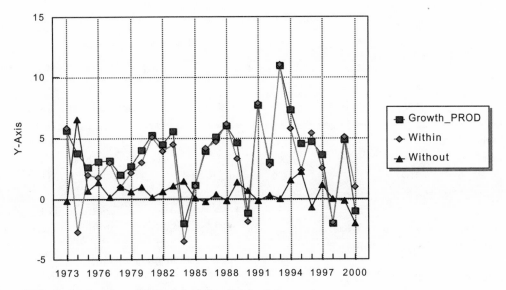

FIGURE 12.7 Decomposition of Growth in Labor Productivity

Rapid economic growth in both these countries has been associated with export-oriented industrialization (EOI) and, initially at least, the use of relatively capital-intensive technologies. Neither country displays a pattern consistent with Kuznets's model; however, this apparent paradox may be explained by examining both the intra- and the intersectoral patterns of income distribution (Chowdury and Islam 1993). Chowdury and Islam argue that a particular kind of labor-market segmentation is important in these two economies. The deterioration in Hong Kong between 1976 and 1981 coincided with the large influx of refugees who found employment in the low-income segment of the labor market. In Singapore in the late 1970s to early 1980s, the government imported foreign workers into selected industries and occupations to overcome domestic labor shortages. Foreign workers could not move freely between sectors and occupations, and this contributed to worsening income inequality. In recent years, high-earning foreign talents may have skewed the income distribution.

In figure 12.9, the Gini coefficients computed using information from the annual labor force surveys were charted. Inequality as measured by the Gini improved during the 1970s. Between 1980 and 2000, there is an obvious upward trend for the Gini

coefficients, indicating worsening income inequality. There are several reasons for the rising trend in the Gini. The restructuring of the economy from 1979—switching from labor-intensive production to more capital-intensive activities—led to jobs with higher remuneration. The spectrum of jobs from the menial to the very skilled has increased over the years. Moreover, the education system has been able to increase the enrollment of students in various fields of study and has resulted in increased technical and professional employment. In the 1960s, only about 3 to 4 percent of each cohort of the population had tertiary education. This proportion has rapidly increased over the years. Currently, 20 percent of each cohort will have university-level education, while another 40 percent will have diplomas from one of the four polytechnics in the country.

The Gini coefficient may not fully describe the actual inequality in Singapore. First, the Gini is based on individual personal income and not on household income. Second, only labor income is included. Third, the government has implemented several measures and policies to mitigate the adverse effects of income inequality. Over the years, it has been able to make use of the budget to help low-income households. By virtue of the fact that

TABLE 12.7 Decomposing Labor Productivity Growth by Sector

Period	Total	Manufacturing	Construction	Commerce	Transportation and Communications	Finance and Business	Community Services	Others
1973–1975	4.18	0.65	0.47	0.74	0.66	0.99	0.64	0.03
1976–1980	3.01	1.51	−0.10	0.27	0.89	0.33	0.07	0.05
1981–1985	2.94	−0.55	0.92	−0.00	0.43	1.42	0.71	0.01
1986–1990	3.79	1.90	−0.86	0.88	0.63	0.78	0.45	0.00
1991–1995	6.96	1.38	0.80	1.53	0.81	1.71	0.67	0.07
1996–2000	2.06	0.67	0.09	0.27	0.47	0.17	0.36	0.02
Percentage Distribution								
1973–1975	100.0	15.5	11.3	17.6	15.8	23.7	15.4	0.8
1976–1980	100.0	50.1	−3.5	9.1	29.5	10.9	2.2	1.7
1981–1985	100.0	−18.8	31.3	−0.0	14.7	48.1	24.3	0.4
1986–1990	100.0	50.2	−22.6	23.2	16.6	20.6	11.9	0.1
1991–1995	100.0	19.8	11.5	22.0	11.6	24.6	9.6	0.9
1996–2000	100.0	32.5	4.5	13.3	22.7	8.4	17.3	1.2

86 percent of households live in the public housing estates managed by the government's Housing Development Board, the state provides rental and utilities rebates as well as waiver of conservancy charges to low-income households. Furthermore, the assistance provided by the government has some aspect of being progressive in the sense that households living in larger apartments are given lesser rebates and concessions than households in smaller apartments.[11]

The latest effort made by the government to share the national wealth to strengthen community cohesiveness is the New Singapore Shares (NSS) scheme. A basic package of 200 to 1,400 New Singapore Shares—depending on income for those who are employed, and on housing type for those who are not employed (the self-employed will receive according to their housing type, unless they qualify for less according to their income level)—has been distributed to citizens. The allocated shares will receive a guaranteed dividend for a fixed number of years, plus bonus payments when the economy does well. These shares will also be immediately redeemable for cash, though not all at once. The scheme costs S$2.7 billion and is very much welcomed by the citizens, especially in light of the current economic downturn.

As indicated in table 12.8, the share of labor income in the GDP has increased from less than 40 percent in the mid-1960s to almost 50 percent in 2000. Currently, only about two-thirds of the GDP

may be attributed to indigenous factors of production. The manufacturing sector that spearheaded the industrialization drive has not diminished in importance. It still contributes about a quarter of the GDP. The declining labor share in the manufacturing sector indicates that Singapore has moved away from labor-intensive manufacturing industries. More importantly, the manufacturing sector remains a site of new innovations and products.

Conclusion

Singapore is one big experiment in capital liberalization. Inviting capital inflows in the form of FDI has yielded many positive benefits. But such outcomes have not come about by abiding to unrealistic neoclassical principles. Indeed, the government has intervened in many aspects to rectify and avoid the negative consequences of liberalization as emphasized by the structuralists.[12] Singapore may have embraced the neoclassical "capitalistic" principle in promoting production, but is more cautious about relying on neoclassical precepts to ensure equitable distribution and rising living standards for its citizens.

As a very small economy, Singapore's remarkable growth in the last forty years has been achieved by taking the international environment as given and maximizing its national product by adjusting domestic structures and erecting institutions that best utilize its meagre resources. Economic development involves structural change. If structural change is a continuous process in growing economies, it follows that adjustment, too, is not a once-and-for-all set of changes but a continuous process that raises fundamental questions about the relationship between short-run and long-run objectives, between policy instruments and goals, and ultimately about the substance of development goals themselves.

Growth and structural change are strongly interrelated. Policy can try to anticipate structural change or accelerate it by removing obstacles and correcting market failures. Policy can also hamper growth by blocking the required changes in the structure or by attempting to dictate them as in Cambodia in the 1970s. As the Soviet experience showed, forced industrialization can accelerate growth, but only for a while and at a very high cost.

Successful development involves two issues, economic flexibility (Killick 1995) and the sequence of development. Flexibility, adaptability, and a capacity to transform are essential for the smooth progression of growth and structural change. Flexibility and adaptability have become more important today as developing countries face more competition from a large number of more developed and newly industrialized economies than in the beginning of the twentieth century. Furthermore, international pressure and trends in structural change are more intense than in the past.

While the pace of structural changes intensifies, the timing and sequencing of change are crucial for good performance. Mosley, Harrigan, and Toye (1991) advocate the following trade, exchange, and capital market liberalization sequence:

1. Liberalizing imports of critical capital and other inputs
2. Devaluing domestic currency to a competitive level, while simultaneously restraining monetary and fiscal expansion to curb inflation and convert a nominal devaluation to a real devaluation
3. Promoting exports through liberalizing commodity markets, subsidies, and other schemes
4. Allocating foreign exchange for maintaining and repairing infrastructure for production increases
5. Removing controls on internal interest rates to achieve positive real rates, and expanding loan agencies to include farmers and small business entrepreneurs
6. Reducing public sector deficits to eliminate reliance on foreign loans at banking standards without decreasing real development spending, and reforming agricultural marketing to spur farmers to sell surplus

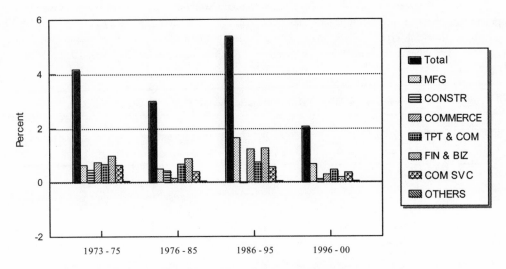

FIGURE 12.8 Decomposition of Labor Productivity Growth by Industry

FIGURE 12.9 The Gini Coefficient for the Singapore Economy

7. Liberalizing other imports, rationalizing tariff structure, and removing price control and subsidies to the private sector
8. Abandoning external capital account control

Singapore seems to have followed the sequence quite closely. So far, the country appears to have coped with structural changes and international shocks. However, it has to continue to nurture its flexibility in response to the changing international competitive environment.

The international and regional economic environment has changed quite significantly since the 1997 Asian financial crisis (AFC). Many of the economies in Southeast Asia were adversely affected by the AFC and have yet to restore to full health. The recovery of these highly electronic-dependent economies was hampered by the global slump in electronic demand in 2001. Meanwhile, there are new challenges posed by the rapid growth of the Chinese economy. While Singapore emerged relatively unscathed from the AFC, the global slump in electronic demand and the economic slowdown in the United States dragged Singapore into a recession in 2001 (with a 2.2 percent contraction in GDP).

In meeting the challenges ahead, Singapore's economic structure is poised for change. A high-powered Economic Review Committee (ERC), chaired by the deputy premier, has been set up to review and chart new economic strategies for Singapore. The ERC, made up

TABLE 12.8 Wage Share and Indicators on Equity Conditions

	National Labor Share	% of GDP Indigenous	% of Resident in HDB	Manufacturing Value-Added as % of GDP	Manufacturing Labor Share	Growth in Manufacturing VA/L	Growth in Manufacturing Real Wage
1966	n.a.	90.9	24.0	15.3	47.4	4.5	0.4
1970	n.a.	81.6	35.9	19.9	47.9	2.6	2.2
1975	36.6	76.7	54.8	23.8	45.8	−3.0	10.5
1980	38.7	69.3	74.1	29.1	39.1	6.9	−1.9
1985	49.6	74.7	84.0	23.3	50.0	3.8	8.0
1990	45.5	69.5	87.0	27.1	41.9	4.4	9.2
1995	42.8	67.5	86.0	24.8	39.7	7.2	2.9
2000	49.9	66.0	86.0	26.5	29.2	13.0	2.6

of members from the private and public sector, has the mandate to review all existing regulations and government schemes and to seek new measures to facilitate greater enterprise, efficiency, and resilience in the economy.

In its budget statement, the government has announced its acceptance of the ERC's recommendation to reduce the corporate tax rate and the top income tax rate from 24.5 to 20 percent over a period of three years. This fiscal measure aims to maintain Singapore's competitiveness in attracting and retaining talent. More importantly, it is hoped that this measure will bring in foreign investment that will continue to expand jobs and income. Switching to a greater reliance on indirect tax, the Goods and Services Tax (GST) is being raised from the current 3 percent to 5 percent. To counter the usual regressive tendency of such indirect taxation, an "offset package" composed of public housing rental rebates, higher allowance paid to government pensioners, and rebates on utilities and conservancy charges will be implemented to help lower-income households.

It is recognized that future economic growth will have to be more dependent on productivity improvement via science and technology development. Human and intellectual capital and the adept utilization of knowledge will be critical to long-term economic viability. The Manpower Upgrading for Science and Technology (MUST) program that supports the continuous upgrading and training of research scientists, engineers, and technopreneurial talent provides study grants to suitable candidates. Concerted effort has been made to promote R&D and entrepreneurship. In 2000, the gross expenditure on R&D reached S$3 billion (1.9 percent of the GDP) with more than 25,000 R&D personnel engaged in R&D activities. Furthermore, there is the US$1 billion Technopreneurship Investment Fund that provides venture capital for new start-ups. Currently, there are more than 500 such companies. Changes in laws that stigmatized bankruptcy and business failure, tax treatment of employee stock options, and relaxing rules to help start-ups operate from housing premises are some of the major initiatives to promote a hospitable environment for new technology business to flourish. Under the S&T 2005 plan, the Singapore government has committed S$7 billion over the next five years to identify and build world-class science and technology capabilities to strengthen and seed growth sectors that are globally competitive in the new economy. In particular, the key areas of focus are biomedical sciences, infocommunications, chemicals, and microelectronics.

Ongoing efforts were made to improve market access, enhance trade facilitation, and strengthen Singapore's position as an international trade hub. ASEAN has advanced the completion of the ASEAN Free Trade Area (AFTA) from 2008 to 2002. This target, as of January 1, 2002, was successfully met as the six original signatories to the AFTA agreement reduced their tariffs on goods traded among them to no more than 5 percent. Countries (Vietnam, Cambodia, Laos, and Myanmar) were given more time to complete their tariff reduction. Furthermore, ASEAN ministers have also endorsed the protocol to liberalize trade in services among member countries beyond those undertaken by member countries under the General Agreement on Trade in Services (GATS) of the World Trade Organization (WTO). ASEAN leaders at the ASEAN-China Summit held in December 2001 endorsed the proposal for a Framework on Economic Cooperation and to establish an ASEAN-China FTA within ten years. It is an FTA that will create a huge market with 1.7 billion consumers, a regional GDP of about US$2 trillion, and total trade estimated at US$1.23 trillion. This will offer immense business opportunities in trade and investment for enterprises in ASEAN and China.

Singapore pursues bilateral free trade agreements (FTA) as a complementary strategy for global trade liberalization. An FTA with New Zealand was concluded in August 2000 and became effective from January 1, 2001. Negotiations have concluded for another two FTAs, one with Japan and the second with the European Free Trade Association (EFTA), consisting of Iceland, Liechtenstein, Norway, and Switzerland. Negotiations with the United States, the EU, Mexico, Australia, and Canada are also underway. At the multilateral level, Singapore participated in the fourth WTO Ministerial Conference held in Doha, Qatar, in 2001 where a new round of multilateral trade negotiations was launched.

The free flow of capital as well as talent into and out of the economy is expected to continue and increase in the future. Singapore aspires to become an international business hub. New institutions and policies will have to be designed and continuously reviewed to ensure that citizens also reap the benefits of even greater capital liberalization and increased labor mobility across national boundaries.

Notes

1. Examples of the contrary view include Taylor (1993) and Mosley, Harrigan, and Toye (1991).

2. An industrialization program was drawn up by a United Nations team. A 1961 United Nations Report laid the groundwork for Singapore's first development plan, covering the period 1961–1964. More detail on Singapore's development history can be found in Low et al. (1993).

3. ASEAN stands for the Association of Southeast Asian Nations. It is a regional grouping that was formed in 1967 by five countries: Indonesia, Malaysia, Philippines, Singapore, and Thailand. Later in the 1980s and 1990s, the membership of ASEAN was increased to ten to include Brunei, Vietnam, Laos, Myanmar, and Cambodia.

4. Limited domestic market and focused efforts in promoting export-oriented investment and enterprises resulted in direct exports expanding at a faster rate than output. In the manufacturing sector, the ratio of direct export to output increased from 43 percent in 1966 to 58 percent in 1975, 63 percent in 1985, and 64 percent in 2000. The balance of trade in goods and services in the balance of payment turned from a deficit S$1.7 billion (29.8 percent of GDP) in 1970 to a surplus of S$19.6 billion (12 percent of GDP) in 2000.

5. Government participation in industry may take one of the two organizational forms: as a statutory board or as a limited liability company (LLC). A statutory board is created by special legislation and is empowered to perform specific functions. It is managed by a board of directors with representation from government ministries, the private sector, professional organizations, and other groups. A limited liability company owned by the government is incorporated under the Companies Act, like any other private business enterprise. Government-owned LLCs may be private or public. The government participates in the equity capital of industrial enterprises either directly or indirectly.

6. The Central Provident Fund (CPF) is a mandatory national fund set up during the colonial period in 1955 with the original purpose of providing for the needs of the elderly and the disabled. Employers and employees have to contribute a certain percentage of a monthly wage to the member's CPF account. Currently, employees contribute 20 percent, while employers contribute 12 percent of their wage to the CPF. For workers above fifty-five years of age, the contribution rates are reduced by almost half. This is done as part of the overall program to encourage employers to retain workers beyond the retirement age.

7. Where Y is GDP, C and G are respectively private and public consumption expenditure, I_P and I_G are respectively private and public investment, X is exports, and M is imports.

8. The import propensity ratio can exceed 100 percent because of the preponderance of Singapore's entrepôt activities. In the decomposition analysis, entrepôt activities are excluded. Hence, domestic exports and retained imports are used in the computation. Total exports are the sum of domestic exports and re-exports. Similarly, retained imports are total imports minus re-exports.

9. Where E is the economically active population, L is the total number of persons employed, and U the number of unemployed persons.

10. The Kuznets hypothesis postulates that for a developing country, inequality will rise as per-capita income rises. As the economy becomes more developed, inequality will begin to fall. Hence, an inverted U-shape graph will result when inequality is plotted against per capita income.

11. According to the *Economic Survey of Singapore, 2001*, published by the Ministry of Trade and Industry, the total cost of offering rebates on maintenance services, rental, and utilities to low-income HDB households is estimated to be S$433 million. Assuming that this amount is distributed to workers earning less than S$1,000 per month, the Gini coefficient for the year of 2000 will be reduced from 0.4999 to 0.4395, similar to the Gini of the late 1970s.

12. Neo structural thinking explicitly recognizes the shortcomings of earlier structuralist analyses. Such shortcomings include limited concern with short-run macroeconomic management, especially with respect to monetary and fiscal policy; an inability to devise medium-term policies to link national development objectives with planning; the neglect of public enterprises management efficiency; and overconfidence in the virtues of government intervention in the economy, combined with an urban-industrial bias in terms of interventions (Rosales 1988).

References

Amsden, A. 1989. *Asia's next giant: South Korea and late industrialisation.* Oxford: Oxford University Press.

Bitar, S. 1988. Neo-conservatism versus neo-structuralism in Latin America. *CEPAL Review* (34):218–36.

Chowdury, A. and I. Islam 1993. External shocks and structural adjustments in East Asian newly industrialising economies. *Journal of International Development* 5(1).

Killick, T., ed. 1995. *The flexible economy: Causes and consequences of adaptability of national economies.* London: Routledge.

Low, Linda, Toh Mun Heng, Soon Teck Wong, Tan Kong Yam, and Helen Hughes. 1993. *Challenge and response: Thirty years of the Economic Development Board*. Singapore: Times Academic Press.

Mosley, P., J. Harrigan, and J. Toye. 1991. *Aid and power: The World Bank and policy-based lending*. New York: Routledge.

Pang, E. F., and A. H. Tan. 1981. Employment and export-led-industrialisation: The experience for Singapore. In *The development of labor intensive industry in ASEAN countries*, edited by Rashid Amjad. Geneva: International Labor Organisation.

Rosales, O. 1988. An assessment of the structuralist paradigm for Latin American development and the prospects for its renovation *CEPAL Review* (34):239–59.

Taylor, Lance, ed. 1993. *The rocky road to reform*. Cambridge, Mass.: MIT Press.

von Alten, Florian. 1994. *The role of government in the Singapore economy*. European University Studies. Berlin: Peter Lang.

Wade, R. 1990. *Governing the market: Economic theory and the role of the government in East Asian industrialization*. Princeton, N.J.: Princeton University Press.

13

The Distributive and Macroeconomic Impact of Liberalization in Thailand

Bhanupong Nidhiprabha

1. Introduction

Since the early 1970s, Thailand has undergone structural changes in its production, employment, and trade structure. Trade liberalization altered the production pattern by raising the output share of manufactured products from 15 percent in 1970 to 30 percent in 2000. By 1980, the output share of manufactured products had exceeded the share of agricultural products (see figure 13.1a). The relative importance of the agricultural sector in Thailand has been declining throughout the last three decades. It should be noted that the share of non-tradable goods in total output did not increase as much as the share of the other sectors. The transfer of resources between the traditional and modern sectors predominantly dictated the structural output change. After the 1990s, the transformation process slowed down.

At the same time, the share of manufactured exports in total exports rose rapidly at the expense of the share of agricultural export products. The crossover point occurred in 1984, four years after the crossover in the production structure (see figure 13.1b). A sharp declining trend in the agricultural export share and a sharp increasing trend in manufactured exports took place after the baht devaluation in 1984. After 1993, the structural changes in output and exports slowed down substantially. Capital liberalization induced huge capital inflows, thereby raising the price of non-traded goods with respect to the price of traded goods. Investment and production in non-traded sector became more attractive. The shares of output and employment in the non-traded sector have been gradually rising over the years.

Trade liberalization affects resource allocation. As the terms of trade between manufacturing and agricultural products rose, resources were reallocated to the manufacturing sector. By 2000, the agricultural sector still held the largest employment share. The manufacturing sector, which has a higher capital/output ratio than the agricultural sector, cannot absorb all the labor released from the agricultural

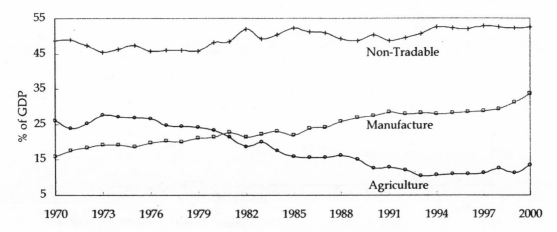

FIGURE 13.1a Structural Changes in the Thai Economy, 1970–2000 Production

sector. The employment share in the agricultural sector declined substantially after 1990 (see figure 13.1c), while the labor share in the manufacturing sector did not rise as fast. It was the non-tradable sector that absorbed labor migration from the rural areas.

Trade and exchange rate policy must have had an important effect on the changing structure of the Thai economy as well as on income distribution. The relative income shares between different sectors depend on relative employment shares, productivity differentials, and the terms of trade among different sectors.

The manufacturing sector gained from rising productivity through imported capital goods financed by cheap credit and overvalued exchange rates. If public spending on education is not sufficient to raise productivity in rural areas, income disparity becomes worse. Moreover, when the terms of trade between agricultural products and manufactured products follow a declining trend, the relative income shares of farmers in rural areas will be smaller. Trade reform creates enormous expansion in the demand for skilled labor in urban areas. Given the above scenario, as the relative employment share of the agricultural labor sector declines, one would expect that income inequality becomes worse as real per capita income rises. It is possible, however, that in some periods, one observe some improvement in income distribution. This can happen during commodity booms when export prices of rice, rubber, and sugar increase so much that they offset the declining relative shares of productivity and employment.

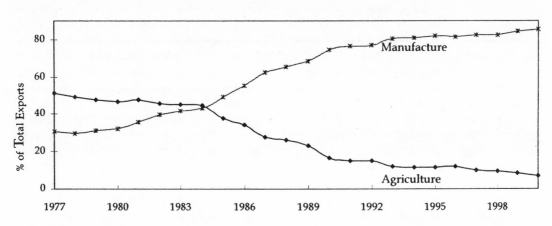

FIGURE 13.1b Exports

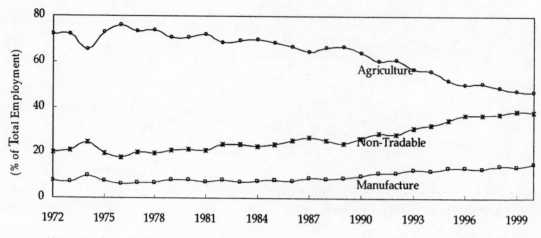

FIGURE 13.1c Employment

It is widely accepted that the benefits of economic development in Thailand have not sufficiently trickled down to the poor. During the past three decades prior to the currency crisis in 1997, real per capita income had continuously increased. Although poverty had declined sharply as a result of rapid economic growth, income inequality has become a major focus in economic development planning. During the few years before the crisis broke out, inequality had reached its peak and showed a sign of slowing down—as if the country had reached the turning point of the inverted U-shaped Kuznets relationship.[1]

In the aftermath of the 1977 crisis when output declined by 10 percent, surprisingly, income inequality did not rise back to its previous level. Evidence indicates that the relationship between the income level and inequality must be complex, involving other factors. As pointed out by Bruno, Ravallion, and Squire (1996), the effect of growth on inequality can go either way. Cross-country data indicate that growth has no systematic impact on inequality. Similarly, Bowman (1997) did not find that distribution necessarily deteriorates with economic growth in poor countries before it can improve. The results were contingent on several other factors including what type of policy was applied.

This chapter explores the macroeconomic impact of liberalization in Thailand and its complex relationship with growth, poverty, and income distribution. The rest of the paper is organized as follows.

Section 2 discusses Thailand's macroeconomic performance during the period of trade and capital liberalization (1970 to 2000). Section 3 analyzes the components of aggregate demand by employing a decomposition analysis. Section 4 contains the decomposition of employment and sectoral labor productivity. Section 5 examines the relationship between income distribution and external liberalization. Section 6 investigates the impact of social policy on poverty and distribution. Section 7 concludes.

2. Liberalization and Macroeconomic Performance

Thailand's rapid income growth may be attributed to investment, consumption, and export booms. The development strategy shifted from import substitution in the 1960s to export promotion through investment promotion policy in the 1970s. The ratio of tariff revenues to imports was 18 percent in 1970. By 2000, the ratio declined to a level that was less than 4 percent (see figure 13.2a). The declining effective tariff rate trend signifies the reduction in import protection, thereby exposing importable sectors to competition with foreign goods. The country should enjoy higher welfare levels from gains in trade and specialization, provided that resources can be relocated to the sector that has comparative advantage.

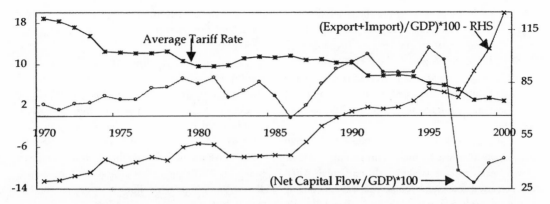

FIGURE 13.2a Liberalization Indicators Degree of Openness and Average Tariff Rate, 1970–2000

It should be noted that the process of trade liberalization was interrupted when the government was hard-pressed for revenue and when the country suffered from a balance of payments crisis. There were some periods when tariff rates were raised to curb imports and to enhance revenues. Nevertheless, the process of trade liberalization continued even after the crisis. In the near future, some manufactured goods imported from Southeast Asian countries will not be subject to any tariff rate. There seems to be no turning back for Thailand toward its previous inward-oriented development strategy of the 1960s.

Since exports have been a major driving force for the economy, the government has earnestly pursued export promotion by providing incentives to exporters. Investment and tax privileges, export tax rebates, and financial subsidies through cheap credit policy

have been given to exporters. As a result, both exports and imports have been rising more rapidly than the GDP level. The degree of openness, as measured by the value of total external trade divided by GDP, has been increasing rapidly (see figure 13.2a). From 27 percent in 1970, the exposure to external trade rose to 120 percent in 2000. The 1997 currency crisis and subsequent recession neither severed nor diminished Thailand's trade linkages.

In terms of capital liberalization, in 1991 the Thai government accepted the IMF Article VIII. Capital controls were relaxed to allow the free flow of capital. In 1993, the government permitted financial institutions to offer offshore banking facilities to domestic borrowers. The motivation behind this was to establish Bangkok as a financial center in the region so that the cost of borrowing for investment would be cheaper. Net capital inflows rose sharply in the mid-1990s,

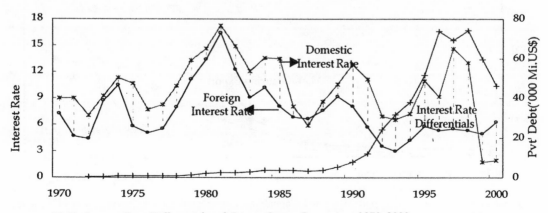

FIGURE 13.2b Interest Rate Differential and Private Sector Borrowing, 1970–2000.

providing substantial resources for bank lending and investment. The ratio of net capital inflows to GDP was 2 percent in 1970, climbing to 10 percent in 1990, and reaching its peak in 1995 (see figure 13.3). Except for capital flight after 1997, both indexes of the degree of openness indicated a trend of increased globalization with trade reform and capital control relaxation.

As long as the domestic interest rate is higher than the foreign interest rate, there is an incentive for the private sector to borrow abroad. In particular, when the perceived foreign exchange risk was low during the fixed exchange rate regime, capital flows increased substantially after 1990, resulting in massive private debt accumulation in the period prior to the currency crisis (figure 13.2b). In 1996, the commercial banks' share of foreign borrowing in total private net capital inflows amounted to 27 percent. The corresponding share of private non-bank foreign borrowing was 30 percent. A considerable part of these inflows were short-term debts. Furthermore, portfolio investment and non-resident baht accounts amounted to 19 and 16 percent respectively. Long-term capital flows in the form of foreign direct investment accounted for only 12 percent of inflows. The maturity structure of capital inflows lead to vulnerability—a sudden shift in confidence might lead to a sudden outflow of capital. In addition, the overindebtedness of the private sector also increased the degree of vulnerability. It should be emphasized that foreign debts were mainly created by the private

sector, since the government ran a budget surplus throughout the boom period prior to the 1997 currency float.

Capital flows in the form of both foreign direct investment and foreign borrowing led to capital accumulation in export-related sectors as well as an increasing degree of import dependency. Many manufactured exports such as electronics and computer parts and components have low value-added. Foreign investment flows into the electronics industry during the 1970s and 1990s were the highest among all sectors that attracted foreign direct investment. The industry itself accounted for 35 percent of Thailand's total exports. In 2000, the electronics industry, one of the highest job creation industries, employed 460,000 workers. The low educational level of the average Thai worker in this industry makes it impossible for the electronics industry to create high value-added products. Computer-related products assembly plants employed labor-intensive technology that cannot generate high value-added from labor inputs. Assembly plants of hard disks, monitors, and semiconductors cannot generate value-added greater than 20 percent of their sale values. The dependency on imports in CPU, memory chips, and copper-clad assembly make the local content of this industry as low as 20 percent of the input requirement. The import dependency of exports leads to a high correlation between exports and imports. Thus a surge in exports is also accompanied by a sharp increase in imported raw materials, as can be seen from figure 13.3.

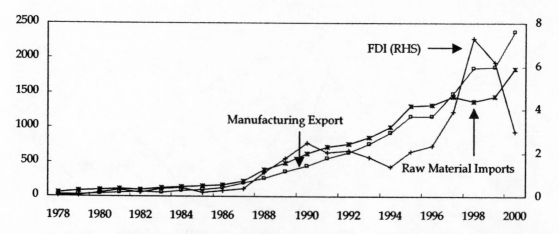

FIGURE 13.3 Manufacturing Exports, Imported Capital and Intermediate Goods (bi.Baht), and FDI Inflow (bi.US$), 1978–2000

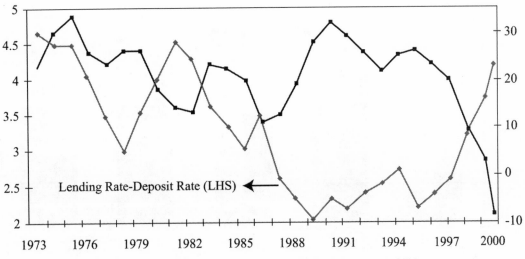

FIGURE 13.4 Interest Rate Spreads and Bank Credit to the Private Sector, 1970–2000

Similarly, a fall in exports is followed by a reduction in imports.

Foreign direct investment increased sharply after 1994, reaching its peak in 1998. The surge in FDI reflected the movements of foreign funds lured by fire sale prices. A large part of the surge in FDI in 1998 was the result of brownfield investment through acquisitions of several ailing Thai banks. Although no new employment was generated, this type of FDI saved some workers from being laid off due to the possible closing down of bad banks.

During the booms, Thailand experienced current account deficits, but the surplus in the capital account was high enough to cause a balance of payments surplus. With the fixed exchange rate, international reserves rose rapidly, reaching almost $40 billion, until mid-1997. Under the fixity of the baht to the U.S. dollar, the expansion of the monetary base fueled by capital inflows led to lending booms and inflationary pressures.

Prior to the crisis, there was an attempt by the Bank of Thailand to sterilize capital inflows. Nevertheless the attempt was futile owing to the lack of government bonds and the high cost of issuing Bank of Thailand's bonds during the period of tight money markets. The amount of the BOT bonds was small compared to the huge capital inflows. After the crisis, tight monetary policy was pursued under the guidance of the IMF and the monetary base contracted sharply after 1998.

The interest spread between banks' lending and deposits rates remained high in the periods before and after capital liberalization. Bank efficiency, measured by the narrowness of the interest spread, did not increase as expected. This is not surprising since banks were able to obtain external funds at a lower cost. During the property booms of the early 1990s, world interest rates were at low levels. Banks did not foresee immediate foreign exchange risks, thereby borrowing heavily from abroad and ignoring mobilizing funds from domestic sources. As figure 13.4 shows, the spread did not fall below 3 percent and its trend was rising both before and after the crisis. The widening interest gap after the financial crash was due to the cost related to non-performing loans, while the widening interest gap before the currency crisis was caused by excess demand from high-risk and high-return investors. To sum up, capital liberalization did not bring about a more efficient allocation of financial resources. The excessive credit expansion in the late 1980s was a leading indicator of banking failure in the 1990s.

Bank lending booms are usually leading indicators of economic crisis. Margin loans and property loans feed into asset price bubbles. The overvaluation of assets cannot exist without credit expansion. As figure 13.4 suggests, bank loans expanded by 30 percent in the year before the crisis broke out. Then lending abruptly contracted as banks could not find qualified borrowers. The contraction in bank credit has

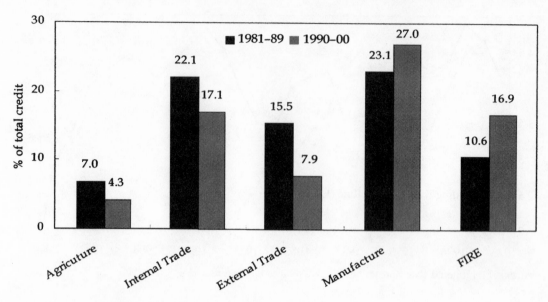

FIGURE 13.5 Credit Allocation by Commercial Banks, 1981–2000.

prolonged the recovery of the debt-deflation economy. In 2001, bank credit continued to decline by 6
percent from the previous year. Capital liberalization
can lead to unsustainable growth. Capital convertibility alone does not guarantee long-term growth
with stability. The institutional infrastructure must be
altered in such a way that countries that undertake
liberalization can minimize the related cost of financial reforms.

One may compare the period before and after
external liberalization. During the period 1981–1989,
the share of bank credit allocated to the agricultural
sector was 7 percent, while the manufacturing and the
finance, insurance, and real estate (FIRE) sectors received 23.1 and 10.6 percent of total credit, respectively. It is clear from figure 13.5 that after the
launching of financial liberalization, both manufacturing and non-traded sectors obtained a greater
share of bank credit, while the share of agricultural
credit declined to 4.3 percent during 1990–2000. If
money capital and physical capital are complementary, the increase in the bank credit allocated to the
manufacturing and FIRE sectors would imply higher
capital/labor ratios and higher labor productivity.

Nevertheless, the concentration of bank credit in
some sectors such as the property sector and other non-
traded sectors can lead to financial fragility. By borrowing foreign loans in the short term and by long-term

lending to domestic borrowers in baht, commercial
banks became more vulnerable to external shocks. The
mismatching of maturity dates and currencies are a
classic form of technical mismanagement. It calls for
close monitoring and supervising by bank regulators,
in addition to stringent rules on capital adequacy to
prevent future crisis. These are some of the preconditions for successful capital liberalization. As pointed
out by Taylor (1998), financial crises are caused by
destabilizing private sector profit seeking when policy
and circumstances provide the preconditions and the
regulatory authorities are acquiescent.

There are various adverse consequences of capital
inflows. While the demand for both traded and non-
traded goods rises because of monetary expansion,
the supply response from the non-traded sector will
be sluggish because of limited endowments. The
rapid rise in the prices of the non-traded sector relative to the traded sector leads to appreciation in the
real exchange rate.

One can employ the ratio of the producer price
index (PPI) to the consumer price index (CPI) as a
proxy for the real exchange rate. Since the consumer
price index contains services, the CPI should track the
movement of non-traded goods, while the producer
price index would capture changes in the price of
traded goods. Between 1991 and 1996, the price of
non-traded goods rose faster than the price of traded

goods (by about 2 percent annually). Thus, the continued real appreciation led to the loss of competitiveness and increasing pressure on the Bank of Thailand to defend the fixed exchange rate. After the float, the real exchange rate—as measured by the ratio of traded to non-traded price—depreciated annually by about 1.57 percent in 1997 and 1998.

3. Decomposition Analysis of Aggregate Demand

As discussed earlier, import dependency has increased over the course of economic development in Thailand, since export commodities require imported capital goods and raw materials. Foreign direct investment and imported capital goods are directly related. There is empirical evidence from cross-sectional studies of developing countries provided by Jong (1995) suggesting that imported capital goods and foreign direct investment during 1965–1985 contributed to higher economic growth. Nevertheless, Singh (1986) argues that imported capital goods cause trade deficits and subsequently lead to economic crisis as in the case of Mexico. Indeed, among the three leakage parameters presented in figure 13.6a, the import propensity coefficient was consistently higher than the other parameters. Except for the period of turmoil in 1997 and 1998, the period after capital account liberalization witnessed a

strong growth in imports accompanied by an economic boom.

The leakage parameter from private savings, on the other hand, exhibited a relatively more stable trend than import propensity. The large drop in consumption in 1988 confirmed that during the period of uncertainty, households held back their spending, thereby aggravating output contraction. The 1998 output contraction and subsequent declines in output growth below the previous growth path decreased tax revenue. This is shown by the declining tax propensity parameter. Figure 13.6a indicates that during the rapid growth era between 1985 and 1995, tax revenue increased faster than gross output. Consequently, the pressure on the current account and price stability can be mitigated. The movement of the tax leakage parameter reflects the outcome of fiscal automatic stabilizers.

Gross output can be decomposed into the weighted average of three own multiplier components shown in figure 13.6b. The weights are the proportions of each leakage parameter to the total value of all leakage parameters. Exports and investment were the important driving forces of the Thai economy, because of the rising importance in the saving and import propensities. The rising level of the investment/saving ratio after capital liberalization signals that the alarmingly large trade deficit financed by foreign savings may be destabilizing in the future. The rapidly rising own multiplier of government spending

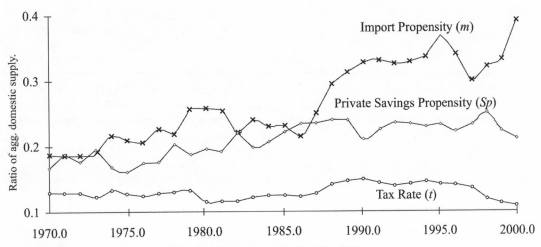

FIGURE 13.6a Decomposition Analyses: Aggregate Demand, 1970–2000
Leakage Parameters: Private Saving, Import, and Tax Propensities

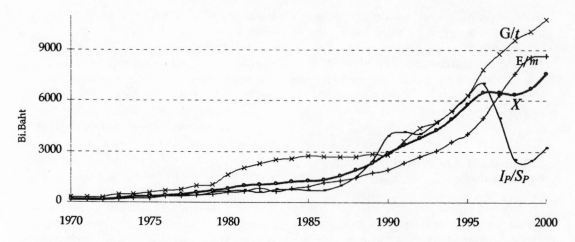

FIGURE 13.6b Effects of Own Multipliers (Investment, Government Spending, and Exports) on Output, 1970–2000

suggests that fiscal policy can be effective during an economic slump.

If the income elasticity of demand for imports is high, the trade deficit during the boom can turn into surplus during the bust. Figure 13.6c illustrates this point. The robust U.S. economy in 1999 and 2000 boosted Thai exports, bringing back the growth rate from –10 percent in 1998 to 4.5 percent in the following year. The investment/saving gap is a mirror image of the trade gap when the fiscal budget is balanced. The current account would have widened

much more if the government had run budget deficits. The collapse of private investment means that imports of capital goods were not necessary since the underutilization of plants and equipment is widespread.

Figure 13.7 reiterates the point that excessive investment cannot occur unless there are financial resources obtained from financial institutions. The boom-bust cycle of credit can be captured by the change in private credit. Thus the cyclical movement in the claims on the private sector predetermines the excess of

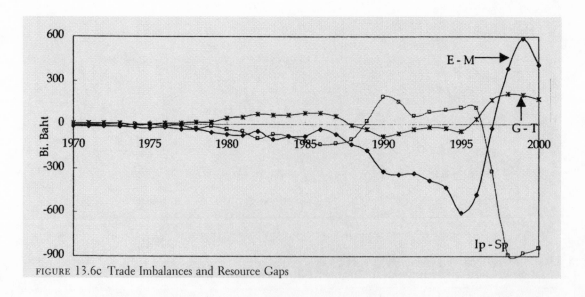

FIGURE 13.6c Trade Imbalances and Resource Gaps

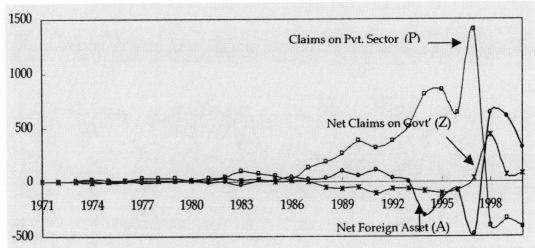

FIGURE 13.7 Net Change in Financial Claims by Banking Sector: Net Foreign Assets, Private Sector Credit, and Net Claims on Government, 1970–2000

investment over private savings. Since the government ran budget surpluses prior to the year 1997, the net claims on government were negative, because the government used cash balances to early retire public debt. The change in net foreign assets is dictated by the position of the current account and net capital flows. Capital flight was apparently strong between 1997 and 2000. Capital control relaxation can lead to a surge in capital inflows as well as massive capital flight. Too much and too fast capital inflows can be destabilizing.

Prior to the currency crisis, Thailand had experienced continued inflows of foreign capital through foreign borrowing. The net capital inflows in 1996 amounted to 9.9 percent of GDP. The inflows reversed into capital flight throughout the late 1990s and continued into the early 2000s. At the highest level of capital flight in 1998, the net capital outflows reached 13.9 percent. Bank and non-bank private sectors reported heavy capital flight: around 11.3 and 3.7 percent of GDP respectively. Nevertheless, the severity of capital outflows was attenuated by foreign direct investment and portfolio investment throughout the crisis period and after the recovery in the early 2000s.

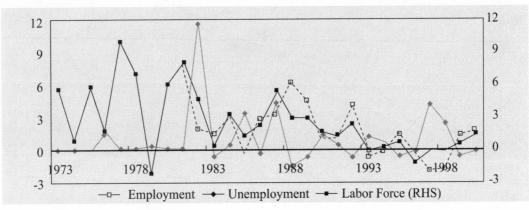

FIGURE 13.8a Decomposition Analysis: Employment, Labor Productivity, and Wage Growth Rates of Labor Force, Employment, and Unemployment, 1972–2000[1]

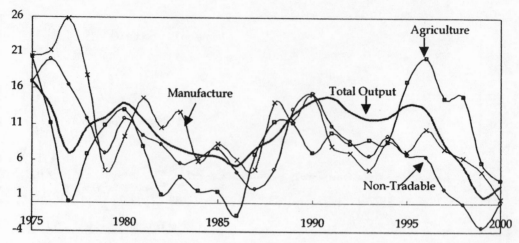

FIGURE 13.8b Sectoral Productivity Growth (3 Years Moving Average) 1972–2000

4. Decomposition Analysis of Employment and Productivity

The growth rate of labor force, employment, and unemployment are shown in figure 13.8a. The rate of change of unemployment depends on the difference between the rates of change of unemployment and employment plus the difference between the rate of change of the employment share and the rate of change of the labor force participation. It is hypothesized that the faster the rise in unemployment, the higher the degree of income disparity. As such, rapid economic growth indirectly affects income distribution through its impact on employment generation.

The productivity growth rate of the entire economy was positive between 1975 and 2000. However, there was negative growth in the agricultural sector in 1986

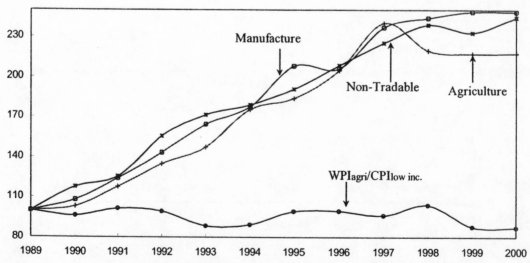

FIGURE 13.8c Wage Gap between Agricultural and Non-agricultural Sectors, and Rural Terms of Trade, 1989–2000

TABLE 13.1 Poverty Indicators: Quality of Life

Urban Population (% of total)	Adult Literacy Rate	Education Enrollment Ratio (% of Relevant Age Group)		Life Expectancy at Birth	Infant Mortality (per 1,000)	Under 5 Mortality (per 1,000)
		Primary	Secondary			
15 (1975)	82 (1974)	79 F (1977) 86 M	25 (1975)	59 (1970–1975)	74 (1970)	102 (1970)
17 (1980)		97 F (1980) 100 M	29 (1981)	58 (1975)	57 (1975)	
18 (1984)	86.7 (1985)	97 F (1983) 101 M	20 (1987)	65 F (1982) 61 M	49 (1980)	40 (1987)
22 (1989)	89.9 (1990)		28 (1988)	66 F (1984) 62 M	38 (1990)[a]	
23 (1992)	94.6 (1993)	97 F (1993) 98 M	33 (1990)	71 F (1990) 66 M	33 (1995)	37 (1992)
22 (2000)	95 (1998)		48 (1997)	72 F (1998) 66 M	29 (1998)[a]	37 (1998)

Source: World Bank, *WDR* (various issues); and World Bank, *World Table* (various issues).

a. Source: WWW.adb.org/Documents/EDRC/statistics/.

Note: F = female; and M = male.

and in the non-tradable sector in 1999 (see figure 13.8b). Since the productivity growth of total output is the weighted average of the difference in output growth and the employment growth rate, the structural changes in output and employment as depicted in figure 13.1 would have an important impact on productivity change. In the early 1970s, output and employment growth in the agricultural sector would dominate overall productivity. But after capital liberalization in the 1990s, movements of output and employment in the non-tradable sector explained the variation in the productivity change of the overall economy. Output expansion in the traded sector is related to commodity booms. A slump in the world prices of rice, sugar, and semiconductors would have a detrimental impact on the expansion of output in both the agricultural and manufacturing sectors. If changes in productivity affect the value of the marginal product of labor, income distribution is also affected by productivity changes.

The analysis of income disparities can begin by examining the wage gap between the agricultural and manufacturing sectors. Then I can proceed by explaining the wage gaps between the non-traded, the agricultural, and the manufacturing sectors. Wage gaps between the agricultural and manufacturing

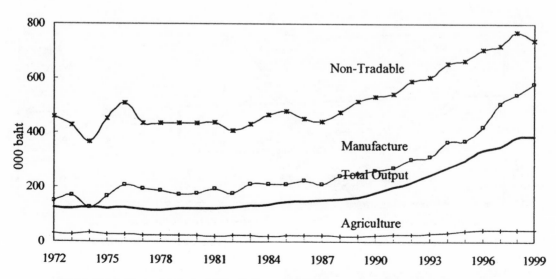

FIGURE 13.8d Capital/Labor Ratio by Major Industry, 1972–99

sectors can be captured by the trend of the wage rates of the two sectors, as shown in figure 13.8c. The period when the three lines of wage rates converge should be one of reducing income inequality. The years 1991, 1994, and 1996 should be the years of improving income equality. However, after the financial shock in 1998, the wage gaps between the three sectors widened. The widening (narrowing) gaps should roughly correspond to the rising (falling) value of the Gini coefficient (see table 13.1). The poor in rural areas are adversely affected if the terms of trade of their products turn unfavorable for them. The rural terms of trade are calculated by using the ratio of the agricultural producer price index to the low-income consumer price index. The rural terms of trade are shown in figure 13.8c. When the terms of trade turned against the rural poor, inequality should rise such as in 1992, 1999, and 2000. These were the years when the Gini coefficient edged upward. On the other hand, 1998 saw a marginal decline in inequality as the rural terms of trade were favorable to the poor.

Figure 13.8d illustrates the time trend of capital accumulation in the agriculture, manufacturing, and non-tradable sectors. The overall capital/labor ratio increased gradually after the period of trade liberalization in the 1970s. After the push for capital liberalization since 1990, the capital labor ratio increased dramatically. The service sector or the non-traded sector has the highest K/L ratio. In contrast with the rising trend of the K/L ratio in the manufacturing

sector, the K/L ratio in the agricultural sector increased marginally. As a result, there have been widening productivity discrepancies between the rural sector and the urban sectors containing both manufacturing and non-traded sectors. After the 1997 crash, the K/L ratio in the service sector has been declining. Because of uncertainty, overcapacity of physical capital, and the lack of credit, investment expenditures declined considerably from the boom period. The change in the productivity gap in the late 1990s will undoubtedly affect the distribution of income of workers in the three sectors.

Decomposition analysis of the non-traded sector shows that productivity growth, measured by its three-year moving average rate of change, had been declining since 1990 (see figure 13.9a). The movement of productivity growth in the construction sector was pro-cyclical. Because commerce and service sectors have the highest employment shares (see figure 13.9b), they dominated the movement of the overall productivity of the non-traded sector. The employment share of the construction sector is also pro-cyclical, expanding and contracting in the same manner as investment in the real estate sector. The K/L ratio of the transportation sector is the highest among the four sectors in the non-traded sector (see figure 13.9c). It should be noted that productivity change was negative only in 1998, when GDP growth registered –10 percent. Productivity growth in the commerce sector moved countercyclically in the slump of 1998. The rate of change of overall

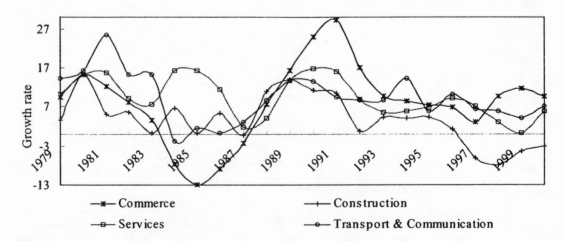

FIGURE 13.9a Decomposition of Non-Tradable Sector Productivity Growth (3 Years Moving Average) 1976–2000

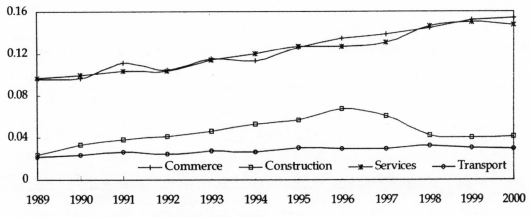

FIGURE 13.9b Employment Share(L_i/L), 1989–2000

productivity depends on the difference between the weighted average of sectoral output growth and the weighted sectoral employment. The rate of change of the overall productivity growth can also be thought of as the weighted average of sectoral productivity growth plus the difference in output share and employment share weighed by sectoral employment growth (see the footnote in figure 13.8b). Thus if productivity differs significantly among sectors, overall productivity growth will fluctuate substantially. Large differences in the output and employment shares of all sectors imply large income disparities.

Between 1980–1989 and 1990–2000, the employment share of the agricultural sector declined from 68.2 percent to 54.1 percent. During the same

period, the manufacturing sector's share of employment was raised from 8.6 to 12.3 percent. For the trading sector as a whole, the employment share declined by 8.7 percentage points. While the share of employment in the traded sector declined, the share of employment in the non-traded sector rose from 23.7 percent to 32.6 percent. The employment in construction rose from 2 percent of the labor workforce in the 1980s to 5.1 percent in the 1990s. The commerce and service sectors were the most successful in generating employment (see figure 13.9b). The agricultural sector has been shedding employment along with its economic development, as depicted in figure 13.1c. Table 13.2 indicates that the sectors that experienced high productivity growth

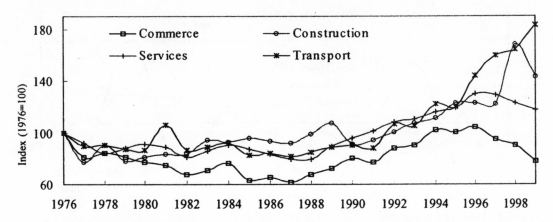

FIGURE 13.9c K_i/L_i ratio, 1976–99

TABLE 13.2 Economic Provisioning

Year	Government Spending (% of GDP) on			Year	Access to Sanitation (% of population)	Access to Save Water (% of population)
	Education	Health	Welfare			
1972–1979	3.2	0.63	0.58			
1980–1989	3.6	0.98	0.56	1982	97	66
1990–1996	3.3	1.2	0.58	1995	98	89
1997–2000	4.4	1.5	0.89	1990–1998	96	81

Source: World Bank, WDR (various issues); and UNDP, HDR (various issues).

Note: According to HPI measures, Thailand is ranked into 29 and the value is 18.7% (deprivation in long and healthy life, in knowledge, and in economic provisioning).

were the sectors that generated the highest numbers of jobs. A slowdown in productivity growth in the construction sector between 1990 and 2000 contributed to substantial job destruction in this business-cycle sensitive sector (see figure 13.9b). Wage flexibility in the non-traded sector mitigated unemployment during the economic slump.

After the financial crash in 1997, the unemployment rate in Thailand rose considerably (but less than the rates experienced in some developed countries such as Australia, Canada, France, and Germany). As discussed earlier, capital accumulation in the non-traded sector was relatively high when compared with the traded sector. Job losses in the non-traded sector were attenuated by falling wage rates.

It is quite clear from figure 13.10a that changes in the wage gap between the non-traded and traded sectors correspond to changes in the productivity gap, with some lags in the pre-crisis period. Wage rate

adjustments take place but not always instantaneously, in line with productivity changes. If the terms of trade of the two sectors remain stable, fluctuations in the wage differential mainly reflect changes in the productivity growth of the two sectors.

Figure 13.10b shows that the number of self-employed increased after 1997, reflecting the layoff from private enterprises. During the booms of the last three decades, cooperative profits rose as a percentage of total national income, while the share of the self-employed continued to decline. The interest share of total income rose with the booms, which needed to be financed by household savings. As the economy slows down, the demand for funds disappears. The liquidity glut drives down the interest rate. One thus observes a declining share of interest income in 1999. This trend would continue well into 2002. As long as there is no solid recovery, there would be no demand for funds to push up the domestic interest rate. Since the wage

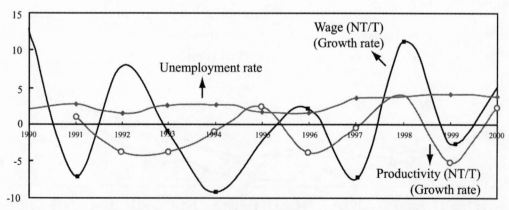

FIGURE 13.10a Income Distribution, Wage Inequality, and Poverty Unemployment Rate, Wage Inequality, and Productivity between Non-Tradable (NT) and Tradable (T) Sectors, 1990–2000

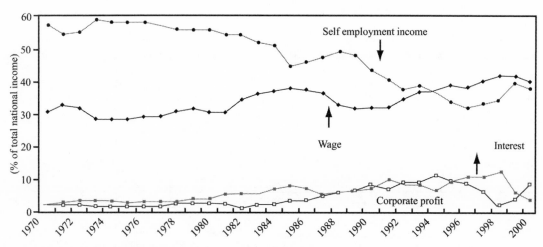

FIGURE 13.10b Distribution of National Income, 1970-2000

share of income continues to rise, the discrepancies among wage earners would be an important factor determining the overall income inequality.

The Lorenz curve, based on all sources of income, is shown in figure 13.11. There was a significant decline in inequality between 1988 and 1998. The Gini coefficient dropped from 0.48 in 1988 to 0.41 in 1998.[2] An increase in inequality in 1999, as shown in figure 13.12, was the result of increasing poverty due to increased unemployment. While the number of people who live below the poverty line declined from 32.6 percent in 1988 to 11.4 percent in 1996, the percentage of the poor rose to 13 and 15.9 percent in 1998 and 1999 (see figure 13.13). It was estimated that there were 1.2 million unemployed in 1999. The figure may increase further if economic stagnation persists. The year 1996 saw the lowest rate of unemployment as well as the lowest poverty level. Economic growth is indirectly related to income distribution. With no growth, people will be pushed into unemployment. The number of the poor or people who live below the poverty line will increase and further tilt income distribution toward the rich.

Figure 13.14 shows that between 1992 and 1998, the terms of trade were in favor of the agricultural

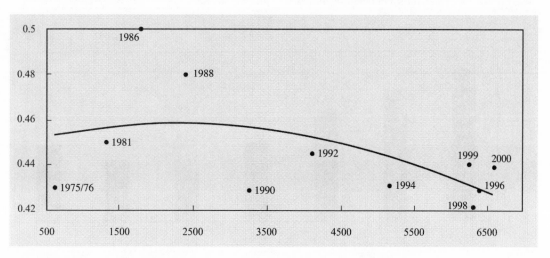

FIGURE 13.11 Economic Growth and Income Distribution, 1975/76–2000

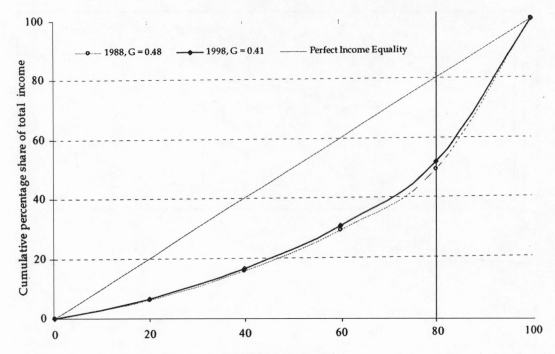

FIGURE 13.12 Distribution of Income Before and After Liberalization

sector, except for the year 1993. The sharp rise in agricultural product prices relative to industrial product prices was beneficial to farmers. Figure 13.14 also traces the trend of the terms of trade between the non-traded and the traded sectors from 1990 to 2000. The movement of the *Pnt/Pt* ratio was in line with the movement of the real effective exchange rate (REER). The *REER* (on the right-hand scale) is obtained from the calculation of the Bank of Thailand; an upward trend indicates the appreciation of the exchange rate. Both indexes pointed to the same conclusion: that international competitiveness deteriorated after capital liberalization. Since the value of the marginal product of labor in the agricultural and manufacturing sectors is determined by international price levels, exchange rate policy is an important factor affecting income distribution.

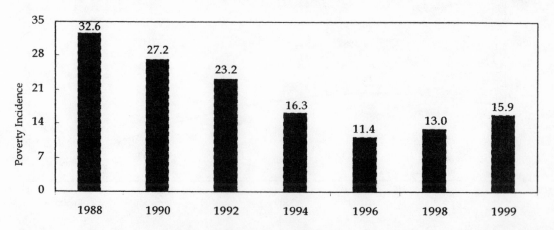

FIGURE 13.13 Population Below National Poverty Line, 1988–2000

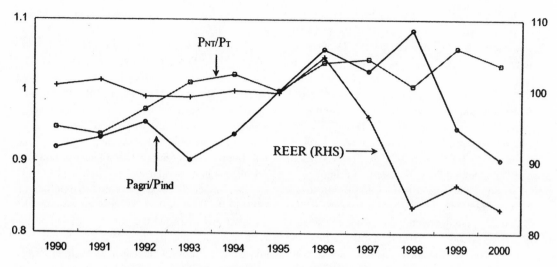

FIGURE 13.14 Relative Prices: Real Effective Exchange Rate (REER), Price Ratios of Non-tradable/Tradable (P_{NT}/P_T), and Agriculture and Industry (P_{agri}/P_{ind}), 1990–2000

The nominal effective exchange rate depreciated by 14.5 percent annually in 1997 and 1998 (see table 13.3). Since the inflation rate in Thailand was higher than the inflation rates of its major trading partners, the real effective exchange rate depreciated by only 10.6 percent. After the foreign exchange markets had regained stability, the REER of the baht appreciated by 3.75 percent in 1999, but lost its ground again in 2000 due to the worldwide strength of the dollar. Currency depreciation in 1998 had a strong redistributive income effect. The nominal wage rate in the traded sector declined by 4.7 percent in 1998, while the nominal wage rate in the non-traded sector experienced a 2.5 percent decline in 1999. The flexibility of both nominal and real wage rates in both sectors kept unemployment at low levels.

5. Poverty, Income Distribution, and Economic Growth

The National Statistical Office conducts its survey on household income every other year. The relationship between the Gini coefficient and the level of real per capita income is shown in figure 13.11. The evidence indicates that during this episode of Thailand's rapid

TABLE 13.3 Poverty Lines, Incidence, Depth, and Severity, and HDI, 1970–2000

Year	National Poverty Line (US$) (Per Person/Day)[a]	Population (%) below Poverty Lines		Poverty Gap Ratio	Severity of Poverty Index	HDI
		National Poverty Line	International Poverty Line ($2/day)			
1988	0.62	32.6		10.4	4.6	0.60 (1975)
1990	0.69	27.2		8.0	3.3	0.64 (1980)
1992	0.68	23.2	23.5	6.8	2.8	0.67 (1985)
1994	0.84	16.3		4.3	1.7	0.70 (1990)
1996	0.96	11.4		2.8	1.1	0.83 (1995)
1998	0.71	13.0	28.2	3.2	1.2	0.74 (1998)
1999	0.78	15.9				

Source: www.nesdb.go.th/Main_Menu/Macro/Devindex_data/dev6.html.

a. National poverty line is converted into baht using annual average exchange rate (baht/$).

economic progress, income inequality deteriorated as economic development proceeded. Figure 13.10a shows the relationship between income level (in domestic currency) against the movement of the Gini coefficient. The rise in the coefficient in 1986 was followed by its subsequent decline in 1988 and 1990. A marginally declining trend continued well until 1998. Then there was a spike in 1999, when the Gini edged upward together with a reduction in income level. As the economy rebounded in 2000, the Gini coefficient was heading toward the southeastern direction.

Atkinson (2001) argues that it is misleading to talk about the inexorable trend of income inequality. Instead, one should discuss the experience of rising inequality as "episodes." Except for a spike in 1986, the inequality and growth tradeoff seems to correspond to Kuznets's thesis that inequality must rise until income reaches a threshold level where improved equality can be observed. For the first time in Thailand's recent economic history, output contracted by 10 percent in 1998. Yet inequality did not rise to the level corresponding with the pre-crisis income level. In fact, the Gini coefficient declined marginally in 1998 despite the increasing number of the poor. The evidence suggests that income inequality is the result of interactions among different factors such as wage adjustment, terms of trade, and sectoral productivity. We need to examine both micro and macro data together with the impact of social policies.

High growth rates have a favorable impact on poverty. High growth years were followed by a drastic reduction in the number of the poor. The percentage of the poor, whose incomes were below the poverty line, declined from 32 percent in 1997 to 11 percent in 1996. When the growth rates in 1982 and 1986 fell below the trend growth path, poverty alleviation in subsequent years was not as effective as during the boom years. In 1998, the percentage of the poor rose to 13 percent, but income inequality declined marginally. The financial crisis must have affected the middle-income and upper-income classes more than the poor.

Figure 13.10b clearly illustrates that rapid growth in GDP helps reduce the poverty level. The growth rate of GDP shows a positive relationship with the income share of the bottom 20 percent. Note also that negative income growth in 1998 did not reduce the income share of people at the lowest rung of the development ladder. However, there seems to be no correlation between growth and income inequality, as shown in figure 13.11.

The percentage of the poor was cut in half from 1972 to 1994. Warr (2000) found evidence that very large reductions in absolute poverty incidence in Thailand, Indonesia, Malaysia, and the Philippines from the 1960s to 1999 were related to high rates of economic growth. If external liberalization is conducive to growth, then it must help poverty reduction. But the relationship between liberalization and income distribution is far more complicated.

The number of the poor rose from 6.8 million in 1998 to 7.9 million in 1998. The 1998 recession led to job losses and increased the number of people who lived below the poverty line. The poverty line was adjusted upward by 19 percent in 1998 (from 1996), while real per capita income fell by almost 14 percent. Poverty lines were calculated based on the cost of living of the poor in both urban and rural areas. Usually the percentage increase in the poverty line exceeds the inflation rates faced by the poor in both areas. If nominal per capita income rises faster than the inflation rate, poverty can be alleviated. But this was not the case in 1998, when nominal income fell along with a rising price level caused by massive currency depreciation. Real income in 1998 declined below its 1994 level, but the number of the poor was still lower than the level in 1994. One cannot deny that per capita income increased at an impressive rate from 1976 to 1996.

People who are grouped at the lowest income percentile are the poor whose income falls below the poverty line. More than half of these poor lived in the agricultural sector. In 1998, 46.5 percent of the poor owned land, 8.9 percent were tenants, and 14 percent were landless laborers. Only 9.4 percent of the poor were laborers in the manufacturing sector. Deininger and Squire (1997) provide evidence supporting the hypothesis that the unequal distribution of assets, more than of income, can be an impediment to rapid growth. In addition, countries with more equal land distribution tend to grow faster. Land and human capital are two crucial factors giving rise to rural poverty. The poor are mainly farmers and farm labors who do not own land and have little formal education. Nevertheless, the problem of inequitable land distribution is not as serious as in some Latin American countries. Therefore one cannot explain rising inequality with land ownership distribution in Thailand.

Income inequality arises mainly from the difference between income earned by farmers and wages and salary earned by workers in the modern sector. Income inequality can be improved considerably if the income gap between rural and urban sectors can be narrowed.

Workers in the non-traded sector earned twice as much as workers in the traded sector, presumably because of the higher values of their marginal product. The capital/labor ratio in the non-traded sector (including FIRE) must be higher than the corresponding ratio in the traded sector (including importables, exportables, and agricultural products). The relative wage rates between the two sectors did not change significantly between 1989 and 2000. Nor did the Gini index move considerably during this period. If the wage rate in the non-traded sector increased substantially relative to the wage rate in the traded sector, one would have observed a significant increase in inequality (see figure 13.8c).

6. External Liberalization and Income Distribution

The average product in the manufacturing sector far exceeded the average product in the agricultural sector. Foreign direct investment in the manufacturing sector must have enhanced the sector's productivity through the importation of capital goods. However, there has been no significant foreign direct investment in the agricultural sector. As the real wage in the manufacturing sector rose, income inequality increased. Furthermore, the declining terms of trade between agriculture and manufactured products aggravated the discrepancies. The conclusion that trade reform hampers rather than helps more equitable income distribution is in sharp contrast with the simulation results from the study done by Sarntisart (1995), which indicates that a move toward free trade would lead to a more equal distribution of income. However, wage inequality rose after trade reform in Mexico (Harrison and Hanson 1999) and also in Chile (Beyer, Rojas, and Vergara 1999). In these studies, foreign direct investment, export orientation, technological change, and openness widened the wage gaps between skilled and unskilled labor.

Capital account liberalization aggravated the problem of inequality. The too-much and too-fast inflows of foreign capital caused consumption and credit booms. Without low-cost funds, bank credit could not have expanded at the astronomical rate seen in the early 1990s. Banks envisaged higher profits from lending to the property sector. They might have suffered from disaster myopia or a linear perception of ever-rising land prices. According to Thai law, land is the only asset that can be used for loan collateral. Capital control relaxation also implies that firms can borrow directly in terms of dollars. Large corporations with high reputations and a low risk rating were able to enter world money markets without restrictions. As such, foreign financial resources were channeled to sectors that tended to be highly capital intensive.

Export-oriented sectors as well as service sectors were among the recipients of cheap credit from abroad. With a high capital/labor ratio, income distribution favored those who worked in these sectors. The ratios of bank credit extended to these sectors relative to their value-added were strikingly different from the corresponding ratio for the agricultural sector. There exists a certain degree of urban bias in commercial banks that tend to mobilize more funds from rural areas and extend proportionately less to the rural sector. Since a larger amount of working capital is required for business with a higher capital/labor ratio, banks tend to favor large borrowers who are more creditworthy than small-scale businesses and farmers with high default risks.

Income inequality is related to inequality in gaining assess to credit. Although farmers are willing to pay higher interest rates, their requests for loans can be easily turned down because of the lack of collateral. Credit rationing is normal practice for Thai banks, even though there is plenty of liquidity in the system. It is not clear whether capital control relaxation can reduce credit rationing in such a way that banks would prefer lending to the liquidity-constrained poor or high-risk and high-return property developers. If capital control liberalization simply reduces credit constraints for the rich, then capital convertibility can worsen income distribution. If capital markets are imperfect, according to Aghion, Caroli, and Garcia-Penalosa (1999), redistributive policies can be growth enhancing. Subsidies to borrowers to gain access to credit markets to enhance human capital can reduce income inequality.

Capital liberalization has an impact on stock market activity. It is believed that by providing liquidity through free entry and free exit, the government can attract more portfolio investment from abroad. The bull market, driven by margin loans and frenzied speculation, reached its peak in 1994. Capital gains were ensured during the bull runs, and they were not subject to any capital gains tax. Nonresident baht accounts increased substantially as they are directly related to portfolio investment. These were short-term volatile capital inflows aiming for stock market speculation. Some of these speculators were traders in foreign institutions that were supposed to possess superior technical capability to analyze the market compared with the locals. As a result, local traders blindly followed the trading activities of foreign institutional investors. It is not unrealistic to assume that speculators in the stock market are the ones in the top income quintile, so it is odd to hear proponents of the securities market argue that stock market development helps equalize income distribution.

7. Social Policy and Poverty Reduction

Income inequality is only one aspect of social inequality. With strong public policy targeted toward people at the lowest income levels, the Gini coefficient may overstate social inequality. Public spending on education, health, and welfare services can mitigate the plight of the poor. Table 13.4 provides a snapshot of the quality of life in Thailand from 1970 to 2000. There is a gradually increasing trend in the urban population, rising from 15 percent in 1975 to 22 percent in 2000. Income inequality reflects differences in living standards in rural and urban areas. The adult literacy rate jumped from 82 percent in 1974 to 95 percent in 1998, thanks to rising public spending on education (see tables 13.4 and 13.5). Government spending on education in the period 1997–2000 was 4.4 percent of GDP, as compared to 3.2 percent in the period 1972–1979. The primary school enrollment ratio increased for both males and females between 1977 and 1993 (see table 13.4). In 1977, the female enrollment ratio was 79 percent, compared with the male enrollment ratio of 86 percent. By 1993, the enrollment ratios for females and males were at 97 and 98 percent, respectively. Since the male-female wage differential depends on

TABLE 13.4 Income Distributions, 1975–1976 to 2000

| | | % Income Share of the Total Income Receivers | | |
| | | | Lowest | |
Year	Gini Coefficient	Lowest 20%	20%/highest 20%	Middle 60%
1975–1976	0.42	5.6	0.11	44.7
1981	0.45	5.4	0.10	43.1
1986	0.50	4.6	0.08	39.9
1988	0.48	6.1	0.12	43.2
1990	0.43	5.9	0.12	43.7
1992	0.44	5.4	0.10	41.7
1994	0.43	5.6	0.11	44.0
1996	0.43	5.7	0.11	44.2
1998	0.42	5.9	0.12	45.2
1999	0.44	5.3	0.10	43.1
2000	0.44	5.5	0.11	43.5

Source: www.nso.go.th/eng/stat/sociotab7.htm.

productivity and education, the reduction in the inequality of the distribution of human capital should have an equalizing effect on income distribution.

As for the secondary school enrollment ratio, it rose from 25 percent in 1975 to 48 percent in 1997. Although the increasing trend is encouraging, the level is still very low when compared with other countries in Southeast Asia. The fact that the secondary enrollment ratio was below 50 percent in 1997 is an indication of the low productivity of the Thai labor force.[3] Low labor productivity implies a low marginal product value and low wage rates. The value-added of labor in the manufacturing sector could have been raised if the government had prioritized public education dating back to the early 1970s.

TABLE 13.5 Percentage of Poor by Region, 1988–1998

Year	North	Northeast	Center	South	Bangkok and Vicinity
1988	32	48.4	26.6	32.5	6.1
1990	23.2	43.1	27.6	27.6	3.5
1992	22.6	39.9	19.7	19.7	1.9
1994	13.2	28.6	17.3	17.3	0.9
1996	11.2	19.4	11.5	11.5	0.6
1998	9.0	23.2	14.8	14.8	0.6

Source: NESDB (1999).

Government spending on health and welfare also gradually increased during the past three decades, from 1.2 percent in 1972–1979 to 2.4 percent of GDP during 1997–2000. Consequently, life expectancy at birth was raised from fifty-nine years in 1970 to seventy-two and sixty-six years for females and males respectively in 1998. Similarly, infant mortality that stood at 74 per 1,000 in 1970 dropped to just 29 in 1998 (see table 13.4). Access to sanitation and clean water was 96 and 81 percent respectively in 1990–1998 (see table 13.5). It might be odd to argue that economic development in Thailand did not improve the welfare of the poor. According to the Human Poverty Index (HPI) that measures the deprivation of knowledge, economic provisioning, health, and life span, Thailand was ranked twenty-ninth in 1999, with the index of 18.7 percent.

As a major exporter of food, Thailand has maintained self-sufficiency in food production. The national poverty line was only 62 cents a day in 1988 and 78 cents in 1999, less than the $1 a day by international poverty standards. The population that lived below the poverty line declined from 32.6 percent in 1988 to 11.4 percent in 1996.

After the economic crisis hit Thailand in 1997, the percentage of the poor increased to 13 percent in 1998, when output contracted by 10 percent. The number continued to rise to 15.9 percent in 1999, despite the GDP recovery (a 4.3 percent growth rate) in 1999. The percentage difference between the poverty line and the mean income of the poor (the poverty gap ratio) also declined from 10.4 percent in 1988 to 3.2 percent in 1998 (see table 13.6). Furthermore, during the same period, the percentage of the ultra poor within the total poor (the severity of poverty index) also declined from 4.6 percent to

1.2 percent. The ultra poor did not suffer much from the economic crisis in the late 1990s. The Human Development Index (HDI) shows that there has been an increase in the quality of human resources in Thailand. Seen in this light, economic development in Thailand cannot be considered a total failure.

Income disparity measured by the Gini coefficient did not change substantially in the last two decades (see table 13.1). Whenever the price of agriculture products increased relative to the price of manufactured products, the income share of the poorest 20 percent was enlarged. This was the case in 1990 and 1998, when the Gini coefficient was reduced to around 0.42. The relationship between the Gini coefficient can be much more complex than the inverted U-shaped relationship between income level and the income inequality index. As table 13.1 suggests, the bottom/top ratio of income quintiles remained remarkably stable between 1975 and 2000. Again, it is premature to suggest that Thailand's economic development increased both per capita income and income inequality.

Table 13.7 presents the regional differences in poverty. The Northeast remains the region with the highest percentage of the poor. There has been a considerable reduction of the poor in all regions. Bangkok has always attracted massive numbers of

TABLE 13.6 Changes in Income Distribution/Factor Income, 1970–2000

Income Earners	1970– 1979	1980– 1989	1990– 1996	1997– 2000
Self-employment	56.6	50.2	37.6	35.7
Wages	30.1	34.4	36.1	43.5
Interest	2.9	6.1	6.3	10.1
Corporate profits	2.4	3.5	6.5	4.1

Source: Author's calculation using the data from www.NESDB.go.th.

TABLE 13.7 Structural Changes in the Thai Economy: Before and after Liberalization (% of Respective Total Value)

	1970– 1979	1980– 1989	1990– 1996	1997– 2000
1. *Production*				
Agriculture	25.7	17.9	11.4	11.6
Manufacture	18.9	23.3	28.3	31.7
Non-tradable	46.7	50.0	50.8	52.5
2. *Exports*				
Agriculture	49.4	37.9	13.3	8.8
Manufacture	30.6	49.4	78.9	83.6
Non-tradable	19.8	12.6	7.7	7.6
3. *Employment*				
Agriculture	72.1	68.9	58.1	48.3
Manufacture	7.4	10.6	11.1	14.1
Non-tradable	20.4	20.5	31.0	37.5

Source: Author's calculation using the data from BOT, *Quarterly Reports* (various issues).

TABLE 13.8 Percentage Rates Changes in Nominal and Real Effective Exchange Rates, Relative Productivity, Wage, and Prices in Tradable and Non-tradable Sectors

	NEER	REER	Productivity (NT/T)	Wage Rate		P_T/P_{NT}
				Tradable	Non-tradable	
1991–1996	–0.95	0.67	–1.48	11.9	10.2	–1.97
1997–1998	–14.45	–10.58	1.7	5.9	7.1	1.57
1999	4.39	3.75	–5.0	0.0	–2.5	–3.31
2000	–4.27	–3.96	2.3	0.1	5.0	2.94

Source: For NEER and REER, www.bot.or.th; and for the rest, author's calculation using the data from BOT, *Quarterly Reports* (various issues).

migrants in search of higher wages and better living conditions. Capital formation has concentrated in this area, resulting in high productivity and wage rates. Bangkok and its surrounding areas have witnessed the greatest reduction in poverty. It should be noted that the degree of labor mobility in Thailand is high, thereby contributing to a reduction in regional income disparity.

An analysis of factor income shares between 1970 and 2000 suggests that the income share of wage earners increased throughout the last four decades. As the degree of urbanization and commercialization increases, the factor income share of wage earners will rise. The share of self-employed workers in total factor income was 56.6 percent in the 1970s, but it was reduced to 35.7 percent because of the modernization of agriculture (see table 13.8). However, the share of self-employed workers could be underestimated since there are a considerable number of workers in the informal sector. The income share of corporate profits is pro-cyclical by nature. This should also be true for the share of workers in the informal sector (which complements rather than substitutes economic activities in the formal sector).

8. Conclusion

To recapture the finding in the previous sections, the period between 1991 and 2000 may be divided into four episodes. The first episode covers the period between 1991 and 1996, when financial liberalization was earnestly undertaken. The second episode took place in 1997 and 1998, the period in which the

financial and banking sectors were marked by turbulence. The third and fourth episodes characterize the return to a positive growth observed in both 1999 and 2000. The year 1999 was in sharp contrast with the year 2000 since the real effective exchange rate appreciated by 3.75 percent in 1999 instead of depreciating by 3.96 percent in 2000.

One of the adverse consequences of the capital inflows induced by capital control relaxation was the upward pressure on domestic prices. Despite the depreciation of the nominal effective exchange rate by almost 1 percent per year between 1991 and 1996, the real effective exchange rate actually appreciated by about 0.7 percent per year (see table 13.9). As noted earlier, the baht float in 1997 reversed the appreciation trend; the real effective exchange rate depreciated by 10.6 percent on average in 1997 and 1998. The real depreciation could have been 14.5 percent had there been no inflation following the currency depreciation. The year 2000 saw the real effective rate depreciate by about 4 percent as a result of the strengthening of the dollar. This volatile movement of the real exchange rate had an indirect impact on income distribution.

If one measures the real exchange rate as the ratio between the prices of traded and non-traded goods, one reaches a similar conclusion about changes in international competitiveness. Shown in table 13.9, the price ratio between traded and non-traded goods is approximated by the price ratio between the producer price and the consumer price indexes. The rate of change of the real exchange rate calculated in this manner corresponds with the rate of change of the REER. Induced capital inflows, through external liberalization, raised the price in the non-traded sector faster than the price in the traded sector (the price in the traded sector is influenced by the law of one price) after trade reform was undertaken.

Productivity differentials in the two sectors also moved in line with the real exchange rate. In the first episode between 1991 and 1998, labor productivity in the traded sector rose faster than in the non-traded sector. Thus, the price of traded goods increased at a slower pace than the price of the non-traded goods, leading to higher incentives for the reallocation of resources in the non-traded sector. Productivity slowdown in the non-traded sector was apparent again in 1999, when the REER and the price ratio between traded and non-traded goods simultaneously declined (see table 13.9). The depreciation of the baht between 1997 and 1998 was essentially an adjustment to its overvaluation during the boom years. By 2000, the short recovery of the Thai economy stabilized the declining productivity in the non-traded sector. There is a positive correlation between the traded to non-traded price ratio and the productivity differential between the non-traded and traded sectors.

The evidence from table 13.9 shows that Thai labor markets are quite flexible. Wage rates in both sectors can be revised downward. For this reason, unemployment caused by declining aggregate demand did not raise unemployment substantially. Nevertheless, unemployment caused by deficient demand affected income distribution since wage cuts were not proportional across sectors.[4] Labor shedding in the non-traded sector in 1998 led to high productivity in this sector relative to the traded sector, where the wage rate was cut by 4.7 percent.

Growth has a strong impact on poverty reduction. If productivity growth is uneven, growth can affect income distribution. On the other hand, income distribution can exert an indirect impact on growth if macroeconomic instability is related to income distribution. High unemployment, hyperinflation, and exchange rate devaluation adversely affect the poor. If external liberalization can enhance growth, while the relationship between growth and inequality can go either way, then the effect of liberalization on inequality may be different from one country to another.

Trade liberalization leads to changes in the employment and output structure. The employment share in the agricultural sector in Thailand is greater than the share in the manufacturing sector. The agricultural share of employment is declining relative to other sectors. The wage share of labor in the agricultural sector will be lower if the marginal product of other sectors rises faster than that of agricultural labor. If the terms of trade of agriculture goods relative to manufactured goods decline, income inequality will increase. Globalization implies that the prices of domestic goods, including the rate of interest, cannot deviate significantly from the international price level. The episodes of rising income inequality may be attributed to the falling prices of agricultural exports. However, rising unemployment may lead to rising income inequality if manufacturing sector labor is not sufficiently absorbed by the traditional sector.

Capital liberalization led to the concentration of capital in the modern sector, thereby raising the capital/labor ratio in the manufacturing, non-traded, as well as FIRE sectors. The agricultural sector was credit constrained and had a low level of capital accumulation. As a result, productivity differentials among sectors led to wage differentials and income inequality. If labor income levels were related to the value of their marginal product, income disparity between urban and rural areas would remain largely unresolved. Public spending on health and education can help mitigate the social costs of external liberalization by equalizing the distribution of human capital. It remains to be seen whether social policy can effectively reduce the adverse consequences of external liberalization.

Appendix 1

TABLE 13.9 Decomposition Analysis of Effective Demand: Leakage Parameters and Own Multipliers

| Year | Leakage Prameters | | | Own Multipliers | | |
	Import Propensity	Private Saving Rate	Tax Rate	Goverment spending/ Tax Rate	Private Investment/ Private Saving Rate	Export/Import Propensity
1970	0.2	0.3	0.1	294.3	86.5	89.2
1971	0.2	0.3	0.1	287.3	80.8	105.4
1972	0.2	0.3	0.1	301.7	86.4	135.5
1973	0.2	0.3	0.1	468.9	120.0	190.1
1974	0.2	0.3	0.1	451.6	186.0	253.3
1975	0.2	0.2	0.1	576.9	202.8	238.1
1976	0.2	0.3	0.1	683.3	193.2	324.2
1977	0.2	0.3	0.1	743.9	258.4	343.1
1978	0.2	0.3	0.1	1,019.3	271.3	416.8
1979	0.2	0.3	0.1	1,033.9	358.8	456.8
1980	0.2	0.3	0.1	1,666.7	421.9	557.0
1981	0.2	0.3	0.1	2,073.1	443.3	649.4
1982	0.2	0.3	0.1	2,282.2	380.2	792.0
1983	0.2	0.3	0.1	2,526.5	472.0	665.3
1984	0.2	0.3	0.1	2,567.9	501.1	829.5
1985	0.2	0.3	0.1	2,772.9	479.2	911.7
1986	0.2	0.3	0.1	2,691.4	484.2	1,194.5
1987	0.2	0.3	0.1	2,673.6	669.0	1,303.3
1988	0.3	0.3	0.1	2,699.1	958.3	1,469.4
1989	0.3	0.3	0.1	2,106.1	1,571.1	1,754.1
1990	0.3	0.3	0.1	2,809.0	2,318.8	1,907.3
1991	0.3	0.3	0.1	3,614.3	2,573.2	2,321.2
1992	0.3	0.3	0.1	4,400.7	2,605.5	2,691.4
1993	0.3	0.3	0.1	4,716.1	2,964.6	3,019.1
1994	0.3	0.3	0.1	5,411.0	3,371.1	3,573.7
1995	0.3	0.3	0.1	6,333.2	4,001.0	4,039.0
1996	0.3	0.3	0.1	7,816.6	4,376.8	4,967.6
1997	0.3	0.3	0.1	8,765.7	3,223.9	6,402.5
1998	0.3	0.3	0.1	9,613.1	1,756.6	7,608.6
1999	0.3	0.3	0.1	10,138.9	1,676.3	8,609.7
2000	0.4	0.3	0.1	10,836.3	2,188.1	8,669.3
1970–1979	0.188	0.269	0.109	586.1	184.4	255.2
1980–1989	0.23	0.300	0.100	2,405.8	2,634.1	1,012.3
1990–1996	0.317	0.33	0.124	5,014	3,173	1,238.4
1997–2000	0.317	0.310	0.100	9,838	2,212	7,822.5

TABLE 13.10 Financial Balance, Equation 5: $dP/dt + dZ/dt + dA/dt = (Ip - Sp) + (E - M) + (G - T) = 0$

Years	D(A)	D(Z)	D(p)	Ip − Sp	E − M	G − T
1970	—	—	—	−22.0	−13.8	5.5
1971	0.6	5.7	2.9	−26.3	−11.6	7.8
1972	4.8	5.6	3.68	−29.4	−10.1	6.8
1973	2.3	0.6	15.38	−39.7	−12.3	5.7
1974	10.7	−4.9	19.23	−40.4	−17.1	−4.0
1975	−2.8	4.9	17.25	−41.4	−24.7	4.7
1976	−0.7	9.6	15.15	−58.7	−17.9	11.7
1977	−5.7	8.5	30.39	−62.7	−31.2	10.1
1978	0.8	9.2	−39.85	−93.6	−34.6	14.9
1979	5.7	8.6	37.17	−93.7	−55.5	17.2
1980	11.4	17.8	12.01	−114.1	−68.0	43.9
1981	−11.3	17.7	35	−143.6	−76.0	49.9
1982	7.4	31	45.7	−193.2	−47.6	70.7
1983	−26.2	8.9	99.1	−188.4	−104.7	62.1
1984	11.7	22.2	74.2	−212.2	−83.4	60.9
1985	9.2	2.5	50.9	−251.1	−80.7	80.3
1986	43.2	15.5	25.3	−282.6	−33.7	77.3
1987	26.8	3.1	128.2	−300.8	−66.8	53.7
1988	38.8	−47.4	183.6	−343.8	−133.0	−5.6
1989	102	−59.5	258.3	−277.4	−179.8	−35.7
1990	60	−51.1	372.4	−200.5	−319.7	−78.3
1991	106.8	−104.2	311.5	−276.6	−339.9	−63.2
1992	35.5	−61.1	373.9	−399.4	−335.6	−31.2
1993	5	−57.7	507.7	−435.0	−381.7	−17.4
1994	−306	−84.3	806.8	−523.7	−430.2	−28.0
1995	−146.4	−106.1	846.4	−598.9	−604.8	−47.9
1996	−82	−68	636.3	−676.7	−480.6	33.3
1997	−482.7	37.5	1,407.9	−1,081.7	−25.9	169.2
1998	631.2	425.4	−401.7	−1,528.6	378.0	209.0
1999	604.1	66.1	−342.3	−1,513.9	582.9	200.4
2000	312.6	72.2	−415	−1,516.5	404.3	174.2
1970–1979	1.6	4.8	18.1	−50.7	−22.8	8.03
1980–1989	21.3	1.2	91.2	−230.7	−87.3	45.7
1990–1996	−46.7	−76	550.7	−311.2	−289.2	−23.3
1997–2000	266.2	150.3	62.2	−1,410.2	334.8	43.6

TABLE 13.11 Decomposition of Labor Force, Employment, and Unemployment, 1973–2000

| Year | Growth Rate of Labor Force, Employment, and Unemployment | | |
	Labor Force	Employment	Unemployment
1973	5.54	5.64	−0.06
1974	0.67	0.68	−0.01
1975	5.80	5.94	−0.08
1976	1.80	1.25	1.56
1977	10.21	10.22	0.07
1978	6.88	6.99	−0.05
1979	−2.15	−2.32	0.19
1980	6.05	6.04	0.07
1981	8.07	8.11	0.04
1982	4.59	1.84	11.80
1983	0.38	1.39	−0.71
1984	3.37	3.15	0.34
1985	1.32	−0.54	3.23
1986	2.26	2.82	−0.39
1987	5.61	3.18	4.31
1988	2.95	6.17	−1.55
1989	2.87	4.48	−0.82
1990	1.69	0.74	1.50
1991	1.20	0.92	0.34
1992	2.34	4.16	−0.76
1993	−0.18	−0.90	1.09
1994	0.24	−0.18	0.50
1995	0.60	1.47	−0.56
1996	−1.20	−1.04	−0.16
1997	−0.21	−2.01	4.09
1998	−0.20	−1.77	2.36
1999	0.51	1.31	−0.64
2000	1.32	1.60	−0.21
1973–1979	4.1	4.05	0.23
1980–1989	3.74	3.66	1.63
1990–1996	0.67	0.74	0.28
1997–2000	0.36	−0.22	1.4

TABLE 13.12 Decomposition of Total Productivity Growth, 1973–2000

Year	Agriculture	Manufacture	Non-tradable	Total Output
1973	35.39	40.41	12.15	23.58
1974	34.00	−10.96	7.33	24.86
1975	−8.56	32.16	31.06	2.53
1976	7.75	42.70	21.60	12.82
1977	1.27	2.83	−3.12	5.57
1978	11.42	7.92	16.65	13.03
1979	19.58	3.13	7.23	17.22
1980	8.18	16.84	11.53	11.73
1981	−4.08	24.03	9.42	6.10
1982	−0.81	−9.52	3.71	8.61
1983	15.56	23.71	3.41	7.90
1984	−9.84	3.09	11.53	3.92
1985	−1.33	−1.71	7.69	7.53
1986	5.84	17.07	−6.38	4.22
1987	15.67	−1.20	4.53	10.92
1988	12.39	26.51	15.87	12.79
1989	5.45	9.43	18.94	13.85
1990	3.21	9.50	11.46	16.70
1991	20.79	5.19	2.07	13.71
1992	1.02	6.47	12.44	8.37
1993	4.73	2.39	5.44	13.02
1994	20.16	17.23	10.40	14.73
1995	26.21	2.07	4.44	13.67
1996	14.72	11.76	4.78	10.94
1997	3.00	9.00	−3.19	0.19
1998	27.02	−1.62	−2.09	4.53
1999	−13.18	6.01	−5.12	−1.62
2000	−4.39	−2.56	7.19	4.44
1973–1979	14.40	16.30	13.30	14.21
1980–1989	4.70	10.82	8.03	8.75
1990–1996	12.93	7.80	7.29	1.25
1997–2000	3.15	2.75	−0.80	1.88

TABLE 13.13 Decomposition of Productivity Growth: Non-tradable Sectors, 1977–2000

Year	Commerce	Construction	Services	Transport
1977	−2.38	−9.39	3.76	7.18
1978	22.51	29.92	6.96	18.46
1979	7.78	−10.05	19.77	17.02
1980	15.43	25.73	19.00	13.28
1981	13.04	−0.75	8.54	46.28
1982	−4.49	−8.37	0.22	−13.68
1983	2.41	9.65	14.02	13.46
1984	−20.66	18.14	34.21	−5.45
1985	−20.71	−26.75	0.57	−3.67
1986	14.74	24.25	−0.50	9.81
1987	−0.87	1.51	5.26	3.20
1988	8.98	7.36	7.48	12.65
1989	40.77	32.77	28.43	25.34
1990	24.96	−6.66	14.67	2.35
1991	22.35	5.18	5.23	0.22
1992	4.05	3.33	6.44	23.13
1993	2.32	4.07	4.85	2.84
1994	18.47	5.11	6.05	16.60
1995	1.64	3.88	9.27	−1.98
1996	0.34	−5.26	12.22	16.03
1997	6.89	−17.24	−0.34	5.11
1998	21.56	−1.23	−3.07	−3.82
1999	6.90	5.16	4.39	10.62
2000	0.66	−13.13	16.05	14.84
1977–1979	9.30	3.47	10.16	14.21
1980–1989	4.86	8.35	11.72	10.12
1990–1996	10.60	1.37	1.67	1.44
1997–2000	9.01	−6.61	4.21	6.68

TABLE 13.14 Decomposition of National (Factor) Income, 1970–1999

Year	Corporate Profit	Interest	Wage	Self-employment Income
1970	2.2	1.7	31.0	57.5
1971	2.6	2.7	32.5	54.0
1972	2.6	2.7	31.9	55.1
1973	2.2	2.6	28.3	58.9
1974	2.2	2.9	28.1	58.0
1975	2.1	2.8	28.9	57.6
1976	2.0	3.4	29.2	57.5
1977	2.3	3.6	29.7	56.9
1978	2.8	3.5	30.6	55.7
1979	2.8	3.7	31.0	55.5
1980	2.6	4.7	30.2	55.6
1981	2.5	5.3	30.4	54.6
1982	1.3	5.5	34.6	54.9
1983	2.1	6.0	36.2	51.6
1984	2.3	7.1	37.0	50.8
1985	3.6	8.2	38.0	44.3
1986	3.7	7.3	37.4	45.7
1987	4.8	5.4	36.3	47.3
1988	5.8	5.4	32.8	49.3
1989	6.6	6.3	31.7	48.2
1990	8.1	8.0	32.2	43.6
1991	7.7	10.0	32.8	40.3
1992	9.0	9.0	34.7	37.8
1993	9.3	8.4	36.9	38.8
1994	11.2	7.4	36.9	36.9
1995	10.2	9.6	38.5	33.9
1996	9.3	11.0	39.7	32.2
1997	6.6	11.5	41.7	32.9
1998	2.7	12.5	44.1	34.6
1999	3.4	6.2	44.8	39.8
1970–1979	2.4	3.0	30.1	56.6
1980–1989	3.5	6.1	34.4	50.2
1990–1996	6.5	6.3	36.0	37.6
1997–1999	4.2	10.0	43.5	35.7

Notes

1. Kuznets (1955) argued that income inequality widens in the early stages of development and narrows in later stages when income rise above certain threshold levels.

2. In the case of Taiwan, where income rose rapidly, the Gini coefficient passed the U-turn in the early 1980s and stabilized around 0.3 (see Hung 1996).

3. According to Lucas (1990), the lack of human capital discourages foreign investment in developing countries.

4. According to the Labor and Social Welfare Ministry, the top ten industries with the highest layoffs between January and July 2001 included electrical and electronics (1.8 percent of industry employees), construction (1.6 percent), commodity and social services (1.3 percent), metals and metal products (6.5 percent), retail and wholesale trade (0.3 percent), and textiles and knitting (0.3 percent).

References

Aghion, Philippe, E. Caroli, and C. Garcia-Penalosa. 1999. Inequality and economic growth: The perspective of the new growth theories. *Journal of Economic Literature* 37:1615–1600.

Atkinson, A. B. 2001. A critique of the transatlantic consensus on rising income inequality. *The World Economy* 24 (4): 433–52.

Beyer, H., P. Rojas, and R. Vergara. 1999. Trade liberalization and wage inequality. *Journal of Development Economics* 59:103–23.

Bowman, K. S. 1997. Should the Kuznets effect be relied on to induce equalizing growth: Evidence post-1950 development. *World Development* 25: 127–43.

Bruno, M., M. Ravallion, and L. Squire. 1996. Equity and growth in developing countries. Policy Research Working Paper no. 1563. Washington, D.C.: World Bank.

Deininger, K., and L. Squire. 1997. Economic growth and income inequality: Reexamining the links. *Finance and Development* 38–41.

Harrison, A., and G. Hanson. 1999. Who gains from trade reform? Some remaining puzzles. *Journal of Development Economics* 59:125–54.

Hung, R. 1996. The great U-turn in Taiwan: Economic restructuring and a surge in inequality. *Journal of Contemporary Asia* 26:151–63.

Jong, Wha Lee. 1995. Capital goods imports and long-run growth. *Journal of Development Economics* 48 (October): 91–110.

Kuznets, S. 1955. Economic growth and income equality. *American Economic Review* 45:1–28.

Lucas, R. E. 1990. Why doesn't capital flow from rich to poor countries. *American Economic Review* 80:92–96.

Sarntisart, I. 1995. Trade liberalization in Thailand: Income distrubutional impact and financing problem. *Asian Economic Journal* 9:261–91.

Singh, Ajit. 1986. Crisis and recovery in the Mexican economy: The role of the capital goods sector. In *Machinery and economic development*, edited by M. Fransman, 246–66. London: Macmillan.

Taylor, Lance. 1991. *Income distribution, inflation, and growth*. Cambridge, Mass.: MIT Press.

———. 1998. Capital market crises, liberalization, fixed exchange rates and market-driven destabilization. *Cambridge Journal of Economics* 22: 663–76.

Warr, Peter. 2000. Poverty incidence and economic growth in Southeast Asia. *Journal of Asian Economics* 11:431–41.

World Bank. 1993. *Poverty reduction handbook*. Washington, D.C.: World Bank.

14

Turkey, 1980–2000: Financial Liberalization, Macroeconomic (In)Stability, and Patterns of Distribution

Korkut Boratav and Erinc Yeldan

1. Introduction

The integration of developing national economies into the evolving world financial system has been achieved by a series of policies aimed at liberalizing their financial sectors. The motive behind financial liberalization was to restore growth and stability by raising saving and improving economic efficiency. A major consequence, however, has been the exposure of these economies to speculative short-term capital movements (hot money) that increased financial instability and resulted in a series of financial crises in these countries. Furthermore, contrary to expectations, the post-liberalization period was marked by the divergence of domestic savings away from fixed capital investments toward speculative financial instruments. These instruments often had erratic and volatile yields. As a result, national economies with weak financial structures and shallow markets suffered from an increased volatility of output growth, shortsightedness of entrepreneurial decisions, and

financial crises with severe economic and social consequences.

It is the purpose of this chapter to identify and study the main stylized facts and processes characterizing the dynamic macroeconomic adjustments in Turkey since the inception of its reforms toward global integration. Under the neoliberal regime, Turkey in the post 1980s has undergone persistent difficulties, wide fluctuations in national income, and conflicting policy adjustments.[1] At the turn of the century, the most striking aspects of the current Turkish political economy are the persistence of price inflation in a crisis-prone economic structure, stubborn and rapidly expanding fiscal deficits; a marginalized labor force, the dramatic deterioration in the economic conditions of the poor, and the severe erosion of moral values along with increased public corruption.[2]

We plan this study as follows: the analytics of macro adjustments of the two distinct (i.e., 1980–1988/1989 and 1989–2000) phases of liberalization is the theme of section 2. We address the modes of accumulation and the resolution of macro equilibria under both periods separately, and highlight the ascendancy of finance over industrial development. We also investigate the nature and evolution of the flows of short-term foreign capital. In particular, we document the detrimental consequences of hot money flows in inducing instability at the onset of the 2000–2001 financial crisis. Section 3 quantifies the macro adjustments via a set of decomposition exercises and traces the evolution of real output and sources of aggregate demand. The deterioration of fiscal balances forms the thematic background of this section. Microlevel adjustments and related decomposition exercises, in turn, are investigated in section 4 for the manufacturing sector. Here we address two separate, yet related, issues: (1) the effect of external liberalization on oligopolistic concentration and price-cost margins; and (2) the patterns of investment behavior under external liberalization. We summarize the distributional effects of liberalization of commodity trade and finance in section 5. Section 6 concludes.

2. Phases of Macroeconomic Adjustment in Turkey

The post-1980 adjustment path started with an orthodox stabilization policy that also incorporated the first structural steps toward a market-based mode of regulation. The shock treatment of 1980, facilitated by the military coup of September and generously supported by international donors, was, to a large degree, successful in terms of its own policy goals. The rate of inflation that had almost reached three digit figures in 1980 was reduced to an average of 33.2 percent in the following two years. The recession was a brief and relatively mild one (the GDP fell by 2.3 percent in 1980). The liberalization of domestic markets eliminated the painful shortages in basic commodities, and the major realignment in relative prices took place relatively smoothly. However, the whole operation was, to a large extent, dependent on the drastic regression of labor incomes. This was realized through the suppressive control of the relations of distribution by the military regime. The first phase of reforms was followed by a gradual move to trade liberalization in 1984 (which culminated in a Customs Union with the EU eleven years later) and the liberalization of the capital account in 1989.

Particularly during the early phases of its inception, the Turkish adjustment program was hailed as a "model" by the orthodox international community, and was supported by generous structural adjustment loans, debt relief, and technical aid. Currently, the Turkish economy can be said to be operating under conditions of a truly "open economy"—a macroeconomic environment where both the current and capital accounts are completely liberalized. In this setting, many of the instruments of macro and fiscal control have been transformed, and the constraints of macro equilibrium have undergone major structural changes.

We provide a general overview of the recent macroeconomic history of Turkey in table 14.1. We identify the 1972–1979 period as the deepening of the industrialization strategy based on import substitution (ISI). This period, often called the second phase of import substitution, was part of the evolution of the inward-looking, domestic demand–led industrialization that dated back to the 1950s. The late 1970s witnessed a vigorous public investment program aimed at expanding domestic production capacity in heavy manufacturing, capital goods (such as machinery), petrochemicals, and basic intermediates. The foreign trade regime was heavily protected via quantitative restrictions along with a fixed exchange rate regime that, on average, was overvalued in purchasing parity terms. The state was both an investor and a producer, with state economic enterprises (SEEs) serving as the major tools for fostering industrialization targets.

During the import-substitution phase, the underlying political economy of the industrialization strategy was a grand, yet precarious, alliance between the bureaucratic elites, industrial capitalists, industrial workers, and peasantry (Boratav, Keyder, and Pamuk 1984). Accordingly, private industrial profits were fed from three sources. First, the protectionist trade regime (often implemented through strong nontariff barriers) enabled industrialists to capture oligopolistic profits and rents from a readily available and protected domestic market. Second, the existence of a public enterprise system that produced cheap intermediates through artificially low administered prices enabled private industrial enterprises (and the rural economy) to minimize material input costs. Third, a repressed financial system (supported by undervalued foreign currencies) enabled cheap financing for fixed capital investments in manufacturing. Industrialists, in turn, "accepted" a general rise in manufacturing wages together with an agricultural support program

TABLE 14.1 Phases of Macroeconomic Adjustment in Turkey, 1972–2001

	Import-Substitutionist Industrialization 1972–76	Economic Crisis 1977–80	Post-Crisis Adjustment 1981–82	Export-Led Growth 1983–87	Exhaustion 1988	Unregulated Financial Liberalization 1989–93	Financial Crisis 1994	Reinvigoration of Short-term Foreign Capital-Led Growth 1995–97	Contagion of the World Financial Crisis 1998	Contagion of the World Financial Crisis 1999	Exchange Rate Based Disinflation and Financial Meltdown 2000	Exchange Rate Based Disinflation and Financial Meltdown 2001
I. Production and Accumulation (Real Rate of Growth, %)												
GDP	6.8	0.5	4.2	6.5	2.1	4.8	-5.5	7.2	3.1	-5.0	7.2	-9.3
Agriculture	1.8	0.5	0.6	0.8	7.8	0.1	-0.7	1.3	8.4	-4.6	4.1	-4.9
Manufacturing	9.7	-0.2	7.9	8.6	1.6	6.0	-7.6	10.2	1.2	-5.7	5.9	-8.5
Fixed Investment:												
Private Sector	11.5	-7.3	-1.0	14.1	29.2	11.9	-9.6	9.5	-8.2	-17.8	15.9	-35.1
Private Energy and Transport.	19.5	-10.6	27.3	7.5	4.2	16.2	-26.2	25.8	-14.3	-31.7	15.6	
Private Manufacturing	10.9	-13.6	4.8	7.7	9.7	14.3	-0.5	4.7	-6.3	-17.5	15.0	
Private Housing	9.0	2.2	-19.6	24.5	50.7	11.2	-24.6	2.9	-1.6	18.6	14.0	
Public Sector	15.4	-1.7	4.8	12.0	-2.3	5.2	-39.5	15.8	13.9	-8.7	19.6	-21.9
Public Energy and Transport.	16.3	0.3	9.5	16.8	-2.6	4.4	-44.6	13.6	14.6	-15.4	26.2	
Public Manufacturing	16.0	1.3	-11.2	-9.6	-11.3	-6.9	-41.4	7.8	19.1	-4.3	20.3	
Manufacturing Sector (Total)	12.0	-9.4	-0.8	3.7	6.6	12.4	-2.5	4.8	-5.6	-17.6	17.0	
As % Share of GNP:												
Savings	20.9	17.3	17.7	19.5	27.2	21.9	23.0	21.1	23.1	19.6	19.9	
Investment	21.3	22.3	18.3	20.9	26.1	23.7	24.4	24.8	24.3	22.3	24.1	
PSBR	5.7[a]	6.9	3.7	4.7	4.8	9.1	7.9	7.2	9.2	15.3	12.5	15.4
II. Distribution and Prices												
Inflation Rate (CPI)	18.4	59.5	35.1	40.7	68.8	65.1	106.3	85.0	90.7	70.5	39.1	68.0
Annual Rate of Change in Exchange Rate (TL/$)	3.9	48.0	45.0	39.7	66.0	50.4	170.0	72.0	71.7	58.2	28.6	114.2
Real Interest Rate on Government Bonds[b]	—	—	—	—	-5.8	10.5	20.5	23.6	29.5	36.8	4.5	31.8

(continued)

TABLE 14.1 (continued)

	Import-Substitutionist Industrialization 1972–76	Economic Crisis 1977–80	Post-Crisis Adjustment 1981–82	Export-Led Growth 1983–87	Exhaustion 1988	Unregulated Financial Liberalization 1989–93	Financial Crisis 1994	Reinvigoration of Short-term Foreign Capital-Led Growth 1995–97	Contagion of the World Financial Crisis 1998	Contagion of the World Financial Crisis 1999	Exchange Rate Based Disinflation and Financial Meltdown 2000	Exchange Rate Based Disinflation and Financial Meltdown 2001
Manufacturing Real Wages[c]	3.1	-1.1	-1.1	-3.9	-7.1	10.2	-36.3	-2.8	3.3[d]	4.6[d]	-8.8[d]	
Share of Wages in Manufac. Value Added (%)	27.7	35.6	24.5	20.6	15.4	21.8	16.1	16.7				
III. Internationalization												
Man. Exports Growth	39.4	14.3	19.7	12.5	14.0	5.1	18.0	14.2	3.2	-5.5	4.9	12.4
As % Share of GNP:												
Imports[e]	11.7	11.2	14.0	15.9	15.8	14.6	17.8	23.2	22.5	21.7	27.2	27.0
Exports[e]	5.3	4.2	8.5	10.8	12.8	9.1	13.8	15.8	13.2	14.2	13.7	20.8
Current Account Balance[e]	-1.4	-3.4	-2.7	-1.9	-1.7	-1.3	-2.0	-1.4	1.0	-0.7	-4.8	2.2
Stock of Foreign Debt	1.4	14.5	27.1	37.8	44.8	35.1	49.6	45.6	50.9	55.7	58.3	75.4

Sources: SPO Main Economic Indicators; Undersecretariat of Foreign Trade and Treasury Main Economic Indicators; SIS Manufacturing Industry Surveys.

a. 1975–76 only.

b. Annual average of Compounded Interest Rate on Government Debt Instruments deflated by the whole sale price index.

c. Wage earnings of workers engaged in production. Private manufacturing labor data cover enterprises employing 10+ workers.

d. Refer to unit wage costs in ($) obtained from production workers in private manufacturing.

e. Including luggage trade after 1996.

that induced the domestic terms of trade in favor of agriculture.

Import substitution reached its limits in 1976 when keeping up the investment drive and financing the consequent current deficits became increasingly difficult. The foreign exchange crisis of 1977–1980, accompanied by civil unrest and political instability, ended with an orthodox stabilization package (1980) and a right-wing military regime (1980–1983).

2.1. Major Turning Points and the Early Phase, 1981–1988/1989

Macroeconomic developments in the post-1980 period may be divided into two phases: 1981–1988/1989 and 1990–2000. The main characteristics of the first phase were export promotion with strong subsidies and gradually phased import liberalization, together with a managed floating exchange rate and regulated capital movements. The gradual but significant depreciation of the Turkish lira (TL) was one of the pillars of the new policy orientation. Severe depression of wage incomes and declining agricultural support measures continued during the years following the military regime. There was also a decisive shift toward a supply-side orientation in fiscal policies.[3]

Domestic financial liberalization was an additional component of the 1980s reforms. The early phase of financial liberalization turned out to be a painful process. The speedy lifting of controls on deposit interest rates and on credit allocation in mid-1980 led to the financial scandal of 1982. The crisis occurred when numerous money brokers (called "bankers") who had flourished by offering very high real interest rates to savers via Ponzi financing schemes went under along with a number of smaller banks. Thereafter, the policy pendulum moved between reregulation and deregulation up till the late 1980s. But the trend, although gradual, was definitely toward the establishment of a liberalized financial system.

In retrospect, the mode and pace of financial reforms during the 1980s progressed in leaps and bounds, mostly following pragmatic solutions to emerging problems. The foreign exchange regime was liberalized early in 1984. Banks were allowed to accept foreign currency deposits from residents and to engage in specified external transactions. An interbank money market for short-term borrowing facilities became operational in 1986. In the following year, the

Central Bank diversified its monetary instruments by starting open market operations. The Capital Market Board, a supervisory and regulatory agency over the capital market, was established, which initiated the reopening of the Istanbul Stock Exchange.

During 1983–1987, export revenues increased at an annual rate of 10.8 percent, and the gross domestic product rose at an annual rate of 6.5 percent. These years were also characterized by the continued erosion of wage incomes—a process that had started early in the decade under the 1980 stabilization package and with the hostile measures against organized labor by the military regime.[4] The suppression of wages was instrumental both in lowering production costs and in squeezing domestic absorption. The share of wage labor in manufacturing value-added declined from an average of 35.6 percent in 1977–1980 to 15.4 percent in 1988 (see table 14.1), and average markup rates (gross profit margins as a ratio of current costs) in private manufacturing increased from 31 to 38 percent (Metin, Voyvoda, and Yeldan 2001a).

The severe deterioration of public sector balances in the late 1970s was brought under relative control during the 1980s. Compared with the crisis years of 1977–1980, the public sector borrowing requirement (PSBR) declined by more than 2 percentage points to 4.7 percent of the gross domestic product (GDP). Thanks to improved public and external accounts during the accelerated growth phase of 1983–1987, the gap between domestic savings and investment rates, which were recorded at 19.5 and 20.7 percent respectively, remained at a manageable magnitude (see table 14.1).

There were, however, adverse changes with respect to the composition of total fixed investments in tradable sectors. In fact, as gross fixed investments of the private sector increased by 14.1 percent during 1983–1987, only a small portion of this amount was directed toward manufacturing. The rate of growth of private manufacturing investments was on the order of half of this figure, at a rate of only 7.7 percent per annum, and could not reach its pre-1980 levels in real terms until the end of 1989. As data in table 14.1 attest, much of the expansion in private investments originated from housing investments that expanded by an annual average of 24.5 percent during 1983–1987.

This resulted in a significant anomaly as far as the official stance toward industrialization was concerned: in a period where outward orientation was supposedly directed toward increasing manufacturing exports through significant price and subsidy incentives, the distribution of investments revealed a declining trend for the sector. The implications of this non-conformity between the stated foreign trade objectives toward manufacturing exports and the realized patterns of accumulation away from manufacturing constituted one of the main structural deficiencies of the growth pattern of the period. The impressive export boom of the 1980s was, thereby, essentially predicated on productive capacities established during the preceding decade. Thus, capacity constraints and limited technological upgrading contributed to the overall deceleration in the export growth of manufactures (by 4.4 percent) during 1989–2000.

The export-led growth path, which was dependent on wage suppression, the depreciation of the domestic currency, and extremely generous export subsidies, reached its economic and political limits by 1988. Regressive distributional policies were crucial to the internal logic of the model; but it was becoming more and more difficult to sustain them within the political and social context prevailing at the end of 1988. Two consecutive years of negative per capita growth and a new wave of populist pressures leading to distributional shocks immediately before the 1989 elections were evidence that the policy model of 1980–1988 had exhausted itself. The way out of the impasse (by accident or design) turned out to be the liberalization of the capital account in August 1989. The full convertibility of the Turkish lira was realized at the beginning of 1990.

2.2. Capital Account Liberalization and Its Consequences

The 1989 benchmark was, indeed, the second turning point in the economic policies of the post-1980 period in terms of both its distributional implications and macroeconomic consequences. The fiscal and financial dimensions of the shift toward populism and capital account liberalization will be reviewed further below. The macroeconomic consequences will be analyzed with regard to four aspects. First, optimistic expectations about financial deepening within the domestic financial markets did not materialize. Second, capital account liberalization made the economy vulnerable to newly emerging financial cycles. Third, substantial leakages from net inflows—that is,

through capital outflows and reserve accumulation—transmuted the conventional linkages between growth, current account balance, and capital flows. And, finally, arbitrage-seeking ("hot money") inflows and outflows began to constitute a rising share of capital movements and contributed to rising external and domestic instability.[5]

2.2.1. Increased Fragility in the Domestic Financial Markets

One can easily trace the drastic effects of the unregulated opening of domestic financial markets and consequent financial deepening in the Turkish economy. Contrary to expectations, the public sector's share in financial markets remained high. The financing behavior of corporations did not show significant change, and credit financing from the banking sector and interfirm borrowing continued. Furthermore, the share of private sector securities in total financial assets fell. Thus, the observed upward trend of the proportion of securities to GNP originated from the new issues of public sector debt, particularly treasury bills. The commercial banking system was the major customer of such securities. The banks, in turn, were operational in marketing the T-bills to private households via repo operations. The repo–reverse repo trading volume, which stood at around US$5 billion in 1997, accelerated rapidly to $221 billion in 2000, or 110 percent of the GNP (see table 14.2). Securitized deficit financing through T-bills and other debt instruments led to an overall increase in real interest rates, including deposit rates. Hence, time deposits/GNP ratios tend to rise after 1996. In fact, with the implementation of positive interest rates and the new possibility of foreign exchange accounts for private households, financial deepening has meant increased foreign exchange deposits with substantial currency substitution. Thus, it can be stated that the public sector securities and foreign exchange deposits were the pioneering symbols of financial deepening in Turkey in the 1980s and 1990s.

As Akyuz (1990) and Balkan and Yeldan (2002) attest based on these observations, the Turkish experience did not conform to the McKinnon-Shaw hypothesis of financial deepening with a shift of portfolio selection from "unproductive" assets to those favoring fixed capital formation. Indeed, throughout the course of these events, Turkish banks became

TABLE 14.2 Financial Deepening in Turkey: Financial Assets and Monetary Indicators (% of GNP)

	1988	1989	1990	1991	1992	1993	1994	1995	1996	1997	1998	1999	2000
I. Securities by Issuing Sectors													
Public Sector	6.9	7.7	5.5	7.4	15.9	16.8	22.7	19.8	35.3	22.9	29.4	38.7	37.5
Government Bonds	3.0	3.9	3.2	1.8	6.8	7.5	4.8	4.4	8.3	8.0	2.5	27.3	32.3
Treasury Bills	4.0	3.3	2.1	5.4	8.7	9.0	16.7	15.4	24.8	14.9	26.9	11.3	5.2
Private Sector	0.9	1.0	1.0	1.0	1.7	3.8	2.1	2.1	1.0	1.0	1.0	1.1	4.6
Shares	0.3	0.4	0.5	0.7	0.5	0.5	1.0	0.5	0.6	0.7	0.8	0.9	2.4
TOTAL	7.8	8.7	6.5	8.5	17.6	20.6	24.8	21.9	36.3	23.9	30.4	39.8	42.1
II. Monetary Indicators													
Currency in Circulation	2.7	3.0	2.9	2.7	2.7	2.6	2.6	2.4	2.1	2.2	2.1	2.6	2.6
M1	8.8	8.5	7.9	7.4	7.1	6.5	5.9	5.0	5.6	4.7	4.3	6.3	6.5
M2	21.1	20.5	18.0	18.5	17.3	14.1	16.2	16.0	18.7	17.9	20.3	28.9	26.0
M2Y	28.4	26.6	23.5	26.5	26.6	23.7	30.7	30.7	36.8	34.5	36.3	51.3	45.4
Total Deposits	15.7	16.6	15.7	15.9	18.3	19.0	24.6	26.0	29.3	27.0	27.7	39.5	33.6
Demand Deposits	3.4	3.4	3.3	2.8	2.5	1.0	0.9	0.7	0.7	0.7	0.5	0.8	0.7
Time Deposits	7.2	8.8	8.3	8.1	8.1	5.3	7.6	8.1	10.5	9.8	11.2	16.3	13.6
FX Deposits	4.2	3.8	3.6	4.7	7.3	12.7	16.2	17.3	18.0	16.5	16.0	22.4	19.3
Banking Sector Credits	17.6	16.1	16.5	12.4	12.7	14.0	13.3	16.5	18.5	21.7	19.4	20.1	20.4
III. Securities Markets:													
Stock Exchange Trading Volume[a]					115	773	5,854	8,502	8,567	21,771	23,202	52,311	36,696
Government Securities Direct Transactions Trading Volume[a]								312	2,403	10,717	8,828	16,509	32,736
REPO—Reverse REPO Trading Volume[a]										4,794	23,704	123,254	221,405

Sources: Central Bank, *Quarterly Bulletins*; SPO, *Main Economic Indicators.*

a. Millions US$.

detached from their conventional functions, and started to act as institutional rentiers. They were able to make huge arbitrage gains when conditions were appropriate (see table 14.3), but became extremely vulnerable to exchange rate risks and to sudden changes in the inflation rate. In their new functions, they gradually emerged as the dominant faction within business groups, especially in terms of influencing and manipulating economic policies.

Some parameters of this process are reported in table 14.3. The net return on speculative arbitrage ("hot money") is given in column 1. This return is calculated as the rate of difference between the highest (nominal) interest rate offered in the domestic economy and the rate of (nominal) appreciation of the foreign currencies. It yields the net return to a foreign portfolio investment, which switches into Turkish lira, captures the interest income offered in the domestic economy, and switches back to the foreign currency at the end-of-period exchange rate. The difference between interest earned and the loss due to currency depreciation is the net earning appropriated by the investor.

The gross inflows and outflows of external credit to and from the banking system are tabulated under columns 2 and 3 of table 14.3, and the net flows of hot money injected into the domestic financial system are listed under column 4. All of these flows are highly sensitive to whether or not the domestic rate of return is positive; the net flows are observed to be of the expected sign. Net flows fluctuated widely, especially between 1993–1995 and 1998–2000. The gross inflows of the banking sector's external credit grew rapidly from $50 billion in 1991 to $120 billion in 1995. After a brief deceleration during 1996 and 1998, they again climbed to $108.6 billion in 1999. Under the disinflation program, the gross inflows and outflows of the banking sector foreign credit were $209 and $204 billion, respectively. This magnitude was in excess of the aggregate GNP in 2000!

A crucial factor behind all these developments was the collapse of public disposable income (which declined by 39 percent in real terms during the 1990s) owing to the emergence of negative public savings from 1992 onwards (see table 14.4, below). This was, essentially, the outcome of borrowing from domestic banks at high interest rates (see table 14.1) so that a rising portion of tax revenues was allocated to interest payments: the ratio of interest payments to tax revenues rose almost without interruption from 28 percent in 1992 to 77 percent in 2000. The magnitudes involved, more or less, made it inevitable that the financial system was directly shaped by the needs and methods of financing the public sector. Table 14.2 above documents this episode. The new issues of securities by the state increased from 6.9 percent of the GNP in 1988 to 38.7 percent in 1999. In contrast, issues by the private sector hovered around 1 percent of the GNP before jumping to 4.6 percent in 2000. Total banking credits as a percentage of GNP, however, actually declined over the initial phase of capital account deregulation and would reach the pre-liberalization share only seven years later, in 1996.

High interest rates offered by government bonds and treasury bills set the course for the dominance of finance over the real economy. As a result, the economy is trapped in a vicious circle: commitment to high interest rates and cheap foreign currency (an overvalued Turkish lira) against the threat of capital flight generates a floor below which real interest rates cannot decline. When adverse developments in the current account balance tend to become destabilizing, the only mechanism left to prevent the specter of a major devaluation and currency substitution and/or capital flight is further upward adjustment in the domestic interest rates.

TABLE 14.3 Arbitrage Returns, Gross External Credits to Banks and Hot Money Inflows (Mn.$)

| | Return on Hot Money[a] | Banking Sector Foreign Credits | | Net Hot Money Inflows |
		Gross inflows	Gross Outflows	
1988	−0.073			−126
1989	0.236			233
1990	0.293			3,139
1991	−0.038	43,186	42,523	−392
1992	0.154	64,767	62,363	2,439
1993	0.045	122,053	118,271	4,478
1994	−0.315	75,439	82,040	−5,913
1995	0.197	76,427	75,626	2,341
1996	0.329	8,824	8,055	2,198
1997	0.278	19,110	18,386	1,166
1998	0.254	19,288	19,225	2,267
1999	0.298	122,673	120,603	2,907
2000	0.133	209,432	204,691	4,863

Sources: Central Bank Balance of Payments Statistics; SPO Main Economic Indicators.

a. $[(1+R)/(1+E)-1]$; R: The highest rate of return offered in the domestic market; E: TL Rate of change of the exchange rate.

TABLE 14.4 Public Sector Balances (Real 1987 Prices, Billions TL)[1]

	1988	1989	1990	1991	1992	1993	1994	1995	1996	1997	1998	1999[2]
Tax Revenues	10,313.8	11,818.9	13,855.2	13,965.6	15,145.1	17,452.2	15,597.0	15,830.0	17,065.0	20,099.2	22,235.4	22,458.0
Direct	3,983.1	5,120.1	5,879.7	6,013.8	6,359.6	7,115.8	6,820.7	6,061.9	6,195.1	7,380.5	9,668.1	9,346.9
Indirect	6,330.7	6,698.8	7,975.5	7,951.8	8,785.5	10,336.4	8,776.4	9,768.1	10,869.9	12,718.7	12,567.3	13,111.1
Factor Revenues	4,612.5	3,987.4	2,805.2	531.3	−70.4	729.2	1,732.1	3,122.4	4,493.9	4,662.1	5,172.9	5,698.9
Current Transfers	−6,077.6	−6,230.8	−5,892.8	−5,272.4	−5,947.8	−9,201.7	−9,504.5	−10,167.4	−13,897.9	−12,894.7	−16,163.6	−18,953.6
Public Disposable Income	9,866.1	10,587.0	12,095.6	10,196.4	9,966.8	9,498.1	8,083.3	8,779.7	7,755.4	11,912.6	9,919.9	7,351.5
Public Savings	4,970.8	3,801.4	3,084.7	613.1	−718.0	−2,660.6	−925.0	−69.0	−1,634.7	854.4	−2,110.2	−7,132.0
Public Investment	−6,147.9	−5,938.0	−7,762.3	−6,516.7	−5,926.4	−7,224.9	−3,071.7	−3,553.3	−5,101.9	−6,570.7	−7,115.6	−6,889.0
Public Sav-Inv Balance	−1,177.2	−2,136.6	−4,677.6	−5,903.6	−6,644.4	−9,885.5	−3,996.7	−3,622.3	−6,736.6	−5,716.3	−9,225.8	−14,020.9
Ratios to GNP (%)												
PSBR	4.8	5.3	7.4	10.2	10.6	12.1	7.9	5.2	8.8	7.6	9.2	15.1
Budget Balance	−3.1	−3.3	−3.1	−5.3	−4.3	−6.7	−3.9	−4.0	−8.3	−7.6	−7.0	−11.6
Non-interest Primary Budget	0.8	0.3	0.5	−1.5	−0.6	−0.9	3.8	3.4	1.7	0.1	4.7	2.1
Gov. Net Foreign Borrowing	2.1	0.8	0.9	0.4	1.6	1.4	−1.7	−1.1	−0.9	−1.5	−2.0	0.6
Stock of GDI's[3]	5.7	6.3	6.1	6.8	11.7	12.8	14.0	14.6	18.5	20.2	21.9	29.3
Interest Payments on:	3.8	3.6	3.5	3.8	3.7	5.8	7.7	7.5	10.2	7.7	11.7	13.7
Domestic Debt	2.4	2.2	2.4	2.7	2.8	4.6	6.0	6.2	9.0	6.7	10.6	12.6
Foreign Debt	1.4	1.4	1.1	1.1	0.9	1.2	1.7	1.3	1.2	1.0	1.0	1.1
Net New Domestic Borrowing/Domestic Debt Stock (%)	41.7	48.5	40.7	41.7	58.6	48.9	53.1	52.4	57.8	52.4	49.5	49.3

Sources: SPO Main Economic Indicators; Undersecreteriat of Treasury, Treasury Statistics, 1980–1999.

1. Deflated by the wholesale price index.

2. Provisional.

3. Government debt instruments (government bonds + treasury bills). Exclusive of Central Bank advances and consolidated debts.

2.2.2. The Emergence of a New Cycle and Financial Crises

2.2.2.1. The Financial Cycle Dominates the Growth Process. This unstable environment is closely linked with the emergence of a new financial cycle that, ultimately, dominates the growth process. Findings presented in table 14.5 depict one similarity and two differences between growth patterns of the 1980s and the 1990s.[6] On the one hand, the quantitative relationship between growth and current deficits remains stable and moderate during the two decades. This finding suggests that the external gap (in terms of the relative magnitude of foreign exchange requirements of given rates of economic growth) was practically unchanged between the two periods.[7]

On the other hand, an important difference is observed between the two decades when looking at the linkages between non-resident capital flows (i.e., NKF(nr), following the notation of table 14.5), current deficits, and growth. During the 1980s, the linkages between these variables appear to be in the direction of growth → current deficits → capital inflows. In other words, a given growth rate generates current deficits that have to be covered by a somewhat larger margin of capital inflows from non-residents. The 1990s appear to have transformed the direction of the

TABLE 14.5 Net Capital Flows by Non-residents (NKF(nr)), Current Deficits (CD) and Growth (g)

	NKF(nr)/ GNP (%)	CD/ GNP (%)	g (%)*
Cumulative 1981–89	1.9	1.0	5.2
Cumulative 1990–99	3.4	0.8	4.2
1990	3.0	1.7	9.4
1991	0.2	–0.2	0.4
1992	4.3	0.6	6.4
1993	7.1	3.5	8.1
Cumulative 1990–93	3.8	1.5	5.5
Bust: 1994	–4.8	–2.0	–6.1
1995	3.5	1.4	8.0
1996	5.4	1.3	7.1
1997	5.8	1.4	8.3
Cumulative 1995–97	4.9	1.3	7.7
Bust: 1998	1.8	–0.9	3.9
1999	4.6	0.7	–6.1
2000	6.5	4.9	6.1

Source: IMF, Balance of PaymentsStatistics and official Turkish data.

*Period averages are logarithmic growth rates.

above linkage into capital inflows → growth → current deficits. Inflows from non-residents gradually become autonomous (incorporating a rising component of "hot money")[8] and, depending on the degree of sterilization, impact domestic demand and uplift the growth rate and, ultimately, generate a higher level of current deficits. When inflows decline, the process is reversed by depleting reserves, monetary contraction, declining domestic demand, and an improved current balance. Hence, one of the crucial consequences of capital account liberalization turns out to be an increased degree of dependence of the growth path on autonomous capital movements.

There is, moreover, another striking difference between the growth paths of the two periods. During the 1990s, changes in the level and direction of capital movements generated a financial cycle of boom-bust-recovery that, in turn, resulted in the rising volatility of the growth rate. Growth during the 1980s— being, to a large degree, independent of autonomous capital flows—was essentially an export-led process supported, at first, by the post-crisis recovery of the early 1980s and, then, by the Özal government's expansionary policy stance (1984–1987). Although the last stage of this episode was stagnation and exhaustion, it was radically different from the bust phase of the financial cycles of the following decade. Indeed, the post-1990 years exhibit four downturns (1991, 1994, 1998–1999, and 2001), the latter three of which also incorporate financial crises of varying intensity, and four booms (1990, 1992–1993, 1995–1997, and 2000). It is also striking that as we move into the twenty-first century, the duration of the mini business cycles seems to have shortened even further. In fact, the growth rate was negative in ten of the sixteen quarters from January 1998 up till the end of 2001.

2.2.2.2. An Anatomy of Financial Crises, Turkish Style. A brief overview of the bust phases of these cycles that incorporated serious banking and/or currency crises, that is, 1994, 1998–1999, and 2001, will be helpful in this context. Tables 14.5 and 14.6 show that it is not possible to diagnose the underlying cause of these financial disturbances without observing the volatility of capital flows. 1994 appears to exhibit the most violent impact in this respect: net flows by non-residents were reversed into outflows reaching 4.8 percent of GNP. The absolute magnitude of the reversal represented by the difference in inflows between the two years, that is, 1994 minus 1993 figures

TABLE 14.6 Net Capital Flows by Non-Residents (NKF(nr)), Recorded Net Capital Flows by Residents (NKF(r)), Errors and Omissions (EO), Current Account Balance (CA) and Reserve Movements (DR)

	NKF (nr)	NKF (r)	CA	EO	DR	NKF (r)/ NKF (nr)	EO/NKF (nr)	DR/NKF (nr)	CA/NKF (nr)
Expansion 1990–93	24,536	–10,333	–9,782	–2,932	–1,489	–0.421	–0.12	–0.061	–0.399
Bust 1994	–6,259	2,409	2,631	1,766	–547	*	*	*	*
1994 minus 1993	–19,090	6,277	9,064	3,988	–239	*	*	*	*
Expansion 1995–97	27,173	–4,832	–7,454	–2,021	–12,866	–0.178	–0.074	–0.473	–0.274
Bust 1998	3,677	–3,453	1,984	–1,991	–217	–0.939	–0.541	–0.059	0.54
1998 minus 1997	–7,623	–742	4,663	603	3,099	*	*	*	*
Boom 2000 (I-X)	15,179	–2,707	–7,598	–2,550	–2,324	–0.178	–0.168	–0.153	–0.501
Bust minus boom in 2000–2001**	–27,595	1,460	7,891	–665	18,909	*	*	*	
1980–1989	15,529	–3,471	–10,408	2,910	–4,560	–0.224	0.187	–0.294	–0.670
1990–2000	74,654	–23,785	–23,746	–5,898	–21,226	–0.319	–0.079	–0.284	–0.318
16 countries 1980–89						–0.228	–0.111	–0.118	–0.543
16 countries 1990+						–0.241	–0.060	–0.268	–0.431

Note: $NKF(nr) + NKF(r) + EO + DR + CA = 0$.

* Ratios are meaningless when NKF (nr) is negative.

** The cumulative values for November 2000 to September 2001 minus the cumulative values for January to October in 2001.

for NKF(nr), equaled –$19.1 billion. Somewhat surprisingly, resident agents (essentially banks) acted in countercyclical fashion by eliminating their assets abroad and allocating funds to cover their losses in Turkey.[9] The net reversal of both non-resident and resident flows in 1994 compared with the 1993 figure was –$12.8 billion (i.e., 9.7 percent of GNP). The magnitude of the reversal forced the government into two consecutive devaluations of the Turkish lira and pushed the economy into a severe (i.e., –6.1 and –5.5 percent in terms of GNP and GDP, respectively) recession.

The 1998 bust also witnessed comparable reversals in capital movements. The net reversal of resident and non-resident flows between 1998 and 1997 reached up to –$8 billion, or 3.9 percent of the GNP. Although a currency crisis was averted, the outcome was the de facto bankruptcy of eight banks taken over formally by the so-called Savings Deposits Insurance Fund, or SDIS (in effect, by the treasury).[10] The burden on the exchequer due to the liabilities of these banks as of July 2001 was estimated to be around $14 billion or 9.3 percent of the GNP. The effect of these events on the productive sectors became visible from the last quarter of 1998, and the economy went into a severe

recession that continued during 1999 when the GNP declined by 6.1 percent in real terms.

The year 2000 witnessed an exchange rate–based disinflation and stabilization program, designed, engineered, and monitored by the IMF. Starting from inflation rates of 68.8 and 62.9 percent at the end of 1999 in terms of CPI and WPI respectively, the program targeted 25 percent and 20 percent inflation rates for the two indices at the end of 2000. Furthermore, it programmed a 20 percent depreciation of the nominal Turkish lira against the basket of 1US$ + 0.77 euro. Upper limits for the net domestic assets of the Central Bank (CB) were set, and the monetary base was to be totally dependent on the purchases of foreign exchange by the CB. Together with lower limits for net international reserves and upper limits for the PSBR as performance criteria and with the exclusion of sterilization as a policy option, the program can be interpreted as a mild currency board (Yeldan 2001b).

The program appeared to be successful in the first ten months of its implementation. Monetary, fiscal, and exchange rate targets were fully met and the IMF praised the Turkish authorities on the successful implementation of the program. Although domestic

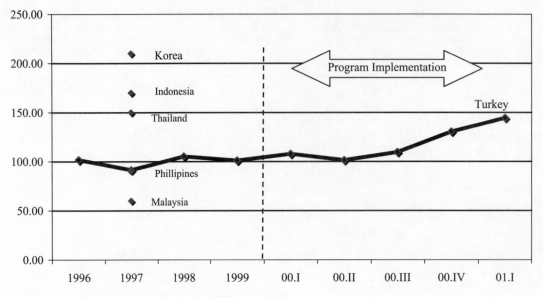

FIGURE 14.1 Short Term Foreign/Debt/CB Reserves (%)

price movements decelerated significantly from February onwards, the decline in inflation was less than the targeted rates of change of price indices and of nominal exchange rates. Between the last weeks of 1999 and 2000, the exchange rate basket rose by 20.3 percent, but rates of change in WPI and CPI indices were 32.7 and 39.0 percent, respectively. Disregarding the price movements of trade partners, these figures correspond to the real appreciation of the Turkish lira by 10.4 and 15.6 percent in terms of the two price indices, respectively.

The appreciation of the domestic currency was further boosted by an explosive growth in net capital flows by non-residents that reached $15.5 billion by the first ten months of 2000. This was reflected in the Central Bank's balance sheet: net external assets increased by 53 percent, and the monetary base by 46 percent between February and mid-November of 2000. In contrast, the wholesale price index rose by (roughly) 22 percent during the same period. Given the "initial success" of the program, risk margins narrowed and real interest rates on government debt instruments (GDIs) rapidly fell from an average of 33 percent in 1999 to practically zero during 2000. A very strong upturn in domestic absorption accompanied by the appreciation of the Turkish lira together with the impact of the Customs Union with EU were the major reasons behind the rapid expansion of the current account deficit to $9.5 billion by the end of

2000 (see table 14.1). This outcome was solely due to the deterioration of the trade balance.[11] By November, IMF officials started to express their concerns about the sustainability of the current deficit[12] and external investors appeared to share the same concern by liquidating their assets in Turkish lira, as international bankers started to call in their short-term loans to Turkish banks.[13]

Although real interest rates on government borrowing had declined to practically zero, short-term inflows continued throughout most of 2000, because strict commitment to nominal exchange rate targets kept generating positive arbitrage rate expectations for banks, which, ex post, averaged 13 percent for the whole year.[14] Even though government bonds with maturities of 12–18 months purchased on lower rates were to generate serious problems for banks in 2001 (after the collapse of the exchange rate and when inflation was, once again, rising), most banks continued to borrow short-term loans abroad during the year.

The ratio of short-term debt to international reserves that had stood at 101 percent at the inception of the program jumped to 152 percent in December 2000. Figure 14.1 portrays the trajectory of the short-term debt/Central Bank Reserves ratio in Turkey and compares it with the data observed in various East Asian economies at the onset of their crises in July 1997. In retrospect, considering the East Asian experiences, Turkey exhibited serious deterioration in

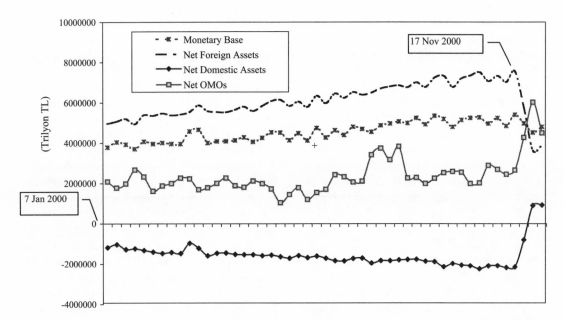

FIGURE 14.2 Monetary Base, Net Domestic Assets, Net Foreign Assets, and Net Open Market Operations (January 7, 2000–December 1, 2000, End-of-Week Observations)

terms of this fragility indicator throughout 2000. Thus, the program succeeded in reducing inflation but not enough to prevent significant currency appreciation. Moreover, it did so at the cost of the increased fragility of the banking system and the external vulnerability of the Turkish economy, as validated by the twin crises of November 2000 and February 2001.

A sudden outflow, as non-residents liquidated their treasury bills and equity assets, started a run against the Turkish lira in November. Additional foreign exchange demand resulted in the erosion of the Central Bank reserves by nearly $7 billion, whose net external assets declined by 52 percent in two weeks after mid-November. The macroeconomic impact was chaotic. As can be seen from figure 14.2, the Central Bank had played the role assigned to it under the program (i.e., the role of a de facto currency board) successfully until November when the first sign of the crisis struck. The monetary base reflected the changes in net foreign assets, while net domestic assets were kept within targeted limits. With the abrupt fall in its net external assets, the Central Bank initially violated the IMF ban on open market operations, and managed to provide additional Turkish lira liquidity to banks. This maneuver, however, did not prevent the monetary base from contracting by 17 percent during the rest of the month, as most of the additional liquidity came back

to the Central Bank as foreign exchange demand. Ultimately, the Central Bank reverted back to the non-sterilization rule, and the ongoing liquidity squeeze was aggravated as overnight interest rates climbed to exorbitant levels.

Short-term policies during the three months between the November and February crises were essentially aimed at preserving the exchange rate anchor at all costs. The reserve level continued to be low till the end of the year and contributed to a severe liquidity squeeze in the banking sector, high interest rates, and contractionary pressures on the economy. An agreement with the IMF late in December included a financial package of $10.5 billion. This funding kept the essential elements of the preceding program intact and replenished reserves early in January 2001.[15] Foreign exchange markets were temporarily stabilized, albeit at interest rates significantly above the pre-crisis levels.

Suppressing foreign exchange demand via exorbitant interest rates was clearly destabilizing. A political skirmish between the president and the prime minister was followed by a second attack on the Turkish lira in late February 2001. As interest rates rose to three-digit figures, the Central Bank had to sell $5.2 billion within two days. This amount roughly equaled the non-residents' net liquidation of Turkish lira securities

(–$3.8 billion) and the amortization of short-term bank loans (–$1.3 billion). The 2000 program officially came to an end as the free floating of the currency was announced on February 22. By mid-May, a more conventional standby agreement with the IMF was finalized. The new program was structured around a long list of so-called structural reforms, which (with the exception of those related to the banking system) had no immediate or even medium-term relevance for stabilization. It also included demand management via fiscal and monetary stringency, but with no targets for the exchange rate.

The impact of capital movements on the 2000–2001 cycle can be observed by the findings in tables 14.6 and 14.7 that, using monthly data, compare the boom phase (January to October 2000) with the bust phase (November 2000 to September 2001) of the cycle. Table 14.6 (row 8) shows the magnitudes involved as capital flows were reversed during the eleven months from November onward: the aggregate shock owing to the reversal in non-resident capital flows in 2000–2001 (i.e., –$27.6 billion) is significantly greater than those observed during the earlier crises in 1994 and 1998–1999. The breakdown of capital flows into non-resident and resident flows in table 14.7 confirms that the drift into financial crisis was predominantly the result of capital outflows originating from non-residents. Outflows from portfolio investments played the most crucial role, followed by the amortization of short-term bank loans. Residents,

particularly in terms of their recorded capital movements, once again acted countercyclically and their net outflows, including the unrecorded (i.e., *EO*) items, declined by $800 million. Even if this factor is included, the magnitude of the reversal between the first ten months of 2000 and the following eight months of all cumulative capital flows—*NKF(nr)*, *NKF(r)*, and *EO*—is an astounding–$27.6 billion!

Dramatic macroeconomic implications follow. The high tempo of inflows by non-residents during the first ten months of 2000 generated a boom with unstable characteristics. As external agents perceived the expansion as unsustainable, capital flows were reversed. The magnitude and suddenness of the reversal determined the depth of the financial crisis and its impact on the growth rate. Hence, in 2001 the economy moved into a depression (–9.4 percent in GNP) that was much more serious than those observed in the preceding crises. The contraction was accompanied by massive layoffs, rising inflation, increased social unrest, and a current account surplus that was, once again, essentially the result of import compression. Hence, as evidence from tables 14.6 and 14.7 shows, it is impossible to grasp the movement into a financial crisis and economic downturn unless we start with the analysis of capital flows.

2.2.2.3. Underlying Causes of Increased External Fragility. There is some confusion in Turkey and elsewhere about the causes of financial crises. As discussed above, the underlying cause in the Turkish case is the impact (and, at times, positive and negative shocks) generated by large, uncontrolled capital movements with a large "hot" component within a fragile financial system. Weak prudential regulation of banks or large public deficits may aggravate the situation, but do not cause the collapse per se. And there is always an individual pretext that triggers the bust. A usual source of confusion is to see the pretext as the cause. Each case is unique in the sense that there are different events triggering financial disturbances. But crisis is ultimately the result of structural fragility generated by unregulated and chaotic capital movements and their impact on the financial cycle, without which the same trigger events would never have resulted in an economy-wide havoc.

To be able to take better account of the disruptive mechanisms of this structural fragility, let us note the well-known dilemmas faced by policy makers in a developing economy with an open capital account.

TABLE 14.7 Capital Movements Before and During the 2000/2001 Crisis (Mn.$)

	2000 (I) to 2000 (X)	2000 (XI) to 2001 (IX)
A. NKF, nonresidents	**15,179**	**–12,416**
FDI	589	2,881
Portfolio	6,789	–9,063
Long-term flows	3,201	190
Short-term flows	4,600	–6,424
B. NKF, residents	**–5,257**	**–4,462**
FDI	–751	–497
Portfolio	–730	76
Short-term, recorded	–1,226	–826
Short-term, unrecorded (EO)	–2,550	–3,215
C. Reserve changes[a]	**–2,324**	**16,585**
D. Current balance	**–7,598**	**293**

Sources: IMF, Balance of PaymentsStatistics and official Turkish data.

Note: $A + B + C + D = 0$

a. "–" signifies increase and vice versa.

On the one hand, as is the case with Turkey currently, fiscal stringency is imposed by the rules of the game and using fiscal tools as a short-run macroeconomic policy option is off the agenda. On the other hand, under conditions of open capital accounts, the monetary authority can independently target either the nominal exchange rate or the interest rate, leaving the determination of the other to the interplay of market forces.

Evidence accumulated from developing country experiences in the last two decades overwhelmingly suggests that a liberalized capital account cannot be launched unless it is expected that a higher rate of return on domestic assets (deflated by the exchange rate) will be realized in comparison with the rate of return abroad. However, such a commitment favoring high domestic interest rates stimulates foreign inflows and leads to the appreciation of the domestic currency, further inviting an even higher level of hot money inflows into often shallow domestic financial markets. As a result, debt-financed public (e.g., Turkey) or private (e.g., Mexico and Korea) spending escalates. In order to accommodate this process, the central bank is forced to hold significant foreign exchange as reserves. In this setting, the only proper role remaining for the monetary authority becomes that of monetary sterilization. Thus, the surge in the aggregate money supply is checked by restricting its domestic component. Consequently, domestic interest rates rise and the cycle recommences. Eventually, the bubble bursts as hot money rushes out of the country, and a series of severe and onerous macro adjustments takes place through very high real interest rates, sizable devaluations, and the severe entrenchment of aggregate demand.[16]

2.2.3. Rising Leakages from Non-resident Inflows

Capital account liberalization resulted in a rising gap between non-resident inflows and the current account during the 1990s, as has already been noted (see the first two rows of table 14.5). Factors contributing to the growing gap are not merely of theoretical interest. The cumulative current account deficit during the 1990s equaled $14.1 billion, whereas Turkey's external debt during the same period had risen from $42 billion to $102 billion—a dramatic increase of $60 billion, far in excess of the financing requirements of the current account. As long as the growth of the external debt is considered

to be a policy issue, the analysis of factors that lead to the detachment of external borrowing and current account deficits becomes important in practical terms. Table 14.6, above, provides the basic quantitative framework for depicting these factors.

The well-known balance of payments (BOP) identity as depicted and defined in equation 1 in this chapter's appendix, that is, $NKF(nr) + NKF(r) + EO + DR + CA = 0$, constitutes the framework of table 14.6. The terms represent, respectively, net capital flows emanating from non-residents, residents' net flows, net errors and omissions, changes in reserves, and the current account balance. The same data can also be presented with slight modifications in terminology. By reversing the signs of the last four terms of the BOP identity, one can decompose the non-resident inflows into current deficits and "leakages" (i.e., recorded and non-recorded outflows by residents, and reserve accumulation). The conceptual framework for both representations is further elaborated in the appendix (see appendix equations 1 and 2).

Table 14.6 shows the striking change that occurs as a result of the liberalization of capital accounts after 1989. The ratios of $NKF(r)$, EO, DR, and CA within net non-resident flows,—that is, $NKF(nr)$—should be interpreted as the share of each type of utilization to which non-resident flows have been allocated. Findings on the values of each of the terms (and of the relevant ratios) during different phases of financial cycles as well as the cumulative sums for the 1980s and 1990s are summarized and analyzed in the following paragraphs of this section.

A negative value for $NKF(r)$ signifies recorded capital outflows by residents. It will be observed that during the 1990s, with the exception of the crisis year of 1994 (when residents acted in countercyclical fashion and engaged in net inflows), $NKF(r)$ was negative. In relative terms, their drain on the capital account was particularly heavy during the financial bust in 1998 (when the current account was in surplus), as recorded resident outflows as a ratio of $NKF(nr)$ rose to 94 percent. Comparing the 1980s with the 1990s, it is observed that capital controls really do make a difference. The ratio of the residents' outflows to non-residents' inflows rose by 10 percentage points from 22 to 34 percent during the latter decade.

Throughout this study, the "net errors and omissions" (EO) item of the BOP statistics is treated as unrecorded capital movements by residents. A negative *EO* value is, thus, considered as capital flight.[17] The liberalization of capital flows should, generally, be expected to transform unrecorded capital movements into recorded items by legalizing the former. This factor, together with improved statistical methods, should result in lower values, at least in relative terms for the *EO* item. This appears to be the case for a sample of sixteen emerging economies[18] during the 1990s, compared with the preceding decade, when the share of capital flight (as represented by negative *EO* values) within non-resident inflows declined from 11.1 to 6 percent (see table 14.6, column 8, last two rows).

The Turkish experience, however, was directly the opposite. During the 1980s the net balance of the *EO* item was positive (i.e., 18.7 percent of *NKF[nr]*), probably owing to the reversal of capital flight that took place during the severe crisis of the late 1970s. This positive contribution would, thereby, offset most of the recorded residents' flows, the cumulative sum of which was negative during the earlier decade (i.e., –22.4 percent of *NKF[nr]*). The 1990s reversed the direction of capital flight by changing the cumulative *EO* item into negative values, and residents' unrecorded capital movements as a ratio of total non-residents' flows were –6 percent. Thus, recorded and unrecorded capital movements by residents (*NKF[r]* + *EO*) together constituted a 40.4 percent drain on the non-residents' inflows—a radical deterioration that can only be understood within the context of the liberalization of the capital account.

Under a regime of controlled mobility of international capital, the adequate level of reserves was traditionally regarded as three or four months of imports for covering the time lags between payments for imports and export receipts, as well as for offsetting temporary disequilibria in the current account. Capital account liberalization radically changed and broadened the criteria of reserve adequacy, and brought forth such indicators as the "ratio of reserves to short-term debt plus the stock of portfolio equity," the "ratio of foreign-assets-to currency (usually M2Y)," and a minimum level in excess of the scheduled amortization of external debt. For example, after observing that "foreign exchange reserves and reserve policy played an important role in the recent financial crises," in 1999 Alan Greenspan suggested that "countries could be expected to hold sufficient liquid reserves *to ensure that they could avoid new borrowing for one year*" (italics added).[19]

These new and drastic adequacy requirements for reserve levels have pushed most developing countries to move into an accelerated rate of reserve accumulation in "normal" periods. The outcome has been an additional and "expensive"[20] drain on non-resident inflows. However, the aforementioned drain of reserve accumulation on net inflows in Turkey does not show much change in the pre- versus post-liberalization years (see column 8 in table 14.6). Period averages, however, were affected by the severe drain on Central Bank reserves in late 2000, which pulled total reserve accumulation for that year to practically zero. Table 14.7 depicts the turbulence in capital movements that adversely affected the Turkish economy during the 2000–2001 crisis. Reserve accumulation amounting to $2.9 billion for the first three quarters of 2000 was reversed during the last quarter, when $2.5 billion in reserves were depleted. If the 2000 data are disregarded, between 1989 and 1999 the net increase in reserves amounted to $19.9 billion, constituting 84 percent of the total increase ($23.8 billion) in the import bill; whereas the similar ratio for developing countries as a whole was 60 percent, which is still considered excessive.[21]

These developments in capital movements during the past decade are not limited to Turkey. For comparative purposes, the last two rows of table 14.6 present the data for sixteen emerging economies (including Turkey) for the two decades. For all sixteen countries as well as Turkey, the share of current deficit financing out of non-resident inflows has declined, but the decline is much more substantial for Turkey (i.e., from 67 to 32 percent) compared with the others (from 54 to 43 percent). During the last decade, the shares of recorded and unrecorded resident outflows have been substantially higher in Turkey and those of reserve accumulation have been similar. These findings suggest that the impact of capital account liberalization in Turkey on the reallocation of capital inflows has been much more substantial than in comparable emerging economies.

2.2.4. Arbitrage-Seeking Short-Term Capital ("Hot Money") Flows

Another disturbing feature of capital flows during the 1990s is the increasing magnitude, both in absolute and relative terms, of hot money flows (see appendix 1 for the conceptual and empirical specification of hot money).

In a developing economy, hot money flows emerge from the arbitrage-seeking activities of rentiers and banks (both non-residents and residents) as well as of firms (essentially residents). The arbitrage returns, defined as the speculative gain for rentiers between the highest (nominal) interest offered in the domestic economy and the rate of (nominal) change in the exchange rate (defined as Turkish lira per dollar), are calculated in table 14.3, above. It should, however, be pointed out that the same variables similarly affect the behavior of banks borrowing abroad and moving into TL assets (e.g., government debt instruments) or firms borrowing in foreign exchange but spending in TL. The rate of return minus the risk premium compared with rates of return abroad determines the direction of hot money flows. Table 14.8 provides empirical findings on hot money movements distinguished between residents and non-residents. The following observations are worth noting.

1. The mere magnitude of gross short-term capital movements must be a source of concern. Columns 2 and 3 of table 14.3, above, report the gross flows of banks' foreign credit acquisitions and repayments for the post-1991 period. Even if we take into consideration that some of these figures include double counting due to the renewal of short-term bank liabilities more than once every year, the relevant magnitudes point at one of the most important sources of instability in the financial system.

2. It was predominantly short-term arbitrage-seeking (i.e., "hot") capital movements that were affected by capital account liberalization in 1989.[22] The net balance of 1990–2000 is negligible (i.e., $262 million). But if we include the dramatic outflows during the recent crisis, the net balance for "hot money" for the 1990–2001 (January–September for the last year) period, thus, turns out to be –$13.1 billion.[23] This is significantly different from the earlier decade when "hot" non-resident inflows were of negligible magnitudes, but reverse capital flight acted as a positive factor in financing current deficits. It is observed that the 1989 turning point affected arbitrage-seeking flows by raising non-resident inflows substantially, particularly during the boom phases of the cycle but, more importantly, by reversing the direction of residents' flows into recorded and unrecorded outflows, exceeding the total of hot money inflows since 1990.

3. Since "arbitrage seeking" is determined by the same variables regardless of the residence of the relevant agent, how can we explain the divergence between the actions of residents and non-residents? Indeed, as briefly discussed earlier, residents had acted in countercyclical fashion during the 1994 and the 2000–2001 crises (see table 14.8). Two (not necessarily mutually exclusive) hypotheses are worth testing empirically: one explanation is that residents might have contradictory expectations about the behavior of exchange rate movements and/or external agents' greater willingness to take "moral hazard–based risks" (this ultimately turned out to be justified). Alternatively, resident rentier behavior may be a transitional

TABLE 14.8 Direction and Magnitude of "Hot Money" Movements from Non-residents and Residents

	Hot Money: Nonresidents (1)	Total Nonresident Flows (2)	(3) = (1)/(2)	Hot Money: Residents (4)	Total Resident Flows (5)	(6) = (4)/(5)	Net Hot Money (7) = (1) + (4)
1990–93	9,664	24,536	0.394	–12,278	–13,265	0.926	–2,614
1994	–5,913	–6,259	0.945	4,212	4,175	1.009	–1,701
1995–97	5,705	27,173	0.21	–3,233	–6,853	0.472	2,472
1998	2,267	3,677	0.617	–3,286	–5,331	0.616	–1,019
1999	2,907	8,646	0.336	–1,333	–2,076	0.642	1,574
2000	4,863	16,362	0.297	–4,572	–6,215	0.736	291
1980–89	2,454	15,529	0.158	213	–561	*	2,667
1990–2000	19,493	74,654	0.261	–19,231	–29,683	0.648	262
2001 (I–IX)	–9,222	–10,283	0.897	–4,100	–3,495	1,173	–13,322
90–01 (I–IX)	10,271	64,371	0.16	–23,331	–33,178	0.703	–13,060

Sources: IMF, Balance of PaymentsStatistics and official Turkish data.

*Ratios are meaningless when signs of hot money and total flows are different.

phenomenon of one-off portfolio diversification, the impact of which will wear off after the first substantial movement abroad is exhausted.

4. The shares of "hot money" within capital flows of both residents and non-residents have risen substantially since the liberalization of capital accounts. For non-residents, the "hot inflows"/total inflows ratio has risen by more than 5 percentage points to 26.1 percent during 1990–2000 as compared with the preceding decade (with, however, a highly fluctuating pattern). For residents, "hot" outflows constitute 65 percent of total outflows during the same period. Hot money movements are much more volatile than other capital flow categories, particularly when crisis periods are included.

5. The 1994 and 2000–2001 data in table 14.8 clearly show the contribution of hot money movements to the emergence and deepening of financial crises. Within eleven months following October 2000, net recorded and unrecorded hot money flows by non-residents and residents reached –$13.3 billion and, to say the least, generated an extremely adverse and destabilizing impact on the economy.

To summarize, the liberalization of the capital account in Turkey in 1989 has pushed the economy into an unstable and risky path in four ways: (1) the fragility of the domestic financial system has increased substantially; (2) the growth path of the economy has become more volatile, subject to a newly emerging financial cycle, and the period between its boom and bust phases has shortened considerably; (3) drains or "leakages" out of inflows have increased in relative terms, and the external debt has grown at a pace totally unrelated with the external financing needs of economic growth; and, finally, (4) arbitrage-seeking and short-term capital ("hot money") flows constitute a rising share of total capital movements from both residents and non-residents, and this phenomenon has begun to destabilize the economy.

3. Economics of Macro Adjustment: Sources of Aggregate Demand

In order to trace the patterns of adjustment to financial liberalization, we will deploy a series of decomposition analyses of macro aggregates of final demand. Since liberalization, there have been substantial swings in the parameters governing the demand

"injections" (such as investments, government expenditures, and exports) and "leakages" (i.e., savings, taxes, and imports).

Much of the variability in aggregate demand in the Turkish economy is induced by the state's fiscal stance. The escalation of public deficits via ever-rising costs of (internal) debt servicing became the dominant element in aggregate demand. The costs of domestic debt servicing were so explosive that, by as early as 1992, public savings had turned into deficits. By 2000, interest costs on domestic debt reached 80 percent of the overall tax income of the public sector. In all likelihood, the disposable income of the public sector, itself, is likely to be negative by the end of 2001.

3.1. Decomposition of the Sources of Effective Demand

We will address these developments utilizing the analytics provided in Godley (1999) and Berg and Taylor (2001) where the following decomposition measure is applied over effective demand. At the sectoral level, total supply, X is given by the sum of GNP, Y, and imports, M. Total GNP, in turn, can be partitioned into private disposable income, Y^p, and public disposable income, Y^G, loosely referred to as aggregate tax income, T. Thus $Y = Y^p + T$.

Goods market equilibrium necessitates the balance of aggregate supply and demand (sum of private consumption, C^p; private investment, I^p; government expenditures, G; and net exports, E-M). Denoting the following "leakage" parameters relative to aggregate GNP as

$$s_p = \frac{Y^P - C^P}{Y}$$

$$t = \frac{T}{Y}$$

$$m = \frac{M}{Y}$$

one can obtain the following version of the (Keynesian) multiplier function:

$$Y = \frac{s_P}{s_P + t + m}\left(\frac{I^P}{s_P}\right) + \frac{t}{s_P + t + m}\left(\frac{G}{t}\right) + \frac{m}{s_P + t + m}\left(\frac{E}{m}\right)$$

Here, I^p/s_p, G/t, and E/m are the direct "own" multipliers of, respectively, investments, government expenditures, and exports. The overall impact of injections is scaled by the corresponding leakages of savings, tax burden, and import propensities.

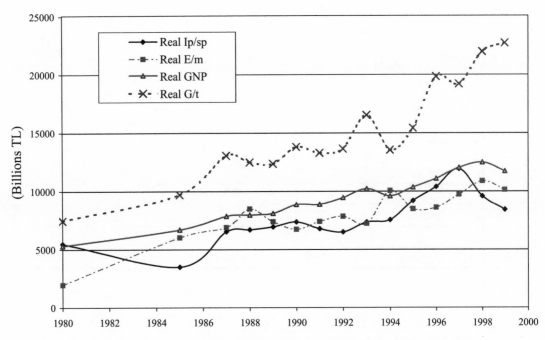

FIGURE 14.3 Decomposition of the Sources of Macroeconomic Demand (Real 1980 Prices)

We portray the evolution of the values of key parameters in figure 14.3. The abrupt expansion of G/t clearly stands out against other demand components. The dismal performance of $I^p/s_p < Y$ discloses the channeling of investable funds away from real fixed investment toward financial speculation targeted at the government's deficit financing and the securitization of domestic debt. Real exports as scaled by the import propensities, E/m, also fall short of GNP throughout the post-liberalization era. The only two exceptions occurred in 1998 and then again in 1994 — both being crisis years during which imports contracted severely.

How dependable is the source of G/t in sustaining growth in GNP? Or, in other words, should we regard the massive injection provided by the G/t as a healthy source of growth? To properly assess the impact of G/t, we further decompose G into its components. We deduct transfer expenditures from G wherein the most important item is interest costs on domestic debt. We then carry out the same analysis by employing G^* as real non-interest government expenditures (on goods and services).

This revision sheds a totally new light over the state's stance as the source of demand. Real non-interest government expenditures, scaled by t (G^*/t),

becomes much weaker as a source of injection in the first half of the 1990s. After 1994, the post-crisis management severely reduced the G^*/t component. Even so, the public sector continued to provide a relatively stronger demand pull compared with exports. Thus, the foreign sector has continuously been a laggard throughout the whole post-financial liberalization era. Private investments behaved comparably at par with public spending during 1994 through 1996. After then, however, investment lost all its impetus as limited domestic savings were channeled to the securitization of the fiscal deficits and financial savings dominated the incentives against fixed investments in the real sector. These patterns are portrayed in figure 14.4.

3.2. Deterioration of the Fiscal Balances

The post-1988 period witnessed a drastic deterioration of the fiscal balances in Turkey. Public sector borrowing requirement (PSBR)/GNP ratios averaged 4.5 percent during 1981–1988 but rose to 10.2 percent in 1991 and averaged 9.4 percent over 1990–1999. By the end of 1999, PSBR reached 15.1 percent of GNP and is anticipated to rise even further in 2001. Before investigating the consequences of this on resource use

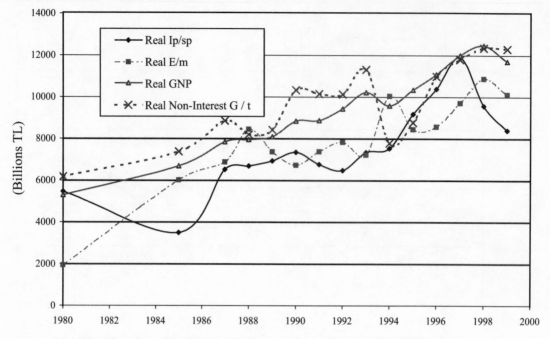

FIGURE 14.4 Decomposition of the Sources of Macroeconomic Demand (Real 1980 Prices)

and income distribution, it will be useful to overview the factors that generated this deterioration.

We document this deterioration in table 14.9, which is based on real values of the fiscal accounts using 1987 prices.

Note that during 1988–1993, the major erosion has occurred in the factor revenues item, that is, in net factor income generated by the state economic enterprise system. Factor revenues of the state declined by 86 percent in five years (in real terms). The real erosion up till 1992 corresponds to approximately 5 percent of the GNP of that period. The swift upward movement in transfer expenditures started in 1992. Between 1991 and 1996, the increase was more than 125 percent in real terms. The major item in this account was interest payments. The rise in domestic debt gave way to a rapid buildup of interest costs.

On the revenue side, tax collections had registered modest improvements in real terms (by 50 percent up till 1993), but they started to decline thereafter (essentially owing to the erosion of direct taxes). The share of indirect taxes in the total rose from 59 percent in 1990 to 64 percent in 1997.

These developments led to a sharp collapse in the disposable income of the public sector, which declined by 45 percent in real terms. As we shall discuss, this decline had devastating effects and generated strong pressures on the provision of public services and/or raised the PSBR to unprecedented levels.

In this context, it is important to note a fundamental change in the financing of the PSBR, compared with the pre-liberalization period of the 1970s and 1980s. Data on the financing patterns of the PSBR suggest that, under the financially repressed conditions of the 1970s and early 1980s, the most direct method of deficit financing was through Central Bank advances (monetization). However, after embarking on the path of structural adjustment, especially with the removal of interest ceilings in a series of reforms throughout the 1980s, the Turkish private sector faced a new phenomenon: positive real rates of interest. Financial institutions and rentiers swiftly adapted to changes in the rates of interest during the 1980s, and the government found it much easier to finance its borrowing requirements from domestic borrowing through issues of government debt instruments (GDIs). This also enabled successive governments to bypass many of the formal constraints on their fiscal operations. Consequently, with the advent of full-fledged financial liberalization after 1988, PSBR

TABLE 14.9 Public Sector Balances (Real 1987 Prices, Billions TL)[1]

	1988	1989	1990	1991	1992	1993	1994	1995	1996	1997	1998	1999[2]
Tax Revenues	10,313.8	11,818.9	13,855.2	13,965.6	15,145.1	17,452.2	15,597.0	15,830.0	17,065.0	20,099.2	22,235.4	22,458.0
Direct	3,983.1	5,120.1	5,879.7	6,013.8	6,359.6	7,115.8	6,820.7	6,061.9	6,195.1	7,380.5	9,668.1	9,346.9
Indirect	6,330.7	6,698.8	7,975.5	7,951.8	8,785.5	10,336.4	8,776.4	9,768.1	10,869.9	12,718.7	12,567.3	13,111.1
Factor Revenues	4,612.5	3,987.4	2,805.2	531.3	-70.4	729.2	1,732.1	3,122.4	4,493.9	4,662.1	5,172.9	5,698.9
Current Transfers	-6,077.6	-6,230.8	-5,892.8	-5,272.4	-5,947.8	-9,201.7	-9,504.5	-10,167.4	-13,897.9	-12,894.7	-16,163.6	-18,953.6
Public Disposable Income	9,866.1	10,587.0	12,095.6	10,196.4	9,966.8	9,498.1	8,083.3	8,779.7	7,755.4	11,912.6	9,919.9	7,351.5
Public Savings	4,970.8	3,801.4	3,084.7	613.1	-718.0	-2,660.6	-925.0	-69.0	-1,634.7	854.4	-2,110.2	-7,132.0
Public Investment	-6,147.9	-5,938.0	-7,762.3	-6,516.7	-5,926.4	-7,224.9	-3,071.7	-3,553.3	-5,101.9	-6,570.7	-7,115.6	-6,889.0
Public Sav-Inv Balance	-1,177.2	-2,136.6	-4,677.6	-5,903.6	-6,644.4	-9,885.5	-3,996.7	-3,622.3	-6,736.6	-5,716.3	-9,225.8	-14,020.9
Ratios to GNP (%)												
PSBR	4.8	5.3	7.4	10.2	10.6	12.1	7.9	5.2	8.8	7.6	9.2	15.1
Budget Balance	-3.1	-3.3	-3.1	-5.3	-4.3	-6.7	-3.9	-4.0	-8.3	-7.6	-7.0	-11.6
Non-interest Primary Budget	0.8	0.3	0.5	-1.5	-0.6	-0.9	3.8	3.4	1.7	0.1	4.7	2.1
Government Net Foreign Borrowing	2.1	0.8	0.9	0.4	1.6	1.4	-1.7	-1.1	-0.9	-1.5	-2.0	0.6
Stock of GDIs[3]	5.7	6.3	6.1	6.8	11.7	12.8	14.0	14.6	18.5	20.2	21.9	29.3
Interest Payments on:	3.8	3.6	3.5	3.8	3.7	5.8	7.7	7.5	10.2	7.7	11.7	13.7
Domestic Debt	2.4	2.2	2.4	2.7	2.8	4.6	6.0	6.2	9.0	6.7	10.6	12.6
Foreign Debt	1.4	1.4	1.1	1.1	0.9	1.2	1.7	1.3	1.2	1.0	1.0	1.1
Net New Domestic Borrowing/ Domestic Debt Stock (%)	41.7	48.5	40.7	41.7	58.6	48.9	53.1	52.4	57.8	52.4	49.5	49.3

Sources: SPO *Main Economic Indicators*; Undersecreteriat of Treasury, *Treasury Statistics, 1980–1999.*

1. Deflated by the wholesale price index.

2. Provisional.

3. Government debt instruments (government bonds + treasury bills). Exclusive of Central Bank advances and consolidated debts.

financing relied almost exclusively on issues of GDIs to the internal market—especially to the banking sector.

The underlying characteristic of domestic debt management was its extreme short-term outlook. Net new domestic borrowings, as a ratio of the stock of the existing debt, rose to almost 50 percent over the 1990s. This ratio increased to 58 percent in 1992, indicating that each year the state had to resort to net new borrowing, reaching half of the stock of debt already accumulated. Thus, the public sector was trapped in a short-term rolling of debt, or Ponzi financing. This clearly unsustainable process contributed to the so-called confidence crisis of the 1990s. For this scheme to work, however, domestic financial markets required the continued inflow of short-term capital inflows. This necessitated a combination of high real rates of interest, along with an appreciation of the lira.

3.3. Decomposition of the Fiscal-Real Linkages

Given that the evolution of the financial sector has mostly been related to the debt-servicing costs of a public sector with unsustainable amounts of debt, it would be illuminating to repeat the above decomposition exercise from the perspective of real-financial linkages.

The equation system introduced in section 3.1, above, can be used to obtain the real-financial balance within the domestic economy:

$$\Delta F_p + \Delta D + \Delta A = (Ip - spY) + (G - tY) + (E - mY)$$

where ΔF_p, ΔD, and ΔA stand, respectively, for the net change in financial claims against the private sector, in the government's domestic debt, and in foreign assets. Clearly, when the balance between the injections and withdrawals of any entity (the private sector, the government, or the rest of the world) is positive, then financial claims against that entity must be rising. So, for instance, when $G > tY$, it means that the government is accumulating debt. (Since in the Turkish context, the government's net foreign borrowing was virtually non-existent during the 1990s—see table 14.8—this meant the buildup of domestic debt.) Similarly, $E < mY$ indicates that net foreign assets of the home country are declining. Since it must be true that at any point in time

$$dFp/dt + dD/dt + dA/dt = 0$$

the expansionary stance of the government $(G > tX)$ must be matched by some other entity increasing its

asset holdings or reducing liabilities. In the Turkish case, this primarily meant the buildup of domestic assets in the hands of the domestic banking sector (with injections of liquidity from the rest of the world via short-term capital inflows). Under these conditions, banks' assets mostly consisted of the domestic debt instruments of the government, while their liabilities were mostly short-term foreign borrowings. This operation by itself deepened much of the fragility already existing in the system due to the mismatch between the maturity and currency compositions of domestic assets and foreign denominated liabilities.

This mismatch, often referred to as short positions of the banking system, reached almost $15 billion or about 7 percent of the GNP by the end of the decade, and increased the vulnerability of the banking system with a high devaluation risk. With the rise of the gap in the open positions of the banking system, the ongoing risk premium of new borrowing increased secularly until net capital flows reversed as in late 1998, and again in November 2000. The necessary adjustments to bring the system back to the financial asset-liability stock-to-stock equilibrium were indeed onerous and painstaking.

Now utilizing the GNP identities once again, let us distinguish private from public consumption as C^p and C^g and I^p and I^g respectively. Disposable income in the private sector channels either into private consumption, C^p, or into private savings, S^p. This works similarly for the public sector. We thus obtain

$$I^P + I^G + E = (Y^P - C^P) + (Y^G - C^G) + M$$

The two terms in the parentheses on the right-hand side reflect, respectively, the private savings and the public savings. Denoting $s_G = (Y^G - C^G)/Y^G$, and using the remaining variables as defined above, we get a version of the decomposition equation above, this time reflecting the investment-saving balances of the respective entities:

$$Y = \frac{s_P}{s_P + s_G + m}\left(\frac{I^P}{s_P}\right) + \frac{s_G}{s_P + s_G + m}\left(\frac{I^G}{s_G}\right) + \frac{m}{s_P + s_G + m}\left(\frac{E}{m}\right)$$

Table 14.10. documents the relevant parameters and the main indicators of the aggregate demand decomposition. The most striking observation is the negative saving performance of the public sector beginning in 1992. This fact alone induces a severe

TABLE 14.10 Sources of Aggregate Demand: Main Indicators and Parameters

	sg	sp	m	t	Real GNP	Real Ip/sp	Real Ig/sg	Real E/m	Real G/t	Real Non-Interest G/t
1980	0.045	0.127	0.120	0.167	5,303.0	5,470.6	10,913.5	1,945.3	7,449.1	3,096.0
1985	0.077	0.210	0.189	0.141	6,688.2	3,494.7	7,778.1	6,017.1	9,701.3	2,981.1
1987	0.066	0.173	0.177	0.160	7,840.5	6,519.8	12,226.4	6,879.4	13,058.5	3,815.4
1988	0.068	0.204	0.176	0.156	7,955.4	6,692.9	9,839.4	8,454.4	12,467.8	3,884.7
1989	0.047	0.174	0.175	0.159	8,084.1	6,931.4	12,626.7	7,366.7	12,354.5	4,687.2
1990	0.034	0.186	0.174	0.167	8,843.7	7,349.5	22,254.8	6,724.2	13,801.9	5,753.1
1991	0.007	0.206	0.165	0.174	8,872.9	6,766.0	94,314.6	7,382.7	13,280.3	6,277.3
1992	−0.008	0.224	0.172	0.182	9,442.7	6,486.8	−77,942.3	7,835.2	13,642.3	6,628.0
1993	−0.027	0.254	0.192	0.181	10,212.7	7,338.3	−27,732.3	7,219.4	16,544.6	7,209.3
1994	−0.011	0.242	0.203	0.188	9,589.8	7,537.5	−31,843.7	10,050.1	13,530.4	5,924.1
1995	−0.001	0.222	0.241	0.171	10,349.7	9,187.0	−465,263.4	8,454.4	15,430.6	6,467.8
1996	−0.017	0.215	0.274	0.169	11,087.3	10,385.2	−34,602.9	8,583.5	19,837.7	7,492.3
1997	0.005	0.205	0.298	0.183	12,007.6	11,912.2	158,963.3	9,713.1	19,215.5	7,883.9
1998	−0.019	0.235	0.272	0.191	12,471.8	9,571.7	−42,055.3	10,880.1	21,992.9	8,108.3
1999	−0.069	0.222	0.266	0.202	11,709.2	8,407.2	−10,582.5	10,116.7	22,725.3	8,697.8
2000	−0.052	0.221	0.309	0.244	13,048.6	9,488.4	−16,655.0	9,977.4	21,740.6	7,439.7

Note: For symbols, see text. Real quantities are in billions TL, deflated by the GNP deflator (1980 = 100).

volatility in the investment patterns, as I^G/s_G ratios become negative after 1992 (with the exception of 1997). This observation pertains despite the secular rise of the tax burden, t. The import coefficient is also observed to rise by almost twofold from 0.12 in 1980, to 0.31 in 2000.

Much of the expansion in I^p/s_p and E/m is absorbed by the negative saving performance of the public sector, and the abrupt financing demands of the government increase uncertainty and risk in the financial markets. It also increases the volatility of the money multiplier as the government calls for many auctions to dispose off its debt instruments.

4. Microlevel Adjustments in the Manufacturing Sector

In this section, we investigate the structural consequences of the post-1980 outward orientation on market concentration and productivity in the Turkish manufacturing industries. To this end, we will refer to recent Turkish literature and report on the concentration tendencies and oligopolistic markup pricing practices prevalent in this sector. Furthermore, we shall employ a new set of decompositions on productivity and employment patterns to reveal the leading/lagging subsectors within manufacturing.

The period under analysis spans the overall transformation of the Turkish economy from domestic-oriented, import-substitutionist industrialization to one emphasizing export orientation and integration with global markets. During this period, manufacturing has evolved as the leading sector, both in terms of the degree of its export orientation and as a focal area where distribution patterns between wage labor and capital have been reshaped.

Independent studies[24] and rudimentary data from official agencies provide (both formal and anecdotal) evidence that one of the major structural deficiencies of manufacturing reveals itself in the rather loose association between export penetration gains and labor productivity, on the one hand; and the dismal patterns of employment, accumulation, and wage labor remunerations, on the other hand. This deformation is, in fact, a perennial feature of the post-1980 structural adjustment era. In their analysis of the decomposition of labor productivity in manufacturing, Voyvoda and Yeldan (2001) report that, since the inception of the structural adjustment reforms and outward orientation, the underlying sources of productivity gains have not significantly altered in this sector. They find that none of the leading export sectors of the 1980s have generated sufficiently strong productivity contributions or admitted strong interindustry linkages to serve as the leading sectors propelling the rest of the economy.

Given this background, there exists considerable evidence on the extent of monopolization and high concentration in the Turkish manufacturing industries. The State Institute of Statistics data suggest, for instance, that the process of export orientation and overall trade liberalization since 1980 has not affected the structural characteristics of the manufacturing industry. Many of the monopolistic sectors either kept their existing high rates of concentration or even suffered from increased monopolization as measured by their CR4 ratios or Hirfindahl indexes. Even among many competitive sectors of 1980, one observes increases in the CR4 ratios by 1996.[25]

These observations suggest that, contrary to expectations, the opening process was unable to introduce increased competition in the industrial commodity markets. Here we attempt to formalize these observations and deduce econometric hypotheses on the patterns of trade liberalization, concentration, and profitability. To this end, we will summarize the results obtained by Metin, Voyvoda, and Yeldan (2001a), who investigated these empirical questions using various panel data procedures. The relevant data cover twenty-nine sub–sectors of Turkish manufacturing for the 1980–1996 period. We focus on three sets of issues: (1) the effect of openness on the extent of market concentration, as measured by CR4 rates; (2) the behavior of gross profit margins (markups) in relation to

openness, concentration rates, and real wage costs; and (3) the behavior of sectoral real investments in relation to markups, real wage costs, and the openness indicator.

4.1. Phases of Macroeconomic Adjustment in Turkish Manufacturing

Table 14.11 summarizes the main indicators of the manufacturing industry under the post-1980 adjustments. To document the extent of the oligopolistic structure of the sector, we tabulate the rate of market concentration in the manufacturing industry subsectors by calculating the shares of the four largest enterprises in the total sales (revenues) of the sector (hence the acronym, CR4). Accordingly, we classify those sectors with CR4 ratios above 30 percent as imperfectly competitive and those having CR4 ratios below this threshold as competitive.[26] Data on other sectoral variables come from the *State Institute of Statistics (SIS) Manufacturing Industry Annual Surveys*. To arrive at "wage rates" and the "average labor product," we have used data on "total wages paid" and "value-added" divided, respectively, by "average number of workers engaged." We have used the sectoral wholesale producer prices in deflating nominal magnitudes.

TABLE 14.11 Evolution of the Turkish Manufacturing Sector under External Liberalization

	Structural Adjustment Reforms 1980–81	Outward-Orientation 1981–88	Unregulated Financial Liberalization 1989–93	Financial Crisis and Reinvigoration of Short Term Capital-Led Growth 1994–97
Competitive Sectors				
Value Added/Total Manufacturing	0.45	0.42	0.51	0.48
Employment/Total Manufacturing	0.58	0.59	0.62	0.65
Ratio of Trade Volume to Value Added	0.39	1.04	0.91	1.46
Share of Public Firms in Value Added	0.15	0.13	0.11	0.04
Share of Wages in Value Added	0.33	0.22	0.23	0.19
Annual Rate of Growth of Real Wages (%)	2.77	−1.88	11.62	−7.92
Annual Rate of Growth of Labor Productivity (%)	26.54	8.83	11.69	−2.01
Gross Profit Margins (Mark-up)	0.28	0.33	0.39	0.38
Noncompetitive Sectors				
Value Added/Total Manufacturing	0.55	0.58	0.49	0.52
Employment/Total Manufacturing	0.42	0.41	0.38	0.35
Ratio of Trade Volume to Value Added	0.67	1.04	0.89	1.59
Share of Public Firms in Value Added	0.62	0.53	0.43	0.42
Share of Wages in Value Added	0.28	0.14	0.21	0.14
Annual Rate of Growth of Real Wages (%)	3.39	−3.15	15.41	−8.28
Annual Rate of Growth of Labor Productivity (%)	83.25	12.71	8.53	3.24
Gross Profit Margins (Mark-up)	0.34	0.46	0.49	0.53

Source: SIS Manufacturing Industry Annual Surveys and Manufacturing Industry Concentration Ratios.

TABLE 14.12

	Open Sectors	Inward-Looking Sectors
Competitive sectors	312, 322, 381, 383	311, 321, 323, 331, 352, 356, 369
Imperfectly competitive sectors	351, 353, 382, 384, 385, 390	313, 314, 324, 332, 341, 342, 354, 355, 361, 362, 371, 372

The periodization of table 14.11 follows the adjustment path of the overall economy as characterized and discussed in table 14.12, above. Given our criterion of distinguishing individual sectors as competitive versus imperfectly competitive based on their CR4 ratios, we observe that eighteen of the twenty-nine sectors fall under the "imperfectly competitive and oligopolistic" group in 1980. Eight of them have CR4 ratios higher than 50 percent. By 1996, there was very little change in these subgroups. As of 1996, the share of value-added in the imperfectly competitive sectors in the manufacturing total reached 51 percent. Furthermore, these sectors employed 31 percent of total manufacturing employment in our database. In contrast, in 1980, the output share of the imperfectly competitive sectors was 55 percent and their employment share was 42 percent.

At the risk of overgeneralization, we can nevertheless confer a tendency for higher markup rates within the imperfectly competitive block. Petroleum refineries (353), soil products (361), and non-metals (369) have the highest markup rates over 1994–1996 (of 1.07, 1.04, and 0.72, respectively). We further observe that growth in real wages has been consistently negative over the 1981–1988 and 1994–1997 episodes, while real wage costs have been on an upward trend under the financial deregulation of 1989–1993. As of 1994–1997, the highest share of labor costs in value-added (0.27) is recorded in manufacture of footwear (324). This is followed by glass products (362) with 0.25, and paper and paper products (341) with 0.24. The dissociation between real wage movements and labor productivity is clearly visible over the classic export-led manufacturing era from 1981 to 1988. Even though real wages seem to have caught up with real average labor productivity over 1989–1993, this pattern falls short of its momentum, and by 1994–1997 real wages start a contractionary trend.

4.2. Econometric Investigation

We now redirect our attention to the econometric investigation provided by Metin, Voyvoda, and Yeldan (2001; hereafter, MVY). We focus on the twenty-nine subsectors of manufacturing based on three-digit ISI-Classification (the ISIC codes and their sectoral identification are laid out in appendix 1, table 14.14).

MVY also rely on the initial classification based on the CR4 ratios introduced above. Accordingly, those sectors that have a CR4 in excess of 0.30 are classified as "imperfectly competitive/oligopolistic" and those with a CR4 of less than 0.30 are classified as "perfectly competitive." On a different spectrum, sectors are regarded as "open" provided that their trade volume (measured as imports plus exports) as a ratio of sectoral value-added exceed 0.50. Sectors with trade volume to value-added ratios of less than 0.50 are regarded as "inward-looking." They carry this classification based on the characteristics of the twenty-nine sectors in 1980. We thus obtain the following tabulation (see appendix 1, table 14.13, for identification of the ISIC codes).

MVY utilize two specifications: they first study the distributional issues and analyze the behavior of gross profit margins (markup rates) in relation to trade liberalization, sectoral concentration, and swings in real wage costs. Secondly, they analyze the patterns of accumulation, and study the behavior of sectoral investment (by destination) against the behavior of markup rates, real wage costs, and openness.

The two essential estimating equations are as follows:

$$MR_{it} = f(\alpha_i, O_{it}, CR4_{it}, RW_{it})$$
$$RI_{it} = f(\alpha_i, MR_{it}, O_{it}, RW_{it})$$

The first implicit function represents the trade orientation and distributional aspects of the manufacturing industry. MR_{it} denotes markup rates, $CR4_{it}$ denotes concentration ratios, O_{it} stands for the "openness" of each sector (ratio of imports plus exports to sectoral value-added), and RW_{it} denotes real wage costs. The second relationship tries to explain the process of capital accumulation using three possible determinants, namely markups, real wage costs, and openness, where RI_{it} is the real investment of each manufacturing industry sector. The index $\{i = 1, 2, \ldots N\}$ refers to the individual unit, and $\{t = 1, 2, \ldots T\}$ refers to a given time period. The coefficients α_i (sector-specific composite term) have two components: α_{i1}, a sector specific intercept, and $\alpha_{i2}t$, a sector-specific deterministic growth trend.

The general form of the econometric specifications is assumed to be linear.

For trade orientation and distribution:

$$MR_{it} = \alpha_i + \beta_1 O_{it} + \beta_2 CR4_{it} + \beta_3 RW_{it} \quad (1')$$

For accumulation:

$$RI_{it} = \alpha_i + \beta_1 MR_{it} + \beta_2 O_{it} + \beta_3 RW_{it} \quad (2')$$

MVY employ panel data estimation on specification (1') in six sets of equations. First, they estimate equation (1') for the whole sample, in other words for $i = \{1, 2, \ldots 29\}$ and $t = \{1980, 1981, \ldots 1996\}$. Then, they take each of the identified cells as one individual group exclusively and redo the estimation. Finally, they distinguish those sectors that were "inward-oriented" in 1980, but became "open" by 1996. That is, sectors $i \in \{2 \text{ and } 4\}$ in 1980 and $i \in \{1 \text{ and } 3\}$ in 1996. This leaves them with the following sectors: {311, 314, 321, 323, 324, 331, 332, 341, 352, 355, 356, 362, 371, 372}. These are classified as "trade adjusters."

4.2.1. Distributional Indicators: Behavior of Gross Profit Margins

We start summarizing MVY's econometric investigation with the analysis of the behavior of gross profit margins (markups). Our highly detailed observations of the markups, as portrayed in table 14.11, reflect a general rise in the average profit margins despite the increased openness and the secular rise in wage costs after 1989.

To test these hypotheses, MVY regress markup rates on openness, concentration (CR4 ratios), and (the logarithm of) real wage costs using the panel data. The econometric results reveal the following relationship for the markup equation when all sectors are considered:

$$MR_{it} = \alpha_i - 0.004\,O_{it} + 0.181\,CR4_{it} + 0.111\,Log\,RW_{it}$$
$$(-5.107) \quad (6.361) \quad (13.108)$$

where α_i is the sector-specific term and t-ratios are given in the parentheses. For the whole sample, the overall coefficient of openness is estimated to be a

mere –0.004. The magnitude, which is found to be statistically significant at the 1 percent level, is nevertheless very small, suggesting that sixteen years of adjustment to foreign integration have not brought about a meaningful change in the market structure of the Turkish manufacturing industry. As such, the speed of adjustment of gross profit margins is revealed to be very slow in spite of import discipline or export penetration, and the technological and institutional barriers to entry seem to persist over the post-1980 reform era.

Concentration rates, however, have a statistically significant and a higher (positive) coefficient of 0.181 at the 1 percent level. Thus, a 1 percent increase in the level of concentration as measured through the CR4 ratio is likely to affect the average profit margin of the sector by +0.18 percent. The a priori expectation that higher concentration levels would be indicative of higher profit margins is confirmed in the aggregate. What is more interesting, however, is that markups do have a positive relationship with respect to real wage costs (with a coefficient of 0.111). These observations suggest that the sector has been characterized by Sraffian dynamics, with the persistence of markups against wage increases. (Also see Boratav, Yeldan, and Köse 2000 and Yentürk and Onaran 1999 for a further assessment of the behavior of markups during the post-1989 wage cycle in Turkish private manufacturing.)

Across the subgroups, we observe that, in general, "open" sectors (as of 1980) have a negative relationship with "openness." "Inward-looking" (as of 1980) sectors, however, display a positive relationship against the same variable. Most importantly, "trade adjusters" carry a coefficient of +0.026 vis-à-vis openness. Thus, for those sectors that were inward looking in 1980, the process of opening could not have been associated with a competitive squeezing of the cost margins (markups). On the contrary, it seems evident that the inward-looking sectors (as of 1980) have adjusted to the new trade environment by way of increasing their profit margins (with an estimated coefficient of +0.026 vis-à-vis openness). Trade adjusters, as a group, displayed positive coefficients in relation to the concentration indicator (CR4) and the real wage costs. Except for the "inward-looking and imperfectly competitive" group, markups have positive relationship with real wage costs under all groups. Thus, generally speaking, it seems that the manufacturing sectors could have responded to the trade policy shocks and real wage costs by increasing their profit margins over the post-1980 reform era.

4.2.2. Investment Behavior and Patterns of Accumulation

Now we turn our attention to the analysis of the behavior of sectoral investment in response to openness, markup rates (profitability), and real wage costs by regressing the logarithm of sectoral real investments against *CR4*, *MR*, and the logarithm of *RW*. The overall effect of profit margins on manufacturing real investment is quite strong, with an elasticity of 0.548. This suggests the presence of strong accelerationist investment patterns in the sector. Openness, though positive, carries a smaller coefficient—0.035 (yet, it is not found to be statistically significant).

MVY's estimated equation was reported as

$$\text{Log}RI_{it} = \alpha_i + 0.548 MR_{it} + 0.035 O_{it} + 0.841 \text{Log} RW_{it}$$
$$(5.956) \qquad (1.439) \qquad (15.063)$$

The most interesting result is the estimated positive elasticity of real wages on real investment with a coefficient of $+0.841$ that is statistically significant at the 1 percent level. In other words, real wages seem to act as an accelerator variable, stimulating real fixed investments in the manufacturing sector, while the effect of openness—as measured by the ratio of trade volume to value-added—has been found to be insignificant. The unorthodox behavior of real wages in stimulating both gross profit margins and real investments in a positive manner suggests the continued importance of domestic demand factors in the Turkish industrial commodity markets. These results concur with the findings of Yentürk and Onaran (1999) that post-1980 Turkish manufacturing followed a wage-led growth pattern.

5. Distributive Impacts and the Cost Structure of Value-Added

Turkey is known to suffer from one of the most skewed income distributions compared with countries that have the same level of development. This outcome is partly the legacy of prolonged import-substitution growth patterns with excessive quota rents and an oligopolistic industrial and banking structure. Other reasons include the relatively stagnant and overpopulated agriculture sector, which has loose linkages to the domestic industry, high rates of immigration due to both economic and political pressures, and unequal access to education.

With commodity trade liberalization in 1980 and then financial liberalization in 1989, there were renewed orthodox expectations toward more equitable forms of distribution of the national product as import-quota rents would be dissipated, and the domestic production structure would be transformed given the signals of efficiency (world) prices. It was further argued that, as the labor-intensive domestic industries shifted toward export markets, labor would be able to increase its factor remunerations in real terms.

These orthodox prescriptions failed to operate, however, as the economy witnessed sharp shifts in the underlying economic polity with the emergence and administration of new modes of surplus extraction mechanisms throughout the course of "liberalization." First and foremost, the pro-liberal stance and the integration process of the domestic economy with world markets did not lead to a more competitive environment in the domestic industry. On the contrary, as discussed in section 4.2 above, concentration rates in most of the outward-oriented sectors (such as food processing, cement, glass production, and ceramics) did in fact rise sharply. Furthermore, the financing behavior of corporations did not show significant changes, and the banking sector became increasingly dissociated from credit financing and intermediation, and its focus evolved into the securitization of domestic debt.

More generally, the post-1980 integration process has invigorated new and intensified distributive tensions as the share of non-wage income in national product rose, the marginalization of labor deepened, existing wage inequalities between skilled and unskilled labor intensified, and social safety nets became increasingly inaccessible.

Let us take a closer look at the increased wage gap between the skilled/organized and the unskilled/marginal segments of the labor force. Köse and Yeldan (1998) categorize "informal/marginal" labor as that part of the employed labor force that is not officially registered under any social security coverage and is also not entitled under the "self-employed or employer" status. Based on the *State Institute of Statistics (SIS) Household Labor Survey* data, Köse and Yeldan report that the ratio of marginal labor to total employment in industry increased to 49 percent in 1994 from 41 percent in 1980. This form of employment was very extensive in traditional sectors like food

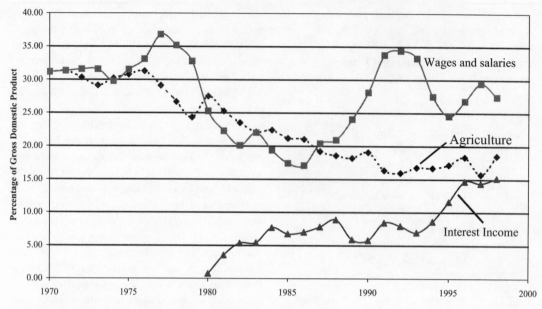

FIGURE 14.5 Functional Distribution of Income, Turkey: 1970–1998

processing, textiles and clothing, wood and furniture, and metal products, where small-scale enterprises have greater importance. Wage data strongly suggest that the wage gaps between the large/small and public/private enterprises widened significantly and exceeded the wage gap magnitudes of the early 1980s. In particular, the highly organized mining and electricity/gas workers improved their relative economic positions significantly. Wages in the clothing industry compared with manufacturing averages, on the other hand, eroded by 20 percentage points over the post-1980 liberalization period (Köse and Yeldan 1998; Boratav, Yeldan, and Köse 2000; Yentürk 1999).

Given the extent of polarization indicated by these numbers, it is clear that the "traditional" explanations of income inequality (such as unequal access to education, unequal distribution of assets and land concentration, and urban bias) are not sufficient in explaining the macroeconomic processes that give rise to such an outcome. Even though generalizations can be misleading, one can nevertheless associate rising income inequality and labor marginalization with the informalization of industrial relations, new technological advances that favor skill-intensive production patterns, and an unequivocal trend toward the dissociation of the financial sector from the productive sphere of the economy, coupled with the concomitant expansion of financial rents.

A careful inquiry along these lines will necessitate a shift of focus toward the functional categories of income and the underlying processes of macro adjustment. We turn to these issues in the next section.

5.1. Indicators of the Functional Distribution of Income: The Evidence

Given data constraints, it is common practice to separate agricultural income from non-agricultural income sources. Among non-agricultural activities, we found it possible to distinguish the following entities: interest income, profits, rental income, and public and private wage income.

Figure 14.5 documents the distributional consequences of the post-1980 financial deregulation episode given this breakdown. The share of interest income within aggregate domestic income is observed to stand around 15.2 percent by 1998, reaching almost the total value-added of agriculture—a sector that houses 45 percent of the civilian labor force. The share of interest income was virtually zero in 1980.[27]

Over the long run, the overall decline in agricultural and wage and salary income is phenomenal: the share of agricultural income fell by almost half in the course of the last three decades. The wage cycle, on the other hand, displays a rising trend in the 1970s and follows a declining course throughout the outward orientation of the domestic economy in the 1980s. The share of non-agricultural wage labor reached its lowest score in 1986 to 17.1 percent from its peak of 36.8 percent realized in 1977. Such an extensive fall clearly reflects the faltering employment response of the domestic industry to significant reductions in real wages. The implication is that the scope for capital-labor substitution has been highly limited in the Turkish economy.

Given this background, it would be illuminating to trace the dynamics of the real earnings of wage labor against (labor) productivity growth over an extended time horizon. In what follows, we decompose variations in the average product of labor and the real wage rate in the Turkish industry to obtain their underlying long-term trends. We make use of the Hodrick-Prescott filtering methods to disintegrate the cyclical variations in productivity growth and wage rates from their respective historical trends. This exercise enables us to isolate the underlying trend paths of the two variables, and to make inferences about the evolution of the wage cycle against the long-term productivity patterns in Turkish industry.

Data for our analysis come from the *Manufacturing Industry Annual Surveys* reported by the State Institute of Statistics. For the "wage rate" series,

we have used "total wage earnings" divided by "total workers engaged in production." The average labor product is derived by dividing "total value added" by the same labor employment magnitude. Both series are deflated by the wholesale price index and are filtered in logarithmic form. The exercise covers the time period 1950 to 1996.

The results of the filter are portrayed in figures 14.6 and 14.7. The units on the y-axis are in real 1963 TL prices in log scale. In figure 14.6, we observe the historical trend of the real average labor product in Turkish manufacturing. The trend has a secular upward slope with an average rate of annual growth of 3.8 percent for the whole time horizon (1950–1996). This is in contrast with the trend of the real wage rate portrayed in figure 14.7. The trend in real wages fluctuates with an increasing trend until mid-1970s, a deceleration between 1980 and 1988, and recovery following 1989. The observed recovery in real wage is clearly the end result of the post-1989 populism that enabled sharp increases in real wages between 1989 and 1993 (as narrated in section 3, above). Given this record of events, it seems plausible to argue that the post-1989 upswing in manufacturing real wages was in fact in line with the real average product of labor as far as the long-term trends of the two series are concerned.[28]

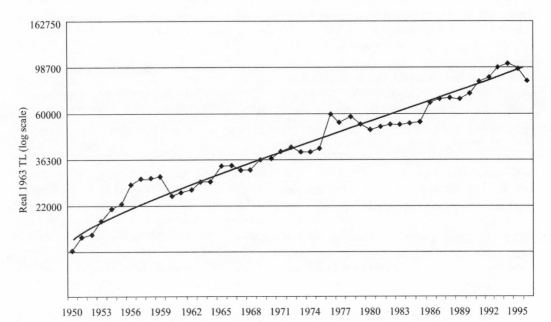

FIGURE 14.6 Real Average Labor Productivity in Large Private Manufacturing: H-P Filtered Trend

FIGURE 14.7 Real Wages in Large Private Manufacturing: H-P Filtered Trend

Fluctuations of the real wage trend follow the political cycle quite closely (as also shown in section 3, above). The fundamental characteristic of this cycle is that it discloses a relatively weak connection between wage remunerations and labor productivity in manufacturing industries. The trend path of real wages clearly signals a break following 1979–1980. This is the era when the domestic economy underwent significant transformation as it sought integration with global commodity and asset markets. The ongoing wage suppression as manifested by the downswing in the wage cycle indicates that adjustments in the labor markets served as one of the main mechanisms in bringing forth this transformation. Implemented under military rule with severe restrictions against collective bargaining and unionization, cost savings on wage labor were instrumental in the extraction of an economic surplus, which, in turn, was oriented toward export markets via a generous export-subsidization program.

From a different perspective, the sharp contrast between the trend of labor productivity against real wage earnings following the 1980 transformation clearly displays the extent of dissociation between the productive sphere of the domestic economy from its indigenous processes of accumulation and distribution. As the internationalization of the commodity and financial markets intensified, the links between savings generation and the productive use of such funds in enhancing capital accumulation—the process of intermediation—were severed. With the complete deregulation of the financial sector and the consequent ascendancy of finance over industry, international finance capital—whose singular goal is immediate financial gain rather than long-term economic development and sustainable growth—was able to assume a dominant role in the economy.

5.2. Decomposition of the Structure of Costs

Given aggregate GNP, we can deduce its components in the following manner. Let PY be the nominal GNP, then

$$PY = iD + rN + \Pi + WpLp + WgLg + A$$

where iD is interest income generated in the economy; rN is rental costs; Π is aggregate profits; $WpLp$ and $WgLg$ are wage costs in the private and public sectors, respectively; and A is agricultural income.

If we add import costs (in domestic currency), eP^*M, we get this breakdown of the costs of aggregate (nominal) supply:

$$PX = iD + rN + \Pi PX + WpLp + WgLg + A + eP^*M$$

where Π is the share of profits in total output.

Let the debt to output ratio be $d = D/PX$, the real import/output ratio be $m = M/X$, and the real exchange rate be $z = eP^*/P$. Denoting $n = N/PX$, $lp = Lp/X$, $lg = Lg/X$, $wp = Wp/P$, $wg = Wg/P$, and $a = A/PX$, we obtain the structural breakdown of the unit costs:

$$l = id + \Pi m + wplp + wglg + a + zm$$

We provide the relevant data and the associated calculations in table 14.3. The breakdown of unit costs is portrayed in figure 14.8.

Aggregate real GNP is observed to rise at an annual average rate of 4.4 percent over 1990–1998. The expansion of the share of interest is phenomenal. The share of iD increased from 0.049 in 1990 to 0.119 in 1998. This translates into an annual increase of 17.7 percent over the same period. Import costs likewise are about one-fifth of the aggregate cost of production. The rise of import costs comes to an average rate of increase of 10.4 percent per annum. The share of wage costs in the public sector fluctuated through the 1990s. From as low as 0.077 in 1988, public sector wage labor succeeded in raising its share up to 0.166 in 1992, but began a rapid decline falling to 0.096 in 1996. Private sector wage cost is observed to be more stable, and its share hovers around 0.10–0.12. Profits are another fairly stable entity in the cost structure,

capturing about a third of unit costs. A decline in the making is visible after 1995, however, as interest servicing costs expand their share at the expense of non-agricultural, non-wage factorial incomes.

6. Conclusion

In this chapter we have tried to identify and study the main stylized facts and processes characterizing the dynamic macroeconomic adjustments in Turkey since the inception of its post-1980s globalizing reforms. The Turkish adjustment experience reveals the process by which a developing market economy is trapped by the demands of integration with world markets and the distributional requirements warranted by such reorientation. The state apparatus became the bastion of privilege regulating the mode of income redistribution within society. The elements of this redistribution involved both direct mechanisms of attaining favorable production and export subsidies, currency depreciation, and wage suppression, as well as indirect mechanisms such as tax evasion on capital incomes and a financial market development strategy that enabled massive income transfers to the rentier class.

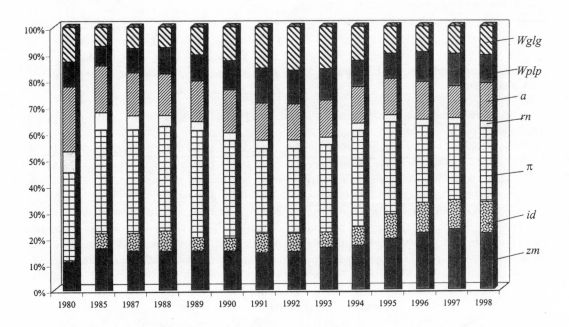

FIGURE 14.8 Decomposition of the Structure of Costs

Our decompositions of the components of aggregate demand reveal that the increased financial demands of the public sector dominate much of the process. Yet government expenditures, swamped as they are by interest servicing costs on domestic demand, do not provide a sustained impetus to the rest of the economy. Furthermore, operating under a regime of open capital markets, the economy is trapped in a vicious circle of high real interest rates, an overvalued domestic currency, and increased volatility in the flows of speculative short-term foreign capital.

Existing data reveal very little structural change in the sectoral composition, market concentration, and behavior of profit margins under the post-1980 Turkish structural adjustment reforms and outward orientation. It is also notable that the sectors that are characterized by high concentration coefficients do not necessarily reflect high shares of public ownership, and that reductions in the share of public companies do not directly lead to an increase in the degree of competitiveness. As such, the change in market concentration is revealed to be very slow in spite of the import discipline or export penetration; and the technological and institutional barriers to entry persist over the post-1980 reform era.

These results suggest the continued importance of domestic demand in the Turkish industrial commodity markets and an overall wage-led growth pattern with both profit margins and real wages acting as accelerationist variables to stimulate fixed investments.

Appendix 1: Capital Movements: Definitions, Data, and Method

The IMF, in its *Balance of Payments Manual, 1993* (5th edition), made a number of changes in the conceptual framework of the capital and financial account of balance of payments (BoP) statistics. As a result, capital movements emanating from residents or non-residents, from non-official (i.e., banks and "other sectors") and official (i.e., general government and monetary authorities) agents, can be distinguished, together with the types of assets and liabilities that constitute the content of capital movements. The quantitative analysis of capital flows in general and "hot money" (i.e., arbitrage-seeking, short-term private capital), in particular, as presented in tables 14.3–7, are based on this improved conceptual framework adopted by Turkish BoP statistics as well.

A Decomposition Based on the Balance of Payments Identity

Let us denote net capital flows emanating from nonresidents by $NKF(nr)$, from residents by $NKF(r)$, net errors and omissions by EO, reserve movements as DR, and the current account balance as CA. The well-known balance of payments (BoP) identity is expressed as follows:

$$NKF(nr) + NKF(r) + EO + DR + CA = 0 \quad (1)$$

For a typical developing economy, the usual signs observed during "normal periods" are $(+)$ for $NKF(nr)$ and $(-)$ for the other terms. This means that residents engage in net recorded capital outflows; errors and omissions are interpreted as reflecting residents' unrecorded capital movements, and the net outcome is capital flight; reserves tend to increase; and the current account chronically generates a deficit. These are not rigid generalizations: in individual years, there may occur net repatriation of nonresidents' assets (i.e., $NKF(nr) \to 0$); residents may engage in net repatriation of their external assets or reverse capital flight may occur (i.e., $NKF(r) \to 0$ and $EO \to 0$); and reserves may decline, or the current account may generate a surplus (i.e., $DR \to 0$ and $CA \to 0$). However, empirical findings for developing countries as a whole or for the subgroup of "emerging markets" have shown that cumulative sums of each of the above categories have generated the "usual" signs for a few years or for the full financial cycle.[29] This observation enables us to reformulate the decomposition of nonresidents' inflows. Let us first reformulate equation (1) as follows:

$$NKF(nr) = -[NKF(r) + EO + DR + CA] \quad (1a)$$

Since the terms in the right-hand side (RHS) of the equation usually have negative signs, let us reverse the signs and rename the terms: $-NKF(r)$ becomes net capital outflows by residents, denoted by $NKO(r)$; $-EO$ becomes capital flight by residents denoted by KFL; $-DR$ becomes reserve accumulation, denoted by RAC; and $-CA$ becomes current account deficit, denoted as CD. It would be helpful if we also rename $NKF(nr)$ without any change of sign as net capital inflows by non-residents, denoted as $NKI(nr)$. Hence, with the signs reversed in the RHS and the terms renamed, equation (1a) is transformed into the following decomposition:

TABLE 14.13 Manufacturing Industry Labor Productivity Decomposition 1981–1996

	Sectoral Labor Productivity Growth Rate	Sectoral Output Share	Sectoral Employment Share	Real Output Growth Rate (g_i)	Employment Growth Rate (n_i)	Net Productivity	Productivity by Reallocation of Labor	Reallocation Weight
Food Manufacturing	1.314	0.104	0.147	1.704	0.168	0.160	−0.035	−0.206
Beverage Industries	0.794	0.029	0.014	0.712	−0.046	0.022	0.000	−0.002
Tobacco Manufactures	3.007	0.042	0.058	0.939	−0.516	0.061	0.042	−0.081
Manufacture of Textiles	1.142	0.112	0.209	1.851	0.331	0.170	−0.109	−0.330
Manufacture of Wearing Apparel	1.690	0.013	0.031	13.026	4.214	0.117	−0.217	−0.052
Manufacture of Wood and Cork Products	1.607	0.007	0.016	1.529	−0.030	0.010	0.001	−0.027
Manufacture of Furniture and Fixtures	5.460	0.002	0.005	17.639	1.885	0.038	−0.014	−0.007
Manufacture of Paper Products	1.904	0.014	0.023	1.997	0.032	0.027	−0.001	−0.035
Printing, Publishing, and Allied Industries	2.074	0.011	0.013	3.743	0.543	0.035	−0.009	−0.017
Manufacture of Basic Industrial Chemicals	1.964	0.078	0.055	2.545	0.196	0.183	−0.008	−0.039
Petroleum Refineries and Petroleum Derivatives	0.546	0.271	0.013	0.466	−0.052	0.140	−0.013	0.243
Manufacture of Rubber Products	1.612	0.015	0.013	2.025	0.158	0.028	−0.002	−0.014
Manufacture of Nonmetallic Mineral Products	1.370	0.066	0.074	1.705	0.141	0.103	−0.013	−0.091
Basic Metal Industries	1.182	0.075	0.093	0.687	−0.227	0.069	0.028	−0.122
Manufacture of Fabricated Metal Products	1.524	0.029	0.049	2.070	0.216	0.054	−0.016	−0.074
Manufacture of Machinery	1.810	0.042	0.062	1.784	−0.009	0.076	0.001	−0.088
Manufacture of Electrical Machinery Apparatus	1.804	0.034	0.039	3.043	0.442	0.089	−0.021	−0.048
Manufacture of Transportation Equipment	2.162	0.044	0.062	3.456	0.409	0.133	−0.036	−0.087
Other Manufacturing Industries	2.382	0.012	0.023	5.436	0.903	0.053	−0.033	−0.037

$$NKI(nr) = NKO(r) + KFL + RAC + CD \qquad (2)$$

The interpretation of the decomposition (2) is as follows: a typical capital-scarce developing country chronically generates current deficits in its external accounts. These deficits as well as additional foreign exchange demands due to residents' (recorded and unrecorded) capital outflows and reserve accumulation can, in the medium run, only be "financed" through net inflows from non-residents. Hence, net inflows from external agents, that is, $NKI(nr)$, are allocated to finance both the "leakages," or "drains," that is, $(NKO(r) + KFL + RAC)$ and CD. Transitionally, some of the terms in the RHS of equation (2) may take negative signs and appropriate interpretations follow. Residents may repatriate their external assets in net terms. Reserve depletion and current surpluses may occur whereby the relevant terms are expressed as negative terms on the RHS. However, the decomposition logic loses its significance when the sum total of the RHS terms, and consequently, $NKI(nr)$ is negative—a phenomenon that can be expected to occur only exceptionally (under serious financial crisis) in a developing country, for example Turkey in 1994, Mexico in 1995, or East Asia in 1997–1998.

It will be noticed that table 14.2 has used the conventional signs of the BoP accounts as expressed in equation 1 rather than the decomposition terminology of equation 2. However, in reading and interpreting table 14.2, it will be helpful to keep the decomposition logic in mind. Hence, the negative values of the ratios in the last four columns of table 14.2, can (after mentally reversing the signs) be read as the shares of the current deficit and the relevant "leakage" items out of non-residents' net capital inflows.

Arbitrage-Seeking, Short-Term, Private Capital ("Hot Money") Movements

Short-term private capital flows, with the exception of trade credits, can be considered as constituting a broad definition of hot money movements engaged by banks, institutional and private rentiers, and firms. Within the new framework of BoP statistics, this broad category may be disaggregated into the following items:

Zero values for some of the items do not necessarily imply the absence of the relevant transborder transaction. Improved recording also results in the change from zero values into positive or negative figures. For example, it is known that non-residents have been purchasing and selling Turkish treasury bills, but they have not as yet been recorded within the correct item (i.e., 4680). The relevant figures are registered elsewhere in the capital account, for

TABLE 14.14 "Hot Money" Items within the Framework of Standard Balance of Payments Statistics

Heading	IMF Code for Non-resident Flows	IMF Code for Resident Flows	Note
Portfolio Investment			
Equity securities	4660 (8) (−518)	4610 (−50) (171)	Investment in equities
Money market instruments	4680 (0) (0)	4630 (0) (0)	Investment in government paper
Other Investment			
Short-term loans to banks	4774 (724) (63)	4724 (−134) (−75)	Bank to bank loans
Short-term loans to other sectors	4777 (586) (419)	4727 (0) (0)	Other sectors = firms and households
Deposit and currency: banks	4783 (−152) (2,303)	4733 (−678) (−752)	
Deposit and currency: other sectors	4784 (0) (0)	4734 (0) (0)	Other sectors = firms and households
Other liabilities and assets: banks	4795 (0) (0)	4745 (0) (0)	
Other liabilities and assets: other sectors	4798 (0) (0)	4748 (−676) (−427)	Other sectors = firms and households
Net errors and omissions	—	4998 (−2,594) (−2,203)	Residents' non-recorded flows

Note: Figures in parentheses are Turkey's 1997 and 1998 values in million dollars for the relevant item.

example within 4783 and/or as another unrecorded quantity within the EO item. (Note that Mexican BoP data show zero values for the 4680 item up till the end of 1993, but register negative values for the following two years [–1.9 and –13.8 billion dollars in 1994 and 1995 respectively] and positive values thereafter. Negative values for the 4680 item in 1993–1994 signify the sale of Mexican government debt papers by non-residents; the earlier purchase of which should have been recorded as positive [instead of zero] values for the same item in the preceding years. Once again, earlier inflows have, evidently, been recorded elsewhere.)

These observations suggest that it is too early to treat individual items of the capital and financial accounts of the BoP statistics in Turkey (and elsewhere) as reliable and undertake a quantitative analysis based on these specific variables. However, the sum total of "hot money" flows emanating from non-residents' as well as residents' "hot" capital movements are, essentially, reliable magnitudes. In other words, the distinction between residents and non-residents in transborder transactions is much more reliable than the specific item in which the specific quantity is recorded. This is the reason for distinguishing "hot money" figures only between residents and non-residents in table 14.3 without going into the individual items behind the two totals.

Notes

1. This observation holds despite the overall continuity of the neoliberal regime with the program of economic liberalization and market-led adjustment put into full force during the early 1980s by the military government and its civilian successors.

2. See Yeldan (1995, 1998) for a discussion on the characteristics of the post-1989 Turkish macro adjustments in terms of the creation and absorption of the economic surplus and a quantitative analysis of the strategic role played by the state apparatus. Önis and Aysan (2000); Cizre-Sakallioğlu and Yeldan (2000); Boratav, Türel, and Yeldan (1996); Ekinci (1998); and Boratav, Yeldan, and Köse (2000) provide similar analyses based on the effects of international speculative financial capital flows on the Turkish economy.

3. Yeldan (2001a), Boratav and Türel (1993), Şenses (1994), Uygur (1993), and Celasun (1994) provide a thorough overview of the post-1980 Turkish structural adjustment reforms.

4. Anti-labor legislation from the early 1980s was effectively utilized by Özal's government up till the late 1980s.

5. See Yeldan (2001a); Ertugrul and Selcuk (2001); Cizre-Sakallioğlu and Yeldan (2000); Balkan and Yeldan (2001, 1998); Selçuk (1997); Boratav, Türel, and Yeldan (1996); Ekinci (1998); and Yentürk (1999) for an extensive discussion of the post-financial liberalization macroeconomic adjustments in Turkey. Metin, Voyvoda, and Yeldan (2001b) study the stylized facts of the macro adjustments using detrending techniques of the business-cycles literature.

6. See appendix 1 of this chapter on definitions, data, and method related to the presentations in tables 14.4–6.

7. The contrast with the boom year of 2000 (when a 6.1 percent GNP growth generated current deficits equal to 4.9 percent of GNP) suggests that complacency on this issue may be premature (see note 8, below).

8. See section 2.2.4 and table 14.7.

9. There was also a significant amount of financial investment by households in the so-called super T-bills (that offered 400 percent interest rates with a three-month maturity) financed by switching from unrecorded forex holdings. Although such currency switching from unrecorded to recorded assets may not incorporate cross-border capital movements, it is reflected as positive values in the "net errors and omissions" item that, in the methodology followed in this paper, are considered as reverse capital flight by residents.

10. Savings deposits were insured at 100 percent since the 1994 crisis. Additionally, a scandalous provision imposed by the IMF during the negotiations for the additional standby agreement in December 2000 extended the guarantee to bankrupt banks' external debts. Hence, international banks' bad loans to Turkish banks are henceforth guaranteed and to be covered by the Turkish exchequer. The "moral hazard" dimension of this provision goes without saying, and there is no estimate on the magnitude involved.

11. During the first eleven months of 2000, exports remained practically unchanged but imports rose by 37 percent, more than doubling the trade deficit to 25 billion dollars. The adverse effects of the 1994 Customs Union treaty with the EU on the trade balance were delayed because of the substantial devaluation that same year, whose protective effects continued to prevail during the following five years of mild appreciation. These favorable conditions were reversed in 2000 not only because of the faster rate of appreciation of the Turkish lira vis-à-vis the currency basket but also because of the depreciation of the euro vis-à-vis the dollar.

12. Yet the realized external disequilibria should have come as no surprise to the IMF. Past experience of

all exchange rate–based stabilization programs show that they initially generate a demand-based expansion accompanied by rising and usually unsustainable trade and current deficits, followed by a contractionary phase— the magnitude of which depends on the size of the earlier external deficits. An overview of such exchange rate–based disinflation and stabilization is summarized in Calvo (2001); Calvo and Vegh (1999); Calvo, Reinhart, and Vegh (1995); Amadeo (1996); Agenor (2000); Akyuz and Cornforth (1999); Diaz-Alejandro (1985); Kaminsky and Reinhart (1999); Frenkel (1995); and Agenor and Montiel (1999, ch. 8). For individual country experiences, see Corbo (1985), on Chile; Patinkin (1993) and Bruno (1993) on Israel; and Frenkel and Fanelli (1998) on Argentina. The IMF itself had access to a series of interim reports and staff papers documenting such possible effects on the financial market. See, for example, Kaminsky, Lizondo, and Reinhart (1998).

13. There were, without doubt, additional complications. The number of banks transferred to the Savings Deposit Insurance Fund kept increasing throughout 2000. Most of their owners faced criminal charges and were arrested. The shock and apprehension of the financial community was aggravated when the newly established Board of Banking Supervision and Regulation called on the banks to reduce the open positions between their foreign exchange liabilities and assets to the pre-set limits by the end of the year. This resulted in additional foreign exchange demand.

14. The weighted average of interest rates on 2000 auctions, that is, 36 percent deflated by 20 percent (i.e., the change in the nominal exchange rate).

15. $8.1 billion in IMF credits between November 2000 and June 2001 financed part of the reserve depletion of $15.2 billion.

16. Elements of this vicious cycle are further studied in Kaminsky and Reinhart (1999); Adelman and Yeldan (2000); Diaz-Alejandro (1985); and are more recently referred to as the Neftci-Frenkel cycle in Frenkel 1998.

17. This interpretation is shared by many researchers. Unrecorded current account operations, for example smuggling as well as foreign exchange movements in and out of the formal sector, without any cross-border transactions taking place are also reflected in the EO item. The latter interpretation appears to be more valid for Africa.

18. The sixteen countries covered are Argentina, Brazil, Chile, Colombia, Egypt, India, Indonesia, Malaysia, Mexico, Pakistan, Peru, Philippines, South Africa, South Korea, Thailand, and Turkey.

19. UNCTAD (1999), 110–11.

20. The differential between the rate at which reserves are borrowed and the return on the international assets at which they are invested represents the net loss on reserve accumulation. This resembles the case of a

head of household in a developing country who borrows from the bank and then puts the borrowed money in a deposit account at the same bank. These two transactions that generate a net loss to the household may appear totally absurd and irrational; but in fact, have a logic of their own if the deposit account is used to "gain respectability" from the consular office of, say, Australia, to which he has applied for a visa.

21. UNCTAD (1999), 108.

22. The only non-hot capital movement that was affected by the 1989 liberalization was, probably, the FDI abroad of residents.

23. Note that period coverage for recent hot money movements in tables 14.7 and 14.7b are different: the former (row 9) covers the first three quarters of 2001, whereas the latter incorporates the last two months of 2000 additionally.

24. See, for example, Boratav, Yeldan, and Köse (2000); Onaran (2000); Yeldan and Köse (1999); Filiztekin (1999); Ercan (1999); Pamukçu and de Boer (1999); Köse and Yeldan (1998); Yentürk (1997, 1999); Uygur (1996); Kepenek (1996); Şenses (1996); Bulutay (1995); and Maraş lioğlu and Tiktik (1991).

25. See, for instance, Metin, Voyvoda, and Yeldan (2001a); Güneş (1996); Kaytaz, Altin, and Güneş (1993); Katircioğlu (1990); and Şahinkaya (1993) for the evaluation of market concentration and patterns of oligopolistic markup pricing in the industrial commodity markets. Güneş, Köse, and Yeldan (1996), in turn, document comprehensive panel data on the degree of concentration in Turkish manufacturing using the standard Input-Output classification for the period 1985–1993.

26. This is the threshold used by Boratav, Yeldan, and Köse (2000) and Yeldan and Köse (1999), where, on a further level of finesse, the sectors that had CR4 ratios between 30 and 49 percent are classified as "monopolistically competitive," and sectors with CR4 ratios exceeding 50 percent are regarded as "oligopolistic."

27. All income data are inclusive of taxes and are in gross terms.

28. See Boratav for a narrative support of this claim.

29. See UNCTAD 1999, table 5.2. Consolidated African data for 1980–1998 generate the same signs except for the EO item, which tends to be positive (UNCTAD 2000, table 3).

References

Adelman, Irma, and Erinç Yeldan. 2000. The minimal conditions for a financial crisis: A multiregional intertemporal CGE model of the Asian crisis. *World Development* 28 (6): 1087–100.

Agenor, Pierre-Richard. 2000. *The economics of adjustment and growth.* London: Academic Press.

Agenor, Pierre-Richard, and Peter Montiel. 1999. *Development macroeconomics.* Princeton, N.J.: Princeton University Press.

Akyüz, Yilmaz. 1990. Financial system and policies in Turkey in the 1980's. In *The Political Economy of Turkey,* edited by T. Aricanli and D. Rodrik. London and New York: Macmillan.

Akyüz, Yilmaz, and Anthony Cornford. 1999. Capital flows to developing countries and the reform of the international financial system. UNCTAD Discussion Paper, no. 143. Geneva: UNCTAD.

Amadeo, E. J. 1996. The knife-edge of exchange rate based stabilization impacts on growth, employment and wages. In *UNCTAD Review,* no. 1. Geneva: UNCTAD.

Balkan, E., and E. Yeldan. 1998. Financial liberalization in developing countries: The Turkish experience. In *Financial liberalization in developing countries,* edited by R. Medhora and J. Fanelli. London, New York: Macmillan.

———. 2002. Peripheral development under financial liberalization: The Turkish experience. In *The ravages of neo-liberalism: Economy, society and gender in Turkey,* edited by N. Balkan and S. Savran. Hauppauge, N.Y.: Nova Science.

Berg, J., and L. Taylor. 2001. External liberalization and policy implications. In *External liberalization, economic performance, and social policy,* edited by L. Taylor. London: Oxford University Press.

Boratav, K., and O. Türel. 1993. Turkey. In *The rocky road to reform,* edited by L. Taylor. Cambridge, Mass.: MIT Press.

Boratav, K., O. Türel, and E. Yeldan. 1996. Dilemmas of structural adjustment and environmental policies under instability: Post-1980 Turkey. *World Development* 24 (2): 373–93.

Boratav, K., E. Yeldan, and A. Köse. 2000. Globalization, distribution and social policy: Turkey (1980–1998). CEPA Working Paper Series, no. 20, February. New York: Center for Economic Policy Analysis, New School University.

Bruno, M. 1993. *Crisis, stabilization and economic reform: Therapy by consensus.* London: Oxford University Press.

Bulutay, T. 1995. *Employment, unemployment and wages in Turkey.* Ankara: ILO/SIS.

Calvo, G. 2001. The economics of sudden stop. Mimeo. University of Maryland.

Calvo, G., L. Leiderman, and C. M. Reinhart. 1996. Inflows of capital to developing countries in the 1990s. *Journal of Economic Perspectives* 10: 123–39.

Calvo, G., and C. A. Vegh. 1999. Inflation stabilization and BOP crises in developing countries. In *Handbook of Macroeconomics,* edited by J. Taylor and M. Woodford, 1531–614. Amsterdam: North-Holland Press.

Cizre-Sakallioğlu, Ü., and E. Yeldan. 2000. Politics, society and financial liberalization: Turkey in the 1990s. *Development and Change* 31 (1): 481–508.

Corbo, V., and L. Hernandez. 1996. Macroeconomic adjustment to capital inflows: Lessons from recent Latin American and East Asian experience. *The World Bank Research Observer* 11 (1): 61–85.

Diaz-Alejandro, C. F. 1985. Good-bye financial repression, hello financial crash. *Journal of Development Economics* 19: 1–24.

Ekinci, N. 1998. Dynamics of growth and crisis in the Turkish economy (in Turkish). *Toplum ve Bilim* (77): 7–27.

Ercan, Hakan. 1999. Non-wage labor cost in Turkish manufacturing industry: An international comparison. In *The burdens related with Turkish labor markets and policies,* edited by T. Bulutay. Ankara: State Institute of Statistics.

Ertugrul, A., and F. Selcuk. 2001. A brief history of the Turkish economy, 1990–2000. *Journal of East European and Russian Trade.*

Filiztekin, A. 1999. Growth and dynamics of productivity in Turkish manufacturing. Mimeo. Istanbul: Koc University, Department of Economics.

Frenkel, Roberto. 1995. Macroeconomic sustainability and development prospects: Latin American performance in the 1990s. UNCTAD Discussion Papers, no. 100, August. Geneva: UNCTAD.

———. 1998. Capital market liberalization and economic performance in Latin America. CEPA Working Paper Series III, no. 1, May. New York: Center for Policy Analysis, New School University.

Frenkel, Roberto, and Jose M. Fanelli. 1998. Argentinian economy in the 1990s. In *Financial Liberalization in Developing Countries,* edited by R. Medhora and J. Fanelli. London: Macmillan Press.

Godley, W. 1999. Seven unstable processes: Medium-term prospects and policies for the United States and the world. Special Report, The Jerome Levy Economics Institute. Annandale-on-Hudson, N.Y.: Bard College. http://www.levy.org.

Kaminsky, G., S. Lizondo and C. Reinhart. 1998. Leading indicators of currency crises. *IMF Staff Papers* 45 (March): 1–48.

Kaminsky, G., and C. Reinhart. 1999. The twin crises: The causes of banking and balance-of-payments problems. *American Economic Review* 89 (3): 473–500.

Katircioğlu, E. 1990. *Concentration in Turkish manufacturing and the factors determining concentration: 1975–1988* (in Turkish). Istanbul: TÜSES.

Kaytaz, E., S. Altin, and M. Güneş. 1993. Concentration in Turkish manufacturing industry (in Turkish). *TMMOB Proceedings of the Congress on Industry*, vol. 1. Ankara: Chamber of Engineers.

Kepenek, Y. 1996. Data on the Turkish labor markets from the view point of its users (in Turkish). *METU Studies In Development* 23 (1): 35–57.

Khakimzhanov, S., and E. Yeldan. 2000. Why are the interest rates so high in Turkey? Paper presented at the METU Conference on Economics, Ankara, September 14–17.

Köse, A., and E. Yeldan. 1998. Turkish economy in 1990s: An assessment of fiscal policies, labor markets and foreign trade. *New Perspectives on Turkey* (18).

Maraşlioğlu, H., and A. Tiktik. 1991. Sectoral developments in the Turkish economy: Production, capital accumulation, and employment: 1968–1988 (in Turkish). Mimeo. Ankara: State Planning Organization.

Metin-Özcan, K., E. Voyvoda, and E. Yeldan. 2001a. On the patterns of trade liberalization: Oligopolistic concentration and profitability: Reflections from post-1980 Turkish manufacturing. *Russian and East European Journal of Finance and Trade*.

———. 2001b. Dynamics of macroeconomic adjustment in a globalized developing economy: Growth, accumulation and distribution, Turkey 1969–1998. *Canadian Journal of Development Studies* 22 (1): 217–53.

Milanovic, B. 1986. Export incentives and Turkish manufactured exports: 1980–1984. World Bank Staff Working Paper, no. 602. Washington, D.C.: World Bank.

Neftçi, S. 1998. FX short positions, balance sheets, and financial turbulence: An interpretation of the Asian financial crisis. CEPA Working Paper, Series III, no. 4, June. New York: Center for Policy Analysis, New School University.

Onaran, Ö. 2000. Labor market flexibility during structural adjustment in Turkey. Istanbul Technical University Discussion Papers in Management Engineering, no. 00/1, January. Istanbul: Istanbul Technical University.

Önis, Z., and A. Aysan. 2000. Neoliberal globalization, the nation-state and financial crises in the semi-periphery: A comparative analysis. *Third World Quarterly* 29 (1): 119–39.

Pamukcu, T., and Paul de Boer. 1999. Technological change and Industrialization: An Implication of structural decomposition analysis to the Turkish economy (1968–1990). *Ekonomik Yaklasim* 10 (32): 5–30.

Patinkin, Don. 1993. Israel's stabilization program of 1985, or simple truths of monetary theory. *Journal of Economic Perspectives* 7 (2): 103–28.

Şahinkaya, S. 1993. Sectoral labor productivity, real wages, and gross profit margins or mark-up rates in manufacturing industry (Turkey 1963–1988) (in Turkish). *Toplum ve Ekonomi* (4).

Selçuk, F. 1997. Consumption smoothing and current account: Turkish experience, 1987–1995." *METU Studies in Development* 24 (4): 519–30.

Şenses, F. 1994. The stabilization and structural adjustment program and the process of Turkish industrialization: Main policies and their impact. In *Recent industrialization experience of Turkey in a global context*, edited by F. Şenses. Westport, Conn.: Greenwood Press.

———. 1996. Structural adjustment policies and employment in Turkey. Economic Research Center Working Paper, no. 96/01. Ankara: Middle East Technical University.

Uygur, E. 1993. *Financial liberalization and economic performance of Turkey*. Ankara: Central Bank of Turkey.

———. 1996. Export policies and export performance: The case of Turkey. Mimeo. Ankara: Ankara University, Faculty of Political Science.

Voyvoda, E., and E. Yeldan. 2001. Patterns of productivity growth and the wage cycle in Turkish manufacturing. *International Review of Applied Economics* 15 (4): 375–96.

Yalçin, C. 2000. Price-cost margins and trade liberalization in Turkish manufacturing industry: A panel data analysis. Mimeo. Central Bank of the Republic of Turkey, Research Department, March.

Yeldan, E. 1995. Surplus creation and extraction under structural adjustment: Turkey, 1980–1992. *Review of Radical Political Economics* 27 (2): 38–72.

———. 2001a. *Küreselleş me Sürecinde Türkiye Ekonomisi: Bölüş üm, Birikim Büyüme.* Istanbul: Iletiş im Publications.

———. 2001b. Türkiye Ekonomisinde Krizin Yapisal Dayanaklari Ya Da Kriz Sürecini Bölüşüm Eksenine Oturtmak Üzerine Temel Değerlendirmeler. *Birikim* (April): 12–25.

Yeldan, E., and A. Köse. 1999. An assessment of the Turkish labor market against its macroeconomics policies. In *The burdens related with Turkish labor markets and policies*, edited by T. Bulutay. Ankara: State Institute of Statistics.

Yentürk, N. 1997. *"Türk Imalat Sanayiinde Ücretler," Istihdam ve Birikim*. Istanbul: Friedrich Ebert Stiftung.

———. 1999. Short term capital inflows and their impact on macroeconomic structure: Turkey in the 1990s. *The Developing Economies* 37 (1): 89–113.

Yentürk, N., and Ö. Onaran. 1999. Do wages stimulate investments? An analysis of the relationship between wages and investments in the Turkish manufacturing industry. Istanbul Technical University Discussion Papers in Management Engineering, no. 99/11, December.

15

Vietnam: External Liberalization, Structural Change, Economic Growth, and Income Distribution

Le Anh Tu Packard

1. Introduction

As aptly noted in the 2001 *National Human Development Report*, Vietnam has undergone a triple transformation: from war to peace, from central planning to market economy, and from isolation to international integration (National Centre for Social Sciences and Humanities [NCSSH] 2001). Moreover, while Vietnam's shift to a more market-oriented economy may seem irreversible to outside observers, the actual reform path has tended to follow an "on-off" policy cycle (Fforde and de Vylder 1996; Packard and Thurman 1996; Riedel and Turley 1999). It is marked by bold policy response under dire economic circumstances when *something* had to be done, and a hesitant stance otherwise.

As with other countries, a severe economic crisis was the catalyst for reform in Vietnam. Faced with near famine, triple-digit inflation, and the collapse of the trading system of the socialist bloc, the government in 1989 launched Doi Moi—a comprehensive program of external and domestic reforms that placed the country squarely on the road to a more market-oriented economy. Almost immediately, the startling transformation of the economy and the improvement in the living conditions of most Vietnamese convinced many that the government's decision to liberalize was correct. Indeed, Vietnam of the 1990s gave every appearance of capturing the promise of external liberalization. From 1989 to 2000, Vietnam's annual GDP growth rate averaged 7.1 percent, one of the highest in the world. Consequently, there is optimism mixed with caution as Vietnam enters a second and even more intense phase of external liberalization and accelerated reforms.

This chapter examines the macroeconomic performance and structural evolution of the Vietnamese economy following the reforms launched by the government in 1989. We compare Vietnam's actual macro- and microeconomic performance to the scenario predicted by external liberalization advocates. The objective is to shed light on several questions.

First, what were the macroeconomic and distributional outcomes observed during the 1990s, and should external liberalization get full credit for these outcomes? Second, will external liberalization help create enough good jobs for a rapidly expanding labor force? Third, can the policy reform be properly described as "true" external liberalization, or was it merely a successful foreign direct investment (FDI) and export promotion campaign in the East Asian tiger tradition? Fourth, why were the socio-economic outcomes in Vietnam more positive compared to some other liberalizing economies? And finally, what can Vietnam anticipate in the second phase of external liberalization in light of its own experience and the experience of other countries?

Not surprisingly, the findings suggest a mixed picture. First, the socio-economic outcome was largely positive because macroeconomic growth and stability was achieved and almost all sectors of society including the poor saw a marked improvement in their living conditions. From 1993 to 1998, the proportion of people living below the poverty line fell from 58 to 37 percent (World Bank 1999). As measured by the Human Development Index (HDI), Vietnam's HDI rose from 0.456 in 1990 to 0.696 by 2000, placing Vietnam in the medium human development category (0.500–0.799), well above expectations given its low per capita income classification ($755 or less).[1] At the same time, disappointingly, productivity gains from labor reallocation between sectors[2] have not been significant, despite a high GDP growth rate, increased labor mobility, and a greater share of the industrial sector in total output. Consistent with this, one sees that although the *level* of employment in industry and construction has risen, its *share* of total employment fell to 12.7 percent during the Doi Moi period (1989–1999) from 13.5 percent during the "subsidy" period (1981–1988). Other unfavorable outcomes include increased social stratification and cutbacks in the delivery of public services during the early reform years as a result of budget constraints.

The answer to the second half of the first question is that external liberalization deserves partial but not full credit for Vietnam's strong macroeconomic performance during the Doi Moi years. Complementary domestic reforms associated with the shift to a market economy,[3] the development of offshore oil resources, and exogenous shocks in the geopolitical environment including domestic institutional reforms in East Asian economies (discussed in section 3) all

played critical roles. It should also be noted that initial policy reforms had an especially potent effect because the economy was operating well below its potential during the pre-1989 "subsidy" period. The extent of resource underutilization[4] and misallocation was such that the institutional changes brought about by the reforms produced substantial increases in output without requiring many additional inputs (Packard and Thurman 1996; Fforde and de Vylder 1996). The primary divide in our analysis is the pre-1989 period when output growth was constrained by a scarcity of imported inputs resulting from the international economic boycott ("before") and the Doi Moi era marked by changes in the post–Cold War international balance of power and Vietnam's more conciliatory foreign policy stance[5] ("after"). The decision by non-CMEA countries to end the trade embargo probably contributed as much to the rapid expansion of foreign trade[6] as Vietnam's actual lowering of trade barriers.

Second, despite gains from trade liberalization, not enough jobs were created in the higher wage sectors of the economy. This was because output growth in the higher value-added sectors was not high enough relative to productivity increases that were required of Vietnamese enterprises to survive the more competitive environment of the 1990s. Thus, even during the period of rapid industrial growth and swift transformation into a very open economy, the industrial sector's contribution to overall employment growth was generally negative or small.[7] This is shown in figure 15.1, which separates each sector's contribution to employment growth. In general, the low productivity primary sector accounted for 60–80 percent of Vietnam's employment growth, with significant contributions from the services sector during 1992–1997. This strongly suggests that despite the high growth rates of the Doi Moi years, the economy continues to operate at below capacity because of the large reservoir of underutilized labor resources.

At the same time, these two factors—the geopolitical sea change and significant resource underemployment—help to explain an interesting puzzle: why the U.S. dollar value of Vietnam's exports grew at an annual average rate of over 26 percent from 1989 to 2000, even though up until 1995, there was a trend rise in the relative price of non-traded to traded goods (the real exchange rate), that brought about an increase in the relative share of non-traded to traded output (shown in figure 15.2). Clearly, there was enough

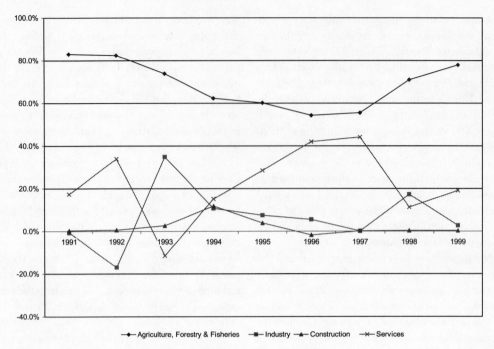

FIGURE 15.1 Sectoral Contribution to Overall Employment Growth

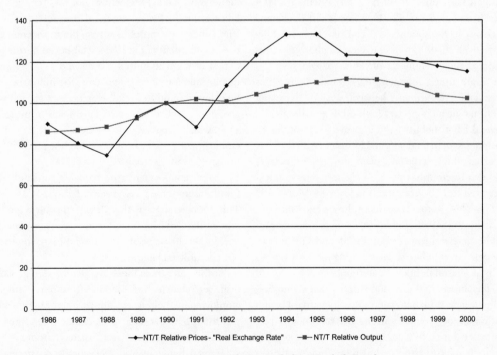

FIGURE 15.2 Relative Price and Relative Output of Non-traded to Traded Goods

slack in the economy, despite widely reported short-ages of skilled labor, to accommodate both greater export demand and greater growth of the non-traded goods and services sectors.

Third, in contrast with other countries, Vietnam's first phase of external liberalization covered the current but not the capital account, and even the current account liberalization was incomplete. For this reason, the Vietnamese economy was spared the volatile swings precipitated by large inflows of highly mobile short-term capital and its abrupt reversal that were experienced by its regional neighbors such as Thailand. Moreover, what took place in Vietnam was managed external liberalization, with some backsliding during the mid-1990s, when the leadership perceived that the country had safely emerged from the economic crisis and therefore felt less pressured to move quickly on the reform agenda. And yet—to take issue with the skeptics—there was much more to Vietnam's reforms than mere FDI and export promotion. As will be discussed in section 5, the 1989 reforms in their totality had a "big bang" transformational impact on the economy and society, involving considerable dislocation of manufacturing output and employment. Moreover, although Vietnam's trade regime is considered to be highly restrictive,[8] actual revenues from external trade (including import and export duties) accounted for less than 3 percent of the total value of imports and exports from 1989 to 1992. At its peak, actual revenues climbed to 7.8 percent in 1995, but by 1999 they had declined to 4.8 percent.[9]

Fourth, an important factor behind Vietnam's more positive experience with external liberalization, in contrast with the experience of many semi-industrialized economies, has to do with the country's own relatively less developed economic status. Although Vietnamese enterprises, both state and private, were initially devastated by cheaper and sometimes better quality imports from neighboring countries, Vietnam—not being semi-industrialized—in the early Doi Moi period did not yet possess the broad range of industries that would have faced bruising competition from foreign imports. The situation would be different in the period of expanded liberalization. The economy has become more developed relative to the early 1990s, and many more enterprises may not survive a significantly less sheltered environment. This brings us to the last question: what are the likely outcomes of the next phase of external liberalization?

The chapter is organized as follows. Section 2 identifies the policy phases and major themes of the post-war period. Section 3 provides a broad historical overview of the Vietnamese post-war economy. Section 4 reviews the state of the Vietnamese economy under the centrally planned/"subsidy" period prior to the launching of the "big bang" reforms. Section 5 describes Doi Moi and the country's socio-economic performance from 1989 to 1993. Section 6 describes the more hesitant post-crisis policy stance period from 1994 to 1997, which witnessed a recovery of state finances, and the slower growth phase from 1998 to 2000 characterized by a sharp drop in foreign direct investment (FDI) associated with the regional financial crisis. Section 7 analyzes shifts in the sources of effective demand. Section 8 analyzes productivity shifts and the decomposition of employment, and relates it to income distribution outcomes. Section 9 reviews social welfare and social policy issues associated with the Doi Moi reforms. Section 10 discusses what may be anticipated in the second phase of external liberalization. Section 11 presents the conclusions.

2. Policy Phases and Major Themes

I distinguish the following episodes marked by broadly homogenous policy packages and economic circumstances:

A. "Subsidy" period: imports are a binding constraint (1981–1988)
B. Liberalization phase I: vigorous reforms (1989–1993)[10]
C. Recovery in state finances/hesitant policy stance (1994–1997)
D. FDI and government revenue fall (1998–2000)
E. Liberalization phase II: Honoring international commitments (2001–)

Table 15.1 presents the main economic indicators associated with these five episodes. During the "subsidy" period, Vietnam was a closed, centrally planned economy heavily dependent on Soviet bloc aid for needed foreign inputs. Overuse of price controls and subsidies, severe restrictions on private sector activity, and chronic shortages of imported intermediate goods and capital equipment were the main factors that constrained investment spending and output growth.

TABLE 15.1 Main Economic Indicators

	GDP Growth (Annual) (%)	Per Capita National Income Growth (%)	Final Consumption as % of GDP	Gross Capital Formation as % of GDP	Agriculture, Forestry, and Fishery (%)	Industry (%)	Services (%)
1975–1980	0.30[a]	−1.9[a]	105.9	20.3	0.80	2.20	−1.50
1981–1988	5.60	3.7	101.5	13.2	4.80	9.10	4.20
1989–1993	6.50	4.6	90.6	17.2	4.10	6.10	8.30
1994–1997	9.00	7.1	81.9	26.2	4.20	13.20	8.80
1998–2000	5.80	3.9	75.7	28.7	4.20	10.50	4.30

Source: Transformations by author; original series from GSO.

a. 1977–1980.

During 1986–1988, largely because of economic mismanagement, the average inflation rate rose to nearly 450 percent. 1989 marked the first phase of trade liberalization and the opening of the economy. An exogenous shock—the collapse of trading arrangements with the CMEA—convinced the government that the only viable option was to embrace vigorous and comprehensive reforms.

The spectacular initial results exceeded expectations. Boosted in 1989 by the huge 87 percent year-upon-year jump in the dollar value of exports, during the 1989–1993 period Vietnam was able to increase its average annual GDP growth rate to 6.5 percent while bringing down the inflation rate to 38.7 percent. On the demand side, the economy's remarkable speed of adjustment was evident in the external sector's overnight rise to dominance, as measured by the climb in the trade to output ratio[11] from 24.7 percent in 1988, to 58.2 percent in 1989, and to 111 percent by 2000 (see figure 15.3). Indeed, IMF economists have noted that Vietnam's openness by this measure is twice the average of all countries eligible for its Poverty Reduction and Growth Facility (International Monetary Fund [IMF] 2002). Another

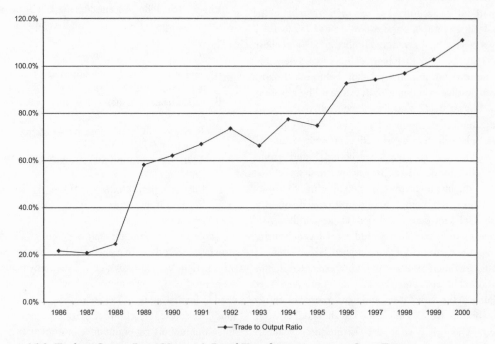

FIGURE 15.3 Trade to Output Ratio: Vietnam's Rapid Transformation into an Open Economy (Nominal Exports plus Imports of Goods and Services as % of Nominal GDP)

measure of the rapidly expanding influence of the foreign sector in the Vietnamese economy is the FDI sector's rising share of gross industrial output, from 2.6 percent in 1989 to 35.5 percent by 2000.

The critical but volatile role of investment spending is another key theme. By 1994, buoyed in large part by the powerful surge in FDI and domestic private sector investment spending, Vietnam successfully emerged from crisis. The nation's capital stock grew quickly as fixed capital formation rose to 24.3 percent of GDP in 1994 from less than 15 percent of GDP during the 1988–1991 period. However, the volatility of the investment cycle was quickly felt when FDI capital inflows dropped precipitously from over US$2 billion in 1997 to an estimated US$700 million in 1999, largely because of spillover effects of the 1997–1998 regional financial crisis that devastated Vietnam's primary foreign investors, the Asian countries.[12]

Changes in the state's fiscal position and fluctuations in the state sector's share of GDP are also key themes with important social policy implications. The state-owned enterprise (SOE) sector's sizeable weight in both export and non-traded sectors explained its speedy recovery during the mid-1990s from the twin woes of government-imposed financial discipline and competitive pressures from foreign imports. Because both export and non-traded goods sectors enjoyed high growth rates during this period, the state sector's share of nominal GDP jumped from its 31.1 percent low in 1991 to 40.5 percent in 1997. Ironically, though not surprisingly, with the rapid economic recovery came a slackening in the pace of reform as politically powerful economic actors successfully lobbied to protect and advance their positions.

More recently, a potentially dangerous erosion of the state's fiscal position has emerged that IMF economists attribute to structural weaknesses in the revenue system. Since 1997, there has been a trend decline in important components of government revenues relative to GDP. This is because in the transition to a market system, the government's ability to tax the emerging non-state sector is still weak, while contributions from the SOE sector as a share of total revenues have been falling. At the same time, the government's prudent fiscal stance during this period has meant a compression of expenditures. According to the IMF, the current expenditure category has been the hardest hit, falling by 4 percentage points of GDP to 13 percent. The cuts in social spending have been severe, and the recurrent expenditures needed to maintain existing public capital assets have been sharply curtailed.

3. Vietnam's Postwar Economy: Overview and Structural Change

The basic story that emerges from macroeconomic data compiled by the Government Statistics Office (GSO) is that Vietnam's slow recovery from the devastation of war, trade embargo, and central planning was accomplished mainly by the efforts of its people with substantial aid from its Soviet bloc allies.[13]

GSO time series data also show that it took *over twenty-five years* for Vietnam to narrow the gap between output and expenditure. When the war ended in 1975, total consumption and investment expenditures exceeded gross domestic output by 37 percent. Imports were 4.6 times greater than exports. The gap between output and expenditure was reflected in the trade deficit, which was largely financed by loans and grants from the Soviet bloc countries (see table 15.2).

During the subsidy period (1981–1988), the Vietnamese central bureaucracy and the CMEA system regulated foreign trade, which consisted mainly of bilateral exchange between Vietnam and

TABLE 15.2 Key Expenditure Indicators as % of GDP

	Final Consumption (%)	Gross Capital Formation (%)	Total Expenditure (%)	Exports/Imports (f.o.b.) (%)	Trade Deficit (%)	Government Current Expenditure (%)	Private Consumption (%)
1975–1980	105.9	20.3	126.3	24.0	22.9	n.a.	n.a.
1981–1988	101.5	13.2	114.7	36.1	12.2	14.4	85.1
1989–1993	90.6	17.2	107.8	86.0	7.5	17.3	73.3
1994–1997	81.9	26.2	108.0	70.2	9.4	17.1	64.8
1998–2000	75.7	28.7	104.4	91.6	4.2	13.1	62.6

Source: Transformations by author; original series from GSO.

individual CMEA countries. With imports acting as a binding constraint, and no domestic production of capital goods, the share of gross capital formation in GDP fell to around 13 percent. The resulting low capital/output ratio and disincentives created by misguided policies (discussed in section 4) stifled labor productivity. However, because the trade embargo effectively turned Vietnam into a closed economy, until 1989 the industry sector did not have to worry about competition from imports, and consequently enjoyed a 9.1 percent growth rate. But labor was not sheltered by the closed economy. During this period, employment in the industrial and construction sector witnessed volatile growth (its share of total employment fluctuated in the 12.1–14.9 percent range) and even experienced a 9.6 percent contraction in 1985.

The phase I liberalization period of vigorous reforms (1989–1993) was impelled by the disintegration of the CMEA, which prompted the drive to find new markets and new trading partners. The centerpiece of Doi Moi's outward orientation was the extremely favorable Foreign Investment Law of December 1987, which set the stage for the emergence of Vietnam's foreign direct investment (FDI) sector. FDI was envisaged to play a key role in Vietnam's growth and transformation. It was the means of upgrading the country's physical infrastructure, and mobilizing external resources for the technological renovation and capacity expansion of Vietnam's SOEs. During this early period it was FDI's potential role as rescuer of financially distressed SOEs that strengthened the bargaining power of foreign investors.

The government's open-door policy coincided with the economic boom in East and Southeast Asia.[14] Domestic institutional reforms in South Korea and Taiwan facilitated outward investment, and they quickly became Vietnam's top largest foreign

TABLE 15.3 Total Registered Foreign Direct Investment Capital (1988–1999), Millions of US$

		%
Singapore	5,867	15.8
Taiwan	4,592	12.4
Hong Kong	3,613	9.7
Japan	3,361	9.1
Korea	3,149	8.5
France	2,136	5.8
British Virgin Islands	1,738	4.7
Russia	1,519	4.1
United States	1,309	3.5
United Kingdom	1,180	3.2
Malaysia	1,121	3.0
Australia	1,114	3.0
Thailand	1,072	2.9
Other countries	5,318	14.3
Total	31,770	

investors. Along with other Asian investors, they were eager to preside over the country's economic takeoff. Indeed, by 1999 the four Asian tigers and Japan accounted for 55.5 percent of total registered FDI capital (see table 15.3). However, these investors were hardhit by the Asian financial crisis in 1997–1998, which led to a sharp fall in FDI flows to Vietnam.[15] From an average annual growth rate of 16.3 percent during the 1994–1997 period, FDI flowed out during the 1998–2000 period (see table 15.4), causing the FDI share of Vietnam's total investment capital to contract sharply to 21.6 percent from 30.6 percent between the two periods.

During the "vigorous reforms" phase, the FDI sector expanded at a phenomenal rate[16] (see figure 15.4 and table 15.4) and FDI gross industrial output recorded average annual increases in excess of 44 percent. The structural composition of FDI inflows continues to change in response to policy incentives and better information about sectors with significant growth

TABLE 15.4 Total Investment Capital by Ownership Sectors

	% Share of Total			Average Annual Growth Rate		
	State (%)	Non-state (%)	FDI Sector (%)	State (%)	Non-state (%)	FDI Sector (%)
1976–1980	n.a.	n.a.	n.a.	6.4	n.a.	n.a.
1981–1988	59.4	40.0	0.6	3.6	7.5	n.a.
1989–1993	40.6	42.0	17.4	26.5	21.3	149.3
1994–1997	42.5	26.9	30.6	13.5	−0.7	16.3
1998–2000	57.8	20.6	21.6	13.3	−1.1	−23.8

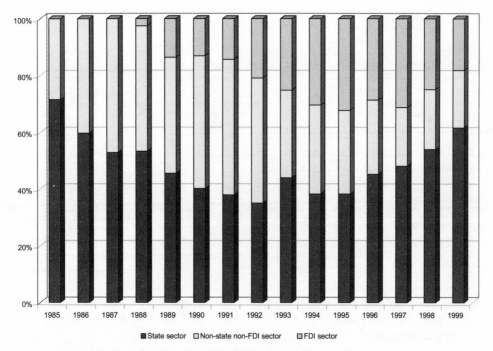

■ State sector   □ Non-state non-FDI sector   ▨ FDI sector

FIGURE 15.4 Share of Investment Capital by Ownership Sectors

potential. Initially, FDI was attracted to the oil and gas sector, which accounted for nearly 37 percent of total FDI disbursement during the 1988–1993 period. But by 1998–2000, its share of FDI flows had declined to less than 15 percent. FDI also flowed to the highly protected import-substitution industries.

According to a joint report of the World Bank, Asian Development Bank, and UNDP (World Bank 2000b), over 50 percent of FDI inflows went to industries with more than 90 percent effective protection rates. Consequently, the share of heavy industry in total FDI flows rose from less than 8 percent during 1988–1993 to nearly 22 percent by 1998–2000. At the same time, manufacturing sectors that better reflected Vietnam's medium-term comparative advantages—light industry, food, and export processing zone production—also saw their combined share rise from 16.5 percent during 1988–1993 to nearly 21 percent by 1998–2000. However, reflecting domestic institutional rigidities and frictions, the agricultural sector's share of FDI inflows has been surprisingly low—given its importance in the economy and strong comparative advantage. The situation is slowly changing, and the agricultural sector's share has grown slightly, from 4.1 percent during 1988–1993 to 8.4 percent in 1998–2000. With respect to the non-traded sector, during the 1998–2000 period,

construction accounted for 9.1 percent, transport and communications for 3.4 percent, hotel and tourism for 8.4 percent, and office and apartment building management for 9.5 percent of total FDI inflows (see table 15.5).

TABLE 15.5 Structural Composition of Foreign Direct Investment

	1988–1993 (%)	1994–1997 (%)	1998–2000 (%)
Agriculture, forestry, and fishery	4.1	5.5	8.4
Oil and gas	36.7	19.5	14.8
Heavy industry	7.9	19.2	21.8
Light industry, food, and EPZ	16.5	22.1	20.9
Construction	3.6	9.0	9.1
Transport and communications	5.3	4.1	3.4
Hotel, tourism	10.3	10.5	8.4
Office property and apartments	3.5	6.8	9.4
Other services	12.1	3.2	3.8

TABLE 15.6 Average Annual GDP Growth Rate by Economic and Ownership Sectors

	GDP (%)	Agriculture, Forestry, and Fishery (%)	Industry (%)	Construction (%)	Services (%)	State Sector	Non-state Sector
1977–1980	0.30	0.80	2.20	–4.60	–1.50	–2.8	2.0
1981–1988	5.60	4.80	9.10	2.50	4.20	6.8	5.2
1989–1993	6.50	4.10	6.10	8.10	8.30	4.3	8.2
1994–1997	9.00	4.20	13.20	14.60	8.80	10.2	8.1
1998–2000	5.80	4.20	10.50	3.10	4.30	5.2	6.2

Source: Transformations by author; original series from GSO.

The "vigorous reforms" phase was also marked by intense competition from imports, particularly in the consumer goods market, impacting relative prices. The price index of traded to non-traded goods fell from 1990 to 1991 (see figure 15.2). The initial losers were Vietnam's state-dominated industrial sector and its employees. At the same time, the state's more tolerant stance toward private sector activity had an offsetting effect. It proved to be sufficient encouragement to push the non-state sector's growth rate to above 8 percent over a prolonged period (1989–1997), from the 5.2 percent average growth rate recorded during the subsidy period (see table 15.6).[17]

Not surprisingly, external liberalization and the transition to a market economy also brought about significant structural change in the monetary and credit spheres that reflected the gradual rise of the private sector. For example, credit to the non-state sectors rose from around 2.5 percent of GDP during the 1986–1993 period to 14.5 percent of GDP by the end of the decade, while net foreign assets as a percent of GDP climbed from 1.8 percent before 1989 to 15.1 percent by the 1998–2000 period (see table 15.7). Moreover, the rapid increase in monetary depth—the ratio of M2/GDP more than doubled from

17.2 percent in the 1986–1988 period to nearly 40 percent by the 1998–2000 period—show that inflation fears have eased. Greater confidence in the financial system is also reflected in the rise in the private sector's savings propensity, and a portfolio shift away from precious metals and stones.

With respect to overall developments in the Vietnamese economy, it is noteworthy that the expected negative link between per capita income and population growth also holds up. The high population growth rate from 1977 to 1988 has been decelerating with higher per capita income growth (see table 15.8). The inverse correlation is especially strong between per capita electricity output and population growth, which is not surprising because per capita electricity output is a reasonably good proxy of a country's level of economic development.

4. The Vietnamese Economy before Doi Moi

While the focus of this study is on the Doi Moi period, the reader should bear in mind Vietnam's turbulent history, and in particular the legacy of colonial rule and devastation from "the twentieth century's longest

TABLE 15.7 Selected Monetary and Credit Variables as % of Nominal GDP

	Net Foreign Assets (%)	Net Domestic Assets (%)	Claims on Non-state Sectors (%)	Claims on State Enterprises (%)	M2/GDP (%)	Dong Liquidity (%)	Currency Outside Banks (%)	Dong Deposits (%)	Foreign Currency Deposits (%)	Inflation Rate (%)
1986–1988	1.8	15.5	2.4	14.6	17.2	16.3	7.7	8.6	0.9	449.1
1989–1993	7.0	18.5	2.5	11.9	26.3	18.4	9.1	9.3	8.0	38.7
1994–1997	5.1	19.1	8.5	10.4	24.2	19.0	8.8	10.2	5.2	8.8
1998–2000	15.1	24.2	14.5	13.3	39.6	29.0	9.9	19.1	10.6	2.9

Source: Author's transformations using original data from IMF, World Bank, and State Bank of Vietnam.

TABLE 15.8 GDP, per Capita Income, and Population (Average Annual % Change)

	GDP (%)	Per Capita National Income (%)	Per Capita Electricity Output (%)	Population (%)
1977–1980	0.2	–1.9	7.1	2.20
1981–1988	5.6	3.7	8.6	2.20
1989–1993	6.5	4.6	13.9	1.80
1994–1997	9.0	7.1	21.8	1.70
1998–2000	5.5	3.9	29.9	1.50

Source: Transformations by author; original series from GSO.

international conflict" (Kolko 1997). The effects of French colonial rule have been well documented, notably by Ngo Vinh Long (1973). While much was made of colonial contributions to developing transportation infrastructure, Long pointed out that regressive asset redistribution under the French and the introduction of the sharecropping system led to decreased soil fertility and much lowered land productivity. Taxation under the French was so notoriously unjust (Long 1973, 62–76) that the national allergy to paying taxes that continues to plague the government today counts among the legacies of French rule. Finally, during World War II, French and Japanese actions resulted in the 1944–1945 famine, which killed about 2 million people.

With respect to the Vietnam-U.S. war, Kolko's (1997) concise enumeration of relevant statistics bears repeating:

> [T]he United States and its allies exploded fifteen million tons of munitions during 1964–72, twice the amount used in all of Europe and Asia during World War Two. It sprayed defoliants[18],which cause cancer, birth defects, and other illness, on a fifth of South Vietnam's jungles, over a third of its mangrove forests, as well as on rice crops. About seven million South Vietnamese... became refugees and were forced into camps and cities... Almost all of North Vietnam's industry, bridges, and transport systems were destroyed...as many as 1,350,000 South Vietnamese civilians were wounded, with death for between a fifth and a third of this number. Over two million North Vietnamese soldiers and civilians were killed— altogether, about three million people died.

The abrupt collapse of the U.S.-backed Thieu regime in 1975 caught the Vietnamese revolutionary forces by surprise. The ruling 1976 Fourth Party Congress opted to impose the North's socialist institutions on the South, and set an unrealistic twenty-year target to switch from small-scale production to large-scale socialist production. The invasion of Cambodia in December 1978 put an end to Chinese and Western aid, and led to a stringent world economic embargo. While the economy's disappointing post-war performance was chiefly attributable to Vietnam's international isolation, the state's decision to curb private sector activity and impose central planning did not improve matters. The Vietnamese Communist Party (VCP) policy during the "subsidy" period was also marked by the neglect of exports, little attention to costs, and the absence of financial discipline (Fforde and de Vylder 1996). An indicator of increasing misery could be seen in the sharp decline in real wages of the average public sector worker, which shrank each year by 14–18 percent from 1977 to 1980. Among the problems facing state-sector employees was that their nominal wages could hardly keep pace with inflation that hovered in the 20 percent range until 1980, when it accelerated past 25 percent (see figure 15.5).

Initially, the state sector dominated gross industrial output. Its share in 1976 stood at 77.4 percent but it fell to 57.1 percent in 1980 (shown in figure 15.6). There are two reasons for this decline. First, since state sector industrial production tended to be more import intensive than non-state production, it was hurt more by the shortage of imported inputs. Second, the non-state sector benefited from a relaxation of controls on its production activities in the aftermath of the devastating war with China. The necessity of having to generate sufficient resources to maintain an army of 1.5 million, at a time when the economic crisis of 1979–1980 was made worse by bad weather (40 percent of the North's rice crops were devastated by typhoons), forced the party to

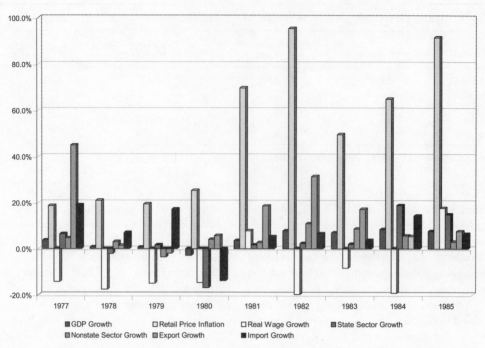

FIGURE 15.5 Key Economic Indicators during the "Subsidy" Period: Evolution of Output, Inflation, Real Wages, Imports, and Exports

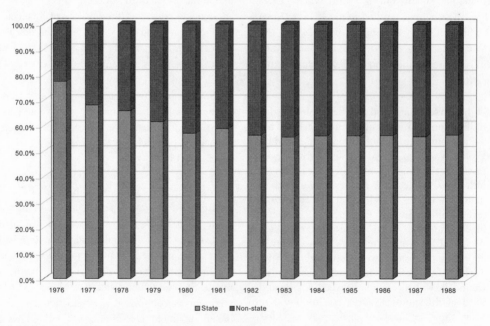

FIGURE 15.6 Gross Industrial Output: State versus Nonstate Share, 1976–1988

adopt pragmatic measures in order to stimulate production.

In January 1981, the VCP introduced the output contract system in agriculture. It allowed farmers to sell all output in excess of the contracted amount of output to be produced in the free market. With respect to industry, a complex "three-plan system" allowed SOEs to produce and sell goods not covered by quotas on a free-market basis (Fforde and de Vylder 1996). The result of these initiatives was a strong surge in agricultural and industrial output, which increased by 10.6 and 9.7 percent respectively in 1982. The output response was greatest in commodity sectors where there was an adequate supply of domestic inputs and strong market demand.

The improved economic performance was accompanied by an acceleration of the inflation rate (from 25 percent in 1980 to 95 percent in 1982)[19] and a large gap between "free market" and "organized market" prices. That gap only narrowed when the latter's price jumped by 102 percent in 1981 and by nearly 142 percent in 1982 (see table 15.9). At the same time, the mini reforms produced a surge in smuggling and speculation activities, and rampant corruption accompanied the slide in state employee real wages. With increased lawlessness came renewed efforts to clamp down. The government once again tried to regulate private trade, expand state and cooperative control of the wholesale and retail sectors, and curb the autonomy of exporters (Riedel and Turley 1999).

Although the Third Five Year Plan (1981–1985) has been described as an "awkward compromise" between concessions to pressures from below and the VCP's bias toward recentralizing (Riedel and Turley 1999), this overlooks the important learning process that eventually led to more comprehensive reforms. Departing from earlier ambitions to rush the nation into large-scale socialist production, the 1982 Fifth Party Congress reduced the number of large-scale projects and gave top priority to agriculture. It acknowledged that a strong agricultural sector was needed to pave the way for the country's eventual industrialization. The bias in favor of the state sector remained, however, and was reflected in its relatively stronger growth performance.

From 1984 to 1988, the economy was in the grip of hyperinflation. The retail price index grew at an annual rate of over 300 percent. It would be misleading, however, to place full blame on the monetized budget deficit, that averaged 6.6 percent of GDP, since the deficit during the vigorous reform (1989–1993) period accounted for 5.8 percent of GDP and yet the authorities managed to bring down inflation to 38.7 percent. The more important culprits behind hyperinflation were wage increases given to government workers, the centralized system of resource allocation that gave rise to persistent shortages and fueled black market trading, and botched anti-inflation policies. Inflation climbed from 92 percent in 1985 to a whopping 775 percent in 1986— largely because of the disastrous currency reform introduced in September 1985. With hyperinflation came widespread hoarding. During the Sixth Party Congress period, the North put five key commodities (rice, sugar, kerosene, fish sauce, and meat) back on the ration list (Fforde and de Vylder 1996). In March 1988 the Central Bank introduced new currency and again botched it. Food prices doubled within a few days, and the dong's value dropped by almost a half (Kolko 1997).

In the period leading to the vigorous reforms phase, the government adopted a series of measures that represented important concessions to free market and private business concerns (Fforde and de Vylder 1996). Provinces and cities were instructed to close internal customs posts. The state monopoly was abolished in the trade of most commodities including food items, gold, and silverware. Permission to conduct import-export business was more widely granted (Tran Duc Nguyen 1991). Major policy decrees issued at the end of 1987 covered foreign investment; land; foreign trade; state industrial management; private, family, and individual sectors; and agriculture (Fforde and de Vylder 1996). These reforms, particularly the land and agricultural reforms, unleashed the productive energies of a nation mostly made up of farmers. Revenues from agricultural exports increased more than fourfold.

TABLE 15.9 Inflation: Average Annual Rate

	Retail Price (%)	Organized Market (%)	Free Market (%)
1976–1980	21.2	3.5	42.2
1981–1985	214.8	90.7	60.2

Source: Transformations by author; original series from GSO.

5. The Doi Moi Phase of Vigorous Reforms

The 1987–1989 macroeconomic crisis—marked by hyperinflation, near famine, severe shortages, the abrupt termination of CMEA assistance, and the loss of markets in Eastern Europe—marked the decisive turning point. The reforms adopted during this watershed year brought about a complete upheaval of the economic system. To gain new trading partners, Vietnam undertook a series of foreign policy initiatives—withdrawal from Cambodia, normalization of relations with ASEAN, China, and Western countries including the United States—that removed the major obstacles to expanded trade with the West and neighboring countries.

A comprehensive program of economic reforms ushered in sweeping changes on many fronts: external liberalization, anti-inflation measures, rural reforms and extensive price liberalization. Resource allocation was improved because imported intermediate goods were valued at market prices, and all state and non-state enterprises were allowed to set the price of their own products. By the end of 1989, the state only retained control over transport, communication, electric, petroleum, and cooking oil prices, but continued to indirectly regulate the price of other essential commodities (such as rice or gold) by buying or selling stockpiles of those commodities.

Without being obliged to by the IMF, the government voluntarily embraced orthodox stabilization measures such as introducing positive real rates of interest and imposing greater fiscal discipline and credit restraint. The structure of the banking system was transformed, with the diversification of both institutions and ownership. By the end of 1992 the expanded banking sector included four state-owned commercial banks, five branches of foreign owned banks, three joint venture banks, twenty-four shareholding banks with varied ownership, and several thousand very small rural and urban cooperatives (World Bank 1993).

Almost immediately, the sweeping reforms produced dramatic results. The decision to raise interest rates achieved the desired effect of restoring confidence in the domestic currency. It also drove up the cost of hoarding goods, and enterprises were forced to dump goods on the market to avoid bankruptcy. Thus, previously stockpiled food, paper, bicycles, and other consumer goods flooded the market, bringing an end to the shortage economy (Vo Dai Luoc 1995), and exerting downward pressure on the price level. The legalization of gold trading also strengthened public confidence, and helped induce changes in the composition of household assets. Meanwhile, the maxi-

devaluation of the exchange rate effectively wiped out the black market for foreign exchange, and was another factor that induced households to shift out of gold and U.S. dollars back into dong-denominated assets. The price of gold, U.S. dollars, and rice all fell, and inflation was brought to a halt by mid-1989. Dong deposits as a percent of GDP jumped from 8.5 percent in 1988 to 14.7 percent in 1989.

During hyperinflation, people minimized their holdings of the domestic currency and kept some of their wealth in rice stocks. In the spring of 1989, more rice was released to the market as there was less need for its function as a store of value. The effect of these portfolio shifts was to bring down the price of rice as well as the price of gold and U.S. dollars, thus clearing the hyperinflation vortex. Meanwhile, additional rice came to market owing to the rural reforms. The abolishment of compulsory delivery of agricultural products to the state at below market prices improved the agricultural terms of trade. The gradual strengthening of property rights, granting of long-term leases, and autonomy (Ronnas and Sjoberg 1991) gave farmers the incentive to boost production and brought about the revival of self-managed family farms. Agricultural output grew by 7 percent in 1989. From being a net importer of food, Vietnam became the world's third largest exporter of rice.

At the same time, the mishmash of policy innovations and inconsistencies in the structure of state-controlled interest rates (see figure 15.7) gave rise to certain anomalies. For example, from November 1989 to December 1990, the very low real rate of interest on commercial bank deposits of enterprises caused many SOEs to depart from the usual custom of depositing their idle funds at the State Bank. Because subsidies to state enterprises had been drastically curtailed, and SOE managers were granted greater autonomy, they resorted to highly profitable financial intermediation by lending out their idle funds to other enterprises at higher rates (Vo Dai Luoc 1995). The upshot of these unofficial lending activities, which the government could not control, was excessive credit and inattention to risk, leading to financial problems and renewed inflation. The resulting sharp increase in the retail price index—of over 67 percent—reversed previous gains. Not surprisingly, this was followed by a contraction in dong deposits to 9.4 percent of GDP in 1990, and an exodus to more inflation-proof foreign currency deposits, causing the latter to rise to 8.8 percent of GDP in 1990.

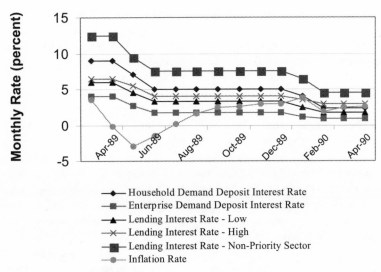

—◆— Household Demand Deposit Interest Rate
—■— Enterprise Demand Deposit Interest Rate
—▲— Lending Interest Rate - Low
—✕— Lending Interest Rate - High
—■— Lending Interest Rate - Non-Priority Sector
⋯◉⋯ Inflation Rate

FIGURE 15.7 Interest Rates and Inflation Rate, April 1989–May 1990

Although hyperinflation was subdued and new trading partners were found, the adjustment costs were considerable. The burden fell on public sector employees who were made redundant. Between 1988 and 1991, the SOE labor force shrank by nearly 30 percent, a total reduction of 794,000 (World Bank 1993). The unemployment problem was further exacerbated because, in addition to a very high labor force growth rate,[20] the economy had to accommodate an additional 500,000 demobilized soldiers and other workers released from the civil service, plus thousands more overseas workers who were repatriated from Eastern Europe and Iraq.

While government assistance helped to ease some of the transition pains, the number of skills training centers established by the government (fifty-five by the end of 1992) and the number of unemployed workers that could be helped was very small relative to the scale of the problem (World Bank 1993).

The burden of adjustment also fell on the state enterprise sector. The hard budget constraint and anti-inflation high interest rate policy increased their debt servicing costs. Their financial situation deteriorated, and they were forced to liquidate inventories and to restructure. Trade liberalization also brought in a flood of imports from China, Thailand, and Japan. It was estimated that only 20 percent of all

SOEs were profitable. About half were loss-makers, and 30 percent underutilized their productive capacity. The industrial sector experienced a 4.3 percent contraction and state sector gross industrial output fell by 7.1 percent. The non-state sector, which had been doing relatively well in 1987 and 1988, also felt the heat. In 1989 and 1990 non-state sector gross industrial output contracted by 4.2 percent and 8.2 percent respectively. The state-sector manufacturing industry was particularly hit hard. In 1989 it contracted by 19.5 percent. The non-state manufacturing sector also contracted, but not as much (by 3.2 percent).

The workers of many financially strapped SOEs went without pay. Meanwhile, production by co-operatives and small handicraft industries and trade organizations also fell (Vo Dai Luoc 1995). In 1989 industrial output fell by 4.3 percent. In addition, with price liberalization, SOEs were no longer able to profit from the difference between official and free market prices. Moreover, their financial difficulties were passed on to the government in the form of reduced SOE contributions to the budget, weakening already shaky public finances. The severity of the budget constraint led to cutbacks in the delivery of public social services. The government stopped investing in infrastructure, which was already dilapidated (World Bank 1993).

Yet the Vietnamese economy managed to emerge from this period of painful structural adjustment with largely positive outcomes. FDI and foreign trade provided an important cushion by stimulating output growth in the primary and tertiary sectors of the economy. Vietnam was spared the severe recessions that marked the early stages of transition in Eastern Europe because, even though its industrial sector suffered large contractions, this sector accounted for a much smaller share of GDP compared with the Eastern bloc countries (Truong and Gates 1996). In addition, Vietnam was able to quickly develop new export markets and change the composition of its trading partners (see figure 15.8). For example, although CMEA partners in 1988 provided 57 percent of Vietnam's imports, by 1991 they provided only 5 percent of imports. It was a similar story for exports. By 1992 Vietnam had restored ties with most Asian countries and the EC nations had resumed aid. It also should be noted that earlier investment in offshore oil production started to bear fruit during this period and the rapid growth of oil revenues helped strengthen the current account.

The composition of Vietnam's exports also shifted during the 1990s, away from unprocessed raw materials toward light industrial goods (see figure 15.9). Rice exports accounted for nearly 16 percent of total export earnings in 1990 but its share fell to less than 5 percent by 2000. Similarly, the share of revenues from crude petroleum exports fell from over 27 percent during 1990–1993 to 18.5 percent by 1998–2000. At the same time, the share of light industry exports have gained in importance, and by 1998–2000, exports of textiles and garments and footwear account for 14.6 and 11.1 percent respectively of total export earnings.

The structural adjustments associated with the Doi Moi reforms brought about a transformation of ownership in Vietnam's business sector, and induced a rise in the investment share of GDP, from a low of 12 percent in 1985 to 14.6 percent in 1989, notwithstanding the recession in the industry sector. The number of domestic non-state enterprises in the industry sector nearly doubled since the 1981–1988 period to over 600,000 by 1988–2000, thanks to policy reforms during the late 1980s that allowed non-state sectors to engage in larger scale agriculture, industry and trade.[21] The more favorable policy stance toward the private sector permitted a boom in private sector activity, especially in the urban informal sector, and boosted its investment spending.

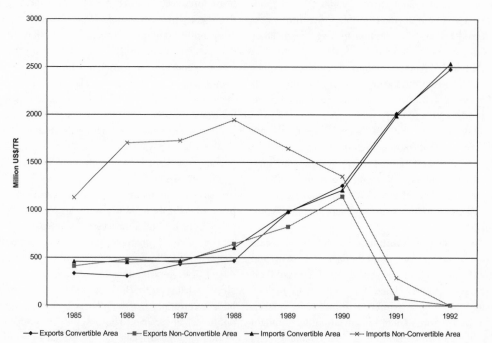

FIGURE 15.8 Trading Partners: Switch to Convertible Areas

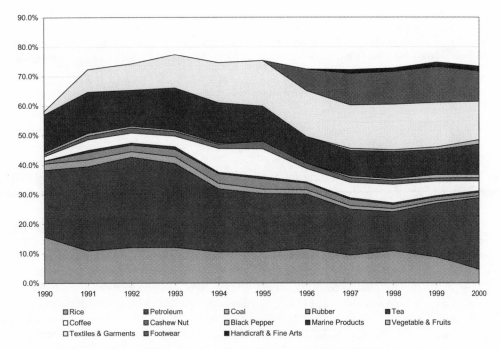

FIGURE 15.9 Merchandise Exports by Commodity as Share of Total, 1990–2000

From 1989 to 1993 private sector investment increased at an average annual rate of over 21 percent, despite receiving very little credit from the formal banking sector. The emergence of urban credit cooperatives, set up to circumvent the rigid banking system,[22] helped fulfill the private sector's credit needs during late 1989 and early 1990. This period also saw the emergence and rapid growth in the number of FDI firms, and major shakeups in the SOE sector. Consolidation and liquidation decreased the total number of SOEs from over 12,000 to less than 7,000 by 1995. In the industrial sector, the number of SOEs fell from over 3,000 during the subsidy period (1981–1988) to around 1,800 by the end of the decade (see table 15.10).

A final note regarding the 1989–1993 phase of vigorous reforms: it is not well known that during this period, a significant shift in the relative price of traded to non-traded goods in favor of the non-traded goods sector (see table 15.11) took place. This was due in part to the government's anti-inflation policy, which favored a relatively strong domestic currency.[23] For this reason, entrepreneurs did not have a strong incentive to enter the highly competitive export market. Indeed, many business managers who were surveyed during this period expressed the view that they could

TABLE 15.10 Number of Industrial Enterprises

| | Average Number of Enterprises | | | Annual Average Growth Rate | | |
	State Owned	Domestic Non-state	Foreign Invested	State Owned (%)	Domestic Non-state (%)	Foreign Invested (%)
1975–1980	2,088			17.5	—	—
1981–1988	3,039	333,060	1	2.2	4.2	—
1989–1993	2,540	411,260	74	−7.8	5.8	236.0
1994–1997	1,919	587,897	478	−2.7	8.1	42.4
1998–1999	1,804	602,850	920	−1.6	0.1	20.6

TABLE 15.11 Traded versus Non-traded Goods Prices, and Export and Import Growth Rates

	Relative Price Traded/Non-traded (%)	Exports (US$) (%)	Imports (US$) (%)	Price of Traded Goods (%)	Price of Non-traded Goods (%)
1987–1988	9.8	14.9	13.1	402.3	357.8
1989–1993	−8.8	27.4	9.7	42.9	57.2
1994–1997	0.2	32.5	32.3	12.3	12.5
1998–2000	2.2	16.4	10.4	7.4	5.1

make more profits at less risk producing for the domestic market, and this was borne out in their business decisions. An unexpected outcome of this shift in the terms of trade was an improvement in the government's fiscal position. The reason: because the state sector accounted for 55.3 percent of non-traded output and only 23.3 percent of traded output (as of 1994), this shift in the terms of trade in favor of the non-traded goods sector contributed to the improvement of SOE finances, and made possible their increased contribution to the state budget. Interestingly, during this period the dollar value of exports continued to rise at the robust rate of 27.4 percent (see table 15.11). One may infer from this counterintuitive development that there was enough slack in the economy so that the two sectors did not have to compete for the same resources, and that the export growth rate probably would have been even higher had the terms of trade favored the traded-goods sector.

6. Recovery in State Finances/Hesitant Policy Stance Phase

By 1994 it became clear that Vietnam had successfully weathered the socio-economic crisis. Inflation was well under control, the economy was sailing along smoothly, and government revenues as a share of GDP climbed steadily and peaked at 24.7 percent from their 1988 low of 11.3 percent. A number of well-connected SOEs were able to offset the loss of state subsidies with FDI funds for joint-venture projects. There was continued progress in normalizing relations with other countries and international institutions. The milestones included GATT observer status, membership in ASEAN, accession to protocols of AFTA membership, normalization of diplomatic relations with the United States, and the establishment of formal relations with the European Union (1995 and 1996). Most bilateral agreements were finalized under the Paris

Club, and creditworthiness was reestablished with the May 1996 agreement in principle to restructure the London Club debt.

The rise in the SOE budgetary contributions increased their influence. With the end of the crisis, the party leadership became more receptive to SOE lobbying for increased protection. They actively debated the merits of adopting East Asian development strategies emphasizing state-managed industrialization. Their partiality for large centralized *chaebol*-style conglomerates was seen in the March 1994 Decrees that established two types of general corporations, with the stated aim of increasing SOE efficiency and ability to compete against foreign firms. The plan was to merge many smaller enterprises under a single management in order to reap economies of scale. Decree 91/TTg established 17 general corporations comprising some 450 SOEs. These conglomerates were in industries deemed to possess comparative advantage or have strategic significance, and their management reported directly to the prime minister. Decree 90/TTg established 74 smaller general corporations covering some 900 SOEs with the objective of achieving gains from concentration in more traditional industries. Critics of this strategy called attention to the risk that these politically powerful conglomerates could become costly and unwieldy bureaucratic nightmares, diverting public resources away from higher priority projects established by the Public Investment Program (PIP) to develop the nation's infrastructure.

As foreign investors began teaming up with well-connected SOEs in import substitution industries, concern also grew that this emerging powerful alliance might lobby for protective tariffs and other import restrictions to shut out lower cost competitive imports. For example, foreign automakers successfully pressured the government to ban imports of cheaper second hand vehicles as a condition for setting up operations in Vietnam. In hindsight, given the acceleration of trade reform in Vietnam, its commitment to eliminate tariff and non-tariff barriers to ASEAN member country imports, and its preparations for accession to the WTO, these concerns may have been unwarranted. Instead, a shakeout in the import substitution industries may be anticipated, and firms with the capacity to compete on a regional basis will come out ahead. One can also expect to see intense political pressure coming from SOEs and foreign-invested firms that may not survive in the more competitive market environment.

The Vietnamese leadership believed that the FDI sector could contribute to economic development through the transfer of technology and management skills, and by opening up new export markets and distribution channels. In this regard, they were not wrong. The FDI sector has helped strengthen Vietnam's export capacity, and its share of exports increased rapidly, from 8.1 percent in 1995 to 21.2 percent in 1998, while its net contribution to the merchandise trade deficit narrowed from slightly over US$1 billion in 1995 to US$685 million in 1998 (see table 15.12).

Although there was considerable liberalization of the current account during the vigorous reforms phase (1989–1993), the government was still inclined to manage trade, and quantitative restrictions and import duties were selectively applied. For example, imports of key inputs such as construction steel, cement, fertilizer, sugar, paper, glass, and petroleum were subject to administrative control in order to reduce trade deficits, protect domestic producers, and conserve foreign exchange. Thus, in May 1997, the government issued a temporary ban on the import of tourism automobiles, motor bikes, writing and print-

ing paper, construction steel, white construction glass of a certain thickness, cement, and consumer goods such as bicycles, fans, sugar, beer, and beverages (Centre for International Economics 1999). An important reason, besides helping domestic producers of these items, was to prevent the trade deficit, which had climbed to 11 percent of nominal GDP in 1996, from worsening. In this regard the government succeeded, because the trade deficit was brought down to 8.1 percent in 1997, 7.3 percent in 1998, and 2.3 percent by 2000.

Revenue from external trade became an increasingly important component of the state budget, growing from 1.3 percent of nominal GDP in 1989 to a high of 6 percent of GDP in 1995 (see figure 15.10). This was when revenues from external trade as a ratio of the nominal value of exports and imports of goods and services peaked at 8 percent. This ratio has since declined to less than 5 percent during the period from 1997 to 1999. According to the IMF, customs duties have fallen by around 0.5 percentage points of GDP since 1998 and account for more than one-third of the decline in tax revenue. At the same time, revenues from SOEs as a percent of nominal GDP have been declining from their peak of 12.1 percent in 1994 to 7 percent in 1999. Figure 15.9 shows a worrisome trend for the government. The decline in SOE and external trade revenue as a percent of nominal GDP has not been offset by increases in other revenue components. For example, VAT collection, as a percentage of GDP, was lower than under the old turnover tax. As a result, government revenues as a share of GDP peaked at 24.7 percent of GDP in 1994, and declined to 16.3 percent in 2000 (see figure 15.11).

Fear of reigniting inflation continues to be the principal consideration behind the government's prudent fiscal stance. For this reason, the decline in revenues as a share of GDP has been accompanied by a similar decline in both current and capital expenditures. This is apparent when we consider the evolution of the budget deficit's share of GDP, from a high of 12.7 percent in 1989 to modest surpluses in 1995 and 1996. However, this fiscal prudence seriously limits the state's ability to provide the public goods needed to enhance economy-wide productivity. It also means that the state has fewer resources to assist the poorest members of society and to provide adequate safety nets for those who are hurt by the redistributional effects of external liberalization.

TABLE 15.12 Foreign Trade by Management Type

	US$ Million		% of Total	
	1995	1998	1995	1998
Exports				
Total	5,448.9	9,360.3		
Central	2,531.2	3,885.8	46.5	41.5
Local	2,477.6	3,491.9	45.5	37.3
FDI	440.1	1,982.6	8.1	21.2
Imports				
Total	8,155.4	11,499.6		
Central	3,475.4	5,672.4	42.6	49.3
Local	3,211.9	3,159.2	39.4	27.5
FDI	1,468.1	2,668	18.0	23.2

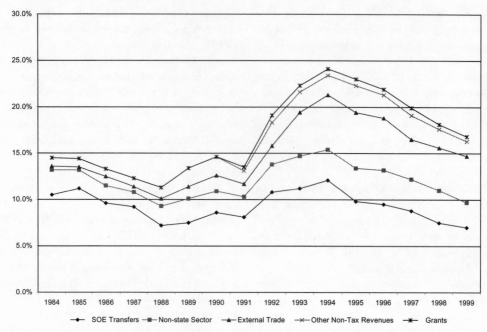

FIGURE 15.10 Revenue Components as Share of GDP (Stacked)

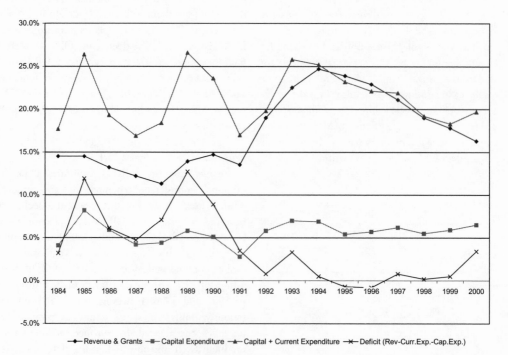

FIGURE 15.11 Revenues and Expenditures as % of GDP

TABLE 15.13 GDP Expenditure Components: Average Annual Growth Rate in Real Terms

	GDP (%)	Consumption (%)	Private (%)	Government (%)	Fixed Capital Formation (%)	Exports of Goods and Services (%)	Imports of Goods and Services (%)
1987–1988	4.8	2.9	2.5	8.6	8.6	–0.8	4.9
1989–1993	6.5	3.9	3.3	10.2	15.8	48.1	21.1
1994–1997	9.0	7.1	7.1	7.6	14.9	20.6	17.9
1998–2000	5.8	3.3	3.7	–0.3	8.3	11.3	8.3

7. Decomposition of the Sources of Effective Demand

In this section, I examine the role of aggregate demand as a determinant of growth. Table 15.13 summarizes the average growth rate of consumption, investment, and exports and imports of goods and services in real terms. Following the decomposition techniques outlined in Berg and Taylor (2001), I consider how the components of effective demand have shifted during the Doi Moi years.

Figure 15.12 highlights the direct "own" multiplier effect of each of the demand components on aggregate supply. It shows clearly that from 1991 on, the most important stimulus came from the private sector, which continuously pumped demand into the system, first because of its negative savings rate, and then later

from its investment spending. During the vigorous reforms period, aggregate investment spending grew on average by nearly 16 percent (see table 15.13), and non-state and FDI industrial investment spending soared (see table 15.4). The private sector injection was also magnified by its very low savings propensity (see figure 15.13), which was calculated as negative prior to 1991.

Public sector retrenchment during the vigorous reform period was characterized by massive labor shedding (the total number of state sector employees fell from 4.1 million in 1987 to 3.1 million in 1991) accompanied by substantial real wage increases for the remaining state sector employees. At the same time, after a prolonged period of real wage declines, the average government worker enjoyed annual real wage increases of 30 percent from 1987 to 1990, which helped to keep private consumption growth in the

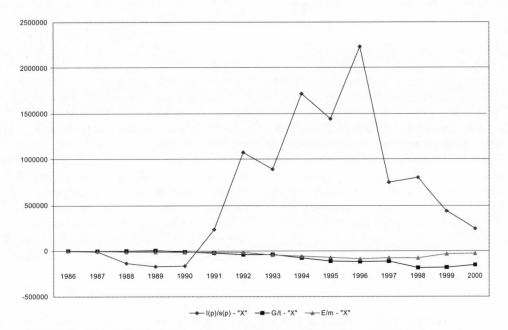

FIGURE 15.12 Sources of Demand: Direct "Own" Multiplier Effects minus Total Supply

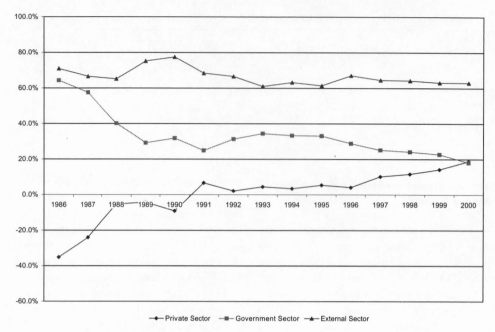

FIGURE 15.13 Leakages: Savings, Tax, and Import Propensities

positive range (see table 15.13). Thus, in contrast with the Eastern European experience, there was no collapse in demand during the vigorous reform phase. Nevertheless, it should be pointed out that private consumption spending was the slowest growth component during this period and its share of GDP declined steeply from over 93 percent in 1986 to less than 77 percent by 1994.

Figure 15.12 also clearly shows that throughout the 1990s, the net stimulus from the public sector has been mainly negative. Real increases in government consumption spending (10.2 percent average annual growth rate from 1989 to 1993) were offset by a rise in government revenues as a share of GDP, as transfers from restructured state enterprises and revenues from external trade contributed to the recovery in state finances discussed earlier (see Figure 15.10). The external sector's negative stance throughout the Doi Moi years was the result of Vietnam's very high import propensity, which cut into demand.

8. Productivity Shifts, Employment Decomposition, and Income Distribution

Table 15.14 and Figure 15.14 summarize the evolution of total employment and its allocation between agriculture, forestry and fishery, industry, construction, and services during the 1990s. While workers in the primary sector (agriculture, forestry, and fishery) account for nearly 70 percent of total employment, this sector's share of total output has declined gradually from over 33 percent in 1990 to less than 24 percent in 1999. During this period its annual labor productivity growth rate averaged only 1.6 percent, which is significantly lower than the other sectors. In contrast, the industrial sector's share of total employment declined from 10.2 percent in 1990 to 9.5 percent in 1999, but its share of total output rose from 19.5 percent in 1990 to nearly 27 percent in 1999, reflecting its much higher labor productivity growth rate of 10.2 percent.

The widening labor productivity growth gap between the primary, industry, and services sector helps explain the growing urban-rural gap documented in the Vietnam Living Standard surveys (VLSS). According to the survey findings, while the overall incidence of poverty declined significantly, from 58.1 percent in 1993 to 37.4 percent in 1998, the reduction in poverty was much greater in urban areas, where it declined from 25.1 to 9.2 percent. Rural areas experienced a smaller decline, from 66.4 to 45.5 percent. Moreover, real per capita expenditure in urban areas grew twice as fast, recording a 60 percent

TABLE 15.14 Main Output, Employment, and Labor Productivity Indicators: 1990–1999

	Output Share in 1999 (%)	Output Average Annual Growth Rate: 1990–1999 (%)	Employment Share in 1999 (%)	Employment Average Annual Growth Rate: 1990–1999 (%)	Output per Worker in 1999 (Millions of Dong at 1994 Prices)	Labor Productivity Average Annual Growth Rate (%)
Total	—	7.7	—	2.7	6.65	4.8
Agriculture, Forestry, and Fishery	23.8	4.3	69.0	2.6	2.29	1.6
	—	—	—	—		
Industry	26.9	12.2	9.5	2.0	18.74	10.2
Construction	7.5	10.4	2.5	2.1	19.56	8.2
Services	41.9	7.2	18.9	3.6	14.70	3.5

Source: General Statistics Office.

increase, relative to rural areas, which recorded a 30 percent increase (World Bank 2000a).

The primary sector workforce largely consists of self-employed farmers and agricultural laborers.[24] Its very low labor productivity supports the view that many agricultural workers are underemployed in a sector dominated by seasonal work. The average time spent on "economic activities" (remunerative work) per year for working-age adults in agriculture was 1,815 hours; in industry it was 2,109 hours and in services it was 2,354 hours (Vu Duc Khanh et al. 2001). One analysis of VLSS noted the extent of underemployment in agriculture "in the fact that the share of employment in self-employed agriculture (61.6 percent in 1997–98) is substantially higher than the share of hours spent working in self-employed agriculture (56.0 percent)" (Bales, Tung, and Cuc 2001). It is very likely that this sector and the informal services sector act as a sink to absorb workers made redundant as a result of downsizing in the state sector.

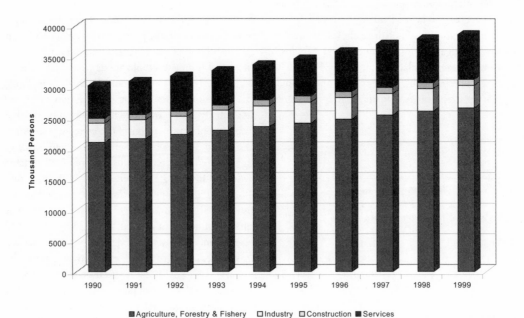

FIGURE 15.14 Total Employment by Sector

From this perspective, the information in figure 15.1, which separates each sector's contribution to overall employment growth, provides additional insight regarding employment shifts between sectors. The first thing to note is the low-productivity primary sector's dominant contribution to employment growth, although its share declined somewhat between 1992 and 1997. It strongly suggests that the economy is operating well below its full capacity level given the large reservoir of underutilized labor resources. The second thing to note is the pronounced shifts in sectoral contributions to employment growth over the decade. For example, the industry sector saw sharp employment fluctuations, which were largely due to the massive restructuring of state-owned enterprises (SOEs) and their greater exposure to a more liberalized and competitive environment.[25] Large numbers of laid-off workers from state enterprises shifted over to the urban services sector during this period and it became the most important contributor to employment growth, especially from 1994 to 1997. It also should be noted that Vietnam's shift to a more market-oriented economy, and the growth of FDI during this period, helped to create new demand for a broad range of consumer and business services.

The evidence from the Living Standard surveys leaves little doubt that, while per capita income has risen and most Vietnamese are better off, the gains from the first phase of reform and external liberalization have largely favored urban, educated, white-collar, and relatively well-off households. Inequality increased by all measures, with the Theil T index[26] recording the greatest change (see table 15.15). The disparity between richer and poorer households was also apparent when comparing real per capita

expenditure between the poorest and the richest deciles. From 1993 to 1998, reflecting their higher income growth, the richest 10 percent of the population increased their spending by 53.3 percent while the poorest 10 percent increased spending by 23.3 percent (Glewwe, Gragnolati, and Zaman 2000).

The greater decline in poverty in urban areas (relative to rural areas) was also accompanied by greater inequality, as measured by the Theil T index, which registered a 6.1 percent rise. In contrast, rural areas experienced less inequality, with the Theil T change in inequality declining by 6.6 percent. The widening urban-rural gap was also seen in the higher concentration of well-to-do families in urban areas: urban households increased their representation in the highest expenditure quintile, from 51.7 percent in 1992–1993 to 68.7 percent in 1997–1998. Educated households also enjoyed a disproportionately larger share of benefits during this period. Among households whose heads were university educated, 13.4 percent lived in poverty in 1992–1993, but by 1997–1998, this rate fell to 4.5 percent. In contrast, 69.9 percent of households whose heads had no schooling lived in poverty in 1992–1993, and this percent declined to 57.3 percent in 1997–1998.

What are the main drivers of Vietnam's productivity growth during the 1990s? Following the decomposition technique suggested by Berg and Taylor (2000), and Syrquin (1986), contributions to productivity growth can be separated into two components. First, there is the pure "own sector" productivity gain, expressed as the weighted output growth rate of that sector minus its employment growth rate (shown as AFF 1, Ind 1, Cons 1, and Services 1 in figure 15.15). Second, there is the contribution to overall productivity growth owing to the reallocation of labor employment across sectors of the economy (shown as AFF 2, Ind 2, Cons 2, and Services 2 in figure 15.15).

The decomposition results are presented in table 15.16 and figure 15.15. Interestingly, at this juncture of Vietnam's economic development, and perhaps for institutional reasons, pure "own sector" productivity gains dominate.[27] In general, the industrial (and to a lesser extent construction and services) sector chalked up significant "own sector" productivity gains. The primary sector ("AFF 2") dragged down the labor reallocation component of productivity gains (see "Net Reallocation Effect" in figure 15.3) because of its large employment share. Indeed, the net reallocation effect did not turn positive until after 1994. It turned

TABLE 15.15 Summary of VLSS Findings on Inequality

Inequality Has Increased By All Measures:

	Theil's T	Theil L	Gini
1992–1993	0.1966	0.177	0.329
1997–1998	0.2302	0.2013	0.352
Percent change	17.1%	13.7%	7.0%

Theil T Changes in Inequality

	Urban	Rural	White Collar
1992–1993	0.1941	0.1365	0.1937
1997–1998	0.2059	0.1275	0.2478
Percent change	6.1%	–6.6%	27.9%

Source: Glewwe, Gragnolati, and Zaman (2000).

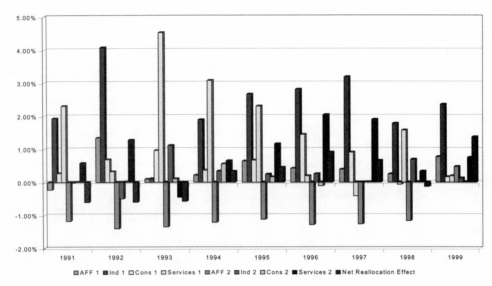

FIGURE 15.15 Decomposition of Productivity Growth into Two Components: (1) "Own Sector" Gains and (2) Gains from Labor Reallocation across Sectors

negative again in 1998 as employment growth in the services sector sharply slowed. In fact, it was primarily the movement of labor into the services sector during the 1990s that contributed significantly to the re-allocation component of aggregate productivity growth, while contrary to expectations, the contribu-tion of the industry sector was disappointingly weak.

Was it possible for industry to play a greater role in job creation? For this to take place, the demand for and supply of industrial output had to have been large enough to offset the effects of massive labor displace-ment in the SOE sector. At the same time, the increasingly competitive business environment of the 1990s forced enterprises to attend more to cost-cutting measures and productivity growth at the expense of job creation. Indeed, Doi Moi's climate of greater fi-nancial discipline made high output growth a man-datory requirement for significant job creation in the industrial sector. As it was, the sector's 12.2 percent annual average growth rate during the 1990s, although high compared to other countries, was not high en-ough to significantly outpace the labor productivity growth that was needed to stay competitive. It may also be argued that the focus on less labor-intensive

TABLE 15.16 Contribution to Overall Productivity Growth Due to Labor Reallocation between Sectors

	Net Reallocation Effect (%)	Agriculture, Forestry, and Fishery AFF 2 (%)	Industry Ind 2 (%)	Construction Cons 2 (%)	Services Services 2 (%)
1991	−0.60	−1.18	−0.01	0.01	0.58
1992	−0.60	−1.40	−0.50	0.02	1.28
1993	−0.57	−1.35	1.11	0.11	−0.45
1994	0.33	−1.21	0.34	0.55	0.65
1995	0.45	−1.12	0.25	0.17	1.16
1996	0.91	−1.28	0.25	−0.11	2.04
1997	0.66	−1.26	0.01	0.01	1.90
1998	−0.13	−1.16	0.69	0.02	0.33
1999	1.37	0.47	0.13	0.02	0.75

import-substitution industries during this period also prevented a greater reallocation of labor to the industrial sector.

The link between employment, per capita output and productivity growth in the industrial sector (excluding construction) and its evolution from 1991 to 1999 is presented in figure 15.16. The reason industry was unable to play a more important role in factor reallocation is also apparent when we compare the per capita output growth path with the labor productivity growth path. To have significant job creation in this sector, per capita output growth must be appreciably greater than labor productivity growth, and this did not happen. Shown in figure 15.16, industry's net effect on employment growth echoes its percent contribution to overall employment growth.

Our analysis of the changing structure of Vietnam's domestic labor market and productivity growth during the 1990s confirms that increased labor mobility between sectors has indeed taken place. During the industrializing stage of developing countries, we expect that reallocation gains associated with shifting labor from low productivity sectors to high productivity sectors would be an important contributor to aggregate productivity growth (Syrquin 1986). However, we find that productivity gains from labor reallocation between sectors have not been particularly significant during this period, except for some

reallocative gains from labor shifting to the services sector. It suggests that Vietnam is still at the very early stage of industrializing and has yet to realize the potential for significant reallocation gains from labor shifting out of agriculture.

We also find that output growth in the higher value-added sectors has failed to outpace productivity growth. As a result, the rate of job creation in the higher wage sectors of the economy has been disappointing. In the meantime, the growing supply of labor is channeled into the low-income low productivity agricultural sector, which is weighed down by chronic underemployment. For this reason, as documented in the two Vietnam Living Standard Measurement Surveys, Vietnam has experienced greater inequality in income distribution during this period of relatively high per capita income growth.

9. Social Welfare and Social Policy Issues

By many measures, including the UNDP's Human Development Index, under Doi Moi Vietnam made impressive gains in poverty reduction, health, child malnutrition, education and other aspects of social welfare.[28] These gains were due in part to the government's long-standing commitment to providing social services. Public expenditure on education as a

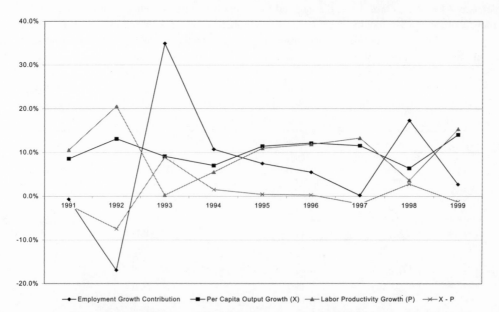

FIGURE 15.16 Industry Sector Employment, per Capita Output, and Labor Productivity Growth

share of GDP rose steadily from 1.3 percent of GDP in 1990–1993 to 2.2 percent in 1998–2000. Public expenditure on health as a share of GDP rose and then fell, from 1.0 percent in 1990–1993 to 0.8 percent in 1998–2000. With respect to education, in 1998 the average expenditure per primary school pupil was 6.8 percent, compared with the East Asian average expenditure of 8 percent per pupil in 1990 (World Bank 2000b).

The trend rise in spending on education from a very low base is striking given Vietnam's significant institutional weaknesses. The country has made considerable progress in increasing enrollments and improving the efficiency and equity of education expenditures (World Bank 2000b). The primary school net enrollment ratio (NER) rose from 87 percent in 1993 to 91 percent in 1998, while the lower secondary school NER rose from 30 to 62 percent and the upper secondary school NER rose from 7 to 29 percent. However, the quality of education varies considerably between different income groups, between urban and rural areas, and between geographical regions. Children from poor families are unable to obtain quality education because they can barely afford to pay regular school fees, let alone the extra cost of private lessons from poorly paid teachers.[29] Ethnic minority children have a disproportionately high repetition and dropout rate (UN Vietnam 1999), the regional variation in student educational attainment is substantial (World Bank 2000b), and the number of instructional hours for primary school students is very low.[30]

The story with respect to health spending and health outcomes is similar. Vietnam's achievements in health have been remarkable and involved a major epidemiological change: the share of communicable diseases in mortality and morbidity dropped sharply from 59 percent in 1986 to 27 percent in 1997.[31] As a result, the infant mortality rate also has fallen steeply from 75 per 1,000 live births in 1983 to about 28.2 during 1992–1996, with an even steeper decline in the child mortality rate. Indeed, with the important exception of child malnutrition, Vietnam's health indicators are much better than expected considering its per capita income level and in comparison with other low-income countries (see table 15.17).

At the same time, there is evidence of a growing gap in the health profile of non-poor relative to poor households (Wagstaff and Nga 2001). During the period from 1983 to 1992, there was little difference between the survival prospects of poor and better-off children in Vietnam. However, the VLSS data indicate that the impressive national reductions in child mortality achieved under Doi Moi have not been evenly spread. The higher income groups saw a large drop in the child mortality rate, but the lower income groups saw little change in their children's survival prospects. Wagstaff and Nga (2001) also find that these inequalities appear to be a recent phenomenon, since they showed up in the VLSS 1998 but not in VLSS 1993 data set. According to the authors, this rising inequality could be explained by (1) differences in immunization and antenatal coverage between the rich and poor, (2) declining access to satisfactory sanitation in the 1993–1998 period among the poorest quartile, (3) the declining proportion of newborns delivered by medical professionals in medical facilities among the poorest quartile, and (4) faster growth of access to safe drinking water among the better off. Not surprisingly, the burden of disease among the rural poor was found to be four times greater than

TABLE 15.17 Social Indicators

Indicator	Unit of Measure	1985	1993	1999	East Asia	Low Income
Health Mortality						
Infant mortality	Per 1,000 live birth	63	42	29	35	77
Under five mortality	Per 1,000 live birth	105	55	40	44	116
Immunization						
Measles	Percent of age group	19	93	96	83	64
DPT	Percent of age group	42	91	95	82	70
Child Malnutrition						
Life expectancy	Years	62	67	68	69	59
Female advantage	Years	3.8	4.5	4.8	3.5	2.2

Source: *Vietnam Statistical Yearbook* (various years); and GSO (1997–1998).

among urban dwellers. According to Dunlop (1999), the Disability Adjusted Life Years (DALYs)[32] lost per thousand people was 1,062 for the rural poor, and only 229 for the urban population. Among children four years and below, the gap was even more dramatic: 4,170 for the rural poor, 150 for urban children.

There are large disparities in health status between different geographical regions. The Central Highlands and Northern Mountainous region have an infant mortality rate of 56/1,000 live births and the maternal mortality rate in the latter region is four times higher than in the lowlands (UN Vietnam 1999). The incidence of non-communicable diseases have risen, while traffic accidents account for 21.6 percent of total mortality in 1997, a big jump from its 1976 level of 2.2 percent (UN Vietnam 1999). Another telling side effect of the transition to market deserves mention: there has been a sharp rise in self-medication and widespread purchase of drugs without a prescription due to aggressive marketing, the easier availability of drugs, and falling drug prices (the medicine price index relative to CPI declined significantly from 1993 to 1997). Antibiotics are among the most commonly dispensed drugs; as a result, antibiotic resistance levels have spread at an alarming rate due to unnecessary consumption, irrational (broad instead of narrow spectrum) and ineffective (short course instead of full course) use. This threatens to undermine Vietnam's ability to control and prevent the spread of many infectious diseases (Tornquist 1999; World Bank 2001a).

10. External Liberalization: Phase II

Vietnam is embarking on a second phase of accelerated external liberalization and far-reaching structural reforms that include banking, SOE, fiscal and public administration reform. The roadmap is defined by explicit commitments to implement the Common Effective Preferential Tariff Scheme (CEPT) of the ASEAN Free Trade Area (AFTA), to honor bilateral trade agreements, particularly with the United States (USBTA), to meet requirements for WTO membership, and to comply with conditions attached to credit provided by the international financial institutions (World Bank and IMF).

The liberalization of the exchange regime includes a phase out of the 50 percent surrender requirement on export proceeds and the removal of all restrictions on current international transfers and payments (IMF

2001). The trade reforms required by the multi- and bilateral trade agreements will bring about an extensive liberalization of trade in both goods and services. There will be major reductions of import tariffs (AFTA tariffs on most tariff lines will be reduced to 20 percent by 2003 and to 0–5 percent by 2006) and phased elimination of quantitative restrictions (QRs). The removal of QRs will lower Vietnam's rating on the IMF's 10-point scale of trade restrictiveness to 6 from its current rating of 9 (IMF 2002). Liberalized trading rights will be extended to foreign-invested enterprises (FIEs). Affiliates of foreign firms located in the ASEAN countries also benefit from the CEPT if they meet the 40 percent intraregional content requirement. The services sector will be wide open to foreign firms, as WTO members will demand equal treatment for U.S. firms under the USBTA, that also sets a timetable for opening Vietnam's domestic banking sector, the non-bank financial services sector, the insurance sector and other services to U.S. firms.

Vietnam's external liberalization and reform agenda continues to be the subject of intense discussion among Vietnamese policymakers and the donor community. Advocates focus on the invigorating effects of opening the economy to foreign competition. They point out that it will stimulate economic growth, improve resource allocation, drive out inefficient producers, discipline domestic producers and foster competition, bring in more effective rules and systems from abroad, provide a counterbalance to domestic monopolies, and protect the government from political capture by interest groups. The expansion of labor-intensive and export-intensive sectors will create more employment and stimulate a more efficient reallocation of resources across sectors (World Bank 2001b). The World Bank estimates that USBTA will make Vietnam a more attractive FDI destination and may boost exports by an additional US$600 million a year. However, more research is needed to test the robustness of these findings. This includes an evaluation of the potential negative impact of various OECD trade barriers and agricultural subsidies (estimated at about US$300 billion per year) on Vietnam's export earnings.

Others in the donor community worry about rapid integration in the context of weak policy capabilities and weak domestic institutions. There is also concern about the absence of adequate preparation.[33] The downside of external liberalization may include deindustrialization, increased price and demand shocks

TABLE 15.18 The *Doi Moi* Reforms

External Liberalization Measures:

- Unification and massive devaluation (by 90 percent) of the exchange rate
- Liberalization of controls on retention of foreign exchange by exporting firms
- Trade liberalization: reduction of tariff barriers and quantitative restrictions
- Foreign trade reforms: state and private firms have easier access to imports and better incentive to export
- Foreign Investment Law to attract foreign investment

Anti-Inflation Measures:

- Introduction of positive real rates of interest
- Budget tightening and greater fiscal discipline
- Credit restraint

Rural Reforms:

- Decollectivization of agriculture
- Return to self-managed family farms
- Long-term leases granted to farmers

Pro-Market Measures:

- Price liberalization: virtual elimination of price controls
- Removal of two-tier price system
- Imported intermediate materials valued at market prices
- Encouraging private sector development: new laws defining the rights and obligations of companies and private enterprises

SOE Reforms:

- Hardened budget constraint; SOEs placed on self-financing basis
- Drastic reduction of subsidies; easy access to cheap credit ended
- Decentralization of decision-making and increased management autonomy

Banking Reforms:

- Separation of central banking from commercial banking
- Diversification of institutions and of ownership
- Foreign participation permitted
- Greater autonomy and independence

Legal Reforms:

- Law on Private Business and Law on Companies approved in December 1990
- Foreign Investment Law amended in 1990
- Law on Central Bank, state-owned banks and credit institutions approved in 1990
- 1992 Constitution officially recognizes multisector economy
- Property rights strengthened with amendment of Land Law in 1993
- Law on Environmental Protection enacted in 1993
- Bankruptcy Law, Labor Code and Law to Promote Domestic Investment enacted in 1994
- Civil Code and Commercial Law enacted in 1995

from abroad, widening income gaps between the rich and the poor and across regions, foreign economic dominance, environmental destruction, excessive resource exploitation, social and political instability, and the loss of cultural and national identities (Ohno 2000).

The government's official position is to acknowledge that the "process of opening up the economy and integrating with the global economy creates many difficulties and challenges for Vietnam" such as having to "deal with fierce competition in international markets while the quality of its development is low, productivity is still not high, and [the economy's] ability to compete is weak." The policy agenda calls for studying the impact of trade policies in order to "adopt effective measures to minimize adverse impacts on the

TABLE 15.19 Chronology

	GDP Growth (%)	Retail Price Inflation (%)	Real Wage Growth (%)	State Sector Growth (%)	Non-state Sector Growth (%)	Significant Events
1976	16.8	21.9	n.a.	n.a.	n.a.	War-devastated economy supported by foreign aid; value of imports are 4.6 times value of exports; Fourth Party Congress decision to impose DRV institutions and central planning methods on South.
1977	3.7	18.6	−14.3	6.4	4.6	Sharp rise in export growth and in state sector investment; surprise withdrawal of Southern currency; VCP takes over property of rich Chinese; measures against Chinese merchant community disrupt rural economy.
1978	0.7	20.9	−17.6	−2.1	3.0	Invasion of Cambodia; end of Chinese and Western aid; private trade suppressed; sharp fall in domestic supplies of imported goods and staples, as agricultural output dropped by 6.4 percent; consumer goods shortage; violating plan directives, SOEs get inputs directly from suppliers.
1979	0.6	19.4	−15.0	1.6	−3.6	Short destructive war with China; economic crisis (1979–1980) compounded by reduction in low price inputs and bad weather; external threat a factor in party decision to relax controls on private sector production and to temporarily abandon drive to collectivize Mekong Delta.
1980	−2.9	25.2	−14.8	−16.9	4.0	Imports fall by nearly 14 percent; 40 percent of rice crops in North destroyed by typhoons; policy U-turn seen in politburo decision to tighten controls on private staples trade. Recentralizing package introduced in 1980–1981.
1981	3.5	69.6	7.7	1.6	2.6	Third Five Year Plan (1981–1985); effort to recentralize while making concessions to bottom-up change in the form of agricultural output contracts and "three-plan system" which lets SOEs produce and sell goods in free market once quotas are met; economy recovers at cost of higher inflation, speculation, smuggling and corruption.
1982	7.7	95.4	−19.9	2.3	10.8	Import shortfall covered by Soviet Union; 81 percent of Vietnam's imports are from the Soviet bloc, up from 52 percent in 1978.

(continued)

TABLE 15.19 (continued)

	GDP Growth (%)	Retail Price Inflation (%)	Real Wage Growth (%)	State Sector Growth (%)	Non-state Sector Growth (%)	Significant Events
1983	6.9	49.5	−8.3	2.0	8.6	Government grants wage increase to state employees; mounting pressure to recentralize.
1984	8.4	64.9	−19.2	18.8	5.6	Food crisis; malnutrition is widespread; UNICEF estimates a daily average calorific ration of 1,900 for the general population.
1985	7.6	91.6	17.6	14.8	3.0	Currency reform introduced in September a disaster; IMF blocks credits to VN; free market prices rise sharply; five key commodities—rice, sugar, kerosene, fish sauce, and meat—are put back on ration list in North; official dong to US$ exchange rate is 1.2 but free market rate is 70.
1986	2.8	774.7	−7.4	1.7	3.7	Doi Moi launched at historic Sixth Party Congress; aid from Soviet Union key source of support for subsidized state sector of economy; greater SOE autonomy encouraged; inflation severely reduces urban household savings; official dong to US$ exchange rate is 14 but free market rate is 261.
1987	3.6	223.1	39.7	5.7	2.1	Abolition of interprovincial trade barriers; rice prices fall; agricultural production fall sharply; Foreign Investment Law enacted; Land Law promulgated; government eliminates subsidies, impose budget controls, adjusts exchange rate and pricing system; hospital and school fees introduced; "contract responsibility system" for SOEs; rationing for many commodities abolished; internal trade checkpoints removed; gap between free market and official prices narrows; official dong to US$ exchange rate is 107 but free market rate is 883.
1988	6.0	349.4	29.1	7.6	4.8	Widespread food shortages; in March State Bank botches introduction of new currency; additional reforms: expanded user rights for farmers; decooperatization of agriculture; increased autonomy for SOEs; foreign trade restrictions eased; separation of commercial and central banking functions.

(continued)

485

TABLE 15.19 (continued)

	GDP Growth (%)	Retail Price Inflation (%)	Real Wage Growth (%)	State Sector Growth (%)	Non-state Sector Growth (%)	Significant Events
1989	4.7	36.0	20.1	−1.8	9.8	Termination of CMEA assistance; comprehensive reforms: unification and devaluation of exchange rate; reduction of trade restrictions; price liberalization; positive real rates of interest rates; anti-inflation measures: credit restraint, budget tightening; SOE weak financial position exposed; SOE transfers to budget declined; massive demobilization involving 500,000 soldiers; decollectivization of agriculture; return to self-managed family farms; SOE reforms include elimination of nearly all direct subsidies and price controls and decentralization of decision making to SOE managers; restrictions on private sector activity reduced; FDI encouraged.
1990	5.1	67.1	31.6	−3.5	11.2	New banking laws separate central banking from commercial banking; Foreign investment law amended; corporate law establishing framework for limited liability and joint-venture company activities approved.
1991	5.8	67.5	9.3	6.6	5.3	Private companies given permission to directly export and import.
1992	8.7	17.5	43.7	10.6	7.5	New Constitution adopted; multisector economy officially recognized; trade pact with EU signed.
1993	8.1	5.2	47.2	9.5	7.1	Land Law amended; Bankruptcy law and Environment Law approved; at November Paris Club meeting, West promises Vietnam US$1.7 billion in loans.
1994	8.8	14.4	24.5	10.4	7.8	U.S. trade embargo lifted; Labor Code enacted; with perception that Vietnam's crisis had ended, reform slowdown; FDI subject to stricter regulation, more selective criteria to have FDI contribute to VN's development objectives re: investment quality, technology transfer, and so on.
1995	9.5	12.7	8.7	9.4	9.6	Law on State-Owned Enterprises approved placing SOEs under direct supervision of Ministry of Finance; National Investment Fund established to provide preferential credit for selected sectors and disadvantaged regions; very slow progress in equitization.

(continued)

TABLE 15.19 (continued)

	GDP Growth (%)	Retail Price Inflation (%)	Real Wage Growth (%)	State Sector Growth (%)	Non-state Sector Growth (%)	Significant Events
1996	9.3	4.5	8.7	11.3	8.0	Eighth Party Congress debates leading role of SOE sector; Law on The State Budget and revised budget classification improved government's capacity to produce better fiscal reports; fiscal transparency strengthened.
1997	8.2	3.6	14.1	9.7	7.1	Asian financial crisis; social unrest in countryside; all barriers against internal trade of rice removed; private enterprises granted licenses to export rice under certain conditions; temporary import bans introduced for selected commodities with large domestic stocks, notably cement, steel, paper, motorcycles, electric fans, beer and other beverages, sugar, and confectionary.
1998	5.8	9.2	−0.6	5.6	3.7	Grassroots Democracy Decree approved; temporary introduction of non-tariff measures and exchange controls to restrain imports and protect domestic production.
1999	4.8	0.1	0.1	4.3	3.7	New Enterprise Law approved; Decree 57 to liberalize export-import rights passed; VAT introduced.
2000	6.8	−0.6	n.a.	n.a.	n.a.	New Enterprise Law becomes effective; bilateral trade agreement with United States signed; Vietnam Stock Exchange opens.
2001	6.8	0.8	n.a.	n.a.	n.a.	IMF and World Bank resume structural adjustment lending to Vietnam.

Sources: General Statistics Office (various years), Kolko (1997), Fforde and de Vylder (1996), Riedel and Turley (1999), IMF (1998) IMF and World Bank (1999), and NCSSH (2001).

liberalization" (61). In this regard, donor agencies, in cooperation with Vietnamese institutions, have launched a variety of research programs to evaluate the possible consequences of external liberalization.[34] In addition, consultants undertaking diagnostic audits of Vietnam's state-owned enterprises (SOEs) have been directed to assess the SOEs' degree of preparedness for trade liberalization. One may reasonably anticipate that the import-substitution industries will experience serious competitive pressure and many will not survive the second phase of external liberalization. This is due in part to the fact that the WTO will no longer allow high tariff ceilings for new members, which means that Vietnam's industrial policy must assume very low tariffs (Kimura 2000).

The preliminary results of the two neoclassical CGE models conducted by donor agencies point to somewhat divergent findings, although the results of both simulations are in agreement that well-to-do urban households will benefit the most from external liberalization. The CGE model of the Vietnamese economy commissioned by the World Bank concludes that the trade reforms will directly benefit the poor (World Bank 2001b), but the effects of tariff removal on nominal household income will not be uniform. The CGE simulation results suggest that the two top urban quintiles and the second top rural quintile will enjoy nominal household income increases in excess of 10 percent, while the poorest rural quintile will enjoy a 2.6 percent increase (World Bank 2001b). Simulation of the MIMAP CGE model find that modest economy-wide efficiency gains from combined tax and tariff reform are accompanied by a sharp redistribution away from rural and poor households, with the greatest benefits going to the richest urban household group. In the MIMAP model, the sharply asymmetric impact of tariff reform among rural and urban household groups are due to differences in expenditure patterns across households as well as differences in the ownership pattern of the factors they hold. Rich and urban households benefit from trade liberalization because their consumption of imported goods is greater than that of poor and rural households. On the income side, the rural work force are hurt most because they hold proportionately more industry specific factors and therefore are less equipped to take advantage of changes in relative prices induced by the tariff reforms (Nguyen and Tran 2000). In order to explain the divergent findings of these two neoclassical CGE models, it will be necessary to undertake a systematic comparison of their model equations and structural relationships in order to determine the differences in their underlying assumptions.

According to the World Bank, trade and SOE reforms will lead to labor redundancy "as some enterprises close and others shed labor in order to improve their efficiency and profitability" (VDR 2002). The effort to shift labor resources to more efficient sectors of the economy is to be facilitated by the Assistance Fund for SOE Rearrangement and Equitization, a safety net established for an estimated 400,000 displaced workers with financing from the World Bank.[35]

11. Conclusion

In summary, Vietnam's remarkably strong economic performance during the first phase of external liberalization and improvement in social welfare is due to the intersection of several critical factors. Emerging from the postwar period of "subsidy" and central planning, Vietnam's open-door policy and far-reaching domestic and external reforms, undertaken from 1989 onward produced far more positive results than those experienced in Eastern Europe and the former Soviet Union.[36] It also made a difference that Vietnam's external liberalization measures during the 1990s were appropriate to the level of economic development, domestic policy capability and state of domestic institutions, at the time. Moreover, the external liberalization measures did not include deregulation of the capital account, and there were times when the government intervened to prevent the current account deficit from rising to unmanageable levels.[37]

At the same time, the successful macroeconomic outcome and significant social welfare gains have been accompanied by a widening income gap between the rich and the poor, between urban and rural areas, and between regions. Preliminary results of simulations of the two CGE models, discussed in section 10, suggest that higher-income groups in urban areas will continue to reap a disproportionate share of the gains from external liberalization.

To address this concern, the CPRGS agenda highlights pro-poor measures[38] to "narrow the social development gap between different regions and population groups" and to "reduce the vulnerabilities of the poor and disadvantaged groups" (CPRGS 2002). The government's ability to carry out these tasks effectively will depend on its capacity to govern and to collect revenues; and it will need to develop effective measures to offset the anticipated erosion in revenues from external trade (associated with extensive tariff reduction) as a share of total government revenues. In conclusion, the second phase of external liberalization places Vietnam on a trajectory that offers great promise at considerable risk, especially if its domestic institutions and enterprises are ill prepared to operate in a more challenging and highly competitive environment.

Notes

I am grateful to Lance Taylor, Erinç Yeldan, Charles Bailey, and Le Anh Son for their comments on earlier versions of this chapter, and to the Ford Foundation and the New School University for their financial support.

1. According to the UNDP, the average HDI of low-income countries is 0.549 (United Nations Development Programme [UNDP] 2001).

2. Typically, significant productivity gains from industrialization are obtained when labor starts to shift out

of agriculture to higher productivity sectors such as manufacturing and services. Thus, a useful measure of progress with respect to industrialization is the contribution to overall productivity of productivity gains resulting from the reallocation of labor when employment shifts from low-productivity to higher-productivity sectors (Chenery, Robinson, and Syrquin 1986).

3. In fact, it is the *combined* effects of external liberalization and the shift to a market economy that led to the outcomes observed during the 1990s, and it is not possible to separate the two deeply intertwined factors.

4. This was owing to institutional rigidities imposed by central planning.

5. This includes the withdrawal of its military forces from Cambodia.

6. With the exception of Kolko (1997), Vietnam analysts in general have not paid much attention to the role of geopolitical factors in clearing the way for Vietnam's rapid growth of foreign trade.

7. The exceptional years were 1993 and 1998 when the industry sector accounted for 34.9 and 17.3 percent respectively of total employment growth during those years.

8. It is rated 9 on the IMF's 10-point scale of trade restrictiveness, where 10 is the most restrictive (IMF 2001, 18).

9. This is a very low figure compared with that of India. Even after liberalizing, India's ratio of import duties to the total value of imports stood at 22 percent in 1997. Taking the peak value attained in 1995, Vietnam's ratio of revenues from external trade to the total value of imports came to 13.8 percent (because of data constraints, I am unable to separate revenues from import duties and revenues from export duties). At the same time, it should be noted that this is an incomplete measure of the actual levels of protection in Vietnam given the existence of quantitative restrictions and other non-tariff barriers.

10. Although the Doi Moi Party Congress was held in December 1986, the actual period of vigorous reform did not begin until 1989.

11. Defined as exports plus imports to GDP.

12. Although press attention focused on foreign investor displeasure with Vietnam's business environment and the slow pace of reforms, the most vociferously unhappy were Western investors who accounted for a relatively small share of total FDI. Thus, it was not so much investor disenchantment, but the straitened circumstances of the East Asian and ASEAN NICs, that was the main reason for the significant drop in FDI.

13. During the early 1980s around 40 percent of the state budget was financed by aid from the Soviet bloc countries (Tran Duc Nguyen 1991). For the first fifteen years after the end of war, the country received minimal outside assistance other than from Soviet bloc countries and some international NGOs.

14. This underscores the time-bound aspect of external liberalization policies. Had the financial crisis hit the Asian Pacific economies only a few years earlier, Vietnam's trade and FDI trajectory would have looked very different, external liberalization policies notwithstanding.

15. The drop in FDI during this period is also attributable to "weaknesses in Vietnam's investment environment" (IMF 1999).

16. Between 1993 and 1997, FDI inflows averaged over 9 percent of GDP per year (IMF 1999).

17. However, the slower (6.2 percent) non-state sector growth rate registered from 1998 to 2000 does not necessarily suggest a return to a less friendly policy stance. Rather, it is a by-product of the Asian crisis.

18. U.S. Ambassador Raymond Burghardt acknowledged that the U.S. military sprayed over 72 million liters of dioxins on Vietnam between 1961 and 1970 (*Vietnam Investment Review* 2002).

19. Several factors contributed to high inflation: first, state sector spending was necessarily large, given the financial burden of maintaining one of Asia's biggest armies. Second, the trade embargo created shortages of imported inputs, leading to supply-side scarcities.

20. This is related to Vietnam's particular demographics: a relatively young population whose big bulge is at the age of joining the labor force.

21. Although until 1989 private enterprises were still banned from export-import operations and banking activities (Vo Dai Luoc 1995).

22. Unfortunately, widespread fraud, facilitated by the lack of prudential controls and general disregard for the law, led to massive bankruptcies estimated at VND 700–800 billion (Vo Dai Luoc 1995).

23. This policy goal was not difficult to achieve thanks to FDI-driven foreign capital inflows.

24. The VLSS 1998 survey (Glewwe 2000) found that nearly 80 percent of the working population are self-employed. Indeed, the largest occupational category is self-employed farmers who make up 59 percent of the workforce. Another 20 percent are the self-employed in the non-agricultural sector. The remaining 21 percent are wage and salary workers who work for the state including state-owned enterprises (8 percent), wholly Vietnamese-owned enterprises including small household businesses (8 percent), joint ventures (about 1 percent), and foreign-owned businesses (0.4 percent).

25. The reforms of 1990–1993 reduced the total number of SOEs from about 12,000 in 1990 to 7,000 by the end of 1993. About 2,000 locally controlled enterprises were liquidated, and another 3,000 SOEs were merged with other SOEs. Employment in the SOE

sector fell from 2.1 million in 1990 to 1.7 million by the end of 1993 (World Bank 1994).

26. For a discussion of the Theil T and Theil L inequality measures, see Theil (1989) and Glewwe, Gragnolati, and Zaman (2000).

27. This is independently confirmed by analysis of the Vietnam Living Standard Surveys, showing that "92% of the reduction in poverty between 1993 and 1998, as measured by the headcount index, is accounted for by improvements in incomes of people who remained in the same sector of employment. Sectoral shifts, that were relatively small during the period, contributed only 8.8 percent to poverty reduction" (Bales, Tung, and Cuc 2001, 56).

28. For example, international health experts consider Vietnam's tuberculosis and malaria control programs to be among the best in the developing world.

29. Many parents claim that the "real teaching" does not take place during regular school hours, but during private sessions organized after regular school hours. This phenomenon, unheard of during the "subsidy" period, has become widespread during the transition period.

30. In terms of instructional hours, the primary school year is only about 660 hours compared to a world average of 880 hours (UN Vietnam 1999).

31. This is due in part to the Expanded Program of Immunization (EPI), which lowered the prevalence rate of polio from 2.6 per 100,000 persons in 1986 to 0.6 in 1996. Similarly, the prevalence of diphtheria in 1996 was only 5 percent of its level in 1986. Neonatal tetanus has been virtually eliminated in most districts, and death from measles has fallen dramatically.

32. The Disability Adjusted Life Year (DALY), a measure of the sickness burden, is the number of years lost due to premature death or sickness.

33. This includes having a clear picture of which industries and enterprises are likely to fail, leading to sudden and destabilizing losses of output and employment.

34. The programs include the following:

- A joint study of Vietnamese industry conducted by the National Economics University (NEU) and the Japan International Cooperation Agency (JICA) with the goal of helping Vietnam "achieve industrialization while vigorously pursuing trade and investment liberalization." The project strategy statement notes that the government has yet to present "sufficiently concrete industrial strategies suitable for the age of integration," and that "candidate industries for promotion (or downsizing)" have not yet been identified.
- Technical assistance and policy research provided by the Multilateral Trade Policy Assistance Program (MUTRAP), an organization financed by the

European Union (EU), to analyze industry competitiveness in the context of WTO accession.

- MIMAP (Micro Impacts of Macroeconomic and Adjustment Policies) research program funded by the International Development Research Center (IDRC Canada), which involves the construction of neoclassical computable general equilibrium (CGE) models to evaluate the efficiency and distributional effects of trade liberalization and tax reform in Vietnam.
- Research commissioned by the World Bank, including a neoclassical CGE model to analyze the effects of Vietnam's proposed trade reform on income distribution and poverty in Vietnam (World Bank 2001b).
- Project on the effects of external liberalization on Vietnam's economic performance and income distribution carried out by the Institute of Socio-Economic Development and Enterprise Management with funding from the Ford Foundation. The project includes the construction of a structuralist CGE model and a comparison of its findings with those of the two neoclassical CGE models.

35. The Fund will finance compensation and retraining for redundant workers. The compensation package will include up to two months of basic salary per year of service, a lump sum payment ranging from VND 5–10 million, plus retraining costs.

36. What also helped was that the ASEAN and East Asian economies were enjoying a period of unprecedented economic boom and therefore were able to play a significant role in boosting trade and foreign direct investment in Vietnam.

37. For example, import restrictions were imposed in 1998 and 1999 to counteract the drop in FDI capital inflows and weak export growth associated with the regional financial crisis.

38. These include improved governance and strengthening of grassroots democracy to ensure better accountability, infrastructure investment in the poorest communities, better health and education for the poor, greater emphasis on agriculture and rural development, and improving the environment for small and medium enterprises.

References

Arnett, Elsa. 2001. A family photo gallery. *San Jose Mercury News*, April 8, 2001.

Bales, Sarah, Phung Duc Tung, and Ho Si Cuc. 2001. Sectoral changes and poverty. In *Living standards during an economic boom: The case of Vietnam,* edited by D. Haughton, Jonathan Haughton, and Nguyen Phong. Hanoi: Statistical Publishing House.

Berg, Janine, and Lance Taylor. 2000. External liberalization, economic performance, and social policy. CEPA Working Paper Series I, Working Paper no. 12, February. New York: Center for Economic Policy Analysis.

Centre for International Economics. 1999. Non-tariff barriers in Vietnam. A framework for developing a phase out strategy.

Chenery, H., Sherman Robinson, and Moshe Syrquin. 1986. *Industrialization and growth: A comparative study.* New York: Oxford University Press.

De Melo, M., Cevdet Denizer, Alan Gelb, and Stoyan Tenev. 1997. Circumstance and choice: The role of initial conditions and policies in transition economies. World Bank International Finance Corporation, October. Washington, D.C.: World Bank.

Fforde, Adam. 1998. Vietnam—culture and economy: Dyed-in-the-wool tigers? Draft paper for ANU Vietnam Update 1998.

Fforde, Adam, and Stefan de Vylder. 1996. *From plan to market: The economic transition in Vietnam.* Boulder, Colo.: Westview Press.

Fukase, Emiko, and Will Martin. 1999a. A quantitative evaluation of Vietnam's accession to the ASEAN Free Trade Area (AFTA). Development Research Group. Washington, D.C.: World Bank.

———.1999b. The effect of the United States' granting Most Favored Nation status to Vietnam. Development Research Group. Washington, D.C.: World Bank.

Fukui, Koichiro, Takao Aiba, and Hiroko Hasimoto. 2000. The significance to Vietnam of membership in the World Trade Organization.

Glewwe, Paul. 2000. Are foreign-owned businesses in Vietnam really sweatshops? *Minnesota Agricultural Economist* (701).

Glewwe, Paul, Michele Gragnolati, and Hassan Zaman. 2000. Who gained from Viet Nam's boom in the 1990s? An analysis of poverty and inequality trends. Policy Research Working Paper, 2275. Development Research Group. Washington, D.C.: World Bank.

Haughton, Dominque, Jonathan Haughton, and Nguyen Phong, eds. 2001. *Living standards during an economic boom: The case of Vietnam.* Hanoi: Statistical Publishing House.

International Monetary Fund. 1998. *Vietnam: Selected issues and statistical annex.* IMF Staff Report no. 98/30, April. Washington, D.C.: IMF.

———.1999. *Vietnam: Selected issues.* July. IMF Staff Report no. 99/55. Washington, D.C.: IMF.

———.2001. *Vietnam: Request for a three-year arrangement under the poverty reduction and growth facility.* March 22. Washington, D.C.: IMF.

———.2002. *Vietnam: Selected issues and statistical appendix.* IMF Country Report no. 02/5, January. Washington, D.C.: IMF.

International Monetary Fund and World Bank. 1999. *Vietnam: Toward fiscal transparency.* Joint IMF–World Bank Report, June 1999. Washington, D.C.: IMF.

Jun, Kwang W., Duc Minh Pham, Victoria Kwakwa, Kyle Peters Jr., and Thang-Long Ton. 1997. Foreign capital flows in Vietnam: Trend, impact, and policy implications. Background paper for the World Bank's Economic Report "Vietnam: Deepening Reform for Growth," November.

Kimura, Fukunari. 2000. Policy measures for industrial promotion and foreign direct investment.

Kolko, Gabriel. 1997. *Vietnam: Anatomy of a peace.* New York. Routledge.

Liljestrom, R., Eva Lindskog, Nguyen Van Ang, and Vuong Xuan Tinh. 1998. *Profit and poverty in rural Vietnam.* Curzon Press.

Lin, Shuanglin. 2000. The decline of China's budgetary revenue: Reasons and consequences. *Contemporary Economic Policy* (October).

Long, Ngo Vinh. 1973. *Before the revolution: The Vietnamese peasants under the French.* Cambridge, Mass.: MIT Press.

Mallon, Raymond. 1997. Mapping the playing field: Options for reducing private sector disincentives in Vietnam. Mimeo.

Matin, Kazi and Duc Minh Pham. 2000. Vietnam trade liberalisation: Following the AFTA programme. *Vietnam Socio-Economic Development* (22).

McCarty, Adam. 1999. Vietnam's Integration with ASEAN: Survey of non-tariff measures affecting trade. UNDP Promoting Vietnam's integration with ASEAN—VIE 95/015. January.

National Centre for Social Sciences and Humanities (NCSSH). 2001. *National human development report 2001: Doi Moi and human development in Vietnam.* National Political Publishing House.

Nguyen Chan, and Tran Kim Dung. 2000. Using CGE model to evaluate tariff policy in Vietnam. Paper presented at the MIMAP Network Conference in Palawan, Philippines, September.

Ohno, Kenichi. 2000. Free trade versus infant industry promotion: The possibility of temporary protection for latecomer countries. November 13. Mimeo.

Packard, Le Anh Tu, and Stephan Thurman. 1996. A model design for Vietnam as an open economy in transition. *ASEAN Economic Bulletin* 13(2).

Riedel, James, and William S. Turley. 1999. The politics and economics of transition to an open market economy in Vietnam. OECD Development Centre Technical Papers no. 152, September.

Syrquin, Moshe. 1986. Productivity growth and factor reallocation. In *Industrialization and growth: A comparative study*, edited by H. Chenery, Sherman Robinson, and Moshe Syrquin. London: Oxford University Press.

Tornquist, Sam. 1999. Vietnam-Sweden health cooperation in the area of drug policy and control. Project Document, April 24. Mimeo. Hanoi: Ministry of Health.

Tran Duc Nguyen. 1991. Vietnam's socio-economic development to the year 2000: Approaches and objectives. In *Socio-economic development in Vietnam: The agenda for the 1990s*, edited by P. Ronnas, and Orjan Sjoberg. Stockholm: Swedish International Development Authority.

United Nations Development Program (UNDP). 2001. *Human development report 2001*. New York: Oxford University Press.

United Nations Vietnam. 1999. *Looking ahead: A United Nations common country assessment of Vietnam*, December. Hanoi: UN Vietnam.

Vo Dai Luoc. 1995. Monetary stabilization: The Vietnamese experience. In *Vietnam in a changing world*, edited by I. Norlund, Carolyn Gates, and Vu Cao Dam. Nordic Institute of Asian Studies. Curzon Press.

Vu Duc Khanh, Vu Thi Thu Thuy, Bui Kim Loan, Le Hong Phong, and Nguyen Quang Phuong. 2001. Labor and employment. In *Living standards during an economic boom: The case of Vietnam*, edited by D. Haughton, Jonathan Haughton, and Nguyen Phong. Hanoi: Statistical Publishing House.

Wagstaff, Adam, and Nguyen Nguyet Nga. 2001. Poverty and survival prospects of Vietnamese children under Doi Moi. September.

World Bank. 1993. *Vietnam: Transition to the market*. September. Washington, D.C.: World Bank.

———.2000a. *Vietnam development report 2001: Vietnam 2010: Entering the 21st century*.

———.2000b. *Vietnam: Managing public resources better: Public expenditure review 2000*. Hanoi: World Bank.

———.2001a. *Growing healthy: A review of Vietnam's health sector*. May.

———.2001b. *Vietnam development report 2002: Implementing reforms for faster growth and poverty reduction*. Report no. 23187-VN.

World Bank et al. 1999. *Vietnam: Attacking poverty*. Joint Report of the Government of Vietnam—Donor—NGO Poverty Working Group. Hanoi:

Index

Page numbers in bold indicate figures or tables.